AS THE TWIG IS BENT . . .

Lasting Effects of Preschool Programs

Members of the Consortium for Longitudinal Studies

E. Kuno Beller
Richard B. Darlington
Cynthia P. Deutsch
Martin Deutsch
Ira J. Gordon*
Susan W. Gray
R. Emile Jester
Merle B. Karnes
Irving Lazar
Phyllis Levenstein
Louise B. Miller
Francis H. Palmer
David Weikart
Myron Woolman
Edward Zigler

*deceased

AS THE TWIG IS BENT . . .

Lasting Effects of Preschool Programs

The Consortium for Longitudinal Studies

LEA LAWRENCE ERLBAUM ASSOCIATES, PUBLISHERS
1983 Hillsdale, New Jersey   London

Lawrence Erlbaum Associates, Inc., Publishers
365 Broadway
Hillsdale, New Jersey 07642

Library of Congress Cataloging in Publication Data
Main entry under title:

As the twig is bent—lasting effects of preschool
   programs.

   Bibliography: p.
   Includes index.
   1. Education, Preschool—United States—Longitudinal
studies. I. Consortium for Longitudinal Studies.
LB1140.23.A8   1983   372'.21'0973   83-5593
ISBN 0-89859-271-2

Printed in the United States of America
10   9   8   7   6   5   4   3   2   1

Contents

v

CHILD PSYCHOLOGY

A series of volumes edited by **David S. Palermo**

Acknowledgments

It would be virtually impossible to individually acknowledge the hundreds of people who contributed to all these studies, some of which stretch back over 20 years. The authors have listed some of the people and organizations associated with their own projects; here we convey our thanks to some who assisted in the collaborative studies that linked these findings together.

The major support for the follow-up studies and their integration came from the Administration for Children, Youth and Families (ACYF), Office of Human Development Services, U.S. Department of Health and Human Services (Grants 90C-1311 and 18-76-07843). Dr. Edith Grotberg, then ACYF's Director of Research and Evaluation, and Dr. Maiso Bryant and Dr. Bernard Brown, of her staff, provided invaluable help and advice in the 7-year period of the follow-up studies. Dr. Brown devoted hundreds of hours of his own time conducting independent data analyses and arranging for the presentation of these data at professional meetings.

Other direct federal financial support came from the Bureau of Maternal and Child Health of the U.S. Public Health Service (Grant MCT-004012-01-0) and from the U.S. Department of Labor (Grant 28-36-80-02). Here again we received valuable advice and critiques from their excellent research professionals.

During two periods the research teetered on the brink of insolvency, as the quantity and diversity of the data overwhelmed our initially too modest expectations of the extent to which subjects and data could be located. On both occasions, the William and Flora Hewlett Foundation came to our rescue and further enabled us to carry out necessary activities that "fell between the cracks" of federal grants regulations. We will be grateful always to Dr. Roger Heyns and to Mr. Ted Lobman of the Foundation staff for their early optimism and continual encouragement.

During the early years of the Consortium, the Education Commission of the States served as our fiscal agent, and Dr. Homer Elserode, then Director of Elementary and Secondary Education, lent his national reputation and gave freely of his time to help us get access to school district data so essential to this research.

We received professional advice, consultation, and critiques from several colleagues who were particularly helpful during the critical period in which we needed to make our decisions on analytic techniques. We are particularly indebted to Dr. Urie Bronfenbrenner and Dr. Steven Caldwell of Cornell University; Dr. Jules Janis of the U.S. Public Health Service; Dr. Robert McCall of Boys Town; Dr. Shirley Moore of the University of Minnesota; Dr. Julius Richmond, then Surgeon General of the United States; and Dr. Virginia Shipman and Dr. Irving Sigel of the Educational Testing Service.

Although all the institutions that participated in this research both waived their normal overhead charges and gave of their facilities, we especially want to recognize the contribution of the New York State College of Human Ecology at Cornell University, which housed the central staff and made available Cornell's library and computer facilities.

Although many people participated in the analyses and dissemination of these data, a few of the central staff played key roles in this work. Dr. Ruth Hubbell was the first staff member; she constructed and field tested the interview schedules and conducted the comparisons of center-based and home-based programs. Dr. Harry Murray carried out the computer analyses of the 1976 follow-up and was succeeded by Dr. Reuben Snipper for the 1980 computer runs. Dr. Jacqueline Royce served as data librarian during the data gathering years and supervised student assistants during the last year of analytic work. Dr. Ann Snipper assisted in the dissemination effort, drafted several of our reports, and maintained liaison with our collaborators. Jane Pedersen and Marjorie Wikerd successively managed our funds and the complicated task of keeping our collaborators supported on budgets that were always too small.

Finally, our special thanks to Dr. Sandra Condry and Jules Marquart, who edited every word of this volume and successfully condensed the original manuscripts to the size of this book, while at the same time earning the acquiescence of our more loquacious colleagues.

Irving Lazar
Richard Darlington

A Tribute to the Consortium

Edith H. Grotberg

The first encounter I had with any member of the Consortium group was in the fall of 1963, and it was with Martin Deutsch. An announcement was posted at the American University, where I was a professor, that Martin Deutsch was bringing a group of preschool children down to Washington, D.C. from New York. He was going to demonstrate in a conference room at the Office of Education the performance ability of some 20 four-year-olds who participated in the Institute for Developmental Studies (IDS) experiment. I attended that session and was amazed at the skills of the young children. They were also quick, alert, totally motivated, and clearly having a great time. Children from families with low incomes and in poverty responded dramatically to a carefully developed program. I never forgot the experience.

The second encounter I had with a member of the Consortium group was in reading some preliminary reports about the Early Training Project directed by Susan W. Gray at George Peabody College for Teachers (later of Vanderbilt University). Dr. Gray responded to a concern of the school system that there was an increasing and progressive retardation surfacing among pupils in the elementary schools. The response was to develop a program of summer intervention for preschool children at the center and home visits during the rest of the year. The children were from families with low incomes and in poverty. Again, the results were impressive and I added that to what I had learned from Martin Deutsch.

As it happened, neither Susan Gray nor Martin Deutsch were part of the Committee which set up the Head Start program in 1965, but their work was its foundation, and I have always thought of them as the inspiration for Head Start.

The other members of the Consortium became well known to me when I was coordinating Head Start research for the Office of Economic Opportunity (OEO).

Edward Zigler was an advisor to Head Start research and in 1970 became the first Director of the Office of Child Development (OCD) to which Head Start was assigned. Kuno Beller, Louise Miller, Merle Karnes, Frank Palmer, and Mike Woolman were, over the years, partially supported by OEO and OCD; others like David Weikart, Ira Gordon, and Phyllis Levenstein were doing research and evaluation for the agencies in addition to developing their own preschool programs.

The members of this group became professional colleagues and friends during the 1960s and 1970s and met with each other at various professional meetings and as members of panels or symposia on preschool programs. They kept up with the issues surrounding preschool programs, especially Head Start. By 1975 they were ready to address the critical issue of the long-term impact of preschool programs.

They readily responded to serious problems facing Head Start in the 1970s. The problems were both from outside and inside the program. Outside was the controversy of whether or not to expand or even to continue the program, as evaluation results were not making a clear-cut case for the long-term benefits of Head Start. Inside was the double bind that if the program proved effective for the long term, it would likely be moved to the Office of Education or to the states. If the program, however, proved ineffective, it would be abolished. Either way the program would be lost to those who saw its unique value in its comprehensive approach, its emphasis on parent involvement, and its responsiveness to local needs. A case had to be made for or against the long-term benefits of preschool programs for children in poverty, even though no other program in the history of education, health, or welfare had ever been required before to justify its existence by long-term benefits.

In 1975, when the problems reached a critical stage, the Research and Evaluation Division of OCD (later the Administration for Children, Youth and Families) became interested in the concept of developmental continuity. This concept encouraged an examination of long-term effects of early interventions and also an examination of patterns of intervention at different periods over time. The two project areas for study were announced for response from the research community. Of the many projects funded in 1976, the Consortium for Developmental Continuity (later the Consortium for Longitudinal Studies) was one. The group had organized and agreed upon a strategy for determining the long-term impact of preschool programs. It selected Irving Lazar as the principal investigator and agreed he had the necessary skills to carry out a study that required careful orchestrating of discrete projects. Dr. Lazar had been one of the earliest consultants to OEO, had been director of child development services for the Appalachian Regional Commission, and had the support and facilities at Cornell University, where he became a professor in 1972, to carry out the study.

By 1977, data were available from the Consortium that, in essence, made the case for early intervention. The results, as described in greater detail in Chapter

13, led to an expansion of Head Start and a major increase in funding support. That is no mean accomplishment and the Consortium group is to be commended. It worked under difficult conditions, with insufficient funds; but the commitment was total, and the results reliable and powerful. Each member and the Consortium as a whole are to be lauded for a job well done.

AS THE TWIG IS BENT . . .

Lasting Effects of Preschool Programs

1 History and Background of Preschool Intervention Programs and the Consortium for Longitudinal Studies

Sandra Condry*
South Lansing Center
Lansing, New York

Introduction

The Consortium for Longitudinal Studies was formed in 1975 to answer the question of whether early education programs had measurable long-term effects on the performance of children from low-income families. This unique collaboration of individual researchers who developed and evaluated early education programs in the sixties has now provided convincing and ecologically valid evidence of the effectiveness of these programs.

This volume is a fitting culmination of the work of the consortium. A chapter by each of the individual researchers is presented. The particular early education program is described, the research design for evaluating the impact of the program is explicated, and the findings are reported and discussed. A chapter on the pooled analyses of the follow-up data from the individual studies offers a summary of the findings of the past seven years' work and, in addition, presents new analyses on the high school and labor market experiences of the eldest of the projects' participants. The final chapter discusses the implications of the consortium findings. The epilogue integrates the findings from the individual studies and the pooled analyses and presents their policy implications.

The present chapter discusses the history and background of early intervention programs and of the Consortium for Longitudinal Studies. The first section summarizes the theories and research of the past 50 years that placed new emphasis on the early development of the child and on the role of the environment in affecting that development. The second section discusses the social and political milieu of the United States in the fifties and sixties that reflected a growing concern for the victims of poverty and led to the establishment of

*During the writing of this chapter, the author was Research Associate at the Foundation for Human Service Studies, Ithaca, New York.

1

Project Head Start. The ensuing debates on the theoretical bases, the implementation, and the effects of Head Start brought into question the efficacy of all preschool intervention programs. It was in this climate that the Consortium for Longitudinal Studies was formed; its purposes and history are described in the third section of this chapter.

THEORETICAL AND RESEARCH BACKGROUND OF PRESCHOOL INTERVENTION PROGRAMS

The development in the 1960s of early education programs for children of low-income families flowed from theories and research in psychology, education, and sociology. The idea that early educational experiences could help low-income children enter the public school system on an equal footing with economically more advantaged children was not new. However, the theoretical basis for this idea had never appeared so strong. Research findings over the previous 30 years suggested that intervention, and particularly early intervention, could have dramatic effects on the subsequent cognitive and behavioral development of children.

The Early Days of Early Childhood Education

Outside American academic circles, the idea of using early education as an instrument to alleviate social problems was well established. The specific use of infant or nursery schools to help children of the poor had been advocated over the years, for instance, by Rousseau in the 1700s and by Pestalozzi in the 1800s (Rusk, 1967).

A well-known early advocate was Maria Montessori (1912). In 1907, she established the Casa di Bambini for deprived children in the basement of a slum apartment house in Rome. Her school was supported by private funds from local businessmen who hoped she would keep unruly children from vandalizing their property while the children's parents were at work. She believed it was possible to modify the young child's cognitive capacity by proper education—not through didactic teaching but rather through the opportunity to learn spontaneously. She developed an individualized approach and stressed sensory training.

Also in the early 1900s, humanitarian Margaret McMillan (1919) founded the "open air" nursery in the slums of England for deprived children. Considerable attention was paid to health as well as to education. In 1918, the government established nursery schools as part of the English national school system. Both the Montessori and McMillan experimental schools achieved considerable success, although their influence on American psychology and education was minor until the 1960s.

Early childhood education has been present in the United States for over a century, but the programs developed in the sixties differed significantly from earlier programs in their emphasis on the cognitive development of low-income children. The United States, for a long time the land of the immigrant, has a history of settlement houses, which generally were established in poor immigrant neighborhoods and were supported by local charities. Although child care has an historic affiliation with services for minorities, these services were not viewed as having academic purposes.

In the 1920s there was an "explosion" of American nursery schools. These appeared at a time when the early years of childhood were being emphasized by Freud (1922) and by Gesell (1929). These nursery schools differed from the earlier day nurseries and child care centers in that they were established to offer educational advantages to the children rather than to free the parents for work. The educational emphasis was on "learning by doing," an idea encouraged by the philosophy of John Dewey (1915), and by the curricula of McMillan and Montessori. Most of these nursery schools were private, although a small number were established within public schools.

Also, a number of laboratory or training nursery schools were established by state and private universities within colleges of education or as separate institutes for child study. Set up in the 1920s, many are still in operation. In addition to caring for children, these laboratory schools were established for teacher training and as research units. It was within the colleges of education in the 1950s and 1960s that several early experimental nursery schools for children of low-income families were established.

Although relevant, the history of American nursery schools and settlement houses cannot account for the dramatic appearance in the 1960s of cognitively oriented preschool programs for poor children. To understand the forcefulness with which these programs were advocated, and the broad acceptance that these programs received, requires a familiarity with American developmental psychology in the 1900s.

Early Views on Intelligence and Development

The history of intelligence testing is central to an understanding of early education in the 1960s. In an influential book (*Intelligence and Experience*, 1961), Hunt traced the intellectual thought and research regarding intelligence in the United States in the twentieth century. He concluded that the traditional view of intelligence as a fixed genetic capacity was not supported by the evidence and that there were convincing theories that viewed intelligence as more responsive to environmental influences than previously had been assumed.

Intelligence as a Fixed Capacity

Hunt pointed out that most textbooks written before World War II accepted the idea that intelligence was a fixed capacity (p. 10). For instance, Burt, Jones, Miller, and Moody (1934) wrote: "By intelligence, the psychologist understands inborn, all-around, intellectual ability. It is inherited, or at least innate, not due to teaching or training [p. 28]."

The idea that intelligence is an inherited capacity followed from Charles Darwin's theory of natural selection (1859) and the broader nineteenth-century furor over the mechanism for changes in the species. Darwin argued that many physical characteristics were inherited and that changes across the generations were due to chance variations, which then were passed on to succeeding generations. This view replaced the earlier Lamarckian notion that characteristics acquired through experience could be passed on to future generations. The theory espoused by Darwin and others was quickly applied to a variety of specific characteristics. The notion of fixedness of a characteristic across generations was extended to cover human intelligence by Francis Galton, Darwin's cousin. In a study of British men, Galton (1869) concluded that genius was inherited because distinguished men tended to come from a small set of families. The fact that the sons of these few families were reared in highly advantaged environments was not considered in this argument.

In the late 1800s, in France, Binet and others developed a test of intelligence to determine which children were likely to profit from schooling. The test was composed of comprehension and reasoning questions. Binet (1905), unlike Galton, argued strongly against the idea that intelligence was fixed. However, his "mental tests" were brought to the United States by Cattell, a student of Galton, and by Goddard (Hunt, 1961, p. 14). Both were ardent hereditarians. Goddard, for instance, administered Binet's test to newly arrived immigrants and, on the basis of test results, recommended that many southern and eastern European aliens be deported due to "feeble-mindedness" (Kamin, 1974).

The view that intelligence is fixed was supported by the testing of school-age children (both cross sectional and longitudinal) after World War I. Although some of the support was artifactual, other data, such as the constancy of individual IQs through the school years, appeared to provide valid support for the belief. There were, of course, individual cases of varying IQ; these were attributed to measurement error (Jones, 1954).

Additionally, evidence was available to support the view that intelligence was determined by heredity. One area of research involved comparisons of the IQ test correlations between pairs of persons of different genetic relationships (see, for example, Elderton, 1923). The prediction was that the more similar the genetic makeup of the persons, the more similar should be their IQs, and investigations generally found such a relation. Although methodologically flawed (Kamin, 1974, p. 61), these and other studies were viewed as providing empirical support for the assumption that intelligence was determined by heredity. (The recent exposure of Sir Cyril Burt's fraudulent work on the IQ testing of twins who were reared separately has belatedly garnered additional disrepute to this area of research; see Hawkes, 1979).

Predetermined Development

A second belief, which encompassed that of fixed intelligence, was that behavioral development unfolds with age and that both physical and behavioral changes are simple maturational processes. Gesell (1929), a prominent proponent of this developmental view, argued that the appearance of behaviors such as sitting, standing, and walking is determined by the maturation of internal controlling mechanisms. According to this view of developmental progress, a particular child sits alone at 7 months because that child is ready to sit alone.

There was research to support this view. Gesell and Thompson (1929) performed several enrichment studies on identical twins. They found that providing one twin with extra practice in some behavior such as climbing or scissor cutting did not appear to have long-lasting differential effects. Dennis and Dennis (1940) examined the effects of the Hopi practice of cradling their infants for the first year of life. Comparisons of the age of walking of cradled and uncradled babies (as recalled by the mothers) were not significantly different. This indicated that deprivation of early motor experience did not delay the onset of walking.

This view, although theoretically motivated and experimentally supported, was challenged even in the 1920s. There were troubling findings that indicated that the environment did have measurable effects on intelligence. Some researchers found that enriching the environment produced positive effects on the organism; others found that environmental deprivation had negative effects. Explaining away these results often required considerable ingenuity.

Evidence for Environmental Effects on the Development of Intelligence and Behavior

Particularly influential among these studies were the "clinically surprising" findings reported by Skeels and Dye (1939). Two infants in a state orphanage were committed to an institution for the mentally retarded because of their extremely low Kuhlman IQs and behavioral lags. They were placed on a ward with "moron" women aged 18 to 50 (with tested mental ages of 5 to 9 years). Six months later, testing showed their IQs to be near normal. Upon examining the ward environment, it was found that each baby had been "adopted" by one woman and also had received considerable attention and affection from the other women on the ward, as well as from the attendants and nurses. On the basis of these serendipitous findings, Skeels set up a more carefully controlled study. A group of 13 young orphans was transferred to similar wards; on subsequent testing they all showed substantial IQ gains. The comparison group of children who remained in the orphanage showed a decrease in IQ over the same time period. These results, although highly suggestive that IQ was affected by environment, were not conclusive because of differences in initial IQ between experimental and control groups. However, when these subjects were adults, Skeels (1966) performed a follow-up study and found important differences between the two groups. The median educational level achieved by the experimental group was 11.7 years, whereas that of the control group was 4.0 years. Of the control adults, one-third were institutionalized at the time of follow-up, whereas none of the experimental group was institutionalized. These ecologically valid, "real world" measures were convincing.

There were also research reports coming from nursery schools that indicated that preschool experiences had measurable effects on intelligence. In one set of studies, Skeels, Updegraff, Wellman, and Williams (1938) established a model nursery on the grounds of an orphanage. During the 3 years of the project, the researchers found that the group of children who attended the nursery school gained in IQ, whereas a matched comparison group of children who remained in the relatively nonstimulating orphanage environment lost in IQ. Methodological problems, however, allowed the findings to be questioned (McNemar, 1940).

A similar study (Wellman, 1940) of noninstitutionalized children also reported IQ gains attributable to nursery school experiences; these findings were discounted on the methodological ground that the positive results were confounded by self-selection of the treatment group and "regression to the mean" (Honzig, Macfarlane, & Allen, 1948).

A set of studies performed by Spitz (1945; Spitz & Wolf, 1946) was particularly influential in convincing child care professionals that intelligence was modifiable. He compared the development of two groups of institutionalized infants. The infants in the first group ($N = 61$) were reared in an unstimulating foundling home environment after separation from their mothers at 3 months of age. The second group of infants ($N = 69$) was reared in a nursery attached to a penal institution for delinquent girls where the mothers were allowed to interact with their infants everyday. Despite the fact that both groups of infants were nutritionally and physically well cared for, the Developmental Quotients (DQ, measured by the Hetzer–Wolf baby tests, 1928) of the two groups diverged dramatically during the first year. The mean DQ for the foundling home infants dropped from 124 to 72, whereas the mean DQ of the nursery infants made a nonsignificant drop from 120 to 105 (an "average" DQ). A more startling measure of the differential effects of these two environments was the mortality rate. During their first 2 years, 37% of the unmothered foundling home babies died, whereas none of the mothered nursery babies did so. This set of studies had methodological defects (Pinneau, 1955); nevertheless, the findings were influential, particularly within the child care community (Reid, 1979).

A study by Dennis (1960) of children raised in an orphanage in Teheran, Iran, contradicted the broader belief that motor development was a purely maturational phenomenon (although earlier work by Dennis and his colleagues had supported this belief). Dennis studied the development of children whose opportunities for locomotor experience were extremely limited throughout infancy and the toddler period. Compared to American children, their motor development was severely delayed. Among the 2-year-olds, 60% were not sitting, and 85% of 4-year-olds were not walking. Among children who were nutritionally well cared for, severe deprivation of locomotor experience led to extremely retarded locomotor· development.

To summarize the environmental arguments, there were several lines of research that seriously questioned the notion that intelligence (as measured by IQ tests) was solely determined by hereditary factors. Rather, the evidence from children who were severely deprived of environmental and emotional stimulation indicated that a child's intellectual and even motor development was affected by the child's experiences. There was also evidence that by enriching a child's environment it was possible to alter significantly the child's IQ and subsequent life experiences.

Theories that Emphasized Importance of Early Development

In addition to the American early childhood research just summarized, theoretical work in psychology was appearing that argued that early childhood was a qualitatively different and particularly important period of life. These theories, especially the works of Hebb and Piaget, did not address the relative importance of heritability, deprivation, or enrichment but rather focused attention on the early years as a time when special learning takes place (or, perhaps, does not take place at all).

These theories were a contrast to the stimulus–response (S–R) learning theory that was prominent in the 1940s and 1950s. S–R theory viewed learning as the association of stimuli and responses and argued that the process of association was essentially the same throughout life (and across species).

D. O. Hebb (1949), in an attempt to bridge the gap between psychological and physiological theorizing on thought, developed an alternative view of learning. An important aspect of his theory was the contention that early learning by the organism (which he termed "primary learning") was qualitatively different from later learning. He suggested that primary learning was slow and incremental and operated to establish perceptual elements, whereas later learning was essentially conceptual in nature and could be noncontinuous (as in one-trial learning). An effect of this theory was to point out the lack of knowledge concerning learning during the early years. Subsequently, other psychologists and neurophysiologists also argued that early learning was very different from later learning. Lenneberg (1967), for example, argued that there was a critical period for the acquisition of language.

A second theory, one that played a more central role in the early intervention programs of the 1960s, was that of Jean Piaget (1926). Although a leader in the study of intellectual development since the 1920s, his work had little impact on

American psychology until the 1950s. Piaget's concern was to understand the development of intelligence in humans. He felt that the problem of intelligence was to discover the child's way of thinking in his/her attempts to comprehend the world. In contrast to the assumption that a specific amount of intelligence was inherited, Piaget argued that two basic functions were inherited: the tendency to adapt to one's environment and the tendency to organize one's processes into coherent systems. The particular ways in which an organism adapted and organized its processes depended on its environment and its learning history.

Piaget's impact on American developmental psychology and early childhood education has been great. He insisted that intelligence necessarily develops through an unvarying series of stages, which was consistent with Hebb's argument that more advanced learning builds on earlier learning rather than replacing it. Also, Piaget's careful longitudinal studies of his own children produced a picture of children who developed intellectually by continually acting on the world. Piaget's theory did not promote a view of intelligence as a fixed capacity, and a possible implication was that an enriched environment would encourage intellectual development.

These theories and research were integrated by Hunt (1961) into the forceful and convincing argument that intelligence was not determined solely by heredity and that development, both intellectual and physical, was not predetermined. Both environmental deprivation and enrichment had been shown to have measurable, sometimes massive, effects on the course of a child's development. Hunt argued that intelligence was plastic and the environment of the child was a critical factor in his/her development.

A third theory that emphasized the importance of early development came from the longitudinal research community. It was well known that IQ scores of young children tended to be more variable than the scores of older children (Jones, 1954). The test–retest fluctuations among young children had usually been attributed to intrinsic unreliability in the test instruments and also to intrinsic validity problems due to the necessity of testing very young children for psychomotor skills versus testing older children for cognitive and verbal skills. Another plausible explanation, however, was that the early IQ score fluctuations were assessing actual fluctuations in intelligence rather than measurement error. The fluctuations could be indicative of a vulnerability to environmental effects (Horowitz & Paden, 1973).

Bloom (1964) developed a general theory of stability and change in human characteristics based on this argument. Using longitudinal and cross-sectional data to support his view, he proposed that development in intelligence, as in height and other human characteristics, was predictable and could be graphically presented as a curve of development. Based on these curves, Bloom argued that just as people achieve half of their adult height by 2½ years of age, they achieve half of their adult intelligence by 4 years of age.

Bloom's (1964) second proposition, which is directly relevant to the discussion here, was that the effect of the environment is greatest during the period of most rapid normal development of the characteristic and its effect is least in the periods of least rapid normal development. Although acknowledging the relative scarcity of evidence on the effects that changing the environment can have on intelligence, he argued, at a practical level, that to ameliorate the effects of environmental deprivation steps should be taken as early in the individual's development as practically possible (p. 89).

In the mid-1960s, Bloom's (1964) propositions extended the argument that the level of a child's intellectual development could be altered by changing the environment. Although some researchers felt he had drawn erroneous conclusions (Elkind, 1969, p. 184), Bloom's proposition that environmental changes early in life were more effective than changes later in life was influential. This view gave impetus to a newly emerging interest in the cognitive and social environments in which children developed. Additional bodies of research in sociology and psychology directly influenced the early-childhood education boom of the 1960s.

Environmental Deprivation in the United States

From the early 1900s there was evidence that certain groups of Americans performed particularly poorly on intelligence tests. By the 1950s there was also abundant evidence that children of low-income families tended to perform poorly on many kinds of academic achievement tests (Anastasi, 1958). In the mid-1960s the U.S. Office of Education undertook a nationwide investigation of the educational achievement of various ethnic and racial groups (Coleman, Campbell, Hobson, McPartland, Mood, Weinfeld, & York, 1966). It reported, for instance, that the average sixth-grade metropolitan black child was more than two grades behind the average metropolitan white child in mathematics, and by twelfth-grade the black youth was 5 years or more behind the white child. The non-metropolitan black child was at an even greater disadvantage. IQ testing produced similar findings of racial divergence with age. Klaus and Gray (1968) termed this "progressive retardation"; M. Deutsch (1967) called it "cumulative deficit."

Although subject to criticism (Brazziel, 1969, p. 204), these findings were particularly salient to psychologists and educators, coming as they did at a time when theories and research indicated that the level of intellectual development was a function of the child's environment. Despite the fact that most of the evidence for intellectual plasticity had been performed on severely deprived children, the implication was easily drawn that the academic failure of poor and minority children could be attributed to environmental deprivation rather than to genetic deficits. This newer view of intellectual development offered great promise for change. A necessary first step was to determine what aspects of the low-achieving child's environment could be contributing to his/her academic difficulties. A second step was to devise a suitable means for preventing or alleviating these deleterious environmental effects. Throughout the 1960s, a number of researchers and educators applied themselves to these problems.

The question of the effects of different environments on the developing child was not entirely new. Since the 1950s there had been research on social-class differences in attitudes and behaviors, which included child-rearing techniques (Davis & Havighurst, 1946). In contrast to the intelligence of the child, the child's personality had long been considered highly malleable and responsive to the social environment.

In the 1950s and 1960s, social-class comparison research was extended to the investigation of social-class differences that could be relevant to cognitive development. Problems intrinsic to this research technique were also adopted. There has been an almost inevitable confounding of socioeconic status (SES) and race, although attempts have been made to separate the two (see Palmer, this volume). The very real heterogeneity of persons within an SES category and the overlap of characteristics across categories tended to be overlooked. The technique of using the (white) middle-class category as the standard for comparison tended to deify that segment of the population, and there was often the implication that middle-class behaviors and values should be the goal of other groups.

This latter tendency within social-class differences research, although a problem when pushed to extremes, was sometimes justifiable. There has been broad agreement that American schools are predominantly middle class—in the way language is used, in motivational aspects, and in values. If an underlying purpose of a study is to elucidate ways in which the child of a low-income family is at a disadvantage in school, then the middle-class family is the appropriate comparison. An obvious alternative solution to the problem—that of changing the schools—was also proposed (Clark, 1965).

Research on social-class comparisons expanded rapidly in the 1960s. Children of lower-class families were found to be at a disadvantage, for instance, in language and number skills (Loban, 1963); in auditory discrimination (Deutsch, 1965); and in attaining conservation—a Piagetian test of the child's ability to recognize that an initial equivalence of amount of two objects is maintained despite a visible but irrelevant transformation (Almy, Chittenden, & Miller, 1966).

The more central problem, of course, was to identify the environmental factors that could account for these apparent cognitive deficits. Appropriate studies were undertaken. For example, an extensive research program by Hess and Shipman (1967, 1968) investigated relationships between parent–child interactions and SES. Among other results, they found class differences in language, in that lower–SES mothers showed a pattern of language restriction and also in teaching behavior, in that working-class mothers made more "imperative" than "instructive" statements. Keller (1963) reported that lower-class parents spent less time in verbal interaction with their children than did middle-class parents.

A conclusion drawn from this research was that lower-class families were "culturally deprived" as compared to middle-class families. An implication was that the academic (and societal) problems of these children could be attributed to effects of their disadvantaged environment rather than to genetic deficiencies.

The terms *cultural deprivation* and *cultural deficit* require some explanation. In a socially and politically influential book, *The Other America* (1962), Harrington argued that the poor in America grow up with a language of poverty, a psychology of poverty, and a world view of poverty that is so radically different from the one that dominates society that the environment was fairly called a "culture of poverty." (The concept of a culture of poverty was developed by the anthropologist Oscar Lewis, 1968.) This notion of a "culture of the poor" resonated with the theories and research on environmental disadvantage. The terms cultural deprivation and cultural deficit were broadly accepted by social scientists in the early 1960s as a succinct formulation of the critical role of environment in some of the social problems associated with poverty.

As this area of research gained a degree of prominence, the terms cultural deprivation and cultural deficit came under attack. Once it became generally accepted that the development of cognitive abilities could be strongly influenced by environmental factors, the meaning of the term cultural deficit lost its contrast with *genetic deficit*. Standing on its own, the term was open to criticism. Not surprisingly, the criticism led to important clarifications of the underlying concept.

It was rightly argued that children from low-income families and from minority groups were not *deprived of culture* but rather were developing in cultures different from that of the white middle class (Baratz, 1969). Cole and Bruner (1972), on the basis of systematic cross-cultural linguistic and cognitive research, argued that cultural differences reside more in differences in the situations to which various cultural groups apply their skills than to differences in the skills possessed by the groups in question. They argued that apparent cultural deficits arise when an individual is faced with demands to perform in a manner inconsistent with his/her past experience. (This argument refers to basic and general skills, not to highly specific skills.) The authors concluded that the job of educators is not so much to develop new competencies as to help children apply their already-developed competencies in the appropriate situations.

Other researchers drew similar conclusions. It was argued that it was the schools and institutions that required reform, not the children (Clark, 1965; Ginsburg, 1972). It was also argued that the cultural deprivation model "blamed the victim" (Ryan, 1971), because the child was seen as deficient and as the source of the problem rather than as the victim of society's institutions that perpetuated inequality and racism (Baratz & Baratz, 1970).

Despite the aptness of these later criticisms, the cultural deficit model was broadly accepted in the early 1960s as the theoretical basis for attempts to alleviate some of the environmental disadvantages of children of low-income families.

The most appropriate strategies for preventing or alleviating the cognitive disadvantages of these children were yet to be determined. However, the developmental theories and research just reviewed suggested that preschool intervention programs for children of low-income families would be particularly effective. It is important to note here that the theories and research alone cannot account for the great number of such programs, which ranged from small research programs to the huge national project *Head Start*. The social and political milieu of the 1960s must receive credit for that, as discussed in a later section.

Experimental Early Intervention Programs

The intellectual, social, and political climate of the 1960s encouraged psychologists, early childhood educators, and social workers to establish preschool programs. These programs shared the basic assumption that environmental factors played an important role in the cognitive and socioemotional development of the child and that early intervention in the life of the low-income child could have significant, positive, long-term effects. The particular type of intervention was not a settled issue (nor were the expected long-term effects). There were a sufficient number of different views of learning and development to support a great variety of curricula. The newness of the field encouraged innovation, as did the availability of financial support from government and private sources.

These new preschool programs differed from each other in many respects: in the age of the child served (from infancy to 4 or 5 years); in the size and composition of the learning unit (from an individual child or child plus parent, to pairs of children, to groups of children); in the length of intervention (from a few months to 3 years or more); and in the type of curriculum (from highly structured and academic to child centered and oriented around free play).

One subset of these preschool intervention programs is of particular concern here; these are the programs which were developed as research projects. These programs were developed and implemented for the purpose of answering specific research questions, such as Are there measurable positive effects of preschool intervention? or Do these possible effects differ by program type? To answer these and other questions, a research design had to be developed that was, in many ways, quite separate from the development of the preschool curriculum and the program itself.

A research design required collection of baseline data, such as child's IQ, level of mother's education, and occupation of head of household. It usually required development of a control or comparison group from the same population as the program group. Hypotheses had to be specified, and measuring instruments or tests had to be selected or developed. A staff of testers and analysts was necessary along with the teaching staff. Those projects with a longitudinal design required plans for keeping contact with participants so that retesting could be performed at specified intervals.

It is worth stressing here that most of these experimental designs placed as much emphasis on the socioemotional development of the children as on their cognitive development. There was recognition that the distinction between the two areas is not especially meaningful at the early stages of development, because the effects of both cognitive and "non-cognitive" experience are likely to be diffuse and general (Hess, 1968). However, as will be seen, cognitive measures have played a more central role than have those in the socioemotional domain. This differential weighting was largely due to the state of the art in measurement. There are intelligence tests that are reliable and standardized and that have considerable predictive validity. Normative data are available and a small subset of tests is commonly selected for use by most researchers.

By contrast, measures in the affective, motivational, and social competence domains have been psychometrically inadequate. There has been a lack of consensus on how to measure social development; that is, there is disagreement on the validity of the tests that are available. Reliability has been a problem. As a consequence, researchers have rarely selected the same measures, which has had the effect of hindering comparisons across studies. Therefore, despite general agreement that socioemotional development was as important a goal of preschool intervention programs as was cognitive development, when it came to assessments based on experimental findings, cognitive effects have taken precedence.

Moreover, intelligence test results have received more attention than other cognitive measures, such as achievement test scores and school grades. Given the intellectual foundation of the intervention programs, this has some justification. For studies that did not follow their participants into the school years, the use of IQ as the cognitive measure is suitable because IQ does correlate with school performance. It is precisely this predictive validity which makes IQ a useful measure. However, the correlation between IQ and school performance is never perfect. The longitudinal studies of preschool programs did not depend on substitute measures for school performance. The clearly stated criterion measure of several of the more carefully designed longitudinal studies was achievement test scores (see Gray, Ramsey, & Klaus and Schweinhart & Weikart, this volume). Nevertheless, the presence or absence of effects on IQ have received inordinate attention over the years. As will be seen, one effect of the consortium work has been to decrease the importance of IQ as a criterion measure.

The earliest of these preschool education programs began operation in the early 1960s (Gray's Early Training Project, the Deutsches' Institute for Developmental Studies, Beller's Philadelphia Project, and Weikart's Perry Preschool Project). Others appeared shortly thereafter. These programs served as models for Head Start, which began in 1965. The research studies varied in the length of time the project participants were followed, ranging from a final assessment at program completion to assessments continuing through the time of high school completion. By the mid-1970s, most of the research projects started in the 1960s were considered completed, although follow-up data collection was planned and being performed by several researchers.

In general, the early results of these studies showed significant IQ gains during the program; at the time of program completion, participating children displayed higher IQ scores than did children who served as controls. A variety of measures also evidenced positive effects on the children's social, motivational, and emotional behavior. The IQ differences, however, tended to decrease after program completion. Later testing, performed when children were in the second to fifth grades (which was generally several years after program completion) tended to show some positive IQ and reading achievement differences between treatment and control children (see Bronfenbrenner, 1974; individual projects in this volume). The apparent fading of the sizable cognitive gains of the preschool participants was a disappointment to those who believed that relatively short-term preschool intervention experiences would have substantial and lasting effects on intellective competence.

Summary and Conclusions

By the early 1960s a variety of studies had been conducted that indicated that the developmental course of intelligence was responsive to environmental factors rather than being totally determined by heredity. There were also theories, from several areas of research, which argued that early development was qualitatively, or at least quantitatively, different from later development. The inference was made that environmental effects on development would be greatest during the early years of development.

During the 1960s, two distinguishable but intertwined lines of research investigated these ideas. Comparisons of the environments of economically disadvantaged and advantaged children found numerous differences. It appeared likely that these differences could account for SES differences found in children's language, achievement motivation, IQ, and other areas of development. Despite the myriad of criticisms, there did appear to be evidence of cognitively relevant differences in the environments of economically advantaged and disadvantaged children. The evidence lent support to the view that IQ and other cognitive performance differences between children from low- and middle-income homes could be attributable at least in part to environmental influences.

The second line of research assessed the effects of experimental early intervention programs which were developed for the purpose of better preparing children of low-income families for school. These studies investigated a variety of hypotheses and found both cognitive and social gains. A common result was that children who had participated in early intervention programs tended to display higher IQ scores than similar children who had not participated. This was evidence that IQ was modifiable. An additional general finding was that these IQ differences tended to decrease and even disappear within a few years of program termination. This could be interpreted as supplementary evidence of the plasticity of IQ. The question of whether the child's IQ changes reflected changes in underlying cognitive capability or were the result of more superficial performance changes was not so easily answered.

The research in the 1960s surrounding early intervention programs could possibly have ended here. Some questions were answered, and many complexities were revealed which showed that other questions were oversimplified and even irrelevant. Indeed, by 1972, many of these research programs were considered completed by the developers. It is necessary to review the social and political milieu of the 1960s and 1970s for an understanding of the renewed importance of these programs in the mid-1970s.

SOCIOPOLITICAL BACKGROUND OF CONSORTIUM FOR LONGITUDINAL STUDIES

The academic concern over the detrimental effects of poverty on children reflected a growing national realization that, in the midst of prosperity, large groups of Americans were impoverished. In part, poverty was becoming visible because of the mass migration of poor white and black families from rural areas to urban and industrial centers. During the 1950s, for instance, 1,400,000 blacks left the South for cities in the North and West where they replaced the two million whites who had fled to the suburbs (Kravitz, 1969, p. 55). Center-city schools were faced with an influx of children who had received poor schooling; children from southern black schools were at a particular disadvantage.

In the influential book mentioned earlier, *The Other America—Poverty in the United States,* Michael Harrington stated that the poor in America constituted 25% of the total population and argued that "being poor is not one aspect of a person's life in this country; it is his life" (1962, p. 162). Harrington (1962) warned that the nation is:

> beginning the sixties with a most dangerous problem: an enormous concentration of young people who, if they do not receive immediate help, may well be the source of a kind of hereditary poverty new to American society. If this analysis is correct, then the vicious circle of the culture of poverty is, if anything, becoming more intense, more crippling, and problematic because it is increasingly associating itself with the accident of birth [p. 188].

This warning received attention within the Kennedy administration. During the 1960 presidential campaign, John F. Kennedy went to West Virginia to seek the electoral support of traditionally anti-Catholic Protestant ministers. He felt particularly indebted to West Virginia for his election and decided that a program to alleviate poverty would be an appropriate sign of concern and gratitude.

Social Activism in the 1960s

The federal government's involvement in poverty programs (an important part of which was Project Head Start) is also attributable to the civil rights movement. The start of the highly visible civil rights movement can be set in 1954 when the U.S. Supreme Court ruled that "separate but equal" public schools were unconstitutional. Efforts to integrate southern schools were undertaken and demands for other forms of racial equality came from individuals and then from groups. In 1955, Rosa Parks in Montgomery, Alabama, refused to sit at the back of the bus. Nonviolent civil disobedience became the principal tactic of this movement. Martin Luther King, Jr. emerged as the leader of these largely black, Southern church-based activities. In 1960, in various communities, blacks, with white supporters, initiated sit-ins at segregated facilities, such as lunch counters and swimming pools.

The Freedom Ballot in 1963 and Freedom Summer in 1964 brought many northern activists to the South to register voters and organize protests. (Unlike the black movement of the late 1960s the early civil rights movement was consciously integrated.) Involvement of the federal government was deliberate. From the beginning, acts of civil disobedience to local laws were appealed to federal courts for ruling on constitutionality. In addition, national guardsmen were repeatedly mobilized to protect civil rights activists, and the FBI was brought in to investigate civil rights violations.

The "march" became an important instrument of nonviolent protest. The great number of marches, usually organized by established civil rights groups, dramatically displayed the scope of support for civil rights issues. A march that yielded direct political effects was the 1960 March on the Conventions. The demonstration at the Democratic Party Convention in Los Angeles forced the inclusion of a strong civil rights plank in its platform. It was during the 1963 March on Washington, which focused on both economic and racial justice, that Dr. King declared, as reported by Boutwell, Callender, Jr., and Gerber, 1965:

> I have a dream that one day this nation will rise up and live out the true meaning of its creed: 'We hold these truths to be self-evident; that all men are created equal' . . . I have a dream that my four little children will one day live in a nation where they will not be judged by the color of their skin but by the content of their character [p. 157].

Dr. King's dream was enthusiastically supported by many Americans. In addition, there was a sense that this dream could be realized. There was the sense that the prosperous, enlightened United States could erase racial discrimination in the laws, in the schools, and in the labor market.

In retrospect, the 1963 March on Washington was the peak of the early civil rights movement. The movement continued as a force through the 1960s and later; however, it was changing—from an integrated movement to a black movement, and from a nonviolent movement to one more dominated by confrontationists. The buildup of the Vietnam War in 1965 did much to splinter groups which were already dividing on other issues (Harrington, 1973). The ghetto riots that began in 1965 were blatant evidence of change. The assassination of Martin Luther King, Jr., in 1968 marked an end to the early spirit of community.

The civil rights activism of the early 1960s built up broad social support among blacks and whites for racial and economic equality. Many believed the crucial issue of the day was to help more people fully participate in the generally prosperous society (Chilman, 1966). The early years of social activism also forced federal involvement in problems that previously had been recognized as the responsibility of state and local governments.

Federal Government Response to Social Activism

The commitment of the Democratic Party and President Kennedy to aid the poor led to the Human Resources Development Act. It proposed some innovative plans, one of which was the creation of Community Action Agencies at the municipal level, through which federal funds for anti-poverty programs would be channeled. However, the Kennedy administration was unable to get the act passed by Congress. President Lyndon Johnson, after Kennedy's assassination, took responsibility for the act by declaring a "war on poverty". Under its new title, The Economic Opportunity Act, it was passed by Congress in August, 1964. The Office of Economic Opportunity was set up within the Office of the President rather than as a branch within, for instance, the Department of Health, Education, and Welfare. This arrangement allowed the director maximum flexibility in establishing innovative programs and in allocating federal funds. The OEO implemented a wide variety of programs, including Community Action, the Job Corps, Neighborhood Youth Corps, Upward Bound, VISTA, Adult Basic Education, Legal Services, programs for the elderly poor, and, of particular interest here, Project Head Start.

Project Head Start

The federal government traditionally has been reluctant to assume responsibility for child care. Politicians know that "the American social system presumes that barring economic disaster or health crisis, a family should and will care for its children without public intervention" (Steiner, 1976, p. 1).

The reticence of the government to intervene in the lives of children can be seen historically in the paucity of programs for children. The Social Security Act of 1935 established a federal–state program of cash aid to dependent children and a small set of child welfare services. In addition, the United States has an interrupted history of publicly supported day care. During each of the World Wars (and also after the Civil War) day care services were provided for the purpose of freeing women for employment. During the Depression, day care centers were opened under the federal government's Works Progress Administration. The primary purpose was to provide employment for unemployed teachers and domestic workers (Lazar & Rosenberg, 1971). As soon as an emergency ended, federal support for a program was quickly eliminated.

The traditional pattern of restraint in the use of public intervention was challenged by the developmental theories and research presented by Hunt, Bloom and others. These works suggested that the existing social policy of intervening in the child's life from six to seventeen years of age did not adequately meet society's responsibility to children. For example, Bloom's (1964) book concluded:

> Put briefly, the increased ability to predict long-term consequences of environmental forces and developmental characteristics places new responsibilities on the home, the school, and the society. If these responsibilities are not adequately met, society will suffer in the long run [p. 231].

This challenge came at an opportune time—when the ongoing war on poverty program was seen to be in need of a comprehensive project that could show quick results (Steiner, 1976, p. 27).

A multidisciplinary planning committee was assembled by Sargent Shriver, the first director of OEO, to "consider the kinds of programs which might be effective in increasing achievement and opportunities for children of the poor" (Sundquist, 1969, p. 147). The panel proposed a comprehensive preschool intervention program which could contribute significantly to meeting the critical needs of development during early childhood.

This proposal received a positive reception. Sargent Shriver was familiar with, and impressed by, Susan Gray's Early Training Project. Mrs. Lyndon Johnson (who became the honorary Chairperson of Project Head Start) had visited the Deutsches' Institute for Developmental Studies Preschool Program in East Harlem (M. Deutsch, 1981). President Johnson was easily convinced of the need for services for the very young; he had at one time been a teacher and school principal for children of poor Mexican-American families in Texas.

The Planning Committee made a series of recommendations which were accepted by the OEO. The program was to contain five components: an education program, with one teacher and two aides for every 15 children, to encourage the development of language skills, self-reliance, and self-esteem; a health program that was to provide complete medical and dental examinations and immunizations; a program of parental involvement as nonprofessional teacher aides and as participants in classes on a variety of subjects, such as child–rearing and English language; a nutrition program which would provide at least one hot meal and one snack each day for the children and nutrition information for parents; and social and psychological services through referral and recommendation by the social services staff. The group agreed to recommend an 8-week summer program for 100,000 children. The decision to forego a small pilot program was made on the basis of the political realities of government support and public interest. The Planning Committee recommendations became the official OEO statement of rationale and objectives.

In late February, 1965, President Johnson announced the establishment of Project Head Start, which would open its doors to children that very summer. Julius Richmond, a noted pediatrition, researcher, and teacher, was named as its director. Letters were sent to 3500 community public health directors, mayors, school superintendents, and social services commissioners announcing the availability of funds for summer Head Start programs. Special, and largely successful, efforts were made to involve the 300 poorest counties in the country.

The response to the announcements was overwhelming, and the projected enrollment was raised several times. A tremendous amount of work was accomplished at both the federal and community levels. Teachers were trained, the Rainbow Series of pamphlets was produced, applications were processed and consultants were sent out to help program organizers. In each community it was necessary to find equipment, hire staff, recruit volunteers, make medical and health arrangements and publicize the program.

Three months after President Johnson's announcement the first programs were underway. In the summer of 1965, more than half a million children were enrolled in more than 13,000 centers. The programs involved 41,000 teachers, 46,000 nonprofessional aides (drawn from the poor), and 256,000 volunteers (Richmond, Stipek, & Zigler, 1979).

The quality of these early programs varied tremendously. Some programs were able to provide well-trained teachers with appropriate materials for small classes. Others were less successful. Nevertheless, enthusiasm was high among both staff and parents (Hymes, 1979, pp. 93–97).

In the fall of 1965, on the advice of the Head Start Steering Committee (formerly the Planning Committee), President Johnson announced that year-round centers for 3- and 4-year-olds would be established in addition to the summer programs. A few such centers opened that fall and, by 1967, 200,000 children attended full-year programs.

Evaluations of Head Start

A recognition of the necessity for evaluation of Head Start was present from its inception. However, Head Start's hurried establishment as a full-fledged national program precluded a closely monitored, carefully evaluated pilot effort. Once Head Start was established, program evaluations were undertaken. In the summer of 1965, Head Start funded a national random-sample postprogram evaluation, using cognitive, linguistic, and affective measures (Planning Research Corporation, 1966). Other evaluations were conducted for the 1966 full-year programs and also for the 1967, 1968, and 1969 programs, using pre/postdesigns and a variety of implementation and outcome measures. None of these were true experimental tests with random assignment of children to treatment and control status. These and additional Head Start findings were summarized by Edith Grotberg (1969), then National Head Start Research Coordinator.

Most studies showed immediate but not durable benefits to the children on aptitude and achievement tests. Grotberg (1969) described a common pattern that she termed "the catch-up effect." During the first 1 to 3 years after program completion, the rate of gain of participants leveled off, then slowly declined. The nonparticipants, upon entering public school, showed a developmental spurt. Although their rate of gain was less steep than among the participants during preschool, that gain was enough eventually to reduce the once highly reliable gap between the two groups to nonsignificant levels. The controls had caught up with the preschool children. For both groups, the final levels suggested poor academic performance—the level of performance predictable from the low SES of the families.

Project Head Start also funded a study of Head Start's impact on community institutions, by comparing health and education services available for children in both Head Start and non-Head Start communities. The Kirschner Associates report, *Community Impacts of Head Start* (1970), found many more identifiable incidents of improved service delivery in the Head Start communities; for instance, health departments had introduced new services for preschool children.

Westinghouse Report

The most widely known of the Head Start evaluations was the Westinghouse Report (Westinghouse Learning Corp., 1969), which was one of the first evaluations funded by the OEO Evaluation Division after Head Start was transferred to the Children's Bureau. It was designed to provide the quickest possible statement of average long-term effects of Head Start, by comparing Head Start children with non-Head Start children on standardized tests 1, 2, and 3 years after entering public school.

The study used a posttest-only design. A sample of 225 Head Start centers across the country was selected, of which 104 agreed to be included; 70% of these centers had provided summer-only programs, and the remainder had provided full-year programs. A sample of children who attended these centers between September 1966 and August 1967, and who at the time of assessment were in first, second, and third grades in the local schools, comprised the experimental groups. A comparison group, which was matched for age and sex, was developed from children in the same grades and schools. The children were administered a series of cognitive and affective tests, the parents were interviewed, elementary school teachers performed ratings of the children, and directors of the Head Start centers were interviewed.

Children who had attended summer-only programs displayed no measurable advantage over comparison children in any area of academic testing. On only two of the cognitive measures did full-year Head Start children score higher than comparison children; these were on the Metropolitan Readiness Tests (administered in first grade) and on two subtests of the Illinois Test of Psycholinguistic Abilities (ITPA). Tests of affective development, which tend to have inadequate psychometric qualities, showed Head Start children did not score higher than comparison children at any of the three grade levels.

When analyses were performed on subgroups of the centers, a few differential effects were found (mainly on subtests of cognitive measures): Head Start children who were in the southeastern United States or core cities, or who were black, tended to score higher than did their matched controls. From parent interviews it was found that parents of Head Start children expressed strong approval of the program and its effects on their children. These differential findings were confirmed by Smith and Bissell (1970), who used alternative statistical tests to attempt to correct for the higher socioeconomic status of the comparison children. They concluded that Head Start was effective for children who needed it most.

The Westinghouse authors (1969) concluded, on the basis of the few main effects, that "although this study indicates that full-year Head Start appears to be a more effective compensatory education program than summer Head Start, its benefits cannot be described as satisfactory [p. 11]."

The first criticisms were made even before the contract to perform the study was announced, and extensive criticism continued for several years after the study's completion. Many Head Start planners and researchers were dismayed by the premise of the research design, which was that Head Start's positive effects should be measurable not only immediately after the program but also several years later. The posttest-only design was criticized for insensitivity, because it precluded development of a true control group through random assignment of children. As it turned out, the children in the comparison group did belong to families of higher socioeconomic status and these preprogram differences had to be adjusted statistically. There was also a lack of documentation about the type and quality of the Head Start programs themselves.

The restricted range of dependent variables was viewed as inadequate for a program with such a broad range of objectives (which included improving the health and nutrition of the children, educating and involving the parents in the community, and improving the social as well as the cognitive competencies of the children). This problem was compounded by the almost complete lack of adequate measures of affective and motivational development, which placed undue emphasis on the cognitive measures. Indeed, an important effect of the Westinghouse Report (1969) for many people was to define the goal of Head

Start as the production of cognitive gains (Datta, 1976, p. 165). The representativeness of the sample was criticized, because more than half of the original sites refused to participate. Although there was a large enough sample of summer-only children to allow generalization, the sample of full-year children was distressingly small.

Despite these criticisms, the Westinghouse study was rapidly performed. The report, drafts of which were circulating in early 1969, announced findings and made recommendations that had several specifiable effects on Head Start (which are treated more fully by Datta, 1976). One recommendation of the report was to phase out summer programs. The shift from summer to full-year programs was particularly dramatic in 1970 when approximately half as many summer programs were funded as the year before; by 1977 there were only 200 summer programs (Richmond et al., 1979). The report was also considered influential in restraining the expansion of Head Start. The total yearly enrollment peaked in 1966 at 725,000 children, of whom 25% were in full-year programs; by 1977, 350,000 children were served, 95% of whom were in full-year programs (Richmond et al., 1979). The drop in enrollment was especially dramatic in 1970 when many summer programs ended.

Another effect of the report's findings was to provide support for President Nixon's plan, in 1969, to change the status of Head Start from operational to experimental. This meant that rather than serving all eligible children, Head Start needed to serve only a small proportion of eligible children (Datta, 1976, p. 137). This status change was related to the administration's decision to move Head Start out of OEO and into the newly created Office of Child Development (OCD) in the Department of Health, Education and Welfare (HEW).

Edward Zigler, the first director of OCD, urged that Head Start become more innovative, and several major experimental projects were undertaken. For example, Home Start, from 1972–1975, trained parents to work with their children in the home. In 1972, the Child Development Associate Program was initiated to train workers in Head Start and day-care centers. (The switch from summer to full-year programs increased the need for trained workers.) It should be recognized that Head Start had been developing innovative programs before the Westinghouse Report (1969). Parent and Child Centers (later, Parent and Child Development Centers) were launched in 1967 to serve children from birth to 3 years, along with their families.

The Westinghouse Report (1969) had other, broader effects on policy makers and on the public, for instance, on evaluation methodology and on attitudes toward the value of scientific evaluations. Some of the broader effects cannot be attributed solely to the Westinghouse Report, however, because other events that occurred during this same period were also relevant.

Criticisms of the Bases of Head Start

In 1969, Jensen reviewed the findings of intervention programs for young children from low-income families and concluded, "compensatory education has been tried and it apparently has failed [p. 2]." He raised again the heredity–environment issue, arguing that this apparent failure should come as no surprise because genetic potential contributed significantly more to intellectual capabilities than did one's environment. Despite arguments that the nature/nurture issue was irrelevant, because even the most staunch hereditarians acknowledged that the environment played some role in intellectual development (Zigler, 1975), Jensen's report appeared to provide theoretical justification for the slim Westinghouse findings. In addition, the Coleman Report on Equality of Educational Opportunity (1966) had concluded that individual differences in academic achievement were more related to family variables (SES and parent education) than to measures of school quality. This reinforced the notion that education was a relatively weak form of intervention. Also during this time, Moynihan (1969), who in 1969 became an advisor to President Nixon, was arguing that the War on Poverty was misconceived. Moreover, by this time, national priorities had shifted to the war in Vietnam and away from social action.

In this environment in the fall of 1970 the Office of Management and Budget (OMB) attempted to cut the Head Start budget. Zigler, as Director of OCD, played a pivotal role in convincing the new Secretary of HEW, Elliot Richardson, to fight OMB for Head Start's survival (Datta, 1976). Parental enthusiasm and community support for Head Start as well as congressional popularity were also important in this struggle, which Richardson won. Head Start funding was not cut in 1971, nor was it cut in succeeding years, although during the 1970s the yearly increases in appropriations rarely kept pace with inflation (Richmond et al., 1979, p. 142). In 1974 another effort to cut Head Start's budget was partially deflected. In 1976 the program was viewed as somewhat secure when a 3-year extension was recommended by the administration and again in 1981 when it was included in the Reagan Administration's "safety net."

Summary and Conclusions

Head Start has provided a comprehensive set of services for a proportion of the nation's economically deprived families. It has encouraged and supported research on early childhood development and initiated a number of innovative service programs. This unique national program developed despite government reluctance to interfere in the traditional domain of the family. This hesitance was overcome by the conjunction of new theories on the developing child and the political purposes of two presidents, who were responding to a relatively brief period of national social concern for the poor. As expected, Head Start became the most favored of the OEO-initiated programs. Both community and congressional support have kept it alive (although often not growing) through some difficult periods.

The relative decrease in federal financial support for Head Start in the late 1960s and the 1970s should be partly attributed to a changing national mood. There were increasing doubts about the federal strategy of financing individual services and encouraging community action and also about the benefits of compensatory education. The Westinghouse Report (1969) was heralded as justification for revising national policy. The report had immediate, specific effects, such as hastening the switch from summer to full-year programs and encouraging a more experimental approach to publicly funded early-childhood intervention. Although designed to provide a definitive conclusion, the Westinghouse Report never recommended the abolition of Head Start.

CONSORTIUM FOR LONGITUDINAL STUDIES

The Westinghouse Report (1969) played an important role in dissuading Americans from the belief that a brief, one-shot preschool intervention effort could permanently offset the debilitating effects of poverty. It did not, however, prove that Head Start was without benefits. Indeed, many preschool supporters were satisfied with more modest goals, such as to improve "the quality of life for the child and the family at the time of preschooling and better equip him to make the entry into primary school [Bernard Van Leer Foundation, 1972, p. 4]." The increased enrollments in a variety of privately supported early childhood education programs during the 1970s, especially among middle- and upper-income families, indicated that many Americans did not require research evidence of the efficacy of preschool programs before making use of their services (Datta, 1976).

It was clear, however, that evidence would be required for there to be continued government support of Head Start. It was generally true that the Westinghouse results, as well as the findings of the smaller, experimental intervention programs, indicated that early positive effects on aptitude and achievement test scores faded after several years. However, this was not proof that all effects had disappeared, particularly given the unsatisfactory measures available for assessment.

Many researchers recognized that it was premature to judge the effects of early intervention programs while the participants were still so young. A stated objective of most programs, less grandiose than breaking the cycle of poverty, was to improve school performance. Jensen (1969), in his review, concluded that, "The proper evaluation of such compensatory education programs should therefore be sought in their effects on actual scholastic performance rather than in how much they raise the child's IQ [p. 59]." Mrs. Lyndon Johnson, when asked in 1965 what the government hoped to gain from Head Start, had replied that they hoped for fewer dropouts from school (Zigler & Valentine, 1979, pp. 45–46). Evidence for such effects was hardly available in the early 1970s.

It was in this atmosphere that the Administration for Children, Youth and Families (ACYF, the successor of OCD) agreed to support a novel evaluative approach to the question of the efficacy of preschool programs. The traditional approach would have been to set up a large longitudinal study of children who were randomly assigned to treatment and control status at 3 years of age. After pretesting both groups, the treatment children would attend a well-documented Head Start program. Ideally, these children would be followed through their high school years. Such an experiment would necessarily require more than 15 years.

A valid substitute for a prospective longitudinal approach would be to collect follow-up data on children who had participated in the pioneer experimental early intervention programs of the 1960s. The research designs and the fact that they served children of low-income families made these programs especially well-suited for assessing the possible long-term effects of preschool intervention programs. ACYF agreed to fund this latter approach through an independent analytical group headed by Irving Lazar at Cornell University.

A literature search was undertaken to identify the set of early experimental programs. A few programs (Gray, Ramsey, & Klaus, this volume; Schweinhart & Weikart, this volume) were engaged in collecting follow-up data, but it was recognized that many programs had not kept in contact with their participants. A high rate of attrition was expected, so the literature search was restricted to programs with a fairly large number of participants. A total of 15 early education studies by 12 research groups was identified. The principal investigators of these groups were approached and all but one agreed to join together to assess the long-term effectiveness of early education.

In 1975 the Consortium for Longitudinal Studies, originally known as the Consortium for Developmental Continuity, was formed as a voluntary association of independent investigators. The aim of the Consortium was to provide a general assessment of the long-term effectiveness of early education across different programs. The members agreed:

1. To send their original raw data to an independent group in Ithaca, New York, for recording, formatting, and independent analysis.
2. To work together to develop a common protocol for the collection of follow-up data from their original experimental and control subjects.
3. To seek out their subjects, collect the common data, and send it to Ithaca for analysis.

In addition, it was agreed that the investigators would be free to collect additional data and to publish analyses of their own studies. In turn, the Ithaca group was to be responsible for the joint analyses and to be free to publish those results. The present volume is the culmination of this collaborative effort.

There have been many advantages to this collaboration. Collectively, the Consortium overcame many of the shortcomings of earlier evaluations. Because the participant programs were designed as research or demonstration projects, control or comparison groups were available for almost all the programs. Detailed data on the children and families had been collected before the programs began and also for several years after program completion. The investigative collaboration allowed collection of common follow-up data and the large sample size permitted analyses not possible with smaller sample sizes. In 1975, the preschool participants were 8 to 18 years old; this meant they had sufficient school experience to allow assessment of their school competence, using ecologically valid measures (such as assignment to special education and graduation from high school). The children were old enough to allow testing for any long-term effects of early experience on attitudes and values.

The diversity of programs provided an unusually broad base for generalization to early intervention programs. These programs served children in several areas of the country, at different ages, for differing periods of time, and with a wide variety of curricula. Although the programs varied tremendously, they all attempted to provide poor children with increasing social and cognitive competence. In a broad sense they were replications—independent tests of the hypothesis that early educational intervention has positive effects on the development of children of low-income families. The value of independently replicated experiments is that chance findings tend to cancel each other out; thus, common findings across projects should be accepted as convincing evidence of an effect.

The disadvantages of this collaboration also merit attention. It is important to look more closely at the effect of statistically canceling out dissimilar findings of different projects. The pooled analyses were designed to allow a low probability that a false hypothesis of a lasting effect would be accepted. This strategy necessarily increased the probability that a false hypothesis of no effect would fail to be rejected. That is, in setting a stringent criterion for a Type I error, the likelihood of a Type II error is increased. In the search for findings that are common across projects, there is the danger of dismissing a real effect in one project as merely a chance variation because it did not occur in several projects.

An unavoidable problem in pooling the findings of originally independent projects was that different projects collected different data. Any analyses of original data across projects were necessarily limited to the measures that were common across the projects. Some questions, including site-specific ones, could not be addressed. For instance, it was not possible to make curriculum comparisons because curricular differences were confounded with subject and site differences. Fortunately, the projects of two Consortium members (Karnes, Shwedel, & Williams, this volume, and Miller & Bizzell, this volume) did compare several curricula.

The present collaboration was also hampered by a restricted budget. In contrast to the millions available in the 1960s for early education, there was relatively little monetary support for an evaluation of preschool effectiveness in the mid-1970s. A common view was that at a time when Head Start's future was shaky this collaboration would provide another "nail in the coffin." The small budget limited the follow-up information that could be collected. Budget restrictions exacerbated the unavoidable difficulties of collaboration; many problems could not be settled to everyone's satisfaction.

Collaboration by so many well-known researchers presented unexpected professional difficulties. Although individual investigators were free to publish reports on their own new findings (and several did), the products of the collaboration (articles, a monograph, and public recognition) tended to be credited to the Ithaca group rather than to the 11 individual investigators. In the academic world, where professional recognition of one's work is the stock in trade, the almost inevitable loss of individual recognition was costly. It is to the credit of the individual investigators that the promise of providing a definitive answer to the question of long-term effects of preschool was worth this loss of recognition.

The work of the Consortium has attained some prominence. As is detailed in the pooled analyses chapter and in each of the chapters of the principal investigators, lasting effects of preschool education have been demonstrated. These effects were not simply on IQs but also on actual school performance and events. The most significant of these positive effects is that children who attended a preschool program, compared to similar children who did not, were less likely to have been assigned to special education classes and less likely to have failed a grade during their school careers.

Because the consortium programs were not actual Head Start programs (with the exception of the Planned Variation Program [Miller & Bizzell, this volume] and the Follow Through Program [Seitz, Apfel, Rosenbaum, & Zigler, this volume]), caution must be exercised in making generalizations to Head Start. These programs were closely supervised and carefully documented in ways that Head Start programs generally were not; however, the Consortium programs were similar to Head Start in terms of the general curricular goals and target population. It is recognized that these experimental early intervention programs are examples of what Head Start could be rather than what it has been.

The Consortium findings have played a role in bolstering Head Start's position. In 1977, Congress increased the appropriation for Head Start beyond that requested by the Carter administration. In early 1981, in the midst of federal budget slashing, President Reagan (1981) announced, "There will be no cut in Project Head Start . . . ." As this chapter is written, Head Start is again threatened with reduction or dismantling. Whether research evidence, congressional support, and general popularity will sustain Head Start remains to be seen.

The Consortium findings also have had a buoying effect on the broader area of early childhood education. Current program developers and supporters are referring to Consortium findings as evidence that their programs will also be efficacious in the long run (Minnesota Council on Quality Education, 1981, p. 51; Caldwell, 1981).

Summary

The Consortium for Longitudinal Studies, formed in 1975, has been a unique collaboration of independent early-childhood education researchers that investigated the question of long-term effects of preschool education experiences on children of low-income families. Original data from 11 different early intervention programs were reanalyzed, follow-up data were gathered on program participants and control group members, and results were statistically pooled. This effort has provided convincing evidence that high-quality preschool education programs had positive, long-term effects on the subsequent school experiences of participating children.

REFERENCES

Almy, M., Chittenden, E., & Miller, P. *Young children's thinking: Studies of some aspects of Piaget's theory.* New York: Teachers College Press, 1966.

Anastasi, A. Heredity, environment, and the question "How?". *Psychological Review,* 1958, *65,* 197–208.

Baratz, J. C. A bi-dialectical task for determining language proficiency in economically disadvantaged Negro children. *Child Development,* 1969, *40,* 889–901.

Baratz, S. S., & Baratz, J. C. Early childhood intervention: The social science base of institutional racism. *Harvard Educational Review,* 1970, *40*(1), 29–50.

Bernard Van Leer Foundation. *Summary Report and Conclusions: Seminar in Curriculum in Compensatory Early Childhood Education.* Jerusalem: Bernard Van Leer Foundation, 1972.

Binet, A., & Simon, T. Sur la necessite d'establis un diagnostic scientifique des etats inferieurs de l'intelligence. *L'annee Psychologique,* 1905, *11,* 191.

Bloom, B. S. *Stability and change in human characteristics.* New York: Wiley, 1964.

Boutwell, W. D., Callender, Jr., W. P., & Gerber, R. E. *Great speeches from Pericles to Kennedy.* New York: Scholastic Book Services, 1965.

Brazziel, W. F. A letter from the South. *Harvard Educational Review,* 1969, Reprint Series no. 2, 200–208.

Bronfenbrenner, U. *A report on longitudinal programs:* (Vol. II: *Is early intervention effective?* DHEW Publication No. (OHD) 74–24, 1974.

Burt, C., Jones, E., Miller, E., & Moodie, W. *How the mind works.* New York: Appleton-Century-Crofts, 1934.

Caldwell, B. *Early childhood education—Once again, born again.* Keynote address to New York State Council for Children Conference, Buffalo, N.Y., May 1, 1981.

Chilman, C. S. *Growing up poor: An overview and analysis of childrearing and family life patterns associated with poverty.* Washington, D.C., U.S. DHEW, Welfare Administration, Division of Research (USGPO), 1966.

Clark, K. B. *Dark ghetto: Dilemmas of social power.* New York: Harper & Row, 1965.

Cole, M., & Bruner, J. S. Cultural differences and inferences about psychological processes. *American Psychologist,* 1972, *26*(1), 867–876.

Coleman, J., S., Campbell, E. Q., Hobson, C. F., McPartland, J., Mood, A. M., Weinfeld, F. D., & York, R. L. *Equality of educational opportunity.* Washington, D.C.: U.S. Government Printing Office, 1966.

Darwin, C. *Origin of the species.* London: Murray, 1859.

Datta, L. The impact of the Westinghouse/Ohio Evaluation on the development of Project Head Start: An examination of the immediate and longer-term effects and how they came about. In C. Abt (Ed.), *The evaluation of social programs.* Beverly Hills, Calif.: Sage Publications, Inc., 1976.

Davis, A., & Havighurst, R. J. Social class and color differences in child-rearing. *American Sociological Review,* 1946, *11,* 698–710.

Dennis, W. Causes of retardation among institutional children. *Journal of Genetic Psychology,* 1960, *96,* 47–59.

Dennis, W., & Dennis, M. G. The effects of cradling practices upon the onset of walking in Hopi children. *Journal of Genetic Psychology,* 1940, *56,* 77–86.

Deutsch, M. The role of social class in language development and cognition. *American Journal of Orthopsychiatry,* 1965, *35*(1), 78–88.

Deutsch, M. Personal communication. May, 1981.

Deutsch, M. *The disadvantaged child.* New York: Basic Books, 1967.

Dewey, J., & Dewey, E. *Schools of tomorrow.* New York: Dutton, 1915.

Elderton, E. M. A summary of the present position with regard to the inheritance of intelligence. *Biometrika,* 1923, *14,* 378–408.

Elkind, D. Conceptions of intelligence. *Harvard Educational Review,* 1969, Reprint Series no. 2, 176–185.

Freud, S. *Beyond the pleasure principle.* (Translated from second German edition by C. J. M. Hubback.) New York: Boni & Liveright, 1922.

Galton, F. *Hereditary genius: An inquiry into its laws and consequences.* London: Macmillan, 1869.

Gesell, A. Maturation and infant behavior patterns. *Psychological Review,* 1929, *36,* 307–319.

Gesell, A., & Thompson, H. Learning and growth in identical twin infants. *Genetic Psychological Monograph,* 1929, *6,* 1–24.

Ginsburg, H. *The myth of the deprived child.* Englewood Cliffs, New Jersey: Prentice-Hall, 1972.

Grotberg, E. *Review of Head Start research, 1965–1969.* Washington, DC: OEO Pamphlet 1608:13, 1969. (ED028308)

Harrington, M. *The other America: Poverty in the United States.* New York: Macmillan, 1962.

Harrington, M. *Fragments of the century.* New York: Dutton, 1973.

Hawkes, N. Tracing Burt's descent to scientific fraud. *Science,* August 17, 1979, *205,* 673–675.

Hebb, D. O. *The organization of behavior.* New York: Wiley, 1949.

Hess, R. D. Early education as socialization. In R. D. Hess & R. M. Bear (Eds.), *Early education: Current theory, research and action.* Chicago: Aldine, 1968.

Hess, R. D., & Shipman, V. Cognitive elements in maternal behavior. In J. P. Hill (Ed.), *Minnesota Symposia on Child Psychology* (Vol. 1). Minneapolis: University of Minnesota Press, 1967.

Hess, R. D., & Shipman, V. Maternal influences upon early learning: The cognitive environments of urban pre-school children. In R. D. Hess & R. M. Bear (Eds.), *Early education: Current theory, research and action.* Chicago: Aldine, 1968.

Hetzer, H., & Wolf, K. Eine Testerie fur das erste *Lebensjahr. Z. Psychol.,* 1928, 107, 62–104.

Honzig, M. P., Macfarlane, J. W., & Allen, L. The stability of mental test performance between two and 18 years. *Journal Experimental Education,* 1948, *4,* 309–324.

Horowitz, F. D., & Paden, L. Y. The effectiveness of environmental programs. In B. Caldwell & H. N. Ricciuti (Eds.), *Review of child development research* (Vol. 3), *Child Development and social policy.* Chicago: University of Chicago Press, 1973.

Hunt, J. McV. *Intelligence and experience.* New York: Ronald Press, 1961.

Hymes, J. L. Head Start, A retrospective view: The founders. In E. Zigler & J. Valentine (Eds.), *Project Head Start: A legacy of the war on poverty.* New York: Free Press, 1979.

Jensen, A. R. How much can we boost IQ and scholastic achievement? *Harvard Educational Review,* 1969, Reprint Series no. 2, 1–23.

Jones, H. E. The environment and mental development. In L. Carmichael (Ed.), *Handbook of child psychology.* New York: Wiley, 1954.

Kamin, L. J. *The science and politics of I.Q.* Potomac, Md.: Lawrence Erlbaum Associates, 1974.

Keller, S. The social world of the urban slum child: Some early findings. *American Journal of Orthopsychiatry,* 1963, *33,* 823–831.

Kirschner Associates. *A national survey of the impacts of Head Start centers on community institutions.* Washington, D.C.: Office of Economic Opportunity, May 1970. (EDO45195)

Klaus, R. A., & Gray, S. W. The Early Training Project for disadvantaged children: A report after five years. *Monographs of the Society for Research in Child Development*, 1968, *33*, (4, Serial No. 120).

Kravitz, S. The Community Action Program—Past, present and future. In J. L. Sundquist (Ed.), *Perspectives on poverty* (Vol. II): *On fighting poverty, perspectives from experience*. New York: Basic Books, 1969.

Lazar, I., & Rosenberg, M. E. Day care in America. In E. Grotberg (Ed.), *Day care: Resources for decisions*. Office of Economic Opportunity, 1971.

Lenneberg, E. H. *Biological foundations of language*. New York: Wiley, 1967.

Lewis, O. *A study of slum culture: Backgrounds for La Vida*. New York: Random House, 1968.

Loban, W. D. *The language of elementary school children*. Champaign, Ill.: National Council of Teachers of English, 1963.

McMillan, M. *The nursery school*. London: Dent, 1919.

McNemar, Q. A critical examination of the University of Iowa studies of environmental influences upon the IQ. *Psychological Bulletin*, 1940, *37*, 63–92.

Minnesota Council on Quality Education. *A study of policy issues related to early childhood and family education in Minnesota. A report to the Minnesota Legislature*. St. Paul, Minn.: Minnesota Council on Quality Education, 1981.

Montessori, M. *The Montessori method*. (trans. Ann E. George, 1912) New York: Schochen Books, 1964.

Moynihan, D. P. *Maximum feasible misunderstanding*. New York: Free Press, 1969.

Piaget, J. *The language and thought of the child*. New York: Harcourt, Brace, 1926.

Pinneau, S. R. The infantile disorders of hospitalism and anaclitic depression. *Psychological Bulletin*, 1955, *52*, 429–459.

Planning Research Corporation. *Results of the Summer 1965 Project Head Start* (Vols. 1 and 2). May 6, 1966. (EDO18250)

Reagan, Ronald. State of the Union message on economic recovery. *Vital Speeches of the Day*, March 15, 1981 (Vol. XLVII), No. 11.

Reid, J. H. In, A. W. Shyne (Ed), *Child welfare perspectives: Selected papers of Joseph H. Reid*. New York: Child Welfare League of America, 1979.

Richmond, J. B., Stipek, D. J., & Zigler, E. A decade of Head Start. In E. Zigler & J. Valentine (Eds.), *Project Head Start: A legacy of the war on poverty*. New York: Free Press, 1979.

Rusk, R. R. *The doctrines of the great educators*. New York: St. Martin's Press, 1967.

Ryan, W. *Blaming the victim*. New York: Pantheon, 1971.

Skeels, H. M. Adult status of children with contrasting life experiences: A follow-up study. *Monographs of the Society for Research in Child Development*, 1966, *31*, no. 3.

Skeels, H. M., & Dye, H. B. A study of the effects of differential stimulation on mentally retarded children. *Proceedings and Addresses of the American Association on Mental Deficiency*, 1939, *44*, 114–136.

Skeels, H. M., Updegraff, R., Wellman, B. L., & Williams, H. M. A study of environmental stimulation: An orphanage preschool project. *University of Iowa Studies in Child Welfare*, 1938, *15*, no. 4.

Smith, M. S., & Bissell, J. S. Report analysis: The impact of Head Start. *Harvard Educational Review*, February 1970, *40*, 51–104.

Spitz, R. A. Hospitalism: An inquiry into the genesis of psychiatric conditions in early childhood, Part I. *Psychoanalytic Study of the Child*, 1945, *1*, 53–74.

Spitz, R. A., & Wolf, K. M. The smiling response: A contribution to the ontogenesis of social relations. *Genetic Psychology Monographs*, 1946, *34*, 57–125.

Steiner, G. Y. *The children's cause*. Washington, D.C.: Brookings Institution, 1976.

Sundquist, J. L. (Ed.). *On fighting poverty. Perspectives on poverty* (Vol. II). New York: Basic Books, 1969.

Wellman, B. L. Iowa studies on the effects of schooling. *Yearbook National Sociological Studies in Education*, 1940, *39*, 377–399.

Westinghouse Learning Corporation. *The impact of Head Start: An evaluation of the effects of Head Start on children's cognitive and affective development.* Executive Summary, Ohio University report to the Office of Economic Opportunity. Washington, D.C.: Clearinghouse for Federal Scientific and Technical Information, June 1969. (EDO36321)

Zigler, E. Has it really been demonstrated that compensatory education is without value? *American Psychologist*, 1975, *30*, 935–937.

Zigler, E. & Valentine, J. *Project Head Start: A legacy of the war on poverty.* New York: Free Press, 1979.

2

The Early Training Project
1962–1980

Susan W. Gray
Barbara K. Ramsey
Rupert A. Klaus
George Peabody College for Teachers
of Vanderbilt University

Introduction

Each sample in the Consortium analyses has its idiosyncratic characteristics as well as points of similarity with the others in the group. Our participants are all black and are from small towns in the Southeast. From the data on demographic and family characteristics presented in Chapter 13 one could argue that our families are possibly the most disadvantaged of the entire Consortium. From any point of view the sample clearly consists of a group of families hard pressed in 1962 to provide a minimum level of adequacy in the daily lives of their children.

The Early Training Project was designed and shaped during the beginning years of the 1960s. The original impetus was the concern of local school officials with progressive retardation observed in the elementary school that at the time served the black children of the town, almost all of whom came from low-income families. The majority of the white children from low-income homes had been zoned into a county school rather than the local city school. Thus, the school officials had no basis of comparison for the black school except the other city schools that enrolled upper-lower- or middle-class whites. We thought the progressive retardation observed was more likely to be a social class phenomenon than a racial one. Because of the makeup of the schools at that time, however, we chose the low-income blacks because we wished to follow them through several years in the city school system.

We saw our task as attempting to answer the question of whether it was indeed possible to offset progressive retardation. Our chosen strategy was to design an intervention ''package'' of variables that appeared to be related to school retardation or progress and would be possible to manipulate. We attempted to plan the

33

intervention package so that it would be feasible to replicate or to adopt on a wide scale, should it prove successful. We decided upon a pattern of intensive intervention periods during the summer months, when both staff and space were more available than in the rest of the year and upon an abbreviated program during the fall, winter, and spring months.

The major intervention phase began in May 1962 and extended through the summer of 1965. After that time only follow-up testing and interviewing were done. The first follow-up phase of the study extended from 1966 to 1968. The second follow-up phase began in 1975 and extended into 1980. At the beginning of this last phase most of the young people were completing their public schooling, and by the end of the period a few were in their third or fourth year of college.

The first follow-up of the study was concerned almost entirely with the question of offsetting progressive retardation. The important criterion was to be school achievement in second grade, and later in the fourth. The high school follow-up, however, was undertaken for somewhat different reasons, although our concern with possible enduring effects of the intervention program remained. About a year before the Consortium on Longitudinal Studies was formed, we began to plan the high school follow-up. At that time there were three topics with which we were primarily concerned. There were also some subsidiary questions of interest.

Our first topic was the one the Consortium has pursued: Are there enduring effects of the early intervention? One feature of our design, discussed later in the chapter, made possible a related query. We had incorporated into our research design a distal control group in a similar but different community. The two communities had diverged over time, or so it appeared, and this change over time would be of interest in group comparisons of long range effects.

A more compelling area of concern was our belief that we were dealing with an intrinsically interesting sample. We had already amassed a sizable data base on a group markedly different from those of the well-known longitudinal studies. The Berkeley and the Fels studies, for example, have dealt with populations characteristically white, middle-income, and scoring well above 100 on intelligence tests (McCall, 1977). Our sample, being black, low-income, and from the Southeast, represented a sharp contrast. In addition, the period from 1962–1980 was a time of particular significance from the standpoint of school desegregation and civil rights legislation. Our children began first grade in segregated schools but, at the beginning of their fifth year, found themselves in almost totally desegregated schools. The mothers could look back on the children's experiences in both kinds of schools. The parents of our sample had been accorded only very limited civil rights in the early 1960s. By the late 1970s situations, although hardly ideal, had improved greatly in terms of employment and participation in the affairs of the communities.

A third major topic was the investigation of early indicators of future school success. Our large data base extended back to the third or fourth year of the children's lives. It would be possible to investigate the relationship of these early measures to the status of the participants in the final years of school.

Other longitudinal issues could be explored as part of our follow-up endeavors, such as the question of stability in intellectual performance, the influence of the sex of the participant on performance, and the nature and stability of parental attitudes over time.

Two publications are available on the first two phases of the study: Klaus and Gray (1968) and Gray and Klaus (1970). The intervention program is also described in some detail (Gray, Klaus, Miller, & Forrester, 1966). A book has been written on the study, one which explores in depth the questions mentioned above and which examines other related issues as well (Gray, Ramsey, & Klaus, 1982).

This chapter presents a condensed version of procedures and major findings of the Early Training Project. Because much of the material on group comparisons, however, may be found in the summary reports on the entire Consortium, we attempt to emphasize those aspects of our study that distinguish it from the others in the Consortium and to present some data on areas investigated by us but not by the Consortium as a whole. Many aspects of the study can receive only a brief mention. Readers who wish to pursue certain issues further are referred to the publications cited.

THEORETICAL BACKGROUND OF THE STUDY

Much of the rationale for the Early Training Project and its approach to problems of inadequate achievement in schools stemmed from the pressing social and educational problems of the late 1950s and early 1960s. It also grew out of the general climate of opinion among developmental psychologists and other early childhood specialists at that time. These elements of its background are shared by other studies in the Consortium, particularly those on which work began prior to 1965, and are described in Chapter 1.

Our first task in designing the intervention program was to attempt to identify those elements of early experience that appeared to be related to the improvement of educability and that we believed might be absent or inadequate in the children's home experiences. Our search was first directed to child-rearing behaviors that appeared to differ in middle- and low-income groups and that at the same time appeared to relate to the greater success in school observed in more favored children. We also examined the more general literature in some depth and met with persons with practical experience in the field and those with relevant research backgrounds. Our intervention package contained two broad and overlapping components. We called the first *aptitudes relating to achievement* and the second *attitudes relating to achievement*.

Aptitudes relating to achievement were broken down into three areas:

1. One area was language, in which we were influenced by some of Bernstein's (1962) early writings, particularly his emphasis on the greater dependence upon contextual cues in the adult-to-adult speech of the working class as compared to the middle class. A reliance on contextual cues may be effective within the home setting but is ill-fitted for school life, where the emphasis is on more generalizable information that can be transferred from one context to another (Cole & Bruner, 1971).

2. Perceptual discrimination is a necessary condition for learning to read. Because our children had appeared inadequate in this respect at the beginning of the program, we stressed the development of perceptual abilities. Many of our children came from homes organized neither temporally or spatially. Temporal disorganization meant little familiarity with orderly sequences of events.

3. Concept development was also emphasized. By this we meant helping the children to learn the simple basic concepts of number, color, shape, position, activity, and the like that are expected to be part of the understanding of entering first graders. Also stressed were classification and the sequencing of experiences.

Attitudes relating to achievement were subdivided roughly into five categories:

1. Motivation to achieve in school-type activities. We had been particularly influenced in our thinking at this point by the work of McClelland (1961) and by the recently published book of Atkinson (1958).

2. Delay of gratification. This variable was chosen on the premise that an ability to delay gratification is a necessary condition of school learning. The findings of Mischel (1961) relating such delay to social-class influences figured in our thinking.

3. Persistence. Like the two previous areas, persistence, the willingness to work for a goal that was not immediately obtainable, is a necessary condition for school achievement.

4. Identification with appropriate achieving role models, an especially important issue for the male children. Thus we planned to provide teachers and assistant teachers who could serve such a function in a general way.

5. An interest in school-type activities. This emphasis was based upon observation in low-income homes. Children who had no familiarity with the common material of first grade classrooms—picture books, phonograph records, crayons, and paper, jigsaw puzzles, and pegboards—will find the school room an alien place.

Such is a rough sketch of our thinking as we planned the intervention program. The program itself, described later in the chapter, consisted of either two or three summers of special group experiences, plus either one or two school years of home visits. This intervention period, including more limited contacts in the first grade, lasted from 1962 to 1965.

The high school follow-up, the main concern of this chapter, was begun when the young people were entering their eleventh year of school. At the end of the fourth year of school, the results of intelligence tests and achievement tests, although still indicating some differences between experimental and control groups, showed less superiority for the experimental group in the fourth than in the second grade. It seemed unlikely that effects would appear at a later date. As the years went on, however, we became increasingly aware that we had in the project a valuable data base for examining the effects of early intervention over time and also for comparison with other longitudinal studies, which for the most part had very different samples. In addition, more assessment tools were available for adolescents and young adults than there had been for young children.

Our original intent was to pattern much of the high school follow-up on our early research. Thus we planned to use tests and interviews paralleling as closely as appropriate the tests of intellective ability and achievement and the parental interview schedules we had administered earlier. We also hoped to use tests of the affective domain if more promising ones were available than what we had found for use with young children. In addition, we planned to interview the young people themselves. School records were incorporated into our research plan because of the interest of the entire Consortium in these ecologically valid indices of school success. Toward the end of high school we could obtain a relatively complete account of school progress in such matters as promotion or retention, special education placement, and grades assigned.

We entered the study without a strong belief that lasting effects would be found. Still, it had been our hope in the early 1960s that the program would set in motion certain processes that could be maintained or even strengthened over time. If our efforts to alter the children's aptitudes for school-type activities were successful, the children might find the program of the school more manageable. The content of the school program would change over time, but the desire to achieve, to persist, and to model oneself after those who achieve in school-type activities might well endure, if such motivations were reinforced by successes along the way. The transactions with one's school peers and teachers would thus be of prime importance in determining whether such motivations would endure. Our program might, we thought, at an older level illustrate the kind of transactional model proposed by Sameroff (1975).

Our initial data base would allow us to ask the question of early predictors of status in late adolescence. The Berkeley and Fels studies (McCall, Applebaum, & Hogarty, 1973) had both accumulated information on early predictors, the Bayley study particularly in relation to intellective performance. With a markedly different sample, we could inquire as to whether early predictors, such as demographic status and early intelligence test scores, played the same role with our sample as they appear to do with middle-class white groups.

A detailed investigation of the performance, the attitudes, and competencies of this particular group seemed valuable to us as documenting some aspects of the life of an intrinsically interesting sample. Not only are our young people different from the longitudinal samples already mentioned, but they have lived through a period of particular significance for southern blacks. Thus, the characteristics of the sample became a chief reason and justification for the detailed follow up.

THE SITE AND THE SAMPLE

The Consortium analyses of the Early Training Project data have been based upon the experimental group and a local control group randomly assigned from the same sample. A second control group was included in our design to allow us to explore the possible spread of effect within the one community.

Tennessee, in which our two communities are located, has been one of the poorer states of the Union. Its support of public education has placed the state close to the bottom over the years. As in much of the South, industrial development was rapid in the period in which our young people were in school.

At the beginning of the study, the city, Town A, in which the experimental and local control groups lived had a population of about 22,000, of which 15% was black. The city has grown and preliminary reports from the 1980 Census lists its population as 32,845 (Bureau of the Census, 1981). It is 35 miles from a central city of about half a million. The educational system is generally considered to be good. When our young people were in elementary school, test scores on the Metropolitan Achievement Test tended to be above national norms (Klaus, 1980).

Largely because of desegregation, which became fully operative in 1968, and partly because of shifts from a city to a county school organization, the Town A children moved from school to school nearly twice as often as those in Town B, the city in which the distal control group lived. They also experienced several curriculum changes in their elementary school years. Desegregation probably had a bearing on the children's school performance, but it is difficult to disentangle it from the other changes in their school experiences. We collected some data, however, on attitudes relating to desegregation from the parents and from the participants. These data are enlightening but too lengthy to report here. They may be found in Gray et al. (1982).

Town B was chosen as the city most similar to Town A within a reasonable travel distance. At the beginning of the study Town B had a population of about 20,000 of which 23% was black. It has shown somewhat less growth than Town A. Preliminary census figures for 1980 show a population of 29,311 (Bureau of the Census, 1981). Different patterns of industrial development have existed over the years. Town A has tended more to light industry, and Town B has a large proportion of heavy industry, especially chemicals. On a highly impressionistic basis Town B seems less attuned to socioeconomic changes since the midcentury than does Town A.

The Auspices of the Study

Throughout the study we have had the full cooperation of the schools. Indeed, the original stimulus for the research was provided by the Superintendent of Schools of Town A. One of the two principal investigators for the original study served as the psychologist for the Town A schools. A more favorable reception and working relationship appeared likely if the study was sponsored by the city schools. To confirm the arrangements the schools became the fiscal agent, and the psychologist in the schools was the director of the study during its intervention phase. In Town B the study was also seen as being sponsored by the schools of Town A; all contacts in Town B were handled through their school officials, particularly through the principal of the school in question. The school system provided the school building, utilities, maintenance, and use of a bus to transport the children. Over the years financial support has come from various federal agencies and private foundations. These funding sources are listed on the last page of the chapter.

The Sample

Our Town A sample consisted of 63 children and their families selected as follows: A house-to-house survey was made to locate all black children born in 1958. Data were collected on housing condition and the last grade completed in school and occupation of both parents. By these criteria our families were well below the usual cutting lines for poverty. With almost no refusals, 63 children aged 3½ to 4½ were selected and divided into three groups by random assignment. The two experimental groups, as explained in the section on design, were later pooled into one group for purposes of analysis during the second follow-up phase of the study.

The distal control group was selected in a somewhat less systematic fashion. A particular area of Town B was chosen in which the families were similar to the ones in Town A. All the children were expected to attend a single school comparable to that of the other town. A house-to-house survey was conducted until we had located 27 families who met our criteria and who were willing to participate. We offered a small monetary inducement to the parents each time a child was tested. Refusals were few.

Comparisons of the groups showed only a few differences. The mothers in the experimental group were older than those in the local control group ($p < .05$, two-tailed). More mothers were employed in the experimental than in the distal control group ($p \leq .05$, two-tailed). They also had more children ($p \leq .05$, two-tailed). For the most part group differences were small, but the distal control group families appeared to be a little more favored. The demographic data for the Consortium samples, as presented in Chapter 13, reveals a picture of the relatively low educational and occupational levels and the large family size of our sample. The imaginative reader can flesh out these bare bones of demographic data into an understanding of the likely constraints of the day-by-day existence of these families in the early 1960s. Put together large families, poor housing, many mothers employed, low educational and occupational levels, and one can begin to comprehend what life was like for the families of our participants.

Similar data were collected in 1976. A certain amount of attrition had occurred. It is discussed in the next section. As a whole the 1976 demographic status of the families was similar to what it had been in 1962. The most conspicuous changes were in employment of mothers. More mothers were employed, and the work had changed. In 1962 all but two who worked were domestic servants, many on a part-time basis. By 1976 only 15% of the working mothers were so employed. We did not attempt to collect income figures, because of a fear of being intrusive. If we judge by the SES level of the employed parents, however, and by interviewers' informal reports on the homes, incomes, although probably modest for the most part, appeared to have improved in current and also in constant dollars.

Participant Location and Retrieval in the Follow-Up Study

Our procedure in locating participants was to find as many as possible through the schools and then to make contacts with the young people and their parents either in person or by telephone. In each of the cities we obtained the services of a recently retired black teacher who was well-known in the community and knowledgeable about the families there. Our two locators obtained written permission both from the parents and from the young people for interviewing and for testing. Among the parents located we had one refusal to be interviewed and four refusals for their child to be tested. From 1975 to 1979, the last time the families were contacted, the retrieval rate, thanks to an assiduous interviewer, steadily improved, so that by the latter date we had some information (at least school records) on 86 of the original 90 participants. The four missing included one child who died and another who became permanently disabled. In 1979, 67 of the 86 were still in their home cities; 10 more still lived in the state.

The high recovery rate in 1979–1980 made possible some enlightening comparisons between analyses based on the full 86 and those based on the 72 recovered in 1975. In general findings were similar, with a suggestion that group differences were less marked in the 1979–1980 sample.

Our study of possible attrition effects was rendered complex by the different testing and interviewing occasions between 1975 and 1980. Differences between participants still in the sample and those lost were calculated for each testing or interview period. To check for possible differential effects we examined the demographic data collected in 1962, the 1962 and 1964 Binets, and Metropolitan Achievement Test scores for 1968. There were few if any indications of differential attrition in the experimental and the local control groups. In the distal group, however, there was evidence of differential attrition for the 1975 testing. The educational level of the lost mothers in the distal control group was significantly lower than that of those retained. Of particular interest in view of the results on intellective performance to be discussed later, the lost participants in the distal group were significantly lower ($p \leq .05$, two-tailed) on six of the seven subtests of the Metropolitan Achievement Tests in 1968. In the experimental group there were significantly more siblings in the lost families.

In summary, our various comparisons within Town A appear to have been little influenced by attrition on the comparative indices we used. Comparisons that involve the distal control group, however, must be made with an awareness of the bias in the retention pattern of that group for some of the years, one that suggests that those recovered in 1975 were somewhat more favored than those not recovered.

THE DESIGN AND THE PROCEDURE

The first two phases of the Early Training Project fell into the relatively neat research design delineated in Table 2.1. All children in all four groups were tested in May prior to the first summer of the assembled program, and all mothers were interviewed. The median age of the children at that time was 3 years and 10 months, all having been born in 1958. The first experimental group attended the summer preschool for 10 weeks. Each week through the rest of the year a specially trained home visitor visited the homes of the first experimental group. The next June the second experimental group also attended the summer preschool, and so on, as shown in the table. During the first grade, a home visitor went to each home in the two experimental groups twice a month. All groups were tested at the end of first grade, and at the end of the second year of school (1966). The first follow-up phase (1966–1968) extended the testing to 3 years beyond any intervention and 4 years beyond the last summer program.

The second follow-up phase was complicated by difficulties in locating participants and in scheduling tests and interviews, perhaps inevitable with longitudinal studies, especially those not originally planned as such. During this phase, data were collected over a 5-year period. Table 2.2 shows the occasions. Where interviews stretched over a good part of a school year, as it did for some of the stragglers, this is indicated in the table (e.g., 1976–1977). All data were collected across all groups.

TABLE 2.1
Layout of General Research Design

Groups	Experimental 1 (E1) (Three summer schools)	Experimental 2 (E2) (Two summer schools)	Local Controls (LC)	Distal Controls (DC)
	Experimental Phase			
1962: Summer	Pretest, summer school, interim test 1	Pretest, interim test 1	Pretest, interim test 1	Pretest, interim test 1
1962-1963: Winter	Home visitor contacts	–	–	–
1963: Summer	Interim test 2, summer school, interim test 3	Interim test 2, summer school, interim test 3	Interim test 2, interim test 3	Interim test 2, interim test 3
1963-1964: Winter	Home visitor contacts	Home visitor contacts	–	–
1964: Summer	Interim test 4, summer school, interim test 5	Interim test 4, summer school, interim test 5	Interim test 4, interim test 5	Interim test 4, interim test 5
1964-1965: Winter	School entrance, home visitor contacts	School entrance, home visitor contacts	School entrance	School entrance
1965: Summer	Immediate post-test	Immediate post-test	Immediate posttest	Immediate posttest
	First Follow-Up Phase, All Groups			
1966: Summer	. . . . Follow-up tests			
1968: Summer	. . . . Follow-up tests			
	Second Follow-Up Phase, All Groups			
1975	Follow-up tests, ... School records			
1975-1976	Parent interview, Participant interview, ... Demographic information			
1976-1977	Parent interview, ... Participant interview			
1979-1980	Participant interview, School records, ... Demographic information			

The Treatment

The second section of this chapter describes the major goals of treatment experience, specified in terms of variables that, on the basis of research and logical analysis, appeared to relate to school achievement. The treatment was derived from these goals.

TABLE 2.2
Major Data Collection Points and Instruments Used

	Treatment Phase				First Follow-up Phase			Second Follow-Up Phase		
	1962	1963	1964	1965	1966	1968	1975	1975-76	1976-77	1978-80
Aptitude										
Stanford-Binet	X*	X*		X	X	X				
Wechsler Individual Scale for Children			X	X	X		X			
Illinois Test of Psycholinguistic Ability		X	X	X	X					
Peabody Picture Vocabulary Test	X*	X*	X*	X	X	X				
Achievement										
Metropolitan Achievement				X	X	X				
Stanford TASK							X			
Affective Domain										
Piers-Harris Self-Concept			X	X						
Rosenberg Self-Esteem							X			
Counselor's Ratings							X			
Demographic Data	X									
School Records							X	X		
Interviews										
Participant								X	X	X
Parent								X	X	X

*Test administered in May and August of these years.

43

Summer Program

The 10-week summer program was systematically planned to foster the aptitudes and attitudes with which we were concerned. Our lead teachers were two experienced black females, both with high motivation to enhance the educability of the children who would be in their charge. Each group of about 20 children had four assistant teachers, either graduate or undergraduate college students, equally balanced as to sex and race. Most of the materials of the program were those common to preschools, with a heavier emphasis on those designed to foster perceptual and cognitive skills. It was not so much the *what* as the *how* of the materials that was important. As an example, 1-inch cubes are often used in preschools. We used them too, and in many ways (the how)—for counting, color recognition, copying designs, learning position names, and even more.

Because our assembled program took place in the summer, space was no problem. Indeed, we had an entire school, relatively new and well-designed, at our disposal. The playgrounds were large and added further scope to our activities. We planned the room arrangements to provide as nondistracting an environment as possible, to make it easier for the children to focus upon their teachers and upon the materials and activities at hand.

The several aptitudes with which we were concerned were mostly promoted during small group sessions with the assistant teacher assigned to a given group of four or five children. Of course, as in any well-run program, these aptitudes were emphasized at other times when the occasion arose. This was especially true of language. Attitudes relating to achievement tended to permeate the entire program. Teachers could try to enhance achievement motivation in almost any activity in which the children were engaged. Can you throw the ball farther next time? Can you put one more block on the top of your tower?

Much of our approach was based on the use of social reinforcement, proceeding over time from physical expressions, such as hugging, smiling, or applauding to verbal expressions and finally, to encouraging the child to internalize reinforcement (Aren't you proud that you could. . . ?).

The Fall-to-Spring Program

The weekly home visits were based upon the same attitude and aptitude variables. The chief purpose of the visits was not to conduct direct teaching of the child but rather to enlist the mother's concern to become herself the teacher of her child over the winter months. Materials were brought for her use, and often simple assignments were given that would involve the joint efforts of the mother and child. As an illustration, in early spring, the mothers joined with the child in measuring how tall the leaves of the daffodils had grown. Our home visitors were mature black women with experience in early education and in group work.

As we look back on the summer classroom activities and winter visits we believe the distinctive character of the program may well have lain in our systematic efforts to enhance the motivations with which we were primarily concerned. Emphasis on attitudes was not incidental to the program but its very heart.

DATA COLLECTION

During the experimental and the first follow-up periods, attention was directed primarily to standardized test performance for the participants and to interviews with the mothers. The important dependent variable was to be school achievement. To serve, however, as marker variables, and to give some idea of whether we were on the right track, we began at pretest time to use individual tests of intelligence and of receptive language. We thought it important to assess some aspects of the affective domain as well. We tried a number of devices—some developed by us—with face validity insofar as our attitude variables were concerned. The limited time and resources prevented us from developing these to a point where they had, as a minimum, adequate reliability. Table 2 presents a layout of instruments used and major data collection points from 1962 to 1980. At each time all groups were tested or interviewed. In the case of the Town A young people, the testing was blind as to program or control status, except as the participants themselves may have revealed that status.

The Specific Instruments

Our choice of instruments in the first two phases are relatively obvious. The Stanford–Binet was our intelligence test of choice because of the availability of comparative data. The Wechsler Individual Scale for Children (WISC) was given in 1964, 1965, and 1966. The Peabody Picture Vocabulary Test (PPVT) was our test of receptive language. The two forms were altered. Later we added the Illinois Test of Psycholinguistic Ability (ITPA) for information on other aspects of language.

We selected the Metropolitan Achievement Test because of its general adequacy and also because of its use in the Town A schools, which would make available a wealth of comparative data. For the affective domain we used a test of cognitive style, Matching Familiar Figures (MFFT) (Kagan, Rosman, Kay, Albert, & Phillips, 1964) in 1964, and an adaptation of the Piers–Harris test of the self-concept (1964) in 1965 and 1966. All tests used in our analyses were administered by the project staff or examiners employed by them.

The interviews during the experimental phase were designed to elicit the following responses from the mothers: perceptions of the general status of blacks in their community, perceptions of their children in the study (especially sources of pride and of concern), and educational and occupational aspirations for their children. The interviews were revised slightly each year to include new questions on the child's progress. The interviews were conducted by experienced black female interviewers.

For the second follow-up phase, use of other indices of the young people's development was made possible by the increasing maturity of the participants, and the accumulation of a large body of data from school records. Our original intent was to select tests that would be adolescent counterparts of the early tests, and to devise parent interviews that posed questions within the same domains of concerns as the earlier interviews. We selected the revised Wechsler Individual Scale for Children (WISC-R, Wechsler, 1974) as being more appropriate than either the Binet or the Wechsler Adult Individual Scale (WAIS) (Wechsler, 1955) for our young people. For assessing achievement we chose a newly published test, the Stanford Test of Academic Skills (TASK) (Gardner, Callis, Merwin, & Madden, 1973), which appeared to be well-constructed, with adequate norms, and which could be administered in a total of 120 minutes. There were three subtests, Reading, English, and Mathematics. In the affective domain we were concerned with obtaining an index of the participant's concept of self, especially feelings of self-worth. We hoped to tap other attitudinal variables through the use of interviews questions. As a test of the self-concept we selected the Rosenberg Test of Self-Esteem (1965), later adopted by the Consortium.

The first interview for the parents was designed to address most of the same areas as the early interviews, but adapted for parents of adolescents. We also added a section on racial attitudes and desegregation. The interview was open-ended. The second interview, administered some 9 months later, was the one developed by the Consortium. It covered some of the same ground in a somewhat different way, but for comparative purposes it was necessary to administer this second interview.

Our first interview with the young people was developed from a number of sources. Much of it came from an interview for adolescents developed at High/Scope (Weikart & Schweinhart, 1976). The items on desegregation and on racism were developed by Cook and his associates (Woodmansee & Cook, 1967). This interview was partly structured and partly open-ended. The second interview was the one developed for use by the Consortium. The third interview was also developed by the Consortium. We added a number of other items in areas that were of interest to us, such as the quality of life, and certain aspects of life course selection.

School records were collected in 1975 and in 1978–1979. We obtained permission to photocopy all records, and extracted the material relevant to our concerns and those of the Consortium.

General Procedures of Data Analysis

During the experimental and the first follow-up periods, our analytic strategy of choice was a repeated measures analysis of variance for all instruments used over a period of time. The analyses were followed by orthogonal comparisons and the use of Duncan's multiple-range test (1955). The details of these analyses may be found in Klaus and Gray (1968).

The second follow-up required different strategies. Because there had been a gap of at least 7 years since the last measures in a domain, and because our measures were not strictly comparable, we used a sex by treatment analysis of variance for test scores, with the two experimental groups pooled. Data derived from interviews and from school records posed other problems as many of them were based on nominal scales and sometimes were simply dichotomous (one either graduated or did not, for example). For the dichotomous data we made use of chi-square with appropriate adjustment for sample size. Other nonparametric techniques were used as appeared most suitable for the particular data set. For the examination of early predictors of status in late adolescence we used an hierarchical multiple regression analysis.

Our chosen significance level was .05, as adjusted for the number of comparisons made, according to the Dunn–Bonferroni correction (Marascuilo & McSweeney, 1977). Most of our statistical hypotheses were nondirectional, that is, two-tailed. One-tailed tests were used only when the history of findings over the years clearly indicated a directional hypothesis was justifiable. These restrictions tended to make our tests conservative ones.

The reader may recall that the two experimental groups and the local control group were randomly assigned from the pool of all families in Town A who met our criteria and had a child born in 1958. Unfortunately, from the standpoint of providing a test of the length of treatment (three summer schools vs. two), the two experimental groups were different on certain criteria that appeared relevant. The estimated income was considerably higher—although still very low—in the second group; almost twice as many fathers were present, and in general the group appeared more favored. By the end of the second summer experience, the two groups were not significantly different on any tests, nor did they appear so at any later date. Because length of treatment appeared to be confounded with demographic status, we decided to pool the two groups and thereby increase our number of experimental children.

FINDINGS

Summarizing the results of a study such as ours within the limits of one section of one chapter necessitates drastic cuts and the elimination of data of possible interest to some readers. At appropriate points we indicate where presentation on such findings may be found in other publications.

Research Questions

There were three general questions with which we were concerned:

1. What lasting effects, if any, of the early intervention program are revealed in differences between the experimental group and each of the two control groups?
2. What variables from the early data base are effective predictors of status in late adolescence?
3. From a descriptive standpoint, what are the participants and their parents like, especially in terms of characteristics revealed in interview data?

The third question must receive relatively short shrift in this chapter because of space limitations. Descriptive data on this sample, however, may be useful for comparative purposes with other longitudinal samples. The information contained in the interviews may be particularly valuable. For example, data on the occupational and educational orientations of young low-income blacks and their parents are meager at present, especially those that are current.

Most of our answers to these questions will be presented in tabular form, with discussions oriented more to the general meaning of the findings. We present findings according to the following domains: intellective development, school performance, educational and occupational orientations, and early predictors of adolescent status. The reader is reminded that the intervention phase extended from 1962 to the fall of 1964, plus a curtailed program in 1964–1965; after that only follow-up assessment was conducted.

Lasting Effects of the Intervention

Most of our analyses, except for those on school records, include the distal control group. For this reason and because we report some additional findings, there may be some small discrepancies between certain of the data present here and the information on the project in the overall Consortium findings.

Findings on Intellective Development

Figure 2.1 presents the findings on the Binet over eight data points, from the pretest to the summer of 1968. These data are presented with the two experimental groups separated. The second group entered the program (except for testing) a year later, a situation that presumably influenced its test scores, at least until after the second summer. Throughout the period the experimental children were sig-

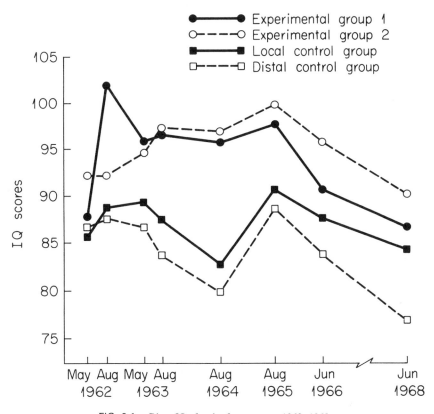

FIG. 2.1.   Binet IQs for the four groups, 1962–1968.

nificantly superior to the combined control group, although it is apparent that the IQs have declined across groups.

Figure 2.2 represents results with the WISC or, in high school, the WISC-R, over four data points. The WISC was first used in May of 1964, just before the final summer program. The combined experimental groups were significantly superior to the combined control group on both Verbal and Performance through the 1966 testing. The two experimental groups were not significantly different from each other, nor were the distal and local control groups different from each other. The inclusion of the WISC-R in the figure is perhaps somewhat questionable, but may be enlightening to the reader. The data reported by Doppelt and Kaufman (1977) suggest that the Performance Scale IQ in the mid-teens would be higher by 6 points on the WISC than on the WISC-R. If 6 points were added to the 1975 scores, the drop from 1966 would be less sharp. In fact, the mean would be almost as high as the one for 1966 in the experimental group. It is apparent in Figure 2.2 that the superiority of the experimental group on the

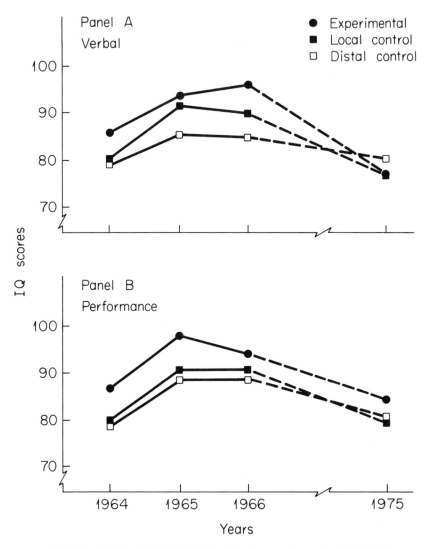

FIG. 2.2.   WISC and WISC-R Verbal and Performance Scores for 1964, 1965, 1966, (WISC), and 1975 (WISC-R).

Verbal Scale no longer existed in 1975. Not only were there no significant differences, but the distal group was a slight bit higher (possibly because of differential attrition).

The mean WISC-R scores are below the WISC-R standardization sample of black children aged 6.5 to 16.5 who came either from the southern region or from families where the head of the household was employed in semiskilled or unskilled occupations (Doppelt & Kaufman, 1977). In the standardization sample, children from homes with either of these two demographic characteristics scored substantially lower than blacks from other regions or other parental occupations. Our lower scores may reflect the combination of both variables. We should also mention that the WISC-R was administered by white female examiners. They were highly skilled and experienced with black adolescents. We would have preferred black same-sex examiners if well-trained ones had been available. Unfortunately, they were not.

Two other tests in this domain were administered during the first two phases, with somewhat similar findings. The Peabody Picture Vocabulary Test (PPVT) was used nine times (with forms A and B alternated) from May 1962 to June 1968. The experimental groups were significantly superior to the control groups through 1966. The Illinois Test of Psycholinguistic Abilities (ITPA) was administered in August 1964 and in the summers of 1965 and 1966. The experimental children were superior to the control ones in the first 2 years, but no longer in the third. Klaus and Gray (1968) give the details of both the analyses, together with information on the ITPA subtests.

Achievement Tests

During the first two phases of the study the Metropolitan Achievement Test was administered in the springs of 1965, 1966, and 1968. Analyses were performed with the two experimental groups separated. The second experimental group was superior, although not significantly so, on every subtest on each of the three occasions. In a somewhat similar fashion the local control group was superior to the distal one, although for them some of the differences were significant. Our original analyses of variance (Klaus & Gray, 1968) had indicated significant F's in 1966 ($p \leq .05$) for word knowledge, word discrimination, and reading. These three subtests were next subjected to orthogonal comparisons, beginning first with the combined experimental groups and the combined control groups. The experimental groups were significantly superior to the controls on the three subtests, ($p \leq .05$). The two experimental groups were then compared; in no case was the second group significantly superior to the first. Next the two control groups were compared. Here the local controls were superior on the four subtests ($p \leq .05$). Inspection suggests that most of the variance in the comparisons was carried by the second experimental group and the distal control group. The reader may recall that the second experimental group, although randomly assigned from the same pool as the first experimental group, tended to be more favored on demographic indices.

The Stanford TASK, given in 1975, has three subtests: Reading, English, and Mathematics. It was administered in small groups by examiners selected by the project staff. The results are given in Table 2.3 in raw score form, and with males and females presented separately. Here a sex by treatment analysis of variance indicated only one significant difference: The females were signifi-

TABLE 2.3
Mean Scores on 1975 Tests of Intellective Performance

	Experimental Group		Local Control Group		Distal Control Group	
	Male	Female	Male	Female	Male	Female
WISC-R						
Verbal Scale IQ	76	78	75	78	75	82
Performance Scale IQ	86	82	82	77	81	81
Full Scale IQ	79	78	77	76	76	80
Stanford TASK: Raw Scores						
Reading	33	41	32	37	41	41
English	31	46	34	39	33	47
Mathematics	22	23	22	21	25	27
N=	18	16	9	9	6	14

cantly superior to the males on the English subtest, a not unexpected finding. We have been unable to find comparative data on southeastern black samples. The level of TASK we used (I) was planned for grades 8, 9, and 10. Examination of the items suggested that this level would be more appropriate for our group than level II. Normative data were available for this form only through the fall of the tenth grade. On these norms the mean scores for the participants on the three subtests ranged between the 16th and the 24th percentiles, and fell below estimated median scores for seventh- and eighth-grade students as based on national group norms (Gardner et al., 1973). This appears congruent with the WISC-R findings. It is clear that our young people in their eleventh year of schooling were not functioning well as a whole insofar as standardized test performance goes. Before we draw conclusions as to their general level of adequacy, however, it would be wise to examine other indices of performance.

School Records

One of the major tasks undertaken by the Consortium as a whole was to obtain and examine school records of the participants in the various studies. Because the school policies in our two towns appeared to differ somewhat in matters of retention in grade, of social promotions, and of policy and availability of special education classes, we restricted our analyses to the experimental and local control groups insofar as such variables were concerned. The data for the 62 young people on whom we had records in Town A are given in Table 2.4. All of the indices are dichotomous. No significant differences were found either in retention in grade or in graduation. The highest percentage graduating (80%) was found for the experimental females. The smallest percentage (50%) was for the local control females. On placement in EMR classes, however, differences were striking. Only two children in the experimental group of 41 were placed in an

TABLE 2.4
Comparisons of Experimental and Local Control Adolescents
on Records of School Progress

	Experimental			Local Control			Test of Significance[a]
	Male	Female	Total	Male	Female	Total	
Retained in grade at least once	17	7	24	6	5	11	NS
Not retained	4	13	17	5	5	10	
Graduated from high school	11	15	25	5	5	10	NS
Did not graduate from high school	10	4	16	6	5	11	
Placed in programs for educable mentally retarded (EMR)	2	0	2	4	3	7	.004[b]
Never placed in EMR program	19	20	39	7	7	14	
N =	21	20	41	11	10	21	

[a]Experimental vs. local control, male and female combined.
[b]Log linear chi square.

EMR class, whereas 7 of the 21 in the control group were so placed, a difference significant at the .004 level.

School grades were available for all groups. Because of variability in the curricula selected (general, academic, or vocational–technical), we calculated the grade point average (GPA) on all areas except deportment (study hall), physical education, band, and chorus. GPAs were computed for grades 9 through 12 (or through the last full year attended for dropouts). There was a slight tendency for the experimental females to be superior to the local control ones. Differences between experimental females and distal ones approached significance ($p \leq .10$, one-tailed, adjusted). Experimental females appeared to maintain higher grade point averages than those in either of the control groups. One must bear in mind, however, that grading policies in the two schools may have differed. Among the males differences were not observed. As a whole grades were low. Only one participant, an especially capable female in the local control group, had a GPA as high as B. In Town A, with the exception of the experimental females, over a third of the young people had failing grades, and a fourth were shown as failing in the distal group.

Nearly half of the young women became pregnant while in school, and carried their children to term. Table 2.5 presents the data on completion of high school for these young women. There was no difference between the two groups in the number who became pregnant. We had not expected such a difference because the early intervention was hardly designed either to reduce or to foster high school pregnancy. A more plausible hypothesis, in view of the motivational components in the early program, was that the pregnant young women in the

TABLE 2.5
Childbearing and Completion of High School

	Experimental Females (N = 20)	Local Control Females (N = 10)
No children born	12	4
One or more children	8	6
High school completion for those bearing children		
Prior to delivery	2[a]	0
After delivery	5[a]	1
Total	7	1
Dropping out among those bearing children		
Prior to delivery	1[a]	3
After delivery	0	2
Total	1	5

[a]Second delivery for one female in each such category.

experimental group would be more likely to complete high school than those in the control group. The difference found was striking. More experimental females completed high school, with a probability level of .006.

Indices of the Affective Domain

One of our two classes of variables was attitudes relating to achievement. We made some attempts to develop our own attitudinal measures for use at the end of the intervention period but met with little success.

Findings for 1962–1968.   During the first two phases of the study, however, we used two instruments worth reporting. One was the Matching Familiar Figures test (MFFT), an index of cognitive style, developed by Kagan et al. (1964). When the experimental children were compared to the two control groups, they showed themselves as more reflective (having a longer latency) than the local control children, but not the distal ones. These findings may point to a slight change in task orientation. As a second test, we used a simplified and shortened adaptation of the Piers–Harris self-concept test (1964) in the summers of 1965 and 1966. No significant differences were found on either occasion, although there did appear to be a weak but consistent trend toward more favorable self-images among the experimental children.

Findings in the Second Follow-Up Phase.   On the Rosenberg Test of Self-Esteem we were unable to find useful comparative data. Tests of personality characteristics hardly lend themselves to the kind of standardization we expect with achievement tests. The mean scores of our young people across groups and across sexes were similar, being between 7 and 8, where a score of 10 indicates a self-accepting response to all 10 items.

The Rotter Internal-External Control Scale (Rotter, 1966) was also administered. We found the usual sex difference, with females being more external in locus of control than males. Our mean scores, between 10 and 13, appear to be more external in orientation than scores reported by others who have studied black adolescents (Ducette & Wolk, 1972).

For the rating scale on social competence, the high school counselor was asked to divide cards into seven piles for each of four characteristics: leadership, productivity, social adjustment, and participation in school activities. Each individual was judged relative to all the other participants with whom the counselor was acquainted. The middle pile was used where the counselor did not have information by which to judge. A series of log linear chi-squares was performed for all four scales. Among the males only one significant difference appeared: The local control males were ranked as more productive ($p \leq .05$, two-tailed). Among the females, however, on each of the four scales the experimental ones received the higher ranking ($p \leq .05$, two-tailed). To our knowledge the counselors were not aware of a participant's status as control or experimental. One must be aware that in these rankings we are dealing with soft data that appear on the basis of a factor analysis to be influenced by certain elements of school achievement. The consistency of the responses on the experimental females, however, is noteworthy.

EDUCATIONAL AND OCCUPATIONAL ORIENTATIONS OF PARTICIPANTS

The interview data we collected over the years is voluminous. In this chapter we restrict ourselves to material on the educational and occupational orientations of the participants, with a brief look at the orientations of their parents. A more extended discussion of the interview data may be found in Gray et al. (1982). The discussion here is based upon questions asked in the 1976 and the 1976–1977 interviews.

Educational Orientations

The educational aspirations expressed by the young people in 1976, and their expectations as recounted the next year were examined. There was only one significant difference when college aspirations of the groups were compared for each sex: Significantly more of the distal control females aspired to attend college (93%) than did the experimental females (47%) ($p \leq .05$, two-tailed). Forty-three percent of the local control females expressed college aspirations; the percentage of males ranged from 17% to 57% within treatment groups. The only groups who expressed in appreciable numbers any aspirations to attend technical or business schools were the two female groups in Town A (approximately 25%). No one expected to attend such schools in the interview less than one year later. The number expecting to attend college was generally lower across treatment groups ranging from 33% to 67% of the males and 33% to 83% of the females. The data were checked for congruence between aspirations and expectations. The level of congruence did not differ markedly among the male groups. Overall, three-quarters of the males expected to attain their educational aspirations. Within the female treatment groups, about four-fifths of the distal control females and half of the experimental and local control females expected to attain their educational aspirations. Where a discrepancy was indicated, responses were about equally distributed between those whose aspirations exceeded their expectations and the reverse.

Occupational Orientations

The 1976 interview contained questions on both aspirations and expectations for future work. The data were first coded according to Duncan's socioeconomic status level of occupation (Duncan, Featherman, & Duncan, 1972). A surprisingly high percentage of responses was not codeable, so responses were reclassified according to the categories: (1) professional/managerial; (2) clerical/sales; (3) craftsmen/foremen; (4) operatives (excluding industry); (5) service workers; (6) factory workers; and (7) construction workers. The proportions of young people aspiring to or expecting to attain white-collar occupations did not differ between experimental and control groups of either sex.

A wide range of occupations was selected by the males. Somewhat more experimental males aspired to white-collar occupations (56%) as compared to the local control and distal control groups (28% and 17%, respectively). Very few of the males in each treatment group expected to attain white-collar occupations (0% to 14%). Their responses classified as white-collar occupations were vague, such as "office work." Probes yielded no elaboration. Among blue-collar occupations the same vagueness prevailed. Less than a fourth of those who named factory work were more specific than the term itself. A quarter to a third did not specify an occupational expectation, although all except one had given an aspiration. Only three of the males expected to reach the exact occupation to which they aspired. Only among those males choosing blue-collar occupations were aspirations and expectations congruent.

Within the female treatment groups, fairly high percentages aspired to white-collar occupations (43% to 80%). The percentages of females expecting to attain professional/managerial or clerical/sales occupations were lower (14% to 47%). The range of occupations tended to be narrower. The familiar teacher-nurse-secretary subsumed the majority of white-collar choices, particularly in the distal control group. All the blue-collar responses could be classified as factory or service work. Among females there was more congruence between aspirations and expectations in white-collar than in blue-collar work. As with the males, differences were not significant. Local control females selected professional occupations only, whereas the experimental ones were as likely to choose clerical as professional work.

The young people's perceptions of occupational opportunities for blacks in the community were also examined. As part of the interview, the young people were asked: (1) What kinds of jobs do most blacks around you have? (2) Are there better jobs than these available for blacks in Town A or B? Occupations named for each question were combined and classified according to the same categories of aspirations and expectations. Factory work was the most frequently mentioned category for both sexes in all three treatment groups (71% to 93%). In each of the male treatment groups, no more than one-quarter named either professional/managerial or clerical/sales occupations. Higher percentages of females, particularly those in the experimental group, named white-collar occupations (28% to 71% for professional/managerial and 40% to 71% for clerical/sales).

A series of binomial tests was performed on the proportions of males and females in each treatment group for whom occupational aspirations or expectations in 1976 or aspirations in 1977 coincided with what they perceived as available jobs for blacks. This yielded three tests for males and females within the three treatment groups. There was a significant positive relationship for the experimental females ($p < .05$, two-tailed) in each of the three possible comparisons. No significant differences appeared for the other female groups and only one for any of the male groups.

These as well as other measures on the educational and occupational orientations of the young people indicate few differences between the male treatment groups. The pattern of findings for the female treatment groups suggests that the experimental females were probably more decisive and realistic than the local control group.

MOTHERS' EDUCATIONAL AND OCCUPATIONAL ORIENTATIONS FOR THEIR CHILDREN

During the intervention period, mothers were questioned each year on aspects of their educational and occupational orientations for their children as part of a more general interview. No evidence was found that the intervention program directly affected the educational and occupational status of the parents themselves or that it influenced their perceptions of occupational opportunities for blacks in the community. Educational and occupational aspirations for their children were similar across treatment groups for both sexes. These aspirations did not seem to follow a developmental cycle. Educational aspirations of mothers for their children appeared unrelated to sex or age of child. In general, the mothers' specific aspirations do not appear to have been affected by either social change or their children's achievements. The predominant responses were college and the professions. The occupational choices differed by sex of child and changed little between the period of their sons' and daughters' childhood and adolescence. Choices were sex-stereotyped and restricted to an extremely narrow range of occupations. Further discussion may be found in Gray et al. (1982).

The information on occupational orientation, although showing little in the way of treatment effects, is of considerable interest from a descriptive standpoint because of the paucity of data upon a sample such as ours.

EARLY STATUS AND PERFORMANCE IN ADOLESCENCE

Two hierarchical multiple regression analyses were conducted with certain indices from our early data base as independent variables or predictors and with two indicators of high school status as dependent variables. One criterion was based on standardized test performance and the other upon meeting certain school requirements. The analyses were performed according to the procedure described by Cohen and Cohen (1975). The length of this chapter militates against a detailed consideration of the findings. Tables 2.6 and 2.7, however, present the analyses for the two criteria; the interested reader can find a more detailed explanation of the procedures and the findings on these analyses and related ones in Gray et al. (1982).

The same sets of independent variables were used in each analysis, and are presented at the left of the two tables. They were selected from among possible early variables as best representing, in approximate chronological order, the early influences for which our data were relatively satisfactory.

The criterion variable in Table 2.6 was based on factor scores for each participant derived from a principal components factor analysis of the two WISC-R scales and the three subtests of the TASK. The table shows two related analyses, one for the entire sample and one for the Town A group only. The two control groups had appeared to diverge over time, and we wished to obtain additional information to help us separate community effects from treatment ones. For the entire group the five sets of independent variables explained 63% of the variance, or 67% for Town A only. With the total sample all sets of variables except sex contributed a significant amount of variance. Although in third and fifth places, respectively, the largest amounts of variance were explained by the pretest Binet (22%) and by the early school set (17%). The treatment variable needs a word of explanation. The elements within the set that contributed most of the variance was the Binet score just prior to first grade entrance. Because the 1962 Binet had already entered the equation, the variance contributed by the 1964 Binet presumably arose from gains or losses during the two year period. In this period, the experimental group had a mean gain of six points, whereas the local and distal control groups had a loss of two and six points, respectively. These differences make it possible that the variance contributed by the 1964 Binet is at least in part an index of whether the treatment "took."

The analysis for the school performance criterion is presented in Table 2.7. The school performance index for each participant was the sum of the z scores for GPA, last grade completed, and number of years in school (an index of persistence). The distributions for the last two variables were markedly skewed but we attempted no transformations. The analyses in this table were based upon the entire sample recovered ($N = 86$). We also analyzed the data with only the 72 participants on whom we had high school test scores. Differences appeared to be slight. With our predictor variables it is not surprising that we could predict the school performance criterion less well. The amount predicted (35%), however, appears to be in line with other predictive studies of academic attainment, as for example, Bachman, O'Malley, and Johnston (1978). Demographic characteristics, the first set, explained 14% of the variance for the full sample, with both father presence and mother's education being significant elements within the set. The fifth set, early school variables, contributed 11%. It is noteworthy in this

TABLE 2.6

Hierarchical Multiple Regression Analysis of Intellective Factor Scores[a]

1975 Sample

Variables	Town A + B, N = 72			Town A, N = 52		
	Cumulative R^2	Increment for sets	Variance due to set elements[b]	Cumulative R^2	Increment for sets	Variance due to set elements[b]
Demographic	.12	.12*		.07		
Father presence			.06*			
Mother education			.04[t]			
Mother employment			.001			
Sex	.14	.02		.09	.02	
1962 Binet	.36	.22**		.37	.28**	
Treatment	.45	.09*		.46	.09[t]	
Sex X treatment interaction			.00			
Treatment group			.005			
1964 Binet			.08**			
Early School	.63	.17**		.67	.21**	
1965 Piers-Harris			.005			.02
1966 Reading comprehension			.013			.01
1968 Grade placement			.012			.001
1968 GPA			.06**			.05*
Total R^2	.63**			.67**		

**$p \leq .01$.
*$p \leq .05$.
[t](trend) $p \leq .10$.
[a]Factor score based upon 1975 WISC-R and three subtests of TASK.
[b]Variance due to set elements not computed when p for sets $> .05$.

TABLE 2.7

Hierarchical Multiple Regression Analysis of School Performance
Criterion Scores: Full Sample[a]

Variables	Town A + B, N = 72			Town A, N = 52		
	Cumulative R^2	Increment for sets	Variance due to set elements[b]	Cumulative R^2	Increment for sets	Variance due to set elements[b]
Demographic	.14	.14**		.12	.12[t]	
Father presence			.05*			
Mother education			.06*			
Mother employment			.001			
Sex	.18	.04*		.17	.05[t]	
1962 Binet	.23	.05*		.22	.05[t]	
Treatment	.24	.01		.24	.03	
Sex X treatment interaction						
Treatment group						
1964 Binet						
Early School	.35	.11*		.35	.11[t]	
1965 Piers-Harris			.02			
1968 Reading comprehension			.002			
1968 Grade placement			.01			
1968 GPA			.05*			
Total R^2	.35**			.35**		

**$p \leq .01$.
*$p \leq .05$.
[t](trend) $p \leq .10$.
[a]Criterion score based on GPA, last grade completed, and number of years in school.
[b]Variance due to set elements not computed where p for sets $> .05$.

61

analysis, as well as in the one on the intellective criterion, that the GPA for a single year in childhood was a significant predictor of high school status. In the discussion section we return to the question of why our analysis of school records showed some conspicuous differences between experimental and control children, whereas treatment groups predicted almost none of the variance on the school performance regression analysis.

DESCRIPTION OF A SAMPLE OF INTRINSIC INTEREST

Secondary analyses of the various studies in the Consortium must of necessity deal with broad issues that cut across projects. Such an overall view is the strength of the procedure. Secondary analyses, however, are not intended to consider idiosyncratic characteristics of samples, the particular configuration of background factors that each represents, the pattern of intervention experiences, or the social context in which a sample passed its growing years. Many of these elements, if not unique, at least vary widely in degree and patterning across samples.

It is in such descriptive data that much of the value of our study may lie. The group is in sharp contrast with the more familiar longitudinal samples. Our families are not only unusual, but they have lived in unusual times. Their experiences with segregated schools and the process of desegregation, their lives in the turbulent 1960s, the rapid industrial development of the region during this period—none of these can now be duplicated. Although it may not be possible to make meaningful quantitative comparison with other groups in other circumstances and times, one's understanding of influences upon development may be enriched by the study of a sample such as ours. The interview data are particularly valuable in this respect, because we have parents' responses from the early years of the study and also contemporaneously with interviews of their children as young adults. Again we refer the interested reader to Gray et al. (1982).

A SUMMARY OF THE MAJOR FINDINGS

The findings of the study fall into five general areas as summarized in the paragraphs that follow.

1. *Intellective Development.*   On individual intelligence tests some effect of the program was discerned through the fourth year; on achievement test batteries significant differences were observed through the second year but not through the fourth. In the eleventh year of schooling no significant differences were found.

2. *Indices of the Affective Domain.*   At no time in the program have we found significant differences on tests of the affective domain, with one exception, MFFT in 1964. High school counselors' ratings, however, on personal–social adjustment consistently and significantly favored the female experimental group.

3. *The Meeting of School Requirements.*   The number of participants placed in special education was significantly smaller for the experimental group. Among the females, the experimental group tended to maintain a higher GPA. All except one of the local control females who became pregnant in high school dropped out, whereas all but one of the pregnant experimental females graduated.

In general, the effects of the experimental program upon success in meeting school requirements appeared in the females, whereas except for special education, the program appears not to have affected the school performance of the males. One must bear in mind, however, that the sample was small, particularly when divided into two sexes and three treatment groups.

4. *Interviews of Participants and Parents.*   The interview data represent a valuable archive for the study of low-income individuals in the 1960s and 1970s. In general they are less useful for treatment comparisons. The study of the youth interviews, however, revealed one consistency of interest from the standpoint of the intervention experience. The experimental females appear to be both more decisive and more realistic in their aspirations and expectations than are any of the other five groups.

5. *Early Predictors of Status in Young Adulthood.*   On a multiple regression equation five sets of early predictors explained approximately two-thirds of the variance in performance on intellective tests given in the eleventh year of school. The significant predictors were early demographic status, pretest Stanford–Binet at age 3½ to 4½, treatment group (especially IQ gain), and early school performance (notably GPA in the fourth year). The same five sets of variables explained about 35% of the variance for a composite school performance score (GPA in high school, last grade completed, and years in school).

THE MEANING OF THE FINDINGS

This section is concerned with an attempt to see how the findings presented in the previous section fit together and what meaning they have for researchers and practitioners concerned with early experience and its impact over time.

Most of the long-lasting effects of the program seem to have been for our sample in the area of meeting school requirements. In the eleventh year of schooling, intellective tests showed no differences in groups, but effects on school performance appear to have endured through the final years of schooling. With the exception of assignment to special education, most of the effects were observed in the females. Why one sex and not the other? Why did the effect last longer on school performance than on test scores? We examine the questions in reverse order.

School Performance Versus Achievement on Standardized Tests

Some of our findings are so striking that we would be inclined to consider them a fluke, except that the significance levels were high, $p = .004$ for special education placement and $p = .006$ for completion of school after childbearing. The gradual waning of differences between experimental and control groups upon standardized tests is not surprising. We calculated once that by age 6 the children in the study would at most have spent 2% of their waking hours in the intervention program. The 2% must be set against life in an environment with the demographic characteristics we have listed. By age 18 the percentage is ⅔ of 1%. Such results appear a miracle unless, indeed, something happened to consolidate and move forward the gains made in the early period. Schooling, whether superb or mediocre, must play an important role in intellective test performance. School achievement in particular is dependent upon continued input of subject matter content day after day, year after year. The schools the young people attended were not poor ones, but they were not exempt from the problems faced by most schools with limited budgets in providing equitable education for all their children. In view of the massive need, what we provided was too little and too soon terminated.

One of our two major classes of variables was attitudes relating to achievement. The possibility that we altered motivational patterns is consistent with our findings. The most striking instance of motivational differences is the return to school after childbirth among the adolescent females. One such experimental female remarked to the interviewer, "I wasn't going to let a little old baby keep me from graduating from high school." The early experiences may have helped the child fit more smoothly into school expectancies, both in terms of behavior and of interest in the activities provided. Such a child might try harder and accomplish more. Thus the child would be more likely to be passed to the next grade and less likely to be placed in special education. During the early years the experimental children were actually achieving at a slightly higher level, as indicated by standardized tests. Teachers might come to look with more favor on them. The clearest suggestion of such a perception occurred in the counselor ratings of the experimental females. If changes were made in the child's and possibly the parents' motivations, and if the child was perceived more favorably by the teachers, one has the makings of a benign spiral that could continue over the years. We do not have clear evidence of such a transactional process, but our findings make its existence at least plausible.

Regression Analyses and Individual Tests of School Performance

We conjecture that one reason the treatment effect appears inconsistent in the two analytic procedures comes from differences in the criterion variable. We did not include special education nor return to school after pregnancy in the regression analysis because both were dichotomous and the second was obviously unsuited for an analysis involving both sexes. Only high school GPA was thus left as common to both analyses. The two kinds of analytic approaches are, of course, entirely different. The more favored status of the experimental females in the school records analyses presumably is reflected partially in the significant contribution of sex to the R-square on school performance.

Differential Effects of the Program on Males and Females

Although the regression analyses did not show a sex by treatment interaction, the comparisons within sex and according to treatment group on school records, counselor's ratings, and educational and occupational orientation suggest the superiority of the female experimental group. Why should the treatment be more effective for the females? During the intervention period we endeavored to make the program meaningful to the small boys, to provide role models for them, to present materials of special interest, and to allow a large measure of vigorous physical activity. We have wondered if we sometimes did too well or rather, without realizing it, may have created a transition problem for the boys when they entered first grade. Were the schools or the homes more responsive to the females? There has been a fair amount of speculation on the possible differential treatment of the male and female child in the black home. Why then, in our sample, should the superiority of the female be observed in the experimental but not the control group? It may be sample vagaries. Yet it may also be that our early treatment, although we did our best to avoid any kind of sex discrimination, enabled the small girl, possibly more responsive to school expectancies and more mature, to use her skills more effectively once she entered public school. The question is intriguing but an answer is not readily available.

The Time and Place in Which the Study Was Conducted

To some extent every study is a product of its time and place. We would like to address two aspects of the issue: What was the impact of the community and the geographic region, and what was the effect of the particular timing—1962–1966?

Our study began in two towns in the Southeast, both with populations under 25,000. The families were black and poor. Segregation in schools and discrimination in employment and social opportunities were the order of the day. In our first interviews the parents appeared relatively isolated and little aware of what was happening with blacks either in their state or in the country. The original planning for the Early Training Project was completed 5 years before the advent of Head Start. It thus coincided with the first stirrings of efforts to enable low-income people to break out of the poverty cycle. It was a time of slowly emerging hopes for the black and the poor.

The Early Training Project was one of the earliest research-oriented efforts to enhance the educability of young children from low-income families. The study achieved national salience among educators and students of child development. Thus it was surrounded with an aura of something new and special—an attitude that affected the research staff, the community, the parents, and later the children themselves. We do not think this cohort effect is the whole story, because there were some clear differences between groups, but the possibility should be taken into account. Such a view of the enterprise may have created a personal climate and motivational patterns that could not easily be duplicated once early education and special programs became more commonplace. As Cronbach (1975) has pointed out, however, the most that a researcher can do is to provide truth for our time. All the Consortium studies were begun in the 1960s, half before 1965. Yet it would be foolish to dismiss the results of these studies as being only the product of the decade in which they were initiated. The experimental–control designs suggest that the timing of a project is only part of the story. Truth for our time is critical, and on it we must build truth for later decades.

A CONCLUDING REMARK ON THE FUTURE OF EARLY CHILDHOOD EDUCATION

How much is it reasonable to expect from even the best designed and executed early intervention program? We were surprised at the lasting effects of our own program. After all, the amount of input was small indeed when seen against the massive impact of other experiences in home and school over a child's growing years. And such positive effects as we found have been modest ones. They have been statistically significant and may have had ecological validity in some instances, and much in the way of direct practical consequences. We and our fellow researchers, for we are not the only ones, can point to savings in school expenditures if children are not placed in special education programs or retained in grade. Or we can take note of what appears to be a more hopeful future for our experimental females. Yet, in our study at least, after participation in a carefully designed program our young people showed a gradual waning in achievement test performance, both in terms of differences in treatment groups and across all groups. Such declines suggest that, as important as our findings of relatively enduring effects may be, they are at best only a start, albeit a consequential one, on the serious educational and social problems that will be encountered by young people who have grown up in poverty.

Those who shape public policy are understandably in search of panaceas. Common wisdom has it that Head Start was oversold in its early years. It would be just as accurate to say that it was oversubscribed. Too much was expected—a result of naiveté, wishful thinking, and political necessity. For the difficult problem of developing sufficient educational and social competence to sustain a person throughout life, or at least to the threshold of adulthood, there are no quick and easy solutions. One is reminded of the tale of Alexander when he would study geometry, how he quickly became impatient with Euclid's systematic exposition and asked for a brief summary. At which point Euclid laid down his scroll and replied: There is no royal road to geometry. Neither is there a royal road to solving the problems of the coming generation of those living in poverty. Society has made some steps along the road, but to travel it to a successful completion will be long and arduous. Our early steps are important, some think critical, but the road must be traveled all its length; we cannot arrive at the goal of enhancing educational and social competence for children and young people without providing that full measure of help and guidance needed at every stage of the journey.

ACKNOWLEDGMENTS

The early phase of the project (1961–1966) was supported by a grant from the National Institute of Mental Health, with some additional funding from 1966 to 1968 from the U.S. Office of Education and the Office of Economic Opportunity. Follow-up was made possible by funding from the Spencer Foundation and the Joseph P. Kennedy, Jr., Foundation and continued through support from the Administration for Children, Youth, and Families, through the Education Commission of the States, and through the Foundation for Human Service Studies.

REFERENCES

Atkinson, J. W. (Ed.). *Motives in fantasy, action and society: A method of assessment and study.* Princeton, N.J.: Van Nostrand, 1958.
Bachman, J., O'Malley, P., & Johnston, J. *Adolescence to adulthood: Change and stability in the lives of young men* (Vol. 6). Ann Arbor, Mich.: Institute for Social Research, 1978.
Bernstein, B. Language and social class. *British Journal of Sociology,* 1962, *11,* 271–276.
Bureau of the Census. *Final population and housing unit counts*—Tennessee, 1980. Washington, D.C.: U.S. Department of Commerce, March, 1981 (# PHC80 - V -44).

Cohen, J., & Cohen, P. *Applied multiple regression/correlational analysis for the behavioral sciences.* Hillsdale, N.J.: Lawrence Erlbaum Associates, 1975.

Cole, M., & Bruner, J. S. Cultural differences and inferences about psychological processes. *American Psychologist,* 1971, *26,* 867–876.

Cronbach, L. J. Beyond the two disciplines of scientific psychology. *American Psychologist,* 1975, *30,* 116–126.

Doppelt, J. E., & Kaufman, A. S. Estimation of the differences between WISC-R and WISC IQ's. *Journal of Educational and Psychological Measurement,* 1977, *37,* 417–424.

Ducette, J., & Wolk, S. Locus of control and levels of aspiration in black and white children. *Review of Educational Research,* 1972, *42,* 493–504.

Duncan, B. Multiple range and multiple F tests. *Biometrics,* 1955, *11,* 1–42.

Duncan, O. D., Featherman, D. L., & Duncan, B. *Socioeconomic background and achievement.* New York: Seminar Press, 1972.

Gardner, E., Callis, R., Merwin, J., & Madden, R. *Stanford TASK: Test of Academic Skills Manual.* New York: Harcourt Brace Jovanovich, 1973.

Gray, S. W., & Klaus, R. A. The Early Training Project: A seventh year report. *Child Development,* 1970, *41,* 909–924.

Gray, S. W., Klaus, R. A., Miller, J. O., & Forrester, Bettye, J. *Before first grade.* New York: Teachers College Press, 1966.

Gray, S. W., Ramsey, B. K., & Klaus, R. A. *From 3 to 20: The Early Training Project.* Baltimore: University Park Press, 1982.

Kagan, J., Rosman, B. L., Kay, D., Albert, J., & Phillips, W. Information processing in the child: Significance of analytic and reflective attitudes. *Psychological Monographs,* 1964, *78,* (1, Serial No. 578).

Klaus, R. A. Personal communication, 1980.

Klaus, R. A. & Gray, S. W. The Early Training Project for disadvantaged children. *Monographs of the Society of Research in Child Development,* 1968, *33* (4, Serial No. 120).

Marascuilo, L. A., & McSweeney, M. *Non-parametric and distribution-free methods for the social sciences.* Monterey, Calif.: Brooks/Cole, 1977.

McCall, R. B. Childhood IQ's as predictors of adult education and occupational status. *Science,* 1977, *197,* 482–483.

McCall, R. B., Applebaum, M. I., & Hogarty, P. S. Developmental changes in mental performance. *Monographs of the Society for Research in Child Development,* 1973, *38* (3, Serial No. 150).

McClelland, D. C. *The achieving society.* New York: D. Van Nostrand, 1961.

Mischel, W. Delay of gratification, need for achievement, and acquiescence in another culture. *Journal of Abnormal and Social Psychology,* 1961, *62,* 543–552.

Piers, E. V., & Harris, D. B. Age and other correlates of self concept in children. *Journal of Educational Psychology,* 1964, *65,* 91–95.

Rosenberg, M. *Society and the adolescent self image.* Princeton, N.J.: Princeton University Press, 1965.

Rotter, J. B. Generalized expectancies for internal versus external control of reinforcement. *Psychological Monographs,* 1966, *80* (1, Whole No. 609).

Sameroff, A. J. Early influences on development: Fact or fancy? *Merrill–Palmer Quarterly,* 1975, *21,* 267–294.

Wechsler, D. *Wechsler Adult Intelligence Scale.* New York: Psychological Corporation, 1955.

Wechsler, D. *Manual for the Wechsler Intelligence Scale for Children.* Revised. New York: Psychological Corporation, 1974.

Weikart, D., & Schweinhart, L. *Youth interview form.* Ypsilanti, Mich.: High/Scope Education Research Foundation, 1976.

Woodmansee, J. J., & Cook, S. W. Dimensions of verbal racial attitudes: Their identification and measurement. *Journal of Personality and Social Psychology.* 1967, *7,* 240–250.

Wylie, R. C. *The self concept: A review of methodological considerations and measuring instruments* (Vol. 1) Rev. ed. Lincoln: University of Nebraska Press, 1974.

3 The Effects of the Perry Preschool Program on Youths through Age 15—A Summary

Lawrence J. Schweinhart
David P. Weikart
High/Scope Educational Research Foundation

The Perry Preschool Project is a longitudinal experiment designed to reveal the effects of early intervention on disadvantaged children. Begun in Ypsilanti, Michigan, in 1962, the study compares an experimental group that received a daily preschool program (with weekly home visits) for 1 and 2 years and a control group that received no intervention program. The study was designed to test the hypothesis that early intervention has a positive effect on how children do in school.

It was not a simple matter to initiate a public preschool program in 1962. State educational policies as well as local school traditions did not encourage such activities. The professional resources needed to support a preschool program tended to be in university laboratory schools and were not readily accessible to the public schools. Yet the potential of early education for the disadvantaged seemed obvious enough. The slow movement toward social change that began in the late 1950s produced a hospitable climate. Eventually, because of this climate, there were changes in the rules and regulations of the Michigan education system that cleared away the legal and administrative obstacles. After 2 years of planning, the Perry Project was launched in October, 1962. Enthusiasm for preschool education became public policy in 1965 when national Head Start was launched to prepare low-income children for entrance into kindergarten on more equal footing with their middle-class peers.

SITE AND SAMPLE

Description of Community

The study was conducted with children born in Ypsilanti, Michigan. The population of the city and township of Ypsilanti, according to the 1970 Census, was 62,732, of whom 13% were black. Here and throughout southwestern Michigan, the principal industry is the manufacture of automobiles, with over 25,000 employees in the Ypsilanti area. The other major activity in the area is higher education, with 25,000 students in Ypsilanti at Eastern Michigan University and Washtenaw Community College and an additional 35,000 students 10 miles away in Ann Arbor (1970 population 99,797) at the University of Michigan. The longitudinal sample was drawn from children who lived in the attendance area of the Perry Elementary School, on the south side of Ypsilanti.

The impetus for the Ypsilanti Perry Preschool Project was the recognition that the local school system, certainly representative of the times, was unable or unwilling to promise even minor reforms to permit low-achieving children some success in school. The failure of the school administration and teachers to adjust the curriculum was seen by David Weikart and others on the special services staff as a factor contributing to juvenile delinquency, to the high referral rate of minority and lower-class children to special services for "treatment," and to the high retention in grade and dropout rate of these children. Because the schools would not, or could not, change, the plan devised by Weikart, his special services staff and the principals was to equip high-risk children with improved abilities to cope with the demands of schooling. This was to be done before the children entered school, because a preschool program would be relatively unencumbered by administrative red tape and districtwide curricular requirements. The staff could concentrate on developing a program that truly served the children.

Description of Sample

The poorest children in the neighborhood were selected for the longitudinal sample, 123 children who entered life with all the odds against their success. Children were selected from five age cohorts born each year between 1958 and 1962 whose names appeared on the family census of the Perry Elementary School or who were referred by neighborhood groups or who found by a door-to-door search. The first criterion for selection was that parents reported a low socioeconomic status.[1] The second criterion for selection was that children's IQs, tested at project entry by the Stanford–Binet Scale, were in the range of 70 to 85.

Parents in the sample had an overall median of 9.4 years of school, slightly less than the national figure for blacks in 1970, but over 2½ years below the overall national figure. Less than one in five of the parents had completed high school, compared to one in two adults (of all races) nationally in 1970. About half the families in the sample were single-head families, compared to one in

---

[1]Socioeconomic status was computed as the sum of scores, standardized within the sample, for: (1) the average of parents' years of school; (2) the father's (or single mother's) employment level; and (3) half of the ratio of rooms per person in the household (Weikart, Bond, & McNeil, 1978).

seven families (of all races) nationally; not surprisingly, single-head families accounted for most of the unemployment among families in the sample. In two out of five families in the sample, no one was employed. When parents in the sample were employed, their employment level was typically unskilled. Half of the families in the sample received welfare assistance, compared to only one in twenty families nationally. They lived in residences that were crowded, with over twice the number of people in the typical American household. When tested at project entry, the children in the sample (in line with the selection criteria) were found to have IQs in the range of 70 to 85, with a mean of 79.

All members of the sample were black, growing up during a period that may come to be seen as an historical watershed for blacks. Living conditions for their parents were not much better than they had been for their grandparents or great-grandparents. They had never really recovered from their heritage of enslavement and the stereotypes used to justify it. Then came the civil rights movement, with its demands for black equality and eventually the laws to back up these demands.

The children of the Perry Preschool study, after the early intervention program, went to schools that were partially subsidized by federal and state compensatory education funds. They witnessed national movements towards school desegregation, open housing, and equal employment opportunity. By 1980 some real progress has been made, not only in the enactment of laws but also in the schooling, housing, employment, and income acquired by some blacks. On the whole, blacks are still far from equality in these categories. However, the absolute barriers of overt discrimination have been removed. As the children of the Perry study become adults, role models for black success are increasing, and the pathways to success are becoming more visible for them.

Assignment of Children to Experimental and Control Groups

Children entered the project in five waves. Each wave of children was a year younger than the preceding wave, with the oldest born in 1958 and the youngest born in 1962. The project began in 1962 with the selection of a group of 4-year-olds designated Wave 0 and a group of 3-year-olds designated Wave 1. The sample was completed over the next 3 years by the annual selection of an additional wave of 3-year-old children—Waves 2, 3 and 4. This wave design allowed the study to employ approximate replications of the basic treatment.

Each year, children in the sample for that year were assigned either to the experimental group or to the control group in such a way as to equate groups on the basis of initial cognitive ability, sex ratios, and average socioeconomic status of the groups. First, the children were ranked by their IQs; even rankings were assigned to one group and odd rankings to the other. Pairs of similarly ranked children were exchanged between groups until the sex ratios and mean socioeconomic status scores for the two groups were equivalent. Then one of these groups was arbitrarily designated the experimental group and the other the control group. In Waves 2, 3, and 4, any child with an older sibling in the experimental group was assigned to the experimental group, and any child with an older sibling in the control group was assigned to the control group. This procedure was meant to ensure that the preschool education received by a child (with the mother's participation) in the experimental group would not have an indirect effect on a sibling in the control group. Finally, in a slight deviation from random assignment techniques, five children were transferred from the experimental group to the control group, rather than dropped from the study, because they were unable to attend preschool or to participate with their mothers in the home visit component of the program. These children came from single-parent families

TABLE 3.1
Demographis Comparisons; Experimental vs. Control Group*
at Project Entry and 11 Years Later

Category	Experimental Group	Control Group	p^a – Var
Number of cases (youths)[b]	58	65	
Gender: Percent female	43%	40%	–
Age at entry–Wave 0	4.4	4.2	–
Wave 1-4	3.3	3.3	–
Number of children in family[c]	5.7	5.8	–
Siblings older than youth	2.8	3.0	–
Stanford–Binet IQ at entry	79.8	78.5	–
Median years of school of Parents			
Mothers	9.9	9.5	–
Fathers	8.6	9.0	–
Families[d]			
Socioeconomic status[e]	8.00	7.92	–
Receiving welfare assistance	55%	45%	
No parent employed	51%	34%	
Two-parent families	54%	51%	–
Mother works	5%	9%	–
Father works	46%	45%	–
Employment level–Skilled	4%	2%	–
Semiskilled	10%	3%	
Unskilled	32%	40%	
Single-mother families	46%	49%	–
Mother works	4%	22%	.002 12.7%

(*continued*)

in which the mother was employed. These procedures finally resulted in an experimental group of 58 children and a control group of 65 children.

Equivalence of the Experimental and Control Groups

The experimental group and the control group were equivalent on a variety of background characteristics, that is, variables that served to locate children and families within the socioeconomic matrix and that could not reasonably be expected to be affected by preschool education. Apparently, the cautious matching procedure employed in this study was sufficient to ensure the equivalence of the two groups.

As shown in Table 3.1, groups were equivalent on all measures of youth

TABLE 3.1 (Continued)

Category	Experimental Group	Control Group	p^a – Var
Families 11 years later[c]			
No parent employed[f]	46%	40%	—
Two-parent families	39%	42%	—
Mother works	10%	6%	—
Father works	32%	38%	—
Single-mother families	61%	58%	—
Mother works	17%	20%	—
Housing			
Person/room ratio	1.20	1.25	—
Neighborhood rating by parent[c] – Excellent	21%	15%	—
Good	45%	46%	
Fair	13%	19%	
Not so good	13%	7%	
Poor	9%	13%	
Family moves since child started school[c] 0	15%	17%	—
1	58%	54%	
2-4	27%	30%	

*Reprinted from Schweinhart and Weikart (1980).

[a]The two-tailed p value, based on the chi-square test, was reported if less than .10, followed by the percent of variance accounted for by group membership.
[b]Data collected at project entry, 1962-65, unless otherwise noted.
[c]Data collected 11 years after project entry, 1973-77.
[d]The 123 youths in the sample comprised 100 families due to siblings; 123 cases were used in these calculations because child conditions are being reported.
[e]SES = scores standardized within the sample for: average of parents' years of school, average parents' levels of employment, and half of rooms per person in households.
[f]Labor force participation of unemployed persons was ignored in these calculations.

background and on almost all measures of family background. The two groups of youths were equivalent in sex ratio, age at project entry, family size, birth order, and IQ at project entry. Families in the two groups were equivalent at project entry in socioeconomic status, median years of school completed by mothers and by fathers, proportion of two-parent versus single-parent families, employment status in two-parent families, welfare status, employment levels of employed fathers, and household density.

When interviewed 11 years later, families in the two groups were equivalent on all of the demographic characteristics measured; proportion of two-parent versus single-parent families, employment status of mothers and fathers in both types of families, household density, neighborhood rating by parents, and number of family moves since the child started school. The only group difference in any demographic characteristic was that, at project entry only, more control group mothers in single-parent families were employed, a difference unquestionably due to the practice of reassigning children with single mothers employed outside the home to the control group. However, the difference in mothers' employment status was temporary, probably only while children were young, because there was no difference 11 years after project entry. The experimental and control groups became, if anything, more alike in demographic characteristics over time.

Subject Location and Retrieval for Follow-Ups

In almost two decades since the end of preschool, there has been almost no absolute attrition of subjects from the sample; that is, they can almost all still be located and assessed. This lack of attrition is reflected in a very low rate of missing data across the 48 measures in the study through age 15. The median rate of missing data across these measures is only 5%. For only 4 measures do missing data exceed 25%. Also, the relative homogeneity of the sample militates against differential attrition across groups. Such low rates of missing data have virtually no harmful effect on statistical analysis.

The lack of sample attrition reflects extraordinary efforts by interviewers and testers skilled in investigating tracking. It reflects the continued cooperation and good will of the community, schools, parents, and the subjects themselves and our continuous contact with members of the sample, almost every year. Also, it reflects a tendency for Ypsilanti residents to remain in Ypsilanti and the surrounding area.

For the four instruments featured in this report, the proportions of missing cases were somewhat higher than was typical throughout the study: 11% on the WISC IQ test and 23% on the California Achievement Test given at age 14; and 20% on the youth interview and 17% on the parent interview given when youths were 15 years old. Table 3.2 presents an analysis of potential differential attrition across groups for these instruments. The first question was whether the experi-

TABLE 3.2
Analysis of Differential Attrition for Age 14—15 Instruments*

Instrument / Group/Status on instrument	N/% of Group	Background Variables				
		Females	Initial IQ	Socioeconomic Status	Single-parent	Mother's schooling
Age 14 IQ	110/89%					
Experimental/Present	54/93%	44%	79.5	8.02	47%	9.4
Control/Present	56/86%	39%	78.0	7.82	50%	9.3
Experimental/Absent	4/ 7%	25%	80.0	7.75	25%	10.5
Control/Absent	9/14%	44%	81.9	8.56	45%	10.1
p		—	—	—	—	—
Age 14 Achievement	95/77%					
Experimental/Present	49/84%	45%	80.0	8.06	48%	9.8
Control/Present	46/71%	39%	78.4	7.80	48%	9.3
Experimental/Absent	9/16%	33%	77.0	7.67	33%	7.7
Control/Absent	19/29%	42%	78.8	8.21	53%	9.7
p	.070	—	—	—	—	.051
Youth Interview	99/80%					
Experimental/Present	44/76%	41%	79.1	8.07	49%	9.7
Control/Present	55/85%	40%	78.4	7.84	51%	9.2
Experimental/Absent	14/24%	50%	81.1	7.79	36%	8.6
Control/Absent	10/15%	40%	79.3	8.40	40%	10.2
p		—	—	—	—	—
Parent Interview	102/83%					
Experimental/Present	48/83%	42%	79.2	8.10	49%	9.6
Control/Present	54/83%	39%	78.7	7.85	50%	9.3
Experimental/Absent	10/17%	50%	81.4	7.50	30%	8.6
Control/Absent	11/17%	45%	77.9	8.27	45%	10.0
p		—	—	—	—	—

*Reprinted from Schweinhart and Weikart (1980).

[a] Chi-square analysis of numbers in groups compares the experimental and the control group. Other tests, based on analysis of variance, compare mean scores in all four groups listed; *p* is listed when it is less than .100.

mental and control groups differed in the proportion of cases for whom data on the instrument were present or absent (see first column of Table 3.2). There were no differences for the IQ test or either of the interviews. However, a larger proportion of the experimental group took the achievement test at age 14 (84% vs. 71%).

When compared on a number of background variables—sex ratio, initial cognitive ability, socioeconomic status, proportion of single-parent families, and mothers' years of school—groups were equivalent on all variables for the IQ test and youth and parent interviews; groups were equivalent on all variables except mother's schooling for the school achievement test. Further analysis of mother's schooling for the achievement test revealed that, although mothers with the least schooling were not represented among experimental group children who took the test, the experimental and control group members who took the test did not differ in their mothers' years of schooling.[2]

It seems reasonable to conclude that differential attrition was not likely to have distorted comparisons of outcomes for the experimental group and the control group for the instruments used in ages 14 and 15.

The same six interviewers were assigned equally to the experimental group and the control group for the youth interviews and the parent interviews. These interviewers each conducted between 11% and 24% of the parent interviews and between 16% and 39% of the youth interviews (except for two of them who interviewed one and two youths, respectively). For the sample as a whole, 88% of the respondents to the parent interview were mothers, 8% were other female guardians, and 4% were fathers; there were no group differences in who was the respondent for the parent interviews.

DESIGN OF STUDY

Treatments, data collection procedures and approach to data analysis are presented in the following paragraphs.

Treatments

Children in the experimental group attended a group preschool program 12½ hours a week (weekday mornings) and were visited along with their mothers at home 1½ hours a week. This routine was maintained for about 30 weeks a year, from mid-October through the end of May. The experimental group in Wave 0 received the program for one school year, the remaining waves for two school years.

---

[2]A statement that groups did not differ on a variable is made in this report only when the probability of chance occurrence of the difference found was greater than 1 in 10 (that is, $p > .100$).

Each year there were 4 teachers responsible for 20 to 25 children in the classroom, a teacher–child ratio of 1 to 5 or 6.[3] The 10 persons who served as teachers during the project were all female; 3 were black. One teacher remained through the 5 years of the project; 3 remained 2 to 3 years; and 6 stayed 1 to 2 years. In addition to the project director (Weikart), an additional 2 or 3 researchers were generally assigned to the project, with 9 persons occupying these positions between 1962 and 1967.

The goal of the Perry Preschool's educational program was to help children acquire the intellectual strengths they would need in school. Throughout the operation of the program, teachers and staff were enthusiastic about this goal and employed a variety of strategies in their attempts to meet it. In the first years, strategies were as likely as not to use paper and pencil and to focus on the alphabet, colors, and shapes. But the traditional nursery school emphasis on direct manipulation of materials also had its proponents. In the second year of the project, the staff learned of the Swiss psychologist Jean Piaget and his explanation of how children's development is related to their experiences. Piaget saw language and rational thought as closely related to sensory and motor experience. Also, a consulting visit from Israeli psychologist Sara Smilansky helped to crystallize the notion that the child should plan some of his or her own activities every day. The teachers' role was to help the child think through and articulate these plans and activities.

The curriculum model that emerged from the Perry Preschool Project (Weikert, Rogers, Adcock, & McClelland, 1971) featured educational extrapolations from Piaget's theories of child development—emphasis on classification, seriation, number, space, and time, as well as on the active learning of the child. However, even before that book was published, the curriculum model continued to evolve toward inclusion of the child in the planning of program activities and towards a focus on learning directly from concrete experience and its expression in language. The Cognitively Oriented Curriculum as it is now conceived and practiced is to be found in the book *Young Children in Action* by Hohmann, Banet, and Weikart (1979).

Data Collection Procedures

This report is based on data collected from or about members of the sample between ages 3 and 15, with its major focus on data from youth and parent interviews collected when youths were 15 and from an IQ test and a school achievement test administered when youths were 14. The sources of data for this report are listed in Table 3.3. Parents completed an initial interview and another interview 11 years later. Youths received IQ tests annually from ages 3 to 10 and

---

[3]By comparison, the National Day Care Study recommended a maximum of 18 preschoolers per classroom and a staff–child ratio of 1 to 7 (Ruopp, Travers, Glantz, & Coelen, 1979).

TABLE 3.3
Sources of Data for This Report*

Topic	Measure[a]	Age of Youth
demographics	Initial Parent Interview	3
	Second Parent Interview	15
	1970 U.S. Census	
group size and chronology	Project Records	
IQ	Stanford-Binet Intelligence Scale (Terman & Merrill, 1960)	3-10[b]
	Wechsler Intelligence Scale for Children (Wechsler, 1949)	14
school achievement	California Achievement Tests (Tiegs & Clark, 1963, 1970)	7-11, 14
school commitment	Ypsilanti Rating Scale, Pupil Behavior Inventory (Vinter, Sarri, Vorwaller, & Schafer, 1966)	6-9
	Youth Interview (based in part on Bachman, O'Malley, & Johnston, 1978)	15
special education	School Records	6-18
social status	Ypsilanti Rating Scale, Pupil Behavior Inventory	6-9
parent on youth's schooling	Ypsilanti Rating Scale, Youth Interview, Second Parent Interview	6-9, 15
school conduct	Pupil Behavior Interview	6-9, 15
	Youth Interview	
delinquent behavior	Youth Interview	15
youth employment	Youth Interview	15

*Based on a table in Schweinhart and Weikart (1980).

[a] Data collected but not reported here included: hospital records, the Maternal Attitude Inventory (from Schaefer & Bell, 1958), the Cognitive Home Environment Scale (from Wolf, 1964, Note 1), the Adapted Leiter International Performance Scale (Arthur, 1952), the Illinois Test of Psycholinguistic Abilities (experimental version; McCarthy & Kirk, 1961), and the Peabody Picture Vocabulary Test (Dunn, 1965). Findings for these data were reported by Weikart, Bond, and McNeil (1978).

[b] A dash indicates *annual* assessments between the indicated ages.

at age 14; they received school achievement tests annually from ages 7 to 11 and at age 14. Two child-rating scales were filled out by teachers at kindergarten, first, second, and third grades. School records from kindergarten through high school were examined. At age 15 youths were interviewed extensively. (A comprehensive assessment at age 19 was completed in 1982 and was being analyzed as this chapter went to print.)

Approach to Data Analysis

Our intent in writing this report was to make it accessible to the widest possible audience, that is, to analyze and present results as simply and clearly as possible, consistent with prevailing standards of statistical methodology. In keeping with this intent, it was decided to allow the experimental design of the study to stand on its own and to present simple tests of group differences rather than to artificially correct for minor group differences through analysis of covariance or multiple regression analysis. It was also decided that, whereas interval variables would be analyzed by parametric tests, nominal and ordinal variables would be analyzed by nonparametric tests.

In some instances, a series of variables of similar nature were summed into a scale. For each scale constructed from the age 14 school achievement test and the age 15 youth and parent interviews, the alpha coefficient of internal consistency was calculated and reported. Further, where variables were collected repeatedly over time, as with teacher ratings or achievement tests, an alpha coefficient over time was calculated and reported. The alpha coefficient is a measure, ranging from .00 to 1.00, of how well the items on a scale (or repeated measures) are measuring the same thing for the respondents in question (Cronbach, Gleser, Nanda, & Rajaratnam, 1970).

For each test of statistical significance, the exact, two-tailed p value was reported if it was less than .100. The p value is the probability that (in this case) the group difference on a variable occurred by chance. When the p value was reported, the percentage of variance accounted for by group membership was also reported. The percentage of variance estimates the magnitude or strength of association between two variables, in this case, between receiving or not receiving preschool education and the outcome variable.

FINDINGS

The Perry Preschool program was found to have a significant and enduring positive impact on the scholastic performance, experience, and commitment of the children it served. Children who attended preschool were also less likely to engage in antisocial behavior in the classroom or the larger community.

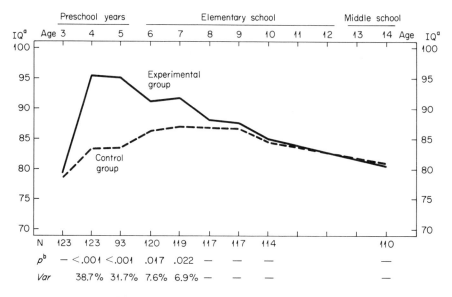

FIG. 3.1.   Cognitive Ability by Group Over Time*

*Reprinted from Schweinhart and Weikart (1980).

[a]Stanford-Binet tests, given at age 3 through 10, have IQs with a national mean of 100 and a standard deviation of 16 (Terman & Merrill, 1960). WISC tests, given at age 14, have IQs with a national population mean of 100 and a standard deviation of 15 (Wechsler, 1949). The a_t, an index of consistency over time for these tests, was .921.

[b]p reported if less than .10, followed by the percent of variance accounted for by group membership.

Effects on Cognitive Ability

As shown in Fig. 3.1, preschool education improved children's cognitive ability during preschool, kindergarten, and first grade.[4] The best evidence for this comes from comparisons between IQs of the experimental group and the control group, because it might reasonably be assumed that the control group pattern would also have occurred in the experimental group had there been no intervention.[4] The experimental group exceeded the control group by 12 IQ points after 1 and again after 2 years of preschool, by 6 points at the end of kindergarten, and by 5 points at the end of first grade (age 7). Contrary to earlier expectations, IQs of the experimental group and the control group were equivalent by the end of second grade and thereafter. At eighth grade (age 14), the Wechsler Intelligence Scale for Children was given instead of the Stanford–Binet because the former

[4]A statement of preschool effect or group difference is made when the probability of chance occurrence of that group difference was less than 1 in 10 (i.e., $p < .100$), with exact, two-tailed p values appearing in the tables.

was judged to be more suitable for older children and provided subtest scores[5] as well as a total IQ. No group differences were found in verbal IQ, performance IQ, or any of the subtests.

The average IQ of the control group rose 9 points from age 3 to age 7, then dropped 6 points by age 14. A part of the initial rise in IQ (we estimate about 5 points) may be dismissed as "regression toward the mean," an upward drift of scores that can be expected when a sample of children is chosen on the basis of low scores (Campbell & Erlebacher, 1975). However, it appears that that control group also experienced real shifts in cognitive ability over time.

Effects on Commitment to Schooling

Within the domain of commitment to schooling, children who had preschool education showed increased motivation during elementary school. At age 15, these children placed a higher value on schooling, had higher aspirations for college, showed greater willingness to talk to parents about school, spent more time on homework, and had a higher self-rating of school ability than the control group.

As shown in Table 3.4, children in the experimental group were rated more highly in school motivation by their elementary school teachers (kindergarten, first, second, and third grades). A similar, though statistically nonsignificant, trend obtained for school potential rated in the same way. The finding on school motivation indicates a greater commitment to schooling during the elementary school years by children who had participated in preschool education.

Youths who had attended preschool placed a greater value on schooling when they were 15 years old compared to youths who did not. Value placed on schooling was measured with a 7-item scale that contrasted the value of schooling in terms of learning and personal worth with experience outside of school. The scale was also used in the Youth in Transition Study (Bachman, O'Malley, & Johnston, 1978).

Table 3.4 also lists findings for items from the youth interview (and one item from the concurrent parent interview) that bear on youths' commitment to schooling. Children who attended preschool were more likely to have thought of going to college. The question on thoughts about college may be regarded as a question about educational aspirations, a topic whose importance has been emphasized by Turner (1964).

Findings on the next two items indicated that youths who had attended preschool were more likely to do homework and spend more time doing it. We have chosen to regard homework primarily as evidence of commitment to schooling,

---

[5]The WISC has five verbal subtests—general information, general comprehension, arithmetic, similarities, and vocabulary—and five performance subtests—picture completion, picture arrangement, block design, object assembly, and coding.

TABLE 3.4
School Commitment of Youths by Group*

Variable	Percentage of Group Reporting		Exp	Ctl	p^b	Var
YOUTH AGES 6-9, RATINGS BY TEACHERS[c] (N = 95)						
School motivation	Score:	39-45	11	0	.087	4.2%
9 items scored 9-45; a_t^d = .829, e.g., shows initiative, alert		32-38	22	25		
and interested in schoolwork, motivated toward academic		25-31	33	25		
performance		17-24	31	41		
		9-16	4	10		
YOUTH AGE 15, SELF-RATINGS (N = 99)						
Value placed on schooling						
7 items scored 7-28; a = .634	Score:	26-28	39	28	.024	5.3%
		23-25	36	34		
		20-22	16	24		
		12-19	9	15		
Have you ever thought of going to college:		Yes	77	60	.077	3.3%
		No	23	40		
Does your schoolwork require preparation by you at home?		Yes	68	40	.006	7.9%
		No	32	60		
How many days a week do you spend outside of school in						
preparation for classes?		0	39	62	.044	6.1%

	Exp	Ctl	p[b]	[c]
1-2	30	20		
3-4	11	9		
5-6	20	9		
Compared with others in your grade, how do you rate yourself in school ability?			.009	7.1%
Much more	9	4		
More	23	15		
A little more	55	40		
A little less	5	26		
Less	5	6		
Much less	5	9		

YOUTH AGE 15, PARENT RATING (N = 102)

	Exp	Ctl	p[b]	[c]
How willing is your child to talk about what s/he is doing in school			.004	8.7%
Enjoys it	65	33		
Talks when asked	29	56		
Doesn't like to	2	7		
Refuses	4	4		

*Based on tables in Schweinhart and Weikart (1980).

[a] Exp = experimental, ctl = control

[b] The two-tailed p value, based on the Mann-Whitney U test, was reported if less than .100, followed by the percent of variance accounted for by group membership.

[c] Scores were averaged across at least 3 of 4 measures at kindergarten, first, second, and third grades.

[d] a_t is the alpha coefficient for the total score, treating reported measures as items; it is an index of consistency of measurement over time.

because actually doing homework probably depends more on student motivation than on teacher assignments. However, it is also possible that, because of various tracking and grouping procedures, children in the control group were actually assigned less homework. Whichever interpretation is valid, or if both interpretations are valid, the findings constitute interesting evidence of the long-term impact of preschool education.

On self-ratings of one's position compared to peers, youths who had attended preschool rated themselves higher on school ability.

Parents reported that youths who had attended preschool were in more cases willing to talk about what they were doing in school; 65% of the experimental group parents said their child enjoyed talking about school, whereas only 33% of the control group parents said this. This greater willingness might conceivably have been due to a better parent–youth relationship, with more communication in all areas, but there were no broader differences found between groups in parent–youth relationship. Greater willingness to talk about school may indicate that youths who had attended preschool were more strongly committed to their school experiences and more willing to take credit for them.

Effects on School Achievement

Preschool education contributed to increased school achievement during the years of elementary and middle school, as indicated in Fig. 3.2. Differences favoring preschool were between 5 and 7% of items passed[6] from age 7 to age 10, but dropped to 2% at age 11. At age 14, there was a highly significant difference of 8% of items passed in favor of children who attended preschool. Reading, arithmetic, and language achievement subtest results followed a similar pattern over time.

A closer examination of the age 14 achievement test suggests that preschool education led not only to improved school achievement but also to greater persistence in carrying out these academic tasks. For each item on the test, the test takers had three alternatives: (1) respond correctly; (2) respond incorrectly; or (3) do not respond at all. The achievement score is based on the number of correct responses—at age 14, 36% for the experimental group and 28% for the control group. Combining correct and incorrect responses produces the number of items attempted—that we are viewing as evidence of task persistence. At age 14 the experimental group attempted 89% of the items, whereas the control group attempted 82%. Or, viewed another way, the nonresponse rate was 11% in the experimental group and 18% in the control group ($p = .004$). Because achievement tests represent academic learning, task persistence is not alone sufficient to explain higher test scores. However, task persistence, direct evidence of commit-

---

[6]Percentage of items passed was selected over other metrics, such as grade equivalents, percentiles, and raw scores, because it focuses attention on the comparison between groups while maintaining some degree of comparability over time.

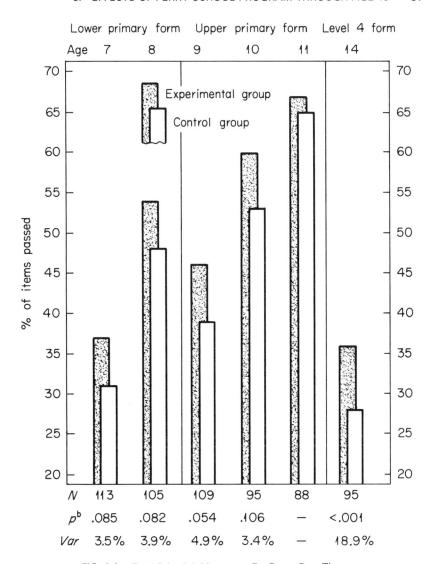

FIG. 3.2.   Total School Achievement[a] By Group Over Time

*Reprinted from Schweinhart and Weikart (1980).

[a]California Achievement Tests (Tiegs & Clark, 1963, 1970). The a_t, an index of the consistency of measurement over time, was .953. The a for the age 14 test (the one test for which a was assessed) was .966.

[b]p is reported if less than .10, followed by the percent of variance accounted for by group membership.

ment to achievement, surely contributes to higher achievement, and higher achievement surely contributes to greater commitment and persistence.

Effects on Placement in Special Education

As this report was being prepared, the complete school records of all members of the sample were examined, from kindergarten through twelfth grade. As shown in Fig. 3.3, by the end of high school 39% of the control group had received special education services for 1 year or more, compared with only 19% of the experimental group.

There were no group differences in the number of years retained in grade; as of eighth grade the sample as a whole averaged .13 years retained in grade. In a previous monograph (Weikart, Bond, & McNeil, 1978), grade retentions were combined with special education placements and regular placements into an overall measure of school success. However, with the passage of time it has become clear that grade retentions were relatively inconsequential for this sample of children. In fact, David Weikart, when he was with the Ypsilanti Public School System (1956–1970), sought to institute a policy of minimal use of grade retention; apparently he was successful.

We view special education placement as a type of reinforcement of the child's student role by teachers and other school personnel. A child who needs special education services certainly ought to receive them, but an unfortunate consequence of this procedure is that the child is labeled as having a more restricted potential and may in fact be dealt with in such a way as to maintain this restricted potential.

Special education placement and grade retention are merely the formal and visible tracking procedures in the school. Rist (1970) observed a variety of grouping procedures leading to differential treatment in classrooms similar to the ones these children attended. Special education placement is yet another grouping procedure and may have the same kinds of undesirable effects which Rist observed.

Effect on Parents' Satisfaction and Aspirations

When their children were 15 years old, 51% of the experimental group parents expressed satisfaction with the school performance of their children, whereas only 28% of the control group parents did so ($p = .014$, Var = 9.9%). There is no reason to assume that parents differed by group in what was required to satisfy them. On the other hand, there is considerable evidence that experimental group children were doing better in school than control group children were doing and were more willing to communicate this fact to their parents.

In a similar vein, 77% of parents of children with preschool hoped their children would get at least some college, whereas only 60% of control group parents had such aspirations for their children ($p = .027$, Var = 5.3%).

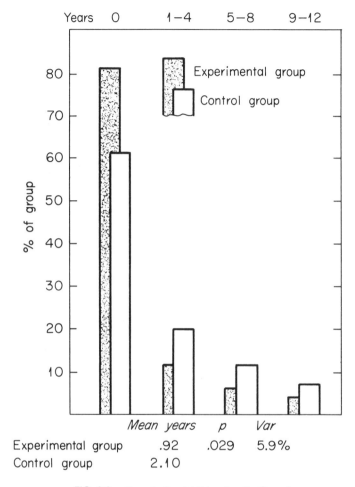

FIG. 3.3.   Years In Special Education By Group*

*Reprinted from Schweinhart and Weikart (1980).
[a]p is followed by the percent of variance accounted for by group membership.

Effects on Antisocial Behavior in School

As indicated in Table 3.5, preschool education led to improved classroom conduct and improved personal behavior as rated by elementary school teachers. Combined, these two factors consisted of 18 categories of antisocial classroom behavior. The categories were originally developed by Vinter, Sarri, Vorwaller, & Schafer (1966) to assess the "predelinquent" behavior of students. They made an effort to insure the validity and significance of this behavior beyond the classroom, that is, in the community.

TABLE 3.5
School Conduct by Group*

Variable	Score Category	Percentage of Experimental Group	Control Group	p^a Var
YOUTH AGES 6-9, RATINGS BY TEACHERS[b] (N = 95)				
Classroom conduct				
12 items scored 12-60; a_t^c = .762	51-60[d]	22	4	.061 3.7%
e.g., does not blame others for trouble,	41-50	48	48	
is not resistant to teacher, does not attempt	31-40	24	41	
to manipulate adults.[d]	21-30	7	10	
Personal behavior				
6 items scored 6-30; a_t = .754	26-30[d]	42	29	.060 3.8%
e.g., lack of absences or truancies, appropriate	21-25	49	57	
personal appearance, lack of lying or cheating.[d]	15-20	9	14	
YOUTH AGE 15, SELF-RATINGS (N = 99)				
School conduct				
9 items scored 5-45; a = .747	30-36[d]	30	23	–
e.g., not skipping class, not coming to	22-29	48	46	
class late or unprepared, not threatening	14-21	20	25	
teachers, not cheating on tests, not copying	10-13	3	2	
assignments.[d]				
How often are you kept after school?	almost always	0	6	.078 3.2%
	often	5	4	
	sometimes	9	17	
	seldom	18	22	
	never	68	52	

*Based on tables in Schweinhart and Weikart (1980).

[a]The two-tailed *p* value, based on the Mann-Whitney *U* test, was reported if less than .100, followed by the percent of variance accounted for by group membership.

[b]Scale scores were averaged across at least 3 of 4 measures at kindergarten, first grade, second grade, and third grade.

[c]a_t is an index of the consistency of measurement over time.

[d]Item phrasing and scores for conduct are expressed positively, so that a higher score means better conduct.

Table 3.5 also shows that, based on youths' self-report data at age 15, preschool education had no apparent effect on the school conduct of teenagers. However, preschool did lead to a reduction in the frequency of being kept after class, with 14% of the experimental group reporting that they were kept after school sometimes, often, or almost always and 27% of the control group reporting that they were kept after school that frequently. As one looks over the categories of school conduct assessed at age 15, one wonders if youths were kept after school for reasons more serious than we were able to ascertain using these categories of school conduct.

Effects on Delinquent Behavior

Preschool education led to a decrease in teenagers' delinquent behavior; we postulate that it did so by strengthening their bonds to schooling. Figure 3.4 portrays the distributions of total self-reported delinquent behavior[7] in the experimental group and in the control group. Wolfgang, Figlio, and Sellin (1972), in their landmark study of delinquency, divided youths into nonoffenders, one-time offenders, multiple offenders, and chronic offenders (five or more offenses). In these terms, the most striking differences in the distribution were that:

1.   Taking nonoffenders and one-time offenders as one combined category, the experimental group had 43% of its members in that category, whereas the control group had only 25%.
2.   The experimental group had 36% of its members in the category of chronic offenders with five or more offenses, whereas the control group had 52%.

Effects on Teenage Employment

Teen-age employment prior to leaving school is a spare-time activity. Almost two-thirds of the sample had a job at one time or another. There was a noticeable though statistically nonsignificant difference between groups in terms of current employment, with 29% of the experimental group and 16% of the control group working. Current employment was during the school year. (Summer employment was not assessed.) These jobs paid an average of two dollars an hour, the legal minimum wage in 1975. The average teen-ager in the sample worked a little over 14 hours a week and had been employed almost a year.

Although it is true that teen-age employment is a marginal, transitional activity, it is also a real-life expression, with economic implications, of such social virtues as task persistence and commitment to success. The trend for a higher proportion of the experimental group to be currently employed is a hopeful sign that the greater success in schooling induced by preschool education will extend to employment and other kinds of success beyond the classroom.

Economic Implications

If early intervention programs demonstrate returns to society on investment, they ought to win the support of public and private investors concerned about the

---

[7]In a technique suggested by Gold (Berger, Crowley, Gold, & Gray, 1975), self-reported delinquent behavior that subjects regarded as trivial was excluded from further data analysis. Examples of such behavior would be fighting or petty stealing from a sibling during childhood.

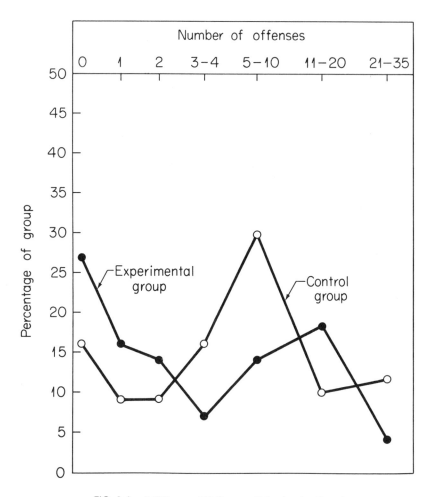

FIG. 3.4.   Self-Reported Delinquent Behavior[a] by Group*

*Reprinted from Schweinhart and Weikart (1980).

[a]16 items; score 0-64; the experimental group scored less than the control group, median test, p = .022, Var = 5.4%.

society. Early intervention programs cost money and are directed at families without enough money to pay for them. If early intervention programs are to exist, they need the support of investors. The Perry Preschool program did demonstrate a substantial return to society on its investment.

An economic analysis of the costs and benefits of the Perry Preschool program was conducted with data collected through 1973 (Weber, Foster, & Weikart, 1978). The approach was that of marginal benefit cost analysis, that is, the differences in expense between the experimental group and the control group were used. Findings were calculated separately for one year of preschool (Wave 0) and two years of preschool (Waves 1 through 4). Because the findings for 2 years of preschool are based on a larger sample (95 children with 48 attending preschool) than the findings for 1 year (28 children with 13 attending preschool), they are more reliable and will be emphasized in this summary. In order to correct for the effects of inflation (which occurred at a certain rate between 1958 and 1973, but might be more or less during some other period), the findings of the analysis were originally presented in 1958 constant dollars. Those same findings are presented here converted to 1979 constant dollars by multiplying them by 251%, the rate of inflation from 1958 to 1979.[8] This conversion did not affect the ratio of costs to benefits.

The benefits of preschool education outweighed the costs. The undiscounted benefits of two years of preschool education in 1979 dollars were $14,819 per child against a 2-year program cost of $5,984 per child (($2,992 per year)—a 248% return on the original investment. The internal rate of return on the investment was calculated to be 3.7%; the internal rate of return is a discount rate that indicates the average earning power of the investment in the project. In other words, the analysis showed that investment in preschool education was equivalent to an investment receiving 3.7% interest over several decades. (The internal rate of return for one year of preschool was calculated to be 9.5%.) There are reasons to believe that this is a conservative estimate, one of which was noted by Grawe (Weber et al., 1978, p. 66) in his commentary on the work—that the analysis did not take into account the effects of inflation: ''If one were to project long-term inflation as unlikely to fall below, say, 5%, then the calculated rates of return would be 14.5% to one year in the project and 8.7% to two years. These values would easily bracket the range of acceptable nominal returns to long-run investments.

The cost estimate employed was the total resource costs, that is, the total public cost of the program plus the total private cost. At least 75% of the cost incurred was due to teacher salaries, which, in 1979 dollars, amounted to $52,670 per year for four teachers, an average annual teacher salary of $13,167. (Teachers were paid according to the local school salary schedule.) In addition to teacher salaries, the school system had the cost of supplies, building maintenance, and the special services support staff (estimated to have spent 10% of their time on the project). Families covered the additional cost of school clothing. There were no transportation costs since the preschool was within walking distance (Weber et al., 1978, p. 33).

Figure 3.5 shows the costs and benefits of 2 years of preschool education by category. In brief, these benefits were: (1) $668 per child from the mother's released time while the child attended preschool, an immediate benefit; (2) $3,353 per child saved by the public schools because children with preschool had

---

[8]Based on the Consumer Price Index of November 1979, seasonally adjusted (Council of Economic Advisers, 1979) and the 1958 CPI (Bureau of Labor Statistics, 1978).

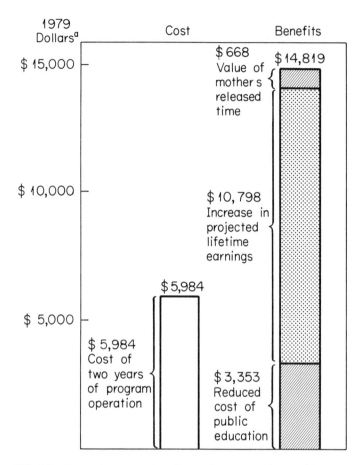

FIG. 3.5.   Economic Costs & Benefits Per Child of Two Years of The Perry Preschool Program*

*Based on Weber, Foster, & Weikart (1978).
aConsumer Price Index of November, 1979, seasonally adjusted.

fewer years in special education or retentions in grade; and (3) $10,798 per child in increased lifetime earnings, projected on the basis of projected educational level using data from the 1970 Census. These benefits are more fully explained below.

Mother's Released Time

While children attended preschool, their mothers' time was released for other activities besides providing care for their children in preschool. Thus the mothers could devote additional time to providing care for the remaining children in the home, to other home responsibilities, possibly to employment outside the home, or to leisure activities. Had there been no preschool, it was assumed that, out of each 2½ hour session, the mother would have spent a total of 1 hour with the child. Over a school year, the average child attended 90% of the 145 preschool sessions, thereby releasing mothers for 130.5 hours a year. However, mothers' time was occupied during the 80% of the 30 scheduled home visits (1½ hours each) that they attended—a total of 36 hours a year. Hill and Stafford (1974) estimated the average wage rate of a homemaker at $1.41 an hour in 1958 dollars, which converts to $3.54 in 1979 dollars. The mothers' time released while the child was in preschool minus the mothers' time occupied by home visits yields a net time released of 94.5 hours a year. Multiplied by $3.54 an hour, the estimated total value of a mother's time released by the program was $334 a year.

Public School Savings

A child who attends a public school in the United States may be treated in one of three ways: (1) he or she may receive regular educational placement, proceeding through school with classmates one grade at a time; (2) he or she may be held back one or more grades, each time joining another group of classmates and proceeding with them one grade at a time; or (3) he or she may be placed in some form of special education, leaving classmates some of the time or all of the time, and being labeled as in need of special help and unable to cope with the normal demands of classroom life. Grade retention essentially doubles the cost of completing a particular grade. According to Weber et al. (1978, p. 46), self-contained special education (total removal from a regular classroom) increased the cost of schooling by 143% during the school year; integrated special education (removal from a classroom part of the time) increased the cost of schooling by 169% per school year; and institutionalized care (school district contribution only) increased costs by 187% per school year. For each program, costs included portions of the salaries of a variety of school personnel (i.e., teachers, principals, librarians, guidance personnel, clerical staff, and aides), salaries of special services staff for special education programs, administration, attendance and health services, plant operation and maintenance, fixed charges, capital outlay, student body charges, governmental aid for instruction programs, and transportation costs. The private resource costs of education were primarily foregone earnings—if an individual were not in school, he or she might have been gainfully employed. Other private resource costs were the cost of books, supplies, school clothes, and so forth.

Based on 1973 findings for education placement, Weber et al. (1978, pp. 43–45) projected the education placements for elementary and secondary school. After correcting for a dropout rate expected to be equal for the experimental and control group (p. 9), overall projections for the number of student years spent in special education (of all types) came to 75.1 years for the experimental group and 167.6 for the control group. Our examination of special education records in 1979 indicated that the actual number of years spent in special education was 55.7 for the experimental group and 153.3 for the control group. The actual rate for the experimental group was 74% of the projected rate. The actual rate for the control group was 81% of the projected rate. Thus, although the projections were somewhat higher than the actual rates of special education placement, the marginal difference was actually greater than the projected marginal difference by 7%. The increase improves the benefit–cost ratio, but by very little. The more important point is that the projected rate of differential placement in special education was actually found to be conservative in its estimate of the economic benefits of preschool education.

Calculating the savings of less expensive schooling on an annual basis, it was found that the marginal benefits for children who attended preschool over those who did not were $3,353 over the course of their schooling, on the basis of data and projections in 1973. The actual marginal benefits are known to have been greater, although the precise dollar amounts depended on actual expenditures during 1973–1980 and remain to be determined.

Increase in Projected Lifetime Earnings

Projected lifetime earnings for members of the sample were based on extrapolations from their special education status and earnings data for black males and females from the 1970 Census (*Occupational Characteristics,* 1973). The Census reports earnings for black males and females by years of school completed, but not by special education status. Therefore the following assumptions were made:

1. If a person spent three-fourths or more of his or her school years in special education, he or she would have earnings equivalent to the median earnings of black males or females with less than 8 years of education.
2. If a person spent one-half to three-fourths of school years in special education, earnings would be equivalent to the median earnings of black males or females with 8 to 11 years of education.
3. If a person spent less than half of school years in special education, earnings would be equivalent to the median earnings of black males and females with a "low 12" years of education. It was assumed for purposes of the analysis that no one would attend college.

Projected earnings took into account the factor of economic growth during the lifetimes of the persons involved. The projected marginal increase in lifetime earnings of the experimental group over the control group was $10,798 per person in 1979 dollars. This benefit alone came close to doubling the initial preschool investment.

Although the relationship between special education status and lifetime earnings should be verified by longitudinal data, there are reasons to believe that it is a conservative estimate. As mentioned above, projected years in special education were an underestimate of the marginal difference in actual years of special education found in 1979. Dropout rates were assumed to be equivalent across groups, although there is a conceptual rationale and some preliminary data (Weikart & Schweinhart, 1979) to suggest that the dropout rate for the experimental group is lower. There is also preliminary data suggesting that some members of the sample are attending college.

Other potential benefits include the reduced rate of delinquency, which will result in savings for the victims of crimes and savings in police and court processing. There is a possibility of savings through a decreased need for welfare assistance and lower rate of usage of various social services. Finally, there is the possibility of an increase in labor force participation, which would render even greater the marginal benefits in projected earnings. These potential benefits remain to be calculated as part of a future benefit–cost analysis.

THE NATIONAL EFFORT AND THE PERRY PROJECT: SOME COMPARISONS AND IMPLICATIONS

The question of the efficacy of early intervention programs is not merely of academic interest; it has direct implications for how the United States government invests financial resources. In the 1979 fiscal year, the federal government alone spent 1.6 billion dollars in programs that brought early childhood intervention to 1.8 million children aged 0 to 5. State and local governments spent at least an additional 20% of this amount ($316 million) in matching funds for most of these programs.

The applicability of the early intervention research of the Consortium for Longitudinal Studies to programs funded in 1979 depends on the extent to which the researched programs are comparable to the currently funded programs. To the extent that a given set of programs resemble the researched programs in population served and program characteristics, it may be inferred that they also produce similar effects. Such an inference constitutes less direct evidence than actual evaluations of the large-scale programs would provide; but given the expense, difficulty, and inevitable criticisms of large-scale evaluations, inferences from smaller studies with experimental designs may in practice be the best guides for decision making.

The Perry Preschool program served disadvantaged children who were found to have low IQs at age 3. The other Consortium programs also served disadvantaged children. Head Start, Title I (of the Elementary and Secondary Education

Act) and Title XX (of the Social Security Act) day care programs are clearly targeted for disadvantaged children. A large proportion of the handicapped children served by preschool programs are classified as educable mentally retarded (with the principal criterion being low IQs), learning disabled, and emotionally impaired, classifications that do not require evidence of organic handicap. In this way they are comparable to the children served in the Perry Preschool program.

The search for discrete program characteristics that are responsible for success continues. Our own speculation has focused on the fact that projects known to be successful have a high degree of quality control—they are closely monitored by directors with high personal investment in the projects, with emphasis on delivery of services as scheduled, training of staff, and a general attitude of experimentation. The essential ingredients are a competent and committed staff whose director is a leader as well as an administrator. (These qualities also lead to success in elementary school programs, as attested to by the research of Edmonds, 1979.) Government regulations have only an indirect relationship to such qualities.

The Consortium programs were not intended to be representative of any particular government program, although the later Head Start programs do resemble Consortium programs in many respects. Their relationship to other programs might best be viewed as exemplary rather than representative, as model programs to inspire others. In this respect, a sports analogy is helpful. Roger Bannister ran the mile in 1952 in less than 4 minutes. His accomplishment was not negated by the facts that no other athlete had ever done it before or that many believed it to be impossible. Today, of course, with proper diet, coaching, improved techniques—and the knowledge that it can be done, all world-class athletes run the mile in less than 4 minutes. Similarly, the fact that some early childhood programs have demonstrated their long-term potential may encourage, inspire, and convince others of the potential effectiveness of their own efforts—and thereby these efforts may be enhanced and made more effective.

Neither is the cost of operating programs like the Perry Preschool program a prohibitive factor. It will be recalled that the per-child cost of operation of the Perry Preschool program, in 1979 dollars, was $2992 per year. The estimated cost per child of operating a Head Start program in 1979 was $2464—including Head Start costs, local costs, and costs covered by other federal programs such as CETA and food supplement programs.[9] It appears that a program like the Perry Preschool could be operated at a rate of expenditure only 21% higher than current Head Start expenditures. Of course the categories of expenditure differ considerably. On the one hand, the Perry Preschool program employed teachers, but it did not employ nurses or social workers. On the other hand, teachers in the Perry Preschool program were paid according to the public school salary schedule,

---

[9]Estimate provided by the staff of the U.S. Administration for Children, Youth, and Families.

whereas current pay for most Head Start teachers is far lower than current public school salary schedules.

Summary

The Perry Preschool Project is a longitudinal experiment designed to reveal the effects of early educational intervention on disadvantaged young people. In this chapter, the effects of the preschool programs were traced from age 3 through age 15.

The study was an examination of the lives of 123 children who were born with the odds against them—poor, apparently destined for school failure, and black in a country that discriminated against blacks. Each year from 1962 to 1965, children were assigned to an experimental group or a control group so as to assure group equivalence in initial cognitive ability, sex ratio, and socioeconomic status. The two resultant groups were indeed equivalent on almost all socioeconomic characteristics of families at project entry and when measured again 11 years later. Children in the experimental group attended a group preschool program 12½ hours a week and were visited at home with their mothers 1½ hours a week. The median rate of missing data across all these measures was only 5%.

The positive effects of preschool education on school performance and antisocial behavior were meaningful and lasting. Improvement in the cognitive ability at school entry of children who attended preschool was indicated by their increased IQs during kindergarten and first grade. Greater school achievements for these children was shown by higher achievement test scores during elementary school and substantially higher scores at eighth grade when compared to control group children. Greater commitment to schooling was shown by a higher value placed on schooling by teen-agers and by several other aspects of commitment to schooling. Reinforcement of a more positive student role for children who attended preschool was represented by more highly rated social development in elementary school, fewer years spent receiving special education services throughout their years in the public schools, and greater satisfaction and aspirations by parents with regard to the schooling of their children. Decreased antisocial behavior at school by children who attended preschool was indicated by more favorably rated classroom conduct and personal behavior during elementary school and by teen-agers' reports of being kept after school less often. Decreased delinquent behavior was shown by lower frequencies of self-reported delinquent behavior and serious delinquent behavior.

Although the Perry Preschool program was not part of a large, government-funding program, there are many similarities between the Perry program and programs such as Head Start. Both target economically disadvantaged children and especially those judged to run a high risk of scholastic failure. The differences in cost between the programs is not great—the Perry program ran $2992 per year per child in 1979 dollars, whereas typical Head Start costs are $2464 per year per child in 1979 dollars.

Economic analysis of the Perry project revealed that the undiscounted economic benefits for two years of preschool were 248% of the cost.

ACKNOWLEDGMENTS

This chapter is a summary of the monograph by Schweinhart and Weikart (1980) entitled "Young Children Grow Up: The Effects of the Perry Preschool Program on Youths Through Age 15." Preparation of this chapter was facilitated by a small grant from the U.S. Administration for Children, Youth, and Families. The research reported is now or has been funded by the U.S. Office of Special Education, the National Institute of Mental Health, the Carnegie Corporation of New York, and the Spencer Foundation.

REFERENCES

Arthur, G. *The Arthur Adaptation of the Leiter International Performance Scale.* Beverly Hills, Calif.: Psychological Service Center Press, 1952.

Bachman, J. G., O'Malley, P. M., & Johnston, J. *Adolescence to adulthood: Change and stability in the lives of young men* (Youth in transition, Vol. VI). Ann Arbor: University of Michigan Institute for Social Research, 1978.

Berger, R. J., Crowley, J. E., Gold, M., & Gray, J. *Experiment in a juvenile court.* Ann Arbor: University of Michigan Institute for Social Research, 1975.

Bureau of Labor Statistics. *Handbook of labor statistics.* Washington, D.C.: U.S. Government Printing Office, 1978.

Campbell, D. T., & Erlebacher, A. How regression artifacts in quasi-experimental evaluations can mistakenly make compensatory education look harmful. In E. L. Struening & M. Guttentag (Eds.), *Handbook of evaluation research,* (Vol. 1). Beverly Hills: Sage, 1975.

Council of Economic Advisers. *Economic indicators,* December, 1979.

Cronbach, L. J., Gleser, G. C., Nanda, H., & Rajaratnam, N. *The dependability of behavioral measurements: Theory of generalizability for scores and profiles.* New York: Wiley, 1972.

Dunn, L. M. *Peabody Picture Vocabulary Test manual.* Minneapolis,: American Guidance Service, 1965.

Edmonds, R. Effective schools for the urban poor. *Educational Leadership,* October, 1979, 15–24.

Hill, C. R., & Stafford, F. Allocation of time to preschool children and education opportunity. *Journal of Human Resources,* 1974, 9, 323–341.

Hohmann, M., Banet, B., & Weikart, D. P. *Young children in action: A manual for preschool educators.* Ypsilanti, Michigan: High/Scope Press, 1979.

McCarthy, J. J., & Kirk, S. A. *Examiner's manual: Illinois Test of Psycholinguistic Abilities, experimental version.* Urbana: University of Illinois, Institute for Research on Exceptional Children, 1961.

Occupational Characteristics. Washington, D.C.: U.S. Government Printing Office, 1973.

Rist, R. C. Student social class and teacher expectations: The self-fulfilling prophecy in ghetto education. *Harvard Educational Review,* Reprint Series No. 5, 1971, 70–110.

Ruopp, R., Travers, J., Glantz, F., & Coelen, C. *Children at the center: Summary findings and their implications* (Vol. 1, Final report of the National Day Care Study). Cambridge, Massachusetts: Abt Associates, 1979.

Schaefer, E. S., & Bell, R. Q. Development of a parental attitude research instrument. *Child Development*, 1958, 28, 339–361.

Schweinhart, L. J., & Weikart, D. P. Young children grow up: The effects of the Perry Preschool Program on youths through age 15. *Monographs of the High/Scope Educational Research Foundation*, 1980. No. 7.

Terman, L. M., & Merrill, M. A. *Stanford–Binet Intelligence Scale Form L-M: Manual for the third revision*. Boston: Houghton Mifflin, 1960.

Tiegs, E. W., & Clark, W. W. *Manual: California Achievement Test, complete battery*. Monterey Park: California Test Bureau (McGraw-Hill), 1963.

Tiegs, E. W., & Clark, W. W. *Test coordinator's handbook: California Achievement Tests*. Monterey, California: California Test Bureau (McGraw-Hill), 1970.

Turner, R. *The social context of ambition*. San Francisco: Chandler, 1964.

Vinter, R. D., Sarri, R. S., Vorwaller, D. J., & Schafer, W. E. *Pupil Behavior Inventory: A manual of administration and scoring*. Ann Arbor: Campus Publishers, 1966.

Weber, C. U., Foster, P. W., & Weikart, D. P. An economic analysis of the Ypsilanti Perry Preschool Project. *Monographs of the High/Scope Educational Research Foundation*, 1978, No. 5.

Wechsler, D. *Manual for the Wechsler Intelligence Scale for Children*. New York: The Psychological Corporation, 1949.

Weikart, D. P., Bond, J. T., & McNeil, J. T. The Ypsilanti Perry Preschool Project: Preschool years and longitudinal results through fourth grade. *Monographs of the High/Scope Educational Research Foundation*, 1978, No. 3.

Weikart, D. P., Rogers, L., Adcock, C., & McClelland, D. *The Cognitively Oriented Curriculum: A framework for preschool teachers*. Urbana: University of Illinois—NAEYC, 1971.

Weikart, D. P., & Schweinhart, L. J. *Preliminary findings on the social and economic adjustment of young adults who completed an experimental preschool*. Paper presented at the annual meeting of the American Educational Research Association, San Francisco, April 1979.

Wolf, R. M. *The identification and measurement of environmental process variables related to intelligence*. Unpublished doctoral dissertation, University of Chicago, 1964.

Wolfgang, M. E., Figlio, R. M., & Sellin, T. *Delinquency in a birth cohort*. Chicago: University of Chicago Press, 1972.

4 The Gordon Parent Education Infant and Toddler Program

R. Emile Jester
Barry J. Guinagh
University of Florida

Introduction

In the summer of 1966, Ira J. Gordon began his Parent Education Project, initiating a series of three intervention programs: *Infant Stimulation Through Parent Education* (PEP), *Early Child Stimulation Through Parent Education* (PEP 2), and *A Home Learning Center Approach to Early Stimulation* (HLC). This chapter is a summary of these three programs and their outcomes 12 years later when most of the children were about 11 years old. Dr. Gordon was the inspiration behind these projects and headed the longitudinal investigation until his death in the fall of 1978. Although the intervention with the children ended in 1970, he continued to study the children and their families through 1977 while at the University of Florida.

Purpose of Study

The purpose of the original education program was to enhance the development of infants through weekly visits to their homes by parent educators who taught mothers activities to carry out during the week with their infants. The parent educators were women from the community with characteristics similar to those of the parents they were visiting. The program was designed to serve children from the age of 3 months until they reached their third birthday, although for experimental purposes some families were not in the program for the maximum time period. The study was centered at the University of Florida at Gainesville. Contact was made with about 550 families in eleven surrounding counties during the entire time of the project.

Although the underlying philosophy for the project remained relatively constant over the years, details in emphasis have changed. In 1967 Gordon stated:

> The purpose of this project is to investigate a way in which early intervention into the lives of babies might break the poverty cycle. The project attempts to simultaneously raise the chance that the infant will reach a higher level of intellectual functioning and that the adult who mothers him will gain in competency and feelings of self-worth [p. 57].

The emphasis was optimistic: The purpose was nothing less than an attempt to modify the so-called "poverty cycle." However, as the project evolved with a better understanding of how difficult it is to "break poverty cycles," less emphasis was placed on breaking the poverty cycle and more on modifying the intellectual functioning of the infants. The focus shifted to implementation of the program and parent education and the Home Learning Centers were seen by project staff as opportunities to apply basic principles of early development in a real life setting. This application is reflected in the specific goals of the Home Learning Center project when the children were aged 2 to 3. These goals were:

1. To sustain a combined home visit and home learning center approach, using paraprofessionals as the key educators of parents who would in turn teach their children.
2. To develop intellectual and personality stimulation materials that could easily be taught to the mother by paraprofessionals and that the mother could then teach her infant.
3. To investigate the continuing effects of such a program as the youngsters reached kindergarten and the beginning of school years.

History of Study

The three parent education programs were longitudinal in design. The first program was for infants up to age 1 and their families and was the Parent Education Program (PEP). The second study, Early Child Stimulation Through Parent Education (PEP 2), was for children up to age 2. The third study, A Home Learning Center Approach to Early Stimulation (HLC), involved 2- to 3-year-olds in small group settings while maintaining the weekly home visit with the family.

Three follow-up studies have been completed on the children and families: School Performance as a Function of Early Stimulation (Guinagh & Gordon, 1976), Middle School Performance as a Function of Infant Stimulation (Gordon & Guinagh, 1978), and Middle School Performance as a Function of Early Intervention (Gordon & Jester, 1980). Therefore, six separate studies covering a period of 14 years form the basis for this chapter.

In the first program, PEP, the major concern was whether such a program was feasible. Would the home visitors or parent educators be accepted? Could a curriculum be developed that the mothers would use? Would the families accept the notion that infants were active learners? These questions were answered with a resounding yes and the project was extended for another year.

The second project, PEP 2, was essentially the same as the first. The children were now between 1 and 2 years of age and the activities were designed to reflect this. There was also an emphasis on what we termed the "language envelope." All the materials taken into the home were introduced to the mothers with the suggestion that they talk with their babies as much as possible while doing the activities. The activities were based heavily on Piaget's theory but also included ideas from the works of Gesell and many others. When the parent educator presented the activity to the mother, the importance of spontaneity, flexibility, a light touch, a warm emotional tone, and of enveloping the child in language were stressed.

At age 2, the HLC added a twice weekly 2-hour "nursery school" for the children in addition to the home visit. The same, or similar, activities were used with the children for both the home visit and in the home learning center. The primary difference was that the home learning centers were equipped much as a typical nursery school might be. There were inlay puzzles, shape toys, books, child-size furniture, and a multitude of other typical nursery school materials. The same paraprofessionals did both the home visits and managed the home learning centers. Each parent educator worked with ten parents by home visitation and directly with their ten children in two groups of five during the nursery school. This phase of the intervention program lasted until the children were 3 years old.

THEORETICAL BASIS AND HYPOTHESES

The first major input in the formation of Gordon's Parent Education Program was the changing view in the 1960s regarding the development of human intelligence. The work of Jean Piaget, particularly his *The Origins of Intelligence in Children* (1952), traced the development of intelligence to the earliest months of life. Intelligence, in Piaget's view, developed only in interaction with the environment. In 1961, J. McVicker Hunt, using many of Piaget's ideas, published *Intelligence and Experience*. In that book, Hunt suggested that intellectual ability was far more modifiable than many psychologists had previously thought. Given the proper environment, one that provided a match with the child's intellectual needs, it was believed that IQ levels could be changed dramatically. In 1964, Benjamin Bloom published *Stability and Change in Human Characteristics* in which he also emphasized the importance of the environment in the development of human intelligence. These were influential ideas and were part of the Zeitgeist that prevailed when Gordon began his attempt to ''break the poverty cycle'' with culturally disadvantaged families.

Ira Gordon, teaching at the University of Florida, was aware that even at age 4, many children from poor homes were already lagging behind their peers from higher socio-economic level homes when compared on cognitive measures. The obvious question could then be asked: if at age 4 there is a difference, why not begin earlier? If intervention were initiated when differences were small or nonexistent, then early intervention in the form of early stimulation should encourage intellectual growth.

A second major interest involved the degree to which the home environment was important to growth of academic skills and their relationship to intelligence. In 1966, James Coleman in *Equality of Educational Opportunity* reported that the quality of the students' home environment had more effect on the variance in achievement scores than the quality of education in the school. Other researchers have since come to similar conclusions (Jencks, Smith, Acland, Bane, Cohen, Gintis, Heynes, & Michelson, 1972; Mayeske & Beaton, 1975). Therefore, it was argued, the place to put a major thrust was with the family. The home was viewed by Gordon as the primary sociialization agent of the child. By helping a mother learn how to provide an educationally stimulating environment for her child, the child might have a supportive environment all the time and not just during the weekly visits. This was the major objective of the Gordon parent education program—parental involvement in the educative process of the child. Parent educators were just that, *parent* educators, and their focus was on the mother.

A third research interest was the use of paraprofessionals as parent educators. Gordon gave much of the credit for this idea to his wife Esther, because she contended that women from similar backgrounds as the population to be served would be better able to communicate due to the absence of social and economic barriers. Levinson and Schiller (1965) and Riessman (1966) had reported that the use of nonprofessionals who were themselves members of the same cultural group was a successful method for increasing communication with the target population.

Although the theories underlying Gordon's assumptions were clear in suggesting that early stimulation or training should produce differences in the intellectual growth of the child, the theories are not useful in predicting the lasting nature of such effects. It is easy to make the inference from the theories that early stimulation would be much like a vaccination that, if given early enough, would prevent the child from future failure. From a developmental perspective, however, this seems unlikely because skills which make a competent 3-year-old are not satisfactory for success when the child reaches age 6. A major assumption underlying Gordon's notion of using parent educators to teach the mothers was that the effect would be to change the family and therefore the environment surrounding the child into one that was more positive for intellectual growth than would be expected in the typical "disadvantaged family." "Both the theoretical foundations and the research foundations supported the development of a stimulation program to be delivered at home in the early years of life so that the family and home might become a more positive learning environment [Gordon, Guinagh, & Jester, 1977, p. 100]." Because the parent educator only visited once a week and left an activity for the parent to do during the week, it was the parent who was to bring about changes in her child by providing a positive learning environment.

Although the goal was to produce a more positive learning environment, the exact nature of that learning environment was not completely specified. Underlying the home visits was the notion that although the parent educator was presenting the activity for the current week there would also be an exchange of ideas that would serve to increase the mother's positive attitude towards learning and intellectual growth. This included the teaching of strategies of intervention with the infant that were expected to continue after the program was over. This intervention by a paraprofessional of similar cultural background as the target population was seen by Gordon (1969) as "a possible way to educate these parents to provide their children with a good start, so that the poverty cycle of these families might be broken [p. 3]." It was assumed that once the mothers and families had acquired a more positive attitude toward the notion that intelligence and, indeed, school success were due to interaction with the environment and were not due to some internal factors over which they had no control, then this attitude would be self-perpetuating and that the enriched environment would be sustained. The assumption was that one could change the motivation patterns from "external" to "internal" and that once changed, these patterns would be permanent. From Gordon, Guinagh, & Jester (1977) "Our goal was to help the child not only to develop skill but also to develop motivation that would outlast the program and get him off to a good start in school [p. 100]."

The Gordon Parent Education Program was innovative on several levels as it sought to combine theory and practice to serve children and their families. Prior to 1966, there were very few programs of an educational nature for children under age 3. Experimental work done with young infants prior to this generally bypassed the parents. Gordon's approach to educating the infant was to do so through the efforts of the infant's family. Thus, the child's primary teacher was considered to be the child's mother and not a "professional" with high level training. The third primary innovation of these programs was the use of paraprofessionals to teach the mothers. Home visits were not especially innovative as these had been done by public health nurses and social case workers for many years. The innovation was in the assumption that optimum outcomes of the visit could be achieved if the visitor was from the same cultural background as the mother being visited. These innovations in intervention into the lives of disadvantaged families led to some specific hypotheses regarding the intervention and its expected outcomes for both the infants and their mothers.

Three basic hypotheses were derived that have remained throughout the intervention and follow-up projects. These were:

1.   Paraprofessionals could teach mothers activities to do with their infants during weekly home visits.
2.   These visits would produce measurable differences in the infants and their mothers.
3.   The effects of teaching the mothers would produce relatively permanent change in their interaction with the child that would have lasting effects into the school years.

Other subhypotheses were included from project to project but these three were consistent throughout the projects.

SITE AND SAMPLE

Description of Community

The projects were conducted in a 12-county area in north central Florida. About half the families lived in Gainesville, a city of about 60,000 at the time of the study in the mid- and late-1960s. The remainder of the families lived in rural settings or very small communities.

The principal employers in the area at the time of the projects were governmental agencies through the Veteran's Administration Hospital, the University of Florida, and Sunland Training Center, an institution for retarded individuals. At that time there was almost no manufacturing or light industry in the counties and the area surrounding Gainesville was primarily agricultural.

Within the community of Gainesville, the economic status varied greatly. About 30% of the population was black and the majority of these families were economically disadvantaged. Racial segregation was still widespread in the community; the University of Florida was an almost totally white institution at that time and had little influence on the black community other than to provide employment. The housing patterns were also segregated.

The white population in the community covered the economic spectrum. Only 20% of white mothers giving birth in the hospital where recruitment occurred met the economic criteria for inclusion in the program. Thus whereas the black population was fairly homogeneous in the surrounding area, the poor white population was from a lower economic level than the majority of the white community. The rural population was just as poor as the urban population. Some of the families were very isolated and were without modern plumbing.

There were few educational opportunities for infants and toddlers in the 12-county area of the study. There were some quality day-care centers, but most of them did not accept infants. The most prevalent group care provided was that of a neighbor taking several infants into her home. Some of these home day-care centers were very well-run whereas others would at best be considered custodial. The idea of parent education as presented by the Gordon Parent Education Programs was a new idea to the families.

Description of Sample

Mothers in the original group were identified at their infant's birth by the obstetrics staff of the J. Hillis Miller Health Center at the University of Florida. The criteria for inclusion were that the family was classified as "indigent" on the hospital records, there was no history of mental illness or retardation in the mother, and it was a single birth with neither a breech or Caesarean delivery nor major complications to either infant or mother. The first sample consisted of 206 mothers and infants born between June 1966 and January 1967. This sample constituted what Gordon referred to as the "pilot" group (Gordon, 1967). Another sample of 131 consisted of babies born between June 1967 and September 1967 and their mothers. These two samples are referred to as the "original sample" with a total size of 397 (Gordon, 1969). The original sample consisted of about 80% black and 20% white families. By the time of the follow-up study at 11 years the proportions had shifted to about 90% black and 10% white, in part due to the fact that some white families had dropped out because they were uncomfortable with being a part of a "poverty" program.

The mothers in the original sample were first contacted at the hospital. During this hospital visit the mothers were told about the project and invited to participate. If a mother agreed to participate she was asked to sign the informed consent form. Sixty of the women refused to sign and no further contacts were made. The mothers agreeing to the weekly home visits were first visited when their infants were 3 months old. By the time of the first home visit random assignments had been made to treatment or control groups.

During the second year of the project, the Home Learning Center (HLC) program was developed that included a longitudinal design following the children to age 6. Later, a decision was made to follow the children's development through 11 years of age. The study design is shown in Table 4.1, and includes a counterbalancing of the effects of time and length of intervention, that is, children could be involved with up to three continuous years of intervention or with other combinations of length and timing of intervention. The children were followed after the end of the intervention so that the long-term effect of the treatment combinations could be assessed.

Beginning in November of 1968 new families with 2-year-old children were added to the longitudinal design for the HLC. One hundred and eighty-six families were contacted who had children born during the same time period as the babies in the original sample. The same criteria for inclusion were used as for

TABLE 4.1
Experimental Design for Longitudinal Study

Group	Years in Program	Treatment Phase Age of Child in Months 3-12	12-24	24-36	First Follow up 48, 60, 72	Second Follow up 123, 132
1. EEE	all 3 years	Home Visit	Home Visit	Home Learning Center/ Home Visit	Test	Test
2. EEC	first 2	Home Visit	Home Visit	Control	Test	Test
3. CEE	second 2	Control	Home Visit	Home Learning Center/ Home Visit	Test	Test
4. ECE	first & third	Home Visit	Control	Home Learning Center/ Home Visit	Test	Test
5. ECC	first only	Home Visit	Control	Control	Test	Test
6. CEC	second only	Control	Home Visit	Control	Test	Test
7. HLC	third only	Control	Control	Home Learning Center/ Home Visit	Test	Test
8. Control	None	Control	Control	Control	Test	Test

the original sample. It was thus assumed that when they entered the project at age 2 the HLC children were much like the original sample. The families were found by searching hospital records, visits to churches, and the parent educators' personal knowledge of families living in the same neighborhoods as the original sample.

Assignment to treatment groups as shown in Table 4.1 was done randomly. The pilot sample (PEP) was divided into two groups, treatment and control. When the next sample (PEP 2) was drawn, families were randomly assigned to control or treatment groups. In addition, part of the original treatment group was then assigned to a control group. This process continued until all the groups in Table 4.1 had been formed. The HLC sample was added when the children in the original sample were about 2 years old. By the time the HLC project was started, all of the group assignments had been made. All intervention ended when the children were age 3, but the children and their mothers were followed on a yearly basis to age 6, then at 10 years and 3 months, and again at 11 years of age.

There were a variety of reasons why families dropped out of the program. The most frequent reason given was "moved"; the next most frequent reason was "refused." The proportion of refusals decreased as the children got older. This was probably because if one were going to refuse to participate, the refusal was likely to happen early after the initial contact rather than after intervention had begun. The numbers of families remaining in the samples at various ages are shown in Table 4.2. The attrition appears to be essentially random and the reasons given for dropping appear to be random with respect to treatment group. After the children were 3 years old, the reasons for dropping were no longer recorded, but attrition that occurred after intervention was primarily because the family could not be located. By the time the children were 11 years of age the total number remaining had dropped to 99 cases. Also, due to scattered instances of missing data for the remaining groups, some of the longitudinal analyses have been performed with fewer numbers of cases. In addition, because of attrition, some of the treatment groups had become so small that meaningful comparisons could not be made. Thus for most of the analyses, experimental groups were combined to make the comparisons meaningful.

DESIGN AND METHODS OF STUDY

Curriculum

The core of the treatment was a weekly home visit with the mother and her infant by a paraprofessional parent educator. During the visit the mother was taught an activity that she was expected to do during the week with her infant. Inasmuch as there were no existing curriculum materials designed expressly for the use we intended, we could not rely upon the work of others. We used four primary

TABLE 4.2
Numbers Remaining in Samples at Project Intervals

Group	Original Sample	Treatment Phase			First Follow up Phase			Second Follow up Phase	
		12 mos.	24 mos.	36 mos.	48 mos.	60 mos.	72 mos.	123 mos.	132 mos.
1. EEE	90	32	29	24	23	26	26	21	19
2. EEC	38	21	18	12	14	12	11	11	9
3. CEE	43	16	10	10	9	9	8	1	1
4. ECE	36	16	12	11	11	11	9	5	5
5. ECC	14	12	11	10	10	11	11	8	8
6. CEC	67	22	17	16	15	16	13	8	8
7. HLC	–	–	82*	59	52	51	50	32	31
8. Control	109	38	69*	50	52	52	51	24	23
Total	397	157	248	192	186	188	179	106	99

*186 families were contacted for the HLC. 121 were assigned to treatment, 51 to the already existing control group, and 14 were not assigned. Attrition reduced the numbers to these values.

sources for our ideas in construction of the basic curriculum. First was Piaget's theory of cognitive development. We selected activities that could be sequenced to match the developmental level of the infants. Many of these activities involved the concept of object permanence. Although some of the activities we used resembled Piaget's descriptions, it is important to note that his theoretical ideas had not been translated into specific curriculum materials. We translated his testing activities into teaching activities. The first series of exercises for the period of 3 to 12 months relied heavily on examples from the exercises developed by Uzguris and Hunt (1966). The activities were designed to be easy to use and easy to evaluate. We attempted to eliminate the pressure of "testing" by the parent educators and mothers but nevertheless some of the activities seemed to be used for this purpose rather than for teaching as they were designed. We further restricted our activities to those that required a minimum of materials. Most of the activities used materials that were readily available to the mothers such as paper bags, milk cartons, cans, cloth scraps, and so forth. We purposely eliminated any but the least expensive store-bought toys. Occasionally we did provide such items as rattles, ribbons, and books.

Our second source for ideas was from laboratory studies with children. Richardson (1932), for example, had worked with what he called "string–and–lure" tests. These were designed to test children's progression in using a string to pull objects into reach. Unfortunately, other laboratory studies did not result in many items although the parent education efforts at the University of Iowa in the 1930s did lend support to our overall efforts. The experimental work with infants tended to be more testing and less teaching.

For our third source, we examined scales of infant development by Bayley (1933), Gessell (1943), and Cattell (1950). A number of learning activities were adapted from these scales.

The fourth source for curriculum ideas was from the general folklore. Many of these ideas were developed with our parent educator staff. Games and rhymes were adapted into learning activities for mothers and children to do together. This was not particularly innovative because mothers have been playing nursery games with their children for many years. It was, however, innovative for this population because many parents were not familiar with such activities.

Several considerations were paramount as we selected materials for inclusion in the curriculum. The following principles were followed in the preparation of the activities:

1. The environment should be responsive. The activities were designed so that the child could see the effect of his actions. When the activity was presented to the mother she was encouraged to be responsive to the child's efforts.

2. The directions for the activity must be explicit and complete. An example is shown in Fig. 4.1. The instructions were intended to provide a complete

POSITION

1. Baby's position: sitting with a flat surface in front of him.
2. Mother's position: beside the baby supporting him.

ACTION

1. Hold a favorite toy out to the baby.
2. When he reaches for it, place it in front of him and cover it quickly, leaving a little of the toy showing.
3. Say, "Where is the toy?" "Find the toy."
4. Repeat actions 1 and 2, but, cover the toy completely.

AIM OF THE GAME

The baby gets the toy after it is completely covered.

PURPOSE

To help the bably realize the permanence of objects.

FIG 4.1.   Example of the instructions and handout used by Parent Educators when teaching activity to mother.

picture to the mother of what she was to do, even to the point of describing the appropriate postures.

3. The purpose for the activity must be clearly stated because we believed it to be very important for the parent to know why the activity should be useful to the child. For example, in Fig. 4.1, the purpose of the activity is "To help the baby realize the permanence of objects."

4. The instructions must clearly state the expected behavior for the infant. If this was not clear, the parent would be unable to determine whether or not the baby's responses were appropriate.

Although much of the curriculum content was based on Piaget, we built activities on the basis of any content that could be converted into a meaningful game that the parent would consider useful and worthwhile. Although not stressed on the written sheet describing the activity that was left with the parent, the parent educators were to stress the importance of "a light touch, of spontaneity and flexibility, and of a warm emotional tone" when working with a child.

Because the Parent Education Programs began when the child was 3 months old and continued until the child was 3 years old, the organization and difficulty level of the content reflected this age span. For the first year of the baby's life the activities were based largely on the normative work of Bayley, Gesell, and Cattell. The activities in the first series were designed to be used when the infant was in a prone or supine position. The next series included items for the baby when in a supported sitting position. In the next series, the infant's position was sitting alone and he or she could lean forward. In the fourth series, we assumed a creeping child and in the fifth, that the children would be walking. Our attempt in sequencing the activities was to provide a variety of activities at each developmental level.

When the children entered the HLC at age 2, the nature of the activities changed slightly. The activities were again organized around the theoretical position of Piaget. These activities were on a more general nature than those for the younger ages and were not so closely age graded. Another change, although we still relied as much on easily found inexpensive materials as we could, was the introduction of educational toys. Their use was primarily in the HLC setting, although occasionally a parent educator would take a toy into the home to be used for demonstrating to the mother how the toy could be used as a learning device and not solely for amusement. The majority of the curriculum activities relied on such easily obtained materials as empty egg cartons, old stockings, and oatmeal boxes and were devised by the professional and paraprofessional staff members. The activities for 2- to 3-year-olds have been published in *Child Learning through Child Play* (Gordon, Guinagh, & Jester, 1972). A revision of the original activities for infants up to age 2 was published in *Baby Learning through Baby Play* (Gordon, 1970).

Parent Educators

The parent educators were recruited from a population similar to that of the disadvantaged mothers in the project. The 15 original paraprofessionals were selected from over 75 applicants. Fourteen had children of their own and all but 2 were high school graduates. Twelve were black and 3 were white; some were in their twenties with education beyond high school. The remainder of the group were older and more matronly who, it was thought, might relate better to the mothers but also might have some difficulty learning the kinds of record keeping necessary to a research project. Some of the women had been employed previously in low-paying jobs such as housekeepers and maids.

Our basic assumption in the use of paraprofessionals was that their personal characteristics would be similar to those of the mothers being visited. It was expected that this similarity would enable the parent educators to establish trust that should, in turn, result in more open communication and permit the collection of data not generally available to the professional. In addition, we believed that the paraprofessional would be able to establish rapport with the parents more readily than would professionals because they would be sensitive to cultural differences perhaps missed by professional staff. We thus made the assumption that our paraprofessionals would enter the program with qualities similar to those of the families being visited. No assumptions were made about their skill level except that training would be required for them to perform their teaching and research roles adequately.

Preservice training of the original 15 parent educators began in the summer of 1966 and lasted for a period of 5 weeks. The goals of this training were to instill in the paraprofessional ways of working with the mother so that she would understand:

1. How to do the activities with her youngster.
2. Why these activities were important for the development of her baby.
3. Why it was important for the mother to do the activities with the baby and not to think of the parent educator as the teacher of the baby.

The training staff was chosen to reflect a broad spectrum of ideas and came from education, nursing, and child psychology. The staff was new to the teaching of women at this educational level and therefore attempted a variety of methods when presenting ideas and material. Experience suggested that one of the more effective educational methods was role playing. Concrete presentations were also found to be an important aspect of the training situation. A large proportion of the preservice training was devoted to teaching the parent educators the activities they would be teaching to the mothers. At first, dolls were used for practice of the activities and the parent educators would role play the mother for each other. As they gained proficiency, infants were brought into the training sessions and the role playing continued. At the end of the preservice training the parent educators knew all the activities, how to present them, and their purposes. They had also practiced teaching the activities and knew how to present them without giving mothers the feeling that they were unknowledgeable or were not caring for their children properly.

Following the preservice training, inservice training sessions were held once a week for the duration of the project. The full day of inservice activities included: (1) administrative chores; (2) general education programs to broaden the parent educators' perspectives on human development and other aspects of daily living; (3) training on matters specific to the job; and (4) evaluation feedback from the project staff. Administrative chores such as filling out travel forms and various project reports were the least popular among our parent educators.

As the projects matured, more time was devoted to the general education aspects of the inservice training. We invited presentations from experts in child development, nutrition, health, the state welfare system, insurance, home economics, and a variety of other topics intended to broaden the general educational development of the parent educators. This was further extended when, toward the end of intervention in the fall of 1969, some of the parent educators took regular classes at Sante Fe Community College near Gainesville for half a day. Regular credit was given for some of their project work, and the courses they took counted toward an associate degree that some of them have since completed.

Specific job training usually consisted of clarification of the learning activities for mothers and their presentation. Although the activities had been learned during the preservice training, review was needed from time to time. In addition, activities were sometimes modified as experience dictated and this had to be discussed with the parent educators after which they learned the details and practiced the activity prior to taking it into the home.

When the Home Learning Centers were added to the program, the parent educators had to learn a variety of new skills. The most important was how to deal with a group of 2-year-olds in a relatively unstructured setting. Although there was a tendency for the parent educators to emulate traditional models for teaching, these did not work too well; when an attempt was made to work with children individually, it was found that not many of our parent educators were able to do this. Sometimes the child did not want to work with the parent educator and sometimes the attempt was frustrated by another child's interruptions. After a little experience we learned that it was best to follow the children's lead and to focus on their interests when in the group setting.

A small proportion of the inservice time was used for presentations from the project staff relating to the progress of the research components of the program to the parent educators. It was found to be important to emphasize continuously the research aspects of the project. The parent educators were much more interested in working with the mothers than they were in collecting research data.

Implementation

Implementation of the home visits and the teaching of the infants' parents by the paraprofessional home visitor closely followed the philosophy of the program: Parents are the primary teachers of their children.

Each parent educator was assigned to ten families and visited the home once a week to teach the mother a learning activity. During the early phases of the project the activities were presented through role playing and with the baby present. The mother and infant were to try the learning activity while the parent educator was present. Although the parent educators had a great deal of autonomy in their activity, they were supervised closely. At least once a week every parent educator met with her supervisor to discuss the prior week's home visits. At that time the next activities to be presented were selected and practiced through role playing. The parent educator and supervisor then had a general discussion of each family's condition and the supervisor made suggestions if they were appropriate.

During the home visit the parent educator reviewed the activity taught by the parent in the previous week. These reviews focused on the appropriateness of the activity for the child. If the child had experienced success and enjoyed the activity, then it was considered to have been appropriate and a new activity was selected for that week. The activity was presented to the mother and a general discussion of the condition of the family followed. Many of these relationships became very warm and close and it was not unusual for a parent educator to have coffee and a snack with a mother before she left the home. Some personal and family problems became apparent during these visits. These were discussed at the next meeting with the parent educator's supervisor, recommendations were made, and the cycle repeated. The implementation could thus be thought of as a cycle from professional to paraprofessional to parent to baby.

As the project moved into its second year, the parents were more sophisticated and the home visits changed slightly. Role playing became almost nonexistent in some families and the assumption was easy to make that the mothers understood and would do the activity with the babies. The adults were becoming more verbal with each other and the child was more frequently in the background. The nature of the visit did not change in the sense that the parent was "taught" and was to deal with the child personally. There was, however, a tendency for the adults to "test" rather than "teach" the child. Many of the activities lent themselves to this because it was easy to see if the child could do them. These kinds of activities were often done a few times and then considered "passed" when the child could do them. As the children became older and more capable of motor activities that could be easily observed, this became more and more of a problem.

This "testing" produced a particular threat to our original philosophy, which was to maintain a high level of interaction between parent and child. Many of the activities were meant to be repeated in ways that would be pleasing to the child.

If the parent assumed an activity was "passed" and the child no longer had to acquire the skill necessary for the activity, there was a tendency to drop that activity and go on to another. Part of this problem was probably the result of our early emphasis on curriculum materials and how to present them to the child. In our training we stressed when a child should be doing an activity rather than simply moving through them as rapidly as possible. It is easy to see how these activities could be interpreted as signs of completion or as tests of particular skills.

Another related problem was that the parent educators often preferred teaching the child rather than the parent. This was, again, probably related to our training. Much of our training was on how the task should be presented to the baby and at what stage of the baby's development the task was appropriate. The parent educators thus knew much more about how to deal with the babies than they did about dealing with the parents. Another reason for this tendency is that babies are usually appealing and cooperative, making that experience more fun than trying to teach a parent who was sometimes tired.

As the Home Learning Centers became established, we also learned a great deal. Placement of the centers in private homes had several advantages. We had no construction or rental costs and the atmosphere was friendly, homelike, and less institutional than most programs. There were, however, some problems. For example, there was a wide range in housekeeping standards among the home mothers. Some homes were always clean and tidy, whereas a few were consistently stale and untidy. It was difficult to maintain a pleasant relationship while criticizing a home mother's housekeeping standards. Project staff attempted to help by showing some of the home mothers how to clean and what products would help. Change of these conditions was not rapid or easy, and there were many setbacks.

A more prevalent problem was with the mother's other children in the home. Our original assumption was that preschool children who lived in the home could simply join into the activities. This was not a valid assumption. In many cases, the home children thought of the toys as belonging to them and they did not want to share them. When their mother intervened or tried to work with other children, jealousy often developed. The problem became severe enough that we required the home mothers to find babysitting for their other children during the Home Learning Center sessions. Many of the mothers objected to this because it meant putting their own children out of the home and also used some of their limited resources. The parent educators insisted that because they had to find sitters for their children, the mothers in the Home Learning Centers should also.

Data Collection Procedures

The children and mothers were evaluated both during and after the intervention phase of the program. Testing and interviews were done annually during the program for purposes of summative evaluation. In addition, children were evaluated almost every time the parent educator made a home visit. This formative evaluation was used for the purpose of planning learning activities for the children. As shown in Table 4.1, the summative evaluation was done annually until the children reached their sixth birthday. After that, testing and some interviews were done when the children were 8, a little over 10, and 11 years old.

The most important variable expected to change in the children as a function of the early intervention project was that of "intelligence." At the beginning of the project there were relatively few standardized tests of intelligence appropriate for infants at 1 year of age. The Griffiths Scale (Griffiths, 1954) was selected because it was the best standardized scale available at the time. By the time the infants had reached 2 years, the Bayley Scales of Infant Development (Bayley, 1969) had been published. The primary advantage in using the Bayley Scales was that the standardization samples were from the United States whereas the samples for the standardization of the Griffiths Scales were from England. When the children reached 3 years of age, the Stanford–Binet, Form L–M (Terman & Merrill, 1960) was used, and again at 4, 5, and 6 years. The children were tested with the Wechsler Intelligence Scale for Children-Revised (WISC-R; Wechsler, 1974) when they were 10 years and 3 months old.

Standardized achievement tests were administered to the children as a part of their school programs. We collected the data from the children's school records. Three different achievement tests were used by the school systems the children attended: the Metropolitan Achievement Test, the Comprehensive Test of Basic Skills, and the Stanford Achievement Test.

The Classroom Behavior Inventory, Short Form (Schaefer & Aaronson, 1965) was completed by the teachers of project children when they were 8 years old. Adjustment to school was judged by analysis of school records, and the files were examined to determine the number of children assigned to special programs. The number who skipped or were retained a grade was also recorded.

One of the most pervasive assumptions underlying the home visit was that the mothers would develop more positive self-concepts and would become more self-directed. This was expected to happen as a result of the mother's improved skills in dealing with her baby because of the instruction by the parent educators. Gordon had developed the *How I See Myself Scale* (HISM) to measure "self concept" (Gordon, 1968). In addition to this scale, the *Social Reaction Inventory* (SRI), developed by Bilker (1970) and adapted for use from Rotter's Locus of Control Scale, was administered to the mothers at each of the evaluation points shown in Table 4.1.

Another assumption underlying the intervention efforts was that the home environment would change in terms of what the family thought was important for the child's intellectual development. It was expected, for instance, that mothers would report such things as more books and magazines in the home and would expect more and better school performance from their children. In order to measure these kinds of constructs, Gordon chose the *Home Environment Review*, which was an adaptation of the Wolf Scale (Garber, 1968; Garber & Ware,

1972). The scale has been divided into nine subscales, each of which assesses a quality of the child's environment with respect to educational activities and expectations. The form was completed by the parent educators at each of the evaluation points shown in Table 4.1.

Some of the data collection was performed by the parent educators. Such instruments as the *How I See Myself* (Gordon, 1969), *Social Reaction Inventory* (Bilker, 1970), and the *Home Environment Review* (Garber & Ware, 1972) were simple enough in their administration that paraprofessionals could be expected to produce valid and reliable results. The children's intelligence tests were administered by trained and qualified graduate students. In the early phases of the project, the test administration took place in a room at the Shands Teaching Hospital at the University of Florida. There was, however, some trade-off in terms of advantages and disadvantages. Although this procedure added an air of credibility for many of the project families, the hospital environment appeared to create a negative reaction for some of them. Therefore, a home of one of the parents was used for testing at ages 3 through 5. From age 6 on, the children were tested at school.

General Approach to Data Analyses

During the early phases of the intervention projects, the principle analyses were *t* tests based on simple comparisons between "experimental" and "control" groups. When the longitudinal plan was adopted and the experimental design was developed in the Home Learning Center project, the appropriate analysis was a repeated measures analysis of variance for all instruments. In the original design both length and timing of treatment were considered to be independent variables and were completely counterbalanced. This resulted in a total of eight groups at the end of the third year of the projects (see Table 4.1).

The original experimental design for the longitudinal study was such that a repeated measures analysis of variance was appropriate for the data. Due to attrition, however, the design became sufficiently unbalanced that such an analysis of all eight groups was no longer appropriate. In order to assess the lasting effects of intervention on the dependent measures better, the original eight groups were recombined into three. This resulted in larger within-cell sample sizes as well as a better balance in the analyses. The first "new" group, which we labeled "longitudinal," consisted of children who were in the program for 2 or 3 consecutive years (groups 1, 2, and 3). The second consisted of children who were recruited for the Home Learning Center (HLC) and for whom data were not collected prior to 2 years of age (group 7). The third group consisted of children who had been assigned to the control group at the beginning of the project along with a smaller group recruited with the HLC children (group 8). The three remaining groups (groups 4, 5, and 6) included so few cases with complete data that we decided to drop them from the analyses.

One result of this recombination of the groups was that the main effects in the analysis due to length and timing of treatment could not be evaluated. The loss of this information, however, was offset by the added power and clarity of the analyses for the remaining three groups. The majority of the more recent analyses have been done with these groups. Only the intelligence test data satisfied the conditions and assumptions underlying the analysis of variance for repeated measures.

Because the children in the project had been tested on three different achievement tests we could not combine the scores directly. Therefore, in most of the analyses of the achievement test data, stanine scores were used. Although these are not as precise as the original test scores, they clearly reflect the relative placement of the children regardless of the test used.

FINDINGS

The broad aims of the investigation were to determine if a parent education approach to intervention into the lives of economically disadvantaged infants and their mothers would be feasible and if there were long-term positive effects on both mother and child. There were a number of subsidiary hypotheses also, as described in the previous section.

Effects on the Child

Intelligence. As noted earlier, the original purpose of the study was to determine if intervention during the early years would have a measurable and lasting effect on the intelligence of children from economically disadvantaged populations. The results of the testings for the eight experimental groups are shown in Table 4.3 The differences among the groups for the first two testings at ages 1 and 2 were not significant; however, by the time the Binet was used when the children were 3 years old, differences were apparent between treatment and control groups. The differences favored children who had been in the treatment for all 3 years, two consecutive years, or the third year only. These differences were maintained until the children reached 10 years of age.

The three recombined groups (longitudinal, HLC, and control) were then subjected to two repeated measure analyses of variance on the IQ test data. One of the analyses was done using all of these data and the other without the WISC-R scores. Both analyses indicated statistically significant differences among the three groups ($p < .05$). When the WISC-R was included in the analysis there was a significant difference across occasions or testings ($p < .001$), and when the WISC-R was excluded this difference disappeared. The results are shown graphically in Fig. 4.2. It is apparent that for all three groups the scores dropped between the Binet tests and the WISC-R. This is probably due to differences in the tests and testers rather than to a "real" drop in intelligence. A study comparing the mean WISC-R Full Scale IQ with the mean Stanford–Binet IQ (1972

TABLE 4.3
Means and Standard Deviations for IQ Tests Given at Ages 1-6
and 10 by Treatment Group

Group		1-Griffiths	2-Bayley	3-Binet	4-Binet	5-Binet	6-Binet	10-WISC-R
					Age and Test			
1-EEE	N	49	20	21	21	25	26	21
	M	110.61	87.2	98.79	98.38	96.60	95.8	89.05
	S	9.26	14.1	16.79	20.14	14.61	13.3	16.51
2-EEC	N	28	10	12	9	11	11	11
	M	110.78	83.7	95.83	99.22	95.27	98.0	85.62
	S	11.48	12.7	14.98	11.53	10.27	12.7	16.60
3-CEE	N	19	8	9	9	9	8	1
	M	111.05	86.8	99.00	98.78	95.22	94.8	97.02
	S	10.35	5.9	13.19	11.11	13.09	6.7	.00
4-ECE	N	18	7	9	8	11	9	5
	M	109.06	80.0	89.89	91.38	91.45	90.4	78.21
	S	12.82	8.6	11.47	12.73	11.32	10.0	6.79
5-ECC	N	11	9	9	9	11	11	8
	M	114.64	86.3	91.67	97.00	97.55	91.3	80.01
	S	9.73	9.17	8.83	14.83	18.65	14.4	10.53
6-CEC	N	24	10	13	12	15	13	4
	M	109.33	91.9	89.85	84.50	86.40	90.5	79.92
	S	8.41	17.7	10.56	10.53	11.46	13.0	14.57
7-HLC	N		37	52	42	48	49	32
	M		87.6	95.01	94.67	92.58	94.8	81.74
	S		14.9	12.98	10.51	10.34	12.2	10.82
8-CON	N	58	41	45	43	52	49	24
	M	106.67	89.3	90.98	89.72	88.81	89.2	77.75
	S	9.26	14.1	11.20	12.27	12.45	9.8	11.40

norms) revealed a two point difference favoring the Stanford–Binet (Wechsler, 1974) for children in the age range covered by the present study. Although this difference is not as large as those found in this study, some of the apparent drop is probably due to the tests used. The differences among the three groups, however, are significant both with and without the WISC-R scores at 10 years. The longitudinal group scored highest, followed by the Home Learning Center group, and then the control group. Differences as a function of group membership have been maintained from completion of the program until children reached 10 years of age. It seems that the longer the intervention, the more the IQ test score is effected.

Achievement. Although IQ tests may be used to predict school performance, they do not measure it. A second hypothesis was that performance on school

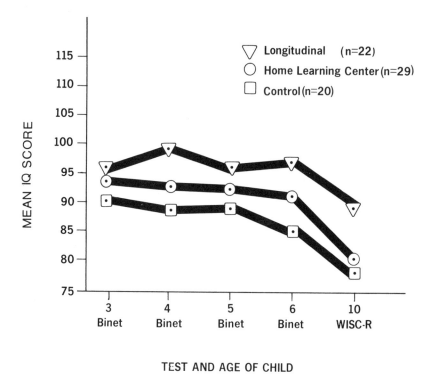

TEST AND AGE OF CHILD

FIG. 4.2.   Mean IQ test scores for Longitudinal, Home Learning Center, and
Control groups from 3 to 10 years of age.

achievement tests would be significantly higher for children in the treatment
groups than in the control groups.

The children were from ten different school districts in the surrounding area
and all did not receive the same achievement tests. Three different tests were
used, although most took the Metropolitan Achievement Test. In addition, children placed in special classes (Educable and Trainable Mentally Retarded) were
not given such tests. Therefore much of the data could not be combined directly.
However, given the assumption that children in special classes would be below
class average, it was then possible to examine the proportions of project children
who scored at or above the grade level they were in. Because of different
entering dates the children were at three different grade levels when these data
were gathered in 1976. In the spring of 1976 project children were in grades 2, 3,
and 4. Few reached grade level on these achievement tests. Although more
project children in the longitudinal group reached grade level than those in the
control group, none of these differences was statistically reliable.

When a less stringent achievement level of only 9 months behind grade level
was used, some of the differences among the groups were significant (see Table

4.4). Reading and math scores produced the largest statistically reliable differences (for reading, $p < .025$ and for total reading, Math Concepts, and Math Problem Solving, $p < .05$).

These achievement data, collected when project children were in the second, third, and fourth grades, tended to support the general conclusion drawn from the intelligence test data that those children who had been in the program were positively influenced and performed better than did their control peers.

In 1978, the project children were in the fourth, fifth, and sixth grades. Achievement test scores were gathered both then and when the children were in

TABLE 4.4
Proportions of Children within Nine Months of Grade Level on
Achievement Tests when in 2nd, 3rd, and 4th Grade in Spring,
1976 by Treatment Group

Test/Subtest[a]	Group			Longitudinal vs. Control	
	Long[b]	HLC[b]	Cntrl[b]	Z[c]	P
Word Knowledge	.452 (14/31)	.222 (8/36)	.286 (4/14)	1.05	n.s
Reading	.387 (12/31)	.222 (8/36)	.077 (1/13)	2.05	.025
Total Reading	.364 (12/33)	.237 (9/38)	.150 (3/20)	1.67	.05
Language	.367 (11.30)	.281 (9/32)	.286 (4/14)	.53	n.s.
Spelling	.483 (14/29)	.343 (12/35)	.308 (4/13)	1.06	n.s.
Math Competence	.419 (13/31)	.457 (16/35)	.286 (4/14)	.85	n.s.
Math Concepts	.452 (14/31)	.257 (9/35)	.154 (2/13)	1.87	.05
Math Prob. Solv.	.419 (13/31)	.278 (10/36)	.154 (2/13)	1.69	.05
Total Math	.394 (13/33)	.297 (11/37)	.200 (4/20)	1.47	n.s.

[a] All tests were the Metropolitan Achievement Test, except Total Reading and Total Math, which included 11 children who took the Comprehensive Tests of Basic Skills or the Stanford Achievement Test.

[b] Numbers in parentheses indicate the number of children within nine months of grade level/number of children with complete test scores.

[c] z comparison of Longitudinal with Controls, one-tailed test.

Note. There were no significant differences between the Home Learning Center and Control groups.

the fifth, sixth, and seventh grades in 1979. Because the data were based on three different achievement tests, stanines were used as a form of standard score so that there could be more complete data for the analyses. The results are shown in Table 4.5 for both years. Proportions of children scoring at or higher than the fourth stanine were compared for the three treatment conditions, i.e., Longitudinal (Long, two or more consecutive years in program), Home Learning Center (HLC, last year in treatment), and Control (Cntrl, no treatment). The differences were statistically significant for four of the 1978 comparisons: Vocabulary, Long > HLC and HLC < Cntrl ($p < .05$); Math, Long > Cntrl and HLC > Cntrl ($p > .05$). Analysis of 1979 data resulted in only one significant difference: Reading, Long > Cntrl ($p < .05$). There were no other significant differences among the groups on achievement test performance.

Placement in Special Classes. A powerful measure of social significance is assignment to special education classes. The term *special education* refers to all classifications of Educable Mentally Retarded (EMR), Trainable Mentally Retarded (TMR), Specific Learning Disability (SLD), and Emotionally Handicapped (EH). The proportions of children assigned to special education during the school years 1974–1975 and 1977–1978 are shown in Table 4.6. The proportions generally favor the treatment groups with the longitudinal group producing the fewest special education children. During the year 1978–1979 the differences still favored the treatment groups but are not large enough to be considered significant.

TABLE 4.5

Comparisons of Groups on Achievement Test Performances in 1978 and 1979 Using Proportions who Scored at Stanine 4 or Higher

	Group			Long vs. Cntrl		Long vs. HLC		HLC vs. Cntrl	
	Long[a]	HLC[a]	Cntrl[a]	z	p	z	p	z'	p
1978 Results[b]									
Vocabulary	.60(25)	.24(34)	.46(22)	1.00	n.s.	2.84	.01	-1.72	.05
Reading	.48(25)	.42(34)	.36(22)	.81	n.s.	.52	n.s.	.36	n.s.
Math	.52(25)	.47(34)	.23(22)	2.06	.025	.38	n.s.	1.84	.05
1979 Results[b]									
Vocabulary	.42(24)	.23(31)	.26(23)	1.13	n.s.	1.52	n.s.	-.30	n.s.
Reading	.63(24)	.45(31)	.35(23)	1.90	.05	1.28	n.s.	.77	n.s.
Math	.54(24)	.45(31)	.48(23)	.44	n.s.	.66	n.s.	-.19	n.s.

[a]Numbers in parentheses indicate the number of children with complete test scores.

[b]Most tests were Metropolitan Achievement Tests; a few children took the Comprehensive Tests of Basic Skills or the Stanford Achievement Test.

TABLE 4.6
Proportion and Number of Children Assigned to Special
Education Programs by Group

Group	1974-1975	1978-1979
Long	.0645	.0909
	2/31	3/33
HLC	.0270	.1250
	1/37	4/32
Cntrl	.2857	.2917
	6/21	7/24

Comparisons:	1974-1975	Long vs. Cntrl, X^2 = 3.16, p < .05
		HLC vs. Cntrl, X^2 = 6.19, p < .01
	1978-1979	Long vs. Cntrl, X^2 = 2.61, p < .10
		HLC vs. Cntrl, X^2 = 1.47, n.s.

School Adjustment.   There were no differences among the treatment groups on such variables as referral for discipline problems or psychological help or for grade retention. It should be noted that Florida schools have had social promotion, and therefore the latter variable is of little value. In addition, the children were rated on the *Classroom Behavior Inventory* (Shaefer & Aaronson, 1965). Ninety teachers in second-, third-, and fourth-grade classrooms filled out the inventory on project children during the school year 1974–1975. The teachers were told the background of the study but were not told what treatment the children received. Analyses of these data revealed no statistically significant differences among any of the groups.

Self-Concept.   The children's version of the *How I See Myself* scale (Gordon, 1969) was administered to the children when they were 6 and 10 years of age. No reliable differences were found as a function of group membership.

Effects on the Mother

Home Environment.   An important expectation was that the child's environment would become more positive as a result of the instruction and suggestions made during the home visits. The *Home Environment Review* (Garber & Ware, 1972) was used to measure seven variables related to the home environment and to parental expectations of the child's schooling. During the early phases of the project there were consistent differences favoring the treatment groups. That is, the mothers of project children reported more books and educational materials in the home, used more positive rewards, were more aware of their children's development, and had higher expectations for their children than did control mothers (Gordon & Guinagh, 1974). These differences had "faded" by the time the children were in middle school (Gordon & Jester, 1980). The only remaining difference was "Awareness of development," with the treatment mothers scoring higher than control mothers ($p < .01$).

Mothers' School-Related behavior.   *The Teacher's Report of Parent Behavior* (Shaefer, 1976) was filled out by the teachers in the public schools for project children's parents. The intent of the scale was to measure the degree to which the mothers were involved in the educational activities of their children. The results showed no difference among treatment groups in the teachers' perceptions of the parents' behavior.

Mother's Locus of Control.   During the course of the study, the mothers were administered the *Social Reaction Inventory* (Bilker, 1970), which was an adaptation of Rotter's Locus of Control Scale. During intervention, there were significant, although small differences in feelings of internality that favored the treatment mothers. These differences faded after the end of intervention. When the children were 6, 10, and 11 years old, there were no significant differences among any of the groups.

Self-Concept.   The mothers were administered the *How I See Myself* Scale (Gordon, 1969) several times during the course of the project. Although it was hypothesized that the mothers would become more positive in their self-perceptions, the data collected using this scale did not support the hypothesis. The data for the first year of the program were summarized in an earlier report with the conclusion "that there was a significant difference between the control and the experimental mothers at entry point in their feeling of Interpersonal Adequacy, the experimental group being significantly lower. Neither changed markedly during the 9-month interval [Gordon, 1969, p. 145]." Although there was an early indication that the scale was not sensitive to change, it was used throughout the project. None of the analyses using this scale indicated any reliable differences as a function of timing or length of intervention.

Summary of Findings

The cognitive and school performance data collected during the course of this project, such as IQ, achievement, and placement in special education classes, supported the hypothesis that those children in the program for two to three consecutive years performed better than control children for as long as 7 years after the active intervention had ended. However, the socioemotional and personality data relating to the mothers and their children, such as teacher ratings and inventories of personality variables, did not show such differences. Even though there were some small differences between treatment and control mothers early during the intervention, wherever these differences occurred they faded shortly after the intervention ceased.

DISCUSSION OF RESULTS

This review of the Gordon Parent Education Program has reported on long-term findings in four different areas: intelligence, academic achievement, placement in special education, and social-emotional adjustment. The most convincing evidence of the program's facilitative effects was intelligence test data that indicated the longer a child was in the intervention the higher was his or her IQ score. As was shown in Figure 4.2, there were differences favoring the longitudinal (2–3 years in program) group up to 7 years after intervention. Children in the program for the maximum length of time (3 years), on the average had an IQ of 91 at 10 years and 3 months of age. This is below the average IQ of 100 but well above the mean IQ score of 78 for the control children.

With regard to school achievement, differences were less obvious. The children who were in the treatment groups, however, generally scored higher than those in the control group. Many of the differences were statistically reliable. Math and Reading Achievement test scores were higher for the longitudinal group on most of the testings and usually were statistically reliable ($p < .05$).

Another indication of facilitative effects of the intervention is the number of children assigned to special education. During 1974–1975, when the children were 10 and 11 years old, there were fewer children from the treatment groups assigned to special education than from the control group ($p < .05$). By the academic year 1977–1978, the percentage of children from the control group assigned to special education was still higher than for the intervention groups, but the difference was significant only at the .10 level. Again, these findings are in the predicted direction and support the hypothesis that intervention into the lives of disadvantaged infants has a positive effect on their later school performance. This effect was observed to be significant up to 7 years after intervention had ceased.

Although some differences were observed between the treatment and control mothers on social-emotional measures such as the Social Reaction Inventory and the Home Environment Review, these differences had faded by 7 years after intervention had ceased. The fact that they were being visited once a week for a fairly extensive time period may have been enough to have helped the mothers look at life and their situation a little more positively than they have since intervention ceased. This is a problem for future investigation.

The best indicator of program effectiveness in terms of dollar values to society may be the children's assignment to special education programs. Project children were assigned to such programs significantly less often than their control peers.

Whatever effect the program had on the child's family that could have produced this outcome was a durable one. The mere fact that fewer treatment children ended up in special classes is a finding that suggests a home visit program such as outlined in this chapter is a valid way to educate parents to help their children in school-relevant areas of functioning.

A CONCLUDING STATEMENT

This chapter has summarized six projects initiated by Ira J. Gordon from mid-1966 until the fall of 1978. The aims of the projects were ambitious and innovative. In 1966 most research involving infants was observational with little or no active intervention. Gordon believed it would be possible to combine a quality intervention program designed to "break the poverty cycle" with quality research. The projects were designed to demonstrate this belief through a longitudinal experimental design that included yearly measurement until the children reached age 11. There is no question regarding the initial issue—the "poverty cycle" cannot be "broken" by a project such as this. It is clear, however, that intervention into the lives of disadvantaged infants can result in reliable performance differences as long as 8 years after the end of intervention. This is a powerful effect and it must be assumed that some of the underlying reason is due to changes in the mothers that, in turn, enhanced the children's school performance.

Although attrition could be cited as a problem in the generalization of these findings, there have been many programs since 1966 that have used Gordon's methods. Although most of these programs have not pursued the infants after intervention, the results are consistent. Program evaluations show distinct advantages to infants resulting from the intervention efforts. Repeated longitudinal research in such projects would help to resolve the significance of the attrition in the Gordon studies.

When the children entered the public schools, new forces acted to modify their behavior and patterns of school achievement. The children's public school experience came on the heels of racial integration with crosstown busing and some social upheaval. It is natural that such variables would interact with home forces to further affect the child. With these and many other external forces acting on the children since intervention ceased, perhaps the most remarkable thing about Gordon's Parent Education Project is that there have been such sustained differences at all.

The most intense intervention for project children occurred when they were less than 3 years old and yet they appear to have been affected in permanent ways. We do not know exactly what produced the differences but we do know that they are permanent and have benefited the children. We also know that no matter what the effect of the program the environmental forces will continued to modify the children as they grow older. We conclude with the words of our friend Ira Gordon (1976): "Each developmental period to some degree predicts the next. But, no one is locked in, in a mechanistic or deterministic sense. Change is not the antithesis of continuity. What we can become, while influenced strongly by the past, is at the same time influenced strongly by the present [p. 122]."

ACKNOWLEDGMENTS

Funding during the first year was from the Ford Foundation. Later funding came from various grants from the U.S. Department of Health, Education, and Welfare: The Children's Bureau; National Institute of Mental Health; and the U.S. Department of Health and Human Services: Administration for Children, Youth, and Families. The University of Florida also contributed in-kind support.

REFERENCES

Bayley, N. Mental growth during the first three years. *Genetic Psychology Monographs.* 1933, *14,* 7–89.

Bayley, N. *Bayley scales of infant development.* New York: Psychological Corporation, 1969.

Bilker, L. *Locus of I-E control expectancy changes in disadvantaged mothers.* Doctoral dissertation, University of Florida, 1970.

Bloom, B. *Stability and change in human characteristics.* New York: Wiley, 1964.

Cattell, P. *The measurement of intelligence of infants and young children.* New York: Psychological Corporation, 1950.

Coleman, J. S. *Equality of educational opportunity.* Washington, D.C.: U.S. Office of Education, 1966.

Garber, M. *Ethnicity and measures of educability.* Doctoral dissertation, University of Southern California, 1968.

Garber, M., & Ware, W. B. The home environment as a predictor of school achievement. *Theory into Practice,* 1972, *11,* 190–195.

Gesell, A. *Infant and child in the culture of today: The guidance of development in home and school.* New York: Harper, 1943.

Gordon, I. J. *A parent education approach to provision of early stimulation for the culturally disadvantaged.* Final report to the Fund for the Advancement of Education established by the Ford Foundation, 1967. Mimeographed.

Gordon, I. J. *A test manual for the How I See Myself scale.* Gainesville, Fla.: The Florida Research and Development Council, 1968.

Gordon, I. J. *Early child stimulation through parent education.* Final report to the Children's Bureau, Social and Rehabilitative Service, Department of Health, Education, and Welfare. PHS-R-306, PHS-R-306(01), 1969.

Gordon, I. J. *Baby learning through baby play.* New York: St. Martin's Press, 1970.

Gordon, I. On the continuity of development. *Childhood Education,* 1976, *52,*(3), 122–128.

Gordon, I. J., & Guinagh, B. J. *A home learning center approach to early stimulation,* NIMH, DHEW, Final report, Grant No. 5 R01 MH 16037-06, 1974.

Gordon, I. J., & Guinagh, B. J. *Middle school performance as a function of infant stimulation.* Final report, ACYF, DHEW, Grant No. NIH-HEW-OCD-90-C-908, 1978.

Gordon, I. J., Guinagh, B. J., & Jester, R. E. *Child learning through child play.* New York: St. Martin's Press, 1972.

Gordon, I. J., Guinagh, B. J., & Jester, R. E. The Florida parent education infant and toddler programs. In M. C. Day and R. K. Parker (Eds.), *The Preschool in Action,* 2nd Edition. Boston: Allyn & Bacon, 1977.

Gordon, I. J., & Jester, R. E. *Middle school performance as a function of early intervention.* Final report to the Child Welfare and Demonstration Grants Program, Administration for Children, Youth and Families, Grant No. 90-C-1309(01), 1980.

Griffiths, R. *The Abilities of Babies.* London: University of London Press, 1954.

Guinagh, B., & Gordon, I. *School performance as a function of early stimulation.* Final report to the Office of Child Development, Grant No. NIH-HEW-OCD009-C-638, 1976.

Hunt, J. McV. *Intelligence and Experience.* New York: Ronald Press, 1961.

Jencks, C., Smith, M., Acland, H., Bane, M. J., Cohen, D., Gintis, H., Heynes, B. & Michelson, S. *Inequality: A reassessment of the effect of family and schooling in America.* New York: Basic Books, 1972.

Levinson, P., & Schiller, J. The indigenous non-professional. *Research Issues*-Research paper No. 6, Division of Research Welfare Administration, March, 1965.

Mayeske, G. W., & Beaton, A. E. *Special studies of our nation's students.* Washington: DHEW, 1975.

Piaget, J. *The origins of intelligence in children.* New York: International Press, 1952.

Richardson, H. The growth of adaptive behavior in an experimental study of seven age levels. *Genetic Psychology Monographs,* 1932, *12,* 195–359.

Riessman, F. *The role of the indigenous non-professional in a community mental health neighborhood service center program.* Paper delivered at the American Orthopsychiatry Association Meeting, 1966.

Schaefer, E., & Aaronson, M. *Classroom Behavior Inventory,* short form, K-12. Prestandardized copy, 1965.

Schaefer, E. *Parent–Professional–Child interaction and involvement second year progress report and proposal for renewal.* Mimeographed, Frank Porter Graham Child Development Center, Chapel Hill, N.C., March 1976.

Terman, L., & Merrill, M. *Stanford–Binet intelligence scale: Manual for the third revision-form L–M.* Boston: Houghton Mifflin, 1960.

Uzguris, J., & Hunt, J. McV. An instrument of assessing infant psychological development. Mimeographed, University of Illinois, February, 1966.

Wechsler, D. *Manual for the Wechsler intelligence scale for children* (Rev. ed.), New York: The Psychological Corporation, 1974.

5 A Comparison of Five Approaches for Educating Young Children from Low-Income Homes

Merle B. Karnes
Allan M. Shwedel
Mark B. Williams
University of Illinois, Urbana Campus

Introduction

Prior to the 1960s, preschool education was primarily the privilege of children from affluent homes, because existing programs were largely private and funded through tuition. Although little research had been conducted to evaluate the effects of these programs on subsequent academic and social adjustment, it was generally believed that such programs helped youngsters meet the expectations of the public schools. Logically enough, the rights of all children to receive the benefits of early education began to receive attention—along with a broad social concern for helping the poor to participate more fully in our society. Thus Head Start was launched by the federal government in the summer of 1965. There was, however, no agreement about the educational approach that would be most effective in helping these children gain the knowledge and skills essential for competing successfully in the public schools. Indeed, Head Start was often referred to as a ''crash'' program.

Concurrent with the initiation of the summer Head Start program, the University of Illinois, with supporting funds for three years from the Cooperative Research Branch of the U.S. Office of Education, established a research center under the overall direction of Merle Karnes to design and evaluate approaches for educating young disadvantaged children as well as to study social and psychological factors in the functioning of disadvantaged children. A number of researchers pursued these objectives.

The studies conducted at the center were reported in three volumes to the federal government in May 1969. Volume I dealt with curriculum development and evaluation. Karnes, Hodgins, and Teska (1969) reported the relative effects of five preschool programs as well as research on such issues as the length of time required to stabilize effective functioning, the strategic age for intervention, the effectiveness of paraprofessionals as classroom teachers, and the role of mothers as the primary change agent. In Volume II, Bereiter, Englemann, and Washington (1969) and colleagues reported their studies of the processes and products of educational intervention. Volume III concentrated on an analysis of family and relatives and on neighborhood and community variables that have bearing on school readiness. These studies were conducted by Farber, Lewis, and Harvey (1969).

The evaluation and follow-up of the children enrolled in the five preschool programs is the only study of the initial project reported on in this chapter. The major goal of that study was to determine the extent to which each of the five programs prepared young disadvantaged children for public school and, if possible, to determine the approach(es) that best accomplished this goal (Karnes, 1973a; Karnes, Hodgins, & Teska, 1969; Karnes, Teska, & Hodgins, 1970).

History of the Study

The University of Illinois has a long history of research with preschool disadvantaged and handicapped children. In the late 1940s, Samuel A. Kirk, Chairman of the Department of Special Education, with supporting funds from the National Institute of Mental Health, U.S. Public Health Service, and the Illinois State Department of Education, in cooperation with the Champaign Community Unit IV Schools, conducted a 5-year research project with young mentally retarded children, most of whom were from low-income homes (Kirk, 1958). Kirk established two experimental groups—one in a community setting and the other in an institution. A control group was identified for each experimental group. Merle Karnes was educational director of the community program and consultant to the institutional preschool. One of the questions Kirk addressed was, "Does preschool training affect the rate of development of such children?" The overall results of the study were positive. Seventy percent of the children in the experimental groups accelerated their rate of mental development. The gains made by the experimental groups during their preschool attendance were markedly superior to those of their counterparts in the control groups who either maintained their previous rate of development or lagged further behind. Kirk therefore concluded that preschool training did make a difference in the functioning of his subjects. During the study it had become evident that an instrument to pinpoint strengths and weaknesses in the area of information processing was needed, and thus the pilot work on the Illinois Test of Psycholinguistic Abilities began.

Because Kirk had answered affirmatively the question "Is a preschool experience better for mentally retarded children than remaining at home?" Karnes did not choose a control/experimental design for her study but decided instead to evaluate several approaches to the education of young disadvantaged children. It was just as well, for so many experimental programs for low-income children were being developed at the University of Illinois during the mid-1960s that the Urbana/Champaign population of approximately 100,000 would not have been large enough to supply 3- and 4-year-olds for a control group. In fact, the Dean of the College of Education established a clearinghouse to prevent researchers from pursuing the same subjects and thus annoying parents.

Because Karnes had worked with young disadvantaged children in the Kirk project and because she was convinced that the Illinois Test of Psycholinguistic Abilities (ITPA; Kirk & McCarthy, 1961) was a viable research instrument to evaluate program effectiveness and to serve as an instructional model for curriculum development, she included the ITPA instructional model in her experimental program, which she called the Ameliorative Program (later referred to as the GOAL program). The ITPA, however, was only one in a battery of tests used to determine program effectiveness.

Five preschool programs were included in the comparative study. These were chosen on theoretical as well as practical grounds to represent levels of structure. The teacher–child interaction was considered to be the paramount ingredient of structure, and the degree of structure was contingent upon the specificity and intensity of that interaction. In other words, as the specificity and intensity of this interaction increased, so did structure. Two programs represented the less structured end of the continuum: the *Traditional* (T) Program and the *Community-Integrated* (C-I) Program. These programs had a similar theoretical orientation, but the Traditional Program included only disadvantaged children whereas the Community-Integrated Program primarily enrolled middle-class children with only two to four disadvantaged children in any one class unit. A third class unit of disadvantaged children was enrolled in the *Montessori* (M) Program, which resembled the traditional nursery school program in many respects but relied on a methodology that entailed considerable structure. The two highly structured classrooms were the *Ameliorative* (A), developed by Karnes and her associates, and the *Direct-Verbal* (D-V), developed by Bereiter and Englemann. Both programs were developed at the University of Illinois and both enrolled only disadvantaged children.

Three of these programs were established in the first year of the study. Seventy-five disadvantaged children were enrolled in two Traditional classes, two Ameliorative classes, and one Direct-Verbal class. In the second year of the study a second Direct-Verbal class was added, and the Montessori and the Community-Integrated classes were begun.

Although the University Foundation had purchased a former elementary school building to house the center, renovation was not completed and classes were housed in churches during the first year. The Traditional classes met in the Champaign Presbyterian Church, the Ameliorative classes in the Urbana Presbyterian Church, and the Direct-Verbal class in the McKinley United Presbyterian Foundation. Thus, staff of the three programs had no opportunity to interact during the school day and the director of the center called no inter-group meetings. Bereiter and Englemann ran their own inservice training, as did Karnes. Only the research directors had offices in the College of Education.

The following year the renovated building, Colonel Wolfe School, was ready for occupancy and the second wave of the Direct-Verbal program was housed there, as was the second-year class of the first wave. Ameliorative subjects now attended public kindergarten and returned to Colonel Wolfe for a 1-hour school readiness program. The Montessori class met in the community-operated Montessori building and the Community-Integrated children attended preschool programs housed in several churches. These last two programs were under private direction and operated independently of the university. Research funds paid for tuition, transportation, and the collection of research data. Children attended school for approximately 2 hours and 15 minutes for a period of no less than 7 or more than 8 months.

Characteristics of Programs

The distinguishing characteristics of the five programs may be summarized as follows:

Traditional Nursery School Program. The promotion of personal, social, motor, and general language development was the major goal of the Traditional Nursery School Program. This program, modeled after the Child Development Laboratory of the University of Illinois, Department of Home Economics, expected teachers to encourage children to talk and to ask questions, to stimulate their interest in the world around them, and to capitalize on opportunities for incidental and informal learning. Typically, teachers were seen moving from one child to another, adjusting their instructions to meet individual needs, asking questions of individual children or, at times, of the entire group, encouraging children to explore and to use materials creatively, and promoting child–child interactions whenever possible.

Outdoor play was an integral part of the daily routine. Indoor play focused on a doll and housekeeping center, a vehicle and block center, and a small toy center that included puzzles, beads, puppets, and books. Periods were regularly scheduled for music and art. Juice time, rest, show and tell, listening to stories read by the teacher, the routine supervision of toileting, and taking off or putting on wraps completed the daily schedule.

The teachers were well aware of the strengths and weaknesses of the children and actively tried to help children overcome weaknesses. This was an adaptation of the Child Development model, because the children in that program came from upper-middle-class homes.

Teacher behavior was characterized by positive reinforcement, encouragement and support, enthusiasm, interest in the activity in which each child was engaging, stimulation of new interests, and expansion of existing interests. Observers noted that children were busily engaged in activities that seemed to be interesting to them. There was a great deal of verbal interaction between children and between teachers and individual children, and observers noted from the very first weeks of school that the children were making gains in language development.

Weekly inservice training with the project director was a consistent characteristic of the program. This training was based on the expressed needs of the teachers. The teacher–pupil ratio was 1 to 5. Teachers had individual conferences with parents, and some parents visited school. Teachers sent notes home to parents when deemed desirable and group meetings were scheduled to interpret the program and to discuss concerns that parents had in common.

During the second year of the project the children who had been enrolled in the Traditional Program went on to kindergarten in their respective school districts. The only contact project staff had with these children or their parents during the second year was to collect data on child progress at the end of the kindergarten year.

Community-Integrated Program.   The theoretical orientation of the Traditional Program also characterized the Community-Integrated Program. As previously stated, two to four children from low-income homes were enrolled in four centers attended primarily by white children from middle- and upper-class homes. The centers were operated by community groups and were licensed by the state. The Community-Integrated Program was included in the study for two reasons:

1. It was felt that it might be an advantage for children from low-income homes who had not mastered standard English to interact with peers who presented good language models; additionally, they would be exposed to the language models of their teachers. By contrast, in the Traditional Program standard language models were provided by teachers only, because the children formed a homogeneous group.

2. At the time of this study, low-income children were being bused from low-income areas to schools made up predominantly of middle-class children. Thus it seemed desirable to evaluate the effects of such an administrative plan on disadvantaged subjects.

The directors of the community centers administered the program. They were responsible for the inservice training of their staff and for parent involvement. Observers noted that the disadvantaged children were not openly rejected by the other children but that they were consistently on the fringes. There was very little interaction between the middle-class and low-income children. For the most part, the middle-class children had never before had a black child in their class and because 67% of the children in the entire preschool study were black, that ratio was also found among the Community-Integrated subjects.

Teachers generally exhibited positive behavior toward all of the children but made little effort to mainstream the children from low-income homes. The ratio of adults to children was at least one to eight, sometimes with a higher proportion of adults.

The major variable, then, in the Community-Integrated Program was social integration with the same general goals of social, motor, and cognitive/language development. The setting was informal, as was true in the Traditional classroom, but Community-Integrated teachers did not differentiate instruction, facilitate integration, or deliberately try to help children overcome weaknesses.

There was no reluctance on the part of the community preschools to enroll low-income children. There were no complaints to project staff about unusual difficulty with any of the children. School contacts with parents were minimal or nonexistent.

Montessori Program.   Including the Montessori program seemed logical since Maria Montessori had developed her methodology with slum children in Italy with reportedly good results. There were those who believed that this approach might be the answer to the major question of this study, "What approach promotes the greatest child progress among young children from low-income families?" The Montessori class was housed in the building where all Montessori classes were conducted. The teacher was a fully trained Montessori teacher, and the class was under the administration and supervision of the directoress. All the materials used met Montessori standards. Project funds paid for tuition, transportation, and the collection of research data. The entire class was made up of low-income children. An aide assisted the trained teacher. The morning began with a health check and toileting. The second activity was what the Montessori teachers referred to as "on the line" activities. The group met for songs, fingerplays, conversations, and exercises. The next half-hour was devoted to a spontaneous choice of approved materials and was followed by a second period devoted to games, musical activities, and stories. The next period, approximately a half-hour, included a life demonstration, juice time, toileting, the silence exercise, and tidying the classroom. The final 10 or 20 minutes of the day were given over to playground activities or supervised short walks. The specific nature of the prepared environment made the level of structure within the Montessori classroom higher than that of the two traditional programs. The level of specific control over what the children did, however, was not as great as that in the Ameliorative or Direct-Verbal programs. Structure in the Montessori program was derived from the prescribed manner in which the child learned from materials rather than from the teacher–child interaction. Persistence to task, development of inner language, and visual–motor development were felt to be important objectives of the program.

Observers in the classroom noted that children tended to work independently of other children. There was very little cooperative play and little verbal interaction between children or between teachers and children. This was especially true when the level and amount of verbal interaction of this program and the two highly structured programs were compared.

Ameliorative Program. The Ameliorative Program developed and directed by Karnes used a psycholinguistic instructional model derived from the clinical model of the Illinois Test of Psycholinguistic Abilities. Because inadequate language skills represented the greatest weakness of the target children, verbalizations in conjunction with the manipulation of concrete materials were considered critical in promoting language development. It was thought that the environment of disadvantaged children did not appropriately develop the skills, knowledge, and attitudes essential for success in schools designed to serve middle-class children (Karnes, Zehrbach, & Teska, 1977). A game format in which children encountered concepts and skills in meaningful context was deemed to be more useful in ensuring permanency of learning than rote drill. When the child was unable to make a verbal response, the teacher supplied an appropriate model. When the child began to initiate such responses, the teacher had an opportunity to modify and expand these verbalizations. Children were divided into three groups according to IQ scores. Each teacher taught three 20-minute structured periods to the same group of five children in language, mathematical concepts, and social studies or science. The remainder of the morning was devoted to music, art, directed play, snack time, and rest.

The teacher–child ratio was 1 to 5. Weekly inservice training was a regularly scheduled part of the program, and parent conferences and visits to school were encouraged. When a child was absent, the teacher made every effort to help the child "make up" the work he or she had missed. Although the development of cognitive/language abilities was felt to be of utmost importance, the development of a healthy and realistic self-concept was also valued as was the development of appropriate interpersonal skills and creativity.

The behavior of teachers was characterized by a positive, accepting attitude toward the children—helping the child develop a good self-concept and self-esteem by demonstrating a genuine appreciation and liking for the child, providing immediate feedback so that the child knew how he or she was doing, fostering the acquisition of effective interpersonal skills, encouraging the child to persist at a task until complete, and encouraging motivation to learn. The developer was committed to the idea that the preschool's role was to build readiness to read; therefore, formal reading was not introduced at the preschool level (Karnes, 1973a, 1973b).

When the children subsequently enrolled in kindergarten in the public schools, they returned to the center each day for 1 hour of teacher-directed activities designed to foster school readiness, especially in reading and mathematical concepts. Project funds provided transportation for the children.

The Ameliorative Program, then, viewed the cause of school failure of low-income children to be the discrepancy between negative experience or the lack of appropriate experiences provided the child by the environment and the experiences needed to ensure success in middle-class schools. Because the name Ameliorative was often interpreted as synonymous with a remedial program, Karnes later changed the name to GOAL, for Games Oriented Activities for Learning.

Direct-Verbal Program.   The Direct-Verbal Program directed by Bereiter and Englemann (1966) involved oral drill in verbal and logical patterns. This strategy was chosen because its originators believed that disadvantaged children were developing adequately in perceptual and motor skills but inadequately in verbal and abstract skills. The ratio of teachers to children was 1 to 5. Each teacher taught a 20-minute structured period in reading, language, or arithmetic. Children were divided into three groups according to IQ. The instructional strategy was to teach the children a rule by rote followed by applications to the rule. These examples were of increasing difficulty.

The program was designed to teach essential competencies in basic English. Teachers began by teaching a basic identity statement that they then applied to familiar objects; for example, "This is a (*chair*). This is not a (*table*)." When this statement was mastered, other language patterns were introduced involving polar sets, plurals, subclass nouns, prepositional phrases, active verbs, personal pronouns, and common tenses.

A kind of patterned drill was also used in the teaching of arithmetic. It was felt that the disadvantaged child could not abstract the principles of arithmetic from everyday life because he or she lacked the verbal and logical sophistication to do so.

Reading instruction was initiated at age 4, and a modified Initial Teaching Alphabet was used to teach reading. The reading staff wrote controlled vocabulary stories for the children to read. Songs were also written by the staff, and these songs were specifically designed to give children additional practice in the language operations they had been taught and in question-and-answer interactions. Thus, the Direct-Verbal program formally trained children in the school subjects of reading and arithmetic with special emphasis on language development.

Principles of behavior modification were used to reinforce appropriate behavior and to extinguish undesirable behavior. Initially raisins were used as reinforcers and later verbal praise was the primary reinforcer. This approach is currently referred to as Direct Instruction, and DISTAR is the curriculum that embodies the Direct Instruction System for Teaching Arithmetic and Reading. The approach is one of the models involved in Follow Through, a program financed by the Federal government.

The children who attended these five preschool programs have been the subjects of longitudinal study over the past 15 years. The original longitudinal study followed their progress through the first several years of elementary school. In 1975, Karnes became one of 13 principal investigators to join the Consortium for Longitudinal Studies, and she began to investigate the long-term effects of these preschool programs. The remainder of this chapter is devoted to these follow-up studies.

RATIONALE FOR THE INITIAL STUDY

At the time the five-approaches study was initiated, it seemed appropriate to investigate the effectiveness of specific interventions rather than to pursue the question of preschool versus no preschool experience for children from low-income homes. Lack of appropriate experiences among these children was felt to inhibit their optimal development, and it seemed apparent that provisions must be made to help such children compensate for deficits accruing from inappropriate or lack of growth-enhancing experiences. About this time psychologists were promoting the notion that intelligence is not fixed and that cognitive development occurs primarily in response to a variable range of experience and stimulation (Ausubel, 1966; Hunt, 1961). Almy (1964) agreed with Hunt and Ausubel and went on to explain that unless the young child is exposed to a wide variety of stimuli that are well matched to the action patterns the child already has available, the development of cognitive abilities will not be maximized.

A number of researchers investigated characteristics of low-income families and their young children. Among these were those who studied the adverse effects of the environment on cognitive development. Reissman (1962) found that these children generally had inadequate perceptual skills; poor orientation to obtaining information was found by Ausubel (1966) and Deutsch (1963); a number of researchers found lags in language development or lack of mastery of standard English: Ausubel (1966), Deutsch (1964), Goldberg (1963), Hess & Shipman (1965), Hunt (1964), Jensen (1963), John (1963), John and Goldstein (1964). Reissman (1962) pointed out that children from low-income homes were poorly motivated to pursue intellectual and school-like activities. Deutsch (1964) contended that the effects of lack of stimulation on intellectual development are cumulative. The longer deficits persist, the more irreversible they become. Because the young child is more pliable and flexible, the implication for early intervention was apparent.

Although early intervention for young children from low-income families held promise, the ingredients of an effective program were yet to be determined. There was, however, a body of research that had implications for program planning, and a number of researchers set about developing and testing various curricula. The University of Illinois was in a unique position to investigate differential effects since Bereiter and Englemann and Karnes were developing experimental programs at the same center and existing preschools in the University and in the larger community represented several theoretical frames of reference. Thus, in the fall of 1965 a comparative study was launched to answer the overriding question, ''What approach(es) is most effective in promoting the growth of children from low-income homes to ensure their successful participation in the public schools?''

Because funding agencies do not usually provide for follow-up studies, data collection during the elementary school years was limited. The last contact made with the subjects was at the fourth-grade level. It was, therefore, with enthusiasm that Karnes became a member of the Longitudinal Studies Consortium in 1975. She was, of course, interested in following up the subjects in her studies, but an even greater motivation to become involved in the Consortium was the opportunity to study the persistent effects of early childhood programming. She felt that if hard data could be made available to legislators and to others in positions of power, the continued funding of programs such as Head Start might be ensured. The follow-up has been informative and challenging, and the authors hope it will prove helpful for future planning and policy making.

SITE AND SAMPLE

The original preschool study and subsequent follow-up studies have been conducted in Champaign–Urbana, a community of 100,000 located in central Illinois. The community, surrounded by an extremely fertile farming region, is the home of the University of Illinois, which has an enrollment of more than 30,000 students. Although the average income in the community is relatively high, a wide range of socioeconomic levels is represented and a low-income population of considerable size has been present for many years. At the time of the original intervention 12% of the population of the Champaign–Urbana area was black and 88% was white. The sample of children selected for the programs consisted of 67% black and 33% white. The University is the largest employer in the area, but there are numerous light industries and small businesses which provide additional employment for unskilled workers. The State of Illinois responds well to the welfare needs of the poor and consequently many low-income families received some support from the state.

The twin cities of Champaign and Urbana maintain separate public school systems of very high quality, both of which offer a wide range of special services for low-income and minority students. At the time of the original early intervention study, however, few programs at the preschool level were available to low-income families. Most preschools and day care centers were privately operated, requiring considerable tuition, and Head Start was just beginning to operate a half-day summer program. During the middle 1960s, however, researchers began to develop programs for early intervention with children from low-income homes; indeed, experimental programs proliferated. During the years of the Karnes early intervention studies, competition was keen among researchers trying to recruit 4-year-old children from low-income homes for these experimental programs. This is the reason that no control (no-treatment group) was constituted for the Karnes study. A child assigned to a no-treatment group would likely be recruited for another experimental program, and it was felt to be unethical in terms of the welfare of the children to deny their participation in programs that might benefit them. A complete discussion of the constitution of a post hoc no-treatment comparison group in 1979 will be presented later.

Sample Selection for the Early Intervention Study

Several methods were employed to find preschool subjects from low-income families for the early intervention study. Families judged to be economically deprived by public aid and school authorities were contacted to learn if they had children within the age range required for the study. Further referrals were sought from these families and from other agencies in the community. Finally, acutely disadvantaged sections of the community were canvassed door-to-door in an effort to locate preschool children new to the area or otherwise unknown to referring agencies. Final eligibility was determined on the basis of detailed home interviews on family background, usually conducted with the mothers of potential subjects. Children selected had to be 4 years old by the first of December to ensure that they would be eligible for kindergarten the following school year. Additionally, they must not have attended a preschool previously.

Children were recruited in two waves: Wave I children were enrolled in the 1965–1966 school year, and Wave II children were enrolled in 1966–1967.[1] All eligible children were administered the Stanford–Binet Intelligence Scale (Terman & Merrill, 1960); on the basis of the IQ scores they were then stratified into three groups. The "high" group consisted of those who scored 100 or above, the "middle" group those who scored between 90 and 99, and the "low" group those who scored between 70 and 89.[2] Class units of 15 subjects each were then constituted. Each unit was comprised of five subjects (one-third) from each of the three IQ strata, and class units were, therefore, comparable in terms of mean IQ. Units also contained comparable race and sex distributions—approximately 67% black and 33% white, and approximately 50% male and 50% female. Each class unit was then randomly assigned to one of the five interventions.

Demographics of Experimental Subject Population

A wide range of demographic information was collected concerning the families of the subjects, including presence of fathers in the household, educational level

---

[1]As described above, there were two Ameliorative classes, two Traditional classes, and one Direct-Verbal class during Wave I. Wave II classes consisted of one Direct-Verbal, one Montessori, and one Community-Integrated class.

[2]Children scoring below 70 or above 120, with a few exceptions, were disqualified from this study on the basis of too great a variability from the majority of subjects in order to combat the "regression to the mean" phenomenon.

and occupation of fathers, educational level and occupation of mothers, family size, and family living conditions. No significant differences were found among the groups on any of these family background variables.[3]

Location and Retrieval of Experimental Subjects for Follow-Up Studies

An extremely high proportion of the subjects in the original preschool study were located and participated in the follow-up studies. More than 94% (116) of the 123 subjects enrolled in the original study completed the preschool year. Nearly 88% (102 subjects) participated in at least some part of the follow-up through the end of grade 3. Follow-up data were obtained for nearly 75% of the 116 subjects in the longitudinal study that took place in 1976 to 1978, a full ten years after the preschool intervention. Data were collected in the 1979–1980 phase of the follow-up study on 86 experimental subjects, again a very respectable 74% of the 116 subjects.

Constitution of a Post Hoc Comparison Group

Two major reasons, both cited earlier, explain why no control (no-treatment) group was established originally. First, Kirk (1958) had already demonstrated that retarded children who attended a preschool program did significantly better on measures of intelligence than children who remained at home; in other words, preschool programming is better than no programming at all. Second, the researchers were reluctant to deny children the opportunity to participate in experimental preschool programs—and many programs were available at the time. From the earliest follow-up, however, the absence of a no-treatment comparison group in the research design was acutely felt, and this lack was again discussed at length in terms of the pooled studies analyzed by the Consortium on Longitudinal Studies.

After collecting follow-up data on the experimental subjects for several years, Karnes and her associates decided to constitute a post hoc no-treatment comparison group in spite of the serious problems such a procedure presented—the impossibility, for example, of ensuring random assignment of subjects to treatment and control conditions. In 1979, a method was devised by which a control group could be established with minimal experimental bias. To fill the required race, sex, and IQ stratifications of the original groups, more children had been tested each year of the study than were placed in experimental groups. Folders of several hundred unused but potential subjects were reviewed, and 58 were chosen based on the following criteria: children were tested during the appropriate time period (1965–1967); they were tested on at least the Stanford–Binet

---

[3]Teska (1969) reported, however, that pretest IQ of the subjects was correlated to several of the background variables, such as father present in the home, father's educational level, and number of siblings.

Intelligence Scale; and there was no clear indication that the child was ineligible for the program.

An effort was then made to locate these 58 subjects, a considerable task in light of the fact that no contact had been made with them or their families since the initial recruitment. Nonetheless, contact was made or school data located for 45, or nearly 68% of these subjects. Data collected on these subjects as well as further analysis of the original family background information revealed that a number of these potential control group subjects had to be disqualified. The largest number of potential control subjects was eliminated because interviews with their mothers or data from their school records indicated that the subjects had in fact attended some other preschool program. A total of 24 subjects remained in the control group after all data had been carefully reviewed.

Demographics of the Comparison Group

In many cases the family background interviews conducted at the time of initial recruitment were found in the folders of the potential control subjects. However, interview data were missing for some subjects, and an attempt was made to collect this information through brief telephone interviews with the mothers of the control subjects. The only significant differences between the control subjects and the experimental subjects are in numbers of siblings (the control group had more) and mean pretest IQ (a lower mean). The lower mean IQ of the control group is understandable because fewer low-income children who scored high on the Stanford–Binet Intelligence Scale could be found than children whose performance placed them in the lower IQ strata. Thus, there were fewer "unused" or "leftover" children with high IQ's eligible for inclusion in the post hoc comparison group. This very important difference between the control group and the experimental groups could be dealt with in two ways. First, the independent variable of pretest IQ could be controlled by means of covariance techniques in analysis of the follow-up data. A second way to deal with this difference would be to use a randomly selected yet comparable subgroup of experimental subjects to contrast with the control subjects. Only covariance techniques were employed in analyses of the follow-up data.

Location and Retrieval of Comparison Group Subjects for Follow-Up

As mentioned above, a very high proportion of control subjects was located for follow-up, especially considering the time that had elapsed without contact. Further, the cooperation given to the follow-up was remarkable since the subjects and their families had no real personal interest in the study as did the families who had participated in the original preschool program. Of the 58 subjects originally selected for possible inclusion in the control group, a total of 38, or 65%, were located and agreed to participate in the Youth Interview and testing.

Of the 24 chosen for inclusion in the control group, follow-up data on at least one measure was collected for 19 subjects, or nearly 80%.

METHODOLOGY

Longitudinal data on subjects in the original five experimental preschool groups were collected in three major phases. The first set was collected in the years immediately subsequent to the preschool intervention, 1966–1971, when the subjects attended kindergarten through fourth grade. The next two sets were collected in conjunction with the joint research study sponsored by the Consortium for Longitudinal Studies. From 1976 to 1978, data were collected on the experimental subjects, the oldest of whom were 17 years of age. After the establishment of the post hoc comparison group in 1979, a third phase of data collection began and was completed in September of 1980; the oldest subjects were then 19 years of age. The following discussions of data collection procedures treat each phase separately. All results are discussed in a later section. Table 5.1 gives a breakdown of the research design across time.

Data Collection from Kindergarten through Fourth Grade

Because the experimental preschool programs had been designed to enhance the subjects' success in school through an early emphasis on cognitive skills and language development, attention focused during the first follow-up on intellectual functioning, language functioning, and school achievement. The Stanford–Binet Intelligence Scale was used as the measure of intellectual functioning because it had been administered as a pre- and posttest during the year of the preschool intervention. Language functioning was measured on the Illinois Test of Psycholinguistic Abilities for the same reason. Measures of school success included both the Metropolitan School Readiness Test (Hildreth, Griffiths, & McGauvran 1949) and the California Achievement Test (Tiegs & Clark, 1963). These tests were administered by professional school psychologists at the end of the kindergarten year, at the end of first grade, and at the end of second grade for subjects in all five groups. Subjects in Wave I were also tested at the end of third grade. In addition to the tests named above, other measures, such as the Frostig Developmental Test of Visual Perception (Frostig, Lefever, & Whittlesey, 1963) and measures of social functioning, were also administered during and after the preschool year.

Data Collection from 1976 to 1978

A major concern in the long-term follow-up was again to determine whether the various programs had had differential effects on school success. This could be

TABLE 5.1
Layout of Research Design and Data Collection

Groups	*Ameliorative*		*Direct Verbal*		*Traditional*
	Wave I	*Wave II*	*Wave I*	*Wave II*	*Wave I*
1965 Summer	Pre-Tests (N = 15)		Pre-Tests (N = 15)		Pre-Tests (N = 15)
1965-66	Preschool Intervention		Preschool Intervention		Preschool Intervention
1966 Spring					
1966 Summer	Post-Tests	Pre-Tests (N = 15)	Post-Tests	Pre-Tests (N = 15)	Post-Tests
1966-67	After-School Program	Preschool Intervention	2nd Year Preschool Intervention	Preschool Intervention	
1967 Spring	Follow-Up	Post-Tests	Follow-Up	Post-Tests	Follow-Up
1968 Spring	Follow-Up	Follow-Up	Follow-Up	Follow-Up	Follow-Up
1969 Spring	Follow-Up	Follow-Up	Follow-Up	Follow-Up	Follow-Up
1970 Spring	Follow-Up	Follow-Up	Follow-Up	Follow-Up	Follow-Up
1971 Spring	Follow-Up		Follow-Up		Follow-Up
1976-77	Follow-Up	Follow-Up	Follow-Up	Follow-Up	Follow-Up
1979-80	Follow-Up	Follow-Up	Follow-Up	Follow-Up	Follow-Up

Groups	*Community-Integrated*	*Montessori*	*Post-Hoc Comparison*		
	Wave II	*Wave II*	*Wave I*	*Wave II*	*Wave III*
1965 Summer			Pre-Tests (N = 8)		
1965-66					
1966 Spring					
1966 Summer	Pre-Tests (N = 15)	Pre-Tests (N = 15)		Pre-Tests (N = 7)	
1966-67	Preschool Intervention	Preschool Intervention			
1967 Spring	Post-Tests	Post-Tests			Pre-Tests (N = 4)
1968 Spring	Follow-Up	Follow-Up			
1969 Spring	Follow-Up	Follow-Up			
1970 Spring	Follow-Up	Follow-Up			
1971 Spring					
1976-77	Follow-Up	Follow-Up	Follow-Up	Follow-Up	Follow-Up
1979-80	Follow-Up	Follow-Up	Follow-Up		

measured directly by examination of school records or indirectly by means of achievement test scores. Of further interest, of course, were the reasons for differential effects that might be found, so it seemed important to collect data that would reveal the subjects' attitudes, family situation, and parental attitudes, as well as global measures of overall intellectual functioning.

Two sets of instruments were used in this phase of the study. One set had been agreed upon by all the investigators in the Consortium and was to be administered by all projects: Parent Interview, Youth Interview, and School Record Form—all designed by members of the Consortium staff. All investigators also agreed to administer the Wechsler Intelligence Scale for Children, Form R (WISC-R) (Wechsler, 1974).

In addition to the Consortium set, Karnes employed four other measures. The Stanford–Binet Intelligence Scale was administered, in addition to the WISC-R, because it had been used in the original and follow-up studies. The Comprehensive Test of Basic Skills (CTB/McGraw–Hill, 1968) was used to obtain measures of vocabulary, reading comprehension, and arithmetical concepts. Attitudes were assessed by means of the Locus of Control (Norwicki & Strickland, 1973), a test designed to indicate the degree to which the subject attributes events that occur to circumstances beyond his or her control, and by the "Arousal Seeking Tendency Instrument" (Mehrabian & Russell, 1974), a measure of curiosity and change-seeking behavior.

These data were collected in several stages over a period of 2 years. First, subjects were located through public school rosters, phone books, calls to related families, and a considerable amount of legwork. The Youth Interview and the WISC-R, the two Consortium instruments, were administered during the first session with each subject. The four additional instruments were scheduled for two or more sessions at a later date. School record information was collected at the local public schools concurrent with the scheduling and testing of subjects. The numbers tested on each measure show a relatively low attrition rate for the subjects; more than 10 years after the original preschool study, nearly 75% of the subjects were located and were willing to cooperate with at least some part of the follow-up study.

Data Collection in 1979 through 1980

The latest phase of the follow-up was characterized by two major changes. First, two new instruments were devised by Consortium staff in order to collect more detailed information about subjects' activities and attitudes and about their school achievement. The 1979 Youth Interview, designed for older subjects no longer in high school, consists of questions about family situation, school achievement, plans for further education, work experiences, attitudes toward self, and leisure activities. The 1979 School Data Form is a comprehensive tool for collecting year–by–year information regarding special educational services, grade placement (or retention), attendance, class rank, and average grades received. These two instruments were to be used with all the subjects in the follow-up since the new information was intended to expand upon as well as update the information collected previously.

The other major change in the 1979–1980 data collection was the addition of the no-treatment comparison group described previously. Time and staff restrictions limited the number of instruments that could be used with this group; however, because most of the data on the experimental subjects had been collected 2 years earlier, comparisons with control data collected at this time would have been spurious in any case. Therefore, only the new instruments, the 1979 Youth Interview and the 1979 School Data Form, were used with the post hoc comparison group. Two additional kinds of information on the control subjects were, however, collected. First, mothers of no-treatment subjects were interviewed briefly over the telephone to provide missing background information on the family and to ascertain whether the subject had in fact ever attended a preschool program. Second, a measure of general intellectual functioning was administered—the Wechsler Adult Intelligence Scale (WAIS) (Wechsler, 1955) because it was appropriate to the ages of the subjects and because it contains a number of "performance" as well as verbal items. Again, because intelligence test data on the experimental subjects were 2 years old and could not be compared to the newly collected data, one group of experimental subjects, the Ameliorative group, was chosen to receive WAIS's at the same time.

The steps taken to collect the 1979–1980 data were similar to those employed in the second phase of the follow-up. Youth Interviews and WAIS's were administered in a single session at the center site for subjects in the post hoc comparison group and in the Ameliorative group. Youth Interviews for subjects who required no further testing were conducted in various locations at the convenience of the subject—at the center site, in the subject's home, and in less conventional locations such as automobiles, parking lots, and restaurants. Phone interviews were conducted with subjects who had moved out of town and with a few subjects who could not otherwise be scheduled. Interviews in most cases were not conducted with subjects until they had graduated or dropped out of high school; thus, much of the interviewing was completed during the summer of 1980. All subjects were paid for the time they gave for interviews and tests. School record data were collected concurrently with the administration of the Youth Interviews and tests.

DATA ANALYSIS PROCEDURES

Throughout the 15-year history of this project, the major research issue had been to identify the preschool program or programs that most effectively equipped low-income children for school success. Thus, the independent or experimental variable has been type of preschool program. At various times other categorical variables—IQ strata, father's presence in the home, or race—have been used as independent variables in conjunction with program variables.

The efficacy of a preschool program was to be judged by success in school, but the concept of school success is multifaceted in nature. Some children are considered successful in school because they participate in extracurricular activities; others are deemed successful because they receive outstanding grades. Recognizing the complexity of the concept of school success, the researchers selected a relatively small number of variables to use as indicators of school success. The major indicators, or dependent variables, included level of intellectual functioning (Stanford–Binet or WISC-R scores), linguistic ability (ITPA), academic achievement (Metropolitan Readiness Tests, California Achievement Tests, California Tests of Basic Skills), social functioning (teacher ratings, self-reports, Locus of Control questionnaire), and academic status (grade level, type and amount of remedial educational services). The choice of particular dependent variable(s) for use in any given analysis depended on the specific research question and the children's age.

In general, during the early phases of the study, data were analyzed using multivariate analysis of covariance with preintervention IQ as the covariate and type of program as the independent variable. For more detailed discussions of statistical procedures, the reader is referred to studies listed in the results section.

By 1979–1980 students from all groups would graduate from high school if they had made normal academic progress. Thus, it was appropriate to collect data regarding school outcomes. In addition, as noted earlier, it had been possible to construct a post hoc no-preschool group that had been tested for entry into the preschool study but had not been admitted. With the addition of this group, researchers could assess long-term effects of intervention versus nonintervention as well as the effects of five types of intervention. The major questions investigated during Phase III were as follows:

1. How did the participants in the five preschool programs and the youngsters in the no-preschool group fare in terms of school performance?

2. Did type of preschool program for low-income children affect overall performance in school?

3. What was the relationship of familial variables, pre-preschool IQ, and post-preschool IQ to overall performance in school?

Various analytical procedures, including analysis of covariance and multiple regression, were used to answer these questions. Dependent measures for school performance included a project-developed index of school success, amount of remedial educational services, graduation rate, frequency of grade retention, suspensions and expulsions, and overall grade point average. As in earlier phases of the study, program type, preintervention IQ, and other demographic characteristics (mother's education, father's education, father's presence during pre-school, race, and sex) were used as independent variables.

RESULTS AND DISCUSSION

Program Effectiveness: Intervention Phase (1965–1967)

The data on immediate differential program effects have been reported exten-sively in the literature (Karnes, 1973a, 1973b; Karnes & Hodgins, 1969; Karnes, Hodgins, & Teska, 1969; Karnes, Plummer, & Lee, 1978; Karnes, Teska, & Hodgins, 1970; Karnes, Teska, Wollersheim, Stoneburner, & Hodgins, 1968; Karnes & Zehrbach, 1975; Karnes, Zehrbach, & Teska, 1972; Karnes, Zehrbach, & Teska, 1974; Karnes, Zehrbach, & Teska, 1977); thus, only a brief review of the data from preschool through third grade is presented. Data analysis procedures are discussed in detail in Karnes, Hodgins, & Teska (1969).

The key indicators of educational progress during the intervention phase were intellectual functioning and language functioning. At the end of the preschool year significant differences were found in intellectual functioning on the Stan-ford–Binet in favor of the Ameliorative and Direct-Verbal groups. These two groups demonstrated gains of approximately 14 IQ points; gains in the other three groups ranged from 5 to 8 points. All children in the A and D-V groups evidenced IQ gains, whereas from 15% to 24% of the children in the other three groups regressed (Fig. 5.1).

Similar results favoring the A and D-V groups over the other groups were found in the area of language development. On the total ITPA scale only the A and D-V groups showed nondeficit performance at the end of the preschool year. On the preintervention assessment of language development, children scored lowest on the subtests for Vocal Encoding, Auditory–Vocal Automatic, and Auditory–Vocal Association. Significant differences at the end of the preschool year favored the A and D-V groups. Preprogram deficits of 6 to 12 months on two of these three subtests were eliminated for the A group. The D-V group eliminated initial deficits on one of these three subtests. The Traditional group also made gains on these subtests but not to the degree achieved by the A and D-V groups. The Montessori and Community-Integrated groups demonstrated stat-ic or regressive performances.

It had been hypothesized that structure was a valid dimension for affecting change; therefore, the five intervention programs were chosen to represent de-grees of structure along a continuum. Findings at the end of the preschool year, however, did not totally support this assumption. Children in the two highly structured programs (A and D-V) generally made the greatest gains; however, children in the T program, low on the continuum of structure, surpassed the gains of the children in the M program, an intervention that entailed greater structure,

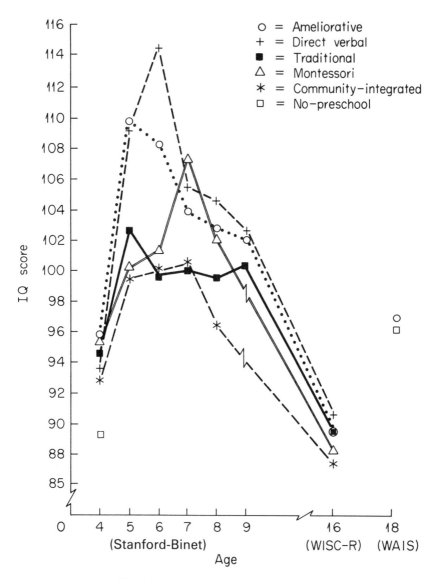

FIG. 5.1   IQ scores by age across six groups.

and those of children in the C-I group, a program with a theoretical orientation comparable to that of the T group.

One explanation of why the Montessori group failed to make the progress of the A, D-V, and T children is that although the "prepared environment" had been carefully planned, the children did not systematically engage in verbalization with each other or with their teachers, as was characteristic of the A, D-V, and T programs. Thus, the emphasis on sensory-motor development without concurrent emphasis on expressive language seemed to result in a somewhat greater lag in language development as measured by the ITPA.

It had also been hypothesized that the C-I group, because of its accessibility to middle-class peer models in language, would evidence greater progress in language than the homogeneous low-income T group, whose only middle-class language models were teachers. Because onsite observations suggest that the children in the C-I group did not interact verbally with their advantaged peers, and only minimally with their teachers, they did not make the progress of children in the T group, who generally experienced a similar curriculum.

It must be pointed out, however, that while the children in the T program made good progress, the A and D-V groups generally made superior performance. Thus, the two highly structured programs demonstrated that when children are directly taught skills and content with a strong emphasis on language interaction, they make superior gains. The A program, for example, taught the skills tapped by the Auditory–Vocal Automatic Test of the ITPA (Grammar), and the A children excelled in this area. In number readiness, as assessed by the Metropolitan Readiness Tests, both the A and the D-V programs directly taught the skills and the children excelled as compared to youngsters in the other three programs.

In summary, at the end of the first year of intervention, children in the two highly structured programs (A and D-V) demonstrated the greatest gains. Children in the T program made more modest gains, whereas children in the C-I and M programs showed the least amount of progress.

Phase I: Follow-Up from Kindergarten through Grade 4 (1966–1971)

The research concern during the first follow-up phase was to monitor group performance in intellectual functioning, language ability, and academic achievement as children progressed through kindergarten and the early primary grades. During the first year of follow-up when the children were kindergarten age, the A group and the first wave of the D-V group continued to receive program-related intervention. Children in the A program attended public kindergartens and returned to the demonstration center for a 1-hour daily program of school readiness activities with a teacher–child ratio of 1 to 6. Children in Wave I of the D-V program did not attend public kindergarten but continued the highly structured program with a teacher–child ratio of 1 to 5 for a second year. Children in Wave II of the D-V group did not continue the structured program for an additional year but instead went directly into kindergarten. The T, C-I, and M children attended public kindergarten only.

Academic performance as measured by standardized achievement tests was assessed throughout Phase I, but only the A, D-V, and T groups were assessed each year. Language functioning was assessed only at the end of kindergarten and first grade for all 5 groups. At the end of kindergarten the D-V group demonstrated a level of language functioning on the ITPA significantly higher than that achieved by the other four intervention groups, who evidenced static or regressive performance. This continued gain in language functioning in the D-V group may have been due to the extra year of highly structured programming with a high teacher–pupil ratio. However, by the end of first grade, the A, D-V, and T groups did not differ significantly on the ITPA.

Reading and math readiness were assessed in kindergarten for all 5 groups. Children in the A and D-V programs had significantly superior performances in number readiness skills (Metropolitan Readiness Tests) to those of children in the other three groups, but only the A group demonstrated significantly superior reading readiness skills (Metropolitan Readiness Tests). Here, too, the continued program intervention during kindergarten appeared to benefit children in both the D-V and A groups.

Tests of reading achievement (California Achievement Tests) were administered to the T, D-V (Wave I), and A groups in the first, second, and third grades. Throughout this period there were significant differences among the groups in reading achievement, but the rate of progress in reading for all groups began to decrease. At the end of first grade, assessment of reading achievement indicated that the A and D-V groups were significantly superior to the T group, with the A and D-V groups functioning approximately one-half year above the T group, which was functioning slightly below grade level. It is interesting to note that the two years of reading instruction provided the D-V children during their preschool years was only as effective as the intensive 1-hour reading readiness support program provided the A children. This follow-up data lends little support for the introduction of formal reading instruction during the preschool years for children from low-income homes.

By the end of the third grade, significant differences in reading achievement remained, but the pattern of differences had changed. At the end of second grade both the A and the D-V groups were significantly higher than the T-group; at the end of third grade, however, the A group scored significantly higher than did the T and the D-V groups. The A group was reading at grade level, while the T and the D-V groups scored at comparable levels, about one-fifth year below grade level. One explanation for the superior reading achievement of the A group may be that this program gave greater emphasis to divergent responses and to the transfer of learning than was true of the other two programs.

In terms of mathematical achievement, significant differences among the groups were found at the end of first grade. The D-V and A groups scored significantly higher on the California Achievement Test than did the T group. Thus, it appears that highly structured programs better prepared children for more formal work in arithmetic at the first grade level, but this advantage was not maintained over the next 2 years.

Because the major question to be answered by the study was which preschool intervention best prepares children for school, it seemed evident at the end of grade one that the two structured programs were the most successful. Nearly half the children in the T program obtained scores on the California Achievement Tests that indicated limited school achievement. Thus, it appeared that potential for initial school success among low-income children is best fostered through a highly structured, teacher-directed preschool program. However, as students progressed in school, the differential effects among the three groups observed on standardized tests of academic achievement became progressively less apparent.

In addition to academic achievement, the intellectual functioning of the five groups was measured throughout Phase I. During kindergarten, children in the D-V program continued to make gains in intellectual functioning (6 IQ points on the Stanford–Binet) and thus evidenced a level of performance that was significantly superior to that of the other groups. The four groups that attended public school kindergarten essentially maintained the gains in intellectual functioning made during the preschool year, and losses or gains did not exceed 3 points. The supportive program given the A group may have been responsible for that group's maintaining the relatively large gain achieved during the preschool year (Fig. 5.1). By the end of the first grade, however, no significant differences were found among groups on the Stanford–Binet. The A and the D-V groups regressed on the Binet, whereas the T and C-I groups remained basically static during the interval, and the M group made slight gains (Fig. 5.1).

IQ scores dropped for all five groups during second grade. The fall in IQ continued through the third grade for the three groups assessed (A, D-V, and T). By the end of Phase I, Stanford–Binet performance indicated that although the initial large gains in IQ scores had been tempered by time, the three groups still showed gains in IQ compared to their preintervention scores.

Standardized measures of academic performance, intellectual functioning, and language development were of primary importance during Phase I, but investigators were also interested in social functioning. Project-developed questionnaires and a modified personality inventory were used to assess social functioning in kindergarten, second, and fourth grade for children from the A and T groups.

At the time of the preschool intervention, one debated issue had been whether a cognitively oriented, highly structured program such as the Ameliorative approach would be as effective in promoting social development as more informal programs such as the Traditional program, which emphasized the development of social skills. Karnes contended that a highly structured, teacher-directed program could also promote social development. At the end of the kindergarten year, a follow-up questionnaire was administered to each child's public school teacher. Kindergarten teachers rated children who had been in the A program significantly higher than those who had been in the T program on items relating to confidence in approaching new tasks and on self-concept. Thus, children enrolled in the T program were rated somewhat lower than children who had attended the A program, despite the fact that one of the major goals of the T program had been fostering social development. This finding was in keeping with that of Weikart, Kamii, and Radin (1966), who pointed out that programs that emphasized language and intellectual development are also effective in promoting social and emotional development. Similar results were found by Domagala (1976), who investigated the social adjustment of children in two of the preschool approaches (A and T) at the second grade level. Children in the highly structured A program attained significantly higher scores on measures of social preference, perceived peer acceptance, and perceived teacher acceptance than did children who attended the traditional preschool. Domagala found no significant difference in the perceived parent attitude between the two groups.

When the children from the A and T groups were in the fourth grade, a 17-item Incomplete Sentence Test designed to tap attitudes and beliefs about self, friends, other people, and school-related activities was administered orally to each child. Results indicated that A subjects had fewer self-conflicts than did T children. There was a trend in favor of the A group, but the difference did not reach statistical significance. Thus, the data suggest that those children experienced somewhat less conflict in school than did those in the T group, and might be somewhat better adjusted.

It was the belief of those associated with the Ameliorative Program that structure helps children discriminate between aspects that need to be learned and less relevant aspects of the school environment; therefore, youngsters in the A group might be able to learn more quickly and easily. In addition, it was felt that children who receive positive reinforcement and who are viewed by significant adults in their lives as learners may become positively oriented toward schoollike tasks and may tend to see themselves as worthwhile, competent individuals. Data up to the fourth-grade level suggest that the Ameliorative Program was at least as enhancing to the social development of children as the Traditional Program.

At the end of Phase I, then, children in all five preschool program groups appeared to be settling into an ongoing school routine with only minimal evidence of cognitive or social differences among the groups.

Phase II: Longitudinal Follow-Up (1976–1977—High School)

By the mid-1970s children in the original five groups were adolescents and, if progressing normally, enrolled in high school. Questions about the differential effects of preschool on intellectual, academic, and social functioning addressed during Phase I were investigated again, but this time from a long-term perspective. Eighty-six youngsters from the original sample ($N = 116$) took tests and were interviewed. A slightly larger number of parents were interviewed to obtain their opinions about the preschool programs and their aspirations and expectations for their children. A complete description of the methodology and findings from Phase II is found in Karnes, Lee, and Applebaum (1979).

These findings can be summarized by stating the groups did not differ in any consistent way from one another. No significant differences among groups were found on the WISC-R. Mean IQ for groups, adjusted for preintervention IQ, ranged from 87.1 to 90.7. Similarly, no significant group differences were found on the following standardized tests: Comprehensive Test of Basic Skills, Locus of Control, and Arousal-Seeking Tendency. Parent interviews, youth interviews, and data from school records also revealed no consistent evidence of persistent differential effects.

The nondifferential data collected during Phase II are in accord with the findings obtained toward the end of Phase I. Differential effects of preschool were becoming less and less apparent as the interval between preschool and data collection increased. Of course, these findings do not mean that the benefits of preschool per se were eliminated; this could be determined only if performance among the five groups could be judged against the performance of a comparable group of adolescents who had not participated in a preschool program. Furthermore, the crucial test for evidence of long-term effectiveness is not so much how students do at age 15 or 16 but rather how they fare on important outcomes such as high school graduation, postsecondary schooling, and job status or income. Information regarding these socially valid indicators of school success could only be obtained after high school graduation.

Phase III: Longitudinal Follow-Up (1979–1980— Post-High School)

The picture of the students that emerged from the data collected in 1979 and 1980 shows considerable variability in terms of overall school performance. Some students had successful secondary school careers with plans for advanced educational study, whereas others exhibited great difficulty in school and eventually left high school without graduating. By the summer of 1980, 60% of the young adults followed up from all five original intervention groups ($N = 102$) had graduated from high school, 10% were still enrolled in high school due to retentions, and 30% had dropped out. Only 47% of the subjects in the post hoc no-treatment group had graduated from high school, 11% were still enrolled, and 42% had dropped out. In this section the progress of all students through their school years will be traced in order to identify patterns of performance among the various groups.

A number of indicators of school performance were examined in order to characterize the performance of the students in each of the six groups. There were no statistically significant differences among the individual groups; however, the relative rankings of the groups across outcome variables provides valuable insights to the impact of the preschool interventions. An overview of the six groups in terms of their graduation status, special educational services, and grade retentions is given in Table 5.2. It will be noted that the Montessori group contained the highest percentage of high school graduates (75%), with the Traditional group a close second (70%). Relatively low rates of high school graduation were found for the Community-Integrated group (43%), the No-Preschool (N-P) group (47%), and the Direct-Verbal group (48%). The rate of high school graduation for students in the Ameliorative group fell in the middle of the six groups (62%). Thus, on this important yet relatively limited measure of school success, students from the Montessori and Traditional groups performed quite well.

Other important indicators of school success are of particular interest, especially in terms of costs and benefits to the individual and to society. Although providing special remedial services is expensive, high dropout rates are apt to translate into even greater costs to the community in terms of unemployment, crime, and failure to actualize individual potential. Retaining students for an additional year at a particular grade level is not only a relatively expensive remedial educational tactic, but it may have a negative impact on a student's self-esteem or on his/her decision to remain in school.

There was a wide variety of special services available at each grade level for students in this study, including remedial instruction, special classes, alternative programs, and ancillary services. One desired benefit of a preschool program would be to reduce the need for such special services among an at-risk population such as the children from low-income families involved in this study. Furthermore, the need for special services can be interpreted as a negative indicator of school success; that is, students who need additional services are not functioning as well in school as students who do not need these services. The data summarized in Table 5.2 indicate that the Ameliorative program was the most efficient in terms of minimizing the need for special educational services among the students. Less than one-third (31%) of the students in this group were ever placed in special classes, with the average length of time in such classes equaling 3.3 years per student. Similarly low rates (33%) were found for students from the Traditional group. In contrast, almost two-thirds (63%) of the students from the No-Preschool group were placed in special classes. Interestingly, although a high percentage of students from the No-Preschool group received services, they did not continue to receive such services for as long a period of time as did the A group (2.5 years). Students from the Montessori, Direct-Verbal, and Community-Integrated groups tended to be in the middle of the six groups in terms of special class placement (42%, 43%, and 42% respectively).

The emphasis on individualization in the Ameliorative and Traditional Programs appears to have minimized potential cognitive–language deficits. The data from the Community-Integrated and No-Preschool groups, on the other hand, suggest that without individualized programming at the preschool level, children with potential cognitive–language deficits will often need special class services at some point in their educational careers.

TABLE 5.2
Group Rankings on Various Measures of Educational Performance

Rank	% of students who were never placed in Special Educational Classes	Average number of Years of Remedial Services for entire group	% of students who were never retained in grade	% of students who have graduated from high school
1	Ameliorative (69%) (N = 26)	No Preschool (2.5)	Montessori (87%)	Montessori (75%)
2	Traditional (67%) (N = 27)	Ameliorative (3.3)	Ameliorative (77%)	Traditional (70%)
3	Montessori (58%) (N = 12)	Traditional and Montessori (4.0)	Direct-Verbal (74%)	Amelioraative (62%)
4	Community-Integrated (58%) (N = 14)	Direct-Verbal (4.8)	Traditional (70%)	Direct-Verbal (48%)
5	Direct-Verbal (57%) (N = 23)	Community-Integrated (6.2)	Community-Integrated (64%)	No Preschool (47%)
6	No Preschool (37%) (N = 18)		No Preschool (56%)	Community-Integrated (43%)

N = total sample size for each performance variable.

Grade retention is another way of identifying students who are experiencing educational difficulties. Although less than 15% of the students from the Montessori Program were retained, almost half (44%) of the students in the No-Preschool group were retained at least once. Retention rates were relatively low for the Ameliorative group (23%) and the Direct-Verbal group (26%). Thirty percent of the students in the Traditional group and 36% of the Community-Integrated group were retained at least once. Typically, grade retention occurred at two points, in the early primary grades and less frequently in high school.

Again, it should be pointed out that although there were no significant differences, there appears to be an inverse relationship between grade retention and high school graduation. Groups with high rates of retention, i.e., No-Preschool and Community-Integrated, had low rates of graduation. Conversely, the group with the lowest rate of grade retention, Montessori, had the highest graduation rate. The special education data suggest that graduation is not strongly related to amount of special class placement. Correlational analyses suggest that high school graduation is more strongly related to rates of retention ($r = .56$) than to rates of special education ($r = .10$).

Composite Index of School Success

Success in school is not an all or none phenomenon; therefore, a wide array of information about school experience was needed to answer questions about the impact of preschool programming and other background demographic variables on subsequent school performance. The following information collected from both school records and individual interviews was weighted and combined to create the composite school success variable: high school graduation (max. pt. = 45) + academic progress through high school (max. pt. = 15) + no need for special educational services (max. pt. = 15) + academic achievement (max. pt. = 15) + acceptable social behavior in school (max. pt. = 5) + future academic promise (max. pt. = 5). The maximum score was 100, which would designate a student who graduated, was never retained, never received special educational services, was ranked in the upper quarter of the class, was never expelled or suspended, and had definite plans to enter a postsecondary educational or vocational institution.

The central issue that motivated this longitudinal follow-up was to determine the degree to which the positive impact of preschool, clearly evident during the early years of elementary school, would persist through high school. As noted earlier, group differences on student performance began to level off toward the middle years of elementary school, at least for the three groups (A, D-V, and T) that were followed through grade four. In general, this leveling process continued into high school, as evidenced by the mean school success ratings presented in Table 5.3. Although the differences between groups diminished over time, each of the groups that received preschool intervention scored higher on the

TABLE 5.3
Composite Indicator of School Success by Treatment Group

Group	Mean School Success Rating
Montessori	77.4
(N = 16)	(15.6)
Traditional	67.4
(N = 26)	(26.9)[a]
Ameliorative	62.6
(N = 24)	(25.8)
Direct Verbal	58.2
(N = 21)	(30.2)
Community Integrated	56.0
(N = 11)	(33.7)
Post Hoc Comparison	55.0
(N = 17)	(32.1)
(F = 1.17, df (5,103), p $>$ .05)	

Note. Composite school success variable = high school graduation + academic progress through high school + no need for special educational services + academic achievement + acceptable social behavior in school + future academic promise. Maximum score is 100.

[a] Standard deviation.

composite school success variable than did the No-Preschool group ($\bar{X}$ = 55). These differences were not statistically significant, but the fact that all five intervention groups, each of which had received a different preschool experience, performed better than the No-Preschool group suggests that preschool does have a positive, long-term benefit in terms of overall school performance.

A close examination of the school success ratings suggests that the children who participated in the Community-Integrated program did not perform much better than did the No-Preschool group ($\bar{X}$ = 56 for the C-I). In fact, if one considers only high school graduation, the No-Preschool group did better than the Community-Integrated group. Perhaps just being in a preschool program is not enough. Observers reported that the children in the Community-Integrated group often remained on the sidelines. This is a good example of how children from low-income families can be placed in middle-class schools without actually being integrated. Ongoing active involvement in the educational and social program of the preschool appears to be a factor that influences the long-term impact of a preschool experience.

Students from the Montessori group received the highest school success ratings ($\bar{X}$ = 77), reflecting their relatively high rate of graduation and low rate of retention, even though this group had higher rates of special class placement than did either the Ameliorative or Traditional groups. Retrospectively, one can theorize that the Montessori emphasis on working independently and persisting to task may have transferred to classroom activities that these students encountered

throughout their educational careers. These students were not necessarily intellectually advanced; in fact, among the five intervention groups they had the
second lowest IQ scores at age 16 (Fig. 5.1). Nevertheless, the ability to work
independently and to persist are qualities that would be viewed positively by
teachers; the ability to persist would certainly benefit students who need to spend
longer periods of time to master course material.

Students in the Traditional and Ameliorative groups also received relatively
high school success ratings ($\bar{X}$ = 67 and 63 respectively), whereas the students in
the Direct-Verbal group were rated slightly lower ($\bar{X}$ = 58). Rates of high school
graduation and length of time receiving special class placement account for the
relative rankings of these three groups.

The data for the A, T, and D-V groups suggest that structured teacher-directed
language programs in preschool are not enough to ensure subsequent school
success. In fact, the school success ratings of these three groups are in reverse
sequence from the emphasis placed on structured language instruction among the
programs. The D-V program, whose patterned drill represented the most highly
structored language programming, demonstrated the lowest rating among the
three. The T Program, which had markedly less structure, earned the highest
success rating of the three. Once again, the transfer from preschool to later
grades may be a key issue. The natural, ongoing teacher–child verbal interaction
that occurred in the Traditional program may be the best way for a low-income
child to acquire the language skills necessary to function successfully in elementary and secondary school. In contrast, the extensive oral drill in language and
logical reasoning utilized in the Direct-Verbal program did not appear to have
much impact on overall school success. As a means of remediating or preventing
language deficits, the structured gamelike approach to language instruction utilized in the Ameliorative approach appeared to help minimize the need for
special education services and to be adequate in terms of impact on overall
school success.

The students in each program were not identical. Although differences among
groups were minimized by the design of the study, the members of each group
differed among themselves in terms of race, sex, pretest IQ, parents' educational
background, and the presence or absence of the father in the household during
the preschool years. The relationship between these background variables and
the composite rating of school success were also investigated.

The correlation matrix in Table 5.4 indicates that neither parental educational
levels nor the presence or absence of the father in the household during the
preschool years correlated with school success. In contrast to these familial
demographic characteristics, certain individual characteristics did correlate with
school success (i.e., sex, preentry IQ, and post-preschool IQ). Females did
better in school than males, and students with higher IQ's at both pre- and post-
preschool tended to do better than students with lower IQ's. The relatively high

TABLE 5.4
Correlation Matrix of Background Variables and School Success

	School Success	Sex	Race	Pre-Entry IQ	Post-Preschool IQ	Age 16 IQ	Father Present	Mother's Educational Level
School success	1.0							
Sex	.22	1.0						
Race	.03	-.03	1.0					
Pre-entry IQ (age 4)	.25	.17	-.30	1.0				
Post-Preschool IQ (age 5)	.27	.13	-.28	.72	1.0			
IQ at age 16	.45	.03	-.36	.62	.61	1.0		
Father present during pre-school year	-.10	-.05	-.22	.19	.13	.04	1.0	
Mother's Educational Level	.06	.03	-.24	.15	.11	.34	.15	1.0
Father's Educational Level	.11	.22	-.24	.11	.14	.28	.08	.35

correlation between preentry and post-preschool IQ suggests that the preschool experience benefited intellectual functioning similarly for children at all IQ levels. One individual characteristic that did not correlate with school success was race. Overall, blacks and whites scored similarly on this index of school performance. A multiple regression analysis indicated that these seven background variables (sex, race, preentry IQ, postentry IQ, father's presence during the preschool years, mother's educational level, and father's educational level) accounted for only 15% of the variability in the school success index. Children from low-income families may do poorer in school compared to children from more affluent families, but within the population of children from low-income families knowledge of background characteristics at the time of entry into preschool may not be helpful in predicting the children that will succeed or fail in their school careers. There are many events or variables that affect subsequent school success that come into play after a child leaves preschool.

Because 90% of the individuals from the six groups have left high school, a picture of their performance would be incomplete without a discussion of their accomplishments outside of school. Unfortunately, most of the individuals had just entered the job market at the time they were interviewed or had only vague plans about additional educational or vocational training. Thus, it is still too early to provide a detailed assessment of group performance during the early years of adulthood. This will be an important area for further research.

SUMMARY OF FINDINGS FOR ALL PHASES

Formal schooling in grades K through 12 makes many different cognitive and social demands on the student. The longitudinal data described in this chapter help to clarify the expectations that educators should have about the contribution that can be made by a child's participation in a well-designed preschool program. Children of varying intellectual abilities from low-income families profited markedly during the time they were enrolled in a preschool program. The largest gains in intellectual and verbal functioning were observed among children who participated in the Ameliorative and Direct-Verbal Programs, with similar but smaller gains for children in the Traditional Program. Gains in intellectual functioning were also observed among those children in the Montessori and Community-Integrated Programs, but gains in verbal functioning were not observed. Clearly, the emphasis of a preschool program affects immediate student outcomes, although it is not always possible to identify the specific program features that facilitate positive gains.

Short-term gains are meaningful only in so far as they translate into continued successful functioning. However, it is crucial to remember that the importance of a gain in one area—for example, verbal ability—is not so much that the child continues to perform well verbally, although that is desirable, but rather that the newly acquired verbal skills enable the child to perfect other skills at some later date, such as the ability to resolve interpersonal conflicts verbally rather than physically. Although this point is obvious, it needs to be emphasized in order to understand long-term effects of preschool.

After children from the five preschool groups entered primary school, gains in general intellectual and academic functioning began to "wear off." By third grade, IQ scores were declining for all five groups, and a reading achievement (which was assessed for only three groups) showed that only one group (Ameliorative) was at grade level and the other two groups (Direct-Verbal and Traditional) were already reading below grade level. Data from the Stanford–Binet provide a revealing insight concerning this "wearing off" effect. By the end of second grade, students from all programs were showing evidence of decline in Stanford–Binet IQ scores, and it is at this point that differences in IQ among the five preschool groups were no longer statistically significant. Thus, the "wearing off" effect appears to be tied to insufficient ongoing support for these children from low-income families. Whereas most groups were relatively stable or declined in IQ between kindergarten and first grade, IQ scores increased considerably for the D-V group, half of whom had received a second year of intensive programming. This finding points to the positive benefits of sustained intensive intervention with children from low-income families throughout the early school years. It should be noted that although the Montessori group made only modest gains in intellectual functioning during preschool, they continued to gain for 2 years following preschool. This sleeper effect may be attributable to persistence to task acquired during the preschool intervention.

By the time the students graduated from high school, marked differences among the groups were no longer apparent. Children from the Montessori, Ameliorative, and Traditional programs performed the best in school, but the differences in school performance among students within the five preschool groups were as great as the differences among the five groups themselves. Background variables such as sex, preschool IQ, and parents' educational level apparently exert a small but lasting influence on school achievement.

The data do not specify conclusively the aspects of a preschool program that are critical for long-term school success. It is evident, however, that one year of preschool is not enough to ensure *high* levels of school success over time among children from low-income families. Nevertheless, the data consistently suggest that students from low-income families who participated in a quality preschool program will tend to perform in school at a slightly higher level than students who never had the opportunity to attend a preschool program.

IMPLICATIONS FOR PRACTICE AND RESEARCH

In the mid-1960s over one hundred young children from low-income families were given the opportunity to participate in one of five preschool programs. After following their progress through the public school system for 15 years and the progress of a group of similar children who did not attend preschool, what has been learned about ways to optimize the educational experience for other children from low-income families? A related question, but no less important, is what remains to be learned about ways to facilitate school success for these children? The following implications for practice and research in early childhood education are drawn from the data obtained over the past 15 years.

1. Participation in a preschool program for children from low-income families has some lasting benefits in terms of overall school success, but 1 year of intervention is not enough to ensure *high* levels of school success.

2. Early intervention can prevent a sizable number of children from being placed in special classes. Placement in special classes is expensive to the taxpayer. Furthermore, the stigma of being placed in a special class may have a deleterious effect on the self-concept of the child. Thus, every effort should be made to prevent children from being placed in a special class if the condition can be remediated in other ways at an early age.

3. A high-quality preschool program can bring about significant improvements for several years in language and intellectual functioning without sacrific-

ing social development. Also, the effects of acquiring readiness skills persist for at least a few years after children leave preschool.

4. No one preschool program demonstrated superior long-term impact over the other four. That both the Community-Integrated and the Traditional programs had similar theoretical orientations but differences in child performance suggest that teacher behavior may be a key variable. Ongoing monitoring of teachers during the implementation of a program is perhaps the only way to ensure that they are following the theoretical and practical components of the program.

5. Preschool programs that are sensitive to individual differences, such as the Ameliorative approach, can minimize the need for special services among children throughout their school careers.

6. Although emphasis on language development is important for preschoolers, task persistence and the ability to work independently, behaviors that were stressed in the Montessori program, may be just as important for long-term school success. In addition, teachers of preschoolers need to make a deliberate effort to help children transfer learning.

7. Merely placing low-income children in a middle-class preschool setting, as was done in the Community-Integrated approach, may not be adequate for these children. Teachers need to understand how to integrate these children into the mainstream setting. Frequent preservice and inservice training should be built into all preschool programs serving children from low-income families.

8. All five preschool programs only minimally involved parents in the education of their children. If parents had been more involved, perhaps the children would have had a better chance of maintaining their gains over time.

9. The data suggest that some children will need to receive continuous or periodic supportive services after they enter elementary school. Children need advocates, either parents or other school personnel, within the school to ensure that adequate supportive services are provided *before* serious deficiencies in critical academic areas become evident.

The longitudinal data collected for this study also raise many issues that should be addressed if educators are to provide the best possible services to children from low-income families.

1. The critical components of a preschool program that facilitate high levels of lasting child progress still need to be delineated.

2. Techniques need to be developed to match both children and teachers to preschool programs.

3. Acquiring skills in preschool is not enough to ensure school success. Ways to encourage transfer of learning between preschool and elementary school need to be identified.

4. Family variables, including school performance of siblings, should be investigated to identify familial patterns that differentiate children who succeed

in school from children who fail. This information can then be used to develop more appropriate parent involvement programs.

5. The longitudinal data suggest that administrative decisions regarding grade retention versus supplying supplemental services may have a differential impact on overall school success. This issue should be examined across a large number of school districts.

6. High teacher–child ratios in preschool appear to be important for individualizing instruction. The effectiveness of alternative ways to establish high adult–child ratios (e.g., using parent volunteers, retired persons, or adolescent volunteers) should be systematically evaluated.

7. The role of self-concept in relation to school performance should be investigated. Valid procedures to assess self-concept and self-esteem among preschoolers need to be developed so that the effectiveness of a preschool program in developing positive self-esteem can be assessed.

8. There is evidence that the effects of preschool begin to decrease during the middle of elementary school. Funding agencies should be encouraged to support follow-up research. In this way, follow-up studies can be built into preschool programs so that educators can identify when and why the gains made during preschool begin to fade. Of course, follow-up research requires funding, and this study shows that educators can learn much by following children as they progress through school.

REFERENCES

Almy, M. New views on intellectual development in early childhood education. In A. H. Passow (Ed.), *Intellectual development: Another look*. Washington, D.C.: ASCD, 1964.

Ausubel, D. P. The effects of cultural deprivation on learning patterns. In S. W. Webster (Ed.), *Understanding the educational problems of the disadvantaged learner*. San Francisco: Chandler, 1966.

Bereiter, C., & Englemann, S. *Teaching disadvantaged children in the preschool*. Englewood Cliffs, N.J.: Prentice–Hall, 1966.

Bereiter, C., Englemann, S., & Washington, E. *Research and development program on preschool disadvantaged children* (Vol. II). Final Report, Bureau of Research, Office of Education, U.S. Department of Health, Education, and Welfare, Project No. 5-1811, Contract No. OE 6-10-235, May, 1969.

Comprehensive tests of basic skills. Monterey, Calif.: CTB/McGraw–Hill, 1968.

Deutsch, M. The disadvantaged child and the learning process. In A. H. Passow (Ed.), *Education in depressed areas*. New York: Teachers College, Columbia University Press, 1963.

Deutsch, M. Facilitating development in the preschool child: Social and psychological perspectives. *Merrill-Palmer Quarterly*, 1964, *10*, 249–263.

Domagala, R. F. *The relationship of two preschool approaches to social adjustment effects at second grade*. Unpublished doctoral dissertation, University of Illinois, 1976.

Farber, B., Harvey, D., & Lewis, M. *Research and development program on preschool disadvantaged children* (Vol. III). Final Report, Bureau of Research, Office of Education, U.S. Department of Health, Education, and Welfare, Project No. 5-1811, Contract No. OE 6-10-235, May, 1969.

Frostig, M., Lefever, W., & Whittlesey, J. R. B. *Developmental test of visual perception.* Palo Alto, Calif.: Consulting Psychologists Press, 1963.

Goldberg, M. Factors affecting educational attainment in depressed urban areas. In A. H. Passow (Ed.), *Education in depressed areas.* New York: Columbia University, 1963.

Hess, R. D., & Shipman, V. C. Early experience and the socialization of cognitive modes in children. *Child Development,* 1965, *36,* 869–886.

Hildreth, G. H., Griffiths, N. L., & McGauvran, M. E. *Metropolitan readiness tests.* New York: Harcourt, Brace & World, 1949.

Hunt, J. McV. *Intelligence and experience.* New York: The Ronald Press Co., 1961.

Hunt, J. McV. The psychological basis for using preschool enrichment as an antidote for cultural deprivation. *Merrill-Palmer Quarterly,* 1964, *10,* 209–248.

Jensen, A. R. Learning ability in retarded, average, and gifted children. *Merrill-Palmer Quarterly,* 1963, *9,* 123–140.

John, V. P. The intellectual development of slum children: Some preliminary findings. *American Journal of Orthopsychiatry,* 1963, *33,* 813–822.

John, V. P., & Goldstein, L. S. The social context of language acquisition. *Merrill-Palmer Quarterly,* 1964, *10,* 265–276.

Karnes, M. B. Evaluation and implications of research with young handicapped and low-income children. In J. C. Stanley (Ed.), *Compensatory education for children, aged 2–8: Recent studies of educational intervention.* Proceedings. Baltimore: Johns Hopkins University Press, 1973. (a)

Karnes, M. B. Implications of research with disadvantaged children for early intervention with the handicapped. In J. B. Jordan & R. F. Daily (Eds.), *Not all little wagons are red: Exceptional children's early years.* Arlington, Va.: Council for Exceptional Children, 1973. (b)

Karnes, M. B., & Hodgins, A. The effects of a highly structured preschool program on the measured intelligence of culturally disadvantaged four-year-old children. *Psychology in the Schools,* 1969, *6* (1), 89–91.

Karnes, M. B., Hodgins, A. S., & Teska, J. A. *Research and development program on preschool disadvantaged children* (Vol. I). Final Report, Bureau of Research, Office of Education, U.S. Department of Health, Education, and Welfare, Project No. 5-1811, Contract No. OE 6-10-235, May, 1969.

Karnes, M. B., Lee, R. C., & Applebaum, L. *A comparison of long-term effects of five early intervention models.* Paper presented at the meeting of the American Educational Research Association, San Francisco, April, 1979.

Karnes, M. B., Plummer, C. M., & Lee, R. C. Immediate, short-term, and long-range effects of five preschool programs for disadvantaged children. Paper presented at the meeting of the American Educational Research Association, Toronto, March, 1978. *Resources in Education* (RIE), August, 1978 (ED 152 043).

Karnes, M. B., Teska, J. A., & Hodgins, A. S. The effects of four programs of classroom intervention on the intellectual and language development of four-year-old disadvantaged children. *American Journal of Orthopsychiatry,* 1970, *40,* 58–76.

Karnes, M. B., Teska, J. A., Wollersheim, J. P., Stoneburner, R. L., & Hodgins, A. S. An evaluation of two preschool programs for disadvantaged children: A traditional and highly structured experimental preschool. *Exceptional Children,* 1968, *34,* 667–676.

Karnes, M. B., & Zehrbach, R. R. Curriculum and methods in early childhood special education: One approach. In *Alternatives for teaching exceptional children: Essays from focus on exceptional children.* Denver, Love, 1975.

Karnes, M. B., Zehrbach, R. R., & Teska, J. A. The Ameliorative approach in the development of curriculum. In R. K. Parker (Ed.), *Preschool in action: Exploring early childhood programs.* Boston: Allyn & Bacon, 1972.

Karnes, M. B., Zehrbach, R. R., & Teska, J. A. The Karnes' preschool program: Rationale, curricular offerings, and follow-up data. In S. Ryan (Ed.), *A report on longitudinal evaluations of preschool programs*. Office of Child Development, Children's Bureau, DHEW Publication, No. (OHD) 74–24, 1974, 95–108.

Karnes, M. B., Zehrbach, R. R., & Teska, J. A. Conceptualization of the GOAL (Game Oriented Activities for Learning) curriculum. In R. K. Parker & M. C. Day (Eds.), *The preschool in action: Exploring early childhood programs* (2nd Ed.). Boston: Allyn & Bacon, 1977.

Kirk, S. A. *Early education of the mentally retarded*. Urbana, Ill.: University of Illinois Press, 1958.

Kirk, S. A., & McCarthy, J. J. *Illinois test of psycholinguistic abilities: Examiner's manual.* Urbana, Ill.: University of Illinois Press, 1961.

Mehrabian, A., & Russell, J. A. *An approach to environmental psychology*. Cambridge, Mass.: MIT Press, 1974.

Norwicki, S., & Strickland, B. R. A locus of control scale for children. *Journal of consulting and clinical psychology,* 1973, 40, 148–154.

Reissman, F. *The culturally deprived child*. New York: Harper & Row, 1962.

Terman, L. M., & Merrill, M. A. *Stanford–Binet intelligence scale*. Boston: Houghton Mifflin, 1960.

Teska, J. A. *Success and failure in five different programs of preschool intervention with culturally disadvantaged children*. Unpublished doctoral dissertation, University of Illinois, 1969.

Tiegs, E. W., & Clark, W. W. *California achievement tests*. Monterey, Calif.: McGraw–Hill, 1963.

Wechsler, D. *Wechsler adult intelligence scale*. New York: Psychological Corporation, 1955.

Wechsler, D. *Wechsler intelligence scale for children–revised*. New York: Psychological Corporation, 1974.

Weikart, D. P., Kamii, C. K., & Radin, N. L. *Perry preschool project: Progress report*. Ypsilanti, Mich.: Ypsilanti Public Schools, 1966.

6 The Louisville Experiment: A Comparison of Four Programs

Louise B. Miller
Rondeall P. Bizzell
University of Louisville

Introduction

Purpose of the Experiment

Our four-program comparison was not designed to determine the effects of preschool versus no preschool, but rather to compare the characteristics and effects of four different programs. It was established by 1968 that significant cognitive gains could be acheived by young disadvantaged children who experienced preschool programs of several different types (Bereiter & Engelmann, 1966; Gray & Klaus, 1965; Gray, Klaus, Miller, & Forrester, 1966; Hodges, McCandless, & Spicker, 1967; Southern & Plant, 1972; Sprigle, Van de Riet, & Van de Riet, 1967; Weikart, 1970; pp. 186–196).

On the basis of the philosophies underlying various programs it was expected that some would have immediate effects on children whereas the effects of other programs (less remedial and more oriented towards providing foundational experiences) might not appear until several years later. For this reason, and in order to check on how lasting any effects would be, the study was designed to be a longitudinal experiment lasting from prekindergarten through second grade. Because different approaches to preschool education reflected different convictions regarding how children learn and develop, it appeared that comparing the effects on children of various programs would not only have practical value but would also provide information about developmental hypotheses. Also, because there was a consensus in the research community that testing IQ was a very limited way to measure the success of programs that were oriented toward longterm development, the experiment was designed to assess other competencies as well as motivation, attitudes, and classroom behaviors.

A second reason for the experiment was the question of whether various programs that sounded so different in goals and philosophies were really very different in respect to what the teachers and children actually did. At the time this study was begun, several other program comparisons were being conducted (Di Lorenzo & Salter, 1968; Erickson, McMillan, Bennell, & Callahan, 1969; Karnes, Hodgins, Teska, & Kirk, 1969; Weikart, 1970), one of which is represented in this volume (Karnes et al.). These program comparisons were true experiments, but in comparing educational programs, the independent variable is quite complex. "Program" includes content, sequence, types of activities, and numerous other aspects of teaching method such as group or individual contact, verbal instruction, demonstration, etc. Other program comparisons had provided descriptions of the programs, but none had been designed for the purpose of examining specific program characteristics and identifying the dimensions on which different programs could be ordered.

The importance of investigating program differences was related to a third question: If there were differences in program implementation and also differences in their effects, what aspects of the programs were crucial? It was the investigation of this link between classroom events—techniques and interactions—and the program outcomes in terms of children's development that most strongly motivated this study.

Because the major dimensions of preschool programs were not well defined, the best strategy appeared to be the selection of a few programs that met several criteria: (1) they represented extreme positions in as many respects as possible; (2) there was evidence of their effectiveness with disadvantaged children; (3) there was ample information regarding their goals and methods; and (4) there were training programs available for teachers and therefore a reasonable prospect for successful implementation. The four programs were: Bereiter–Engelmann (Bereiter & Engelmann, 1966); DARCEE (Gray, Klaus, Miller, & Forrester, 1966); Montessori (Montessori, 1964); and Traditional (*Rainbow Series, Project Head Start,* 1965).

Through the years, we have continued to focus on the original purposes of the study, but have broadened those interests to include questions about the relationships between early and late measures of similar characteristics, the extent to which early measures predict later school achievement, and the combinations of later measures that are related to achievement.

History of the Experiment[1]

Head Start drew many psychologists out of the laboratory and into the field for experimental work. I was one of these. Shortly after the Head Start program was implemented in Louisville, the Urban Studies Center at the University of

---

[1]Bizzell was not on the research team when the study began. Therefore, the first person singular refers to the senior author only.

Louisville was asked to make an evaluation of the program. Because of my interest in both child development and research, I was asked to join a committee to undertake this project.

In 1967, I was quite naive with regard to both field research and early education. As I read the literature, I learned that among professionals who were knowledgeable, there was a great deal of controversy over what experiences should be provided in preschool and how. These controversies were grounded in both philosophical differences regarding education and theoretical convictions regarding the nature of human development, especially cognitive development. I realized that methodological improvements could be made in comparative research and eventually designed an experiment that included several classes in each of several very different programs, random assignment of children to programs, pretesting of children, observations of classroom events, posttesting of children, and examination of the relationships between techniques and outcomes.

A colleague and I met with Dr. Edmund Gordon, then Research Director of Head Start, and he encouraged us to proceed with the experiment described in the following sections.

The experiment was easy to design, but the complexities of implementation quickly became manifest. For example, because of the formalized nature of Montessori training, it was necessary to recruit these teachers from outside the school system. Numerous trips were made to Montessori training programs, but despite the intensive efforts, it was not possible to recruit more than two of them.

We encountered great difficulty in locating and obtaining adequate research instruments to measure such things as curiosity, persistence, and creativity in four-year-olds. After locating a battery called "The Cincinnati Autonomy Test Battery," I contacted Dr. Thomas Banta for permission to use the Curiosity Box, Replacement Puzzle (persistence), and a test of inventiveness called the Dog and Bone. Although it was possible to provide a local carpenter with sufficiently detailed instructions to achieve adequate copies of the last two, the Curiosity Box was much too complicated to describe in such detail. Consequently, it was necessary to fly to Cincinnati and borrow one to use as a model. At the time, there was considerable uneasiness about bombings and hijacking of planes. When I arrived at the ticket counter in Cincinnati carrying a box about $21'' \times 24''$, covered with springs, latches, and other items whose function was not immediately apparent, and was asked "What is this?", the temptation to reply, "It's a curiosity box" was almost irresistible. Fortunately I managed to convince the agent that it was a harmless research instrument.

Somewhat later, the entire study was in jeopardy because of controversies within the local community. At the time the study was getting underway, the Community Action Commission was the delegate agency for Head Start. Strenuous efforts had been made to involve the local residents in the decisions of the Community Action Commission, and in each target area there was a neighborhood council whose approval was required for implementation. Each of the four neighborhood councils had to be presented with the plan. In one of these areas some opposition had developed, the basis for which was never made clear. In that area, the plan passed by only one vote. In another area, the plan was presented on the same night that Louisville's only real riot of the 1960s occurred. As we discussed the study and the council voted, buildings were burning a few blocks away. The only two white individuals at the meeting (my husband and I) were unaware of any disturbance, but after the meeting we were discreetly advised to take a route home that would avoid the troubled area.

At the time of assignment to classes, those connected with the project were besieged by parents who had a preference for one or the other of the four programs and wanted special placement for their child.

During the year, one of the two Montessori teachers (who was experiencing her first year of teaching) became so discouraged that she came close to resigning.

Such problems are certainly not unique to this study. They could be multiplied many times by all those who contributed to this volume. I relate them in the belief that it is important to share with students and others interested in the research something of the personal and social context that characterized the world in which the data were collected.

The study was implemented in the 1968–1969 school year in Head Start (prekindergarten) classes. Classes began in the first week of September and continued through the first week of June. Children were retested each spring through the second grade. We discontinued contact with the children at that point (1972). Details of the original study from the implementation year (1968–1969) through the second grade were reported in 1975 (Miller & Dyer). Therefore, only the major results are outlined in this chapter.

In 1975, we were asked to join the Consortium for Longitudinal Studies (formerly the Consortium for Developmental Continuity) to plan a joint follow-up with other researchers. In the fall of that same year, when our children were entering the sixth grade, an event occurred that in part was unique to this area. For many years there had been a Louisville City School System and a Jefferson County School System. Head Start, in the form of prekindergarten, was concentrated in the city, although there were a few Head Start kindergartens in the county. There had been no *de jure* segration of blacks and whites since the 1950s, but de facto segregation existed because of the concentration of blacks within the city limits. In the same year that busing was inaugurated to integrate the schools, the county and city systems were merged. Although busing itself did produce a few disturbances and protests, it was the combination of busing and total reorganization that produced a time of confusion. Despite heroic efforts and long hours of planning and work, equipment was transferred to the wrong schools, classes were without books, children were left in the wrong places, etc. There is no reason to believe that in our study the effects were greater on one group than another. But the overall achievement levels may have been adversely affected.

By the time the Consortium had completed plans for a cooperative followup, our young people were in the seventh grade. We relocated as many as possible and are currently testing them each spring. As of 1982, they are completing the twelfth grade, and we who began with an interest in preschool programs find ourselves concerned with the characteristics of adolescents.

THEORETICAL ISSUES

Three issues in the area of child development seem to be related to the characteristics of programs:

1. Whether emphasis is placed on the universals in development, i.e., those individual levels and styles or stages of development that are relatively "context-free" (Bruner, 1972), or whether there is an emphasis on the possible developmental lags or deficits that may be typical of certain groups because of the cultural milieu in which development occurs. From the latter perspective, prekindergarten programs are likely to place more emphasis on the remediation of deficits in academic areas and on acceleration of groups to appropriate levels.

2. Whether emphasis with respect to the process of development is placed on accumulation of skills that must be acquired in sequence, or whether the emphasis is on the broader processes of reorganization of understandings and utilization of logical strategies and perspectives. The first emphasis produces a more didactic program; the second is more likely to result in a program that structures the environment to provide challenges and opportunities for exploration and manipulation. The question of whether a preschool program should be evaluated by its immediate effects or by its benefits over a longer period of time is also related to this issue—i.e., immediate gains in specific skills can be expected from some programs but not necessarily from others.

3. The degree to which attempts to accelerate cognitive development can be successful without a corresponding focus on social and emotional development and the development of attitudes and motivations. The breadth of goals in prekindergarten programs varies with the developers' positions regarding this issue.

Educational philosophy is also relevant, of course, to the nature of preschool programs, particularly in respect to the issue of preparation for elementary school. If the pragmatic position is taken that children need to be prepared for first grade as it is currently presented in most public school systems, the prekindergarten program will emphasize two things—the development of preacademic skills and the development of behaviorial characteristics that make children teachable in a large classroom.

Although the larger theoretical issues were not addressed directly in this experiment, they provided the basis for selection of programs and measuring instruments. Different positions on the philosophical issues concerning effective conditions for learning (e.g., the use of negative as well as positive feedback) had resulted in the combination of content and methods in a variety of ways. The challenge was to design an experiment that would permit the assessment of: (1) program positions on dimensions common to all; (2) the impact of different programs in their particular areas of emphasis; and (3) those immediate effects that would be relevant to long-term outcomes in respect to common goals such as school achievement.

The experiment was designed to provide the kinds of information that would generate more specific hypotheses regarding the development of competence and the role that early experiences in classroom settings may have in such development.

In summary, the experiment had three purposes: (1) to determine whether and in what respects the four programs would actually have different characteristics when classroom events were carefully monitored during implementation; (2) to determine whether the four programs would have different effects on children at the end of the implementation year—that is, whether the goals of the more academic programs would be accomplished in IQ and achievement and those of the programs with broader goals would be reached in areas such as motivation and classroom behavior; and (3) if the different programs did accomplish their goals during the implementation year, we wanted to determine whether achievement in later years would be best predicted by early academic success or by the early acceleration of other types of development such as attitudes and nonacademic characteristics.

SITE AND SAMPLE

Community

The experimental programs were implemented within the ongoing Head Start program, which in Louisville at the time the experiment began was a full-day prekindergarten for four-year-olds. There were 48 of these prekindergarten classes in the city, 14 of which constituted the experimental classes.

The four areas of Louisville in which the study was conducted had been designated as "target areas" by the Community Action Commission. These areas were in the central and west central portions of the city where the population was largely black, unemployment was high, income low, and housing ranged from fair to substandard. These areas provided most of the dropouts in the city schools.

Curriculum was under the supervision of the research staff. Special materials required by the four programs were provided by the research project. Regular materials and ancillary services were provided by Head Start. Most of the classes were held inside the school buildings but a few were in trailers or in church buildings. The class day was 6½ hours long, and all children were given a morning snack and lunch. They rested for a period of approximately 1 hour in the afternoon.

Sample

Experimental children were randomly assigned to either regular Head Start classes or experimental classes at each school from the pool of registered applicants. A control group ($N = 34$) was recruited from the same neighborhoods where the experimental classes were located. Twenty-two of them were drawn from the waiting list for Head Start. The rest were located in the neighborhoods

At the end of the prekindergarten year, there were 214 children in the four experimental programs—100 males and 114 females. There were 64 B–E, 64 DARCEE, 33 Montessori, and 53 Traditional children. About half the children's families were receiving some form of welfare. The mean Hollingshead Index of Socioeconomic Status was 63.52, placing these families in the lowest status group. Only 39% of the fathers were living in the household. Most of them were living on approximately $3000 per year and about 90% were black. Experimental program families did not differ from each other on any demographic characteristics.

In the kindergarten year there was a bifurcation of the experimental group, in which some of the children attended a Follow Through program, called Work-Spend. The rest of the children entered regular kindergarten. Because none of the original control group entered the Work-Spend program in the kindergarten year, a second control group was recruited, consisting of children who were attending Work-Spend kindergarten and had not had any prekindergarten experience the previous year. These were cohorts of the experimental sample but were tested for the first time at the end of their kindergarten year. A third group of children were recruited for a B–E kindergarten. These were also children who had not had any prekindergarten experience.

The 34 original control children, 18 males and 16 females, were similar in demographic characteristics to the experimental group with the exception of two factors—more controls were living with both parents, and more of them were white. No demographic data were available on the Work-Spend control group.

Each year the current sample has been compared with dropouts and with the original group on demographic characteristics and on early measures. So far, the results of these comparisons indicate that the retained samples are representative of the original group. Because follow-up had been continuous through second grade, very few children were lost to the study, and the second grade sample was quite similar to the original group. Therefore, the immediate program effects after prekindergarten have been reported in terms of analyses done on the second-grade sample. These results are abbreviated from those reported in the 1975 Monograph (Miller & Dyer). The second-grade sample consisted of 55 B–E, 49 DARCEE, 28 Montessori, 43 Traditional, and 40 control children.

Follow-up Sample

The eighth-grade sample consisted of 108 experimentals and 32 controls. Of the experimentals, 30 were B–E, 29 were DARCEE, 20 were Montessori, and 29 were Traditional. There were 65 males and 75 females. Demographic data became available on the eighth-grade sample (including follow-through controls and the children who had a B–E kindergarten but no prekindergarten) in 1977 from the interview conducted for the Consortium. The Hollingshead Two-Factor Index of Socioeconomic Status (parent education and occupation) for controls was 58.8 and for experimentals 54.7.

In order to determine whether selective attrition had occurred at eighth grade, several analyses were made. The current sample from each group was compared with the dropouts on demographic measures at the prekindergarten point and on end-of-prekindergarten (EPK) levels of achievement (Preschool Inventory—PSI-EPK), end-of-second-grade achievement (California Achievement Test), and IQ at both earlier times (Stanford–Binet). The current samples were also compared with the total sample at the end-of-prekindergarten points in order to determine whether the current differences matched those at the end of the intervention year. There were no significant differences between dropouts and retained children in mother's education or income. The percentage of two-parent families was higher among the retained participants than for dropouts except in Montessori where the reverse was the case. On the Binet, the only differences between dropouts and retained that were larger than the standard error of the mean were for B–E males (5.9) and Traditional females (8.7). In both cases, the retained group was higher. The match between the retained group and the original sample was extremely close except for the percentage of two-parent families in B–E and Traditional where the retained sample was somewhat advantaged compared to the full sample at the end of prekindergarten. Demographic data and performance at the prekindergarten level were known only for the original controls. As was the case with the original sample, these controls had higher incomes and more two-parent families.

DESIGN AND METHOD

The plan called for a 1-year implementation of the four programs in Head Start classrooms and a follow-up for 3 years through second grade. In order to make sure that any differences in outcomes were not due to differences among teachers, four teachers were to be trained in each program style, and replications of the four-program comparison were to be placed in four different areas of the city. Because only two Montessori teachers could be recruited, the four-program comparison was replicated twice. In two areas of the city there were classes in all four programs, and in the two other areas there were classes in three of the programs. Thus, there were 14 classes altogether, four each in B–E, DARCEE, and Traditional, and two in Montessori.

Once the study had been approved by neighborhood councils in all four areas, ten schools were selected, and in all but one school there were enough Head Start classes to provide for a nonexperimental class in addition to the one or more experimental programs provided. These nonexperimental classes were not part of the study but merely provided an alternative to experimental classes for random assignment.

During the second year of the study in 1969–1970, the Louisville City Schools inaugurated a Follow Through kindergarten program in one area of the city. One class from each of the four programs entered this Follow Through kindergarten, a token economy developed at the University of Kansas (Bushell & Brigham, 1971). This particular Follow Through program that was selected by the city school system is referred to as "Work-Spend." All Work-Spend classes were in the same school. The remainder of the children entered the regular kindergarten program. This bifurcation of the longitudinal experiment, although not part of the original plan, produced eight different combinations of prekindergarten and kindergarten experience that continued through first and second grades.

The implementation year of the experiment involved the following phases in chronological order: selection of programs, selection of measures to assess effects, selection of teachers, training of teachers, assignment of programs to sites, registration and assignment of children to programs, pretesting and ratings of children, videotaping of classrooms and in-class monitoring, posttesting of children, development of videotape monitoring instrument, tape monitoring, data reduction, and analyses.

Treatments

Two of the programs (Bereiter–Engelmann and DARCEE) were small-group programs that used didactic methods (direct instruction) to develop foundational skills necessary for school. The content was academic; for DARCEE, it involved association, classification, and sequencing in the processing of information along with the development of motivation to achieve, persistence in tasks, resistance to distraction, and delay of gratification. In B–E, the instructional materials were primarily visual and auditory. In DARCEE, there were also games and many materials to manipulate. Both the Montessori and Traditional programs were oriented towards long-term development and did not involve group instruction. Montessori, however, was a more structured program in that prepared materials were designed to teach language and mathematical concepts whenever the child had progressed through exercises for daily living and sensorial materials. The Traditional program had a much broader emphasis on social and emotional development, whereas Montessori was oriented towards cognitive skills and related attitudes. Traditional also emphasized fantasy and role-playing, Montessori did not. Detailed descriptions of these four programs can be found in Miller and Dyer (1975).

Teachers

Recruitment and Training.   The Montessori teachers were interns imported from Fairleigh Dickinson University. The other 12 teachers were recruited from the pool of regular Head Start teachers on the basis of ability, interest, and probability of completing the training. Teachers were assigned to programs for which they indicated a preference. During the summer preceding the experiment, they were sent to workshops at various universities for training by program experts. For DARCEE, two additional individuals were trained to become Home Visitors. These training programs lasted 8 weeks (4 weeks for the B–E teachers) and the research staff feared that one or more of the teachers would: (1) drop out of the study at the last minute; (2) start but not complete the training; or (3) complete the training but be unable to complete the teaching for a full year. Fortunately, none of these things happened and all 14 teachers fulfilled their obligations, preserving the integrity of the research design. Aides were selected by neighborhood in accordance with Head Start guidelines and were trained by program developers in a 2-day workshop that was held at the University of Louisville just prior to the beginning of school.

Teacher Characteristics.   There were, of course, some biographical differences among teachers, but most of these were unrelated to programs. The Montessori teachers were the youngest and the only two who had completed requirements for a Master's degree. All teachers except one Montessori teacher had at least one year of experience. With respect to personality (16 P.F.; Cattell & Eber, 1957), intelligence (Peabody Picture Vocabulary Test; Dunn, 1965), and attitudes toward teaching (Neill & Bein, 1967), there were no significant differences among teachers in the four programs.

Data Collection: Prekindergarten through Second Grade

Program Monitoring

Five 10-minute tapes were obtained on each teacher throughout the prekindergarten year. The videotaping simply focused on whatever happened to be occurring at the time the videotape technician arrived in the classroom. Monitoring of these tapes was not done until after the end of the school year. The procedure used was based on Bales (1950) and was an attempt to categorize all teacher behavior involving teacher–child interactions during the 10-minute period. The system has been explained in detail elsewhere (Miller & Dyer, 1975). The major categories were role-playing, modeling, exemplification, manipulation, verbal instruction, requests for imitation, requests for performance, and feedback of various types.

A time-sampling procedure for monitoring in class was also used. This procedure assessed the number of groups in the class, the number of children in groups, the number of shifts in group size, the type of group (whether children were doing different things, the same thing, or engaged in a common enterprise), the type of activity going on, the media being used, and the lesson goal. The in-class procedure also replicated the teaching techniques recorded in the videotape procedure, but instead of classifying each act recorded the occurrence of all techniques during a 15-second observation period, thus representing the frequency of use of various techniques. There were five sessions of 2 hours each in each class during the year. A number of classes were monitored by videotape during the kindergarten and first-grade years. No monitoring was done in second grade.

In order to document the correct implementation of the four types of prekindergarten, evaluations of classes and teachers were obtained by experts in each program. For this purpose, a Consultant's Evaluation Form was devised that called for magnitude ratings on a 0–10 scale, where 0 meant "not at all like" and 10 meant "exactly like." These consultants were asked to rate each class on the approximation of such components as teaching techniques, materials, content, sequence, and other aspects of the program.

Program Effects

Constructs.   The tests initially given to the children reflect the variation in goals among the four programs insofar as this was possible. For example, tests of IQ and achievement were selected and it was expected that the more academic and didactic programs would produce greater immediate gains on these measures. Tests of curiosity, persistence, and inventiveness, and the rating of classroom behavior were selected in the hope that these instruments would assess the immediate goals of the more individualized and less didactic programs (or in some cases a more deliberate attempt to teach motivations and attitudes related to learning).

More important than the question of the immediate impact of these four programs was the question of whether and how their experiences in the programs would affect the performance of the children in later years. Because two of the programs (Traditional and Montessori) were oriented towards long-term goals, and because the prekindergarten intervention consisted of only 1 year, we expected that the effects of these two programs might become apparent only after a few years of school.

A further consideration in the selection of instruments was the possibility of finding early measures, or combinations of measures, which would be predictive of school success and competence in later years. Although we believe the tests used in 1968–1969 were the best we could obtain at the time, the lack of adequate measures of many aspects of children's functioning at ages 4 and 5 was painfully obvious. For example, there was no standard way to obtain scores on achievement motivation, intellectual curiosity, or the aspects of cognitive development identified by Piaget.

Specific Instruments.   In the implementation year, two cognitive tests were given to all children: the Stanford–Binet to measure IQ and the Preschool Inventory (PSI; Caldwell, 1968) to measure specific achievements such as vocabulary and knowledge of the world. To measure motivations and attitudes, several tests were selected from the Cincinnati Autonomy Test Battery, designed to assess "self-regulating behaviors that facilitate effective problem solving" (Banta, 1970, p. 424). These were the Curiosity Box (a construction with numerous interesting manipulative and visual items on it) to measure the tendency to explore; the Replacement Puzzle (a type of jigsaw with some permanently fixed pieces forming a space within which the removable pieces must fit, a puzzle usually unsolvable within the time limit) to measure persistence and resistance to distraction; the Dog and Bone (a board with a house on each corner, a fixed bone, and a movable dog) to measure the generation of alternative solutions to the same problem (i.e., getting the dog to the bone). In addition, the Behavior Inventory (Hess, Kramer, Slaughter, Torney, Berry, & Hull, 1966) was completed by both teachers and aides on each child. This is a rating scale which assessed timidity, independence, aggression, achievement motivation, and verbal-social participation (V-S-P). As an additional measure of achievement motivation, the Face sheet of the Stanford–Binet was used to provide estimates by testers of the adequacy of test-taking behavior and attitude. To assess perceptual development, the Early Childhood Embedded Figures Test (Banta, 1970) was given, a series of designs in which the child must find a standard figure embedded. A sample of six children from each class were also given an arithmetic test designed for the Bereiter–Engelmann program, the Basic Concept Inventory also designed for the Bereiter–Engelmann program, and a test called the Parallel Sentence Production (Stern, 1968) that calls for construction of sentences describing pictures slightly different from a standard (e.g., "This skinny lady is sitting on a big chair. Tell me about *this* picture." Child responds: "This fat lady is sitting on a little chair.")

Tests were readministered each year through second grade, except the PSI. Achievement was assessed in kindergarten by the Metropolitan Readiness Test and at first and second grades by the California Achievement Test.

Procedures for Testing.   The Stanford–Binet testers were advanced graduate students or professional psychologists. The remainder of the tests were divided into two batteries given by different groups of graduate students who were given 12 hours of training by the research staff. Scheduling was done in such a way as to make certain that children in different programs were tested by a variety of testers. A 6-month test–retest interval was maintained. In order to avoid a spurious increase due to familiarity with being tested and the experience of a few weeks of school, the first tests were not given until about 8 weeks after the beginning of school. This decision meant that we did not have a pre-intervention test, but it provided a conservative baseline for examining program effects. The Stanford–Binet was given last for all children after they had taken the other two batteries. Both teachers and aides completed the Behavior Inventory on all children after 8 weeks of school and again at the end of the school year. The supplementary tests to the subsample was given only once at the end of the year.

Through second grade all tests were administered by the research staff in April and May of each year except for the achievement tests, which were obtained from the public schools. The Behavior Inventory was completed by kindergarten, first-, and second-grade teachers.

Data Collection: Sixth through Eighth Grades

Instruments used in follow-up from 1976 onward were selected by the entire Consortium; available funds permitted only the testing of IQ, obtaining interview data on both students and their families, and school achievement and other school data such as grades, retentions, and assignment to special education. Subjects were relocated, interviewed, their parents were interviewed, school achievement test results were obtained, and from 1977 to the present IQ testing has been done each spring and school achievement data obtained each fall. Testers and other aspects of procedure were similar to those in Phase I.

The Consortium agreed to use the WISC-R rather than the Stanford–Binet. For our particular study, therefore, the WISC-R and the Stanford–Binet have been given in alternate years, beginning with the WISC-R at seventh grade. Achievement test data have been obtained for sixth grade onward, because these scores are not available until the fall or early spring after the year in which they were administered.

Analyses: Prekindergarten Through Second Grade

Prekindergarten Program Characteristics

In order to determine whether, and how, the four programs differed from each other the data from the two types of observation procedures were divided into three types of classroom activity: classroom structure, child activity, and teacher activity. Discriminant analyses were performed on each set of variables to determine which ones differentiated the programs. Discriminant analyses also provided scores for the classes within each program allowing examination of the degree to which classes in the same programs were alike.

Prekindergarten Program Effects

At the end of second grade, multivariate analysis of variance with classes nested within programs was used to examine program effects in the prekindergarten year. In analyses involving controls, these were divided into "wait listed" and "not wait listed" in order to provide a class factor and determine whether the two types of controls differed. The dependent variables were grouped into three sets for analysis: the main battery, consisting of tests given to all children at the beginning and at the end of prekindergarten; the Behavior Inventory, available only on experimentals; and the supplementary battery, consisting of tests administered only to a sample of experimental children. On the Behavior Inventory, the timidity, independence, and achievement motivation scores were very highly correlated and seemed to reflect the child's attitudes towards working at tasks. Therefore, they were combined into one score called "Ambition."

The variance from these analyses was partitioned into contrasts. Those of greatest interest were: comparison of all experimental groups combined with the controls; comparison of the two most structured and didactic programs (B–E and DARCEE) with the other two (Montessori and Traditional); and comparison of the two programs that were highly individualized and academic but also emphasized noncognitive goals (Montessori and DARCEE) with the other two programs (B–E and Traditional). Whenever both fall and spring scores were available, repeated measures analysis of variance was used. These analyses tested for program differences averaged across both fall and spring data points as well as for change from fall to spring. Sex was included as a factor.

Kindergarten through Second Grade Program Effects

In the follow-up of the children through kindergarten, first, and second grades, we examined: (1) differences between the Work-Spend and Regular programs, and interactions between Work-Spend Regular and prekindergarten experience; and (2) continued effects of the four prekindergarten programs regardless of subsequent experience. For the Follow Through comparisons, separate analyses were performed at the end of each year on the scores of those children who had continuous exposure to Work-Spend or Regular programs rather than one analysis over several years. In order to determine the long-term effects of the four prekindergarten programs, scores of all children in a given program were combined, regardless of whether they had regular kindergarten, Follow Through, no kindergarten, or entered a parochial kindergarten or some other type of program. The stability of the various prekindergarten effects was then examined through repeated measures multivariate analysis of variance on each variable separately over the 4-year period. The analyses included the two factors of prekindergarten experience and sex. Lasting program effects were reflected in significant main effects for the prekindergarten program contrasts.

Analyses: Sixth Through Eighth Grades

Results for these years have utilized the eighth-grade sample. The data for these years were examined for differences among the four programs, comparison of all experimentals with controls, sex differences and interaction of sex with program, and trends over time. For program comparisons at seventh grade, separate 4 × 2 (Head Start Program × Sex) analyses of variance were performed on WISC-R Full Scale, Verbal, and Performance IQ. Verbal IQ was more correlated with all achievement subtests than was Full Scale IQ. Therefore, on achievement, separate 4 × 2 analyses of covariance were done using verbal IQ as the covariate for each subtest. At eighth grade, analyses were similar, using the Stanford–Binet.

To compare experimentals with controls, three groups of "no Head Start" children were combined for a control group—the original controls (the comparison group recruited in the fall of the intervention year), the Follow Through controls (added at the kindergarten point), and the class of B–E children who had a B–E kindergarten but no prekindergarten experience and who were omitted from analyses at second grade. IQ was examined by a 2 × 2 analysis of variance (Head Start/no Head Start × Sex). Achievement was analyzed by 2 × 2 analyses of covariance using WISC-R or Stanford–Binet IQ as the covariate. Trends over time have not been analyzed statistically and are given descriptively.

Most of the results reported on achievement concern the composite "Reading" score which consists of the Vocabulary and Reading Comprehension subtests and the composite "Math" score which consists of the Math Concepts, Math Applications, and Math Computation subtests. The separate subtests were also analyzed and in some cases these are reported also.

In the case of IQ tests, which were administered by the research team, almost all scores were available on those recovered in any one year. Therefore, only scores on children with complete data from prekindergarten onward were used. On achievement test data, N's vary from year to year and from test to test. Because these scores were obtained from school records, missing data were distributed in such a scattered fashion that very few children had complete achievement scores at every point from kindergarten through eighth grade. In order to provide satisfactory N's, all data available on each test each year were used.

FINDINGS

Prekindergarten Through Second Grade

Program Characteristics

Our first major question was, "Did the four programs differ in actual classroom events?" In order to determine whether the programs as implemented were congruent with the prescriptions of the developers, the ratings of consultants were examined. All ratings were above the midpoint of 5, with most ratings being well above the midpoint, indicating that consultants viewed the programs as having been adequately implemented. With regard to program differences, discriminant analyses of the observation data from the in-class procedure indicated the following: in respect to classroom structure, there were really only two treatments (programs)—one teacher-directed, fast-paced, and group–oriented (B–E and DARCEE) and the other child-centered, slow-paced, and individualized (Montessori and Traditional). Specific teaching techniques obtained by monitoring of the videotapes also discriminated the four programs in various ways. In general, there were two programs in a group format that were teacher-directed, fast-paced, didactic, and used high amounts of positive reinforcement: One (B–E) had higher requests for group performance, more teacher modeling, more setting of academic standards, and more error correction; the other (DARCEE) gave more verbal instruction, more requests for individual performance, and less error correction. There were two child-centered, slower-paced programs in an individualized format. One (Montessori) gave more information to individuals and less reinforcement—either positive or negative. The other (Traditional) had little didactic teaching and many requests to individual children, primarily for modification of social behavior, and high amounts of negative reinforcement aimed at behavior control. Children in this program were primarily conversing and role playing, typically imaginary games.

A two-dimensional plot of Functions B and C from the analysis of child activity variables obtained from the in-class observation procedure is shown in Figure 6.1. This figure plots activities of children rather than teachers. Figure 6.1 demonstrates that there were four distinct programs ranging from high verbal recitation and low role playing, to the reverse with programs ordered: B–E, Montessori, DARCEE, and Traditional. Montessori was also characterized by high amounts of manipulation and conversation by children.

The answer to our first question was clear: The four programs did differ in a number of ways in actual classroom behavior of both teachers and children.

Program Effects

Our second question was, ''Did the four programs have different effects on children?''

Prekindergarten.   As a whole, the experimental children were higher on the Stanford–Binet IQ, Preschool Inventory, persistence, and curiosity than controls. Experimentals improved more on Preschool Inventory (achievement) and on curiosity.

B–E and DARCEE versus Montessori and Traditional: B–E and DARCEE were superior on the Stanford–Binet. The two didactic programs also produced higher scores on arithmetic, Basic Concept Inventory, and Parallel Sentence Production.

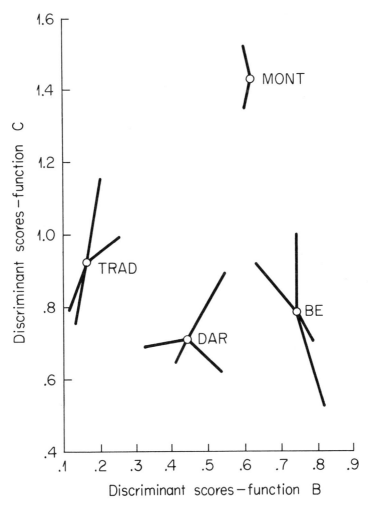

FIG. 6.1.   Two-dimensional Plot of Child Activity in Four Programs

Note: The abscissa represents increasing amounts of verbal recitation and decreasing amounts of role playing (Function B); the ordinate represents increasing amounts of manipulation and conversation (Function C).
(Open circles represent program means).

B–E and Traditional versus Montessori and DARCEE: The B–E and Traditional children scored below the controls on the Dog and Bone (inventiveness), whereas the Montessori and DARCEE children scored above controls.

B–E and Montessori versus DARCEE and Traditional: Traditional and DARCEE were higher in verbal-social participation and showed more change in ambition.

Sex: Females were higher on the Stanford–Binet; males were higher on curiosity and males improved more on the Dog and Bone.

Single programs: DARCEE had a greater change in ambition ratings and ratings on verbal-social-participation. Traditional children changed more in the direction of greater aggressiveness.

In general, the effects of the programs were different and were in line with program goals. The B–E and DARCEE programs improved performance in academic areas; DARCEE also affected motivational measures such as ratings of achievement motivation by testers, and ambition and verbal-social-participation ratings by teachers and aides; Montessori improved in inventiveness and curiosity; Traditional children were high in verbal-social-participation.

The wait-listed controls did not differ from the rest. There were some class differences within programs, the most consistent of which was in B–E. Two of the B–E classes had higher scores than the other two on IQ, Dog and Bone, Preschool Inventory, and Face Sheet ratings.

Kindergarten.   Most of the children who entered the Work-Spend Follow Through continued in this program through third grade. Although Work-Spend had little effect on the tests in the main battery or the ratings made by teachers, there was a decided advantage to those children on achievement in the kindergarten year (Metropolitan Readiness Test). Some combinations of Work-Spend kindergarten with prekindergarten program were more effective than others, and the effects of these different combinations were discussed in the earlier report (Miller & Dyer, 1975). B–E children were the most adversely affected by going into the regular (nonacademic) kindergarten, DARCEE the least affected.

By the end of kindergarten (actually the beginning of the first grade), the Montessori children were high in two subtests of the Metropolitan Readiness test: alphabet and numbers. Program order was maintained on the Dog and Bone with Montessori and DARCEE high, Traditional and B–E low. Program order on IQ was somewhat reversed with Montessori high and B–E low, although these differences were not statistically significant. IQs had declined in all programs, but more steeply in B–E.

First grade.   At the end of first grade, experimentals were still superior to controls on achievement (California Achievement Test) and mostly above the national norms. By the end of first grade, the achievement test superiority of the Work-Spend children had disappeared.

Second grade.   At the end of second grade, all experimental were below national norms on achievement. Montessori, B–E, and controls were superior to other groups on reading (California Achievement Test). The highest group was Montessori males. Montessori and controls were highest on IQ, specifically Montessori males and control females. DARCEE and Montessori children continued to be high on divergent thinking, whereas B–E and Traditional children were still low. Traditional children remained low on curiosity. DARCEE and Traditional children were higher in verbal-social-participation (Behavior Inventory ratings by teachers) over the 4 years, particularly DARCEE. Over the 4-year period, IQ declined in all groups, but the decline was steeper for B–E children and for females in the four program groups.

Findings: Sixth Through Eighth Grades

For the eighth-grade sample, no significant differences were found between program and control children on either IQ or achievement except for one achievement subtest at seventh grade (math applications) on which controls were higher. Both sex main effects and Sex × Program interactions were found, and these are discussed below. All results reported as "significant" had a *p* value of .05 or less, two-tailed. Table 6.1 shows IQ and achievement test means for seventh grade by program and sex, and Table 6.2 shows these means for eighth grade.

With males and females combined, no significant main effects for program were found at either seventh or eighth grades. To answer the more practical question of the children's current standing in terms of national norms, the numbers of those at or above the 50th percentile were examined. As shown in Table 6.3, in both seventh and eighth grades only a very small number of these children were achieving this well—about 18% and 15% of the sample in reading at seventh and eighth grades, respectively, and 15% and 12% of the sample in math. It is interesting, however, that in every case half or almost half of these normally achieving middle school children were from the Montessori preschool program.

Sex Differences

IQ. From the analyses of variance on the WISC-R at seventh grade, there was one Sex × Program interaction. This interaction occurred on Verbal IQ and the Montessori males were high (see Table 6.1).

Achievement. In general, examination of the achievement means indicated that females were similar, particularly in B–E and Traditional, whereas males differed according to original Head Start experience—with the greatest difference occurring between DARCEE and Montessori. However, a significant Sex × Program interaction occurred only on vocabulary at seventh grade.

DARCEE females were higher than males and Montessori males were higher than females. Although the interaction did not reach significance on the subtests other than vocabulary, similar discrepancies existed in both years (Tables 6.1 and 6.2). Sex main effects occurred at seventh grade on reading comprehension,

TABLE 6.1
Means and Standard Deviations for WISC-R IQ and Stanford Achievement
Percentiles[a] for Seventh Grade[b], by Program and Sex[c]

WISC-R Full Scale IQ		B-E	DARCEE	MONT	TRAD	ALL EXP.	CONTROLS
Females	$\bar{X}$	80.9 (17)	87.4 (11)	85.5 (11)	84.7 (18)	84.2 (57)	88.3 (18)
	S.D.	11.6	10.0	6.2	10.3	10.0	16.1
Males	$\bar{X}$	85.5 (13)	83.2 (18)	89.8 (9)	87.2 (11)	85.8 (51)	86.9 (14)
	S.D.	10.1	11.6	15.1	16.4	12.9	11.6
All	$\bar{X}$	82.9 (30)	84.8 (29)	87.4 (20)	85.6 (29)	85.0 (109)	87.7 (32)
	S.D.	11.0	11.0	11.0	12.7	11.4	14.1
WISC-R Verbal IQ							
Females	$\bar{X}$	80.7 (17)	84.5 (11)	80.3 (11)	81.9 (18)	81.5 (57)	85.7 (18)
	S.D.	13.2	11.0	9.2	11.7	11.3	13.8
Males	$\bar{X}$	84.7 (13)	80.6 (10)	92.7 (9)	84.0 (11)	84.5 (51)	85.5 (14)
	S.D.	13.4	12.0	15.2	17.0	14.3	10.3
All	$\bar{X}$	82.4 (30)	82.1 (29)	85.9 (20)	82.7 (29)	82.9 (108)	85.5 (32)
	S.D.	13.2	11.6	13.5	13.7	12.8	12.2
WISC-R Perf.							
Females	$\bar{X}$	82.6 (17)	92.5 (11)	93.4 (11)	90.5 (18)	89.1 (57)	93.3 (18)
	S.D.	10.1	9.9	6.9	12.2	11.0	17.0
Males	$\bar{X}$	88.8 (13)	88.8 (18)	88.2 (9)	92.5 (11)	89.5 (51)	91.2 (14)

All	S.D.	12.6	13.3	18.0	15.7	14.2	13.4
	X̄	85.3 (30)	90.2 (29)	91.1 (20)	91.3 (29)	89.3 (108)	92.4 (32)
	S.D.	11.5	12.1	12.9	13.4	12.5	15.3

Stanford Achievement
%iles—Total Reading

Females	X̄	27.7 (13)	33.3 (9)	23.2 (11)	27.4 (15)	27.6 (48)	26.9 (15)
	S.D.	24.4	19.5	19.4	24.8	22.1	22.6
Males	X̄	24.4 (9)	8.8 (15)	31.6 (9)	28.0 (6)	20.6 (39)	20.8 (12)
	S.D.	20.0	10.8	25.8	20.4	20.4	21.3
All	X̄	26.4 (22)	18.0 (24)	27.0 (20)	27.6 (21)	24.5 (87)	24.1 (27)
	S.D.	22.3	18.7	22.3	23.1	21.6	21.9

Total Math

Females	X̄	27.8 (13)	31.9 (9)	30.1 (11)	19.0 (13)	26.7 (46)	29.7 (15)
	S.D.	21.9	25.0	27.2	16.0	22.3	22.4
Males	X̄	23.3 (11)	13.5 (12)	39.0 (8)	28.0 (6)	24.3 (37)	17.0 (11)
	S.D.	16.2	10.3	24.2	19.0	19.0	12.2
All	X̄	25.8 (24)	21.4 (21)	33.8 (19)	21.8 (19)	25.6 (83)	24.3 (26)
	S.D.	19.2	19.9	25.7	17.0	20.8	19.5

[a] national norms.
[b] eighth-grade sample.
[c] N's within parentheses.

TABLE 6.2

Means and Standard Deviations of Stanford-Binet IQ and Stanford Achievement Percentiles[a] for Eighth Grade[b] by Program and Sex[c]

Stanford-Binet IQ		B-E	DARCEE	MONT	TRAD	ALL EXP.	CONTROLS
Females	X̄	84.0 (17)	88.3 (11)	85.7 (11)	85.7 (18)	85.7 (57)	92.7 (14)
	S.D.	12.6	11.4	12.8	12.0	12.0	13.5
Males	X̄	89.9 (13)	83.5 (18)	92.7 (9)	88.2 (10)	87.8 (50)	87.4 (14)
	S.D.	9.5	11.1	15.8	14.5	12.5	11.7
All	X̄	86.6 (30)	85.3 (29)	88.9 (20)	86.6 (28)	86.7 (107)	90.0 (28)
	S.D.	11.6	11.3	14.3	12.7	12.2	12.7
Stanford Achievement %iles—Total Reading							
Females	X̄	28.6 (12)	32.5 (8)	24.4 (10)	16.8 (14)	24.6 (44)	32.1 (16)
	S.D.	25.6	22.4	21.3	16.4	21.4	21.9
Males	X̄	19.6 (8)	14.3 (9)	38.5 (8)	24.3 (7)	23.9 (32)	31.1 (7)
	S.D.	11.3	11.2	28.5	27.6	21.8	24.8
All	X̄	25.0 (20)	22.9 (17)	30.7 (18)	19.3 (21)	24.3 (76)	31.8 (23)
	S.D.	21.1	19.1	24.9	20.4	21.5	22.2
Total Math							
Females	X̄	29.0 (13)	32.5 (8)	27.1 (9)	20.9 (13)	26.8 (43)	31.8 (16)
	S.D.	24.5	26.2	24.2	13.4	21.6	21.3
Males	X̄	25.0 (8)	12.8 (8)	44.1 (7)	22.9 (7)	25.7 (30)	20.9 (8)
	S.D.	9.9	12.8	25.9	15.6	19.6	24.0
All	X̄	27.5 (21)	22.6 (16)	34.6 (16)	21.6 (20)	26.4 (73)	28.2 (24)
	S.D.	20.0	22.4	25.6	13.8	20.7	22.3

[a] national norms.
[b] Eighth-grade sample.
[c] N's within parentheses.

TABLE 6.3
Numbers of Children At or Above the 50th Percentile on National
Norms for Total Reading and Total Math of the Stanford Achievement
Test for Seventh and Eighth Grades[a]

	B-E ($N = 17$)	DAR ($N = 16$)	MONT ($N = 16$)	TRAD ($N = 17$)
7th Grade Reading Total	2	1	5	4
8th Grade Reading Total	1	2	5	2
	B-E ($N = 17$)	DAR ($N = 16$)	MONT ($N = 16$)	TRAD ($N = 18$)
7th Grade Math Total	3	2	5	0
8th Grade Math Total	2	2	4	0

[a]Subjects who had both scores on each test, only.

math computations, spelling, language, and total reading with females higher. At eighth grade, sex was significant only on language. It should be noted that similar analyses of the seventh and eighth grade results, using the larger sample available at the end of tenth grade, produced statistically significant results for many of the indications present in the data reported here on this smaller sample. (Miller and Bizzell, 1983).

Trends Over Time

IQ.   Two trends found at the end of second grade were of particular interest with regard to IQ over the 10-year period of this study: a greater decrease in IQ for females than for males, and a greater decrease for B–E children than for the other program groups. Means for the eighth-grade sample from the first testing early in the Head Start year (beginning of the prekindergarten year) through eighth grade are shown in Table 6.4 by sex and program. In this sample, the B–E decline had apparently leveled off, but the decline for females was still in evidence. Examination of Table 6.4 shows that Montessori females declined 15.3 points, but the males from this program had increased slightly and were superior to all other groups.

Achievement.   The trends in achievement plotted in Fig. 6.2 show that children from all four programs were below the 50th percentile in seventh and eighth grades. The superiority of Montessori males was evident at kindergarten on the Metropolitan Readiness Test and from second grade onward in both reading and math. The seventh grade was the lowest point for all groups.

Summary of Findings

There were three main areas of interest in which results were found: sex differences; Sex × Program interactions; and trends over time.

194

TABLE 6.4
Mean IQ's by Program and Sex from Beginning of Head Start to End of
Eighth Grade for Subjects on Whom Data for All Years Were Available

Program	(N)	Beg. PreK	End PreK	K	1st	2nd	7th[a]	8th	Difference End of PreK - 8th
Bereiter-Engelmann									
Females	(17)	92.9	99.2	95.8	90.1	83.8	80.9	84.1	-15.1
Males	(13)	97.1	100.5	93.2	93.1	90.2	85.5	90.0	-10.5
All	(30)	94.7	99.8	94.7	91.4	86.6	82.9	86.7	
DARCEE									
Females	(11)	100.0	97.5	92.2	92.0	89.1	87.4	88.3	-9.2
Males	(18)	94.7	95.8	93.8	94.2	89.4	83.2	83.5	-12.3
All	(29)	96.7	96.4	93.2	93.4	89.3	84.8	85.3	
Montessori									
Females	(11)	92.4	101.1	94.8	94.6	89.2	85.5	85.7	-15.3
Males	(9)	89.1	91.7	91.3	92.8	96.6	89.8	92.7	+1.0
All	(20)	90.9	96.8	93.3	93.8	92.5	87.4	88.9	
Traditional									
Females	(18)	92.1	99.4	93.4	91.1	88.8	84.7	85.7	-13.7
Males	(10)	91.3	96.0	97.9	97.5	94.3	88.2	88.1	-7.9
All	(28)	91.8	98.2	95.0	93.4	90.8	86.0	86.6	
Total									
Females	(57)	93.9	99.3	94.2	91.7	87.5	84.2	85.7	-13.6
Males	(50)	93.6	96.3	94.0	94.3	91.9	86.0	87.8	-8.5

[a] WISC-R administered at seventh grade; Stanford-Binet IQ given at all other time points.

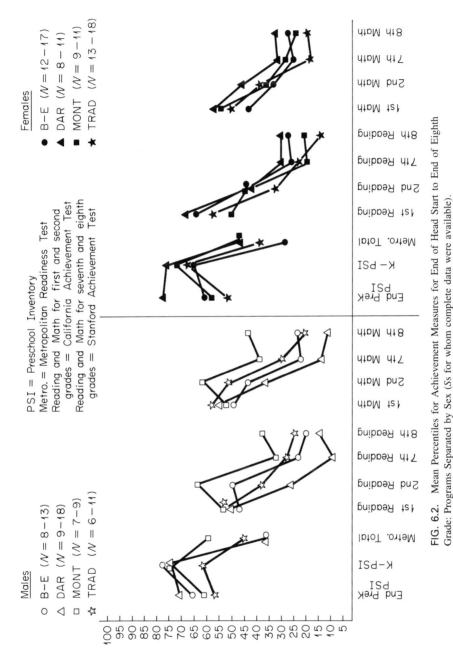

PSI = Preschool Inventory

Metro. = Metropolitan Readiness Test

Reading and Math for first and second
grades = California Achievement Test

Reading and Math for seventh and eighth
grades = Stanford Achievement Test

Females

● B-E (N = 12 - 17)
▲ DAR (N = 8 - 11)
■ MONT (N = 9 - 11)
★ TRAD (N = 13 - 18)

FIG. 6.2. Mean Percentiles for Achievement Measures for End of Head Start to End of Eighth
Grade: Programs Separated by Sex (Ss for whom complete data were available).

195

Females were generally superior to males on the Stanford Achievement Test battery, particularly at seventh grade. In general, the data indicate that males differed according to preschool experience with the greatest difference occurring between Montessori (high) and DARCEE (low). Females were similar across program groups.

The trend toward a decline in IQ that was present at the end of second grade for the B–E group leveled off at the eighth grade, but the decline for females appeared to be continuing. All program groups declined in IQ over the period with the exception of Montessori males who increased slightly. The fact that these boys were not simply a selected sample of originally brighter children is shown in Table 6.4, which presents IQ's by program and sex from the first available point—early in the prekindergarten year.

Stanford–Binet IQ at eighth grade was somewhat higher than WISC-R IQ at the seventh grade for all groups. Two trends are of interest for achievement: Montessori male superiority, and a slump for all groups in achievement at seventh grade. The second trend may be due to the change from the Intermediate Battery to the Advanced Battery Level 1 of the Stanford Achievement Test.

DISCUSSION

Our major purpose was to compare four prekindergarten programs with each other, determine whether and how they differed in actual classroom events, what their effects were, and how their effects were related to the methods and components of the programs. The results certainly indicated that the programs were not equivalent. They differed on many dimensions—from amount of group work to type and frequency of reinforcement. The experiences that these 4 year-olds had in their first classroom depended heavily upon which program they encountered. The four programs also had different effects, both in their immediate impact, and on school achievement and IQ as late as the eighth grade. For example, the prekindergarten year produced the typical advantage for didactic programs, but in middle school the advantage occurred for Montessori. Montessori superiority in later years is confirmed by Karnes' (Chapter 5, this volume) finding of a lower retention rate for these children, highest school success ratings, and the highest percentage of high school graduates.

In our study, the differences among program effects seem to have occurred for boys rather than for girls. Within programs, sex differences were most pronounced in Montessori and DARCEE. On achievement tests, the middle school advantage for the Montessori children, for example, existed primarily for boys. The DARCEE program produced consistently higher achievement test scores for girls than for boys. This latter result is confirmed on Gray's sample as reported in Chapter 2 of this volume, and on different criteria indicating that the sex differences are meaningful for this program rather than an artifact of a particular sample or assessment procedure. Overall superiority for females was found in our study as well as in Karnes' (Chapter 5, this volume).

The problems encountered in attempting to link specific techniques or classroom behaviors to outcome measures have been discussed fully in our 1975 monograph. Essentially the differential effectiveness of the four programs and the consistency among classes in the same program were methodological barriers to any attempt to relate specific program variables to outcomes. Therefore, our third question regarding the crucial components of the programs remained unanswered. On the basis of a second field study (Begab, Haywood, & Garber, 1981) combined with the results of this one, we have suggested that drill and didactic instruction may not be the most effective techniques to use with 4-year-olds. Karnes also points out in her chapter that "extensive oral drill" did not seem to have much impact on overall school success." But more specific recommendations regarding the crucial elements of preschool programs will require further research.

For the entire experimental group combined, the effects of the programs studied in this experiment were not as encouraging as those found by some of the other investigators in this Consortium. Because of a demographic advantage, our control group is not the best group to use for comparison, and there were very few eligible children in Louisville who did not enter Head Start in 1968. Record-keeping procedures in the public schools have not yet permitted us to separate our experimental group from the remainder of this particular population in order to compare the effects of regular Head Start with our particular program implementations. It is therefore difficult to know to what extent these programs as a whole had a beneficial effect. For the most part, none of them succeeded in raising school performance at the middle school level to national norms. At seventh grade, on the average, about 16% were at or above the 50th percentile.

Consortium results however (Chapter 13) leave little doubt that the average effect of the interventions used was beneficial. Results from several of these independent investigations are congruent, and the conclusions reached converge on a number of areas in which research is badly needed. These have been outlined by Karnes (Chapter 5, this volume) and include our emphasis on identifying the crucial components of preschool programs, finding techniques to match children to programs, and learning more about the links between early aptitudes and attitudes and later school success.

ACKNOWLEDGMENTS

This experiment was supported at various periods by the Office of Economic Opportunity, the National Institute of Child Health and Human Development, the Office of Child

Development, the Administration for Children, Youth and Families, and the Education Commission of the States. Currently, the follow-up is supported by the National Institute of Child Health and Human Development.

We are grateful to the many individuals who have contributed so much to this research throughout the years—colleagues, students, teachers, and consultants—and regret that there is not space to acknowledge each by name.

REFERENCES

Bales, R. F. *Interaction process analysis: A method for the study of small groups.* Cambridge, Mass.: Addison-Wesley, 1950.

Banta, T. J. Tests for the evaluation of early childhood education: The Cincinnati Autonomy Test Battery (CATB). In J. Hellmuth (Ed.), *Cognitive studies I.* New York: Brunner/Mazel, 1970.

Begab, M. J., Haywood, H. C., & Garber, H. L. *Psychosocial influences in retarded performance.* Vol. II: *Strategies for improving competence.* Baltimore: University Park Press, 1981.

Bereiter, C., & Engelmann, S. *Teaching disadvantaged children in the preschool.* Englewood Cliffs, N.J.: Prentice-Hall, 1966.

Bruner, J. S. Poverty and Childhood. In R. K. Parker (Ed.), *The Preschool in Action: Exploring Early Childhood Programs.* Boston: Allyn and Bacon, Inc., 1972, pp. 7–35.

Bushell, D., Jr., & Brigham, T. A. Classroom token systems as technology. *Educational Psychology,* 1971, *11,* 14–17.

Caldwell, B. M. *Preschool Inventory. Experimental edition—1968.* Princeton, N.J.: Educational Testing Service, 1968.

Cattell, R. B., & Eber, H. W. *Handbook for the Sixteen Personality Factor Questionnaire. 'The 16 P.F. Test.' Forms A, B, and C.* Champaign, Ill.: The Institute for Personality and Ability Testing, 1957.

Di Lorenzo, L. T., & Salter, R. An evaluative study of prekindergarten programs for educationally disadvantaged children. *Exceptional Children,* 1968, *35,* 111–119.

Dunn, L. *Peabody Picture Vocabulary Test. Expanded manual.* Circle Pines, Minn.: American Guidance Service, 1965.

Erickson, E. L., McMillan, J., Bennell, J., & Callahan, O. D. *Experiments in Head Start and early education: Curriculum structures and teacher attitudes.* Washington, D.C.: Office of Economic Opportunity, Project Head Start, 1969.

Gray, S. W., & Klaus, R. A. An experimental preschool program for culturally deprived children. *Child Development,* 1965, *36,* 887–898.

Gray, S. W., Klaus, R. A., Miller, J. O., & Forrester, B. J. *Before first grade.* New York: Teachers College Press, 1966.

Hess, R. D., Kramer, D., Slaughter, D., Torney, J., Berry, D., & Hull, E. Techniques for assessing cognitive and social abilities of children and parents in Project Head Start. Report on Research Contract OEO-519 with the Office of Economic Opportunity, University of Chicago, 1966.

Hodges, W. L., McCandless, B. R., & Spicker, H. H. *The development and evaluation of a diagnostically based curriculum for preschool psychosocially deprived children.* Indiana University, 1967. (ERIC Document Reproduction Service No. ED021 948).

Karnes, M. B., Hodgins, A. S., Teska, J. A., & Kirk, S. A. *Investigations of classroom and at-home interventions. Research and development program on preschool disadvantaged children.* Vol. 1. Washington, D.C.: Office of Education, 1969.

Miller, L. B., & Bizzell, R. P. Long-term effects of Four Preschool Programs: 6th, 7th, & 8th Grade Effects. *Child Development,* 1983, 54.

Miller, L. B., & Dyer, J. L. Four preschool programs: Their dimensions and effects. *Monographs of the Society for Research in Child Development,* 1975, *40*(5–6, Serial No. 162).

Montessori, M. *The Montessori method.* New York: Schocken, 1964.

Neill, R. D., & Bein, S. L. *An attitude scale for teachers of the culturally disadvantaged. Head Start Louisville and Jefferson County Community Action Commission Evaluation.* Technical supplement No. 2. Louisville, Ky.: University of Louisville, 1967.

Rainbow Series, Project Head Start. Washington, D.C.: Office of Economic Opportunity, 1965.

Southern, M. L., & Plant, W. T. Effects of cognitively structured small group activities upon cognitive functions of pre-first-grade programs for culturally disadvantaged children. *Journal of Genetic Psychology,* 1972, *121,* 11–20.

Sprigle, H. A., Van de Riet, V., & Van de Riet, H. *A sequential learning program for preschool children and an evaluation of its effectiveness with culturally disadvantaged children.* Paper presented at the annual meeting of the American Educational Research Association, New York, 1967.

Stern, C. Evaluating language curricula for preschool children. *Monographs of the Society for Research in Child Development,* 1968, *33*(8, Serial No. 124), 49–61.

Weikart, D. P. A comparative study of three preschool curricula. In J. E. Frost & G. R. Hawkes (Eds.), *The disadvantaged child.* Boston: Houghton Mifflin, 1970.

7

The Harlem Study: Effects by Type of Training, Age of Training, and Social Class

Francis H. Palmer
Academy of Senior Professionals
Eckerd College

Introduction

Early in the morning after Martin Luther King was killed, the first three taxis hailed in Manhattan would not take me to the Harlem Training Center on 126th Street. The fourth complied after a threat of report to the hack bureau. Smoke rose over Harlem. Fires burned in every block. Looting was rampant as thousands of people ranged through the streets only partly contained by the usual constabulary reinforced by a battalion of special police.

By six that afternoon 36 three-year-olds had completed their scheduled 1 hour of individual instruction at the Harlem Training Center. Of the 40 instructors, drivers, and support personnel of the Center, 39 came to work. One, Dr. Ann Haeberle Rees, walked four blocks from the subway station at 125th and Lenox Avenue. She was 8 months pregnant.

More important than curricula or fine facilities, it is people like these who make a difference in the course of children's lives. Now in their midteens, the 240 two- and three-year-olds involved in that program are only half as likely to have failed a grade in school as their peers in that school district. Their IQs remain significantly higher and, on the average, they score 1 year ahead of their peers on reading and arithmetic achievement tests.

To say that people are most important is not to say that curricula and facilities are unimportant. Those characteristics imply programs, and programs provide the vehicle for caregivers and children to interact.

Purpose of the Study

The Harlem Study was not conceived to bring fine people into contact with poor children but to determine whether one program of early educational intervention had durable effects on subsequent school performance. The Zeitgeist of the mid-1960s was that any program that intervened at an early age and provided a rich environmental experience would have significant effects on poor children (Deutsch, 1965). As a consequence, many intervention programs were initiated and some did make desired changes. But most were designed without control groups, so that changes due to the program could not be separated from changes due to the passage of time. More were not documented, so that what was provided for children is not a matter of record. Almost certainly there were many ingenious programs initiated then that, because their effects were not evaluated and the program not well-documented, remain lost for the body of knowledge about the programs that are best for children.

The Harlem Study was originally designed to determine whether a well-conceived program had durable effects. Due to support from the National Institute of Child Health and Human Development, it could afford not one control group but two. As will be seen, that second control group significantly influenced what could be said about the results.

A second purpose of the Harlem Study was to determine if minimal intervention, defined as 2 hours weekly for a period of 8 months, would have durable effects. It asked not whether 10 to 20 hours weekly in nursery school conditions would have effects but whether 2 hours weekly could have durable effects.

Finally, the study was designed to determine whether intervention at age 2 was more effective than intervention at age 3 and whether effects were more discernible among lower-class children than among middle-class children.

Antecedents of the Study

Knowledge about the long and rich past of early childhood programs in America had little to do with the conceptualization of the Harlem Study. Those who planned it had no experience in that formidable practice. Other factors primarily contributed to its conceptualization.

The most important factor that motivated the study was the animal literature on the effects of early experience, notably the research of Harry Harlow with rhesus monkeys (1958). The animal research demonstrated that rats, cats, dogs, and monkeys who were deprived of sensory stimuli early in life did not develop as normal animals do and that their ability to learn was diminished. Harlow's work showed that effects from early sensory deprivation were not limited to physical growth and learning ability but to affective and social development as well. From those studies, a series of hypotheses was developed about the relationship between cognitive development and early separation from the mother (Palmer, 1969b). Those hypotheses influenced the treatment of children in the Harlem Study.

Secondly, I have been with the Social Science Research Council as staff psychologist during a period when exciting breakthroughs were occurring in developmental behavior. I became convinced that much of what we had learned from animals had implications for children; that cognitive and affective development were closely related; and that although we had learned much from classical learning theory, theory alone was insufficient for developing programs for children.

Thirdly, with the same Ann Rees mentioned earlier, I had published a monograph on factors related to change in mental test scores, a synthesis of data from the longitudinal studies of development conducted at Berkeley, the Denver Child Research Council, and the Fels Research Institute in Yellow Springs, Ohio (Rees & Palmer, 1970). From those early studies, a methodology was suggested to determine the durability of effects of early intervention by comparing treatment children with control children over successive annual assessments until they were in the elementary grades.

The result was a study that was substantially different from most other programs with respect to the amount of time the child was exposed to the intervention. But considering the inexperience of the investigators at the time with traditional preschool procedures, the ambience for children within the Harlem Center became surprisingly the same. In other words, the investigators learned what experienced early childhood people already knew.

Finally, the political Zeitgeist of the 1960s accepted as a matter of faith that social programs would interrupt the cycle of poverty. Our knowledge about children suggested that we could make a difference in children's lives, and the War on Poverty provided the funding to prove it.

It should be added that once the treatments were planned and the study initiated, no changes in the Harlem Study occurred. Changes were made in some of the procedures used by the staff as when, for example, it became practice to change the sex of the next instructor if a child was having a difficult time. However, the treatments themselves did not change in spite of the fact that there were many inclinations to do so. A salient illustration of how the original assumptions were adhered to resulted from the early recognition that greater parental involvement would probably have benefited the program. Despite temptation to increase parental participation in the treatments, the original design was adhered to. As a consequence, the results of the Harlem Study speak to the effects of a program in which parental participation was not emphasized, no matter how desirable that appeared to be.

THEORETICAL BACKGROUND AND RESEARCH QUESTIONS

There are three current issues that are implicit in the Harlem Study and in most of the other studies represented in this book. Those three issues are sometimes called ''hypotheses,'' which they are not, because of their global nature and our inability to test them directly.

The Deficit Hypothesis

The deficit hypothesis was in favor in the early 1960s, but its meaning has changed. It evolved from some of the pioneering work with children and their environments (Dennis & Najarian, 1957; Goldfarb, 1945; Hunt, 1961; Skeels & Dye, 1939; Spitz, 1945) and from the animal literature on early development (Palmer, 1969a). Originally, the deficit hypothesis suggested that there were critical periods in the development of the organism when it benefited most from specific experiences. Those experiences were initially defined as exposure to sensory stimuli, but later the concept was broadened to include emotional and social stimulation. To obtain maximum benefit from stimulation, some times were better than others for a child to have that experience. A good experience for the child was defined as one that made him better equipped to adapt to the culture in which he lived. If he did not have the opportunity to learn from certain experiences, he suffered a deficit. In general, it was argued, poor children missed the opportunity to learn basic concepts more often than middle-class children. A good intervention program would provide those experiences. More specifically, if 90% of 24-month-old children already knew the concept *on top of*, those who had not acquired the concept were considered to have a deficit. In 1964, the deficit hypothesis was as simple as that.

The deficit hypothesis has fallen into disfavor for reasons that are more social and political than because the original meaning of the hypothesis was disproved. Those opposed to the deficit hypothesis say that it implies a lack of intelligence. They say it implies a single standard for what intelligence is and a single culture to which the child should adapt, and they argue that intelligence and adaptation are defined by the standards of the middle-class American culture. Just because a child is not adroit at one demand of that culture does not mean that he/she is not intelligent or that he/she cannot adapt well to another culture. There is indeed much to criticize about the deficit hypothesis if it is defined in that manner.

If one can demonstrate that a child must understand Concept A before he can acquire Concept B and defines the lack of experience necessary for learning A as a deficit that precludes the learning of B, however, then no implication of a lack of intelligence is made. In that sense, the deficit hypothesis is a valid interpretation of studies of early childhood and of early animal experience. When the Harlem Study was designed, the deficit hypothesis was as valid as it is today.

The Inoculation Hypothesis

The inoculation hypothesis has a slightly different history than the deficit hypothesis. The present concept was derived and is used as a mildly denigrating attempt to characterize studies that suggest that a short, intense experience in the child's life may have durable effects. Those who use the term usually do so critically, implying that nothing durable can occur from a single or short-term experience. The term, borrowed from epidemiology, was rarely used by developmental investigators 15 years ago.

In one sense, the denigrators of the inoculation concept are, of course, correct. Sustained experiences usually have more pronounced long-term effects. It is a defensible political position designed to justify sustained programs that provide continuous intervention. But does that suggest that we should expect little from programs of short duration or of minimal input?

To deny the possibility of phenomenon for politically useful reasons is good politics but bad science. The animal literature is replete with examples of significant effects following short or one-time exposure. Intuitively, we know that some of our most vivid experiences have been of short duration, frequently in one-to-one situations with another person. Other sciences, biology for example, accept the existence of durable effects from a single experience. Psycholinguists are conducting experiments on the effect of rare events in language development. To reject the inoculation hypothesis is scientifically indefensible even if it is politically effective.

Environmental Change Hypothesis

A third hypothesis current today (Bronfenbrenner, 1979) is that significant effects will not be found where programs emphasize instruction to the child. Only by restructuring the family, the immediate community, and the larger society will we see a truly significant change in the development of children. This implies radical changes in the society to which the child must adapt, and most would argue that some radical changes would benefit children. However, changing the larger society is a bit beyond the developmental psychologist's influence. And the child, even if he becomes instrumental in changing the society as an adult, must first adapt to the environment as it is. If, for example, one believes that children would benefit by being less competitive and less hostile, one could develop programs with that goal. But if the child is to adapt to the larger culture, he must learn to deal with competition and hostility.

Most or all of the studies included in this book were conceived in the belief that if a child does better in school, he will adapt to the larger culture more effectively. They do not imply that if the world were different, the child might not be even better off. The argument that changes in the family, the community, and the larger culture would be more effective in changing the child does not refute the validity of the question: Can children be changed effectively without changing the world around them? That is the question to which the studies in this book are directed regardless of the extent of parental involvement in particular programs.

Those three issues cannot be brought to final test in any single study, but a single study can provide data relevant to each issue.

Research Questions

The Harlem Study assumed that there were certain basic concepts that children needed to know before they could acquire more complex concepts associated with adaptation to our society, and that the earlier those concepts were learned the better. That assumption was confounded with another assumption manifest in the research design: that children of middle-class families would know more of those concepts at the beginning of training than children of lower-class families. Given that, the research was designed to answer another question: Did the intervention most influence the middle- or lower-class child? The study provides evidence related to the deficit hypothesis.

It appears that the Harlem Study may speak to what is called the inoculation hypothesis as well. Each of the 240 children was instructed individually twice weekly for 50 minutes over the approximately 7 months that instruction was offered. The average child obtained a total of 45 instructional periods. In the universe of preschool instructional programs, 45 hours of instruction would probably qualify as a minimal input.

The Harlem Study is also relevant to whether child-oriented intervention can be effective without deliberate involvement of the family, community, or larger society. The treatment families were requested to attend the program the first six times the child visited and were encouraged to visit as often as was convenient. Some came frequently and others never came, not even for the first six sessions. The intent of that degree of family involvement was to provide the parent with the opportunity to observe precisely what experience the child was having, with the hope that it would create trust in the program. That parents were involved is not questioned, else they would not have continued to bring the child to assessments over a period of 15 years. To have a study in which parents are not involved with a program for their child is inconceivable, although a lesser degree of parental involvement is necessary if the focus is on stimulating the child as compared to restructuring the child's social environment.

Three other questions were explicit. Did the carefully constructed curriculum dealing with fundamental concepts have significant effects when compared with a control group of children who attended the training center on the same schedule with the same instructors and materials? Did children derive greater benefit from being age 2 or age 3 when the program began? Did the age of participation and types of intervention have different effects on children whose parents were lower and middle class?

Predesign Decisions

To answer those questions, there were other considerations that had to be resolved before a research design could be decided upon:

1. How many subjects would be lost between the end of training and completion of the first grade? Clearly, effects could be determined only with children available for assessment at elementary school age. Furthermore, chances were that attrition would not occur equally in each condition in the research design. Therefore, to have a sufficient sample available for final data collection, the highest attrition rate anticipated in any cell of the design, rather than the average attrition across cells, dictated the number of subjects in each cell. Mostly by guess, a 50% attrition rate was set as the maximum we would expect in a given cell. Consequently, twice as many children would have to begin the program as were needed for assessment at school age.

2. In general, girls in elementary school have higher IQs and higher reading and arithmetic achievement scores (Rees & Palmer, 1970). To include both sexes would introduce another variable in the research design and require twice the number of children. In the Harlem schools, boys do not do as well as girls and get into more trouble. For that reason, boys were studied rather than girls.

3. How would we know that the instructors in one training condition (Concept Training group) were not better or worse than the instructors in the other (Discovery or participating control group)? It was decided that each instructor would teach an equal number of children in each group.

4. If instructors taught two training conditions, how would we know that they followed the procedures for each condition when appropriate? It was decided that each instructor would be monitored to determine the extent to which instructors followed the appropriate procedure. This proved to be a wise decision. Instructors taught five children per day, and there was confusion initially about the use of the two procedures. By monitoring instructors' behaviors, those errors were quickly corrected.

5. Should the nonparticipating control group be pretested along with the participating controls (Discovery) and Concept Training groups? Good research design would answer "yes." However, the design already required a sample of 120 2-year-olds in 1966, 120 3-year-olds in 1967, and 70 nonparticipating controls. An average of eight visits, or 8 hours per child, was estimated for the pretesting at age 2. Participating children would require 960 hours of pretesting before the program began. If the 70 controls were pretested as well, 1520 hours of pretesting would be required before the 2-year-old training began. Staff, resources, and facilities prohibited that. Consequently, after discussing the matter with an advisory group representing the National Institute of Health, the decision was made to assess the control group for the first time the following summer when they were 2 years and 8 months old and compare them with the experimental group at the same age.

6. Did we need separate, nonparticipating control groups for those children trained at age 3? An ideal design would include an additional control group. Again, facilities, staff, and funding prohibited that. The decision was to have the

nonparticipating controls assessed first when they were 2 years and 8 months and again at 3 years and 8 months. They would serve as controls for both those trained at 2 and at 3 years of age.

Decisions of design were a balance between what was ideal and what was possible. If 30 subjects were required in each cell of the design, and if we varied type of training, age, and social class and had a nonparticipating control, the design would have required 300 children. If girls had been included and a separate control group for those trained at age 3 an additional 360, or a total of 660 children, would have been needed for that ideal design. From the time that decision was made, the investigators knew that not pretesting the nonparticipating controls and not having a separate control group for those trained at age 3 would present problems for data analysis. Those problems proved surmountable.

7. It was recognized that some children would have other preschool experience after the Harlem Program ended and before they entered school. How could we be certain that program mothers would not place their children in later preschool programs more often than control mothers? Clearly, one could not ask mothers to avoid subsequent preschool programs.

It was decided to monitor the children's participation in programs after they left us. If children in one cell of the design were less frequently placed in later programs, we would encourage mothers in that cell to provide subsequent preschool experience and would aid them in that effort. The concern was unwarranted, however; control mothers, for example, were as likely to provide later preschool experience as participating mothers. If it had not been monitored, we would never have known whether subsequent preschool education had biased our results.

SITE AND SAMPLE

The Harlem Community: 1964–1977

In September of 1966, the last donated tile was laid on the floor of the Center and the huge mural on the reception room wall was finished by the black artist who charged no fee. The staff watched the first 24-month-old boy struggle up the 20 steps to the second-story machine shop that had become the Harlem Training Center. The child had his mother by one hand and his driver by the other. He was in awe of the entire procedure. But he was not so much in awe as the staff, each of whom imagined 120 more such struggles to come, twice weekly, for 8 months.

The day before, the captain of the 20th Police Precinct had briefed the staff on the Harlem community, its myths, and its realities. The block on which the

Center and the Precinct were located, between Amsterdam and St. Nicholas on 126th Street, was a relatively trouble-free block, partly because of the police presence but mostly because the residents had been there for years and took care of each other.

Much of Harlem is a ghetto and many of the people who live in it are very poor. However, not everyone in Harlem is poor. High rise apartments, like sentinels of order in the night, existed for a substantial middle class. Some residents were wealthy: Successful businessmen, lawyers, and television producers live in Harlem, too.

Between 1964 when the boys in our study were born and 1977 when they became 13 years old, Harlem changed. Landmarks vanished. The mood in Harlem changed. It can be said, of course, that the mood of New York and even the whole country changed, but in Harlem the change was different.

Perhaps the best way to compare the change in Harlem over a decade is with the two blackouts. New York City had major blackouts in 1967 and 1977. The lights went out, the subways did not run, and people got stuck in elevators for hours. Many people think that the first blackout was New York's finest hour. People who had never said a courteous word to a stranger were offering help to casual acquaintances in the darkened, late-afternoon streets. People who could not get home just settled down in the nearest bistro, next to strangers. During the blackout, the New York City Police reported that the crime rate had been the lowest in several decades. People were so nice to each other that the next day they acted embarrassed about it.

The night of the blackout in 1977 had the highest rate of arrests that the police had experienced in decades. Same city; same people, mostly, but mobs roamed the streets and looted the darkened stores of anything that could be carried. It was as if people still felt like suckers for being so nice a decade before, and had vowed that if the opportunity came again they would rip off what they could. Of course the worst looting was in Harlem, and the people who suffered the most were black.

The boys in the Harlem Study were 3 years old at the time of the first blackout, and they were 13 at the time of the second blackout. By the time they were 13, 24% had failed a grade in school, which is bad. However, in 1976 in the Harlem public schools, more than 50% of the boys failed at least one grade by the time they were 13. The boys who had the training were a little bit better off, but most still lived under conditions not likely to reinforce their slight advantage.

Description of Sample

To covary type of training, age of training, and socioeconomic status, to allow for attrition of subjects, and to maintain an adequate non-participating control, the design of the research called for 30 subjects to a cell as follows:[1]

		Training	Discovery	Control
At age 2:	Lower class	30	30	30
(1966)	Middle class	30	30	30
At age 3:	Lower class	30	30	
(1967)	Middle class	30	30	

Attrition of two kinds can influence the results of a longitudinal study: attrition during the selection of subjects and attrition from the beginning of a program to the time that assessments occur. The latter can bias subsequent comparisons between experimental and control groups, as when one group loses more subjects than the other. In that case the responsibility is on the investigator to demonstrate that the disproportionate loss did not bias the results. Data related to attrition during subject selection is important for defining precisely the population that was studied. The subject selection process in the Harlem Study is given in some detail for three reasons: it communicates the effort needed to select a sample, the characteristics of which are known; it defines the sample precisely; and it provides evidence about the movement of Harlem families during the period 1964–1965.

Depending on the birthdate and type of training given to the children, the resulting subsamples were termed Alpha (to be trained at 2 years), Gamma (to be trained at 3 years), and Beta (nonparticipating controls). Table 7.1 shows the dates on which various actions were taken for each sample.

Steps in the Procurement of Subjects

Birth Record Search. Initial information about subjects was obtained from birth records at Harlem and Sydenham Hospitals and at New York's Bureau of Vital Statistics. Harlem and Sydenham are city hospitals and, not surprisingly, a large proportion of subjects ultimately identified as lower class were born in one or the other. The Bureau of Vital Statistics was particularly important for the identification of subjects, later classified as middle class, who were born in private hospitals.

The potential subject pool was formed from birth records meeting the following criteria: both parents black; birth weight over 5 pounds; not a multiple birth; mother's age between 15 and 45; mother not a drug addict nor in advanced state of syphilis; no indication of any clear-cut abnormality in child at birth; and residence at birth north of 80th Street in Manhattan. That process yielded 953

---

[1]The late Leonard Kogan, then professor at the City University of New York, contributed significantly to the design of this study.

TABLE 7.1
Dates at Which Actions Were Taken on Alpha, Gamma,
and Beta Samples

	Alpha	Gamma	Beta[a]
Birthdate	Aug-Oct, 1964	Aug-Oct, 1964	Nov-Dec, 1964
Birth Records Copied	April-May, 1966	April-May, 1966	April-May, 1966
Names to Post Office	May, 1966	May, 1966	May, 1967
Interviews Assigned	June-Aug, 1966	July-Aug. 1967	June-July, 1967
Child Initially Assessed	October, 1966	October, 1967	July, 1967
Age at Training	2-0 to 2-8 years	3-0 to 3-8 years	—

[a] Beta Controls were assessed annually, beginning in July, 1967, to coincide by age with post assessment for Alpha and Gamma.

healthy children at birth as potential subjects for the Alpha and Gamma groups and 512 for the Beta.

Preliminary classification by socioeconomic status was made from the birth records on the basis of the father's occupation. Where the father was listed but not as husband of the mother, where no father was identified, or when no occupation was available, initial classification was unknown (U). Initial classification by social class is shown in Table 7.2a. The final definition of middle and lower class is described later in this section.

Post Office Search.   In 1965 the United States Post Office provided a service which greatly facilitated the selection procedure. The names and addresses of 1465 mothers whose children had birth record information which met our criteria were sent to the Post Office. The Post Office confirmed those families that lived in the same place as they had when the child was born and provided changes of address for those who had moved to another location in Harlem and had notified that office. Table 7.2a shows the number of families sent to the Post Office for Alpha and Gamma (953) and for Beta (512). Table 7.2b shows the number the Post Office could locate: 579 Alphas and Gammas and 270 Betas. Twenty months after birth, 39% of Alphas and Gammers were unlocatable. Twenty-nine months after birth, 47% of Betas were unlocatable.

These data from the selection process are informative about what Myrdahl (1944) called the American underclass—the shifting and rootless proportion of our population without permanent housing or steady employment. Big city mayors have called our attention to the underclass as well, arguing that the census underestimates how many there are. Furthermore, if we assume that those children whose birth records were eliminated because they did not meet our criteria would probably be even more difficult to locate, and that an unknown number of

TABLE 7.2
Attrition During Subject Selection:
Birth Records to Program Participation

Stage of Selection		Alpha & Gamma		Alpha Revisited[a]	Beta
(a)	*SES from Birth Records*				
	Middle Class (MC)		208	NA	121
	Lower Class (LC)		359		190
	Unknown (U)		386		201
	Total		953		512
(b)	*Located by Post Office*				
	Middle Class		132	NA	64
	Lower Class		238		97
	Unknown		209		109
	Total		579		270
	% of (a)		61%		53%
(c)	*Interviews Assigned*	260	250	64	265
(d)	*Interviews Attempted*				
	Middle Class	61	61	16	52
	Lower Class	100	103	21	73
	Unknown	9	81	21	82
	Total	260	245	58	207
	$ of (c)	100%	98%	91%	78%
(e)	*Interviews Achieved*				
	Middle Class	5	50	11	38
	Lower Class	81	80	12	49
	Unknown	77	64	10	44
	Total	213	194	33	131
	% of (d)	82%	79%	57%	63%
(f)	*"Yes" at Interview*				
	Middle Class	44	38	9	30
	Lower Class	63	72	6	38
	Unknown	68	55	6	32
	Total	175	165	21	100
	% of (e)	82%	85%	73%	76%
(g)	*"Yes" at Scheduling*				
	Middle Class	33	29	5	26
	Lower Class	42	46	2	31
	Unknown	50	40	3	17
	Total	125	115	10	74
	% of (f)	71%	70%	42%	74%

(*continued*)

TABLE 7.2 (Continued)

Stage of Selection		Alpha & Gamma	Alpha Revisited[a]		Beta
(h)	Began Assessment				
	Middle Class	32	29	4	22
	Lower Class	38	46	2	30
	Unknown	49	40	3	16
	Total	119	115	9	68
	% of (g)	95%	100%	90%	92%
(i)	Unknowns Assigned LC/MC				
	Middle Class	20	20	2	10
	Lower Class	29	20	1	6
	Total	49	40	3	16
(j)	Sample at Assessment				
	MC: From (h)	32	29	NA	22
	From (i)	20	20		10
	From Alpha Revisited		NA	6	NA
	Other[b]	4	0		0
	Total	56	55		32
	LC: From (h)	38	46	NA	30
	From (i)	29	20		6
	From Alpha Revisited	NA	3		0
	Total	67	69		36
	Total N for Sample	123	124		68

[a] Alpha Revisited was a subset of Alpha subject pool who, for one reason or another, were not available for training at age two, but were subsequently recruited for training as part of Gamma sample.

[b] Four mothers in pool assigned to Gamma heard about program and requested that their child be included in Alpha for two-year-old training. They were accepted to increase the number of MC children in Alpha.

children are born outside hospitals and without medical care, we can surmise that the urban undercalss comprises a proportion of our population greater than the 7%–10% that is generally estimated.

Assignment of Interview. The pool of potential subjects for Alpha and Gamma ($N = 579$) were sent letters informing them of the study and stating that they would receive more information in the near future. Nine letters were returned as not known at the address. Of the 570 families who presumably had received our letter, 260 were randomly assigned to Alpha and 310 to Gamma. Gamma parents would be interviewed and the children would be trained 1 year later.

One year later when the Gamma sample was recontacted, an additional 60 families had moved out of the area or were unlocatable, providing a potential sample for Gamma of 250 instead of 310. Our experience with the Alpha selection raised concerns about the size of that potential sample, and 64 subjects designated Alpha Revisited were added as potential Gamma subjects. Those 64 families had not been assigned for interviews the year before, or had been contacted for the Alpha sample but had not participated because the child was sick at the time, or because at age 2 the parents thought him to be too young. They are first shown in the selection process in Table 7.2c.

All 270 Beta non participating controls located by the post office were sent letters of initial contact. Five were returned as not known at that address. All the remaining 265 were assigned to interview because it was anticipated that a smaller percentage of Beta would volunteer for the study. Their children were not to be offered a program but only periodic assessment.

A comparison of attrition from birth record to assignment of interview for Alpha and Gamma on the one hand and Beta on the other shows that 54% of Alpha and Gamma and 52% of Beta were ultimately assigned to interview.

Interviews Attempted.   Interviewers were white graduate students and research assistants who had been given detailed instructions on how to approach the families. If the mother was home and indicated that she would like to have the child participate, she was asked to sign a statement of interest. If neither parent was home a message was left. The message stated that someone had called to discuss the program, gave a phone number and name to contact, and if the home appeared to belong to the very poor, a dime was left with the message. Homes of Alpha and Gamma families were visited five times before attempt to contact ceased. Fewer visits to the homes of Beta families were required to recruit an adequate number of potential participants.

Interviews Achieved.   Parents were told that we were studying "children's learning" in one-to-one relationships between instructor and child, and that the program would last 8 months (Alpha and Gamma) or 4 weeks (Beta assessment). Transportation, but not money, was offered.

Table 7.2e shows that of the interviews assigned, 82% of Alpha, 79% of Gamma, and 63% of Beta were achieved. The lower percentage of Betas was probably due to the fact that fewer than five visits were used before an adequate sample was available.

"Yes" at Interview.   Table 7.2f shows that of the interviews achieved, 82% of Alpha, 85% of Gamma, and 76% of Beta signed the statement of interest. The slightly lower percentage of Betas signing the statement of interest was presumably due at least partly to the fact that no program other than assessment was offered.

"Yes" at Scheduling.   Several weeks after parents had signed the statement of interest they were contacted again for scheduling. Parents were informed that their child would attend two 1-hour sessions weekly, and were given choices with respect to days of the week and hours of the day. Of those who had signed the statement of interest, 71% of the Alphas, 70% of the Gammas, and 74% of the Betas came to the Harlem Center, were oriented in greater detail, and scheduled their child twice weekly at specific times of the day.

Began Assessment.   Of those who scheduled their children, 119 Alphas (95%), 115 Gammas (100%), and 68 Betas (92%) began assessment. Those included 49 Alphas, 40 Gammas, and 16 Betas who had been classified as "SES Unknown" until additional information had been obtained at interview and at scheduling (Table 7.2i). Four additional Alphas were added for reasons indicated in Table 7.2j, and six additional Gammas were added from the Alpha Revisited category. The final sample sizes as assessment began were: Alpha, 123; Gamma, 124; and Beta, 68.

Of those parents who were interviewed, 58% of Alpha, 64% of Gamma, and 52% of Beta ultimately participated in assessment. A larger percentage of middle-class Alpha (62%) than lower-class (50%) who were interviewed began assessment, but a smaller percentage of middle-class Beta (49%) than lower-class Beta (54%) began assessment. No difference existed by social class among Gamma subjects.

Characteristics of Final Sample

Socioeconomic status (SES), age, occupation, and education of parents were examined to determine if any of those variables differed significantly across cells of the research design.

Table 7.3 shows the distribution by Hollingshead score for the final sample. That the mean educational rating for all subjects was 4.54 as compared to the mean occupational category of 5.7 shows the sample was underemployed for the level of education.

Table 7.4 shows the sample distribution and average score measured by the Hollingshead Two Factor Index of Social Position. Clearly, that distribution is skewed toward the lower end. For the purposes of our study, we arbitrarily defined "middle class" as Hollingshead I–IV and "lower class" as Hollingshead V. This roughly divided the distribution in half, but with a slightly higher proportion of participants in our lower category (V) because greater attrition was anticipated in that group.

Distributions for age, education, and occupation of mother and father are not shown because of constraints on the length of this chapter. However, no significant differences existed by sample on any of those measures.

TABLE 7.3
Distribution of Sample on Occupation and Education of
Head of Household

Hollingshead Score	Occupation			Education		
	Alpha	Beta	Gamma	Alpha	Beta	Gamma
	Prop. (N)	Prop. (N)	Prop. (N)	Prop. (N)	Prop. (N)	Prop. (N)
1	.01 (1)	.03 (2)	.00 (0)	.02 (2)	.03 (2)	.00 (0)
2	.05 (6)	.03 (2)	.03 (4)	.03 (4)	.00 (0)	.05 (6)
3	.02 (2)	.01 (1)	.05 (6)	.08 (10)	.10 (7)	.10 (13)
4	.14 (17)	.09 (6)	.20 (25)	.35 (45)	.41 (28)	.39 (48)
5	.08 (10)	.13 (9)	.13 (16)	.28 (34)	.26 (18)	.26 (32)
6	.25 (31)	.38 (26)	.19 (23)	.16 (20)	.13 (9)	.02 (3)
7	.46 (56)	.32 (22)	.40 (50)	.07 (8)	.06 (4)	.02 (3)
Mean	5.87 (123)	5.71 (68)	5.60 (124)	4.62 (123)	4.51 (68)	4.48 (124)
		Mean = 5.7				

Note: Hollingshead Occupation Scale: 1 - professional, higher executive; 2 = business manager; 3 = minor professionals; 4 = clerical, sales; 5 = skilled manual workers; 6 = semi-skilled; 7 = unskilled worker/unemployed.

Hollingshead Education Scale: 1 = completed graduate school; 2 = college graduate; 3 = partial college; 4 = high school graduate; 5 = partial high school; 6 = completed 7-9th grade; 7 = less than 7 years of schooling.

TABLE 7.4
Distribution of Sample by SES Rating

Hollingshead ISP	ALPHA (N = 123)[a]		BETA (N = 68)		GAMMA (N = 124)[b]	
	Number	Prop.	Number	Prop.	Number	Prop.
I (11-17)	1	.01	1	.01	0	.00
II (18-27)	6	.05	3	.04	3	.02
III (28-43)	5	.04	5	.07	13	.10
IV (44-60)	42	.34	23	.34	42	.34
V (61-77)	69	.56	36	.53	66	.53
Mean Hollingshead (N)	(110)	59.58	(68)	58.0	(123)	57.11

Note: Index of Social Position rating is computed from 7 times occupation plus 4 times education, so that I = Upper Class, II = Upper Middle, III = Middle, IV = Lower Middle, and V = Lower.

[a] Complete data on Alpha sample was available for 110 participants.

[b] Some data in the Gamma sample is for 123 subjects instead of for 124. One subject did not complete the assessment, and therefore is not counted as having participated in the program.

Discussion of Subject Selection and Sample Characteristics

Were there significant differences among Alpha, Gamma, and Beta in the selection process? The post office located 61% of the identified potential pool for the Alpha and Gamma and 53% of the Beta. However, the Beta post office search occurred several months later after birth so that additional attrition would be expected. Of those interviewed, 58% of Alpha, 64% of Gamma, and 52% of Beta actually participated in the program. The lower percentage for Beta was anticipated, because the annual assessment was expected to be less attractive to parents than the full program. Consequently, a smaller percentage of Beta for whom birth records existed actually participated, but that lower percentage was foreseen because of the nature of the study. Whether that smaller percentage of Beta subjects who participated made for a bias in subsequent assessment results is unlikely. If the Beta mothers who participated were more motivated to provide educational input for their child, the selection process would work toward diminishing differences between Alpha and Gamma, and Beta at subsequent assessments.

Were middle-class mothers more likely to have their child participate than lower-class mothers? Sixty percent of the middle-class parents categorized from the birth records were located by the post office, and 61% of those categorized lower-class were located. Of those who were interviewed, 41% of the middle class and 39% of the lower class ended with their children in the program. Thus, it appears that no difference existed between middle class and lower class with respect to the results of the selection process.

The significant difference between heads of household on education and occupation, when put into the perspective of the Hollingshead norms, indicates clearly that the Harlem black parents of our subjects were better educated than they were employed. It suggests that to tell a black school boy in Harlem that if he finishes high school he will get a better job is, in the Harlem vernacular, "the old perfume."

No significant differences existed among Alpha, Beta, and Gamma with respect to the background variables—social class, education and occupation of the parents and head of household, or age of parents. That data provided a basis for confidently assigning subjects randomly (abba) by lower class and middle class to the Concept Training and Discovery groups. Random assignment within samples and social-class groups was done on the basis of scores at initial assessment on the Concept Familiarity Index, which is described later.

DESIGN OF STUDY

Three conditions, or treatments, characterize the Harlem Study. Initially, those three conditions were conceived as one experimental and two control groups:

1. Concept Training, where a curriculum was devised and organized to teach specific concepts using specific procedures.

2. Participating controls, children who would attend the center with identical schedules, procedures, and staff, but who would not be exposed to the Concept Training curriculum.

3. A nonparticipating control group, selected from the same population pool and assessed annually, but who did not participate in either program described previously.

The participating control group in 1964 was unique for large programmatic studies. It was used to determine if the Concept Training contributed effects greater than those on controls who had identical center experiences except for the curriculum itself. The participating control group was called the Discovery group as a matter of strategy. Instructors were not informed that the Discovery group was a control for Concept Training in the belief that they would be more equally committed to two separate interventions. However, after the initial postprogram assessment, it became clear that the Discovery group as well as the Concept Training group was superior to the nonparticipating controls. Thereafter, the Discovery group was accepted as an intervention, and its role as a control for the effects of Concept Training remained unimparied.

Concept Training Group

Regardless of the language or culture of their environments, young children develop in highly similar environments. Objects are hard and soft, wet and dry, rough and smooth, etc., and are represented by adjectives in the English language. Prepositions, on the other hand, describe the relationship between one concept or word and another. The block is on top of the box, the penny is under the rug, or the chair is next to the table. *Hard, wet, rough, on top of, under,* and *next to* are concepts almost all children learn sooner or later. They are the building blocks for more difficult, subsequent concepts.

The selection of concepts to be included in the curriculum and the sequencing of those concepts by difficulty was the result of previous studies at the Harlem Research Center and evidence obtained from the assessment of Alpha at age 2. Initially, a large number of prepositions and adjectives representing concepts such as described above, and more complex concepts such as *more than, many,* and *same,* were selected from the speech of children ages 2 to 4. Situations were contrived to determine whether or not a child knew those concepts. If, for example, when asked "show me the big one," the child could choose correctly between a big and a little block, a big and little ball, and a big and little truck, he was credited for knowing the concept *big.* By testing many children on 96 such items, the percentage of children who knew a concept at a given age was determined. From those studies we learned many things important for curriculum development. For example, concept knowledge at age 2 is to some extent stimulus bound. A child might choose correctly the big ball over several successive trials but not choose correctly the big block or truck. This occurred far more frequently than chance would lead one to expect. Consequently, the curriculum emphasized teaching a concept in a variety of situations and with different materials. Based on these studies we selected the concepts to be taught at age 2 and age 3, and sequenced the concepts according to difficulty.

Sequencing by difficulty was aided by data on the acquisition of the same concepts by several hundred 2- and 3-year-old children in Antigua and Puerto Rico. The order of concept attainment did not vary greatly between those two cultures and our own.

The curriculum developed for the 3-year-old sample (Gamma) was more difficult than that for the 2-year-olds (Alpha). Some concepts used in the curriculum at age 2 were known by 90% or more children at age 3, and these easier ones were dropped from the older curriculum. Also, item analysis of the 2-year-old assessment revealed ineffective items, and the materials or procedures used for testing such concepts were changed.[2]

The stages in the development of the Concept Training condition can be summarized as follows:

1. Assessment of all program participants to determine the relative difficulty of concepts for the entire population as well as for each individual child.
2. Ordering of the concepts by meaning and by difficulty.
3. Specification of the steps to be used in teaching each concept.
4. Determination of how instructors could best teach each concept.
5. Establishment of criteria for acquisition of a concept.
6. The development of lesson plans and progress sheets to be used by instructors.

Participating Controls (Discovery Groups)

As stated previously, what will subsequently be referred to as the Discovery group was originally designed as a participating control group. Subjects in the Discovery group were not exposed to the structured training obtained by the Concept Training group, but all other conditions of training were identical: one-to-one interaction with the same instructors, the frequency of visits and length of sessions, the materials with which the child played, and the facilities used. Parents were encouraged to observe the first six sessions and were welcomed thereafter.

Instructors were trained not to initiate conversation with the children in the Discovery group, but rather to respond to the child when he sought a response verbally or by gesture. Even when responding to such a request by the child, the instructor was not to use the words related to the concepts used in the structured

---

[2]The revised curriculum can be obtained from Palmer and Associates, Suite 602, 255 Dolphin Point Rd., Clearwater, Florida 33515.

training. However, as long as the child persisted in inquiring about an object or subject, the instructor was to respond and elaborate.

Thus, when the child and the instructor were playing with the materials at hand, if verbally or by gesture the child centered his attention on a particular object and desired a response from the instructor, the instructor would continue to respond about that object or subject as long as the child was interested. For example, if the child approached the instructor with a block in hand and asked, "What's this?" or by gesture asked for the instructor's attention, the instructor might respond, "That is a block, See, there are several blocks on the floor." If the child returned to the blocks and resumed playing, the instructor initiated no further conversation. If, however, the child persisted with the block, the instructor might say, "That is a blue block; let's see how many blue blocks you can find." If he remained interested in the blocks, the instructor would develop games with the blocks, but he would never develop games that taught the concepts used in the structured training.

The children in the Concept Training and Discovery groups approached their training sessions eagerly. Normally the center was quiet, with eight 2- and 3-year-olds in their cubicles with their instructors. However, bedlam reigned from 10 minutes before the hour to each hour. Eight 2-year-olds came up the stairs with their drivers and those mothers, fathers, siblings, or grandparents who had decided to come and watch that day, and eight 2-year-olds burst from their training cubicle to be met by an equal assortment of others.

Nonparticipating Controls

The nonparticipating control group first attended the center at age 2 years 8 months (2–8). Once the children were judged to be adapted to the center and ready for assessment, they were administered the same battery of measures as the Concept Training and Discovery groups. After the initial assessment, the nonparticipating controls were tested at ages 3–8 and 4–8 after the experimentals had completed their assessment, thereby equating the average ages of the control and experimental groups. The nonparticipating controls accumulated an average of 20 hours of assessment in the center before they began attending elementary school, which did not differ significantly from the experimental groups.

DATA COLLECTION PROCEDURES

Preschool Data Collection (1966–1969)

Concept Training and Discovery groups were compared to the nonparticipating control group (Beta), as well as to each other, after Alpha children completed their 7-month training (at 2–8) and again after Gamma children completed their training (at 3–8). Beta served as a control for both Alpha and Gamma. While

Alpha and Beta were being assessed one year after their initial assessment, Gamma was being assessed for the first time. All three groups were reassessed 1 year later at 4–8.

In planning the preschool assessment three aspects were explicitly addressed:

1. The need for a comprehensive test battery that included the specific concepts taught in the Concept Training group as well as content not related to the curriculum.

2. The need for adapting each individual child to the testing situation prior to assessment, particularly those controls who were new to the Harlem facility.

3. The need for minimizing experimenter, or assessor, bias.

Measures of Performance: Age 2–0 to 4–8

The measures used from age 2–0, before Alpha began training, through age 4–8—the last annual assessment before the subjects entered school—are shown in Table 7.5. Some measures were standard, norm–referenced tests (Stanford–Binet); some were borrowed (e.g., embedded figures from Kagan); some were comprised of a combination of elements of already existing measures [Simple Perceptual Discrimination used both the Seguin Form (1866) and Kohs' Blocks (1923)]; and some were devised by the staff (e.g., the Concept Familiarity Index, Sequence, and Persistence). The battery each year varied as a function of the age of the children at the time of the assessment.

Great care was taken to help each child become comfortable and relaxed in the testing situation. During the adaptation period, the child became familiar with the center and its personnel and, most importantly, learned to interact with another adult when the mother was absent. The children differed greatly in their rate of adaptation. Some boys, particularly at age 3–0 and above, appeared ready for assessments on their first visit, whereas others required six or seven visits.

The project was careful to set up safeguards to avoid any assessor bias. During the first 2 years, examiners who had never been involved as instructors were hired and trained. At the two final preschool assessments (3–8 and 4–8 years), some project personnel performed assessments, but a child was never tested by his former instructors.

Data Collection: Elementary Grades (1973–1978)

The Harlem Study lost funding for continued data collection when the subjects were 5 years old and received none until 1975 when it obtained a grant from the Education Commission of the States to support follow-up of the entire sample.[3]

---

[3]Additionally, in 1971, 100 names of project children were sent to another research project sponsored by Dr. Roy John of New York Medical College. His study of visually evoked potential required first-grade subjects with a recorded history of preschool cognitive development. The names were randomly selected and included a proportion of the experimental and control groups. The results are not reported here.

TABLE 7.5
Preschool Battery of Performance Measures*

ASSESSMENT MEASURES	2-0ᵃ	2-8, 3-0ᵇ	3-8ᶜ	4-8ᵈ
Language Facility	X			
Concept Familiarity Index	X	X	X	X
Stanford-Binet		X	X	X
Peabody Picture Vocabulary Test (PPVT)		X	X	X
Persistence at a Boring Task		X	X	
Embedded Figures		X	X	
Sequence		X	X	
Simple Perceptual Discrimination		X	X	
Motor Battery		X	X	
Labeling		X	X	
Location Discrimination		X		
Positional Discrimination			X	
Simple Form Discrimination		X		
Varied Form Discrimination		X	X	
Color Discrimination		X	X	
Body Parts		X		
Body Positions		X		
Delayed Reaction		X		
Form Problems			X	
Grouping			X	
Sorting			X	

*Table reprinted from Palmer & Siegel, 1977.
Note. Content and administration of tests vary with age.
ᵃ The 2-0 battery was administered to Alpha sample only.
ᵇ The 2-8, 3-0 battery was administered to Alpha, Beta, and Gamma samples.
ᶜ The 3-8 battery was administered to Alpha, Beta, and Gamma samples.
ᵈ The 4-8 battery was administered to Alpha, Beta, and Gamma samples. Additional measures used at 4-8 were: WPPSI, Alphabet Knowledge, Seriation Tasks, and Classification.

Subsequently, the project became part of the cross-study analysis of the Consortium for Longitudinal Studies.

Data collection for grades 3 and 4 was limited, constrained by the problem of relocating subjects, loss of personnel who had been associated with the study for years, and other factors related to the absence of support. Efforts to locate subjects by mail and through hired tracers of family movement were just partly successful. More rewarding was the search of the central records of the school system when they were made available in 1976. The individual class records for all 75,000 of the fifth-grade students in 1975 were reviewed. Subsequently, fourth-grade records in 1975 were also checked to identify those children who had failed a grade.

Once a boy had been identified in a class by birthdate and name, his school was contacted and his parents located. Permission was obtained from the parents to obtain school records for norm-referenced reading and arithmetic tests, which were administered routinely to all students by the school system. Data about retention in grade were obtained from class results.

Sufficient funds were not available to test the entire sample at ages 10 and 12. The Wechsler Intelligence Scale for Children (WISC) was administered to one subset of boys when the subjects were age 10 and to the remainder of the boys at age 12 (WISC-R). Interviews with the child and mother were obtained at the time that the child was administered the Wechsler. The boys were paid 10 dollars for reporting to the Harlem Research Center, taking the Wechsler, and for being interviewed.

Some Consortium projects have chosen to collect data on other measures such as placement in special education classes. However, this was not feasible for our project because of the vagueness of criteria and the inconsistency in assignment to special education classes from year to year in New York.

FINDINGS

Results will be presented for evidence related to the training experience, pre-school assessments at ages 2–8, 3–8, 4–8, and for the elementary grades. Annual assessments occurred for grades 4 through 8, but space prohibits more detailed description here. Primarily, results will be reported in the form of multiple analysis of variance or t tests.

Evidence Related to the Training Experience

Attendance

Training began for the first children on October 3, 1966, and by December 31 over 2800 hours of individual instruction had been provided. During that 3-month period, the percentage of children who arrived for scheduled appointments was 77.6%. That figure improved slightly to 79% from January 1 until May 1967, when training was terminated, at which time more than 7500 hours had been provided. Thus, there was no decrease in attendance as the training continued. The average child attended 45 training sessions.

Average attendance for all program children during the training sessions was 80%. No significant differences existed between attendance of lower-class and middle-class children (78% and 79%) or between Concept Training and Discovery Training (78% and 82%).

Of the 123 Alpha children who began training in October, 110 completed the program and posttraining assessment. No parent stated that the reason for dropping out was dissatisfaction with the program. Some parents did say they found that their child was too young and, from what we knew of those children, we agreed with the mother. Not all children at 24 months of age are sufficiently developed to participate in a program such as that offered by the Harlem Center. Of the 13 children who dropped out, more than half were children who had not completed the pretraining assessment (Borden, 1971). Borden's study showed that concept acquisition at 24 months was a good indicator of whether or not the child would continue in a program.

Instructor Performance

Because procedures differed significantly for Concept Training (CT) and Discovery Training (DT) treatment, one can ask, "Did the instructors differentiate their behavior accordingly?" Eight instructors were observed with 2 DT and 2 CT children ($N = 32$). Observers had no contact with the children or the instructors prior to the time of making observations. Each observation lasted 30 minutes during which observers alternated between 15 seconds of observation and 15 seconds of recording. Table 7.6 presents the results for the 11 behaviors observed.

These data show that instructors did interact with the children in manners consistent with the procedures for the CT and DT treatment. For example, verbal interaction on information related to the curriculum between the child and instructor was consistent with CT and DT procedures. Categories 2 and 3 show that verbal interaction not related to the curriculum occurred more in CT than DT, but the number of casual comments did not differ significantly. Categories 6 and 8 show that nonverbal behavior for maintaining rapport and attentive watching behavior were greater for DT, as might be expected if the instructor was denied the opportunity to interact verbally.

Similar monitoring studies were performed throughout training at age 3 (Gamma group) with similar results.

Preschool Assessments (2–0 to 4–8 years)

Pretraining Assessment at Age 24 Months

In 1966, not a great deal was known about measuring the performance of the 24-month-old child. There were real questions about the reliability of measurement taken so early in life; that is, to what extent would a measurement taken at one time yield the same result as a measurement taken a week or a month later? Validity of measurement was also in question; to what extent did the child's responses indicate what he knew? The pretraining assessment was originally conceived as a means of obtaining a rough measure of what the child already knew so that training could begin at his level of development. Assessment could also provide data for the reliability that validity questions.

Two measures were administered to participating children: Concept Familiarity Index, which provided a measure of concepts already known; and Language Facility, which measured words he could speak or understand.

TABLE 7.6
Instructor Behavior by Treatment Group

		Concept Training (N = 16)		Discovery Training (N = 16)	
		Median No. of Responses	Range	Median No. of Responses	Range
1)	Verbal Interaction Info-related to Curr.	82.0	10-124	0.0	0-5
2)	Verbal Interaction Info-not-related to Curr.	16.0	0-41	8.5	0-22
3)	Verbal Interaction Casual Comments	31.0	3-73	25.0	7-81
4)	Verbal Interaction Rapport Maintaining	1.0	0-7	0.0	0-5
5)	Verbal Interaction Punitive	2.0	0-14	0.0	0-5
6)	Rapport Maintaining Nonverbal Interaction	19.5	4-60	25.5	4-64
7)	Participating Nonverbal Interaction	10.5	3-24	5.5	1-30
8)	Attentive Watching Behavior	16.0	4-48	46.5	24-58
9)	Preparation for Activity	2.0	0-6	.5	0-3
10)	Teacher Focused	2.0	0-6	1.0	0-13
11)	Inattentiveness	2.5	0-6	.5	0-15

Concept assessment responses were scored "correct," "incorrect," and "no response." For a given item, the instructor attempted to obtain a response on three occasions before the "no response" was scored. The correlation between "no response" and total score was .03, indicating that the number of "no responses" was not predictive of a child's total score.

The boys required 3 to 14 one-hour sessions to complete assessment. If a child had not completed assessment after 14 sessions, assessment was terminated and training began. Nine of the 123 children at age 2–0 did not complete assessment. An additional 11 children completed either concept or vocabulary assessment, but not both. Thus, complete assessment data is available for 103 children, and assessment on at least one of the two measures was available for 114.

Was the test a reliable measure? For 2-year-olds, the Kuder Richardson reliability was .74. We concluded that the test yielded reasonably reliable information about what concepts children knew at age 2.

The correlation between number of sessions to complete assessment and total score was .07, indicating practically no relationship between the two. We concluded that the number of sessions required to complete assessment was not a valid indicator of how much the children knew. This conclusion was later proven to be incorrect in the study by Borden (1971), which showed that completion of assessment did have predictive value for subsequent program performance, particularly for those who never completed assessment.

Five of 54 middle-class (MC) and nine of 69 lower-class (LC) children did not complete concept assessment. The average number of sessions to complete concept assessment was 9.00 for the MC children and 7.77 for LC. Thus, although a slightly higher percentage of LC than MC children did not complete assessment, the LC children took, on the average, fewer sessions to finish. LC children had slightly more "no responses" than the MC children: an average of 5.80 (of 92 items) compared to an average of 4.79.

No significant difference existed between the average score of the MC (35.53) and the LC (34.94) groups on the concept assessment, nor was there a difference between those children assigned to CT (34.13) and DT (33.06).

A slight but not significant difference in favor of the MC (mean = 21.98; SD = 10.81) over the LC (mean = 19.89; Sd = 9.59) existed on the vocabulary measure. The ability of the CT and DT groups to label and discriminate between objects and actions was practically identical (20.83 versus 20.93, respectively).

Assessment at Age 2 Years–8 Months (Alpha and Beta)

Alpha Concept Training (CT) and Discovery Training (DT) groups were assessed immediately after training ceased. Beta controls were assessed after Alpha, equating for the difference in age. The 2–8 assessment provided for comparisons between CT and DT, lower class (LC) and middle class (MC), and the nonparticipating controls (Beta).

The order of assessment for CT and DT was determined by attendance. Those assessed first had the greatest number of sessions in training. This provided the opportunity for children with the most absences to have several additional training sessions before assessment.

The Concept Familiarity Index (CFI) used at 2–8 was derived from the data obtained from concept assessment at age 2. Using the difficulty level of items at age 2 and the biserial correlations between item and total score, the measure was reduced from 92 items to 50. Thirty-six items were unchanged from the 2–0 scale; 14 were modified or new. At age 2–8, the CFI obtained a Kuder Richardson reliability of .72. Test–retest reliability was .74 when the same person administered the measure twice to the child. Since Beta controls were unfamiliar with the center, preassessment adaptation procedures for them were identical to those used for Alpha at age 2.

The results of the multiple analysis of variance of the 2–8 assessment are shown on Table 7.7. The Concept Training (CT) and Discovery Training (DT) groups outperformed Beta controls significantly on a number of individual measures. No significant differences, however, existed between CT and DT, with one exception: the Concept Familiarity Index for which CT had been trained. Although the average CFI score of the CT group was significantly better than DT

TABLE 7.7

Multiple Analysis of Variance of Test Scores of Alpha and Beta at Age 2 Years - 8 Months

Measures	Alpha Concept (N = 51) Multivariate F = 3.25** Univariate F	Alpha Discovery (N = 44) R = .53** Discriminant Coefficient	Alpha Concept Multivariate F = 6.01** Univariate F	Beta (N = 57) R = .62** Discriminant Coefficient	Alpha Discovery Multivariate F = 2.25* Univariate F	Beta R = .45* Discriminant Coefficient
1. Body Parts	.03	.14	3.60	.17	2.89	-.12
2. Persistence	1.46	.04	3.37	.07	.42	-.01
3. Concept Familiarity Index	6.64*	.88	37.31**	.80	8.96**	.17
4. PPVT	-2.15	.45	.55	-.37	4.06**	-.25
5. Sequence	3.40	.19	5.25*	-.09	.23	-.18
6. IQ (S-B)	-3.37	-.80	5.58*	-.32	14.54**	.60
7. Delayed Reaction	2.24	.44	4.10*	.20	.17	-.16
8. Simple Perceptual Discrimination	1.00	.13	21.66**	.38	8.97**	.45
9. Motor Performance	2.80	.38	16.18**	.31	3.96**	-.06
10. Labeling	-0.07	.03	11.40**	.17	12.10**	.51

*p < .05
**p < .01

227

(30.6 to 27.5, $p < .05$), the DT group significantly outperformed the controls as well (27.5 to 23.8, $p < .01$), in spite of the fact that DT had not been trained on the concepts. DT had higher IQs than CT (95.45 to 91.24) but not significantly so.

On a separate analysis reported elsewhere (Palmer, 1970), middle-class children were, on the average, higher than lower-class children on each measure in the battery but in no case was that difference statistically significant.

Assessment and Training at 3 Years (Gamma)

Selection and assignment procedures for the Gamma sample whose training began at age 3 were identical to Alpha trained at age 2. The same assessment battery was used for the Gamma at 3–0 as had been used for Alpha and Beta 4 months before. The Gamma at 3–0 completed assessment in 8.67 hours, over an hour less than had been needed for Alpha and Beta at 2–8. Perhaps their capacity for responding more quickly speaks to the significant difference 4 months can make for the 3-year-old child. No significant differences existed between CT and DT groups or between LC and MC in hours needed for assessment, although the LC children again averaged less than the MC children (8.58 to 8.76).

The Gamma pretraining assessment revealed one unexpected finding which influenced subsequent analyses: the Beta controls averaged 86 on the Stanford–Binet IQ at age 2–8 and the Gamma averaged 92 at age 3–0. These differences on the Binet between the Gamma and Beta samples are statistically reliable. Are they due to attrition or simply "the luck of the throw" in the random assignment of the subjects? The Consortium analysis concluded that it represents a difference in the original sample (Consortium, 1980, p. 161). That fact suggests using analysis of covariance to correct for these differences. Such analyses were described in some of our earlier reports. However, we have since decided not to control these differences, for reasons to be described shortly.

It is worth noting that the Gamma sample IQs at 3–0 were not only higher than those of the Beta controls at 2–8, but they were also higher than the Alpha sample after training at 2–8. The Alpha and Gamma samples were developed by random selection from the same subject pool born between August and September. In effect, they were a single sample until assignment to Alpha and Gamma. Identical selection procedures were used for the Beta controls; the only difference was that they were born 2 to 3 months later. For the Gammas to have scored higher before training than the Alphas did after training suggests that the difference may have been due to the different response abilities that boys have at age 2–8 as compared to 3–0. From the time those differences were shown to exist at age 3–0, all subsequent analyses controlled for IQ at ages 2–8 and 3–0.

Assessment at Age 3 Years–8 Months (Alpha, Beta, and Gamma)

Of the 121 Gamma children who began training in the fall at 3–0, 99 completed training and assessment at 3–8. Parents of the 22 who dropped out cited family problems and other reasons not different from those who had dropped out during Alpha training, except that fewer stated that their child was too young. Average attendance for Gamma was 81%, and no significant difference existed for dropouts among the CT and DT or the LC and MC groups.

The 3–8 assessment was modified from the 3–0 battery because some measures used at 3–0 were too easy for the child at 3–8 and so were dropped as other measures were added.

The Gamma sample was assessed when they had completed training and was followed by Beta and Alpha. Assessing more than 200 children took longer than 2 months and continued to the end of July. That was a mistake because, as the summer wore on, fewer parents remained in the city, and the Alphas, who were assessed last, suffered the greatest attrition. Reflecting the order of assessment, 97 of 99 Gamma children (97%), 52 of 68 Betas (76%), and 64 of 108 Alphas (59%) completed the 3–8 assessment. No significant differences in the number lost were found when comparisons were made by type of training and social class.

Earlier reports from this project reported the results of analyses of covariance comparing the Alpha and Gamma groups to the Beta control group, controlling for differences in IQ scores at ages 2–8 and 3–0. Those analyses showed a general pattern of superiority of the Alpha and Gamma groups over the Beta controls. However, further reflection suggested that despite their positive results, these analyses had been biased in the conservative direction. The comparisons of Alpha to Beta had been conservatively biased because the only IQ measure available to serve as a covariate was a posttreatment measure for the Alpha group. Thus, controlling for this measure would actually "control out" much of the positive effect of the treatment. The comparisons of Gamma to Beta had been conservatively biased because pretest IQ had been measured at age 2–8 for Beta and at age 3–0 for Gamma. The age standardization of the Stanford–Binet may be weak enough at these very young ages so that the difference being controlled was not a real difference but merely an artifact of the age of testing. Therefore, for this chapter it was decided to replace these analyses of covariance by simple t tests.

As shown in Table 7.8, at 3 years–8 months, Alpha significantly outperformed Beta on four of the nine measures. Gamma significantly outperformed Beta on six of the nine measures. In no case did Beta significantly outperform Alpha or Gamma.

No significant differences existed between Alpha Concept Training and Alpha Discovery Training on any single measure or across the battery of tests. Nor did significant differences exist between Gamma Concept Training (GCT) and Gamma Discovery Training (GDT) except for the CFI where GCT performed better. GCT had just completed concept training when the assessment occurred. Neither Alpha nor Gamma showed significant differences on any measure by social class.

TABLE 7.8
T Tests of Group Differences at 3 Years - 8 Months

MEASURE	Alpha vs Beta Group Differences (2.59/.43)** t	Gamma vs Beta Group Differences (3.34/.42)** t
1. IQ (Stanford-Binet)	1.179	2.416*
2. PPVT	.858	.497
3. Sequence	1.710	1.675
4. Concept Familiarity Index	2.679**	4.001**
5. Persistence	-.796	-1.901
6. Labeling	1.798	2.752**
7. Form Problems	2.129*	2.784**
8. Simple Perceptual Discrimination	3.309**	3.981**
9. Motor Performance	2.121*	2.219*
	df = 114	df = 147

Note. For Alpha, N = 64; for Beta, N = 52; for Gamma, N = 97.
*$p < .05$.
**$p < .01$.

Assessment at Age 4 Years–8 Months (Alpha, Beta, and Gamma)

The last preschool assessment in the Harlem Study was conducted in the summer of 1969 when the children were 4 years and 8 months old. The Alphas had completed training 2 years before and the Gammas 1 year before.

In the summer of 1969, 214 children were assessed: 70 Alphas, 44 Betas, and 96 Gammas. The percentage of children originally assessed in 1967 (Alpha and Beta) and in 1968 (Gamma) was Alpha, 65%; Beta, 65%; and Gamma, 97%. In some instances, a child not assessed at 3–8 (Alpha and Beta) was assessed at 4–8. No differences in losses were found by type of training or social class.

As shown in Table 7.9, at 4–8 Alpha significantly outperformed Beta on four of the nine measures. Gamma significantly outperformed Beta on seven of the nine measures. In no case did Beta significantly outperform Alpha or Gamma.

Significant positive correlations existed between socioeconomic status and performance on most measures at 4–8 for most samples. No significant SES differences existed by type of training across the assessment battery or for any individual measure when Alpha and Gamma were analyzed separately or combined. That lack of difference served as justification for the Ithaca group to combine the two groups under program children in its analysis (Lazar & Darlington, 1982).

Elementary Grade Results (To 13 Years Old)

It will be recalled that the 110 Alphas and 99 Gammas had completed their training and posttraining assessment. In addition, 68 Betas had been assessed for the first time at age 2–8. Thus, the potential subject pool for follow-up analysis in the schools was 277.

In July of 1977 partial or complete data were available for IQ, reading and arithmetic scores, and retention-in-grade data for 240 of the 277 children (87%). That figure is slightly lower than previously published results (Palmer & Siegel, 1977) because the potential subject pool was diminished by 16 children who were known to have moved out of the state or died. Thus, there were 37 subjects in the pool whose whereabouts were unknown.

Resources were not available to administer the WISC to all 240 children or to conduct all the child/parent interviews. Subjects tested and interviewed were selected randomly within cells from the pool of participants who had been located.

Attrition

In 1977–1978, data were analyzed to determine if subjects found differed from those not found on the Stanford–Binet IQ administered at 3–8 and by the social class index originally used to categorize subjects. No significant differences were found for IQ. The combined experimental groups (Concept and Discovery Training) found and not found did not significantly differ ($t = .98$; df

TABLE 7.9
T Tests of Group Differences at 4 Years - 8 Months

MEASURE	Alpha vs Beta Group Differences (4.32/.52)** t	Gamma vs Beta Group Differences (3.24/.43)** t
1. PPVT	-.189	1.339
2. IQ (Stanford-Binet)	1.027	3.406**
3. IQ (WPPSI)	1.052	2.901**
4. Seriation: Model	2.934**	2.756**
5. Seriation: Memory	3.534**	5.116**
6. Concept Familiarity Index	1.385	2.635**
7. Classification	2.093*	2.764**
8. IQ Verbal	-.371	1.248
9. IQ Performance	2.655**	4.396**
	df = 112	df = 138

Note. For Alpha, N = 70; for Beta, N = 44; for Gamma, N = 96.
*$p < .05$
**$p < .01$

= 211; p = .20), nor did the Beta controls (t = .33; df = 57; p = .20). Analysis by social class was determined by chi square (χ^2 = .114; df = 1; p = .70) and did not differ.

Given that attrition analyses have been reported by the Consortium for Longitudinal Studies, attrition will not be reviewed here in detail. Those analyses showed that no selective attrition resulted as a function of the following variables:

1. Final sample as a function of original sample by program children and controls.
2. Final sample as a percentage of original sample for parent interview or child interview.
3. Final sample as a percentage of original sample for WISC-R.
4. Attrition as a function of mother's education.
5. Attrition as a function of original Hollingshead scores of social class (Consortium, 1978).

Scholastic Achievement and IQ Test Results

Data showing that all program children combined (Alpha and Gamma Concept and Discovery Training groups) outperformed the Beta controls on IQ, on reading and arithmetic achievement, and in frequency of never being retained in grade have been reported elsewhere (Consortium, 1978). Analyses presented here concern the effects of type of training (Concept versus Discovery), age of training (Alpha versus Gamma), and social class on various outcome measures.

Type of Training. On arithmetic achievement tests, the combined Concept Training and Discovery Training groups outperformed Beta controls by 8.3 months in the fifth grade (t = 3.39, df = 179, p = .001). But when the arithmetic performance of CT and DT were compared, no significant difference existed between the two treatments. (Arithmetic achievement tests were not administered by the New York Public School System from 1976 to 1978, so test scores are not available for grades 6–8.)

The differences between program (CT and DT) and control children's reading achievement scores increased annually until grade 7, at which time program children were 1 year ahead. The difference at grade 7 was statistically significant [$F(1, 166)$ = 7.91, p = .005]. The two training groups, CT and DT, did not differ significantly when 59 CT and 69 DT were compared in grade 8, nor had they in earlier assessments.

The Wechsler Intelligence Scale for Children was administered to one subset of children at age 10 and to the other at age 12. The combined program children scored 6 points higher on the IQ test than did control children (t = 2.63, df = 175, p = .005). Most of that difference was contributed by a 9-point average difference on the Performance Scale. No significant IQ differences existed when CT and DT were compared.

By grade 7, significantly more control children than program children were retained in grade ($p = .01$, $N = 195$). Again, no significant differences were found between CT and DT. However, when CT and DT were compared separately with the controls, CT and controls were significantly different ($\chi^2 = 9.27$, df $= 1$, $p = .01$) but the DT and control difference only approached significance ($\chi^2 = 1.70$, df $= 1$, $p = .10$). There is the suggestion, then, that Concept Training is slightly more effective than Discovery Training in providing the child with benefits associated with not failing a grade in school.

Age of Training.   No significant differences by age of training (Alpha versus Gamma) were found for arithmetic and reading achievement, IQ, or retained in grade.

Social Class.   Despite the fact that less than 10% of the original sample of Harlem boys would have been classified as middle class by national norms, strong and persistent differences were found by social class on every measure. For IQ test scores, persistent differences between LC and MC existed in every cell of the design. Middle-class children scored significantly higher than lower-class children when compared on the arithmetic scale of the Metropolitan Achievement Test in grade 5. Significant differences by social class were observable on reading scores beginning in grade 3 and persisting through all tested grade levels. In grade 8, ANOVA main effects for program and control children were highly significant [$F(1, 179) = 12.15$, $p < .001$]. Vocabulary and Comprehension subscales were also significant ($p = .007$ and $p = .002$, respectively). However, although analysis revealed that MC program children outperformed MC control children ($t = 2.06$, df $= 76$, $p = .05$), no significant differences existed between LC experimental and LC controls (although LC experimental children displayed higher mean scores).

When comparisons were made between Concept and Discovery Training groups within each of the two social classes, there was a significant difference between the middle-class CT and DT groups [$F(1, 175) = 6.43$, $p = .001$], but no such difference was found between the lower-class groups. Considering the skewed social-class distribution of the sample, these findings suggest that there is a level of socioeconomic status below which the two treatments do not differ.

The retained-in-grade measure is the most revealing about the relationship between social class and training. At grade 8, middle-class program children were significantly better than controls ($\chi^2 = 17.01$, df $= 1$, $p = .001$), but lower-class program and controls did not differ ($\chi^2 = .35$, df $= 1$, $p = .50$). At grade 9, middle-class program children outperformed middle-class controls ($\chi^2 = 4.95$, df $= 1$, $p = .03$), but no difference existed between lower-class program and control groups.

DISCUSSION

The Harlem Study shows that two types of training at ages 2 and 3 produced significant effects on subsequent arithmetic, reading, and IQ scores and on being retained in grade. The analysis by the Harlem staff has been confirmed by the cross-study analysis of the Consortium for Longitudinal Studies. The purpose of this chapter was to examine differential effects of the major variables in the research design: type of training, age of training, and social class.

The two treatments did not have consistent differential effects. The Concept Training curriculum was more strongly related to avoiding retention in grade by grade 9, but both treatments were effective toward that end. There are, however, some practical advantages of the Concept Training curriculum over the Discovery procedure. The curriculum is published and available with explicit instructions for its procedures. The Discovery Training was conducted by instructors specially trained in its procedures, but no curriculum exists. The procedure of not responding to a child until the child requests attention by gesture or by voice is difficult for most instructors to follow. Consequently, for pragmatic reasons, we recommend the Concept Training curriculum. However, the evidence from this and the other studies reported in this volume is that a variety of programs can provide similar effects, provided the procedures for selecting, training, and supervising staff are carefully implemented.

Age of training made no discernible difference in the Harlem Study either. Certainly, age of training is probably not as important as the level of development of the child. Neither this study nor the studies by other members of the Consortium can be definitive on the best age to begin training, or on the best type of training. This should not be surprising, since these questions are probably too simplified. The best answer is probably that some children respond to a program better than others, and that knowledge regarding appropriate matching of child characteristics with characteristics of programs is what is needed. The same is probably true for the age of the child. On the average, some programs may be better for children at age 2, and others at age 3. The revised Harlem Curriculum (Palmer, 1978) has recognized this and provides many more free play situations at age 2.

The Harlem Study does show that a minimal intervention produces durable effects. We suspect that the one-to-one situation is the primary reason that an average of 45 hours of intervention at age 2 or 3 provided substantial benefits more than a decade later, but the evidence on this is not direct. The one-to-one situation worked, but we do not know that one-to-two or one-to-four might not have worked with the same treatments.

Not only did the minimal intervention have durable effects, but those effects were as widespread and as significant as other Consortium studies that provided many more hours of intervention. Perhaps the so-called inoculation hypothesis is more valid than is presently supposed. Perhaps there are some things the 2– and

3-year-old can learn in a relatively short time that persist in his subsequent behavior.

The study raises some points about the deficit hypothesis as well. If one accepts that suggestion in its original meaning, namely, that the child must learn A before B, and the earlier he learns A the better off he is, there may be validity there as well.

The Harlem Study suggests that a program that primarily emphasizes the child as compared to the child and his culture can have beneficial effects. No one could argue that changing the family and the community as well as the child might not do more for subsequent scholastic performance, but the fact is that a program aimed primarily at the child does have durable effects. Of the programs in the Consortium, the Harlem Study had less parental input than the average program, and its effects were as positive as the other programs. We believe that to have parents involved should contribute more, but data are needed to show this.

ACKNOWLEDGMENTS

This study was supported by grants from the National Institute of Child Health and Human Development (HD 02253), the Education Commission of the States, and the Administration for Children, Youth, and Families.

Too many have participated in this study over 18 years to acknowledge separately. One, Dr. Ronald Siegel, is particularly appreciated for his participation over that entire period.

REFERENCES

Borden, B. C. *Concept level, separation behavior and preschool performance of three-year-olds.* Unpublished doctoral dissertation, City University of New York, 1971.

Bronfenbrenner, U. *The ecology of human development.* Cambridge, Mass: Harvard University Press, 1979.

Consortium for Longitudinal Studies. *Lasting effects after preschool.* Washington, D.C.: U.S. Government Printing Office, DHEW Publication No. (OHDS) 79-30178, 1978.

Consortium for Longitudinal Studies. *Persistence of preschool effects: Status, stress and coping skills.* Year 2 report, Grant No. 90-C-1311(03) from the Administration for Children, Youth, and Families. Office of Human Development Services, DHHS, October 1980.

Dennis, W., & Najarian, P. Infant development under environmental handicap. *Psychological Monographs,* 1957, *71,* No. 7.

Deutsch, M. The role of social class in language development and cognition. *American Journal of Orthopsychiatry,* 1965, *35,* 78–87.

Goldfarb, W. Psychological privation in infancy and subsequent adjustment. *American Journal of Orthopsychiatry,* 1945, *15,* 247–255.

Harlow, H. F. The nature of love. *American Psychologist,* 1958, *13,* 673–685.

Hunt, J. McV. *Intelligence and experience.* New York: Ronald Press, 1961.

Kohs, S. C. *Intelligence measurement—A psychological and statistical study based upon the block-design tests.* New York: Macmillan, 1923.

Lazar, I., & Darlington, R. Lasting effects of early education. *Monographs of the Society for Research in Child Development,* 1982, *47* (1–2, Serial No. 194).

Myrdahl, G. *An American dilemma.* New York: Harper & Row, 1944.

Palmer, F. H. Inferences to the socialization of the child from animal studies. In D. A. Goslin (Ed.), *Handbook of socialization theory and research.* New York: Rand McNally, 1969. (a)

Palmer, F. H. Learning at two. *Children,* March 1969, *16,* 55–57. (b)

Palmer, F. H. Socioeconomic status and intellective performance among black preschool boys. *Developmental Psychology,* 1970, *2,* 4.

Palmer, F. H. One to one: A concept training curriculum for children ages two to five. Stony Brook, N.Y.: Early Intellective Development, 1978.

Palmer, F., & Siegel, R. Minimal intervention at ages two to three and subsequent intellective changes. In M. C. Day & R. Parker (Eds.), *Preschool in action.* Boston: Allyn & Bacon, 1977.

Rees, A., & Palmer, F. Factors influencing change in mental test scores. *Monographs of Developmental Psychology,* 1970, *3* (2, Pt. 2).

Sequin, E. *Idiocy and its treatment by the physiological method.* New York: Wood, 1866.

Skeels, H. M., & Dye, H. B. A study on the effects of differential stimulation on mentally retarded children. *Proceedings and Addresses of the American Association on Mental Deficiency,* 1939, *44,* 114–136

Spitz, R. A. Hospitalism: An inquiry into the genesis of psychiatric conditions in early childhood, Part I. *Psychoanalytic Study of the Child,* 1945, *1,* 53–74.

8 The Mother–Child Home Program of the Verbal Interaction Project

Phyllis Levenstein
John O'Hara
John Madden*
The Verbal Interaction Project, Inc.
Adelphi University

Introduction

The Verbal Interaction Project (VIP) turned to the family as the primary resource and home base for its preschool Mother–Child Home Program. The senior author's major interest in starting the program in 1965 was to develop a method to prevent the all-too-frequently observed school disadvantage of low-income children by tapping the rich educational potential of the mother–toddler relationship. Public education was, and is, an opportunity structure that is open to all, rich or poor. The aim of the program was to guide parents to help children escape the adult consequences of poverty by preparing them to utilize fully this valuable resource. The purpose of the research to be described was to test the program's effectiveness in preventing school disadvantage.

The Verbal Interaction Project developed the Mother–Child Home Program as a minimal intervention method to aid low-income parents to enhance the early cognitive and emotional socialization of children in their own families. In brief, the program consisted of specially trained "Toy Demonstrators" conducting weekly or semiweekly home play sessions with mother and toddler together around gifts of toys and books called Verbal Interaction Stimulus Materials (VISM). The method avoided didactic, intrusive instruction. Instead it relied upon, and aimed to strengthen, family relationships while fostering the children's intellectual ability to deal with later academic tasks. In essence, it sought to enhance the capacity of poor families to fulfill a basic function of family life.

The program's first full year of operation and research was in 1967–1968 after a year of pilot research. The program was developed into what is essentially

---
*Now at the Pennsylvania State University, York Campus

237

its present form in 1968, and it has been in operation, and under research, continuously since that time. The method was intended to support the mother (and through her, the family) in fostering the intellectual and social-emotional development of her child. A number of features of the program collectively distinguished it from contemporaneous intervention efforts. These features were that it: (1) was conducted in the home and addressed the mother and child as an interacting, mutually supportive social system; (2) actively involved the mother in one-to-one parent education without direct teaching or unrequested counseling; (3) permanently assigned toys and books as self-motivating curriculum materials that would be reliably available in the home as the focus of verbal interaction techniques; (4) demonstrated to the mother a simple, structured yet flexible curriculum of verbal interaction techniques using these toys and books; (5) used nondidactic home interveners to model curriculum techniques with the toys and books; (6) began when the child was 2 years and continued to age 4; (7) provided explicit descriptions of method and chronology; and (8) operationalized, through explicit policy and practice, a respect for families' rights by actively maintaining an awareness of their wishes and concerns and by responding to them, particularly the rights to privacy, independence, and confidentiality.

The program was kept as simple as possible. College education and prior work experience were not required of the Toy Demonstrators so that it would be possible to implement the program outside the research project with its highly motivated and highly skilled staff. In its implementation at 81 sites, almost all replications have included the program's explicit key elements and thus have demonstrated a very high degree of program integrity.

History of the Study

The program originated in 1965, when a private family service agency on Long Island (Family Service Association of Nassau County, New York) became concerned about the large high school dropout rate in a poverty area served by the agency. The senior author was consulting psychologist to the agency at the time. She agreed to develop a preschool program designed to prevent this problem and to evaluate its effectiveness by systematic research methods. An early version of the Mother–Child Home Program evolved from this, and a 1965–1966 pilot research study with 12 subjects showed positive verbal effects (Levenstein & Sunley, 1968). Based on this modest start, the first full study of the Mother–Child Home Program (MCHP) began in 1967, under the direction of the Verbal Interaction Project (VIP) created for this purpose.

The investigation of the program's effects, through formative and summative research, continued for 10 annual cohorts totaling 653 mother–child dyads during 12 years in VIP's model program and for 2000 dyads in program replications throughout the country. The first six cohorts (1967–1972) were in a quasi-experimental research design in which treatment variations were generally assigned to intact groups. The subsequent four cohorts (1973–1976) were in true experimental research designs in which individual dyads were randomly assigned to treatment variations. The 1973 shift in research design was accompanied by a focus in the study on measurement of maternal interactive behavior as a program outcome (through a videotape method to be later described).

THEORETICAL BASES AND HYPOTHESES

The program's basic assumption was that cognitive and social-emotional growth is fostered, and future educational and emotional problems prevented, by the preschooler and mother exchanging language (the symbols for events and concepts) and other positive interactions, around interesting, conceptually rich materials. (''Mother'' may be any adult who has a primary, enduring relationship with the child.) The interaction should be playful, not didactic, for maximum effect on the child and on the mother–child relationship (Clarke-Stewart, 1973, Clarke-Stewart, Vanderstoep, & Killion, 1979; White, 1963), and it should include ''the experts'' as little as possible.

The program was intended as a minimal method that enhanced the relationship of mother and child while leaving it basically intact. The importance of the spontaneous interactive element of the mother–child relationship to the child's growth was stressed by Bronfenbrenner (1974): ''In the early years of life the psychological development of the child is enhanced through his involvement in progressively more complex, enduring patterns of reciprocal, contingent interaction with persons with whom he has established a mutual and enduring attachment [p. 26].''

The program ideas were developed from an interdisciplinary network of theory and investigations concerning the often overlapping roles in the child's intellectual development of language, of sensory-motor development, of representational competence in general, of play, and of the emotional and social context of early family relationships in which these changes occur. Details of the theory may be found in Levenstein, 1975, and in Levenstein, 1977. Limitation of this space allows here only a brief acknowledgment of our profound indebtedness to the work of Brown (1958), Bruner (1964), Cassirer (1944), Hebb (1949), Hess and Shipman (1965), Hunt (1961), Sapir (1921–1962), and Vygotsky (1962).

An early home-centered intervention experiment (Irwin, 1960) demonstrated its effects on language through the mother's reading of stories to her child, thus utilizing the enhancement of mother–child interaction in its conative as well as cognitive aspects. Many mothers, particularly those of the college-educated, middle-income group, carry on such ''intervention'' spontaneously, as part of a now well-known ''hidden curriculum'' of the family. Schaefer, indeed, suggested that early, basic informal home education be given a name—"ur-Education"—and be recognized as a legitimate supplement to conventional academic education (1970).

Implicit in Schaefer's concept is the inseparability of the mother–child emotional interchange from the cognitive interaction, the intermingling of cognitive stimulation and deepening of the attachment between the mother and child. The futility of trying to separate the two factors conceptually in their deprivation consequences was demonstrated by Bronfenbrenner (1968), in his well-documented review of the effects of early deprivation on humans and animals. Six years later, in his 1974 review of early interventions, Bronfenbrenner commented about the Mother-Child Home Program: "The strategy addresses processes not in the child but in the two-person system which sustains and fosters his development. Moreover, since it is the product of mutual adaptation and learning, the system exhibits a distinctive *hand-in-glove* quality, and thereby an efficiency, that would be difficult to achieve in non-enduring relationships [p. 27]."

Research Questions

The research studies to be described in this chapter were follow-ups to early findings on the effectiveness of the MCHP. In the initial findings (Levenstein, 1970) MCHP children were reported to show IQ gains of 17 points and gains in verbal IQ of 12.2 points. Although this was very promising, two questions were raised concerning the stability and generalizability of the initial results. First, would program graduates maintain their initial gains into the school years and specifically into the educationally significant third grade (Kraus, 1973)? In addition, would these initial cognitive gains translate into normal third grade school performance? Second, would the kinds of results obtained for initial research groups hold up in more stringent research designs? The initial findings were on the outcomes from quasi-experimental research designs. The second question was directed toward the possibility of replicating those results in a series of true experimental research comparisons. A third question was also posed: Would maternal as well as child effects be demonstrated in a true experimental research design? The third, in regard to maternal effects, had been previously explored only with program mothers. The true experimental research design provided the first opportunity to raise the question for both program and control mothers.

SITE AND SAMPLE

The Verbal Interaction Project was (and is) located in Nassau County, a fast growing Long Island suburb of New York. By the 1970 census the county's population had become one of the largest in the United States, almost one and a half million persons. It was also close to being the wealthiest county in the country, having a median family income exceeded by only two others, one in Maryland and one in Virginia.

The establishment of a program for the economically disadvantaged in Nassau County seems incongruous. However, development of the Mother–Child Home Program to serve families in Nassau County filled a pressing need. Embedded within the general affluence were pockets of poverty in which the educational consequences of being poor were experienced not too differently than in the slums of inner cities. These poverty pockets stood out on county census maps that contained census tracts color-coded to show family income level. The average family income for the three tracts was $9709, as compared to $37,896 for the three richest census tracts a few miles away. The poorest tracts also contained the largest number of families living at or below the poverty level. These tracts and these families were the target of the Mother–Child Home Program.

As expected, the schools within the poverty areas showed high rates of children suffering from educational disadvantage that became more evident as the children progressed through the primary grades. Preventive preschool programs were badly needed, along with hard research data documenting program effectiveness. The Verbal Interaction Project responded to that need with the development and research of the Mother-Child Home Program.

Sample Selection and Assignment Procedure

The basic sample selection criteria, although there were some minor variations from year to year, were: (1) eligibility for low income housing; (2) residence in rented housing; (3) occupation less than skilled; (4) neither parent with an education above high school; and (5) child's testability in English. Most participants were black, reflecting black overrepresentation in these poverty areas.

The specific recruiting techniques used to identify potential subjects and assignment procedures varied from 1967 to 1978. In early years (programs begun in 1967–1972) many dyads resided in low-income housing projects. Initially, they were recruited by letter when the children were 2 and 3 years of age. This was followed by door-to-door canvasing in low-income housing projects. After 1968, many lived outside of the housing projects. The research from 1967 to 1972 followed quasi-experimental research designs in which random assignment was used to designate areas as experimental or comparison. Individual subjects were recruited for either treatment or comparison groups, with the stipulation that *within* a specific housing project both treatment and comparison dyads would not be recruited; this step was taken to avoid potential diffusion of treatment to comparison dyads. Entry age requirements were broad enough to allow siblings to be included in some of the quasi-experimental groups. The younger siblings were excluded from all analyses to satisfy assumptions of independence of observations in the analyses. For dyads entering from 1973 to 1976, dyads were randomly assigned to treatment or control status. Potential participants were identified from referrals by public and private agencies, private individuals and from school census lists.

Through the years several treatment variations have been used and are described later. The reader might wish to consult the overview presented in Table 8.1.

TABLE 8.1
Description of Treatment and Control Groups by
General Design and Entry Year

Group Name and Treatment Identification[a]	Entry Year	Treatment Type
Quasi-experimental groups		
One-Year Treatment Groups		
Group 1: T67-I	1967	Program I only
Group 2: T67-I + Short II	1967	Program I and a very short version of Program II
Group 3: T67-C_1 + I	1967	Program I preceded by a placebo treatment
Two-Year Treatment Groups		
Group 4: T68-I + II	1968	Program I and Program II
Group 5: T69-I + II	1969	Program I and Program II
Group 6: T70-I + IID	1970	Program I and Program II with fewer home visits
Control Groups		
Group 7: C_2-67	1967	A test only comparison group
Group 8: C_4-67	1967	A test only comparison group
Group 9: C_5-72	1972	A test only comparison group
True experimental groups		
Group 10: T73-I + II	1973	Program I and Program II
Group 11: C73	1973	A test only control group
Group 12: T74-I + II	1974	Program I and Program II
Group 13: T74-VO I + II	1974	Program I and Program II but VISM Only (VO) - no home sessions
Group 14: T75-I + II	1975	Program I and Program II
Group 15: C75	1975	A test only control group
Group 16: T76-I + II	1976	Program I and Program II
Group 17: C76	1976	A test only control group

[a] Treatment Identifications are abbreviations which have three components: (1) identification as a treatment or control group, by the letters "T" or "C" respectively, (2) entry year—the years of 1967 through 1976 are represented by "67" through "76", and (3) treatment received (for treated groups only) where "I" means Program I, "II" means Program II, "D" means drop in the number of home visits, "VO" means VISM only were given with no home visits.

Quasi-Experimental Designs

Between 1967 and 1972, variations of a basic 1-year and of a basic 2-year program were followed. In addition, several comparison groups were tested. The reader interested in more specific detail is referred to Madden, Levenstein, and Levenstein (1976).

One-Year Treatment Groups. Three groups that entered in 1967 received variations of a 1-year program. In Group 1, the child was 3 years old at entry, and participated in the MCHP for one year only (Program I). In Group 2, the child was age 2 at entry, and was given Program I plus a short version of Program II (the second program year) lasting about 9 instead of 46 home sessions. These two groups were recruited from the same housing project in a location here referred to as Area A. Group 3, recruited when the children were 2 or 3 years old, received a placebo treatment consisting of home visits and non-VISM gifts for 1 year and then received Program I in the second year. This group was recruited from a housing project in what is referred to here as Area B.

Two-Year Treatment Groups. Three groups, entering in 1968 through 1970, received variations of the full MCHP. Children in all three groups were 2 years old at entry. Group 4, entering in 1968 from housing projects in Areas A and B, received both Program I and Program II. Group 5, entering in 1969 from projects in Areas A and B as well as from nonproject residences, also received the full program. Group 6, which entered in 1970 and was recruited from project and nonproject residences in Areas A and B, received Program I and a version of Program II in which home visits were reduced from twice to once weekly.

Comparison Groups. There were three comparison groups in the quasi-experiments. Group 7, entering in 1967 and recruited from census Area C, included 2- and 3-year-old children. Another group of 4-year-olds (Group 8) was recruited from Area A in 1967. Group 9 was recruited in 1972 when the children were 6 years by applying program selection criteria to the first grade of a school in Area A.

True Experimental Designs

In research conducted from 1973 to 1975 (four cohorts) the full MCHP was contrasted with various comparison treatments. Each year a factorial design was used to control for important demographic variables such as sex and sampling site. The purpose of this procedure was to balance these variables across treatment conditions. From 1973 to 1975, dyads were individually recruited for a "lottery" whose alternatives were the MCHP or some other services described later. In 1973, 1975 and 1976, the groups receiving the full MCHP (Groups 10, 14, and 16) were compared with control groups (Groups 11, 15, and 17) that received only an evaluation service. In 1974, Group 13 was a comparison treatment: a VISM-only program in which the toys and books were delivered on a regular schedule without home sessions during the 2 years. This group was compared with Group 12 receiving the full MCHP in 1974.

The four cohorts were recruited from four new locations in Long Island, referred to here as Areas W, X, Y, and Z. The 1973 cohort was selected from Area W, the 1975 cohort from Area X, the 1974 cohort from both Areas W and X, and the 1976 cohort from all four areas.

The 1976 research design was intended to eliminate reactive effects of the dyads' knowledge that they were participating in an educational experiment. All families were initially recruited for our "Early Screening Program" consisting of a series of vision, speech, and hearing tests as well as a developmental screening that included IQ testing. The MCHP was not mentioned at this point. Eligible families were then contacted by a letter from the Nassau County Department of Social Service requesting permission to give their names to the VIP's sponsor at the time, the Family Service Association. This procedure did not produce enough prospective program participants, so, in addition, dyads were recruited from the same sources used in earlier years.

In all four years, dyads were randomly assigned to MCHP or control conditions. However, except for the 1974 Control Group, the evaluations were the only intervention for the control dyads. In all years except 1975, children were pretested on standardized IQ tests.

Demographics of Sample

Tables 8.2 and 8.3 present demographic data for all MCHP and comparison groups. The groups are labeled by their treatment identifications to provide continuity with outcome analyses described later. The variables presented are those usually associated with low-income status. Because of major design differences between quasi and true experimental years, the data are separated by design type, with Table 8.2 for quasi-experimental groups and Table 8.3 for true experimental cohorts. In quasi-experimental years, subject groups are organized by treatment variations. In true experimental years, subject groups are organized by entry year, because in each year subjects were randomly assigned to one of two groups, usually one program and one control (except in 1974, when two treatment variations were used). The demographic data on both Tables 8.2 and 8.3 pertain to data only for those subjects available for outcome analyses. For the quasi-experimental groups, it was for subjects available for third grade follow-up. For the true experimental data, it was for those subjects available for testing immediately after Program II (when the children were approximately 4 years). This was done to provide continuity with outcome analyses. The figures are presumed to be fairly representative of the original total samples; attrition analy-

TABLE 8.2
Demographic Characteristics for Quasi-Experimental Program
and Comparison Families

		Child		Father			Mother		Family
	N	Age at Entry (Years)	% Male	Years of School	% Occup. 6 or 7[a]	% Always Present	Years of School	% Rec'd. Welfare	Number of Children
				One-Year Treatment Groups					
Group 1	9	3	33.3	9.9	88.9	66.7	10.5	22.2	1.4
Group 2	10	2	50.0	9.8	100.0	80.0	11.6	33.3	2.7
Group 3	7	2 + 3	85.7	9.8 (5)	85.7	71.4	10.4	14.3	2.7
				Two-Year Treatment Groups					
Group 4	14	2	28.6	11.0	64.3	50.0	10.6	57.1	1.7
Group 5	18	2	50.1	9.4	61.1	61.1	9.5	50.0	1.8
Group 6	21	2	59.1	9.3	77.3	77.3	10.3	22.7	2.1
				Comparison Groups					
Group 7	12	2 + 3	75.0	10.3	75.0	91.7	11.3	8.3	2.1
Group 8	10	4	50.0	10.3 (9)	71.4 (7)	20.0	10.6	60.0	3.4
Group 9	27	6	48.1	9.6 (18)	100.0 (9)	25.9	10.2	80.0 (25)	3.0

Note: The N is not the N at entry but the N as of follow-up testing when child was in third grade.
Descriptive statistics are presented only for these Ss since outcome analyses are reported for
these Ss. The numbers in parentheses are the number of cases for which data were available
when the N was not that of the total follow-up N listed in the first column.

[a] Hollingshead scales 6 or 7 (unemployed, unskilled, semi-skilled); these figures include available data
for absent fathers not meeting occupational criteria for entry into the program. Occupational levels
of *absent* fathers above semi-skilled did not keep dyads from eligibility.

ses performed comparing subjects who dropped out of the study with those
retained in the study have provided no good evidence that attrition acted to create
differences between study groups.

Most of the group means and proportions for Table 8.2 demographic items are
as expected for a low-income sample. The average level of father's education
was below high school graduation, from mid-ninth to mid-eleventh grades, but
higher than that sometimes reported for poverty groups (Klaus & Gray, 1968).
Most fathers in the sample were in low-status occupations (unskilled or semi-
skilled) or were unemployed. This was the pattern for all groups, but it was less
true for the 2-year group than for others, which raises a question of group
equivalence on this variable. Two-thirds of the fathers in the total sample were
living in the home, but here there was wide variation among the groups; for
instance, within the comparison groups there was a range of 20% to 92%.

The average level of mother's education was a little higher than that of fathers

TABLE 8.3

Demographic Characteristics of True Experimental Program and Control Families

Group	N	Child		Father			Mother		Family
		Age at Entry (Months)	% Male	Years of School	% Occup. 6 or 7[a]	% Always Present	Years of School	% Rec'd. Welfare	No. of Children
Group 10 (Program)	18	26.4	56	9.1 (16)	62.5	33	10.1	83	3.3
Group 11 (Control)	16	25.8	56	11.2 (13)	69.2	33 (15)	10.9	62	2.2
Group 12 (Program)	22	25.5	50	10.7 (21)	58.8	36	11.4	68	3.0
Group 13 (VISM only)	26	24.7	50	11.5 (21)	71.4	27	10.8 (25)	69	2.9
Group 14 (Program)	17	26.6	35	11.7 (15)	88.2	59	11.4	53	2.2
Group 15 (Control)	12	24.8	58	10.1 (9)	85.5	58	11.4	50	1.8
Group 16 (Program)	29	25.3	45	11.3 (22)	61.9 (21)	24	11.2	66	1.9
Group 17 (Control)	26	26.4	38	11.3 (19)	82.3 (17)	15	11.3	69	1.7

Note: The N listed is not the N at entry but the N as of post-testing. Descriptive data are presented only for these Ss since outcome analyses are reported for these Ss. The numbers in parentheses are the number of cases for which data were available when the N was not that of the total follow-up N listed in the first column.

[a] Hollingshead scales 6 or 7 (unemployed, unskilled, semi-skilled); these figures include available data for absent fathers not meeting occupational levels of *absent* fathers above semi-skilled did not keep dyads from eligibility.

and ranged from ninth to eleventh grade. About one-third of the mothers in the total sample were receiving welfare aid, but there was great variation among the groups, ranging from 7% to 80% of mothers on welfare. The proportion of mothers receiving welfare in every group was roughly similar to the proportion of fathers absent from the home.

Some preexisting group differences appear in Table 8.2, apart from the treatments. Group 9 was consistently lower than the other groups on demographic variables.

On Table 8.3, the true experimental groups appear quite similar demographically. The main differences appear to be associated with year rather than treatment status (e.g., the number of children in the family seems to drop from 1973 to 1976, perhaps due to the decreasing age of the participating mothers). Within each entry year, groups seem quite similar, with few exceptions. In 1973, the treatment group contained mothers and fathers with slightly less education than the control group. The group was slightly higher in the proportion of welfare recipients and in number of children. None of the differences were statistically significant.

Subject Location and Retrieval

All located children who had been in the cohorts under investigation were included in the follow-up evaluations, even if they had received less than their full intended treatment. In the immediate postprogram evaluation, 77% of the MCHP dyads and 73% of the comparison dyads across all groups were available for testing, representing fairly low attrition rates. The 1975 cohort demonstrated an unuaually high level of attrition (50% in the control group) and indications of bias in the reasons for attrition. In the third-grade follow-up, the Verbal Interaction Project was successful in retrieving 83% of the dyads who had initially entered the project as MCHP dyads and 86% of comparison group participants. The most frequent reason that dyads were unavailable was that they had moved, although a few dyads refused to participate in posttesting.

Location of families who had moved was often difficult. Relatives, neighbors, schools, post offices, and other resources were enlisted in the search. Fortunately for the follow-up, although perhaps not for the families, the moves were usually within a relatively narrow geographical range, from one poverty area in Nassau County to another. Mothers almost always cooperated in giving written permission to allow schools to release information about their children and providing written permission for the children to be driven to the VIP office for follow-up evaluation.

Immediately after a child's evaluation, the mother was informed of her child's developmental progress. Few children demonstrated problems; however, mothers of those who did were given information about community resources and concrete help in seeking the latter, regardless of their program or control status.

DESIGN OF STUDY

Program Treatment: The Mother–Child Home Program

The Mother–Child Home Program (MCHP) is based in the child's home, with twice-weekly, half-hour home sessions over 2 school years. Usually the child's starting age is two. The number of sessions is geared to the mother's needs, with a maximum of 46 per year. Home visitors ("Toy Demonstrators") model techniques for the mother from a structured curriculum and involve the mother and child together in play. Materials consist of 12 books and 11 toys (VISM) given to the child each year in weekly installments. The cognitive curriculum is broken down into a Guide Sheet for each. The Guide Sheet is intended for the Toy Demonstrator, but it may also be used by the mother. All Guide Sheets list the same core concepts (e.g., colors, shapes) and related behaviors (e.g., matching, imaging), but examples of each from the related book or toy are given to encourage the adult to devise more examples of her own. The books and toys (chosen on 37 specific criteria, of high quality, and commercially available) and the Guide Sheets are progressively more complex.

The Toy Demonstrators are women, paid or volunteer. They need no work experience or education beyond high school. They learn their program skills from a program director with a college degree in an initial eight-session training workshop, which is followed by weekly meetings and individual supervisory conferences. After involving the mother early in the home session, they gradually fade into the background; the mother is free to adopt the modeled behavior, or not, as she wishes. The Toy Demonstrators may not directly teach or counsel the mother.

The 46 home sessions during each year roughly follow the local school calendar for both Program I (first year) and Program II (second year), for a total of about 23 hours of the dyad's time with a Toy Demonstrator each year, aside from the time mothers might spend outside of the sessions playing and reading with their children each day (activities suggested to the mothers but not stressed).

The two broad aims of the theory-based curriculum are parent education and children's cognitive–socioemotional preparation for the school experience. The goals are both cognitive and affective: (1) to enhance the mother's parenting skills and self-esteem; and (2) to foster the conceptual development of the child, along with the growth of his or her psychosocial skills.

The many concrete details of the program have been described elsewhere (Levenstein, 1975). The reader is referred to this source for such specific aspects as the program's written cognitive and affective curriculum; the experience, training, and activities of required program personnel, including the supervision of Toy Demonstrators; the choice of curriculum materials; and the involvement of parents.

Partly because MCHP details have been made explicit in articles and in program manuals, almost all of the 81 MCHP replications have demonstrated close, well-documented fidelity to the model program. This program integrity may also be attributed to the VIP's formal system of aiding MCHP implementation in local sites. The system's training and supervisory procedures include films, videotapes, and more than 100 different technical materials distributed and explained at training institutes.

Data Collection Procedures

Formative Research

The rate of 1973–1976 mothers' accepting participation in the true experiments "lotteries" (taking a chance on receiving the program) was dramatically lower than 1967–1972 mothers' acceptance of a direct invitation into the program. An average of only 48% of mothers in the four true experimental cohorts were willing to join in a subject pool, knowing that there would be later randomization into MCHP or non-MCHP groups of subjects; 85% accepted a quasi-experimental treatment.

Anecdotal and quantitative data demonstrated the enthusiastic acceptance of the Mother–Child Home Program by both children and mothers assigned randomly into MCHP treatment. The children's enthusiasm was reported informally to be a regular feature of home sessions. Both kinds of data also attested to the program's popularity with mothers. For example, when offered the MCHP, almost 100% of mothers in each cohort accepted it. Further, in each of the program's 2 years only about 15% of appointments were not kept. Attrition of subjects—usually caused by families moving out of the area, or mothers' prohibitive work hours—was about 15% during the first program year and 25% by the end of 2 years.

Close monitoring of program delivery facilitated the early detection and correction of drift away from the MCHP's intended method. Extensive qualitative and quantitative data on the method's operationalization documented that program integrity was maintained in every year of model program operation. It included features that remain unique to the MCHP, in spite of the proliferation of home-based early childhood programs since the program's full inception in 1967: the requirement for home visitors' modeling techniques rather than direct teaching or counseling; the gifts of curriculum materials (carefully selected toys and books); a written method and curriculum; and explicit safeguards against the program's own possible intrusiveness into families.

Summative Research

Summative evaluations provided the data for judging the short- and long-term effectiveness of the Mother–Child Home Program. Although data collection for specific groups varied, the data reported here were collected approximately at these times: (1) pretest for all groups when the children were about 2 years old; (2) immediately postprogram, when children were almost 4 years old for true experimental groups; and (3) follow-up, when children were about 8 years old and in third grade (quasi-experimental groups).

At pretest, all mothers were interviewed to acquire demographic data. A standard interview form developed at the VIP was used for this purpose. In the true experimental groups, except for Groups 14 and 15, the Cattell Infant Scale of Intelligence and the Peabody Picture Vocabulary Test (PPVT) were administered to the children.

True Experimental Groups.   At postprogram testing, the intelligence of children was again tested on the Stanford–Binet. In all groups, except Groups 16 and 17, PPVT IQ was also obtained. Parenting skills of mothers in Groups 12 to 17 were rated on an instrument called the Maternal Interactive Behavior Scale (MIB). The scale was developed at the VIP and consists of ratings on 10 categories of maternal interactive behavior based on a 10-minute videotaped play session. Rating categories included maternal interactive behavior such as: (1) gives label information; (2) verbalizes actions; (3) stimulates divergent use of toy; (4) questions or solicits information other than "yes" or "no", and (5) does not reply to child's vocalizations. Videotaping was done at the project office as part of the posttesting procedure.

Quasi-Experimental Groups.   At third-grade follow-up children were assessed on intellectual, cognitive, and social-emotional skills. Intelligence was measured via the Wechsler Intelligence Scale for Children (WISC) for all groups. Reading and arithmetic achievement skills were measured on the Wide Range Achievement Test (WRAT) for all groups except comparison Group 9.

Social-emotional skills were measured on a VIP-developed instrument called the Child Behavior Traits (CBT), which was completed by the child's teacher in the spring of third grade. Teachers were blind to children's treatment status. Examples of CBT information concerned whether the child was well organized in work and play, tolerated necessary frustration, accepted or asked for help when necessary, and refrained from physically aggressive behavior toward others. The CBT also provided a wide range of data on school performance, yielding indices of academic problems, grade failure, and special class placement based on third grade performance. CBT socioemotional data were available for all groups except comparison Groups 8 and 9. Information on academic problems was available for Groups 4, 5, 6, and 9. Indications of special class placement and grade failure were available for all groups except 1 and 8.

Data Collection Procedures for Summative Research

Data were collected in three ways: by VIP staff at the VIP office, in the dyad's home, and by the child's teacher at school. All cognitive testing, including general and verbal intelligence measures and achievement testing, was done at the VIP office by experienced testers who were blind to the child's treatment status. All dyads were transported to and from the office by VIP staff.

In addition to cognitive evaluation, the Maternal Interactive Behavior (MIB) videotape session also took place at the VIP in a room set up for that purpose. The setting for the videotaping was a rather bare playroom furnished with a child's table and two chairs for mother and child, toys on the table, and a videotape camera in one corner operated by cable. The recorder operated and monitored the taping in a room next to the playroom to reduce reactive effects of the procedure. The only instructions given to the mother regarding what she should do during the session were "(child's name) may play with the toys and you may help in any way you like." She was not given any explicit instructions on how to intereact with her child.

Overall Approach to Data Analyses

Group comparisons reported here are based on treatment assigned and intended rather than treatment actually received. Families who received much less than the amount of treatment intended are included in the analyses.

The analysis strategy was different for quasi-experimental groups than for the true experimental groups. The purpose of the analyses of quasi-experimental data was to test the long-term effectiveness of the MCHP. The groups were organized into three treatment levels according to the amount of treatment they received (2, 1, or no years of MCHP). Because groups within treatment levels were distinct, often starting in different years and receiving variations in treatment, they were not simply combined for analysis purposes. Instead, groups were contrasted with all 1-year treatment groups and with all 2-year treatment groups in hierarchical analyses of variance. Control Group 9 was omitted from some data analyses because its demographic status seemed low enough to put it at an unfair disadvantage in comparison with program groups and because comparable measurement points were not available for all variables. This was a conservative approach, especially when it is noted that Group 7 was included in the analyses even though its demographic status was higher than that of program groups. The quasi-experimental program/control comparisons were performed to see whether or not the preliminary substantial short-term effects of the MCHP, reported by Levenstein (1970), had been sustained into third grade.

The purpose of the analyses of true experimental data was to see if earlier results could be replicated within a more stringent research design. An added purpose of the true experimental analyses was to test the effects of the MCHP on parenting skills, using the MIB instrument. Such data were not available for earlier groups. For true experimental years, analyses of variance and covariance provided comparisons between MCHP and control groups in 1973, 1975, and 1976. In 1974 the comparison was between two forms of treatment.

FINDINGS

Long-Term Results Based on Quasi-Experimentsl Data

IQ had been a primary outcome measure in earlier analyses (Levenstein, 1970). The program's ultimate goal was not to change IQ but to prevent school problems, so actual school performance was of chief interest. In follow-up "actual school performance" was operationalized into the following outcome measures: (1) reading and arithmetic achievement; (2) evidence of classroom social-emotional competence; (3) teacher evaluations of academic problems; (4) indices of grade failure; and (5) indices of special class placement. IQ was also an outcome measure at follow-up. Each of the variables is discussed in the following, and all are presented in Table 8.4.

Intellectual Development: IQ Scores.   WISC IQ scores were analyzed in a hierarchical ANOVA, the acronym for analysis of variance (Kirk, 1968) comparing 2 years of treatment (Groups 4, 5, and 6) with 1 year of treatment (Groups 1, 2, and 3) and no treatment (Groups 7 and 8).

The combined mean IQ for the 2-year treatment groups was 100.17 and the mean IQ for the 1-year treatment groups was 100.12. The mean IQ for the control groups was 96.41. The differences between groups receiving the same kind of treatment were small enough to permit pooling of group variance with within-cell variance. The treatment effect in this analysis was not statistically significant, F (2,98) = .96. Thus the almost 4-point superiority of MCHP groups over control groups can not be interpreted as a program effect. Further, this finding suggests that initial postprogram significant IQ effects (Levenstein, 1970) did not extend to third grade. As stated previously, the 1972 control group, Group 9, was omitted from the analysis. (However, if it had been included, the combined mean of control groups would have been 95.02 and the approximately 5-point difference between treated and control groups would have been statistically significant).

WRAT Reading Achievement.   The same statistical approach used to test IQ effects was used in tests of Wide Range Achievement Test results. The combined mean reading achievement for the 2-year MCHP groups was 99.87 and for 1-year groups was 95.81. The combined mean for the control groups (again excluding Group 9) was 90.18. The effect of treatment was statistically significant whether error terms were pooled ($F(2, 98) = 4.71, p < .05$) or not pooled (F (2, 5) = 7.47, $p < .05$).

The data show an influence of length of treatment, with the mean for 1 year of treatment being 5.63 points higher than the control groups and the mean for 2 years of treatment being 9.79 points higher. Furthermore, the mean of 99.87 for the 2-year treatment groups meets the national mean of 100 on this subtest

(Schaie & Roberts, 1970), whereas the mean of the control groups was almost 10 points lower than the national mean.

WRAT Arithmetic Achievement.   For arithmetic achievement, the mean for combined 2-year treatment groups was 101.91 and the mean for 1-year treatment groups was 95.23. The control groups had a mean of 91.64. The treatment effect was significant whether error terms were pooled (F (2, 98) = 6.89, $p < .01$), or not ($F(2, 5) = 8.49, p < .05$).

The mean for 2-year treatment groups was 10.27 points higher than that for the control groups and slightly higher than the national mean of 100 on this subtest (Schaie & Roberts, 1970). Again, the mean for 1-year treatment groups was between the other two groups.

CBT Classroom Social-Emotional Competence.   Again, a hierarchical ANOVA was used to test teacher ratings of social-emotional competence. The control group mean for this analysis, however, was based only on Group 7 and 58.25. The 2-year MCHP groups had a mean of 63.27 and the 1-year MCHP groups a mean of 61.68. Although the MCHP groups scored higher than the control group on this measure, indicating better social-emotional competence, the treatment effect was not statistically significant ($F(4, 81) = 1.33$). Hence the null hypothesis (of no treatment effects) could not be rejected.

Teacher Ratings of Academic Competence.   In addition to social-emotional competence, third-grade teachers also rated children on three measures of academic competence: (1) presence of severe academic problems; (2) special class placement; and (3) grade failure. These data are also presented in Table 8.4. The estimation of program effects on these variables was complicated by several factors. Missing data was a severe problem. Although a full set of data was available for the 2-year treatment groups, data were available for only two of the three 1-year treatment groups and for only two of the three variables for these groups (see Table 8.4). No data were available on severe academic problems. Missing data was even more of a problem in the control groups. No data were available for Group 8, and for Group 7 no data on severe academic problems were obtained. Thus very little data were available for the principal control groups in testing treatment effects. A full set of data were obtained for Group 9, the control group eliminated from most of the analyses described thus far, for reasons previously discussed. Another problem complicating these comparisons was the considerable variation of groups within treatment classifications (e.g., ratings of the percentage of children with severe academic problems range from 14% to 32% in the 2-year MCHP groups). Hence combining data across treatment classifications must be regarded with caution.

To obtain some estimate of treatment effects, chi-square analyses were performed comparing the proportions of subjects in each treatment level (2-year, 1-

TABLE 8.4

Mean (or %) Cognitive, Academic, and Socioemotional Scores for
Quasi-Experimental Program and Control Children in Third Grade

Group	N	WISC IQ	WRAT Reading	WRAT Arithmetic	CBT Socioemotional	Severe Academic Problems	Special Class Placement	School Grade Failure
Two-Year Treatment Groups								
Group 4	14	102.79	101.29	100.21	70.36	14%	14%	8% (N = 13)
Group 5	18	98.39	97.33	99.72	62.23 (N = 16)	32% (N = 19)	11% (N = 19)	11% (N = 19)
Group 6	21	99.95	101.10	104.90	59.33	29%	10%	10%
Combined: Two-Year Treatment	53	100.17	99.87	101.91	63.27 (N = 51)	26% (N = 54)	11% (N = 54)	9%
One-Year Treatment Groups								
Group 1	9	96.67	91.56	91.22	61.78	—[a]	—	—
Group 2	10	97.70	99.60	98.30	67.10	—	0%	20%

Group 3	7	108.00	95.86	96.00	52.50 (N = 6)	—	—	17% (N = 6%)	50% (N = 6)
Combined: One-Year Treatment	26	100.12	95.81	95.23	61.68 (N = 25)	—	—	6% (N = 16)	31% (N = 16)
Control Groups								
Group 7	12	96.50	89.42	91.83	58.25	—	—	38% (N = 13)	15% (N = 13)
Group 8	10	96.30	91.10	91.40	—	—	—	—	—
Group 9	27	93.89	0	0	—	48% (N = 27)	7% (N = 27)	37% (N = 27)
Combined: Control (excluding Group 9)	22	96.41	90.18	91.64	—	—	—	38% (N = 13)	15% (N = 13)
Combined: Control (excluding Group 9)	49	95.02	—	—	—	48% (N = 27)	18% (N = 40)	40% (N = 40)

[a] A dash (–) indicates that no data were available for that group.

year, control) rated as having severe academic problems, as being placed in a special class and as having failed a grade. Group 9 was included in these analyses, with full knowledge of the problems introduced, to provide some control comparison for severe academic problems and so that comparisons on the other two variables would not be limited to one control group (Group 7).

For teacher ratings of *severe academic problems,* the difference between the combined 2-year treatment groups and the control group (26% vs. 48%) was statistically significant [χ^2 (1) = 4.0, p < .05]. The difference seems to be real in that the highest percentage so rated of any single 2-year treatment group was 32%, far below the 48% of the control group (see Table 8.4).

Comparisons for proportions of *special class placement* (at any time) were among 2 years of treatment, 1 year of treatment, and control groups (11%, 6%, and 18% respectively). There were no significant differences among these proportions [χ^2 (2) = 1.56, p < .05], although control group 7 was much higher in special class placement with 38%. All other groups were considerably lower than that.

Finally, in terms of *grade failure* (at any time) the comparisons were again between three levels of treatment. The 2-year treatment groups had 9% grade failure compared to 31% in the 1-year treatment groups and 30% in the control groups. The difference was statistically significant [χ^2 (2) = 7.42, p < .05]. Although significant this difference must be regarded with caution because there was considerable within-treatment classification differences, particularly in the 1-year treatment and the control groups (see Table 8.4).

In sum, teacher ratings of academic competence revealed a significant effect of the 2-year program on several academic problems and on grade failures, but no difference in special class placement. These results must be considered suggestive, because Group 9 was included in these analyses, and there were considerable within-treatment classification differences.

Short-Term Results Based on True Experimental Data

Tests for replication of initial MCHP effects with true experimental designs sought comparisons between groups on Stanford–Binet and PPVT IQ for children and on maternal interactive behavior. For these true experiments, comparisons between groups were generally kept within each entry year, because these subjects were randomly assigned to MCHP and control groups in 1973, 1975, and 1976 and to two forms of treatment in 1974. These data are presented in Table 8.5.

Stanford–Binet IQ.   IQ analyses were divided into three sets of comparisons. In the first set the 1973 and 1976 comparisons were between MCHP children (Groups 10 and 16) and no-treatment controls (Groups 11 and 17), where pretest Cattell IQs were available as covariates for all subjects. In the

TABLE 8.5
Mean General IQ, Verbal IQ, and Maternal Interactive Behavior
Scores for True Experimental Program and Control Groups
Immediately Post-Program

Group	N	Stanford-Binet IQ	PPVT IQ	MIB
1973 Cohort				
Group 10 (Program)	18	102.8	88.17	_[a]
Group 11 (Control)	16	101.1	87.63	–
1974 Cohort				
Group 12 (Program)	22	103.2	90.55	323
Group 13 (VISM only)	26	105.3	92.04	216 (N = 25)
1975 Cohort				
Group 14 (Program)	17	101.3	96.59	252
Group 15 (Control)	12	108.3	94.50	178 (N = 9)
1976 Cohort				
Group 16 (Program)	29	107.0	–	267 (N = 25)
Group 17 (Control)	26	101.1	–	156 (N = 23)

Note. All figures are based on the column *N* unless otherwise specified.
[a] A dash (–) indicates that no data were available for that group.

second analysis, the 1975 MCHP children (Group 14) were compared with no-treatment controls (Group 15) where no pretest IQ was available. In the third analysis of the 1974 cohort, two alternate treatment forms were compared, a full 2-year version of the MCHP (Group 12) and a VISM-only treatment (Group 13), which had toys and books without home sessions.

The first analysis of Groups 10 and 16 versus Groups 11 and 17 was a two factor analysis of covariance, with entry year and treatment as the independent variables. The covariate, used to partially correct for pretreatment group differences and for attrition, was pretest Cattell IQ scores, adjusted for age because Cattell and age were correlated. The effect of treatment was significant [F (1, 84) = 4.92, $p < .05$] with a mean difference of 5 points in favor of the MCHP children. The effect of entry year and the interaction of that variable with year were not significant.

The ANOVA for the 1975 cohort (Group 14 versus Group 15) failed to reveal any significant effect of treatment although the mean difference was in favor of the control group. However, the unavilability of pretest IQ scores prevented correction for the effects of attrition that was unusually high in the cohort, almost 36% overall and 50% from the control group.

There was also no difference between the full MCHP (Group 12) and the VISM-only treatment (Group 13) in the 1974 cohort's analysis of covariance. Again age-adjusted Cattell IQs were used as the covariate.

PPVT IQ.   PPVT scores were available at pretest and posttest for the 1973 and 1974 cohorts and at posttest only for the 1975 cohort. Because each year represents somewhat different comparisons, each was treated separately. For the 1973 comparison, an analysis of covariance failed to reveal any treatment effects. Similarly for the 1974 comparison no significant effects were observed. For the 1974 comparison, there was an interaction between treatment and area of residence such that the treatment effect was larger in one area than another. PPVT scores for full MCHP children were slightly higher than those for VISM-only children.

Maternal Interactive Behavior.   MIB data were available for the groups entering in 1974, 1975, and 1976. For the purposes of these analyses, total scores were used as dependent measures. The score was the sum of nine positive items of maternal interactive behavior minus one negative item. Total MIB scores are presented in Table 8.5. Higher means represent more positive maternal interactive behavior.

For tests of MCHP effect on maternal interactive behavior, all three cohorts provide a treatment-control comparison, because the 1974 VISM-only group did not have interactive behavior modeled for them by Toy Demonstrators. The 1975 and 1976 cohorts had actual no-treatment control groups.

Tests of treatment effects using ANOVA in the 1974 cohort (Group 12 versus 13) did reveal an overall significant effect for treatment [$F(1, 36) = 12.17$, $p < .01$]. The full MCHP group's mean MIB total score was 107 points higher than the mean for the group that received VISM only (see Table 8.5). In the 1975 cohort (Group 14 versus 15), the 74 point difference between MCHP and control mothers was not statistically significant [$F(1, 14) = 3.38$, $p < .10$]. However, as with IQ analyses, high attrition makes this finding difficult to interpret. For the 1976 cohort (Group 16 versus 17) the 111 point difference between MCHP and control mothers was statistically significant [$F(1, 14) = 3.38$, $p < .10$]. However, as with IQ analyses, high attrition makes this finding difficult to interpret. For the 1976 cohort (Group 16 versus 17) the 111 point difference between MCHP and control mothers was statistically significant [$F(1, 44) = 14.61$, $p < .01$].

Thus in two out of three cohorts, participation in the MCHP significantly increased positive maternal interactive behavior. In the third cohort, differences were in the expected direction but failed to reach statistical significance.

MIB scores were relatively uncorrelated with children's IQs ($r = .11$). Thus, IQ effects do not seem to be mediated by the maternal behaviors measured by the MIB. The lack of relationship may, in part, be due to the fact that both IQ and

MIB were measured immediately postprogram. Therefore, recently changed maternal skills may not have had the opportunity to influence child competencies yet. Only follow-ups of mother–child dyads will answer this question. The VIP is currently engaged in such follow-ups.

OVERALL SUMMARY AND MEANING OF FINDINGS

The purpose of the research described in this chapter was to study the effects of the Mother–Child Home Program developed by the Verbal Interaction Project. Altogether, the investigation has covered 12 years. The complete data included 328 children and their mothers in 10 annual cohorts. The research designs were quasi-experimental for the first six cohorts (entering from 1967 to 1972) and experimental for the last four cohorts (entering from 1973 to 1976). It assessed the short-term effects of the program and—even more important—its long-range effects into the school years.

One of the more striking findings of the research is that, in the quasi-experimental data, reading and math achievement scores seem to be a linear function of the amount of treatment received, as had been IQ at age 5 (Madden, Levenstein, & Levenstein, 1976). The available evidence also suggested that advancement in school grades and teachers' judgment regarding the presence of severe academic problems were also related to MCHP participation. These two latter comparisons required the use of a control group (Group 9) that may not have been demographically comparable to other groups. This problem was not present in the achievement test comparisons. In all of these relatively direct measures of one of the original program goals—reduction of school disadvantage—the results are statistically and educationally significant.

Early postprogram IQ scores had initially been used to predict these criteria, yet WISC IQ differences among the groups at third grade were not significant. What seems to have occurred here is the "fade-out" of IQ effects described by Campbell and Frey (1970); but what they did not predict, effects on school-related behavior, seem to have taken the place of these diminished IQ effects. On closer inspection, it may be inappropriate to speak of "fade-out" or even to test for its presence because the "fade-out" refers to a difference between Stanford–Binet at age 4 and WISC at age 8. The results do indicate that IQ differences at age 4 predicted achievement test differences and, probably, better performance in school at age 8, according to both teachers' and administrative criteria. Thus, the quasi-experimental data provide direct evidence of success in meeting program aims of reducing school disadvantage.

The primary weakness of the quasi-experiment was that program variations were delivered to intact groups, making it difficult to determine whether the results were a consequence of preexisting group differences. Table 8.2 does indicate some group differences on demographic variables, but, with the exception of Group 9, these differences did not vary systematically with treatments or with differences in outcomes. Thus, the data do not suggest any plausible reason for differences in outcomes other than differences in treatments received. (See Madden, Levenstein & Levenstein, 1976, for further evidence on this point.) On the other hand, confident assertion that the effects resulted from the program requires a way of estimating what the results would have been had the treated groups not received the MCHP. To increase this confidence and to obtain a better knowledge of the immediate effects of the MCHP, the true field experiments were conducted.

Based on analyses of the experimental cohorts entering the program between 1973 and 1976, we estimated a program effect on Stanford–Binet of between 1 and 9 points. If the cohort entering in 1975 were included, the hypothesis of no effect on IQ could not be rejected. However, the 1975 cohort is not likely to provide a good estimate of program effects because of its unusually high amount of attrition (50% in the control group) and because of signs of bias in the reasons for attrition. Furthermore, because this was the only experimental group not pretested, it was impossible to obtain a good estimate of the effects of attrition on outcomes. It also appears that the effects of the MCHP on IQ were not significantly different from the effects of the VISM-only treatment. Thus, our best experimental estimate is of a significant short-term effect of the MCHP on IQ, but an effect that cannot be discriminated from that of a VISM-only treatment and an effect that is appreciably less than the short-term effects estimated from the quasi-experiments. Thus, these IQ effects do not provide the same basis for prediction of later effects on school performance as did the quasi-experimental IQ effects.

On the other hand, the true experiments did reveal an effect on Maternal Interactive Behavior scores. Although this effect was not significant (again) in the 1975 cohort, it was significant over all groups combined, and it was a sizeable effect. Their performance on this program-referenced measure indicates that, overall, program mothers understood and were able to produce the kind of interactive behavior that the Toy Demonstrator had modeled for them. These MIB effects were relatively uncorrelated with IQ, and they were largest in the 1974 cohort in which the MCHP and the VISM-only treatments were contrasted, the same comparison in which there was no IQ difference. These facts support the possibility that the IQ effects observed in the experimental groups were not mediated by MIB but were a direct consequence of exposure to the program. What will now be interesting to observe is whether MIB differences will mediate later IQ or school performance differences as hypothesized by the theory that defines the program.

Of course, these data, as in any field research, contain several possible sources of error and bias. The quasi-experiments have the weakness that it is difficult to be sure that group differences in outcomes were caused by the program and not by initial differences between groups. On the other hand, the field experiments may suffer from a lack of generalizability due to volunteer effects in recruiting and other reactive effects of experimental arrangements. Rosenthal and Rosnow (1975) reported that a cluster of characteristics reliably differentiate volunteers from nonvolunteers, among them that volunteers expect to be favorably evaluated, are more interested in the topic under investigation and are more intelligent than nonvolunteers. They also noted how rapidly the margin of error increases as the proportion of nonvolunteers increases even slightly. Recruiting for an experimental lottery or for a health screening program produced far lower rates of acceptance (48% overall) than when specific treatments were offered in the quasi-experiments (85% overall). Although the experimental families are not demographically more favored, it is possible that such a selection process could yield a group of mothers better prepared to take advantage of available resources to benefit their children. Not only would the program be more effective with such mothers, but they might take better advantage of a VISM-only treatment, of evaluations without treatment, or of alternate community resources. Further, the IQs of both program and comparison groups, even when they are brought into line with current Stanford–Binet norms, are above these expected for the untreated target population. This is consistent with expectations for volunteer sample bias. Thus the generalizability of these results to the general low income population may be limited by such effects.

To the extent that results in the quasi-experimental and experimental designs do not agree, they do not compensate for each other's methodological weaknesses. Nonetheless, both designs provided evidence for the short-term effects of the MCHP on IQ, although for effects of different magnitudes. The quasi-experiments provided evidence for long-term effects on important outcome criteria, although it remains to be seen whether these will eventually be found in the experimental designs. Of considerable importance, it has now been demonstrated that the maternal behavior that is the focus of the program can be modeled successfully in an ongoing, long-established service program. The nature of this effect and its eventual consequences define the current area of inquiry for the Verbal Interaction Project.

Implications of Findings for Policy, Practice, and Research

It has been previously indicated that the MCHP can be reliably provided as a coherent, inexpensive, minimal intervention program in a wide variety of settings and across an extended period of time. The research described in this chapter provides objective evidence for its effectiveness. In short, it is a social program that is both validated and feasible for implementation on a local, state, or national level.

The results offer no final proof that the MCHP will or will not produce specific effects in every setting. They do, however, offer good evidence that the desired maternal behavior can be successfully modeled in the Program. The best evidence derived from this program (as well as from other programs discussed in this volume) indicates short-term effects on IQ. The data also provide at least a partial basis for predicting long-term effects of the MCHP on school performance.

It is a reflection of the obduracy of social problems that a program continues to be needed to assist parents in helping their very young children to take full advantage of later educational opportunities. The Superintendant of the Chicago schools, Dr. Ruth Love, recently stated: "If we could get parents to read to their little children 15 minutes a day, we could revolutionize the schools [Hechinger, 1981, p. C5]."

Fifteen years ago, the Verbal Interaction Project developed the Mother–Child Home Program mainly to accomplish this simple purpose. The overriding goal was not to revolutionize the schools but to help families take best advantage of whatever public schools can offer. Above all, the program's purpose was to support low-income families in the cognitive and emotional socialization of their preschool children. Needless to say, this family function had long preceded the very existence of schools in any society. The necessity for supporting it will continue as long as poverty is with us and families continue to be society's most fundamental socializing unit.

ACKNOWLEDGMENTS

Supported for development and research of the Mother–Child Home Program by Marion R. Ascoli Fund; Carnegie Corporation of New York; Children's Bureau, U.S. Department of HEW; Education Commission of the States; Foundation for Child Development; General Mills Foundation; Grant Foundation; National Institute of Mental Health, U.S. Department of HEW; Administration for Children, Youth, and Families; North Shore Unitarian Society Veatch Program; Rockefeller Brothers Fund; and Surdna Foundation; and for research of the dissemination of the program by Rockefeller Brothers Fund and the U.S. Office of Education.

REFERENCES

Bronfenbrenner, U. Early deprivation: A cross-species analysis. In G. Newton & S. Levine, (Eds.), *Early experience and behavior.* Springfield, Ill.: Charles C. Thomas, 1968.

Bronfenbrenner, U. *Is early intervention effective?* Office of Child Development, U.S. Dept. of Health, Education, & Welfare, 1974.

Brown, R. *Words and things.* Glencoe, Ill.: Free Press, 1958.

Bruner, J. S. The course of cognitive growth. *American Psychologist,* 1964, *19,* 1–15.

Campbell, D. T., & Frey, P. W. The implications of learning theory for the fade-out of gains from compensatory education. In J. Hellmuth (Ed.), *Disadvantaged child.* (Vol. 3). New York: Brunner/Mazel, 1970.

Cassirer, E. *An essay on man.* New Haven: Yale University Press, 1944.

Clarke-Stewart, K. A. Interactions between mothers and their young children: Characteristics and consequences. *Monographs of the Society for Research in Child Development,* 1973, *23* (6 and 7, Serial No. 153).

Clarke-Stewart, K. A., Vanderstoep, L., & Killian, G. Analysis and replication of mother–child relations at two years of age. *Child Development,* 1979, *50,* 777–793.

Hebb, D. O. *The organization of behavior.* New York: Wiley, 1949.

Hechinger, F. A. *A hopeful view on resurgence of urban schools.* New York Times, July 21, 1981.

Hess, R., & Shipman, V. C. Early experience and the socialization of cognitive modes in children. *Child Development,* 1965, *36,* 869–886.

Hunt, J. McV. *Intelligence and experience.* New York: Ronald Press, 1961.

Irwin, O. C. Infant speech: Effect of systematic reading of stories. *Journal of Speech and Hearing Research,* 1960, *3,* 187–190.

Kirk, R. *Experimental design: Procedures for the behavioral sciences.* Belmont, Calif.: Brooks/ Cole, 1968.

Klaus, R., & Gray, S. The early training project for disadvantaged children: A report after five years. *Monograph of the Society for Research in Child Development* 1968, *33,* (4, serial No. 120).

Kraus, P. E. *Yesterday's children.* New York: Wiley-Interscience, 1973.

Levenstein, P. Cognitive growth in preschoolers through verbal interaction with their mothers. *American Journal of Orthopsychiatry,* 1970, *40,* 426–432.

Levenstein, P. Message from home. In M. J. Begab & S. A. Richardson (Eds.), *The mentally retarded and society: A social science perspective.* Baltimore: University Park Press, 1975.

Levenstein, P. The Mother–Child Home Program. In M. C. Day & R. R. Parker (Eds.), *The preschool in action* (2nd ed.) Boston: Allyn & Bacon, 1977.

Levenstein, P., & Sunley, R. Stimulation of verbal interaction between disadvantaged mothers and children. *American Journal of Orthopsychiatry,* 1968, *38,* 116–121.

Madden, J., Levenstein P., & Levenstein, S. Longitudinal IQ outcomes of the Mother–Child Home Program. *Child Development,* 1976, *47,* 1015–1025.

Rosenthal, R., & Rosnow, R. L. *The volunteer subject.* New York: Wiley-Interscience, 1975.

Sapir, E. *Culture, language, and personality.* Berkeley: University of California Press, 1962 (Originally published, 1921).

Schaefer, E. S. Need for early and continuing education. In V. M. Denenberg (Ed.), *Education of the infant and young child.* New York: Academic Press, 1970.

Schaie, K., & Roberts, J. *School achievement of children 6–11 years as measured by reading and arithmetic subtests of the Wide Range Achievement Test.* Series II, *103,* National Health Survey, National Center for Health Statistics, Public Health Service, DHEW Publication, 1970.

Vygotsky, L. S. *Thought and language.* Cambridge, Mass.: MIT Press, 1962.

White, R. W. *Ego and reality in psychoanalytic theory.* New York: International Universities Press, 1963.

9 The Micro-Social Learning Environment: A Strategy for Accelerating Learning

Myron Woolman
Director
Institute of Educational Research
Washington, D.C.

Introduction

Around their sixth year, most American children enter the elementary school environment. They face, usually for the first time, a requirement to satisfy the institutionally imposed learning goals established by the school curriculum. School achievement testing indicates that a child who is unable to satisfy the curricular standard of first grade is not likely to meet the standards of later grades. Conversely, those children who meet the requirements of first grade are likely to perform well at successively higher grade levels (Arnold et al., 1977; Harckham, Gunning, & Waldron, 1971; Marco, 1973; McClellan, 1973; Turner, 1978). Children who do poorly in school are less likely to adapt to the economic and social requirements of adulthood (Kohen, 1973; Mott & Shaw, 1978; Robison, 1980; Rodriguez, 1980; Sewell & Hauser, 1975; Vargas & Woolman, 1980).

The work of Coleman (1966), Jencks, Smith, Ackland, Bane, Cohen, Gintis, Heyns & Michelson (1972), and others makes it evident that those children whose families differ culturally and are poorer economically than the middle-class norm are significantly less likely to satisfy curricular standards than those whose familial language and behavior is consistent with curricular expectancies that combine economic, cultural, and language patterns. For Hispanic children, it is especially difficult to make the transition into the elementary school curriculum.

Purpose

The basic thesis underlying the design of the Micro-Social Learning Environment can be stated simply: If children enter school fully prepared to meet the demands imposed by the first-grade curriculum, their subsequent progress through successive school grades will be improved markedly, as will later adult adjustment. The prime objective of the Micro-Social Learning method is elementary school readiness.

The Micro-Social Learning Environment was designed as an educational life simulation system to develop, in a carefully organized fail-safe learning environment, those response capabilities necessary to meet typical first grade curricular standards. The basic concept was adapted from the writer's experience in the design of flight and missile simulation and training methods to ensure a pre-established performance level on completion of training (Woolman, 1955, 1960).

The primary task was to design the classroom space, materials, equipment, procedures, and methods of interaction between the children, and between the teachers and the children, so as to evolve a society of learners who shared the same basic goals. What we sought was to provide a situation in which each child would perceive, as his or her first priority, maintaining and improving status position in the reference group (the other students). Mobility in their own society could only be achieved through learning the language and behaviors that were imbedded in the Micro-Social curriculum. This preelementary curriculum was designed to transfer fully, so that graduates would satisfy the requirements of first grade in elementary school.

In essence, a life simulation approach adapted to the preschool environment was designed to ensure that children from lower socioeconomic backgrounds learned, in a stage-by-stage fashion, the language, behavioral control, social interaction skills, and motivation to meet the standards of the typical first grade classroom.

THEORETICAL BASE AND HYPOTHESES

Several basic assumptions underlie the Micro-Social Learning Environment.

The Cultural Continuity Assumption

Contrary to the position advocated by Jensen, namely that IQ scores are manifestations of some underlying genetic potential called "intelligence" (Jensen, 1969), the writer holds that although genetic endowment varies in every group of human beings, measures of performance such as IQ tests and other performance indices, for children lacking neurological defects, are primarily a matter of adaptation to different family learning systems. Stable cross-generational performance on such tests occurs mainly because children learn to satisfy similar language and behavioral requirements as did their family.

The Preelementary Learning Envelope

Although every human being has a personality distinguishable from every other, during the first years of life children are necessarily dependent on their parents or other adults. In this human crucible, children learn to become themselves in the course of a continuing process of interaction with adults, who act not only as role models but as generators of language, attitudes, beliefs, values, and expectations. Children evolve complex sets of responses to obtain goals by acting so as to satisfy their needs from those on whom they are dependent for food, language, comfort, and love. Over time, they learn to respond in ways that are reacted to favorably by those who mediate their life support; each child adapts to the personalities of parents and siblings; the availability of space, food, toys, social access; and observed modes of communication—the whole forming an idiosyncratic pattern of response (the Preelementary Response Envelope) to maximize his or her satisfactions and to minimize tensions.

Each family differs to a degree from every other, even those sharing the same cultural matrix, as to the emphasis and priority assigned to different values, beliefs, traditions, attitudes, and ceremonies. That is, each evolves a familial/cultural envelope that is similar to but distinguishable from every other, although remaining within the same culture. As used here, Hispanic, Native American, and ghetto families all evolve familial/cultural response envelopes.

The rewards obtained by the child in the course of familial interaction differ widely from family to family, based on differences in the availability of stimulation and feedback from parents (see Table 9.1: The Family As A Learning System, A Scale—Environmental Richness); the requirements and importance of language (B Scale—Symbolic Exchange); the sensitivity and reaction of the parents to activities related to the child (C Scale—Parental Response Thresholds); and the timing, contingencies, and quality of the parents' responses to what the child does (D Scale—Parental Responsivity). Even children in families that share the same basic cultural histories possess shades of difference in their underlying values and beliefs and evolve idiosyncratic patterns of manifest language and behavior.

The four learning dimensions presented in Table 9.1 are intended to illustrate the infinite variety of response envelopes that can evolve within families sharing the same culture and even the same roof. The major purpose of Table 9.1 is to present the view that in any family that registers a pattern in which scores on each of the four dimensions is three or above, the children should have little or no

TABLE 9.1
The Family as a Learning System

Scale Values	A Scale Environmental Richness (Levels of Stimulation)	B Scale Symbolic Exchange (Meaningfulness)	C Scale Parental Response Thresholds (Reactivity Modes)	D Scale Parental Responsivity (Feedback Modes)
Level 1	HOME AS CAPSULE Family is isolated and does not interact with outsiders.	VERY LITTLE MEANING Verbalizations rare and responses are brief and often mono-syllabic.	VERY LOW THRESHOLD Parents provide desired goal stimulus immediately rather than tolerate noise or tension-producing activity.	NO FEEDBACK Parent behavior unloving and self-determined. Overt behavior of child has no impact on parent attitude or behavior.
Level 2	NEIGHBORHOOD CAPSULE Family interacts only with itself and other families within narrow social and geographical area.	HIGH AMBIGUITY Verbalization is guarded. Meaning is opaque and listener must guess at meaning and emotional content. Speech interactions very rare.	MINIMAL TOLERANCE Parents usually provide desired goal stimulus rather than tolerate noise or tension-producing activity.	ACCEPTING-UNRESPONSIVE Parent behavior is loving but self-determined and child has little impact. Rigid parent behaviors are only slightly affected by child's responses.
Level 3	COMMUNITY LEVEL Family interacts with other families and individuals within the community area.	PARTIAL AMBIGUITY Verbalization is often guarded but has wide range. Interpretation is sometimes given	MODERATE TOLERANCE Parents provide desired goal stimulus but child often fails to achieve it because of noise or	DUTIFUL-FLEXIBLE Parent behavior maintains warmth and is responsive to child. Standards are reasonable and

(continued from previous page)

Level				
	...child is aware of own success or failure.	...tension-producing activity.	...spontaneously but usually in response to direct question.	
Level 4	**ACCEPTING-FLEXIBLE** Parents attentive and responsive. Respond selectively to needs quickly based on child's response. Flexibility adapts as child matures.	**HIGH THRESHOLD** Parents usually resist producing goal stimulus under duress of noise and tension-producing activity and tend to respond when child is socially adaptive and non-destructive.	**FULL COMMUNICATION** Speech is informative. Language has wide range of tone and content. Sustained responsive interactions in speech.	**INTER-COMMUNITY LEVEL** Family interacts with other families and individuals in other geographic locales.
Level 5	**RESPONSIVE DEVELOPMENTAL** Parents are loving and supportive and highly responsive to child and apply shifting standards to increase skill levels. Planning done to ensure growth in abilities under conditions of adequate success probability.	**FLEXIBLE THRESHOLD** a. Parents resist response to to tension-producing activity. b. Parents provide alternative, socially-accepted modes for obtaining goal. c. Parents systematically provide goals for verbal and adaptive behaviors. Verbal interactions are sustained.	**INTERACTIVE COMMUNICATION** Speech is informed and has high symbolic content. Great facility with language, both common and literary. Responsive to shadings of meanings ensure comprehension.	**MOBILE INTER-SOCIAL** Family has wide social interactions across groups and in varying locales and cultures.

language difficulty later in elementary school. However, in the many cases where one or more dimensions are properly evaluated as being two or below, later language problems are highly probable. Many patterns, such as "home as a capsule" (A Scale—Level 1), "high ambiguity" (B Scale—Level 2), "minimal tolerance" (C Scale—Level 2), and "no feedback" (D Scale—Level 1) offer little chance that language skills will be learned well enough in the home to provide a sound basis for adequate performance in elementary school.

It should be noted further that even in those cases where scores on one part of the scale are high and others low, there could be problems in language and behavioral development. A highly mobile, socially diverse family (A-5) with "low thresholds" and "little feedback" (C-1 & D-1) may not offer sufficient opportunity for language development for the child to become proficient. Conversely, low scores on the A Scale with relatively higher scores on other scales will not necessarily prevent development, as responses that produce desired goals could occur through friends, neighbors, teachers, or other nonfamily members. Where children obtain satisfactions through verbalization, rather than through sulking, crying, or other nonverbal responses, language proliferates. The child learns that language is a tool to reduce tensions and attain goals with minimal expenditure of time and energy.

Though families lack neatly defined goals and objectives, and contain no recognizable curricula or lesson plans, the family does in fact contain an infinite variety of circumstances in which children learn to obtain goals to satisfy their physiological and social needs. The way others react produces the learning envelope that ultimately will determine how well and with what degree of ease a child can satisfy the curricular imperatives of the elementary school.

In this analysis, the reason that IQ scores and other cognitive indices tend to be higher for high-SES (socioeconomic status) families than for low-SES families is that high-SES family child-rearing practices and styles tend to favor language learning. Table 9.1, in all four dimensions, is intended to reflect optimal high-SES child-rearing styles at scale values of three and above. In general, it is assumed that high-SES families possess greater richness in the physical environment (A Scale); high-SES families are more responsive and rewarding to their children's use of language that can be used in elementary school (B Scale); high-SES parents are more patient and selective in reinforcing especially those verbal behaviors that converge on the social norms and expectations of elementary school (C Scale); and finally, high-SES parents usually have more time to be vigilant, sensitive, and emotionally responsive to their children's language and behavioral development in ways that are consistent with elementary school expectations (D Scale). The argument here is that optimal child-rearing conditions are more likely to be found in high- than low-SES families, but it is important to recognize that SES is not a perfect predictor of these conditions—in the general population, substantial numbers of low-SES families would score higher than some high-SES families.

Preelementary Readiness Paradigms

Learning that takes place in a school is more limited and directed than learning that occurs in the family. The school is concerned with transferring a limited spectrum of socially approved skills and knowledge sanctioned by the society (the curriculum).

The preelementary school readiness paradigms are an effort to illustrate simply the problem of transferring responses learned by children in the home to the curricular imperatives presented by the elementary school. The curricular imperatives are shown outlined in heavy black to indicate both stability and consistency of school curricula. Figure 9.1 (upper) shows three 6-year-old children (A, B, and C) at school entry. The children are assumed to be identical in terms of age, natural endowment, and general learning capability and are assumed to be English-speaking. Each has developed a similar number of responses, appropriate to his or her own familial situation, from birth to the sixth year. In other words, their response envelopes are the same shape and magnitude. However, the three children differ in elementary school readiness because of differences in what they have learned in their families.

In the lower illustration, a Preelementary Readiness Environment is interposed. This interposition occurs immediately prior to school entry. It is essentially a method of transition to ensure that children, regardless of familial differences, possess the skills necessary to meet first-grade curricular imperatives by the time they are 6 years old.

The Preelementary Readiness Environment spans all the children. Note that in the lower figure there is no barrier line at the elementary school entry point. This is intended to indicate that children who complete the system would possess transferable skills to meet the curricular standards of first grade. In this sense, the Preelementary Readiness Environment can be viewed as analogous to a ground simulator that ensures that all responses to fly an aircraft preexist, because it is often too dangerous to learn pilot skills in the air (Glaser, 1964).

The Micro-Society Assumptions

It is assumed that a specialized learning environment that would develop the response capabilities required to meet first-grade curricular standards could be devised for children regardless of their familial learning. Such a system would require that children themselves perceive the necessity to radically upgrade their language capabilities and modify their behaviors. For this to occur, a much more responsive and dynamic classroom environment than that usually provided for preschoolers would be necessary. Such an environment would require:

1. Establishing the class members as a reference group.
2. Assuring that personal goals and reference group goals are based on the

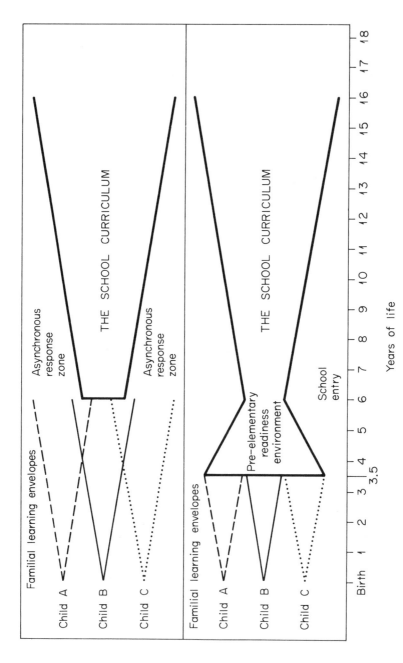

FIG. 9.1. The two pre-elementary readiness paradigms.

condition that individuals become upwardly mobile through language learning and effective, appropriate social interaction.

3. Providing a physical space, materials, methods, and procedures that maximize the opportunity to respond autonomously as individuals and as group members, with minimal dependence on teachers or other adults, so as to increase independence and improve self-image.

The underlying theory is based on the reinforcement position of E. L. Thorndike and B. F. Skinner: namely, that learning occurs as a consequence of the satisfactions that take place when tensions or drives are reduced. However, instead of using deprivation of food, water, or sex to generate drive levels, as is done routinely in animal studies, the necessary tensions to generate human responses are assumed to occur in the strivings to satisfy group norms when learners perceive themselves to be members of a reference group. The classroom was organized, materials developed, and methods of interaction established to make the class of children into a unified society, which shared the same basic goal of maintaining or improving one's position in the classroom society. This could be done only through mastery of the learning materials.

The writer's fundamental purpose was to make the accumulation of a substantial English vocabulary a goal, shared by all classmates. The method used was to make perceived status gain contingent on vocabulary accumulation and to make feelings of self-satisfaction an outcome of recognition by other children, rather than of approval by a teacher or aide. The essential requirement was to generate an unabating source of motivational energy or drive, which would be nurtured and stabilized as a consequence of success.

Food, water, cakes, and M&Ms, like teacher nods, pats, and smiles, ultimately lead to satiation and avoidance. In this writer's experience, the only inexhaustible reinforcer is the unquenchable desire to maintain and/or improve one's position in one's own society. In designing the Micro-Social Learning Environment, the aim was to produce an unending series of games, played with different partners, where the prizes were skills in manipulating language terms and related activities, rather than in the nonlanguage behaviors used in motor activities, such as skipping rope or playing jacks. The central problem was to obtain enough involvement to activate children to learn language terms while interacting, rather than being entertained by listening to a teacher read, a recording, or television. Unless the children did perceive themselves as a reference group in which their own status was important, it was apparent to the writer that the entire project would fail.

Relevant Literature

Much of what was incorporated into the Micro-Social Learning Environment originated, as might be expected, in previous experience.

The fact that it was possible and sometimes necessary to establish skills in one situation to be used in a second was strongly impressed on the writer when he was a member of the design team for the B-47 Ground Simulator (Woolman, 1969). A simulator is essentially a device to develop, under carefully controlled conditions, complex responses that can then be transferred to a second situation under conditions of minimal risk of error. Simulators are especially useful where the second situation is intolerant of error, as in an airplane or spacecraft where certain classes of error are lethal. The metaphor here is that the school curriculum is analogous to an airplane; of course the penalty for high error rates in school is not a fiery crash but rather chronic inability to satisfy society's standards for participation in its economic, political, and cultural mainstream.

A simulator provides the advantage that subskills can be learned separately before they are combined in a later stage. In an aircraft, for example, altitude control can be learned to high precision before requiring students to make turns to compass headings. When each of these subskills has been learned separately, then students may be required to make turns with minimal loss or gain in altitude. By designing the simulator as a learning system, it is possible to select and emphasize subskills, to combine and integrate them, and to evaluate performance carefully under conditions where errors are correctable, costs are low, and patience infinite.

Basically, the Micro-Social Learning Environment was viewed as a simulator in which we could help develop the responses required to meet the next life stage, the elementary school.

The seminal study underlying the Micro-Social Learning Environment was conducted for the U.S. Department of the Army. In this study the writer had the opportunity to organize a missile training system as a microsociety in which members could gain status (promotions, authority, transfers, etc.) through increasing their proficiency, using specifically designed learning materials to make this possible in the onsite situation (Woolman, 1960).

The use of paired learners acting as partners in a total group structure was designed to provide social interaction, a microsociety, and a human feedback mechanism, while substantially increasing the response frequency potential of a group. This concept was tested in diverse situations: It was an important aspect of the success of the missile project, and it appeared to function well in literacy projects in a prison and in various urban and rural settings (Woolman, 1960, 1965, 1967).

In the Micro-Social Environment (as well as in later U.S. Job Corps programs and a vocational trades project in West Africa), learners physically moved from module to module as they mastered successive levels of skill and knowledge. The intent was to make movement in space from module to module a substantial reward by making its achievement highly perceptible to the individual and, above all, highly visible to all members of the microsociety (Woolman, 1976).

A self-instructional program developed for Bell Laboratories of AT & T tested the value of the Progressive Choice Method as a tool to aid in the learning of complex concepts. A study conducted by Holt and Valentine of Bell Labs produced statistically significant positive results for the method when compared with a matched control sample (Holt & Valentine, 1963; Woolman, 1962a, 1968).

Hypotheses

The prime hypothesis was that socially and environmentally disadvantaged children with severe English language deficits (but no neurological defects) who experienced the Micro-Social Learning Environment for an average of 24 months for 2½ hours per day would perform as well in elementary school as the general population of children in the school system.

A corollary to this hypothesis was that children with experience in the Micro-Social Learning Environment would show significant gains on standard tests such as the Wechsler Intelligence Scale for Children (WISC), the Peabody Picture Vocabulary Test (PPVT), and the Goodenough Intelligence Test.

SITE AND SAMPLE

By agreement with the state of New Jersey, the selection criteria were: (1) children of parents classified as migrant workers; (2) children should be free of known neurological or sensory defects; and (3) children should be at least 36 months of age.

Demographics

The 135 children initially tested in the Micro-Social Learning Environment were, for the most part, the children of agricultural workers, classifiable as New Jersey State migrants. Forty-three, or 32%, were children of stationary migrants. Formerly part of the migrant stream, they had settled in Vineland, New Jersey, during the previous 5 years, working as agricultural laborers. Of these 43 families, 11 were on welfare and supplemented their income by picking crops and working in canning plants.

There were 32 seasonal migrant families who worked picking crops during the agricultural season only. Of these, 18 received welfare payments and used their migrant labor income to supplement their welfare checks. In addition there were 39 families on welfare who stated that they occasionally worked on farms or in food processing plants to supplement welfare monies; this required a more sporadic level of effort than that of the seasonal migrant. There were 9 children whose parents also worked in the fields and in processing plants, but were not on welfare. Three of the remaining 12 were the children of Micro-Social teachers who requested inclusion of their own children. The parents of the final nine were at a higher socioeconomic level; their children entered the program at the request of the Vineland School System because of psychological or social problems. Thus, of the 135 children initially in the Micro-Social Learning Environment, 123 (91%) were in a low-socioeconomic level, and of these, 66 families (54%) were on welfare.

The mean yearly income of the 123 migrant families was $4997; that is, for the 4.49 members of the average family, $21.40 was available per family member per week. For the 12 middle-income families, the mean income was $10,141; nonmigrant families received more than twice the weekly income per family member.

Behavioral Characteristics

Behaviors at the outset were characterized by running, fighting, screaming, biting, throwing, and crying; these behaviors tended to become epidemic. If one child ran, laughed, cried, jumped, threw objects, or crawled on the floor, that activity would stimulate an increasing wave of children to act out similar patterns. There were also several withdrawn, nonverbal children, who retreated to walls and corners for up to 6 weeks. In addition, several children spent most of the first few weeks (one child persevered for several months) simply crawling about on the classroom floor. Teacher reports on initial language skills were that more than half the children spoke Spanish as their primary language, and a substantial number (55%) could not speak English at all.

Although the writer had seen much disorganized behavior while working on projects to develop language skills in mentally handicapped children and schizophrenic adults, confidence that the rationale and methods would be operative with migrant children was seriously shaken during the first week of the project. The lack of communication, levels of aggression, and depth of withdrawal of these children were beyond anything previously anticipated or witnessed (Woolman, 1964; Woolman & Davy, 1965; Woolman & Grotberg, 1966).

DESIGN OF STUDY

Treatment

The objectives of the Micro-Social Learning system are to:

1. Sharply increase language skills, including the development of cognitive language capabilities. This objective was operationalized as the acquisition of 2000 words in seven language areas.

2. Develop reading skills to provide a method of expanding language in the home and community setting. Children were to learn to read 300 basic words.

3. Produce skills in social interaction with peers and adults.

4. Provide increased motivation to achieve goals and interpolated subgoals and to restrain impulsive and aggressive behaviors.

Attainment of these objectives was to be accomplished through intrinsically motivated work by the children within a classroom society. Pairs of children acquired a specified set of language terms through stories and workbooks in the modular space and then strengthened their grasp of the language terms through activities performed in the Life Simulator Space. Progress through the curriculum sequence was made socially visible by the children's movement from module to module. Movement to each successive module required cooperative social interaction and mutual assistance because both children were required to demonstrate 100% mastery of a workbook before either could move forward (Woolman, 1970a, 1970b).

Physical Layout

An abandoned supermarket was converted into three classrooms, a playroom, and administrative offices. Each classroom was outfitted with one-way mirrors and microphones to allow visual and auditory access by parents, visitors, other teachers, and evaluators.

A classroom was divided into two parts, the Modular Learning area and the Life Simulator area (see Figure 9.2). In the modular area, the children sat at five modules arranged to form an arc across the classroom. Each module was divided into three sections by separator panels. Within each section there were two scalloped indentations, angled so that each pair of children partially faced each other. The modular area was conceived as a "language pump" to produce an ever-greater pool of associative, class, and cognitive terms.

The Life Simulator space was divided into a simulator room, a free time room, and art rooms. Simulator space equipment consisted of a clothing wheel, large blocks, modular knock-down house, etc. The free time and art rooms contained tip-proof easels, easel pads, and a variety of other art-related materials. There were more than 200 activities, each related to a specific module and language area. The activities available to learners increased as new vocabulary was mastered at the modules.

The program was scheduled for 12 months per year. At the outset, children entered classes at the rate of six per day. Each classroom held 30 children (six at each of the five modules) and was used for two classes per day of 2½ hours each, allowing a maximum student capacity of 180 children. There was a 20-minute snack break to assure that each child had milk and some solid, nutritious food.

During the 4 years of program operation, more than 300 children participated.

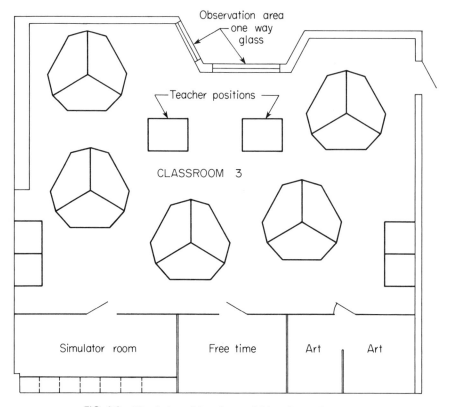

FIG. 9.2.   The design of the micro-social learning environment.

The duration of attendance of these children ranged from 6 to 36 months and averaged 24 months.

Teaching Staff

There were four teachers who rotated responsibilities every 2 months; a teacher was responsible for one of the three classrooms or served as Center Administrator. This system of rotation was instituted for several reasons. First, rotation was a device to minimize the child's dependency on adults and to make unambiguous the fact that progress and mastery were an outcome of each child's personal efforts. The assumption was made that students who maintained progress regardless of the particular teacher or aide would perceive their progress as a consequence of their own efforts rather than as an outcome of special efforts by an adult. Second, rotation was used as a device to maintain system standards and integrity. The assumption was made that teachers would try harder to maintain the child-centered methods and procedures and to limit idiosyncratic interventions if they knew that their class would soon be the responsibility of another teacher. Finally, rotation provided a means of avoiding an administrator or principal who, over time, could reinterpret and distort the methodology. Center administration was limited to activities relating to student attendance, welfare counseling, and administration of activities relating the Center to the larger school district. A Staff Training Guide as well as in-service training were provided to all teachers.

The teacher served as controller and choreographer of the system. She organized the flow; shifted partners; set the children into motion; evaluated their performance; directed the teacher aide and parent aide; and, above all, maintained the dynamic flow of the children so that they perceived themselves as being in an active state of growth.

Parent Involvement

The outreach component consisted of the following elements:

1. One parent of each child was expected to participate as a parent aide 1 day per month.

2. Observation rooms with one-way mirrors and microphones opened on each classroom so that parents could see and hear their own children at any time.

3. Parents were routinely asked to attend meetings where questions were answered regarding school activities, and parents provided their views on the impact of the program on their children.

4. All completed language learning workbooks, and the Life Simulator activity materials were made available to the children to take home as a means of linking the classroom to the home.

5. Reading skill development was integrated into the language learning system so children could help parents with reading English. This skill was quickly put to use in supermarkets and in the reading of highway signs.

Curriculum

The program focused on four skill pools, each containing segments in which terms related to a particular subject were learned. These four were the Behavior Pool, the Speech Pool, the Reading Pool, and the Related Content Pool.

Behavior Pool.   Initial learning consisted of the language to be used and the procedures to be followed in the Micro-Social classroom. Children learned where to hang their coats, how to find the module in which they should be seated, what to do in the module, and how and when to ask questions of the teacher or aide. These and similar necessary behaviors were taught in order to free the children of feelings of apprehension or inadequacy as they entered the learning activities.

The Behavior Pool initially stressed the interactions between children in the course of using the learning materials. New behaviors (such as monitoring and checking work) were taught only after partner-interaction skills had been mastered. The first segment of the Speech Pool was the medium for developing the rhythm and pattern of these behaviors.

Speech Pool.   This consisted of a fundamental vocabulary that projected outward in successive stages from the self, to the home, to the larger world beyond. The segments of the Speech Pool covered these topics: common forms; body parts; food; household (clothing, family, and related objects); nature (plants, animals, and weather); community and classroom; and other lands.

Reading Pool.   This involved the Progressive Choice Reading Method materials that were woven throughout each workbook in each segment of the Speech Pool (Edwards, 1965; Grotberg, 1967; Roth, 1966; Woolman, 1962b).

Related Content Pool.   Immediately prior to first grade entry, the child moved into the Related Content Pool, which covered elementary mathematics and science concepts and procedures. In addition, children learned the behaviors necessary to satisfy first grade classroom requirements. Over a period of 1 month, first-grade classroom procedures were fully simulated.

Modular Area Procedures.   The behavior, speech, and reading skills were developed primarily in the Modular Area. The Modular Area was designed to provide children with an opportunity to develop speech through:

1. Use of the language learning workbooks.
2. Continued access to another learner under conditions of partial privacy.
3. A variety of situations that stimulated verbal interactions between partners.
4. Responsibility for each partner to assist the other in achieving language-related goals.

As children completed their workbooks at a given module, they moved to the next module of a different color where they completed another workbook. The movement from module to module was a socially visible sign of progress (a subgoal). The movement in space was evidence of mastery and was also a means of attaining genuine status, as children who reached a given module attained ''monitor'' status, which allowed them to help partners below their level in the program.

The children learned about their new environment, the partnering process, and the words related to lines, shapes, and colors—all Behavior Pool skills. Their initiation into the flow and interaction of the speech and reading aspects of the program was achieved in the course of learning "ideographs," which are picture directions designed to tell each partner what to do on each workbook page. (See Fig. 9.3).

The workbook pages were typically organized into four or six rows. Each row was preceded by a △ or a □. The child facing the △ sign at his seat completed the △ rows; likewise, the child facing the □ completed the □ rows. On completion of a page, partners switched workbooks. The first child checked the work on the □ rows and also completed the unfinished △ rows; the partners did the converse. The partners then again exchanged workbooks and continued on to the next page unless the ideograph on the page was a raised hand, which meant they were to call the teacher or aide for an evaluation of their work. All evaluations

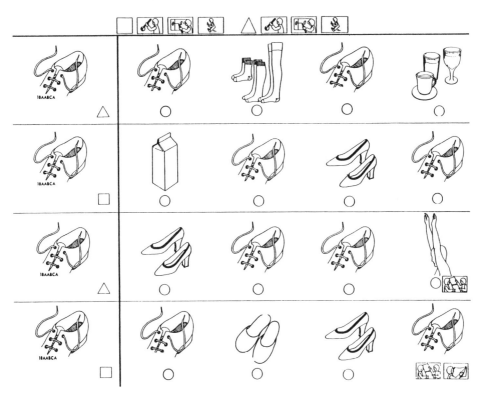

FIG. 9.3.   An illustrative workbook page. The △ and □ forms on the left of each row tell the children which row to work on. Other ideographs provide additional directions. In this case children fill in dots to match a standard.

were of the work of both partners, rather than of each student individually. This was to assure that students would assist each other to learn.

The workbooks were the primary vehicle for the development of the Speech and Reading Pool skills. Children acquired the goal words in the body parts segment, then the words in the foods segment, and so on. Lastly, the children progressed to the Other Lands segment, which functioned as a review of all previous speech segments in the context of ethnic and cultural comparisons.

The procedure for the Modular Area work was as follows:

1. The instructor or an aide read an illustrated story that accentuated the segment's goal words. All words have a referent that has a specifiable function.

2. The story line was then picked up and presented in small segments that were coordinated with each workbook. The children listened to the story segment and pronounced each goal word (approximately 10 words per segment).

3. Using the workbooks and working in pairs, the children matched illustrations of the goal words with standard illustrations. Then, by following a different set of ideographs, the children identified each of the illustrations with the appropriate term (goal word). This involved pointing to each term, asking the question, "What is this called?", and moving on only when the proper term was given. After switching workbooks, reviewing each other's work and completing the page, the partners were signaled to raise their hands for a check-out before going on to the next level. The check-out was given to both partners. It was required that each make 100% correct responses before continuing forward in their workbooks.

Next, the function of each term was given and the learners were to demonstrate understanding of the functional value of the terms. The children responded to a fairly complex illustration by naming the illustrated objects and indicating how those objects were functioning in that context. After being checked out by the teacher, the children were ready for the next story segment. Interspersed among the goal-word tasks in the workbooks, letters of the alphabet were introduced. Children learned to print and read certain of the goal words from each speech segment.

4. The children progressed through the series of evaluations built into the system. As they completed successive segments of the program, they moved from module to module, changing their roles and responsibilities in the process.

5. As the learners mastered the terms in a workbook and demonstrated both comprehension and an ability to verbalize, they proceeded to the Life Simulator Space section of the classroom.

Though the fact was never announced or even mentioned directly, within weeks after operations began, the children were aware that movement from module to module was "the thing to do." Though partners changed frequently (no pair could be together for more than a week) and children were free to walk about, converse, and move to the Life Simulator, the child's own intrinsic motivation to participate in the flow and movement of the classroom provided "structure" to the modular area. There was little necessity for the teacher to assign tasks or resort to authority to direct children to their work.

Life Simulator Area.   The Life Simulator functioned as the "free response" section of the classroom. It occupied about one-fourth of the classroom area and contained an extensive assortment of activities, toys, and materials that were keyed to the learning workbooks used in the modular area. For example, after the children mastered colors and forms, they made Indian-style headdresses from construction paper, each feather in a color they had recently learned. Similarly, after they mastered the terms and illustrations of the parts of the body (168 terms), they made a cutout puppet of their own bodies. Children were free to leave their modules and enter the Life Simulator space on their own initiative. The only barrier was that their activities and games were limited to the workbooks they had mastered at their modules.

In addition to games, toys, and art materials, the Life Simulator area contained plastic replicas of fruits, vegetables, vehicles, animals, male and female people, and other figurines representing a variety of ethnic groups and cultures. Kits were designed or purchased so that children could lay out towns at the appropriate point in the program. Site visits to bakeries, supermarkets, generator

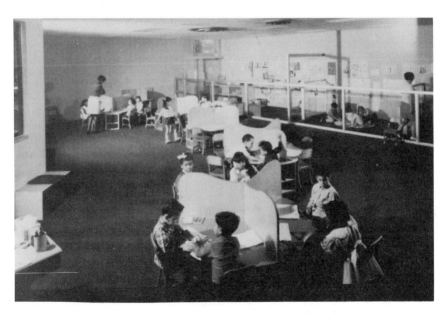

FIG. 9.4.   Micro-Social Learning classroom in session.

plants, newspaper offices, and police and fire stations took place only after the appropriate language base made the trip intelligible.

It should be stressed that the Life Simulator space was not a playroom (though it superficially appeared to be one). The Life Simulator served the following functions:

1. It provided an incentive for progress in the modular workbooks since a completed workbook was the "open sesame" for entering new activities.
2. It provided a means of enriching and actualizing the new forms and language terms learned in the workbooks by relating them to objects which could be seen, touched, manipulated, and colored.
3. It provided a means of transition from two-dimensional workbooks to three dimensions by engendering an awareness of different types of buildings, vehicles, equipment, and functions prior to actual outreach to the community.
4. It provided a means of increasing the precision, depth of meaning, and satisfaction in language use by offering activities that required the use of language terms in speech with others, thus enhancing social interaction.
5. It provided a means of relieving possible feelings of tension by enabling learners to move, on their own volition, from the structured activities at the modules to the less structured activities found in the Life Simulator space.

The sine qua non of the Life Simulator space was to increase the realism of language by providing three-dimensional objects associated with new words. The space was also used to make it self-evident that through words one can remove mystery and confusion and increase opportunities for satisfaction.

Summary

The primary objective of the program was to develop a high-efficiency learning system for disadvantaged (but not organically impaired) preelementary school children. For such children, the learning system needed to provide the opportunities for overcoming severe language deficits as well as behavioral and/or emotional problems. The purpose underlying the design of this physical classroom and these learning materials, methods, and procedures was to establish a social system amongst children in which language learning was perceived as a shared value of prime rank. It was hypothesized that at the end of 24 months of participation, children in the system would be able to meet the standards required in first grade.

FINDINGS

The evaluation of the Micro-Social Learning Environment utilized a longitudinal, multimethod approach, incorporating both quantitative and qualitative data and evaluating process as well as outcome. Evaluation data were collected in three phases: (1) preprogram; (2) during the program; and (3) 1976 follow-up (when most subjects were in the fifth or sixth grade). Five types of data were collected: standardized test data (phases 1 and 2), school competence data (phase 3), parental evaluations (phase 2), teacher evaluations (phase 2), and professional educator evaluations (phase 2). The school competence data were utilized to test the primary hypothesis of the research; the standardized test data to test the corollary hypothesis; and the parental, teacher, and professional educator evaluations to assess process as well as outcomes.

The evaluation of the program was not the responsibility of the project team. The evaluation of the standardized test data was the responsibility of the New Jersey Department of Education. The evaluation of the school competence data was the responsibility of the Consortium for Longitudinal Studies central staff (Consortium, 1977). The parental evaluation was conducted by a parent group. The teacher evaluations were administered by project personnel. Finally, the professional educator evaluations were conducted by Research for Better Schools (1970), under contract to the New Jersey State Department of Education. This use of independent objective evaluation was included in the writer's arrangement with the State in order to minimize the possibility of bias in selection and test administration. This approach to evaluation also meant, however, that the writer relinquished control over the implementation of the evaluation design. This lack of control over design implementation affected the standardized test score analyses, as explained in that section.

School Competence Data

Because the primary purpose of the Micro-Social Learning Environment was to prepare the child to meet the requirements of the school, the most appropriate evaluation outcomes would be indicators of whether the child was actually meeting the requirements of the school. The major indicator selected for analysis was whether the child had ever been retained in grade between elementary school entry and 1976, when the child was in fifth or sixth grade.

Because there was no equivalent control group (see next section), it was decided to compare program children with the general school population. A random sample of the children who had entered first grade one year earlier than the experimental children was selected for comparison. Because the school population included middle- as well as lower-socioeconomic class children, whereas the program children were, for the most part, children of Hispanic-surnamed migrants, the hypothesis to be tested was that no more of the program children (61.3% Hispanic-surnamed would have been retained than were retained in the general school population (25.7% Hispanic-surnamed). Results are shown in Table 9.2. By seventh grade (expected grade level), 32.0% of the program children had been retained in grade at least once, as compared to 34.7% of the earlier cohort. This difference was not significant. The program thus prepared the children to meet minimal school requirements (at least on this measure) as well as did the general school population.

A second comparison was also possible, utilizing just Hispanic-surnamed children. In creating the random sample of the previous cohort, Hispanic-surnamed children were oversampled, yielding a total of 62 children (26 in the random sample reported in Table 9.2 plus 36 additional children in the oversample). This oversampling permitted a comparison of Hispanic-surnamed program children with a random sample of Hispanic-surnamed children from the previous cohort. This comparison provided a control for English-speaking ability, ethnicity, and socioeconomic status. The hypothesis to be tested in this comparison was that fewer Hispanic-surnamed program children would be retained than were Hispanic-surnamed children from the previous cohort. Results are shown in Table 9.3. Only 32.8% of the Hispanic-surnamed program children had been retained, as compared to 62.9% of the sample of Hispanic-surnamed children in the general school population.

Thus, the evidence from the grade-retention-outcome measure strongly indicates that the Micro-Social Learning Environment increased the ability of high-risk children to meet the minimal requirements of the elementary school.

Standardized Tests

The corollary hypothesis that the Micro-Social Learning Environment would result in significant increases in standardized test scores was tested through a one-group pretest–posttest design. The original design for this component of the evaluation was a pretest–posttest with a matched comparison group selected by the New Jersey Department of Education.[1] This design was never implemented, however, and so the available results in this area are based on the weaker one-group design. As noted by Cook and Campbell (1979, pp. 100–102), a one-group pretest–posttest design fails to eliminate a number of threats to validly inferring the effect of the program. The most prevalent of these threats are history, maturation, test–retest effect, instrumentation, and regression to the mean. The threat of history is that events other than the program occur between the pretest and the posttest, and some of these events may affect the outcomes. In the case of the MSLE, the author was intimately concerned with the running of the program and was aware of no extraneous events that would have confounded

---

[1]The initial design of the study was to collect a complete sample of pretests on each child entering the center. Additionally, a group of 180 matched controls was to have been given the same battery. Both groups were then to have been posttested. Unfortunately, without notice to the writer, this agreed-upon design was changed during implementation. After a small sample of control children had been tested, the school system staff unilaterally decided that there would be no further control testing. As the writer, by agreement, was not directly involved in this data collection, the information on the missing control data was not conveyed to him until some months later. Only 13 controls were tested, and only mean scores (without standard deviations) were reported to the writer by the state.

TABLE 9.2
Retention in Grade:
Program Children Versus General School Population

	Not Retained	Retained	Total
Program N	132	62	194
(%)	(68.0)	(32.0)	
General Population N	66	35	101
	(65.3)	(34.7)	

$x^2 = .113$
$p = 0.74$

results. Maturation is ruled out as a threat to validity because the tests employed are standardized by age. Further, because the tests were given less than one year apart, the threat of instrumentation (i.e., changes in the test instrument) seems unlikely. Data from the untreated control groups from other consortium projects show little evidence of an IQ test–retest effect among low-income populations.

The final threat listed by Cook and Campbell (1979)—regression to the mean—requires a bit more discussion. Regression to the mean, which is the tendency for those selected at extreme points on a fallible pretest to regress toward the mean on the posttest, poses a problem for the pretest–posttest design only if the subjects were selected as low scorers on the pretest from a larger population. In that case they would regress upward toward the mean of the larger population purely as a statistical artifact of the imperfect pretest–posttest correlation. However, the Micro-Social subjects were selected primarily from a population of Hispanic-surnamed migrant children and not on the basis of low pretest scores. Hence, there is no reason to believe that the children's posttest scores would regress upwards toward a high population mean. Put another way, the subjects were chosen from a population whose mean IQ test score is below the national norm; therefore, despite the fact that the subjects' mean is below the national WISC norm, they would not be expected to regress upward to the national norm.

TABLE 9.3
Retention in Grade for Hispanic-Surnamed Children:
Program Children Versus General School Population

	Not Retained	Retained	Total
Program N	80	39	119
(%)	(67.2)	(32.8)	
Population N	23	39	62
(%)	(37.1)	(62.9)	

$x^2 = 13.886$
$p < .001$

In sum, despite the weakness of the one group pretest–posttest design in general, in this particular research most of the plausible threats to the validity of the design can be ruled out by the considerations listed above. Perhaps more importantly, as will be seen, the results are consistent with the results of the other phases of the evaluation.

The design was implemented as follows. All children entering the MSLE were pretested on the Wechsler Intelligence Scale for Children (WISC),[2] Peabody Picture Vocabulary Test (PPVT), and Goodenough Intelligence Test. A random sample of 29 children was selected from the program to receive posttesting at approximately 8 months after pretesting.[3] Posttest scores were compared with pretest using the t-test procedure. Results are shown in Table 9.4. The mean posttest WISC IQ of 88.8 represented almost a 10 point increase over the mean pretest IQ of 79.2 ($t = 5.14$; $p < .01$).[4] Similarly, for both the PPVT and the Goodenough, posttest means were significantly higher than pretest means.

In addition to the standardized tests, results were available on a Learning Effectiveness Scale for a sample of 93 children. The LES is a rating scale developed within the project to obtain teacher evaluations of the children on three subscales: Environmental, Verbal Fluency, and Situational Involvement.[5] The score consists of the difference between the rating of the child and the rating of what the teacher expects to be normal for a child of that age. Results are shown in Table 9.4. As can be seen, the posttest rating was significantly higher than the pretest rating ($t = 14.16$; $p < .001$).

In sum, the results from both the WISC and the Learning Effectiveness Scale

---

[2]With reference to the tests employed, at first glance it might appear that WPPSI rather than the WISC should have been used in the pretest, and, in fact, the project has been criticized for not using both the WPPSI and the WISC. It appeared wiser to use the WISC alone, even for children below five, because the two tests differ in items, raw values, and scaled values and are based on data from different age groups with unknown cultural and economic differences in the standardization samples.

Though both WPPSI and WISC are Wechsler scales which generate IQ scores, there is no proof that the scores lie along the same dimension. We therefore could not have grouped IQ scores of children across both tests nor could we use difference scores if children had taken first one test and then the other. On the other hand, by using WISC scores for all children, we could use raw and converted scores for grouped calculations using both obtained and difference scores. This was done following a t test, indicating no difference between children above and below 60 months. The fact that the WISC is not scored for children below 60 months does not affect raw scores on the same scale, and a conversion formula could therefore be used to adjust IQs in proportion to the number of months below 60.

[3]The posttest is actually an intermediate test because it was administered before the termination of the program.

[4]The control group of 13 showed no change in mean IQ score. (The mean score was 80 at both testing points.) Because the state did not supply either standard deviations or individual scores, it was not possible to utilize this data in conjunction with the program group data to test statistically the hypothesis of no change relative to the control group.

[5]The Learning Effectiveness Scale was published as the Social Effectiveness Evaluation Form (copyright 1963, Myron Woolman).

TABLE 9.4
Mean Pretest-Posttest Comparisons on
Intelligence Tests and Learning Effectiveness Scale

Criterion Test	N	Mean Pretest Score	Mean Posttest Score	Mean Difference Score	t	p^a
Wechsler-Bellevue Intelligence Scale For Children (Full Scale)	29	79.2	88.8	9.6	5.14	<.01
Peabody Picture Vocabulary Test	29	68.3	79.3	11.0	3.02	<.01
Goodenough Intelligence Test	27	74.0	80.6	6.6	2.57	<.05
The Learning Effectiveness Scale (LES) (Full Scale)	93	3.2	5.8	2.6	14.16	<.01

$^a p$ values are one-tailed.

indicate program effectiveness and are consistent with the results of the school competence analyses.

Parents' Reactions

It was evident within the first months that parents were deeply committed to the Micro-Social Learning Environment. They frequently visited the observation rooms to watch their children and the classroom in progress. The monthly meetings were uniformly well-attended, with more than 100 parents attending with their children. Latecomers invariably had to accept standing room.

The Parent Survey (Fig. 9.5) was conducted (in Spanish where applicable) by the parents themselves through their elected Parent Advisory Group. The survey took place without the prior knowledge of the writer. Its spontaneous origin and independence from the project, the school system, and the state give these data an unusual character. After being shown the pile of returns, the writer suggested that the parents calculate percentages for the responses (as shown inserted in the survey form).

It should be noted that most parents (70%) had other children in public school. Also, 46% of the parents stated that their children did not speak English on entry (which cross-checks within 10% with the estimate by the teachers). Also, 94% of the parents stated that their children spoke English better (Item 6) and 98% indicated that their children had an increased vocabulary (Item 8). In Item 11, 92% of the parents held that they would keep their children in the center if the program went to higher grades. Fully 100% of the families stated in Item 14 that

Fig. 9.5   Parents evaluation summary.

MICRO-SOCIAL LEARNING CENTER
PARENTS SURVEY

Please fill out and return tomorrow (Circle One)

1. How did you hear about the Micro-Social Learning Center? _____.
2. Do you have any children in public schools? Yes   70%   No   30%
3. How do your children at the Center compare with other children (at same age level)? Same   46%   More advanced   33%   (No Comment   21%)
4. How long has your child been at the Center? _____.
5. Did your child speak any English when he started at the Center?
   Yes   54%   No   46%
6. Does he speak more English now? Yes   94%   No   6%
7. Does he express himself better at home? Yes   95%   No   5%
8. Has his vocabulary increased? Yes   98%   No   2%
9. Does your child show more confidence in himself? Yes   92%   No   8%
10. Has his behavior improved? Yes   92%   No   8%
11. Would you like your children to continue at the Center if there were higher grades? Yes   92%   No   8%
12. If this program's enrollment started at 3½ years of age, would you enroll your children? Yes   87%   No   13%
13. Would you recommend this program to others? Yes   100%   No _____
14. Do you think your child has benefited from this program?
    Yes   100%   No _____
    COMMENTS: 1. Request for report cards
                2. Request for summer vacations
                3. All others were favorable and expressed praise for the program. Most of the comments came from Spanish speaking families who noted that English is not spoken in the home and were grateful that their child had the opportunity to learn English before entering public school.

Parent's signature _____

---

their own children had benefited. The summary comments by the parent survey group are interesting to note. The one at the very bottom of the page, that most parents were grateful that their children were at last learning English, was reminiscent of dozens of statements to the writer who was frequently thanked by parents for doing what they themselves were unable to do—give the children enough understanding of English so they would not have to work in the fields when they grew up.

The survey was conducted more than a year after the center began operation. At the monthly meeting that followed, parents who had not yet obtained or completed their forms vociferously requested and began to complete them. Perhaps a dozen approached the writer offering to fill them out immediately and often to express vehemently the position that the "Micro," as they call the center, was giving their children exactly what they most wanted them to have.

Teacher Reactions

After 5 months of operation each of the teachers responded anonymously to a questionnaire. The teachers were asked to describe their impressions of the effects of the program in terms of various outcomes. Their answers to two of these questions are summarized below with some illustrative quotations.

> The first question asked them to describe: The effect of the Micro-Social Learning Method on the speech and comprehension of the children you have taught. Please indicate the effect on children who had no problems, children with speech problems, and children from homes where Spanish or another language was used. Be as specific as possible.

Most of the teachers responded that those with no speech problems were making good progress, although one simply noted that "Many of the children coming into this program have had some type of speech problem." Three of the teachers commented that the program increased the self-confidence of children with speech problems. Two others noted some progress but said that these children still had speech problems. One teacher did not specifically mention children with speech problems. All teachers but one stated that Spanish-speaking children were speaking more English, particularly in interaction with the teachers. One teacher did not specifically mention Hispanic-surnamed children.

The complete response of one of the teachers is given below:

> The Micro-Social Learning method has affected the speech and comprehension of the children in several ways.
>
> 1. Those children who had no problems verbalizing are now able to construct more meaningful sentences, speak more clearly and more precisely.
> 2. Those who had speech problems still do; however, given specific goal words to say, they have shown progress (pronouncing by repeating after the teacher).
> 3. The Spanish-speaking children who came in with no English vocabulary have really progressed—not only using goal words but by being partnered with an English-speaking child."

Another question asked for a description of:

> The effect of the Micro-Social Learning method on the social interaction of the children you have taught. Please relate to their level of activity in speaking to each other, helping each other, play activity with each other, and their enjoyment of social games and the construction of expressive materials. Please indicate your view of possible changes in interactions between the children and you as the teacher and the aides.

All teachers observed an increase in social interaction among the children. The full response of one teacher is as follows:

At the beginning of the program the children acted in isolation but in very short order the organization of the classroom and of the play equipment required that they help each other. At the present time they play and work together very cooperatively. Their relationship to the teacher and aides is a very interesting and unique one in my view. They seem to regard the adult or adults in charge as a resource person to turn to for instruction or explanation. The children's progress or happiness does not seem to be hooked to any one teacher or personality. This is demonstrated by the easy way in which the children seem to adjust to all of the adults in the program and to the frequent rotating of teachers in the classroom.

In responding to the other items on the questionnaire, the teachers agreed that the program had a calming influence on the originally more aggressive children, and all but one agreed that the program had increased the children's attention spans. Finally, in a retrospective question, most teachers indicated that their original reactions to the program, both in their training period and in the first weeks of operation, had been skeptical but that in the ensuing months and program had convinced them of its value.

The opinions of participants in the program have often been dismissed as "too subjective" to be of value in program evaluation. In recent years, however, such experts in evaluation as Donald Campbell have come to advocate the use of such data as an important component of evaluation (Campbell, 1974). The observations of the persons who actually taught in the MSLE should be given careful attention in assessing the overall impact of the program.

Illustrative Professional Reactions

In addition to the teacher reactions, a number of professional observers viewed the Micro-Social Learning Environment and reported on its activities. Each observer possessed differences in theoretical viewpoint, both from each other and from the rationale underlying the Micro-Social Learning Environment. The theoretical basis underlying the Micro-Social Learning Environment project, the procedures, techniques, equipment, and materials were only briefly explained, often by staff in the time available. Professional reactions to the performance of the children were generally favorable. The professionals were particularly impressed with the system for reinforcing interactions among the children although some had criticisms of specific curricular elements.

The following statement is excerpted from a reaction by the Director of the Institute for Family and Child Research at Michigan State University, made by letter to the Commissioner of Education for the State of New Jersey:

> The effectiveness of the micro-social system developed by Dr. Woolman is, I'm sure, being evaluated in many ways and I shall be most interested in the results of these empirical efforts. I think it is fair to say, however, that the micro-social

dyadic system he has developed, is one of too few unique, experimental approaches toward maximizing appropriate affective and social development in young children.

DISCUSSION

The direct concern of this project was to create a classroom learning environment (the Micro-Social Learning Environment) that could assist in upgrading the performance of preelementary children whose severe language deficits and problem behavior made it improbable that most would be able to meet the demands of elementary school.

The Micro-Social Learning System sought to establish a peer group society in the classroom, in which progress in meeting the learning standards established in the curriculum became the basis for improving one's standing and upgrading one's self-image. The design required children to work together in pairs, using specially designed learning materials in a classroom that provided a Modular Learning area and a Life Simulator space. Its fundamental objective was to help children develop the language base, reading skills, and social behavior required to meet teacher and curricular expectations required for success in the typical first grade classroom. These were:

1. Knowledge of 2000 words in seven language areas.
2. Ability to read 300 basic words.
3. Ability to interact with others easily and naturally as a subordinate, peer, and superordinate.
4. Ability to maintain progress and restrain impulsive behaviors and aggression in the face of barriers to achievement.

Summary of Findings

The primary hypotheses were that preelementary-age children experiencing the Micro-Social Learning Environment for 6 months or more for 2½ hours per day would gain on early criterion measures and later perform as well as the general population of children in the school system. The findings exceeded expectations. There were three standard criterion measures: the Wechsler Intelligence Scale for Children, the Peabody Picture Vocabulary Test, and the Goodenough Intelligence Test. The results indicated that children obtained substantial and statistically significant gains on these measures after experiencing 8 months in the Micro-Social Learning Environment. Data obtained from the Vineland School System after the Micro-Social Learning Study was completed showed no significant difference in rates of retention between Micro-Social graduates (32.0%) and a random sample of Vineland school system students (34.7%). However, when a second comparison was made using only Hispanic-surnamed children, 32.8% of the Hispanic-surnamed MSLE children had been retained, as compared to 62.9% of the sample of Hispanic-surnamed children in the general school population.

Teachers shifted from initial apprehension tinged with animosity to full-hearted acceptance within 8 weeks. Three teachers requested that their own mainstream children become members of the Micro-Social classroom. Teachers, in their own evaluations taken in the fifth month of operation, reported that all children were speaking in English, although at the outset 55% were evaluated as speaking only Spanish. Teacher ratings on the Learning Effectiveness Scale showed sharp and significant improvement in ratings on each of the three sub-scales. At a subjective level, teachers, parents, the State of New Jersey, and outside evaluators reacted positively to the Micro-Social classroom environment.

Obviously, the results of a single demonstration, with or without a control group, cannot be definitive. It is unfortunate, nevertheless, that the agreed-upon control data was not obtained at the outset of the study, as initially arranged with the State of New Jersey and the City of Vineland. In our effort to assure objectivity and limit any possible tendency toward bias through using our own staff to obtain the measures, we lost an important source of comparison both then and in years to come. In retrospect, it is clear that this error was due to three factors: the failure to appreciate the volatility of state budgets; the very slim control exercised by the State Department of Education over local school districts; and the rapid shift in high-level staff at both the state and local levels. This being stated, we should also recognize that the data we did obtain indicated a far greater improvement than expected in this initial demonstration.

CONCLUSIONS

1. Children with Micro-Social experience showed significant gains in standard tests of language and intelligence, as predicted.

2. Children with Micro-Social experience progressed through the school system as well as the general population of children, as predicted.

3. Hispanic children with Micro-Social experience performed significantly better than Hispanic children lacking Micro-Social experience.

4. A carefully controlled study to evalute the Micro-Social Learning Environment should be made, comparing Micro-Social with other existing methods of preelementary readiness, such as Head Start.

5. Steps should be taken to test methods of generalizing Micro-Social classroom techniques to general education from the elementary through the university level.

Implications for Future Application

To this writer, the study clearly indicated that young children can rapidly learn to view themselves as members of a society in a classroom context and will learn those skills that the society has established as necessary. Where these agreed-upon goals are language and social interaction, given the necessary environment and materials, the children will sustain responses over extended periods of time to conform to the social norms of their own reference group. In the course of this social conformity they will acquire the specific language and behaviors de-manded of them as group members. When these language and behaviors conform to curricular requirements, disadvantaged students will show substantial progress in satisfying the academic standards imposed by a curriculum.

The real questions that remain are, first, if a large-scale demonstration project were set up to test the Micro-Social Environment under conditions in which children were in matched experimental and control groups, would the findings obtained be replicated? In this writer's view such a study would probably show greater gain for Micro-Social graduates because there were, in the study de-scribed, several avoidable problems that probably depressed the amount of gain achieved.

Secondly, could Micro-Social learning environments be developed to meet elementary, junior high school, high school, and university requirements? To some extent this question is now in the process of being tested. The writer has recently tested a 5-day, high-responsivity classroom environment for Job Corps resident advisors, using many Micro-Social techniques. The results were strong-ly positive as measured by the reactions of students and the sponsoring govern-ment agency.

The writer's view is that although generalization to different curricular topic areas would require some flexibility and imagination, there are no inherent problems that would act as barriers to the spread of Micro-Social methods. The only question is whether it actually works as well as intended. To determine this is simply a matter of committing the necessary resources to set up comparison studies at different levels under carefully controlled conditions accompanied by a well-articulated and objective method of evaluation.

Obviously, the Micro-Social Learning Environment is neither proved in itself nor does it prove the validity of the assumptions on which it was based. The fact that the outcomes supported the hypotheses does suggest that additional work to test the underlying assumptions is justified.

At a more practical and immediate level, even in its present state, "Micro" does appear to offer a useful supplement to Head Start and day-care programs at little cost, as staff and facilities already exist. It would appear sensible to evalu-ate whether, and/or to what degree, children in such existing facilities would benefit subsequently in elementary school. A more extensive longitudinal, experimental-versus-control study of the Micro-Social Learning Environment is warranted.

ACKNOWLEDGMENT

This study was funded by the New Jersey State Department of Education. Carl C. Marburger, Commissioner of Education.

REFERENCES

Arnold, L. E. et al. Prevention by specific perceptual remediation for vulnerable first graders. *Archives of General Psychiatry,* 1977, *34* (11), 1279–1294.

Campbell, D. T. *Qualitative knowing in action research.* Kurt Lewin Award Address, Society for the Psychological Study of Social Issues, Meeting with the American Psychological Association, New Orleans, September 1, 1974.

Coleman, J. S. *Equality of educational opportunity.* Washington, D.C.: U.S. Government Printing Office, 1966.

Consortium on Developmental Continuity. *The persistence of preschool effects.* Final Report, Grant No. 18-76-07843 from the Administration for Children, Youth, and Families, Office of Human Development Services, U.S. Department of Health Education and Welfare, 1977.

Cook, T. D., & Campbell, D. T. *Quasi-experimentation: Design and analysis issues for field settings.* Chicago: Rand McNally College Publishing Co., 1979.

Edwards, T. L. The progressive choice reading method. In John Money (Ed.), *The Disabled Reader.* Baltimore: John Hopkins University Press, 1965.

Glaser, R. Implications of training research for education - Theories of learning and instruction. *Yearbook of the National Society for the Study of Education* (Part 1). Chicago: University of Chicago Press, 1964.

Grotberg, E. H. *Progressive choice reading instruction in Prince Edward County school system.* (Report to the Office of Economic Opportunity [Grant No. VA-CAP 66-9201/1] and the State of Virginia). Washington, D.C.: Institute of Educational Research, 1967.

Harckham, L. D., Gunning, A. F., & Waldron, C. *Multiple prediction of reading achievement in grades 1 through 4 using kindergarten measures.* Paper presented at the annual meeting of AERA, New York, 1971.

Holt, H. O., & Valentine, C. G. *An exploratory study of the use of a self-instruction program in basic electricity instruction.* Murrayhill, N.J.: Bell Telephone Labs, Inc., 1962.

Jencks, C. M., Smith, H., Ackland, M. B., Bane, M., Cohen, D., Gintis, H., Heyns, B., & Michelson, S. *Inequality: A reassessment of the effect of family and schooling in America.* New York: Basic Books, 1972.

Jensen, A. R. How much can we boost IQ and scholastic achievement? *Harvard Educational Review,* 1969, Reprint Series No. 2, 1–23.

Kohen, A. I. *Determinants of early labor market success.* Columbus: Center for Human Resource Research, 1973.

Marco, G. L. *A comparison of selected school effectiveness measures based on longitudinal data* (ETS Report No. ETS-RB-73-20). Princeton, N.J.: Educational Testing Service, 1973.

McClellan, L. *A longitudinal study of factors which are predictive of reading success of low socioeconomic children in the seventh year of school.* Conference Paper, National Reading Conference, 1973.

Mott, F. L., & Shaw, L. B. *A comparison of female high school graduates and dropouts.* Columbus: Center for Human Resource Research, 1978.

Research for Better Schools, Inc. *An evaluation of the Micro-Social Learning Center in Vineland, N.J.* Philadelphia, 1970.

Robinson, D. *The youth unemployment problem: facts and figures.* (Vice President's Task Force on Youth Employment). U.S. Department of Labor, Employment and Training Administration, 1980.

Rodriguez, J. F. *Youth employment: A needs assessment.* (Vice President's Task Force on Youth Employment). U.S. Department of Labor, Employment and Training Administration, 1980.

Roth, J. A. *Progressive choice method.* Book Production Industries, Cleveland, Ohio: Penton Publishing Co., 1966.

Sewell, W. H., & Hauser, R. M. *Education, occupation and earnings: achievement in the early career.* New York: Academic Press, 1975.

Skinner, B. F., *The Behavior of Organisms: An Experimental Analysis.* New York: Appleton, 1938.

Thorndike, Edward L., *Educational Psychology,* Volume 2: *The Psychology of Learning.* New York: Teachers College Press, 1914.

Turner, R. R. Locus of control, academic achievement and follow-through in Appalachia. *Contemporary Educational Psychology,* 1978, *3,* 367–375.

Vargas, P. G., & Woolman, M. *Research issues in hispanic youth employment: an analysis in equity.* Paper presented at the National Conference on Hispanic Youth Employment, Washington, D.C., 1980.

Woolman, M. *Evaluating flight performance.* (Air Training Command, Final Project Report, MCAFB-TAID-55-1), 1955.

Woolman, M. *On-site training of guided missile operators.* (Technical Report 64). Alexandria, Va.: Human Resources Research Organization, 1960.

Woolman, M. *Programming for conceptual understanding.* (Report to the Communications Social Science Research Department of Bell Telephone Laboratories, Inc.). Murray Hill, N.J., 1962. (a)

Woolman, M. *The programming of reading skills: The progressive choice reading method.* Washington, D.C.: Institute of Education Research, 1962. (b)

Woolman, M. Cultural asynchrony and contingency in learning disorders. In Jerome Hellmuth (Ed.), *Learning Disorders* (Vol. 1). Seattle, Washington: Special Child Publications of the Seattle Sequin School, Inc., 1965.

Woolman, M. Training for adulthood in a Job Corps Center. *Phi Delta Kappan,* 1967, *48,* 433–436.

Woolman, M. Psychology and the functional illiterate. *New Outlooks in Psychology.* New York: Poers and Baskin, Philosophical Library, 1968.

Woolman, M. Operational context training for Nike operators. *Operational Context Training in Individual Technical Skills* (HumRRO Tech. Rep. 35-39). Alexandria, Va.: Human Resources Research Organization, 1969.

Woolman, M. *The micro-social learning system.* (American Institute of Research for the U.S. Office of Education, OE-20148, Catalog No. HE5.220:20148). Washington, D.C., 1970. (a)

Woolman, M. *A systems approach to pre-school education.* (An Analysis for OEO, Division of Planning, Research and Evaluation). Washington, D.C., 1970. (b)

Woolman, M. Manpower training: the tool station skill development system. *Modern Government/ National Development* (Vol. 17, No. 7). Westport, Connecticut: Intercontinental Publications, September 1976.

Woolman, M., & Davy, R. A. *Developing symbolic skills in the mentally retarded.* (Progress Report to the National Institute of Mental Health, Project No. 1010). Washington, D.C., 1965.

Woolman, M., & Grotberg, E. Theory and techniques of speech training of schizophrencis. *The Speech Teacher,* 1966, *15,* 279–285.

10 Long-Term Effects of Projects Head Start and Follow Through: The New Haven Project

Victoria Seitz
Nancy H. Apfel
Laurie K. Rosenbaum
Edward Zigler
Yale University

Introduction

Purpose of Study

The long-range effects of early educational experiences are difficult to determine for at least two reasons. From the viewpoint of scientific study, one common problem is that children's later educational circumstances usually resemble their earlier ones. Middle-class children typically attend middle-class schools for the duration of their schooling; the same continuity generally exists for inner-city children attending inner-city schools. Thus to single out for study the effects of some particular educational period is often not feasible.

A second problem—again from an experimentalist's viewpoint—is that children are not randomly assigned to the kinds of school or classrooms they attend. Rather, curricula, teachers, and facilities are usually made available in some selective manner reflecting some mix of demographic and personal characteristics. Thus, although there is compelling face validity to the notion that the kinds of educational experiences children receive are important determinants of their later academic skills, suprisingly little hard scientific evidence can be provided to document either the truth or falsity of this belief.

The issue is of more than academic interest when the population of children in question typically performs poorly in school. Poverty and educational failure tend to be linked both in the United States and elsewhere (Ogbu, 1978). The possibility that this link could be broken through early intervention was one of the bases for the creation of the Head Start program in the mid-1960s. The subsequent establishment of the Follow Through program was intended to provide economically disadvantaged children with an even more extensive period of continuous early intervention.

299

The present study is an evaluation of the long-term (postprogram) effects of a particular Follow Through program on the children who attended it. Because the program was of a specific and limited duration (from kindergarten through third grade) and because it provided some unusual qualities not present in the inner-city schools to which children returned afterwards (e.g., small adult–child ratios, and socioeconomic and ethnic integration), the problem described earlier of educational continuity was not present for Follow Through children in this particular study. A comparison in later years of Follow Through graduates and their classmates who did not attend Follow Through can potentially provide interesting information about effects of a certain kind of schooling for children's first few years in school. Because the methodology is longitudinal, the emergence of any differences can be traced directly over a long period, and such theoretical issues as "fade-out" (for intervention children) or "catch-up" (for nonintervention children) can be directly addressed.

The problem of selection presented greater difficulties. This study was quasi-experimental in that children were not assigned randomly to attend Follow Through and non-Follow Through classrooms. Although such a design does not render impossible the task of separating selection effects from treatment effects, it does make the task more difficult (Cook & Campbell, 1979; Seitz, 1980). The present authors have no theoretical axe to grind in believing that intervention of the kind offered by this Follow Through program either should or should not prove effective in changing children's long-range educability. Rather, we believe that it is important to ascertain as fully as possible what, if any, the effects of such a program may be. With a quasi-experimental design, such a task is challenging. We have therefore examined a variety of sources of information in order to make the best possible assessment of the relative roles of selection versus treatment in accounting for the results of the present study. As we will show, we believe that these results are most plausibly explained as true effects of the treatment.

History of Study

The study began in the fall of 1967 with all children who had just completed Head Start and who were enrolled in Project Follow Through in Hamden, Connecticut. This was the first year of operation for the Follow Through project. At the beginning of the project, these kindergarten children were therefore the only children attending Follow Through, and the staff and procedures were new as well. At the same time, the investigators also formed a control group of children, some of whom had had Head Start and some of whom had not, who were enrolling in inner-city kindergartens in New Haven. Both the Follow Through and control children were tested until the children were completing third grade, at which time a new group of cross-sectional control children was also tested. When the longitudinal samples of children were of sixth-, eighth-, and tenth-grade age, we retested them, and in the twelfth grade, these children were interviewed and their school records were examined.

In 1968, a second wave of Head Start graduates enrolled in Follow Through. These children were tested during their subsequent attendance at Follow Through. At the end of the third-grade year, the children who had completed the intervention program were compared with a newly selected cross-sectional control group of randomly selected children from an inner-city school serving the same neighborhood in which many intervention children resided. These samples were tested during fourth, fifth, seventh, and ninth grades. In eleventh grade, we interviewed these Follow Through and control children and examined their school grades and attendance records. We are in the process of obtaining their twelfth-grade school performance data.

In addition to low-income inner-city children, the Follow Through project also enrolled children from middle- and upper-middle-class families who resided in suburban areas near New Haven. The resulting SES and ethnic mix in kindergarten was therefore substantial, with approximately half the children enrolled in Follow Through coming from advantaged and half from disadvantaged homes. We have studied longitudinally through the twelfth grade a number of these advantaged children from both the Wave 1 and Wave 2 cohorts. The present report, however, is limited to results from the low-income samples. We will report data on the effects of Follow Through attendance on the advantaged children in a separate paper at a later time.

The two waves of low-income children in the present research report differ in two important respects. First, Wave 1 children experienced both the positive and negative special effects of being the first children to enter a newly established program. Children who are part of the first class of a new institution are not an ideal group with whom to evaluate the effects of the program, as both the high esprit de corps and the relative inefficiency of newly mounted programs are well known. This fact was one of the major reasons for the decision to replicate the study with the second wave of Follow Through entrants.

A second difference between the Wave 1 and 2 Follow Through samples is due to changes in procedures by those of us who evaluated the project. The evaluation of Wave 1 children at the end of the Follow Through intervention period was conducted only upon those children who were in third grade at the time. Because this procedure was followed for both Follow Through and control children, the validity of group comparisons was not affected. However, the nature of the population to whom results could be generalized was limited by this procedure to inner-city children who are academic survivors for the first few years of their school experience. This procedure probably also affected the assessment of gender differences both within and across the Follow Through and control groups, because the samples of boys in all schools were relatively more pruned by retention in grade than were the samples of girls. For the Wave 2 children, the samples studied at the end of the Follow Through intervention period were all of third-grade age regardless of the grade in which the children were actually enrolled.

The present study can therefore be regarded as two studies, with similar methodology but with somewhat different samples. In the study of Wave 1 children, we assess the postprogram effects of Follow Through attendance on inner-city children who were able successfully to complete their first 4 years of school without being retained in any grade during this period. In the study of Wave 2 children, we examine the postprogram effects of Follow Through on a more typical group of inner-city children.

THEORETICAL BASE

The number of studies of the immediate effects of early intervention has been very large. More than a decade ago, reviewers located over 1000 such studies to examine (Hawkridge, Chalupsky, & Roberts, 1968). Although serious methodological shortcomings rendered many of these studies uninterpretable (Campbell & Erlbacher, 1970; Hawkridge et al., 1968), a handful of well-designed and well-executed studies have now provided a data base for reviews of what is known concerning relatively short-term effects of intervention programs (Bronfenbrenner, 1975; Day & Parker, 1977; Gray & Wandersman, 1980; Horowitz & Paden, 1973; Palmer & Anderson, 1981; Ryan, 1974; Stallings, 1975; Weikart, 1981). According to these reviews, positive effects of intervention programs for disadvantaged children are often found on measures of cognitive performance administered at the end of the programs. Variations in the specific curricula children receive also appear to be capable both of being reliably documented (Miller & Dyer, 1975; Stallings, 1975) and of producing somewhat different measurable effects on the children.

Fewer data exist concerning the persistence of effects. Optimistic expectations concerning possible long-term effects were dealt an early blow by a research report suggesting that any immediate benefits of Head Start "faded out" within 3 years after the children's attendance in the program (Cicirelli, 1969). This study was criticized for serious methodological shortcomings (Smith & Bissell, 1970; White, 1970). especially for having employed cross-sectional sampling. But the concept of "fade-out" has remained a tenacious one despite more positive findings from more carefully designed studies (Darlington, Royce, Snipper, Murray, & Lazar, 1980; Lazar, Darlington, Murray, Royce, & Snipper, 1982).

Clearly, longitudinal data (such as are provided by the more recent studies) are essential to ascertain long-term effects and whether they persist, fade out, or, perhaps, increase over time. (See Clarke & Clarke, 1981, and Seitz, 1981, for contrasting views on the possibility of finding the latter kind of "sleeper effects" in intervention research.) The present study, with its longitudinal methodology, is relevant to the general debate concerning the persistence of intervention's effects.

A second issue that remains relatively underinvestigated concerns the social and behavioral effects of intervention. As Zigler and Trickett (1978) have discussed, children's social competence is of particularly great interest to societal decision makers. Specifically, Zigler and Trickett recommend that measures of social competence should include at least four components. The first component concerns children's physical well-being. (By this criterion, the Head Start program has been very effective in delivering health care to poor children [Kirschner Associates, 1970; North, 1979].) The second component is an index of cognitive functioning (such as an IQ test). Third, there should be one or more achievement measures to indicate how well a child is satisfying societal demands. These could include school performance measures, and also, as children mature, information about teen-age pregnancy, involvement in juvenile delinquency, whether the individual is in school rather than a dropout, in the appropriate grade in school, or self-supporting rather than on welfare. The fourth component of a social competence index should be the measurement of motivational and personality attributes.

One indication of the growing sophistication of intervention researchers is that estimates of social competence effects are increasingly being reported. One noteworthy example is provided by Darlington and his colleagues in their analyses of results of 11 different preschool intervention programs involving a total of over 1000 children (Darlington et al., 1980). Although there was no overall increase in IQs as a function of early intervention, the investigators discovered a significant effect on school performance. By late adolescence, children who had received early intervention were more likely to be in the school grade appropriate for their age; control children were more likely to have been placed in special education classes or to have repeated one or more grades. Thus, despite the absence of IQ effects, there were indications of increased competence in school as a function of early intervention. Again, the data in the present study are relevant to the ongoing issue of the possible social competence effects of early intervention.

SITE AND SAMPLES

Description of Community

At the time this study was begun, the city of New Haven was a growing, moderate-sized city. According to the 1970 United States Census Bureau figures (U.S. Bureau of the Census, 1972) its population was approximately 138,000. Ethnic diversity was moderate: 72% of the population was white, 26% black, and

2% other. Unemployment was estimated at 4.3% for males over 16; the majority of workers were employed by business and industry (approximately 80%), another 14% worked for some level of government, and 5% were self-employed. The median income for all families, in 1970 dollars, was approximately $9000. Nine percent of all families were receiving public assistance, and 13% of all families were considered to be below the federal poverty line. The median number of years of schooling completed was 11.7 years, and 48% of the population were high school graduates.

The city and its immediate neighbor to the north, Hamden, Connecticut, made an early and substantial investment in innovative educational programs. In New Haven, for example, very active recruitment for Head Start centers was begun soon after the inception of the program. By 1970 there were 16 Head Start centers in New Haven. In Hamden, the establishment of the Hamden–New Haven Cooperative Education Center made possible several experimental programs, from enrichment for gifted and talented adolescents to facilities for children whose native language was not English. The Hamden–New Haven Coop also provided the physical and administrative facilities for the Follow Through program that is the focus of the present investigation.

A variety of other education programs also were initiated by New Haven parents and school personnel. An active voluntary busing program (Project Concern) existed for several years for inner-city elementary school children to attend schools in towns near New Haven. Projects such as ''Right to Read'' and ''Focus'' (an individual tutoring program) were widely implemented in New Haven schools. Implementation of such programs has, in fact, been so extensive that many of the original control children were dropped from this study because their schools had introduced so many special programs during the years while the Follow Through children were attending Follow Through (Abelson, Zigler, & DeBlasi, 1974).

The presence of a large university has also been a factor affecting the degree of community exploration of early educational programs. Two well-known examples are an elementary school intervention project (Comer, 1980) and an infant intervention program (Provence, Naylor, & Patterson, 1977). In general, the community has been unusually active in educational experimentation and in providing special opportunities for its children.

Description of Samples

An overview of all low-income samples and the times they were evaluated is provided in Figure 10.1. [Middle-class Follow Through (FT) and non-Follow Through (NFT) samples are omitted from the present report.]

Wave 1. The initial group of subjects was 68 children attending FT kindergartens and 72 children attending kindergartens in four (NFT) schools. All the

FIG. 10.1. Overview of low-income samples and testing occasions in the longitudinal evaluation of Head Start and Follow Through Intervention in New Haven.

	Kinder-garten		1st Grade		2nd Grade		3rd Grade		4th Grade		5th Grade		6th Grade		7th Grade	8th Grade	9th Grade	10th Grade	11th Grade	12th Grade
	F[1]	S	F	S	F	S	F	S	F	S	F	S	F	S						
FT Wave 1 (N = 35) (born 1962)	x	x	x					x					x	x		x		x		x
NFT Wave 1a (N = 27) (born 1962)	x	x	x					x					x	x		x		x		x
NFT Wave 1b (N = 74) (born 1962)								x												
FT Wave 2 (N = 31) (born 1963)	x	x	x					x	x	x	x	x			x		x		x	
NFT Wave 2 (N = 37) (born 1963)	x	x	x					x	x	x	x	x			x		x		x	

FT Children at FT; NFT Children in other Public Schools | All Children in Public and/or Private Schools of their Family's Choice

[1]F and S denote Fall and Spring testings, respectively.

305

children resided in New Haven, Connecticut, and all were from economically disadvantaged families, defined as follows: (1) lived in low-income housing; (2) parents had no more than a high school education; and (3) parents were employed as semiskilled or unskilled workers or were unemployed. The FT group was recruited for the program by soliciting parents in several low-income areas. The NFT groups were made up of all the economically disadvantaged children (using the same criteria as for FT) in one classroom from each of four schools located in similar low-income areas.

Upon completion of the intervention 4 years later, 35 of the original FT children and 27 of the original NFT children were completing third grade in these schools. Three of the original FT children and three of the original NFT children (all boys) were held back in kindergarten or first grade and were dropped from the longitudinal samples. One NFT classroom of 24 children was dropped from the study because of the introduction of a tutoring program in the school. The others who were dropped had withdrawn from these schools during the course of the study and were not relocated.

At the third-grade testing, 74 cross-sectional control children were recruited from three different third-grade classrooms, one in an inner-city New Haven school, one in an outlying racially integrated New Haven school, and one in an inner-city school that had no form of enriched programs yet available and was located in another, larger, Connecticut city. These children represented intact third-grade classrooms with no selection of children within classrooms. Like the Wave 1 FT children, these children were in the school grade appropriate for their age. This group of children (NFT Wave 1b) was studied at one time only, at the completion of third grade.

Wave 2.   The initial sample consisted of 65 low-income children attending FT kindergartens. The children met the same criteria for selection as those in Wave 1. Upon completion of the intervention 4 years later, 41 of these children were still enrolled in the FT program. As with the previous wave of subjects, some of the children had not been promoted on schedule. These children (6 boys and 1 girl) were not dropped from the sample but were tested even though they were enrolled in second grade. Although all 41 of these children have been studied longitudinally for the entire postprogram period of this study, we report data for only 31 of them in order—as we explain more fully below—to permit the clearest possible postprogram comparison with a group of NFT children.

A separate NFT group was not recruited by the original team of investigators during the early years of this study. At the time the Wave 2 FT children were completing third grade, we randomly selected a group of 45 children from all children of third-grade age who were attending one of the schools that had provided longitudinal NFT children for Wave 1. This school served a mostly black, low-income area of New Haven.

Although Abelson and her colleagues (Abelson, 1974; Abelson, Zigler, & DeBlasi, 1974) did not find effects of Head Start persisting into third grade for the Wave 1 children, analyses for Wave 2 children did show significant effects of Head Start attendance (Seitz, Apfel, & Efron, 1978). Head Start attendance could not, therefore, be ignored in postprogram analyses for Wave 2 children, but neither were the numbers of children involved large enough to form a reasonable Head Start × Follow Through design. Therefore, the four boys and three girls in the NFT sample who were Head Start graduates and the three boys and three girls in the FT sample who were not were dropped from the sample. (These children have been tested, but their data are not included in the present analyses). Because the NFT Wave 2 sample was all black, the small number ($N = 4$) of FT white children's data are also not reported here. Finally, one NFT child was found to have been a FT dropout; she was eliminated from the sample entirely. The data reported here therefore provide a comparison of black, inner-city, low-income children who received 5 years of early intervention beginning with Head Start and those who received no intervention at all (samples FT Wave 2 and NFT Wave 2 in Fig. 10.1).

Analyses of Selection and Attrition

Selection.   Because children were not randomly assigned to the FT and NFT conditions, it is particularly important to consider how those children who enrolled in the FT program compared on demographic data and test performance with the NFT children whose parents chose to send them to their own neighborhood school. It is also important to compare the two waves of FT children for possible indications of differential selection in the 2 years of the program.

Analyses were reported by Seitz et al. (1978) of comparisons of Wave 1 and Wave 2 FT children and Wave 1 NFT children on demographic data (parental education, number of siblings, intactness of family, and preschool experience) as well as for test performance on the Screening Test of Academic Readiness (STAR) and the Peabody Picture Vocabulary Test (PPVT). These analyses showed that children who attended FT were more likely to have attended a prekindergarten program (Head Start) than were children attending NFT schools (74% versus 33%, respectively, $p < .001$). Mothers of Wave 1 FT boys were also found to have completed more years of education than mothers of Wave 1 NFT boys (11.5 years versus 10.3 years, respectively, $p < .01$). No other FT–NFT differences were significant.

Because NFT children in both Wave 1 and Wave 2 were selected on the basis of neighborhoods, it is possible to compare the neighborhoods in which these children resided with those from which FT children came in order to assess similarity of general neighborhood environment for the different samples. Table 10.1 presents a comparison of neighborhood characteristics for the samples in the

TABLE 10.1

Comparison of FT and NFT Children's Neighborhoods on Demographic Data[a]

	% Black	Median School Years Completed	% High School Graduates	% Single Parents	% Owner Occupied Units	% Vacant Units	% Over- Crowded	% Below Poverty Line	% Receiving Public Assistance	% Sub- Standard Units
Wave 1										
FT (N = 35)	38	10.9	44	16	20	4	11	14	31	2
NFT (N = 27)	12	10.9	42	6	52	3	9	8	13	1
Wave 2										
FT (N = 31)	51	10.9	44	17	25	5	11	17	35	3
NFT (N = 37)	81	10.9	42	18	31	5	11	13	47	2

[a] United States Bureau of the Census, 1970 Census Tracts (U. S. Bureau of the Census, 1972).

present report. These figures were obtained by determining the census tract in which each child lived on the basis of his or her home address. United States 1970 census tract data on a number of demographic variables were then recorded to describe the child's neighborhood. The data in Table 10.1 represent the mean values on these variables for the neighborhoods in which each sample of children were living. As Table 10.1 shows, the home neighborhoods for Wave 1 NFT children were somewhat more advantaged than those in which other samples of children were residing. Specifically, the Wave 1 NFT neighborhoods were more characterized by owner-occupied living quarters, by intact families, and by a lesser percentage of residents receiving public assistance. As Table 10.1 also shows, the neighborhood matching provided by NFT Wave 2 was generally quite close to that for the FT Wave 2 group except for ethnic diversity.

A comparison of the samples on known or probable demographic data is provided in Table 10.2 As described earlier, FT Wave 2 children in the present report are all black, because all NFT Wave 2 children were black. This fact did not reflect sampling error. Rather, although some white children lived in the NFT Wave 2 sample's neighborhoods, parents of these children tended to enroll their children in a local parochial school. The public school serving the area had a 98% black enrollment at the time the NFT Wave 2 sample was chosen, and the ethnic composition of the sample reflects the ethnic composition of the school.

Attrition During the Program. Examination of the FT low-income samples as a whole revealed a relatively high attrition rate of 37% for boys and 51% for girls. Most of the loss occurred at the end of the kindergarten year and was due to the exit of white children from the FT program (approximately 70% of low-income white children did not remain for the full 4 years). The rate of attrition for black low-income children alone was less severe: 74% of the black low-income boys and 55% of the black low-income girls who enrolled in kindergarten com-

TABLE 10.2
Comparison of FT and NFT Children on Known or
Probable Demographic Data

		Percent Black	Years of Parental Education	% From Single-Parent Homes
Wave 1				
FT	(N = 35)	86	11.1	31
NFT	(N = 27)	67	9.7	4
Wave 2				
FT	(N = 31)	100	11.1	19
NFT	(N = 37)	100	(10.9)[a]	(18)[a]

[a] Estimate from 1970 Census Tract Data (U.S. Bureau of the Census, 1972).

pleted the full 4 years of the program. For black children, the pattern of loss was also gradual rather than abrupt.

In the NFT Wave 1 sample, 27 of the 72 original low-income children remained at the end of third grade. Much of the loss was due, however, to the researchers' decision to drop one of the NFT schools from the study rather than reflecting the actual nonavailability of subjects. With the deletion of this school, the original low-income Wave 1 NFT sample had 48 children, and the percentage of children lost was 44%, a figure roughly comparable to the loss in the low income FT samples.

Comparisons were reported by Seitz et al. (1978) between the early (kindergarten and first grade) performance of children who completed the FT program and those who did not. For Wave 1, only 2 of 30 such comparisons were significant, both tending to suggest that children who dropped out of the FT program may have been somewhat less academically capable than those who remained. In the NFT sample as well, what few indications of differential loss existed also suggest the loss of poorer, rather than better, students. In Wave 2, only 4 of 30 comparisons were significant, suggesting a trend towards loss of more capable boys (two comparisons) and less capable girls (two comparisons). In general, the picture conveyed was that despite the many measures on which survivors and nonsurvivors were compared, very few differences emerged. It seems reasonable to conclude that for the FT children whose post-FT performance is the focus of the present investigation there was no large or consistent attrition bias during the program.

Attrition Following the Program.   In the post-FT period, attrition was minimal for both FT and NFT children and in both waves through the seventh- and eighth-grade testing occasion. Two years later, many children were located but did not agree to be tested. (Most, however, gave permission to have their school grades and attendance records examined.) In the eleventh and twelfth grades, the retention rate was again higher because children were interviewed rather than tested. We shall denote the exact number of children seen on each occasion in the results section.

METHOD

School Programs

Follow Through.   The FT program was conducted by the schools of New Haven and Hamden, Connecticut, and was physically located in a school in Hamden. The curriculum and guiding philosophy was selected following consultation with parents and was based on an educational model identified with the Bank Street College of Education (Maccoby & Zellner, 1970). The FT classes were composed of no more than 20 children. At least two full-time staff (head teacher and assistant teacher) were present at all times for an adult–child ratio no larger than 1:10.

The features that most markedly distinguish the FT program from programs in the NFT schools in the study were: (1) an individual rather than a group-oriented approach; (2) an explicit interest in the social-emotional development of the child; and (3) an emphasis on learning how to learn through the mastery of underlying principles and concepts. These features led to more frequent contacts between teachers and individual children in FT classrooms than in NFT classrooms. They also resulted in the use of a broad array of teaching methods, for the manner in which a lesson was conducted in an FT classroom depended on the needs, interests, and ongoing responses of the children in that classroom, rather than on a preset curriculum or technique. The FT program emphasized verbal communication skills. In addition, adult–child relations were oriented specifically toward fostering children's self-esteem and interpersonal trust.

Several features of the FT project other than curricular aims were distinctive. First, it was socioeconomically and racially integrated, especially in the kindergarten classrooms. The school was located on the grounds of a former college campus and was somewhat removed from residential areas. An important consequence of this fact was that all of the children attending the school were transported by bus. No children were outsiders being brought to another group's home territory. The FT project thus constituted an unusual situation in providing socioeconomic and racial integration on psychologically neutral territory.

The socioeconomic level discrepancy was generally large: low-income children came from homes where the head of the household was an unskilled worker or unemployed, whereas middle income was defined by homes where the head of the household was skilled, clerical or managerial, or professional. In many instances the middle-income children were from upper-middle-income families where the household head was a physician, lawyer, or college professor.

Because the Bank Street approach employed an open classroom model, children were not assigned to desks but were free to move about the room to interact with other children. The opportunity for frequent interactions with peers probably increased the effective amount of integration within the classroom. Student diversity within each classroom was maintained through a deliberate policy. The median percentage of low-income children in the classroom was 59%, with a range of 35–81%. The median percentage of black children in the classroom was 68%, with a range of 53%–82%. Diversity was high in the first 2 years but only moderate during the children's last 2 years at the school because of lessened enrollment of middle-income white children.

Non-Follow Through. The NFT schools served neighborhoods that were demographically and economically similar to those of the economically disadvantaged FT children (Abelson et al., 1974; Table 10.1 this volume). Most of the schools were in inner-city neighborhoods with predominantly minority populations. One school was in a noninner-city New Haven area with an ethnically diverse population. Children attending this school either came from low-income families residing in a public housing project or from more advantaged families in the surrounding neighborhood.

Initially, the New Haven schools had similar, traditional public school programs. Classes were larger than in the FT program; classroom teachers seldom had outside assistance. Lessons were usually organized for each class group as a whole, with the exception of reading, which was taught in small groups.

During the second year of the study, class sizes were reduced and a number of experimental projects were initiated in the New Haven schools. In two inner-city NFT schools, low-achieving children began to receive individual tutoring (several NFT children in the present study were tutored). Some children were bused to schools in middle-class neighborhoods (five of the original NFT children were dropped from the study for this reason). The noninner-city school in the socioeconomically mixed neighborhood was not involved in these projects, but the facilities of this school were greatly expanded and an extensive program of extracurricular activities was initiated.

The programs of these NFT schools thus changed in some significant respects during the course of the study. Although the pedagogical approaches used in the classrooms continued to reflect the group-oriented, didactic model that has traditionally been followed in public schools, the range of educational opportunities that were available to the children broadened considerably. It was primarily because of these changes that the NFT school located in another city was added to the cross-sectional study (NFT Wave 1b). As the children in this NFT school had not received any special remedial or enrichment programs, they provided a sample of comparison children with a more traditional type of inner-city school experience than the children in the other NFT schools.

Measures

Academic Achievement.   Academic achievement at the beginning and end of kindergarten was measured with the Screening Test of Academic Readiness (STAR; Ahr, 1966). The STAR is a group-administered instrument designed to appraise general information, conceptual maturity, and perceptual-motor development in preschool- and kindergarten-aged children. Academic achievement in Grade 1 was assessed with the Metropolitan Achievement Tests, Primary I Battery, Form A (Bixler, Durost, Hildreth, Lund, & Wrightstone, 1958–1962). This group-administered battery includes four tests: Word Knowledge, Word Discrimination, Reading Comprehension, and Arithmetic.

Because NFT children took school-administered Metropolitan Achievement Tests twice a year during the last 2 years of the study, they became considerably more familiar with these instruments than did the FT children. For this reason, a different instrument was employed for all children in Grade 3 to measure academic achievement—the Peabody Individual Achievement Tests (PIAT; Dunn & Markwardt, 1970). The PIAT is an individually administered test that requires approximately 45 minutes and provides measures of mathematics, reading recognition, reading comprehension, spelling, and general information. An overall academic achievement measure is based on the sum of these parts. The test has the advantage of having been standardized on a reasonably representative cross section of the school population of the United States. The reliabilities of the subtests are satisfactorily high, ranging from .68 to .94 at the third-grade level and .63 to .86 at the tenth-grade level. The reported median test–retest reliability coefficient for the PIAT tests over the grades involved in the present investigation is .76 (Dunn & Markwardt, 1970). The PIAT has been administered from Grades 3 through 10 in this study.

In addition to academic testing, children's academic success has been measured according to the school's perception of their performance. Collection of these data is still in progress and results will be reported in a later paper.

Intellectual Abilities. Form B of the Peabody Picture Vocabulary Test (PPVT; Dunn, 1965) has been used to investigate verbal intellectual development throughout the study. The PPVT is an individually administered test that assesses verbal conceptual knowledge independent of reading ability. In addition, for Wave 1 children, the individually administered Picture Arrangement Test of the Wechsler Intelligence Scale for Children (WISC; Wechsler, 1949) was administered in Grade 3 to assess the children's nonverbal, problem-solving abilities.

Other Measures. A number of measures of motivation, attitude towards self and school, and problem-solving style were administered to the Wave 1 children in first and third grades. These measures (Abelson et al., 1974) included a nonverbal and a verbal task from the Torrance Test of Creative Thinking (1966), a measure of imitativeness versus self-reliance in problem solving (Zigler & Turnure, 1964), a measure of impulsivity based on latencies in solving the Picture Arrangement Test of the WISC, an Attitude Towards School Questionnaire (ASQ; Klein & Strickland, 1970), and a self-image measure constructed by the researchers (Abelson et al., 1974).

From fifth grade on, both waves of children have received a semistructured interview. The interview has become increasingly involved as the children have grown older and more articulate. The most recent version (administered to eleventh and twelfth graders) requires approximately 45 minutes. The interview is partially forced-choice, to permit easier scoring and to avoid stereotyped, uninformative socially desirable responses (e.g., asking the name of the person's favorite books rather than whether the person likes to read), and it is partially open-ended to facilitate an easier flow of communication. Because results from this interview will not be presented in the present report, it is not described further here.

In fourth grade, the Wave 2 children received a measure of linguistic competence in standard and nonstandard (black) English. This task investigated imitative recall for sentences conforming to the grammatical rules of standard English versus parallel sentences conforming to the rules suggested for nonstandard English (Baratz, 1970; Fasold & Wolfram, 1970). Given that the FT children had attended an integrated school program whereas the Wave 2 NFT children had attended a nearly all black, all low-SES school, the linguistic measure was administered to ascertain whether this difference in peer group exposure would have effects on the children's language. For this particular measure, a comparison group of white middle-class fourth-grade children was also tested. Results were reported in Seitz (1975).

Finally, the Wave 2 FT and NFT children, and MA- and CA-matched groups of middle-class children, were tested twice during their fourth-grade year on an extensive battery of problem-solving and effectance motivation tasks based on tasks developed by Harter and Zigler (1974), and by Yando, Seitz, and Zigler, 1979. Some of these measures were also given to both Wave 1 and Wave 2 FT and NFT children when they were in sixth and fifth grades (respectively, for the two waves). In the present report, however, these data are not presented, as analyses are not yet completed.

Procedure

Intelligence and academic achievement tests were administered in accordance with the standardized instructions given in the test manuals. For Wave 1 children through third grade, the testing was carried out by 12 female examiners (four for the kindergarten testing, three for the Grade 1 testing, and five for the Grade 3 testing). Group testing took place in the classrooms with one of the examiners presenting the test items and two or three others serving as proctors. (Teachers assisted the proctors, except during the Grade 3 administration of the ASQ when school staff were excluded from the classrooms.) Children were taken out of their classrooms for individual testing. The individual testing followed a schedule that ensured that every examiner tested both FT and NFT children on each measure and that no child was individually tested more than once by the same examiner.

For all children in the postintervention periods, and for Wave 2 children beginning in third grade, all tests have been individually administered. Five different examiners, all young white women, highly experienced in testing and interviewing children, have carried out the testing (one for the Wave 2 third-grade testing, one for the Wave 2 fourth-grade testing, one for the fifth–sixth-grade testing of all children, one for the seventh–eighth-grade testing of all children, and one for the ninth–tenth- and eleventh–twelfth-grade testing of all children). Each examiner tested both FT and NFT children. Detailed testing procedures for measures other than standardized tests are described elsewhere (Abelson et al., 1974; Seitz, 1975; Seitz et al., 1978; Seitz, Apfel, & Rosenbaum, 1981).

Wave 1

Abelson et al. (1974) have published extensive data for comparisons made during and at the completion of the FT program for the Wave 1 children. We summarize these findings briefly here.

Kindergarten and First Grade.   In kindergarten, no FT–NFT comparisons were significant. In the first-grade comparisons, Abelson et al. (1974) found that FT children had significantly higher PPVT IQ scores than did NFT children (100.3 versus 88.2, $p < .01$). FT children were also significantly more communicative during testing than were NFT children ($p < .01$) and they had higher verbal creativity scores on the Torrance tests ($p < .05$). FT and NFT children did not differ on academic achievement measures in Grade 1.

Third Grade.   In the third-grade tests, both longitudinal and cross-sectional control subjects were employed. The pattern of findings that emerged was nearly identical with the two different kinds of control groups. In the present summary we follow the conservative strategy of describing those results found significant in comparisons with both control groups. Table 10.3 summarizes the results of unweighted means Program (FT versus NFT) $\times$ Sex analyses of variance performed on the third-grade data.

As Table 10.3 shows, the FT children scored higher on several academic measures and were more involved in the testing situation, as indicated by making more appropriately curious comments during testing than did NFT children. Boys scored higher than girls on two academic measures and had a more reflective (rather than impulsive) problem-solving style on the WISC Picture Arrangement Test.

Third Through Twelfth Grades.   Results from the third- through tenth-grade analyses have been published elsewhere (Seitz et al., 1981); therefore we summarize them briefly here.

As reported by Seitz et al. (1981), analyses on PIAT data have been performed upon deviation raw scores. That is, each subject's raw score performance is subtracted from the score that should have been earned based upon the grade level appropriate for the child's age and years in school. (Children who had at some time failed to be promoted were thus judged according to the level at which they should have been achieving.)

Repeated measures analyses of variance were performed on the data from third through eighth grade. For the reduced sample tenth-grade comparisons, *t* tests were performed.

TABLE 10.3
Summary of Findings for Comparisons of Wave 1 FT and NFT
Groups at End of Grade 3[a]

Measure	Program	Sex	Program X Sex
Peabody Picture Vocabulary Test (PPVT)	FT > NFT[b]	boys > girls	ns
Weschler Intelligence Scale for Children—Picture Arrangement	FT > NFT[b]	ns	ns
Peabody Individual Achievement Test (PIAT)—Mathematics	FT > NFT[b]	ns	ns
PIAT—Reading Comprehension	ns	ns	ns
PIAT—Reading Recognition	ns	ns	ns
PIAT—Spelling	ns	ns	ns
PIAT General Information	FT > NFT[b]	boys > girls	ns
Problem-solving latency	ns	boys > girls	ns
Attitude Towards School Questionnaire (ASQ)—Academic Work	ns	ns	ns
ASQ—School authorities	ns	ns	ns
ASQ—Overall attitude	ns	ns	ns
Student self-image	ns	ns	ns
Comments on Procedures	FT > NFT[b]	ns	ns
Requests for Help	ns	ns	ns
Comments on Meaning	FT > NFT[c]	ns	ns

[a] From Abelson et al. (1974)
[b] $p < .05$
[c] $p < .01$

Analyses of school attendance, grades in school, and interview data for the tenth- and twelfth-grade testing periods have not been completed. These data will be presented in a later report. Because gender differences are considerable, data are presented separately by sex.

Boys. Of the 21 FT and 13 NFT boys in the Wave 1 longitudinal samples, 19 and 12, respectively, were tested 5 years later in eighth grade. There were three gaps in these data: One NFT boy had refused testing on the PIAT in third grade; 2 FT boys had been lost at the sixth-grade testing. As current data were available for these subjects, estimates of their missing scores were made by linear interpolation for the sixth-grade data, and linear extrapolation for the third-grade data.

Group × Time (third, sixth, and eighth grade) unweighted means ANOVAs were performed on each of the PIAT subtest scores and on the PPVT scores. Following significant ANOVA results, post hoc comparisons of each group at each time were made by Satterthwaite's method (Winer, 1971, pp. 529–531). Significant FT–NFT differences were found on the mathematics subtest and on the general information subtest. Figures 10.2 and 10.3 show the performance of the two groups of children at each time.

As Fig. 10.2 shows, the FT boys consistently scored higher than did the NFT boys in mathematics. The difference was significant ($p < .05$) only in the third-grade testing. Tenth-grade attrition was substantial (14 FT and 10 NFT boys were tested), and involved the loss of higher-scoring FT graduates. Nevertheless, the gradual loss in mathematics achievement by FT graduates was probably a genuine result, and not an artifact of attrition. If estimates are made for the missing subjects on the basis of their past performance, the tenth-grade data resemble the sixth and eighth with the FT children higher but not significantly so. At the eighth-grade level (with the larger samples) the approximate grade levels represented by the raw scores are 7–4 for FT and 6–4 for NFT children.

As Fig. 10.3 shows, in general information FT boys have consistently scored higher than NFT boys. The difference was significant only at the sixth-grade

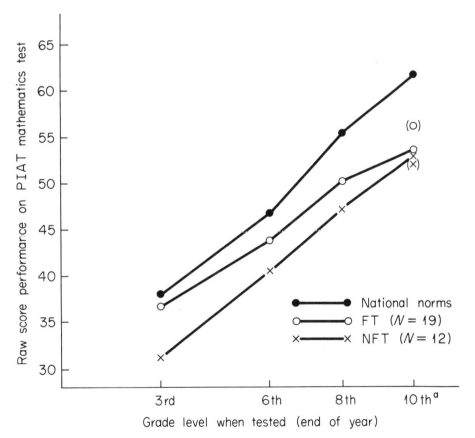

FIG. 10.2. Performance of Wave 1 male longitudinal samples on PIAT mathematics subtest.

[a]Tenth-grade values are based on 14 FT and 10 NFT. Values in parentheses are estimates for the full samples of 19 FT and 12 NFT.

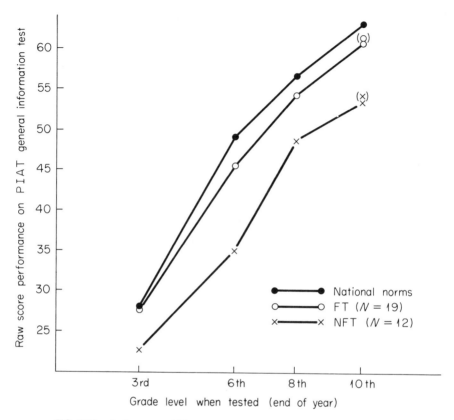

FIG. 10.3.   Performance of Wave 1 male longitudinal samples on PIAT general information subtest.

^aTenth-grade values are based on 14 FT and 10 NFT. Values in parentheses are estimates for the full samples of 19 FT and 12 NFT.

level ($p < .05$). (With the slightly larger full third-grade Abelson et al. sample, the third-grade difference had also been significant.) The tenth-grade attrition was not selective; that is, the lost subjects were not unusually high or low scorers on this measure. The FT–NFT difference approached significance ($p = .11$, two-tailed). With estimates for the missing subjects' performance (and thus a larger N) the difference also approached significance ($p = .06$, two-tailed). Given the consistency of the direction of effect and the fact that, averaged across time, the program effect was significant, we choose to interpret this finding as a significant one-tailed test effect. At the eighth-grade level (with the larger samples) the approximate grade levels represented by the raw scores are 8–2 for FT and 6–5 for NFT children.

   For purposes of later discussion, Fig. 10.4 presents findings on the reading comprehension PIAT subtest. As Fig. 10.4 shows, FT and NFT boys have performed similarly at all testings. At the eighth-grade level (with larger samples tested), the approximate grade level represented by both FT and NFT boys' raw scores was 7–3 (about 1½ years below grade level).

Table 10.4 presents the mean PPVT IQ test performance at each testing for all groups of subjects. For the Wave 1 boys, none of the FT–NFT comparisons was significant. (The slight attrition from the full Abelson et al. third-grade sample rendered the present third-grade comparison nonsignificant.)

Girls. Of the 14 FT and 14 NFT girls in the Wave 1 longitudinal sample, 14 and 12, respectively, had complete test data in sixth and eighth grades. Group × Time unweighted means ANOVAs revealed no significant differences between the groups at any times. In mathematics, however, NFT girls' performance declined significantly over time ($p < .05$), whereas the FT girls' performance did not. In eighth grade, the mathematics comparison approached significance

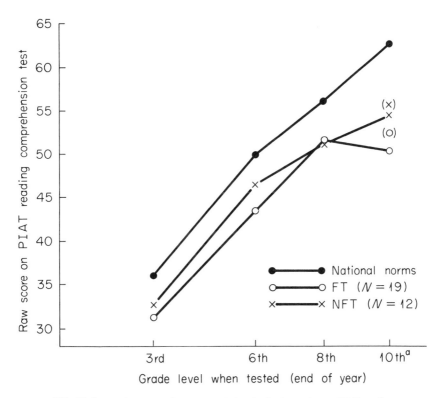

FIG. 10.4.   Performance of Wave 1 male longitudinal samples on PIAT reading comprehension subtest.

[a]Tenth-grade values are based on 14 FT and 10 NFT. Values in parentheses are estimates for the full samples of 19 FT and 12 NFT.

TABLE 10.4
Peabody Picture Vocabulary Test IQs for Longitudinal Samples of Follow Through and Non-Follow Through Children

Wave 1

	Boys				Girls			
	Follow Through (N = 19)		Non-Follow Through (N = 12)		Follow Through (N = 14)		Non-Follow Through (N = 12)	
Grade	$\bar{X}$	SD	$\bar{X}$	SD	$\bar{X}$	SD	$\bar{X}$	SD
3rd	100.6	12.2	95.2	11.8	89.6	10.1	88.3	13.1
6th	99.0	13.5	88.8	14.7	84.1	14.3	86.1	12.7
8th	97.5	13.8	89.5	16.2	86.4	17.0	92.0	17.1
10th[a]	96.8	14.0	94.4	20.1	86.6	21.6	84.8	16.3

Wave 2

	Boys				Girls			
	Follow Through (N = 20)		Non-Follow Through (N = 17)		Follow Through (N = 10)		Non-Follow Through (N = 18)	
Grade	$\bar{X}$	SD	$\bar{X}$	SD	$\bar{X}$	SD	$\bar{X}$	SD
3rd	91.0	11.8	93.2	11.4	95.4	8.0	87.6	7.4
4th	93.2	10.5	93.5	9.2	95.6	7.1	91.9	9.9
5th	88.0	8.1	87.0	9.1	95.2	14.6	84.8	13.3
7th	86.8	11.3	89.4	15.7	93.4	11.9	84.8	15.5
9th[a]	85.7	12.2	83.8	11.9	98.3	13.8	88.8	17.1

[a]For missing subjects, the data for 10th and 9th grades include estimated scores equal to the subject's average IQ over all previous testings. In all groups, the data for subjects actually tested were nearly identical to data with estimates included.

(FT$\bar{X}$ = −4.4 versus NFT $\bar{X}$ = −10.2, p < .10), a finding that is noteworthy given the previous absence of any differences between the groups. The approximate grade equivalents corresponding to the raw scores were 7–0 and 6–0 for FT and NFT girls, respectively. In tenth grade, the difference in mathematics continued to favor the FT girls; attrition, however, rendered inderminate whether this difference was reliable (10 FT and 11 NFT girls were tested in tenth grade).

Wave 2

Early Findings.   No kindergarten and first-grade comparisons are possible with the NFT Wave 2 sample. However, because the sample was redefined to eliminate white children and non-Head Start graduates, and because it includes children who had early school failure, a comparison of Wave 2 and Wave 1 longitudinal samples was made. Table 10.5 presents a summary of these comparisons.

As Table 10.5 shows, the girls in the two waves did not differ significantly on demographic variables or on kindergarten measures. At the end of the first grade,

TABLE 10.5
Mean Values on Demographic Variables and Early School
Performance for the FT Longitudinal Samples Studied Since
the Completion of Intervention

| | Wave 1 | | Wave 2 | |
| | Boys (N = 21) | Girls (N = 14) | Boys (N = 21) | Girls (N = 10) |
Measure				
Percent from Single Parent Home	24	43	24	10
Number of Siblings	2.6	3.1	3.0	2.4
Father's Education in Years	10.4	11.1	11.0	10.3
Mother's Education in Years	11.8[b]	11.2	11.4	11.6
STAR IQ, KG Start	88.6	93.1	93.3	91.1
STAR IQ, KG End	96.4	101.3	94.4	105.0
PPVT IQ, KG Start	90.9[a,b]	75.4	78.9	88.9
PPVT IQ, KG End	101.2[a,b]	88.4	92.0	93.0
PPVT IQ, Grade 1 End	103.5[a,b]	94.2[c]	93.5[b]	103.6
MAT Word Knowledge, Grade 1	1.7	1.7	1.5	1.9
MAT Word Discrimination, Grade 1	1.8	1.8	1.8[b]	2.4
MAT Reading, Grade 1	1.6[a]	1.7	1.3[b]	1.7
MAT Arithmetic, Grade 1	1.6	1.7	1.5	2.0
MAT Word Knowledge, Grade 2	2.5	2.4	2.1[b]	2.8
MAT Word Discrimination, Grade 2	2.7	2.9	2.5	3.4
MAT Reading, Grade 2	2.3	2.4[c]	2.4[b]	3.1
MAT Arithmetic, Grade 2	2.7[a]	2.5	2.3	3.0

[a]Difference between the means of the boys in the two waves is significant, p < .05 or better.
[b]Difference between the sexes within the wave is significant, p < .05 or better.
[c]Difference between the means of the girls in the two waves is significant, p < .05 or better

the Wave 2 girls had higher PPVT IQ scores than did the Wave 1 girls; in second grade, the Wave 2 girls had higher reading scores than did the Wave 1 girls. The boys in the two waves differed on a number of variables. The Wave 1 boys had higher PPVT IQs than did the Wave 2 boys in both kindergarten and first grade. They also had generally higher academic achievement test scores in grades 1 and 2 than did Wave 2 boys, with the difference attaining statistical significance on two of the eight measures.

The overall picture appears to indicate that the girls in the two waves were initially very similar, but responded differently to the FT program. The boys who have been followed since third grade show differences that appear to reflect having dropped children with early school failures from the Wave 1 sample. (Because this was done in both FT and NFT groups, boys in both FT and NFT Wave 1 samples were generally higher scorers than were girls.) In the Wave 2 samples, the sexes were initially comparable. Differences favoring girls began to appear at the end of grade 1 and were clearly evident on a number of school achievement measures in grades 1 and 2.

Third Through Twelfth Grade Academic Data.   Results from the third-through ninth-grade academic testing that have been reported elsewhere (Seitz et al., 1981) will be summarized briefly here. As for the Wave 1 children, analyses of academic data were performed on raw score discrepancy values. Unweighted means repeated measures ANOVAs were performed for third- through seventh-grade data. In ninth grade, when attrition became a problem, *t*-test comparisons were employed. Interview data, school status information, and results from early motivational tests will be reported in a subsequent paper as analyses are not yet complete.

Boys.   Of the 21 FT and 18 NFT boys tested in third grade, 20 and 17, respectively, had complete data at the fourth-, fifth-, and seventh-grade follow-ups. Analyses revealed significant group differences on the mathematics test of the PIAT. Post–hoc comparisons of group means by Satterthwaite's method revealed one significant result: Follow Through boys scored significantly lower ($p < .0 5$) than did non-Follow Through boys in mathematics at the end of third grade. The small attrition was not random, as the lost NFT boys had scored poorly on this test. For the full sample of 21 FT and 18 NFT boys the difference was not significant. At later testings the two groups did not differ significantly. This change reflects the fact that the Follow Through boys improved significantly over time ($p < .01$) in their performance, whereas the non-Follow Through boys did not change significantly over time. For the ninth-grade achievement test data none of the *t*-test comparisons was significant with or without estimates for scores of missing subjects.

Girls.   All 10 FT girls were tested each time. Of the 19 NFT girls, 18 were tested in fourth and fifth grades, 17 in seventh grade, and 15 in ninth grade. The girl who was lost in fourth and fifth grades was relocated in seventh and ninth grades, and one girl lost in seventh grade was relocated in the ninth. Early missing scores for these two subjects were estimated by linear interpolation. The cell sizes for the analyses of third- through seventh-grade data were therefore 10 for the Follow Through graduates and 18 for the non-Follow Through graduates.

Significant group differences were found on three measures: mathematics, general information, and the PPVT IQ. Figures 10.5 and 10.6 show the achievement test performance of the two groups. (The PPVT data were reported in Table 10.4.)

As Fig. 10.5 shows, FT girls consistently scored significantly higher in math-

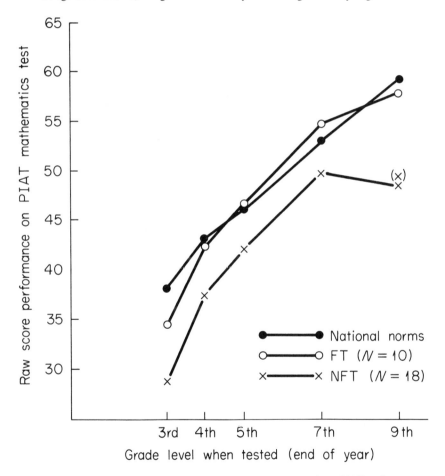

FIG. 10.5.   Performance of Wave 2 female longitudinal samples on PIAT mathematics subtest.

aNinth-grade values are based on 10 FT and 15 NFT. Value in parentheses is an estimate for the full sample of 18 NFT.

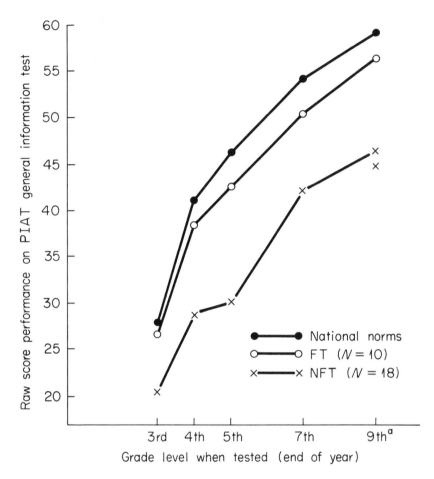

FIG. 10.6. Performance of Wave 2 female longitudinal samples on PIAT general information subtest.

ᵃNinth-grade values are based on 10 FT and 15 NFT. Value in parentheses is an estimate for the full sample of 18 NFT.

ematics. The differences were significant in third and in seventh grades ($p < .05$ in each case). The t-test comparison of the ninth-grade data also showed a significant ($p < .05$) difference in favor of the FT girls, with or without estimates for the four missing subjects. The approximate grade equivalents for the ninth grade raw scores are 9–2 and 6–5, respectively.

As Fig. 10.6 shows, the pattern was similar for general information. FT girls scored significantly better than NFT girls in fourth ($p < .05$) and fifth ($p < .01$) grades. The small attrition was selective, involving the loss of a poorly performing NFT girl. With the full sample of 19 NFT girls the third-grade FT-NFT comparison was also significant ($p < .05$). In the ninth grade the difference approached significance ($p = .08$, two-tailed). With estimates made for the missing four subjects, the difference attained significance ($p < .05$). The approximate grade equivalents corresponding to the ninth-grade raw scores are 8–4 and 5–8, respectively.

For the PPVT IQ test performance, FT girls scored significantly higher than did the NFT girls in fifth grade. (Means and standard deviations were reported in Table 10.4.) The remaining comparisons were not significant. The small attrition was selective, involving the loss of a poorly performing NFT girl. For the full third-grade sample the FT mean of 95.4 was significantly greater than the NFT mean of 87.2 ($p < .05$.) A t-test comparison of the means for the two groups in ninth grade showed no significant difference between the FT and NFT subjects with or without estimates of missing subjects' IQs.

Linguistic Testing. In fourth grade, linguistic comparisons were made among FT children and low-income and middle-income NFT comparison children who had attended segregated black and white schools, respectively. The FT children performed significantly differently from each of the two comparison groups. On standard English, black, low-income NFT children made the most errors; white, middle-class NFT children made the fewest. FT children made more errors than white, middle-class children but fewer than the low-income NFT children who had attended a racially homogeneous school ($p < .01$ for each comparison).

MEANING OF FINDINGS

Our results indicate that an extensive period of school-based intervention during the child's first few years of school can have measurable lasting benefits for at least some groups of children. For two groups of children—Wave 1 boys and Wave 2 girls—general information scores have been significantly higher for FT than NFT children several years after termination of the intervention. The Wave 2 girls have also shown lasting effects of the early program on their mathematics achievement for at least 6 years after leaving the program.

If early effects are also considered, all groups of FT children (both boys and girls in both waves) have been significantly different from NFT children at one occasion or another. In Wave 1, during the intervention phase, both boys and girls in FT and higher creativity scores and showed better communication skills during testing than did NFT children. In Wave 2, on linguistic testing soon after the intervention had ceased, both boys and girls who had attended FT showed greater competence in standard English than did low-income NFT controls.

In terms of long-range effects, a consistent finding in both waves was that the FT group whose scores were superior to those of their NFT controls revealed their superiority in the areas of mathematics, general information, and PPVT IQ. There was also consistency in the failure to find any influence of FT on reading performance. One implication of this pattern of findings is that these results are not the consequence of having tested groups of Wave 1 FT boys and Wave 2 FT girls who were simply bright and high achievers in general. The clearest evidence for this can be seen among the Wave 1 FT boys who scored near grade level on the most recent general information test (3 years ahead of the NFT boys) but who have consistently failed to exceed the NFT boys on reading comprehension. Other evidence exists in the preschool performance of the children. At the end of kindergarten, the mean PPVT IQ of the Wave 1 boys was 103.5 and of the Wave 2 girls was 93 (Seitz et al., 1978).

Our results indicate no fade-out of Follow Through program effects on general information 6 to 7 years following termination of the program. For the groups in which this effect was found the children were achieving near national norms; some children scored considerably higher. It is interesting that this effect continued to be found even though each child had attended at least two other schools since third grade and the total number of different schools ever attended by the children in the samples (and therefore potentially contributing some effect) was over 100. There appears to have been something about the program—perhaps the open classrooms, the many field trips, the small classroom unit—that has stimulated the kind of awareness represented in the continued high general information of some groups of its graduates.

The mathematics results are also interesting. Two of the four groups of Follow Through graduates were superior to the children in their respective control groups at the end of the program. The remaining two groups of graduates showed significant improvement over time whereas the children in the comparable control groups did not. Again, there may be an explanation in the nature of the Follow Through project. The mathematics curriculum was an unusual one, designed by a Chinese consultant to include many activities traditional in Oriental homes, such as paper folding and the creation of complex geometrical string designs. The children also cooked in the classrooms and were often required as exercises to manipulate fractions within such practical contexts as increasing and decreasing recipe quantities. The teaching of geometrical and quantitative concepts was thus perhaps more concrete and practical—as well as more playful—than is usually the case. Among the Wave 2 girls, evidence of the effectiveness of this instruction was clear 6 years later. In ninth grade, the FT girls were scoring near grade level and three years higher than the NFT girls.

The loss of mathematics achievement among boys in Wave 1 appears to reflect lack of exposure to appropriate high school mathematics classes rather than loss of aptitude for mathematical reasoning. Tenth-grade performance on the mathematics subtest of the PIAT requires knowledge of algebra and geometry. Yet, although approximately 90% of the middle-class graduates of the Follow Through program had taken algebra and geometry in high school, only 6 of the 14 Wave 1 low-income boys we tested had taken algebra or geometry by their tenth-grade year. (The proportion was similar among the NFT boys.) Two capable Follow Through graduates with PPVT IQs of 110 and 120 and scores in mathematics near grade level were taking "business math" rather than algebra. The two highest scoring boys in the PIAT mathematics test (with 11–0 and 12–9 grade level performance) earned a D and an F, respectively, in their algebra courses because of chronic truancy. There appears to be a definite underutilization of mathematical talent among these low-income high school boys. In short, the picture is not one of fading talent but of diminishing use of talent.

As the mathematics example shows, gender differences were important in the present study. The most likely explanation of the sex differences in the findings for the two waves is the fact that the Wave 1 children when tested in third grade were confined to academic survivors while the Wave 2 children were not. The present study is really two studies: in Wave 1, of children who were able to complete the first three school grades without failing a grade, and in Wave 2 of a more typical group of inner-city children. Such a fact might well be responsible for the reversed direction of sex effects found in the two waves if boys who survive academically their first few years of school are somewhat brighter than are the girls in their classrooms. This would be the case if boys whose performance is questionable are less often given the benefit of the doubt in school promotion than are girls. There is evidence in our study that the boys in Wave 1 (both Follow Through and non-Follow Through) were indeed brighter than were the girls in Wave 1 from kindergarten on and that the Wave 1 Follow Through boys were brighter than were the Wave 2 Follow Through boys. Each Follow Through group was initially similar to its non-Follow Through control, but there were overall sex differences in the two waves.

An implication of the Wave 2 results—with an all black, inner-city sample containing both academic successes and failures—is that among such samples girls are more affected by educational intervention of the kind provided in the present study than are boys. As Table 10.5 shows, the boys and girls in Wave 2 were initially comparable, began to differ by the end of kindergarten, and became progressively more different during the intervention. Following the intervention, the girls have maintained their advantage over the boys. These findings (as well as the loss in mathematics achievement for Wave 1 boys) lead us cautiously to suggest that the factors that cause inner-city boys to achieve poorly in school are less easily affected by school-based intervention than are the factors that cause inner-city girls to achieve poorly. Such factors as peer pressure, early school failure, the belief that academic success is not masculine, or disillusionment with the educational enterprise may diminish the success of school-based intervention for inner-city boys.

Because the design of this study was quasi-experimental, it is important to consider whether selection rather than treatment might have accounted for the findings. Among Wave 1 boys, maternal education was somewhat higher for

Follow Through than for non-Follow Through boys. In all samples, FT children were more likely to have attended preschool programs than were NFT children.

Given the time of recruitment (1966 and 1967), the likelihood of selective bias reflected by differential preschool attendance seems less of a problem than it would be today. At that time, recruitment was active in neighborhoods where Head Start centers were being established. Parents of Head Start children were therefore usually sought out actively and encouraged to enroll their children rather than being parents highly motivated to seek out a community resource for their children. The non-Head Start children tended to be from neighborhoods in which Head Start centers had not yet been established, so that nonattendance did not reflect low parental motivation.

A particularly compelling argument against invoking some hypothetical selection bias, however, is its lack of parsimony in accounting for the pattern of findings. If FT parents were simply better educated and more motivated, it is difficult to understand why their children did not read or spell better than did the NFT parents' children. Rather, it seems more reasonable that the educational curriculum given the intervention children was unusual in stimulating mathematics achievement and general information about the world. The fact that the children were better in these areas *without* being higher achievers in other areas (e.g., both they and comparision children read equally poorly) is easier to explain on the basis of specific educational experiences than on the basis of parental selection.

Abelson's (1974) data are also relevant to this argument. Abelson examined what became of Head Start graduates who returned to public schools immediately after the Head Start year in comparison with those who received the additional intervention of Follow Through. At the end of first grade, Head Start graduates, regardless of whether they were attending Follow Through, had higher PPVT IQ scores than did public school non-Head Start graduates in the same grade. This effect could reflect either selection or program differences. Two years later, the Head Start children in public school had shown ''fade-out'' whereas the Head Start children receiving Follow Through continued to maintain their advantage. It is hard to explain this pattern on the basis of selection. If the Head Start children who returned to public schools were ''select'' they should have continued to maintain higher IQs. If they were less ''select'' than the children whose parents sent them both to Head Start and Follow Through, they should not have performed comparably at the beginning and end of Head Start and 2 years later in first grade.

One persistent problem in the present study, as well as in other studies of long-term effects, has been low statistical power to detect those effects. Sometimes effects are sizable enough to have practical importance; yet the power to detect them is dangerously small. For example, in the PPVT IQ data, for Wave 2 girls in ninth grade there was a 10-point difference (better than the half a standard deviation that most evaluators consider ''practically significant''). This difference was also obviously replicable over time and represented a level for the Follow Through girls higher than their kindergarten performance. Yet with N's of 10 and 18, the power to detect this size effect is only about .35 (Cohen, 1977). In short, there is a .65 probability of failing to detect a true population difference of substantial magnitude. With an alpha of .05 and a beta of .65, one should expect a beta error.

If one takes statistical power into consideration, the pattern of results reported in the present study does not change, but the confidence one can place in the findings increases. Rather than interpreting the mathematics findings for the Wave 2 girls as if the effect faded then reappeared as a sleeper effect, the simpler explanation is that these FT girls have consistently had higher mathematics performance to a degree that has real-world consequences and that with low power this effect is detected at some times but not at others. The same is true for the general information performance in Wave 1 boys and Wave 2 girls. The only true fade-out in achievement has been mathematics for Wave 1 boys (as discussed earlier).

OVERALL SUMMARY

In terms of the outcome variables that are of greatest interest, it is too early yet to ascertain the results of the Head Start and Follow Through intervention for the children in the present study. The data presently being gathered (for Wave 2) concerning high school graduation will complete the planned battery of information for the study. We shall soon be analyzing results on this variable as well as on career plans, teen-age pregnancy, known incidence of delinquency, and the other social competence variables we have been assessing.

Although the present document is an interim report, several conclusions do seem reasonable. One is that "fade-out" is not necessarily a fact of intervention programs. Where effects were found, they continued to be found for a number of years, despite children's attendance at many different postprogram schools. And, when an effect did disappear, the reasons for the loss seemed more to reflect an inadequacy in the postprogram education the FT graduates received than an actual loss in the cognitive ability being assessed.

A second general conclusion is that raising poor children's academic performance—even to the level of national norms or above—provides no guarantee that these children's future educational careers will adequately reflect their talents. It is disturbing to find that capable high school children do not necessarily use their abilities in the classroom and that their grades sometimes do not reflect their actual level of knowledge (based on independent tests). Much research conducted by the present authors and their colleagues has suggested that poor children perform less well than they might for a variety of motivational reasons (Seitz, Abelson, Levine, & Zigler, 1975; Zigler, Abelson, & Seitz, 1973; Zigler,

Abelson, Trickett, & Seitz, in press; Zigler & Butterfield, 1968). To the degree that educational failure in later years is determined by motivational rather than cognitive problems, interventions aimed at improving cognition alone are likely to be relatively inefficient.

When large-scale center-based intervention programs were initiated in the 1960s, the optimistic expectation was that they would raise disadvantaged children's academic achievement substantially, across all areas, and to the level of national norms. This expectation has not been fulfilled. Instead, some groups appear to respond to educational intervention, while others do not. Our findings are consistent in this regard with those reported by Stallings (1975) and by Miller (1981). Furthermore, improvement occurs in some areas but not others and the level of improved performance in some cases reaches the national average, although in most cases it does not. The most important question—how these children fare as adults—remains to be answered by the data we are presently collecting.

ACKNOWLEDGMENTS

This study was supported by Grant PHS-90-C-912 from the Administration for Children, Youth, and Families and Research Grant HD-03008-13 from the National Institute of Child Health and Human Development. We wish also to acknowledge the cooperation of the New Haven and Hamden Schools and the many principals and teachers whose helpfulness and enthusiasm have made this study both possible and rewarding.

REFERENCES

Abelson, W. D. Head Start graduates in school: Studies in New Haven, Connecticut. In S. Ryan (Ed.), *A report on longitudinal evaluations of preschool programs*. Vol. 1. *Longitudinal evaluations*. Washington, D.C.: U.S. Department of Health, Education, and Welfare, 1974.

Abelson, W. D., Zigler, E., & DeBlasi, C. Effects of a four-year Follow Through program on economically disadvantaged children. *Journal of Educational Psychology*, 1974, 66, 756–771.

Ahr, A. E. *Screening test of academic readiness*. Skokie, Ill.: Priority Innovations, 1966.

Baratz, J. C. Teaching reading in an urban Negro school system. In F. Williams (Ed.), *Language and Poverty: Perspectives on a theme*. Chicago: Markham, 1970.

Bixler, H. H., Durost, W. N., Hildreth, G. T., Lund, K. W., & Wrightstone, J. W. *Metropolitan Achievement Test series*. New York: Harcourt, Brace, & World, 1958–1962.

Bronfenbrenner, U. Is early intervention effective? In M. Guttentag & E. L. Struening (Eds.), *Handbook of evaluation research* (Vol. 2). Beverly Hills, Calif.: Sage Pub., 1975.

Campbell, D. T., & Erlbacher, A. How regression artifacts in quasi-experimental evaluations can mistakenly make compensatory education look harmful. In J. Hellmuth (Ed.), *Compensatory education: A national debate*. Vol. III of *The disadvantaged child*. New York: Brunner/Mazel, 1970, pp. 185–210.

Cicirelli, V. G. *The impact of Head Start: An evaluation of the effects of Head Start on children's cognitive and affective development*. Washington, D.C.: National Bureau of Standards, Institute for Applied Technology, 1969.

Clarke, A. D. B., & Clarke, A. M. "Sleeper Effects" in development: Fact or artifact? *Developmental Review*, 1981, *1*, 344–360.

Cohen, J. *Statistical power analysis for the behavioral sciences* (rev. ed.). New York: Academic Press, 1977.

Comer, J. P. *School power: Implications of an intervention project*. New York: Free Press, 1980.

Cook, T. D., & Campbell, D. T. *Quasi-experimentation: Design and analysis issues for field settings*. Chicago: Rand McNally, 1979.

Darlington, R. B., Royce, J. M., Snipper, A. S., Murray, H. W., & Lazar, I. Preschool programs and later school competence of children from low-income families. *Science*, 1980, *208*, 202–204.

Day, M. C., & Parker, R. K. *The preschool in action: Exploring early childhood education programs*. (2nd ed.). Boston: Allyn & Bacon, 1977.

Dunn, L. M. *Peabody Picture Vocabulary Test*. Minneapolis: American Guidance Service, 1965.

Dunn, L. M., & Markwardt, F. C. *Peabody Individual Achievement Test*. Circle Pines, Minn.: American Guidance Service, 1970.

Fasold, R. W., & Wolfram, W. Some linguistic features of Negro dialect. In R. W. Fasold & R. W. Shuy (Eds.), *Teaching standard English in the inner city*. Washington, D.C.: Center for Applied Linguistics, 1970.

Gray, S. W., & Wandersman, L. P. The methodology of home-based intervention studies: Problems and promising strategies. *Child Development*, 1980, *51*, 993–1009.

Harter, S., & Zigler, E. The assessment of effectance motivation in normal and retarded children. *Developmental Psychology*, 1974, *10*, 169–180.

Hawkridge, D. G., Chalupsky, A. B., & Roberts, A. O. H. *A study of selected exemplary programs for the education of disadvantaged children*. Palo Alto, Calif.: American Institute for Research, 1968.

Horowitz, F. D., & Paden, L. Y. The effectiveness of environmental intervention programs. In B. M. Caldwell & H. N. Ricciuti (Eds.), *Review of child development research* (Vol 3). Chicago: University of Chicago Press, 1973.

Kirschner Associates, Albuquerque, N.M. *A national survey of the impacts of Head Start centers on community institutions*. Washington, D.C.: Office of Economic Opportunity, May, 1970. (EDO45195)

Klein, S. P., & Strickland, G. *The child's attitude toward school*. Los Angless, University of California, Center for the Study of Evaluation, 1970. (ERIC Document Reproduction Service No. ED 048 324)

Lazar, I., Darlington, R., Murray, H., Royce, J., & Snipper, A. Lasting effects of early education. *Monographs of the Society for Research in Child Development*, 1982, *47* (1–2, Serial No. 194).

Maccoby, E., & Zellner, M. *Experiments in primary education: Aspects of Project Follow-Through*. New York: Harcourt Brace, 1970.

Miller, L. B. Prevention through early education: Effectiveness of selected components. In M. J. Begab, H. C. Haywood, & H. L. Garber (Eds.), *Psychosocial influences in retarded performance*. Vol. II. *Strategies for improving competence*. Baltimore, Md.: University Park Press, 1981.

Miller, L. B., & Dyer, J. L. Four preschool programs: Their dimensions and effects. *Monographs of the Society for Research in Child Development*, 1975, *40*, (5–6, Serial No. 162).

North, A. F., Jr. Health services in Head Start. In E. Zigler & J. Valentine (Eds.), *Project Head Start: A legacy of the war on poverty*. New York: Free Press, 1979.

Ogbu, J. U. *Minority education and caste: The American system in cross-cultural perspective*. New York: Academic Press, 1978.

Palmer, F. H., & Andersen, L. W. Early intervention treatments that have been tried, documented and assessed. In M. J. Begab, H. C. Haywood, & H. L. Garber (Eds.), *Psychosocial influences in retarded performance*. Vol. 2. *Strategies for improving competence*. Baltimore, Md.: University Park Press, 1981, pp. 45–68.

Provence, S., Naylor, A., & Patterson, J. *The challenge of daycare*. New Haven, Conn.: Yale University Press, 1977.

Ryan, S. (Ed.). *A report on longitudinal evaluation of preschool programs* (Vol. 1). Washington, D.C.: U.S. Department of Health, Education, and Welfare, 1974. (Publication No. [OHD] 74–24).

Seitz, V. Integrated versus segregated school attendance and immediate recall for standard and nonstandard English. *Developmental Psychology*, 1975, *11*, 217–223.

Seitz, V. Intervention and sleeper effects: A reply to Clarke and Clarke. *Developmental Review*, 1981, *1*, 361–373.

Seitz, V. A methodological comment on "The problem of infant day care." In E. Zigler & E. Gordon (Eds.), *Day Care: Scientific and social policy issues*. Boston, Mass.: Auburn House Publishing, 1982, pp 243–251.

Seitz, V., Abelson, W. D., Levine, E., & Zigler, E. Effects of place of testing on the Peabody Picture Vocabulary Test scores of disadvantaged Head Start and non-Head Start children. *Child Development*, 1975, *46*, 481–486.

Seitz, V., Apfel, N. H., & Efron, C. Long-term effects of intervention: The New Haven Project. In B. Brown (Ed.), *Found: Long-term gains from early intervention*. AAAS 1977 Selected Symposium 8. Boulder, Colorado: Westview Press, 1978.

Seitz, V., Apfel, N. H., & Rosenbaum, L. K. Projects Head Start and Follow Through: A longitudinal evaluation of adolescents. In M. J. Begab, H. Garber, & H. C. Haywood (Eds.), *Prevention of retarded development in psychosocially disadvantaged children*. Baltimore, Md.: University Park Press, 1981.

Smith, M. S., & Bissell, J. S. Report analysis: The impact of Head Start. *Harvard Educational Review*, 1970, *40*, 51–104.

Stallings, J. Implementation and child effects of teaching practices in Follow Through classrooms. *Monographs of the Society for Research in Child Development*, 1975, *40* (7–8, Serial No. 163).

Torrance, E. P. *Torrance Tests of Creative Thinking*. Princeton, N.J.: Personnel Press, 1966.

United States Bureau of the Census. *Census of population and housing: 1970 Census tracts*. Final Report PHC (1) - 142 New Haven, Connecticut SMSA. Washington, D.C.: U.S. Government Printing Office, 1972.

Wechsler, D. *Wechsler Intelligence Scale for Children*. New York: Psychological Corporation, 1949.

Weikart, D. P. Effects of different curricula in early childhood intervention. *Educational evaluation and policy analysis*, 1981, *3*, 25–36.

White, S. H. The national impact study of Head Start. In J. Hellmuth (Ed.), *Disadvantaged child* (Vol. 3). New York: Brunner/Mazel, 1970.

Winer, B. J. *Statistical principles in experimental design* (2nd ed.). New York: McGraw-Hill, 1971.

Yando, R., Seitz, V., & Zigler, E. *Intellectual and personality characteristics of children: Social class and ethnic group differences*. Hillsdale, N.J.: Lawrence Erlbaum Associates, 1979.

Zigler, E., Abelson, W. D., & Seitz, V. Motivational factors in the performance of economically disadvantaged children on the Peabody Picture Vocabulary Test. *Child Development*, 1973, *44*, 294–303.

Zigler, E., Abelson, W. D., Trickett, P. K., & Seitz, V. Is an intervention program necessary in order to improve economically-disadvantaged children's IQ scores? *Child Development*, in press.

Zigler, E., & Butterfield, E. C. Motivational aspects of changes in IQ test performance of culturally deprived nursery school children. *Child Development*, 1968, *39*, 1–14.

Zigler, E., & Trickett, P. K. IQ, social competence, and evaluation of early childhood intervention programs. *American Psychologist*, 1978, *33*, 789–798.

Zigler, E., & Turnure, J. Outer-directedness in the problem solving of normal and retarded children. *Journal of Abnormal and Social Psychology*, 1964, *69*, 427–436.

11

The Philadelphia Study: The Impact of Preschool on Intellectual and Socioemotional Development

E. Kuno Beller
Freie Universität Berlin, Federal Republic of Germany with Robert Davis, Bonny Fatell, David Graham, John McNichols, Sidonia Roy, and Marcene Root.

Introduction

The immediate and prolonged effects of preschool experience on psychological development have been the subject of controversy for many decades. In the first half of this century, the controversy centered around the nature/nurture issue and the status of intelligence tests as measures of ability or performance (Honzig, 1948; Wellman, 1940). During the second half of the century the issue resurfaced with the same vehemence but in a different context. The new focus was provided by Jensen (1969) in his critique of compensatory education, particularly for black and lower-class children in America.

The subject of this controversy has never been purely scientific. Whether a person is psychologically inferior because of genetic programming or because of the lack of opportunity to learn and develop competences has been closely linked to decision making in the area of social policy and financial investment in the education of children. In the 1960s, the Johnson Administration mounted a major effort to make up for the lack of opportunity of socially and economically disadvantaged children. This movement took its cues from the conclusions of social scientists like Hunt (1961) and Bloom (1964), as well as from the prevailing realization following World War II that the gains of privileged societies, as well as segments within societies, are not tenable as long as ignorance, poverty, and violence remain viable forces (Harrington, 1962).

Several years after the onset of this effort, Jensen and others maintained that investment in compensatory education was a failure and could not yield the returns that this investment in education hoped for. However, in addition to contemporary criticism of both the studies Jensen selected and his interpretations

333

of them, the fact that Burt's early studies have been discredited has removed a major foundation of the hereditarian argument (Hawkes, 1979; Kamin, 1974).

A more direct attack on the effectiveness of preschool experiences for socially and economically disadvantaged children was undertaken by Cicirelli in his Westinghouse study (1969). The results of that study have been questioned for its neglect of controlling the quality of educational programs it evaluated and the limited yet global criterion measure it employed to evaluate the short-term effects of Head Start. Notwithstanding this criticism, investigators have continued to rely on one or another IQ test coupled with one of the standardized academic achievement tests as their main criteria in the evaluation of early intervention programs. Although understandable, this practice leaves us with very limited information about the impact of preschool on the development of children.

In order to estimate what a person might do with his/her intellectual aptitude and academic skills, it is important to assess attitudes toward learning and motivation to meet intellectual challenge. On the basis of such reasoning the present study includes these two aspects of intellectual development in its investigation of the impact of preschool experience. Even within the area of intellectual aptitude we found it desirable to assess a range of intellectual functioning that encompassed verbal, performance, expressive, and receptive measures.

Most neglected in the evaluation of preschool effects has been its impact on socioemotional development. The major problems of contemporary society are linked to socioemotional issues—both in their narrow and wide senses. The rapid and immense progress in natural science and technology that reflect a high state of intellectual achievement has left man in an almost primitive stage with regard to the prevalence of prejudice over tolerance, of mistrust over trust, of fear and a sense of helplessness over a sense of competence and courage, and of violent over nonviolent ways of dealing with frustration and conflict. The existence of disadvantaged segments of society reflect not as much a low state of intellectual development as a lack of the effective use and integration of intelligence in socioemotional development. The continued prevalence of low self-esteem, a sense of helplessness, inequality, impulsiveness, and other forms of low ego development contribute as much to school failure as the lack of academic skills. Therefore, the assessment of the impact of preschool on socioemotional development is, in our opinion, indispensable to the evaluation of its effectiveness.

On the basis of these considerations we designed an evaluation of the effect of preschool experience that emphasized a comprehensive view of intellectual and socioemotional development.

This view affected our choice of the independent variables as well. Preschool versus no preschool seemed to us a less differentiated view than length of preschool, which became our primary independent variable. Moreover, as we progressed in our evaluation study, we became more oriented towards the interaction of length of preschool with other variables for studying its effect on development. We chose sex and family background as the two demographic variables and their interacting effects with length of preschool as the framework for our evaluational scheme. In that way we tried to come closer to the question: Which children benefit in what way from more or less preschool experience?

SITE AND SAMPLE

Description of the Community

The children in this study were drawn in 1963 from four public schools located in an urban slum area of North Philadelphia. Blacks constituted 71% of the population in the target area. Residents were employed mainly in unskilled and semi-skilled jobs, with a small proportion of people in clerical positions. There was a hard-core group of black residents without any real work histories and with a low level of employability. The employment problem was further intensified by automation and out-migration of industry that curtailed the number of unskilled and semiskilled jobs available. The median income was $3383. Twenty-seven percent of the housing was classified as "deteriorated" or "dilapidated" in comparison to 13% in the rest of the city.

Description of the Sample

Each of the four schools opened a nursery program for 15 four-year old children. Applicants were recruited by sending notes that announced the opening of this program to parents of all pupils attending each of the four schools. The criteria used to identify "eligible" children were: born in 1959 (i.e., age 3 years and 7 months to 4 years and 6 months); children without serious physical or mental handicaps. Among the applicants from each of the four schools, 15 children were selected randomly for enrollment. These 60 children constituted the Nursery group. Ninety percent of the children were black and all came from low-income families.

Fifty-six of the original children graduated to kindergarten in the same four public schools in which they had attended nursery school. At that time kindergarten was not an integral part of the Philadelphia school system. Approximately 40% of parents with children eligible for kindergarten took advantage of this opportunity, whereas the remaining parents did not send their children to school until first grade.

The Kindergarten group consisted of 53 five-year-olds who entered the same kindergarten classes as the nursery children; however, they had no prior nursery experience. These children were selected from a larger group to approximate the age, sex distribution, and ethnic backgrounds of the children in the Nursery group.

The majority of children in these two groups graduated from kindergarten to first-grade classrooms in the same four schools in which the original programs started. Children in these two groups were assigned to first-grade classrooms in each of the four schools in such a way that an equal proportion of children from both groups would have the same teachers. This was done to control for any differential effects of educational experience due to differences between class-rooms and teachers.

From the first-grade classrooms in which these children were enrolled, a third group of 52 children who had no prior preschool experience was selected. Again these children were selected to be comparable to the ages, sex distribution, and ethnic backgrounds of children in the Nursery and Kindergarten groups. At the end of first grade, the study participants totalled 163; these children are termed the "original sample."

All three groups of children were again kept together within the same class-rooms and with the same teachers during the second grade. After that time, however, so many children had transferred to different schools in the city that it was not practical to continue the battle of keeping the few remaining children in the same classrooms. However, all children were followed up each year to the end of the fourth grade although the total sample had spread to 80 different schools in the city of Philadelphia. One hundred and fifty children or approx-imately 90% of the 163 children in the original sample were reached in 1969 at the end of grade 4. Follow-up was terminated at that point and resumed 6 years later.

Demographic Data

Because this study employed a quasi-experimental design it was important to test comparability among our three groups of children, especially on variables that might produce effects that would be expected to result from preschool experi-ence. The first set of variables thus investigated consisted of the IQ scores of children when they entered the study. The second set of variables consisted of ten demographic background characteristics of the children and their families.

Three intelligence tests were administered to the children at time of entry into the study (nursery, kindergarten or first grade): the Stanford–Binet, the Peabody Picture Vocabulary, and the Goodenough Draw-A-Man tests. Results showed that there were no significant IQ differences among the three groups when each began its school experience. More detail is provided in a later section.

Demographic data were collected by means of an interview when the children entered the program. Because these data from the original groups were in-complete, a second interview was carried out in 1976 to obtain a complete set of information about demographic variables at the time of entry into the program. The information sought in these interviews consisted of father present or absent in the home, parental employment, sex and birth order of the child, the number of siblings, the number of rooms in the home, head of household occupation, and mother's and father's educational level. (These data are presented in Table 11.1.)

There were no statistically significant differences among the three entry

TABLE 11.1
Distribution of Demographic Characteristics for Three Groups of
Children at Time of Entering Nursery, Kindergarten or First Grade
(1976-77 Followup Sample)

			School Entrance Groups		
Variables	All Groups	Nursery	Kindergarten	First Grade	Chi-Square
	(N) %	(N) %	(N) %	(N) %	
Male	(58) 50.4	(20) 48.8	(20) 55.6	(18) 47.4	0.75
Female	(47) 49.6	(21) 51.2	(16) 44.4	(20) 52.6	
Black	(100) 88.5	(36) 87.8	(31) 88.5	(33) 89.2	0.98
White	(13) 11.5	(5) 12.2	(4) 11.4	(4) 10.8	
Father Present in Home	(75) 73.5	(29) 74.4	(23) 74.2	(23) 71.9	0.97
Father Absent	(27) 26.5	(10) 25.6	(8) 25.8	(9) 28.1	
Mother Employed	(38) 38.4	(10) 27.0	(15) 50.0	(13) 40.6	0.15
Mother Unemployed	(61) 61.6	(27) 73.0	(15) 50.0	(19) 59.4	
	(N) Mean	(N) Mean	(N) Mean	(N) Mean	F-Ratio
Birth Order	(104) 3.4	(39) 3.5	(32) 2.9	(33) 3.7	0.85
Number of Siblings	(92) 3.6	(36) 3.4	(27) 3.3	(29) 4.2	1.19
Number of Rooms in Home	(104) 6.9	(39) 7.1	(32) 6.7	(33) 6.7	0.86
Head of Household Occupation[a]	(86) 5.9	(30) 5.7	(28) 5.9	(28) 6.3	2.39
Mother's Educational Level (years)	(90) 10.7	(36) 11.1	(28) 10.8	(32) 10.1	1.7

[a] Hollingshead Occupational Scale (1957).

337

groups on the 10 demographic measures. Thus, numerous indicators of initial status failed to reveal any differences among the three groups. Therefore, there appears to be strong support for the conclusion that these three groups were drawn from a homogeneous population with regard to variables relevant to this study.

Follow-Up Sample

In 1975, as part of the Consortium follow-up, a major effort was exerted to retrieve as many study participants as possible. Several difficulties were encountered: (1) the school system had not kept full records of children's addresses; (2) we were not given permission to contact the study participants directly because of considerations of privacy; and (3) more than one-third of the addresses that were available in the school records were incorrect at the time we resumed our follow-up. A series of search strategies were developed that required a great deal of time and detective work to trace lost participants. Over a period of 2 years we were able to locate 130 of the 163 children in the original sample. There were many broken appointments and a number of refusals of the family to cooperate in making appointments.

Because of these additional difficulties we were able to get complete data for only 107 participants in the 1976 follow-up and for 117 participants in the 1977 follow-up. Complete school records were obtained for 127 out of the 130 relocated participants. Five more subjects were located out of town who were willing to cooperate, but we lacked the funds to carry out these follow-ups. Thus, although we were able to locate 80% of our original three groups (from the end of first grade), we were able to obtain complete school records for 78% of the original sample and complete follow-up information for 72% of the original sample.

Attrition analyses on the Nursery and Kindergarten groups showed that there was no differential attrition between our retrieved and lost subjects on the original IQ scores.

METHOD OF STUDY

Nursery Program[1]

The nursery program was concerned with the children's curiosity for discovery, stressing personalized handling of the children by their teachers. An emphasis was placed on developing a program geared to each child's readiness so as to avoid the premature introduction of concepts and practice in skills that might

---

[1]The nursery program was supervised by Gay Faddis of the Department of Elementary Education of Temple University.

have a negative influence on the child's interest, cooperation, and attitudes. The program attempted to establish a proper balance of self-initiated and structured activities. The structured part of the program was designed to extend the children's knowledge of their surrounding world and to help them develop the kinds of perceptual discriminations and foundation skills that would facilitate their readiness to benefit from educational programs when they entered formal schooling. The content of the program concentrated on language facility, auditory and visual discrimination, listening and paying attention, conceptualizing, gaining information about the environment, motor coordination and control, and self-esteem.

In all, the program was child-centered in the sense that an adult provided the child with opportunities to choose from a variety of learning resources, and learning was shaped around the child's needs and preferences. The adult accepted and appreciated divergent reactions of the child and permitted the child to arrange his/her own individualistic sequences rather than urging the child to follow prescribed ways.

Teachers often sent short notes home telling about something of interest to the parent: the child's adjustment; the program; or some bit of information that was ''good news'' and served to keep the home and school in a positive relationship. A small booklet containing information of help in planning for their children over the summer was given to the parents at the end of the year. It also listed the various services that were available to families, including welfare and recreation.

The classes operated 4 days a week. On the fifth day, the teachers were engaged in in-service training, making home visits, and working closely with parents, home-school coordinators, the social worker, and other school personnel.

Staff and Training

Each nursery classroom had one head teacher and one assistant teacher. The head teacher was a fully accredited teacher with previous early childhood teaching experience, who was selected from the staff of the Philadelphia public schools. The assistant teacher, in every case, was a liberal arts graduate with no teaching experience. The selection of the assistant teacher as a nontrained teacher was intended to encourage persons with teaching potential to meet the challenge of educating disadvantaged children.

A social worker and four home–school coordinators were employed to offer social services to the parents and children. These coordinators were people who lived in the neighborhood of the school. Their major function was to help establish a close relationship between the nursery school and the families through home visiting and helping families with housekeeping and management problems. A health program was instituted to secure physical examinations, immunizations, and treatment.

The total teaching staff met with the project director one afternoon a week to develop guidelines for avoiding routinized teaching. The in-service training program was carried out with these primary objectives:

1. To emphasize the school's responsibility to enrich the lives of children from low-income families.
2. To help teachers understand basic nursery school procedures, the special needs of these children, and their strengths that could be utilized in the school setting.
3. To help teachers develop the ability to identify deficits in the total group and in individual children and provide compensatory learning experiences in the preschool program.
4. To experiment with and evaluate specific techniques and curriculum materials for helping the students develop the abilities, skills, and motivation to learn necessary to meet successfully the demands of the classroom.
5. To help teachers recognize the necessity of working with the parents of the children.

Kindergarten and First-Grade Programs

The educational philosophy of the supervising staff for the kindergarten program was exactly the same as for the nursery program. However, there were some major differences between the two programs. The teacher–child ratio changed from 1:15 to 1:25. The program ran 4 hours a day for 5 days a week throughout the school year. Although there was a home–school coordinator available in every kindergarten class, there was a less intensive effort to involve parents in the program than in the nursery group. Planning and supervisory time was greatly reduced. The first grade classrooms were regular formal schooling programs.

These changes from nursery to first grade are probably characteristic of average schools in the United States that include preschool programs. There tends to be a change from individualized, need-oriented teaching to an emphasis on formal, group teaching that is more achievement- and product-oriented. For that reason we considered our study to be one of the effects of earlier or later exposure to an organized educational program rather than an evaluation of a special preschool intervention program. In comparison to the other projects reported in this volume, our preschool programs were most similar to Karnes' "traditional" program (Karnes, Shwedel, & Williams, this volume).

Data Collection Procedures

Table 11.2 outlines the basic areas in which data were collected, the methods and instruments of assessment, and the developmental points or ranges at which data

TABLE 11.2

Areas in Which Data Were Collected, Methods and Instruments of Assessment, Developmental Range at Which Data Were Collected

Areas	Methods and Instruments	Developmental Range[a]
I. *Demographic*	Interview	MCh and A
II. *Intellectual and Academic Areas*		
1. Aptitudes		
a) General Intelligence	Stanford-Binet IQ Test	MCh to LCh
b) Passive Language	Peabody Picture Vocabulary Test	MCh to LCh
c) Performance	Goodenough Draw-a-Man Test	MCh to LCh
2. Achievement		
a) School Grades	School Records	MCh to A
b) General Academic Performance	Teacher Comments on Report	MCh to A
c) Retention in Grade	School Records	MCh to A
d) Completion of High School	School Records	A
e) Higher Education College	Interview	A
3. Attitudes and Motivation toward:		
a) School and Learning	Teacher Judgments on Bipolar Scales	LCh
	Interview	A
b) Intelligence Tests	Tester Ratings on Bipolar Scales	MCh and LCh
III. *Social, Motivational and Emotional Areas*		
1. Attitudes toward:		
a) Self	Piers-Harris Self Concept Scale	LCh and A
b) Self and Society	Interview	A
c) Sex and Family Roles	Interview	A
d) Work and Occupation	Career Maturity Inventory	A

(continued)

341

TABLE 11.2 (*Continued*)

Areas	Methods and Instruments	Developmental Range[a]
2. Values	Attitude Scale	
a) Moral Judgment	Piaget Stories of Moral Dilemmas	LCh and A
3. Motivation		
a) Dependent Striving	Observational Ratings	MCh
b) Dependency Conflict	Observational Ratings	MCh
c) Autonomous Achievement Striving	Observational Ratings	MCh
d) Aggression	Observational Ratings	MCh
e) Nurturance	Jackson Personality Research Form	A
f) Achievement	Jackson Personality Research Form	A
g) Endurance	Jackson Personality Research Form	A
4. Ego Development and Ego Function		
a) Stages of Ego Development	Loevinger Ego Development Test	A
b) Reflective-Impulsive Style	Kegan Matching Familiar Figure Test	LCh and A

[a] MCh = Middle Childhood (4-6 years); LCh = Late Childhood (7-10 years); A = Adolescence (17 -19 years)

were collected. The following will describe briefly the constructs and the method or instrument used for measurement. Further details about the instruments and data analysis are presented with the results.

Intellectual Functioning

In this area we assessed aptitudes, achievement, attitudes and motivation.

Aptitude.   Three IQ tests were selected to assess (to varying degrees) verbal, performance, expressive, and receptive aspects of intellectual functioning. The three tests were the Stanford–Binet Intelligence Test (Terman & Merrill, 1960), the Peabody Picture Vocabulary Test (Dunn, 1959) and the Goodenough Draw-A-Man Test (Goodenough, 1962). These tests were administered annually to each child from time of entry into the project to the end of fourth grade. Pretesting was always carried out several months after school entrance so as to avoid obtaining artificaly low pretest scores due to a child's unfamiliarity with school.

The Stanford–Binet Intelligence Test is a comprehensive battery of items that includes both verbal and nonverbal functioning, comprehension and expression, and inductive and deductive reasoning. The strength of this test lies in its comprehensiveness, which is in accord with its theoretical objective of obtaining a measure of "general intelligence." The Goodenough Draw-A-Man Test is primarily an expressive performance measure of intelligence. It does not require verbal skills on the part of the testee and, as a measure of intelligence, it is probably less affected by the cultural differences and educational background of the child than verbal tests of intelligence. Whereas the Draw-A-Man Test primarily measures expressive intelligence, the Peabody Picture Vocabulary Test measures essentially receptive intelligence via passive language. This test has been used widely in evaluative studies of educational programs for disadvantaged children and thus provided the opportunity to compare our findings with those of other studies.

Achievement.   In the assessment of intellectual achievement we obtained measures of the child's day-to-day functioning in the classroom as well as more global measures that are suitable for assessing long-range achievement. The child's day-to-day achievement was assessed by means of grades and teacher comments on the child's report cards from first to twelfth grade. Because the children transferred to so many different schools, few teachers were aware of the preschool experience of the children; hence, these data tended to be unbiased in relation to the hypotheses being tested. These data were obtained annually for each child from the files of school records.

The more global measures of academic achievement were retention in grade, completion of high school, and attendance in college. The first two were assessed through school records, whereas the third was assessed by interview.

Assignment to special education classes was not a meaningful measure in our study because of Philadelphia school policy. Analyses of grade retention data are presented in this report. Data on high school completion and college attendance are presented in the pooled analyses chapter in this volume.

Intellectual Attitudes and Motivation.   The child's positive or negative attitudes toward school learning were assessed by asking teachers at the end of first and second grade to select sets of three children who represented the extremes of two bipolar dimensions: best to worst attitudes to study and learning, and most positive to most negative attitudes toward school. In addition, the child's motivational and emotional reactions to the yearly individual intelligence testing situations were assessed. Seven-point scales were developed by the present writer for the following dimensions: cooperative to resistant, involved to uninvolved, and low to high persistence. These scales were scored by the examiner following each individual testing period from nursery through the third grade.

Social, Motivational, and Emotional Functioning

A major and probably unique aspect of the present study was the effort made to get a comprehensive and detailed assessment of effects of preschool on social, motivational, and emotional development.

Attitudes.   Attitudes were assessed with regard to self, self and society, sex and family roles, and work and occupation. A general description of the measures follows, and a more detailed description is presented in the results section. Attitudes towards self were assessed by means of the Piers–Harris Self-Concept Scales (Piers & Harris, 1964) in fourth and tenth grades. Attitudes towards self and society were assessed in eleventh grade as part of an interview intended to assess ''quality of life.'' An inventory of attitudes toward sex and family roles was designed for the present study to assess contemporary versus traditional attitudes towards sex roles, both inside and outside the family structure. Attitudes toward work and occupation were assessed through the Career Maturity Inventory Attitude Scale (Crites, 1973). It was administered in the eleventh grade.

Moral Judgment.   Piaget (1932) formulated a general developmental sequence of moral reasoning through which the child progresses. He developed moral dilemmas in 18 stories that were presented to children to assess their development of moral judgment. A modified version of these stories (Seltzer & Beller, 1969) was presented to our children in the fourth and tenth grades. The fourth grade responses were analyzed according to Piaget's criteria and yielded only total moral judgment scores. For the tenth grade assessment, an inquiry was carried out to elicit responses relevant for a more detailed analysis. A technique was designed to distinguish five specific aspects of moral judgment: attitudes toward: (1) authority; (2) distributive justice; (3) expiatory versus restitutive punishment; (4) immanent justice; and (5) consequences versus intentionality.

Motivation.   In order to assess the effect of preschool on motivation, a series of motivational variables were selected and studied in first grade and also toward the end of high school. In first grade the motivational variables were dependent striving, dependency conflict, autonomous achievement striving, and aggression. These variables were assessed through observational ratings in the classroom by participant and nonparticipant observers. Dependent striving was measured by the frequency with which a child sought help, attention, recognition, physical contact, and nearness; dependency conflict by the frequency of vacillation, indirectness, and inhibition in the expression of dependency needs; autonomous achievement striving by the frequency of initiating, persisting, and completing activities by oneself, by showing tension reduction at the completion of autonomous activities, and by enjoying doing things by oneself; aggression by the frequency of physical attacks, threatening and derogating of others, and destroying or damaging materials. These measures had been used in a series of studies, details of which are contained in previous publications (Beller, 1959; Beller, Adler, Newcomer, & Young, 1972).

Motives were assessed again towards the end of high school by means of the Jackson Personality Research Form (Jackson, 1974). We selected four scales from this personality test to present in this chapter: nurturance, achievement, endurance, and aggression.

Ego Development and Ego Function.   Ego development was measured in the eleventh grade by means of the Loevinger Sentence Completion Test (Loevinger, 1970). This instrument attempts to distinguish successive stages of ego development in areas of impulse control, interpersonal style, conscious preoccupations, and cognitive style. The instrument to assess a specific ego function was Kagan's Matching Familiar Figures Test (Kagan, 1965), which is designed to measure reflectiveness–impulsiveness. This instrument was administered in the fourth and eleventh grades.

Analytic Procedures

The major tests used in the analyses of the data were analysis of variance, *t*-test, chi-square test, and product-moment correlation. All significance levels reported were two-tailed; a *p*-value $\leq .05$ is termed significant, and a *p*-value $\leq .10$ approaches significance. All analyses involved a three-point continuum of 2 years, 1 year, and no preschool. This last point is important for two reasons. First, most studies have used a dichotomy of preschool/no preschool or intervention/no intervention. Secondly, the findings reported in this chapter had a different data base than findings reported on this program in the pooled analyses chapter. The pooled analyses of the Consortium dropped the no-preschool group (first grade) in order to fit the data into a dichotomy of prekindergarten versus kindergarten. Any differences between the findings of this chapter and the Beller findings in the pooled analyses chapter are due to this decision.

Like other studies reported in this volume we investigated interacting effects. However, with one exception, we limited ourselves throughout to first order interactions. That is, we pooled over other variables whenever we analyzed the interaction of a given variable, such as sex, with length of preschool. This decision was dictated by the consideration that when one uses interaction or multiple regression procedures the sample base shrinks considerably and the findings become less powerful. Future analyses of our data will use the multiple regression technique.

RESULTS

The present report is not a final report of all the data collected because their analyses are not yet completed. A further limitation of the present report is that breakdowns by sex and family background that constitute an important part of our analysis have not been completed for all data reported here.[2]

Intellectual Functioning

Aptitude

From our simultaneous use of three intelligence tests we discovered both similarities and differences among the three groups at entrance to the study and in response to the different lengths of preschool experience. Inspection of Figs. 11.1–11.3 shows that our three school entrance groups did not differ from each other on their mean IQ scores when they entered nursery, kindergarten, or first grade. When tested by one-way analyses of variance, the differences among the three groups were not only statistically insignificant, but also below 3 points and therefore within the standard error of measurement.

Another major finding revealed by these graphs is that the absolute level of the child's intellectual functioning at school entrance varied as a function of the intelligence test used. On the Draw-A-Man Test (see Figure 11.3), the original groups of children performed only slightly below the average for the standardization group, that is, the average score was about 98. On the Stanford–Binet, the IQ score of each of these groups was about 91, that is, at the lower end of the

---

[2]Demographic data were not complete at the time of an earlier report (Beller, 1974). The findings included in the earlier report are summarized here only for main effects. Interactions for these data will be analyzed and reported at a later point.

normal range when compared to the standardization group. On the PPVT, the initial level of intellectual functioning was considerably more depressed than on the other two tests because the average IQ score was approximately 82 for the Kindergarten and First Grade groups when they entered school. Thus, depending on the type of test used as the basis for generalization, one might say that the initial level of intellectual functioning of these children ranged from slightly below average to subnormal. The clear implication of this finding is that any generalizations concerning the intellectual functioning of disadvantaged children must be qualified depending on the test used.

A major research question concerned the impact of length of preschool on intellectual aptitude. Initial exposure to school resulted in a greater increase of Stanford–Binet IQ score over the period of 1 year when the child entered school earlier rather than later (see Fig. 11.1). The first year increase was over 6 points (92.1 to 98.6) for the Nursery group, whereas the first year increase for the Kindergarten group was over 3 points (91.2 to 94.4). For the First Grade group there was, if anything, a slight decrease (from 89.9 to 88.6). These change scores differed significantly when tested by an analysis of variance ($F = 10.98$, df $= 2/159$, $p < .01$). The conclusion from these findings is that the first year impact on the level of intellectual functioning is greater the earlier an economically disadvantaged child is exposed to an organized program of education

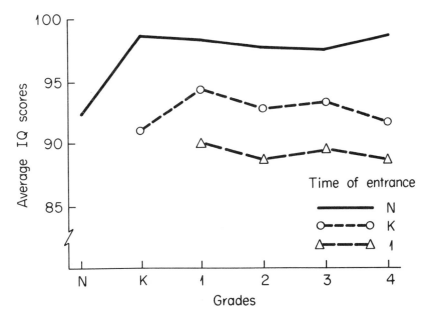

FIG. 11.1.   Stanford–Binet IQ scores across grades of groups entering school at Nursery (N), Kindergarten (K), and First Grade (1).
Note. Original samples with group N's ranging from 46 to 58.

(between 4 and 6 years of age). However, this conclusion is limited to the Stanford–Binet IQ scores; an opposite finding of a delayed effect on the Goodenough IQ scores is described later.

When we consider the prolonged impact of educational intervention (that is, to the end of the fourth grade), it is evident that it also differed markedly as a function of the test employed (and the dimension of intellectual functioning being measured). It can be seen in Fig. 11.1 that the Stanford–Binet test scores, and the differences among the three groups after the initial changes, remained remarkably stable from year to year. The differences among the three groups from first to fourth grade were statistically significant ($F = 6.71$, df = 2/429, $p < .01$). Although all children started school with similar low-average Stanford–Binet scores, those children with the longest preschool experience were the only ones to reach an approximately average level of intellectual functioning on this widely used and well-standardized test. It should be emphasized that the testers were blind to the child's preschool experience and the team of testers changed from year to year.

An analysis of variance carried out on the Peabody Picture Vocabulary IQ scores of children from the first to fourth grade yielded similar results (see Fig. 11.2; this test was first administered to the Nursery group during kindergarten).

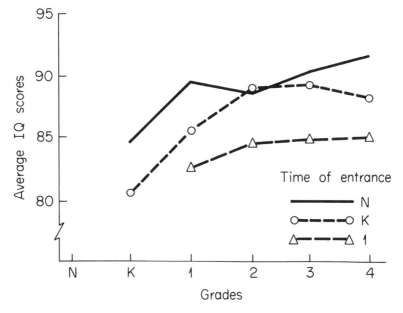

FIG. 11.2. Peabody Picture Vocabulary Test scores across grades of groups entering school at Nursery (N), Kindergarten (K), and First Grade (1).
Note: Original samples with group *N*'s ranging from 46 to 58.

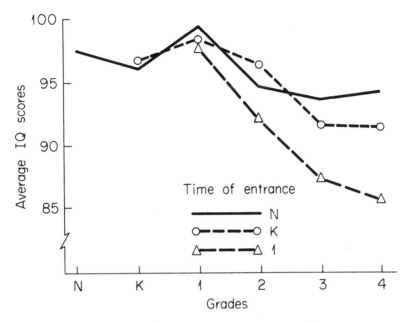

FIG. 11.3.   Goodenough Draw-A-Man IQ scores across grades of groups entering school at Nursery (N), Kindergarten (K), and First Grade (1).
Note. Original samples with group *N*'s ranging from 46 to 58.

Although the difference among the three groups were less marked than were
those on the Stanford–Binet, the differences were in the same direction and
statistically significant when tested by an analysis of variance for repeated measures ($F = 3.40$, df $= 2/414$, $p < .05$).

When we turn to the results of the Goodenough test (see Fig. 11.3), the
outcome differed from those of the first two tests. In contrast to the S–B and
PPVT scores, the three entrance groups showed no initial response to schooling
and did not differ until after first grade on the Goodenough scores. Moreover,
instead of the overall increase of IQ scores on the S–B and PPVT, we find a
steady overall decline of Goodenough scores from first to fourth grade. This
decline was statistically significant ($F = 26.50$, df $= 2/426$, $p < .01$). The major
finding relevant to the effect of length of preschool was that the decline was
proportional to the timing of school entry; that is, after first grade the scores
declined more steeply from first to fourth grade the later the child entered school.
These findings suggest that a later start in school will result in a greater decline of
performance on this particular test.

It is clear from the foregoing that the employment of multiple criteria is
valuable in the evaluation of both initial and prolonged effects of early educational intervention on disadvantaged children.

Achievement

School Grades.[3]   The data for analyzing relationships between preschool experience and academic achievement in the classroom were collected from school records. Our analyses were limited to five major subjects: arithmetic and reading (from first to fourth grades), and spelling, science, and social studies (from second to fourth grades).

Findings were analyzed separately for boys and girls because differences appeared between the two groups. The findings for girls were in the predicted direction for each of the five subjects from grade 1 or 2 through grade 4. Significant differences were found among the three groups, over the three or four grades, for reading, spelling, science, and social studies ($p < .05$), whereas for arithmetic the difference approached significance ($p < .10$). The differences among the three groups of girls decreased by the fourth grade and lost significance, although thereafter the order remained consistent. We conclude that girls with earlier and longer preschool tended to receive better grades than girls with less or no preschool.

The findings from first to fourth grade were much less consistent for boys than for girls. The major difference among entrance groups was the superiority in grades for boys who had attended preschool (nursery school or kindergarten) as compared to boys who had no preschool. Boys with preschool differed significantly from boys without preschool on spelling ($p < .05$), and this difference approached significance on reading and social studies ($p < .10$).

One can conclude from these findings that 1 or 2 years of preschool produced prolonged effects on the school grades of girls from low-income families. The findings for boys, although generally in the predicted direction, were less marked and less consistent.

General Academic Performance.   This measure was based on teachers' comments that appeared on the children's report cards annually from first through eleventh grade (see Table 11.3). As in the case of school grades, such data are not standardized measures of achievement, yet they represent very real and important feedback to the children and their parents. Teacher comments were tallied separately for academic achievement and conduct. Comments about conduct were not amenable to analysis due to the low frequency with which they occurred; that is, there were only 34 comments for 115 subjects over a 12-year period. Over the same period teachers wrote 581 comments on the academic performances of these subjects. The comments were classified as follows: "getting better," "good," "getting worse," "needs improvement," "bad," and "average."

---

[3]For detailed results, see Beller, 1974.

TABLE 11.3
Distribution of Teacher Comments on Academic Achievement
of Pupils with Different Lengths of Preschool Experience

| | School Entrance Groups | | | |
	Nursery	Kindergarten	First Grade	Chi-Square
		All Subjects		
Positive	80	54	56	
Negative	39	44	50	5.61*
		Males		
Positive	30	14	17	
Negative	18	26	27	8.31**
		Females		
Positive	50	40	39	
Negative	21	18	23	<1

$*p \leq .10$

$**p \leq .05$

For the present analysis, the comments were dichotomized into positive (good, getting better) and negative (bad, getting worse, needs improvement) types of responses while excluding the "average" comments. As can be seen in Table 11.3, children with the longest preschool experience received the greatest number of positive and the least number of negative comments. The differences among the three groups approached significance in the total sample ($\chi^2 = 5.61$, $p < .10$), and was significant for comparisons among boys ($\chi^2 = 8.13$, $p < .05$). Thus, the impact of 2 years of preschool can be seen over 11 years of formal schooling. Many different teachers in different schools recorded their favorable impressions of these children over the years and most likely established a positive cycle of pupil achievement and teacher recognition (Beller, 1973).

Retention in Grade. As pointed out earlier, the children in this study attended over 80 elementary schools and more than 25 high schools in the city of Philadelphia. The vast majority of these schools were attended by economically disadvantaged children and the criteria for retention tended to be lax and varied from school to school. Nevertheless, retention is an important criterion of academic achievement or failure. It not only results from poor academic performance, but once it has occurred it may be a determining factor in subsequent academic failure and poor adjustment to school.

The results of the analyses are summarized in Table 11.4. It can be seen that although more preschool experience tended to result in less frequent retention, this relationship did not reach significance for the entire sample. However, when the groups were broken down by family background some linear negative relationships emerged between length of preschool experience and retention in

TABLE 11.4
Distribution of Retained and Non-Retained Pupils with
Different Lengths of Preschool Experience

| | School Entrance Groups | | | |
	Nursery	Kindergarten	First Grade	Chi-Square
		All Subjects		
Never Retained	22	16	14	
Retained a Grade	19	17	24	2.32
		Males		
Never Retained	8	7	5	
Retained a Grade	12	10	12	<1
		Females		
Never Retained	14	9	9	
Retained a Grade	7	7	12	2.42
		Father Present		
Never Retained	18	10	7	
Retained a Grade	10	10	16	5.79*
		Father Absent		
Never Retained	4	4	5	
Retained a Grade	7	3	5	<1
		Employed Parents		
Never Retained	17	12	7	
Retained a Grade	9	12	18	7.19**
		Unemployed Parents		
Never Retained	5	2	5	
Retained a Grade	8	1	3	1.52

$*p < .10$
$**p \leq .05$

grade. For children from parent-employed families, retention in grade decreased significantly as length of preschool experience increased. The same pattern approached significance for children from father-present families.

Although some data have been collected on high school completion and on college attendance, at the last data collection period one-third of our sample was still in high school. It was decided to postpone any analyses of the effects of preschool experience on these two dependent variables until all subjects in our study had left high school. However, see the pooled analyses chapter for later findings on these youths.

Intellectual Attitudes and Motivation

Attitudes Toward School and Learning. In order to assess the impact of preschool experience on attitudes toward school and learning during the elementary grades, the teacher in each classroom with children from our study was asked to select two sets of three children in his/her classroom who manifested: (1) best and worst attitudes toward study and learning; and (2) most positive and most negative attitudes toward school. The four sets from each teacher were examined to find whether children from our study were included. These data were collected only during the first two grades of elementary school. The outcomes of chi-square analyses showed that length of preschool experience was related to a child's attitudes toward school and learning. In both areas, the three school-entrance groups differed significantly both in first and second grades (chi-squares ranged from 6.01 to 9.07, df = 2, $p < .05$). Children with preschool experience were most frequently represented in groups characterized as having the best attitudes toward learning and school and, conversely, least often represented in groups characterized by the worst or most negative attitudes toward learning and school.

Motivation to Succeed on Intelligence Tests.   In order to obtain a broader assessment of the child's achievement motivation in an intellectual performance situation, we obtained measures of the child's reactions in individual intelligence testing situations. Each tester rated the child's attitudes during each testing situation from first to third grade with regard to cooperation, involvement, and persistence. The results of analyses of variance showed that children with preschool experience were significantly more cooperative, more involved, and more persistent in their efforts in the testing situations than were children without preschool experience (F = 6.25, df = 2/114, p < .01; F = 5.33, df = 2/114, p < .01; F = 3.42, df = 2/114, p < .05 in that order).

These above findings show that preschool experience significantly affected not only intellectual aptitude and academic achievement but also children's attitudes toward learning and school and their motivation to succeed in formal test situations.

Social, Motivational, and Emotional Effects

Attitudes

Self-Concept.   Attitudes toward intellectual and school status were assessed in fourth and tenth grades by means of a standardized instrument, the Piers–Harris Self-Concept Scale. This scale also addressed several other areas of attitudes towards self, such as behavior or conduct in school and home, physical appearance, and attributes related to popularity, anxiety, happiness, and satisfaction.

Length of preschool experience had more significant effects on self-concept in tenth grade than in fourth grade. Presence of father produced significant positive effects on self-concept scores in the fourth grade but not in the tenth grade. Employment of parent, regardless of preschool experience, had no effect on self-concept scores in the fourth- or tenth-grade assessments.

Interactions between family background variables and preschool experience occurred rarely in fourth grade but frequently in tenth grade. The outcomes of the analyses of variance are presented fully in Table 11.5 for the tenth grade sample,

TABLE 11.5
Tenth Grade Self-Concept Scores for Pupils with
Different Lengths of Preschool Experience

Piers-Harris Self-Concept Scale	School Entrance Groups			F-Ratio
	Nursery	Kindergarten	First Grade	
All Subjects	(N = 41)	(N = 36)	(N = 38)	
Conduct	15.7	15.1	15.5	<1
Intellectual - School	14.7	13.8	12.1	5.82***
Physical Appearance	9.1	9.1	7.8	4.21** (**)[1]
Anxiety	8.9	9.0	8.5	<1
Popularity	10.0	9.9	8.9	3.75**
Happiness - Satisfaction	7.9	8.1	7.8	<1
Composite Score	64.0	62.9	59.4	2.52*
Males	(N = 20)	(N = 16)	(N = 20)	
Conduct	14.9	15.0	15.6	<1
Intellectual - School	14.6	13.9	13.0	1.27
Physical Appearance	9.1	9.3	8.1	1.53
Anxiety	9.8	10.1	9.1	1.50
Popularity	9.8	9.9	9.1	1.29
Happiness - Satisfaction	8.0	8.1	8.1	<1
Composite Score	64.3	63.9	62.9	<1
Females	(N = 21)	(N = 16)	(N = 20)	
Conduct	16.6	15.3	15.4	2.51*
Intellectual - School	14.8	13.7	11.3	4,62**
Physical Appearance	9.1	9.0	7.6	2.58* (*)[1]
Anxiety	8.1	7.7	8.0	<1
Popularity	10.1	10.1	8.9	2.42* (**)[1]
Happiness - Satisfaction	7.9	8.2	7.5	<1
Composite Score	63.7	61.5	56.9	2.40*
Father Present	(N = 29)	(N = 28)	(N = 27)	
Conduct	16.1	14.9	15.6	1.81
Intellectual - School	15.1	13.8	12.6	3.06*
Physical Appearance	9.5	9.0	8.1	2.18
Anxiety	9.2	8.9	8.3	<1
Popularity	10.1	9.8	9.0	1.90
Happiness - Satisfaction	8.4	7.9	7.6	1.50
Composite Score	65.3	62.1	59.7	2.22
Father Absent	(N = 10)	(N = 8)	(N = 9)	
Conduct	14.6	15.1	15.6	<1
Intellectual - School	13.8	13.1	12.0	<1
Physical Appearance	8.2	9.6	6.9	2.87*
Anxiety	8.3	9.1	9.2	<1
Popularity	10.0	9.9	8.9	1.80 (*)[1]
Happiness - Satisfaction	6.5	8.5	8.5	6.96***
Composite Score	60.2	62.7	60.5	<1

(continued)

TABLE 11.5 (*Continued*)

Piers-Harris Self-Concept Scale	School Entrance Groups			F-Ratio
	Nursery	Kindergarten	First Grade	
Employed Parents	(N = 30)	(N = 28)	(N = 27)	
Conduct	15.8	14.8	15.4	1.38
Intellectual - School	14.8	13.5	12.4	3.87**
Physical Appearance	9.3	9.1	7.9	3.15** (*)[1]
Anxiety	9.3	9.0	8.4	<1
Popularity	10.1	9.7	9.0	2.14
Happiness - Satisfaction	8.2	8.0	7.7	<1
Composite Score	64.7	61.8	59.5	2.18
Unemployed Parents	(N = 9)	(N = 3)	(N = 5)	
Conduct	15.3	16.3	16.2	<1
Intellectual - School	14.1	15.3	13.0	<1
Physical Appearance	8.6	9.6	7.2	<1
Anxiety	8.1	8.7	9.4	<1
Popularity	10.2	11.0	9.0	2.70* (*)[1]
Happiness - Satisfaction	7.0	9.0	8.8	3.40*
Composite Score	61.5	67.0	62.2	<1

*$p \leq .10$

**$p \leq .05$

***$p < .01$

[1] Indicates a positive effect of preschool experience in fourth grade.

whereas significant findings for the fourth grade sample are indicated in the places where they occurred.

It can be seen that preschool experience alone produced a marginally significant effect on the composite self-concept score in the tenth grade for all subjects. Groups with more preschool experience received higher scores than the groups with less preschool experience. Of the self-concept subscores, significant relationships were observed among the three entrance groups on three of the six cluster scores. Specifically, on intellectual and school status there was a positive linear relationship with length of preschool. On the clusters of physical appearance and popularity, the major difference derived from the higher scores of adolescents who had one or two years of preschool experience compared with adolescents with no preschool experience.

As seen in the second and third parts of Table 11.5, the Self-Concept Scale picked up significant effects of preschool experience on girls but not on boys.

In adolescents from father-present and parent-employed families (at the time when the child entered school), length of preschool produced fewer effects but in the same directions as for all subjects. Children with 2 years of preschool from single-parent homes were less happy with themselves, but those with 1 or 2 years of preschool tended to have a more positive self-image with regard to their physical appearance. Children of unemployed parent(s) with 2 years of preschool compared to 1 or no years tended to rate themselves as less happy, whereas those with 1 or 2 years of preschool tended to rate themselves as more popular. It can be concluded from these findings that preschool experience had a prolonged and somewhat delayed effect on the self-concept of these children, and that this effect varied with the sex and family background of the children.

Attitudes Toward Self and Society.   One of the questions on the eleventh-grade interview asked whether a subject felt that he or she had an effect upon society. Of all youths, 40% felt that they were having an impact upon society and this applied more to males (52%) than to females (27%). The adolescents most frequently described their influence in terms of their own jobs (30%), helping other people (28%), and participating in the economic/political force (18%). The relationship between length of preschool experience and the feeling that one has an effect upon society was marginally significant for the whole group. Whereas 50% of the Nursery group and 44% of the Kindergarten group gave positive responses to this question, only 25% of the First-Grade group did so.

Attitudes Toward Sex and Family Roles.   The Sex and Family Roles Inventory was designed for the current study. It consists of 49 four-point Likert-type items that measure sex role attitudes in four areas: equality in jobs and education, home versus career for women, sex roles within the home, and maternal responsibilities. High scores indicate a contemporary as opposed to traditional view of sex roles, that is, greater equality, shared responsibility between the sexes, and greater emancipation of women.

The effects of preschool experience and family characteristics on attitudes toward sex and family roles were analyzed by means of one-way analyses of variance. The results of the analyses are presented in Table 11.6. Although subjects with the longest preschool experience tended to have the more contemporary attitudes toward sex and family roles, the analysis of preschool effects did not reach significance for either the entire group or for males and females separately. However, when the groups were separated on the basis of family background variables, several significant effects emerged. In the father-present and parent-employed groups, adolescents with the longest preschool experience manifested significantly more contemporary attitudes on the total score, as well as for the clusters home versus career for women and sex roles within the home, and approached significance on equality in jobs and education. The father-absent and parent-unemployed sets yielded no relationship between preschool and contemporary versus traditional attitudes although the N's were quite small. Family backgrounds of an intact family and of employed parent(s) appear to enhance the likelihood that 2 years of preschool experience will result in the development of more contemporary rather than traditional attitudes toward sex and family roles and toward equality in jobs and education among economically disadvantaged adolescents.

TABLE 11.6
Sex Role and Family Role Inventory Scores for Subjects
with Different Lengths of Preschool Experience

Sex and Family Roles Inventory	School Entrance Groups			
	Nursery	Kindergarten	First Grade	F-Ratio
All Subjects	(N = 40)	(N = 32)	(N = 35)	
Equality in Jobs/Education	34.73	33.19	33.11	1.18
Home vs. Career for Women	31.65	29.81	29.69	1.12
Sex Roles within the Home	38.50	35.47	36.71	1.28
Maternal Responsibilities	26.73	24.94	26.97	1.99
Total	131.60	123.41	126.49	1.40
Males	(N = 19)	(N = 16)	(N = 18)	
Equality in Jobs/Education	33.16	32.81	31.40	<1
Home vs. Career for Women	30.16	29.06	29.17	<1
Sex Roles within the Home	35.47	35.00	37.33	<1
Maternal Responsibilities	26.11	25.06	27.28	1.20
Total	124.90	121.94	125.17	<1
Females	(N = 21)	(N = 16)	(N = 17)	
Equality in Jobs/Education	36.14	33.56	34.94	1.18
Home vs. Career for Women	33.00	30.56	30.24	<1
Sex Roles within the Home	41.24	35.94	36.06	2.26
Maternal Responsibilities	27.29	24.81	26.65	1.17
Total	137.67	124.88	127.88	1.58
Father Present	(N = 29)	(N = 20)	(N = 23)	
Equality in Jobs/Education	34.72	32.00	32.174	2.66*
Home vs. Career for Women	32.14	27.60	29.09	4.35**
Sex Roles within the Home	39.07	33.35	35.91	3.76**
Maternal Responsibilities	26.41	23.80	26.48	2.58*
Total	132.35	116.75	123.65	4.31**
Father Absent	(N = 9)	(N = 8)	(N = 7)	
Equality in Jobs/Education	34.33	34.38	36.86	<1
Home vs. Career for Women	30.22	32.88	33.14	<1
Sex Roles within the Home	37.44	38.88	41.29	<1
Maternal Responsibilities	27.11	26.00	28.71	<1
Total	129.11	132.13	140.00	<1
Parents Employed	(N = 30)	(N = 25)	(N = 27)	
Equality in Jobs/Education	34.77	32.16	32.44	2.56*
Home vs. Career for Women	32.20	28.52	29.22	3.11**
Sex Roles within the Home	38.97	34.08	35.89	3.25**
Maternal Responsibilities	26.03	24.08	26.67	2.30
Total	131.97	118.84	124.22	3.29**
Parents Unemployed	(N = 8)	(N = 3)	(N = 3)	
Equality in Jobs/Education	34.13	37.00	40.67	1.63
Home vs. Career for Women	29.75	34.00	37.33	1.50
Sex Roles within the Home	37.63	42.00	48.67	1.28
Maternal Responsibilities	28.63	27.33	30.00	<1
Total	130.13	140.33	156.67	1.41

$*p \leq .10$
$**p \leq .05$

Attitudes Toward Work and Occupation. The Crites Career Maturity Inventory was selected because its underlying view or approach is that attitudes toward work and occupation reflect a developmental process rather than a one-time event. The scale (Crites, 1973), consisting of 47 true/false statements, was designed to assess the general level of maturity in an individual's career development. In addition to a composite score, the instrument provides an indication of development along the following five dimensions of the decision-making process: decisiveness (commitment to a specific career choice); involvement (active participation in choosing a career); independence (self-reliance in making career decisions); orientation (attitude toward work values—task versus pleasure-oriented); and compromise (realism of vocational choice).

One-way analyses of variance were performed to investigate relationships between length of preschool experience and sex and family background variables on the maturity of attitudes toward work and occupation. Although subjects with 2 years of preschool tended to have the higher, that is, more mature attitudes toward work, significant differences in that direction were found only on the total score and on the subscale independence for the total group and also for the father-present and parent-employed groups. Thus we might conclude that our data yielded some evidence for a relationship between length of preschool experience and maturity of attitude toward work and occupation, particularly when the preschool experience lasted for 2 years and when the subjects came from father-present and parent-employed families.

Moral judgment

The 18 Piagetian stories were read to subjects in the fourth and again in the tenth grades. In the tenth grade the subjects' responses were followed with an inquiry. Responses were tape-recorded, transcribed, and scored according to the instructions of the *Maturity of Moral Judgment Manual,* (Beller, McNichol, & Root, 1979). Scores were calculated for each moral judgment story and summed to yield a total score. In addition, mean scores from stories that represent a single moral development issue were combined to form five cluster scores. The median interrater reliability was $r = .86$.

One-way analyses of variance were conducted to determine the effect of length of preschool experience on moral development in middle childhood and adolescence. The results of the analyses are presented in Table 11.7, although the cluster scores of attitudes toward authority, distributive justice, and intentionality versus consequences are not included because they yielded no significant findings. Because only one of the breakdowns yielded a marginally significant difference in fourth grade, the table contains detailed results only for the tenth grade sample. Neither presence of father, employment of parents, nor sex of youth by themselves affected maturity of moral judgment in the fourth- or tenth-grade assessments.

As seen from the results for all subjects, that is, regardless of sex and family background breakdowns, groups with longer preschool experience scored signif-

TABLE 11.7
Selected Tenth Grade Mean Moral Judgment Scores for Pupils
with Different Lengths of Preschool Experience

| | School Entrance Groups | | | |
	Nursery	Kindergarten	First Grade	F-Ratio
All Subjects	(N = 41)	(N = 36)	(N = 38)	
Expiatory - Restitutive Punishment	5.2	4.4	4.1	3.53**
Immanent - Non-Immanent Justice	9.4	8.2	7.9	7.07***
Total Moral Judgment	40.5	37.4	36.1	6.58***
Males	(N = 19)	(N = 20)	(N = 18)	
Expiatory - Restitutive Punishment	5.1	4.0	4.1	2.00
Immanent - Non-Immanent Justice	9.3	8.6	8.1	1.87
Total Moral Judgment	40.6	38.4	36.1	2.38* (*)[1]
Females	(N = 21)	(N = 18)	(N = 18)	
Expiatory - Restitutive Punishment	5.2	4.9	4.1	2.02
Immanent - Non-Immanent Justice	9.6	7.8	7.8	6.04***
Total Moral Judgment	40.5	36.2	36.2	5.92***
Father Present				
Expiatory - Restitutive Punishment	5.4	4.4	3.8	4.66**
Immanent - Non-Immanent Justice	9.4	8.3	8.1	4.03**
Total Moral Judgment	40.7	36.3	35.4	8.27***
Father Absent	(N = 9)	(N = 8)	(N = 8)	
Expiatory - Restitutive Punishment	4.4	4.4	4.9	<1
Immanent - Non-Immanent Justice	9.9	8.4	7.1	4.39**
Total Moral Judgment	40.3	41.0	36.2	1.38
Employed Parents	(N = 29)	(N = 28)	(N = 26)	
Expiatory - Restitutive Punishment	5.1	4.5	4.1	2.03
Immanent - Non-Immanent Justice	9.5	8.3	8.0	5.32***
Total Moral Judgment	40.4	37.5	35.7	5.23***
Unemployed Parents	(N = 8)	(N = 3)	(N = 4)	
Expiatory - Restitutive Punishment	5.5	3.7	4.2	<1
Immanent - Non-Immanent Justice	9.5	7.7	6.7	3.21*
Total Moral Judgment	41.5	37.7	34.6	1.80

*$p \leq .10$
**$p \leq .05$
** $p \leq .01$

[1] Indicates positive effect of preschool experience in fourth grade.

icantly higher than the groups with less preschool experience on total moral judgment and on the two cluster scores of expiatory versus restitutive punishment and immanent versus nonimmanent justice.

When these comparisons were carried out separately for each sex, the effect of length of preschool was more powerful for females than for males. There was a significant effect of 2 years of preschool on the total score and on the cluster score of immanent versus nonimmanent justice in tenth grade females.

The introduction of the two family background variables produced a number of significant effects of preschool on the maturity of moral judgment. Length of preschool related significantly and positively to more mature moral judgment on the immanent versus nonimmanent justice category in all breakdowns except unemployed parents where the relationship was marginally significant. Youths with longer preschool experience from parent-employed families also yielded higher total moral judgment scores, whereas such subjects from father-present families also gave significantly more mature responses on total judgment and the cluster expiatory versus restitutive punishment.

Motivation

Motivational variables were assessed both in the first and eleventh grades. Although this report includes all the data on motivational variables assessed in first grade, only those eleventh-grade variables that appeared to be comparable or related to those assessed in first grade are included here. This decision was dictated by limitation of space.

Four motivational variables were assessed in the first grade: dependent striving, dependency conflict, autonomous achievement striving, and aggression. Data on these variables were obtained through repeated observational ratings by participant and nonparticipant observers in the classroom (Beller, 1959, 1972).

The three motivational variables assessed in eleventh grade and reported here were nurturance, achievement, and endurance (persistence). The data on these variables were obtained through administration of the Jackson Personality Research Form (Jackson, 1974) which consists of 16-item scales. Each scale can be treated as distinct because each contributes uniquely to the assessment of individual functioning in a given area.

Relationships between length of preschool experience and the first-grade motivational variables were analyzed by means of one-way analyses of variance and are presented in Table 11.8. As can be seen from the first part of Table 8, for all children differences between the groups were significant for autonomous achievement striving and aggression (p = < .05) and approached significance for dependency motivation and conflict (p = < .10). Children with any preschool experience had significantly elevated scores on autonomous achievement striving and children with 2 years of preschool significantly elevated aggression. Although the directions of these relationships appear in both boys and girls they reach or approach significance only in boys.

Turning to the last part of Table 8 it becomes evident that how preschool experience affected these motivational variables depended on the family background of the child. As in the total group, children of employed parents with the longest preschool experience were significantly elevated on aggression and mar-

TABLE 11.8
Average Motivation Scores During First Grade for Groups
with Different Lengths of Preschool Experience

Motivational Variables	School Entrance Groups			F-Ratio
	Nursery	Kindergarten	First Grade	
All Subjects	(N = 31)	(N = 29)	(N = 35)	
Dependent Striving	4.30	3.56	3.72	2.91*
Dependency Conflict	3.55	3.95	4.25	2.62*
Auton. Achiev. Striv.[1]	4.35	4.29	3.41	3.74**
Aggression	4.54	3.56	3.44	4.59**
Males	(N = 18)	(N = 18)	(N = 18)	
Dependent Striving	4.59	3.94	3.78	2.03
Dependency Conflict	3.71	3.83	4.72	3.25**
Auton. Achiev. Striv.	3.94	4.56	3.33	2.38*
Aggression	5.00	3.94	3.89	2.77*
Females	(N = 13)	(N = 11)	(N = 17)	
Dependent Striving	4.62	3.55	3.94	2.10
Dependency Conflict	3.54	4.09	4.00	.58
Auton. Achiev. Striv.	4.62	4.18	3.47	1.60
Aggression	4.08	2.82	2.94	2.35
Father Present	(N = 19)	(N = 11)	(N = 21)	
Dependent Striving	4.47	4.00	4.33	.542
Dependency Conflict	3.42	3.77	4.52	4.05**
Auton. Achiev. Striv.	4.63	4.54	3.52	2.35*
Aggression	4.47	3.38	4.19	1.75
Father Absent	(N = 6)	(N = 3)	(N = 6)	
Dependent Striving	4.67	2.67	2.83	3.72*
Dependency Conflict	4.17	3.33	4.17	.411
Auton. Achiev. Striv.	3.33	5.67	2.83	2.73
Aggression	4.50	2.68	1.68	7.54***
Parents Employed[2]	(N = 20)	(N = 17	(N = 25)	
Dependent Striving	4.75	3.75	4.12	2.96*
Dependency Conflict	3.65	3.82	4.40	1.96
Auton. Achiev. Striv.	3.35	4.53	3.60	1.64
Aggression	4.70	3.35	3.84	3.25**

*$p \leq .10$
**$p \leq .05$
***$p \leq .01$

[1] Autonomous Achievement Striving.
[2] In the Unemployed Parents group the *N*s were too small for analysis.

TABLE 11.9
Mean Jackson Personality Research Form Scores on Selected Subscales
for Groups with Different Lengths of Preschool Experience

| | School Entrance Groups | | | |
	Nursery	Kindergarten	First Grade	F-Ratio
All Subjects	(N = 36)	(N = 31)	(N = 30)	
Nurturance	11.56	9.94	10.80	2.26
Achievement	10.94	9.45	9.50	3.56*
Endurance	10.33	9.48	9.27	1.28
Males	(N = 17)	(N = 15)	(N = 15)	
Nurturance	10.29	9.93	11.47	<1
Achievement	10.59	10.07	10.53	<1
Endurance	10.00	10.40	10.00	<1
Females	(N = 19)	(N = 16)	(N = 15)	
Nurturance	12.68	9.94	10.13	5.21**
Achievement	11.26	8.88	8.47	6.69**
Endurance	10.63	8.63	8.53	3.56*
Father Present	(N = 26)	(N = 20)	(N = 19)	
Nurturance	11.85	9.50	10.79	3.38**
Achievement	11.39	9.35	10.00	3.75**
Endurance	10.50	9.30	9.42	1.09
Father Absent	(N = 8)	(N = 7)	(N = 7)	
Nurturance	11.25	11.57	11.14	<1
Achievement	9.75	9.43	8.43	<1
Endurance	9.50	9.14	10.43	<1
Employed Parents	(N = 26)	(N = 25)	(N = 23)	
Nurturance	11.58	9.84	10.96	2.18
Achievement	11.23	9.24	9.57	4.07**
Endurance	10.39	9.32	9.70	<1
Unemployed Parents	(N = 8)	(N = 2)	(N = 3)	
Nurturance	12.13	12.50	10.33	<1
Achievement	10.25	11.00	9.67	<1
Endurance	9.88	8.50	9.67	<1

*$p < .10$
**$p < .05$

ginally higher on dependent striving. The effect of preschool experience on elevated aggression and dependent striving emerged again in children from father-absent families while the effect of preschool experience on elevated autonomous achievement striving and on lower dependency conflict appeared only in children from father-present families.

The analyses of relationships among preschool experience, family background and motivational variables in the eleventh grade sample are reported in Table 11.9.[4] The analyses of the three entrance groups without any further breakdowns show a marginally significant effect of 2 years of preschool on elevated achievement motivation. When the groups are separated by sex, it is evident that in females 2 years of preschool experience resulted in significantly higher nurturance and achievement motivation and in marginally significant higher endurance than one or no years of preschool experience. On the family background variables we find that for children of father-present families, 2 years of preschool is related to higher nurturance and achievement, while for children of employed parent(s), 2 years of preschool is related to higher achievement.

Finally, one of the motivational variables assessed in first grade was used as a control variable to address the question: Which children benefited more from preschool experience? This was done by investigating the interaction of autonomous achievement striving with length of preschool experience on average IQ scores from first to fourth grade.

All first grade subjects were divided into those above and below the median on autonomous achievement striving (AAS). This analysis was based on first grade AAS scores because it offered the first opportunity to compare children with 2 years, 1 year, and no preschool. Group comparisons were then carried out separately among the high- and among the low-autonomous children. The outcomes of these comparisons are presented in Fig. 11.4 and 11.5. It is clear from these figures that early educational intervention had a quite different effect on the economically disadvantaged child depending on whether he/she was high or low on autonomous achievement striving. For children who were high on autonomous achievement striving in the first grade, length of preschool experience showed no differential effects on intellectual performance from the first to the fourth grade on either the Stanford–Binet or the Peabody Picture Vocabulary Test. In other words, high autonomous achievement children who did not start school until first grade continued to perform as well on two intelligence tests as those who had 2 or 1 year(s) of preschool experience.

A radically different picture emerged for children who were low on autonomous achievement striving at first grade. These children were greatly handicapped in their intellectual functioning as a result of not having had the preschool experience. The differences among the three low-autonomous entrance groups were statistically significant when tested by analysis of variance, both on the Stanford–Binet ($F = 5.06$, df $= 2/44$, $p < .05$) and on the Peabody Picture Vocabulary Test ($F = 3.35$, df $= 2/44$, $p < .05$). Another finding that can be seen in Fig. 11.4 and 11.5 is that the children who had the earliest educational

---

[4]The scales of autonomy and of aggression were not included in the present analysis because Jackson defined these variables differently than we did in our study.

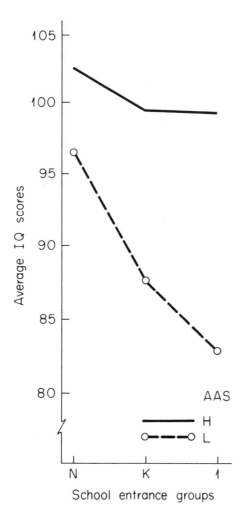

FIG. 11.4. Stanford-Binet IQ scores of high (H) and low (L) autonomous achievement striving (AAS) groups entering school at Nursery (N), Kindergarten (K), and First Grade (1). *Note.* Sizes of groups ranged from $N = 11$ to $N = 20$.

intervention, that is, children in the Nursery group, were least affected by their motivational disadvantage because the differences between high- and low-autonomous children in their performances on the Stanford–Binet and Peabody Picture Vocabulary Test were both statistically insignificant and much smaller than the differences in intellectual performance between any other pairs of high-and low-autonomous school entrance groups. In other words, 2 years of preschool experience prevented in the low-autonomous children the detrimental effects on intellectual aptitude resulting from their motivational handicap. Parenthetically, this effect is not accounted for by the relationship between autonomous achievement and intelligence because a similar comparison among the three entrance groups yielded no significant differences in the proportion of high IQ children. The interacting effect of motivation and length of preschool also was not found on academic achievement from first to fourth grade. Because intelligence tests probably constitute a more enduring measure of intellectual ability than daily performance in the classroom, this interaction effect of a child's motivation and early educational intervention on later intellectual functioning deserves serious consideration.

Ego Development and Ego Function

Stages of Ego Development.   In order to assess the effects of preschool experience on ego development in adolescence, Loevinger's Sentence Completion Test was used. To facilitate statistical analysis of the data, the nine stages of ego development were collapsed into three levels: low (presocial, impulsive, and self-protective); medium (intermediate I, conformist, and conscientious); and high (intermediate II, autonomous, and integrated). Group differences in the distribution of ego development levels were assessed by means of chi-square analyses. The results of these analyses are presented in Table 11.10. It can be seen that the results for the total sample, although not significant, were in the expected direction; that is, subjects with more preschool experience were more likely to be included in the high and less likely to be included in the low levels of

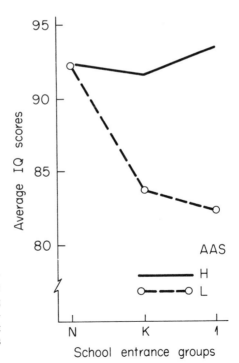

FIG. 11.5.   Peabody Picture Vocabulary Test scores of high (H) and low (L) autonomous achievement striving (AAS) groups entering school at Nursery (N), Kindergarten (K), and First Grade (1). *Note.* Sizes of groups ranged from $N = 11$ to $N = 20$.

TABLE 11.10

TABLE 11.10
Distribution of Low, Medium, and High Levels of Ego Development
for Subjects in Eleventh Grade with Different Lengths
of Preschool Experience

| | School Entrance Groups | | | |
Ego Level	Nursery	Kindergarten	First Grade	Chi-Square
		All Subjects		
Low	5	7	10	
Medium	24	21	21	3.68
High	9	6	4	
		Males		
Low	4	3	6	
Medium	14	9	9	5.19
High	1	5	3	
		Females		
Low	1	4	4	
Medium	10	12	12	11.48**
High	8	1	1	

$**p \leq .05$

TABLE 11.11
Distribution of Reflective and Impulsive Children At Fourth
Grade with Different Lengths of Preschool Experience

| | School Entrance Groups | | | |
	Nursery	Kindergarten	First Grade	Chi-Square
		All Subjects		
Reflective	20	21	9	
Impulsive	18	12	28	11.79***
		Males		
Reflective	15	13	3	
Impulsive	7	7	13	13.29***
		Females		
Reflective	5	8	6	
Impulsive	11	5	15	5.66*
		Father Present[a]		
Reflective	13	12	5	
Impulsive	9	5	14	8.02**
		Employed Parents[a]		
Reflective	15	14	6	
Impulsive	10	5	16	10.15***

$*p \leq .10$
$**p \leq .05$
$***p \leq .01$

[a] In the Father Absent and Unemployed Parents groups the Ns were too small for chi-square analysis.

ego development than subjects with less or no preschool experience. The relationship between length of preschool experience and level of ego development did reach statistical significance for female subjects. None of the family background breakdowns resulted in significant differences. One may conclude that preschool experience had a positive effect on ego development in our sample of female adolescents.

Reflective-Impulsive Style. Kagan's Matching Familiar Figures Test was chosen for the purpose of assessing this area both in fourth and tenth grades. Relationships between length of preschool experience and reflective–impulsive style were analyzed by means of chi-square tests of significance. The outcomes of these analyses are presented in Tables 11.11 and 11.12.

In the fourth grade sample, children with 1 and 2 years of preschool were significantly more reflective than children without preschool. In the tenth grade sample, length of preschool was more linearly related to reflectiveness and impulsivity; however, the effect failed to reach significance. Father presence, regardless of preschool experience, produced no difference in fourth grade and marginally more reflectives in tenth grade. Parental employment, alone, had no

TABLE 11.12
Distribution os Reflective and Impulsive Youths at Tenth Grade
with Different Lengths of Preschool Experience

| | School Entrance Groups | | | |
	Nursery	Kindergarten	First Grade	Chi-Square
	All Subjects			
Reflective	18	11	9	2.35
Impulsive	13	10	15	
	Males			
Reflective	6	6	1	7.40**
Impulsive	7	5	13	
	Females			
Reflective	12	5	8	2.01
Impulsive	6	5	2	
	Father Present[a]			
Reflective	16	7	3	9.49***
Impulsive	5	4	10	
	Employed Parents[a]			
Reflective	14	8	4	5.82*
Impulsive	7	6	11	

*$p \leq .10$
**$p \leq .05$
***$p \leq .01$

[a] In the Father Absent and Unemployed Parents groups the Ns were too small for chi-square analysis.

effect in either grade. When analyzed separately for each sex, the effect of preschool was significant in the fourth grade for males and approached significance for females, whereas in the tenth grade the effect was significant for males only. Father presence, alone produced no difference in fourth grade and marginally more reflectives in tenth grade. Significant and stable effects emerge from the family background breakdowns both in the fourth and tenth grades, although the N's were too small in the father-absent and unemployed-parents groups to allow meaningful analyses. Subjects from father-present families with preschool experience were significantly more reflective than subjects from the same family background without preschool. For youths whose parents were employed during early childhood, the preschool effect was significant in the fourth grade and approached significance in the tenth grade. Here, too, the relationship in fourth grade was one of preschool versus no preschool, whereas in tenth grade, length of preschool became differentiated with 2 years of preschool having the highest number of reflective subjects and 1 year of preschool yielding an intermediate level between the two extreme groups. Although this measure has been sensitive in picking up the effects of preschool experience in middle childhood and adolescence, it differs from most other measures used in this study in that effects of preschool emerged more strongly and more consistently for males than for females.

DISCUSSION

Length of preschool was the main independent variable of this study. A review of the findings presented in this chapter shows that the effects of 1 year of preschool were more variable than those of 2 years or no preschool. This outcome has two implications. First, it would seem that 1 year of preschool experience for economically disadvantaged children such as those in our sample represents a marginal intervention that does not permit firm generalizations about the effect of preschool experience on intellectual and socioemotional development. Secondly, the use of a kindergarten group as a control group for preschool intervention, as was done in the pooled analyses, might have introduced more instability in the findings than the use of another control group like no-preschool prior to first grade.

When we review the effects of length of preschool on measures for which further breakdowns such as sex and family background were not available, the following picture emerges.[5] Intellectual aptitude, which was assessed annually from preschool to the fourth grade, was significantly affected by length of

---

[5]Data collected up to the end of fourth grade have been discussed extensively in a previous report (Beller, 1974). Points contained in the earlier discussion will not be repeated here.

preschool up to the last assessment. Of particular importance is the fact that we used three different intelligence tests and picked up significant preschool effects on two tests, in spite of the fact that correlations between tests ranged from modest to low (i.e., $r = .66$ to $r = .17$).

The findings of preschool effects on the Stanford–Binet and Peabody Picture Vocabulary Tests are in general agreement with findings reported by three other Consortium studies (Gray and Klaus, 1970; Weikart, 1971; Deutsch, Taleporos, & Victor, 1974). All four studies show an initial positive effect of preschool experience on the intellectual performance of economically disadvantaged children. The initial rise is more dramatic but less sustained over time in the studies of Gray and Klaus and of Weikart than in the present study and in that of Deutsch et al. Two factors may have contributed to these differences. The children in both Gray's and Weikart's studies had much lower initial levels of intellectual functioning, particularly those in Weikart's study who were classified as functionally mentally retarded. A less dramatic IQ increase in children in the normal range of intelligence might be more lasting than a dramatic increase in children with initially subnormal IQ levels, especially when the increase is due to a radical but temporary change in environmental stimulation (Karnes, Hodgins & Teska, 1969; Miller, Dyer et al., 1971).

The remainder of the overall effects of preschool will be discussed along with these effects by sex and family background. These additional variables contributed in two ways to the interpretation of the analyses. In some areas—like retention in grade, attitudes toward sex and family roles, achievement and endurance, motivation, ego development, and ego function in adolescence—significant effects of preschool only emerged in the subgroup analyses, for instance, in one sex and not the other and only in subjects from intact and parent-employed families but not from single- or unemployed-parent families. In other instances, the subgroup analyses helped us to understand the meaning of the findings by showing the aspect of the particular variable that was affected by preschool experience. This was the case, particularly in the analyses of effects on self-concept, moral judgment, and motivational variables in first grade.

With regard to sex, the effects of preschool experience were substantially greater on girls than on boys in most of the areas we investigated. Length of preschool had significant effects on school grades for girls from first to fourth grade. The effects on boys were less consistent. Similarly, preschool had a significant effect on girls' self-concept with regard to the intellectual-school subcluster. None of the effects of preschool on the self-concept of boys reached significance. The effect of preschool on maturity of moral judgment in tenth grade was substantial and significant on girls but only marginally significant on boys. Effects on motivation assessed in eleventh grade were clearly stronger for girls than for boys. Preschool tended to raise significantly nurturance and achievement in girls but not in boys. Finally, preschool experience was associated with a significantly higher level of ego development in girls but not in boys.

The much greater effect of preschool on girls than on boys from economically disadvantaged black families may be related to the fact that the mothers in such families tended to assume the responsible role and that 2 decades ago black women had a much greater opportunity to find jobs than did black men. Moreover, this author found evidence that lower-class black mothers were more attentive to and also responded more positively to their preschool-aged girls than to their same-aged boys (Beller, 1967). This may, among other things, have fostered identification of a girl with her mother, who was the more responsible member of the family.

The two areas in which preschool had a greater effect on boys than girls were teacher comments on report cards with regard to academic achievement and reflective-impulsive style. With regard to teacher comments, only the boys with 2 years of preschool showed a significantly higher incidence of positive teacher comments summed over the school years. It is possible that the small nursery groups and 2 years of preschool experience offered these boys sufficient exposure to responsive, nurturant female teachers to interrupt any negative cycles between the mothers and their sons and made these boys more ready for positive cycles of teacher reinforcement and academic achievement. The differential effects may have been due to the greater range of positive and negative teacher comments among the group of boys, whereas all three groups of girls showed approximately twice as many positive as negative teacher comments on academic achievement (see Table 11.3).

Reflectiveness is an important part of academic achievement. The interpretation just offered may apply equally well to reflectiveness. Girls were generally more reflective than boys in the tenth though not in the fourth grade.

These findings over all measures of a substantially greater effect of preschool experience on girls than boys corroborates the findings reported by Gray (Gray, Ramsey, & Klaus, this volume).

The finding that an intact family and parental employment (when the child enters school) sustain or enhance the effects of preschool experience can be interpreted on the basis of the hypothesis that preschool turns children from passive into active learners. It is to be expected that a good many low-income children come home from preschool more curious and more interested in learning than they were before and that this has an impact on the parents and their educational role toward their child. An intact family and employed parents are generally in a better position to respond to this new challenge than are single or unemployed parents. We interpret our results to mean that the child is better able to benefit from the educational process due to the preschool experience depending on whether he or she lives in a family strong enough to support and sustain the child as an active learner. The goal of preschool was to arouse in the child curiosity and motivation to learn, but even intrinsic motivation to learn needs a favorable climate to sustain itself.

In a number of instances the contribution of family background helped us to understand better the effects of preschool experience on the psychosocial development of the child. For example, a child with preschool experience coming from a family in which at least one parent was employed was able to sustain the impact of preschool on a positive self-concept with regard to his or her intellectual status. This effect was not apparent in children of single parents or unemployed parents, who probably could not support and sustain the impact of preschool. Nevertheless, preschool experience did show trends toward a more positive self-image among children of single or unemployed parents. However, the effect emerged in other aspects of self-concept, such as physical appearance or popularity. Another finding that emerged in children with preschool experience from single-parent families appears meaningful to us: Children with 2 years of preschool experience from such families were less happy and less satisfied with themselves than peers from similar families without the benefit of preschool experience. This trend was also apparent for children of unemployed parents. The ability to express such discontent seems to us evidence of strength of facing their plight as the part of society which has the highest unemployment rate and a bleak future. Children without preschool experience—who expressed significantly less unhappiness—may be resigned to their fate or be denying their painful situation. Finally, it needs to be pointed out again that the adolescents with no preschool experience, regardless of their family background, showed a less positive self-image than children with preschool on three subcategories of the test.

As in the case of self-concept, our study revealed a meaningful relationship between preschool experience and family background in its impact on the development of moral judgment. Family factors influenced the effects of preschool in the following ways: Extended preschool experience had a significant positive effect on the development of the overall maturity of moral judgment, on the development of the understanding of justice as not being immanent or magical, as well as a reliance on restitutive rather than expiatory punishment. Apparently, the preschool experience offered these children an opportunity to learn that justice involves rules and circumstances rather than merely magical powers.

The impact of preschool on the development of maturity of moral judgment generally was sustained by both the intactness of the family and the employment or economic self-sufficiency of the parents, but was less apparent in children of unemployed or single parents. The effect of preschool on a greater understanding of the possibility to right a wrong depended only on the presence of both parents, but not on the economic self-sufficiency of the parents. Maybe the opportunity to witness two adults coping with their own interpersonal conflicts and supporting each other may have afforded the child more occasions for experiencing the correction of wrongdoing through restitution than was the case in a single-parent family. Similar factors may have contributed to the finding that preschool experience significantly affected more attitudes toward sharing responsibility in the home in children from two-parent families than in children from single-parent families.

The findings with regard to the overall effects of preschool experience on motivational variables in the first grade have already been reported elsewhere (Beller, 1974). The interpretation offered at that time was that children with preschool experience, especially those with 2 years of preschool experience, were less inhibited in the expression of both positive and negative behaviors. In their critical review of the literature on effects of early day care experience, Belsky and Steinberg (1978) come to the same conclusion.

The additional analyses employing family background variables have thrown new light on the findings that, in the first grade, preschool led to an increase of both positive and negative motivation-related behaviors. Sharp differences appear in these findings when the three groups of first graders are separated into children from intact families and children from father-absent families. Children with preschool experience coming from father-present families are marginally higher on autonomous achievement striving and significantly lower on dependency conflict. The relationship between preschool experience and increased dependency and aggression disappears in this group but emerges again in children from father-absent families. Thus, the earlier interpretation can now be modified in the sense that children who experience greater tolerance of the expression of both positive and negative social behaviors by attending preschool make different use of the more supportive and tolerant environment preschool has offered them depending on their family background.

Negative social behavior like aggression was particularly likely to be elevated in first grade children who came from low-income overburdened single-parent families where frustration of dependency needs is high and opportunities for non-aggressive coping with frustration and conflict are low. By contrast intact families seemed to sustain the higher autonomous achievement striving and lower conflict over expressing dependency needs which resulted from the preschool experience.

Turning to preschool effects on attitudes, motivation and ego function in adolescence, we find that the background of an intact family and employed parents enhances the effects of more autonomy in making career decisions, of higher achievement motivation and greater reflectiveness in coping with problems. It appears that we are dealing here with a pattern of an effective personality which seems to be supported by the combined background of a preschool experience and effective parents who coped successfully with their own personal situation, i.e. keeping the family intact, as well as with their economic situation, i.e. staying gainfully employed.

Finally, while the interpretation of relationships between preschool and family background assigned to the family the role of sustaining positive effects of preschool it is equally possible that children from more intact and more effective families could gain more from their preschool experience.

SUMMARY AND CONCLUSIONS

The 12-year follow-up study examined whether the length of preschool affected the intellectual and socioemotional development of economically disadvantaged children. An attempt was made to carry out a comprehensive assessment of development, to employ multiple criteria and measures in each of the areas studied, and to examine the findings in the context of family background variables.

Length of preschool and preschool versus no preschool related to different aspects of intellectual development (i.e., aptitude, achievement, attitude, and motivation) and of socioemotional development (i.e., attitudes, motivation, moral judgment, ego development, and ego functions). Short- and long-term, immediate and delayed effects were found in both areas of development.

Preschool effects on intellectual aptitude when measured by the comprehensive Stanford–Binet test were greater the earlier the child entered preschool. These effects were immediate; that is, they occurred by the end of the first year of school (nursery, kindergarten or first grade) and were sustained to the fourth grade when measurement ceased. When measured by the Goodenough (performance) IQ test, effects of length of preschool were apparent in third grade and increased in the fourth grade (when measurement ceased).

Effects on academic achievement were assessed in three ways: school grades, teacher comments, and retention in grade. For all three, length of preschool yielded significant effects. Effects of length of preschool on higher classroom grades over the first four grades were more consistent in girls, were more significant in second and third grade, began to level off in fourth grade, and disappeared by the fifth grade. Positive effects on teacher comments on the child's academic progress from first to eleventh grade were marginally significant for children with longer preschool and were significant for boys with 2 years of preschool. The relationship between preschool experience and less retention in grade reached significance among children with employed parents and approached significance among children of father-present families.

The positive effects on attitudes and motivation to achieve intellectually, measured during the first three grades, were due to any amount of preschool versus no preschool, rather than to length of preschool.

Three areas of socioemotional development were assessed with identical methods and content in fourth and tenth grades: self-concept, moral judgment, and reflectiveness-impulsiveness in problem solving. Length of preschool produced delayed effects in the first two areas. Effects of length of preschool were stronger in tenth than in fourth grade on both self-concept and maturity of moral judgment. In both areas these effects were stronger in girls than boys and in pupils from employed- than unemployed-parent families. On maturity of moral judgment, length of preschool effects were stronger on pupils from father-present than father-absent families.

In the third socioemotional area, reflectiveness-impulsiveness, more analyses of preschool effects were significant in the fourth than tenth grades. In the fourth grade, almost all analyses showed significant preschool effects in the predicted direction (for all subjects, males, father-present, and employed parents). The preschool effect on females approached significance, although the Ns were too small to allow analyses of the father-absent and unemployed-parents subsets. These data showed that the Kindergarten group tended to have a particularly high proportion of reflectives so that the preschool effects in most of the analyses (except males) were due to the Nursery and Kindergarten groups versus the First-Grade group. In tenth grade, the analyses of preschool effects on males and father-present groups reached significance, whereas that on employed-parent groups approached significance. In contrast to the fourth-grade results, the tenth-grade Nursery group, in all analyses, had an equal or higher proportion of reflectives than did the Kindergarten group. Therefore, in tenth grade there was a linear association between proportion of reflectives and length of preschool.

Effects on motivational variables were investigated in first and eleventh grades, although methods of assessment and content areas were not identical. In the first grade, children with 2 years of preschool were least inhibited in the expression of aggression and tended to express more dependency needs. Children without any preschool tended to be more conflicted in their expression of dependency needs. Children with preschool were higher than children without preschool on autonomous achievement motivation. When the groups were separated by sex these effects were found only in boys; when the groups were separated by early family background, preschool effects of higher aggression as well as a trend toward higher dependency striving appeared in children from father-absent families. Preschool effects of less conflict over the expression of dependency, as well as a trend toward higher autonomous achievement striving appeared in children from father-present families.

In the eleventh grade, effects of length of preschool were investigated on three motivational variables: nurturance, achievement, and endurance. Significant findings consisted entirely of strongest effects in groups with 2 years of preschool and were as follows: higher nurturance in girls and in youths from father-present families; higher achievement in girls and in youths from father-present and parent-employed families; and a trend toward higher endurance in girls.

The remaining analyses were carried out on socioemotional data collected in eleventh grade only. With regard to attitudes toward one's effect on society, length of preschool had a positive main effect, that is, when the analysis was based on all subjects without any breakdowns into subgroups.

Attitudes toward greater emancipation of women were affected by 2 years of preschool when compared with 1 year or no preschool in subgroups from father-present and parent-employed families. Also, 2 years of preschool resulted in a significantly higher level of ego development among girls.

Finally, putting this study in perspective, the magnitude and range of relationships of length of preschool to later outcomes was much larger than we anticipated. When we look at the findings of the other studies in this volume we arrive at two conclusions: With regard to intellectual aptitudes and academic achievement, our findings are corroborated by others in this volume; with regard to the effects on socioemotional development, our findings await replication because we have explored largely virgin territory.

Two similar conclusions are appropriate for the interacting effects of preschool with demographic and family background variables. With regard to the much greater effect of preschool on girls than on boys from economically disadvantaged black families, our finding is fully in accord with those of Gray's study. However, with regard to the interacting effects of preschool with family background our study awaits replication.

ACKNOWLEDGMENTS

The study was carried out with the support of the Philadelphia Council for Community Advancement through grants from the Ford Foundation, the Office of Economic Opportunity, the Education Commission of the States, and the William Penn Foundation.

REFERENCES

Beller, E. K. Exploratory studies of dependency. *Transaction of the New York Academy of Science,* 1959, *21,* 414–426.
Beller, E. K. *Maternal behavior in lower class Negro mothers.* Presented at the annual meeting of the Eastern Psychological Association, Boston, Mass., April 1967.
Beller, E. K. Research on organized programs in early education. In R. Travers (Ed.), *Handbook for Research on Teaching.* New York: Rand McNally, 1973.
Beller, E. K. The impact of early education on disadvantaged children. In S. Ryan (Ed.), *A report on longitudinal evaluations of preschool programs* (Vol. 1). Washington, D.C.: Office of Child Development, 1974.
Beller, E. K., Adler, P., Newcomer, A., & Young, A. Motivation reinforcement and problem solving in children. In A. Pick (Ed.), *Minnesota Symposium on Child Psychology.* Minneapolis: University of Minnesota Press, 1972.
Beller, E. K., McNichol, J. E., & Root, M. *Maturity of moral judgment manual.* Unpublished manuscript, 1979.
Belsky, J., & Steinberg, L. D. The effects of day care: A critical review. *Child Development,* 1978, *49,* 929–949.
Bloom, B. S. *Stability and change in human characteristics.* New York: Wiley, 1964.

Cicirelli, V. G. et al. *The impact of Head Start: An evaluation of the effects of Head Start on children's cognitive and affective development*. Washington, D.C.: National Bureau of Standards, Institute for Applied Technology, 1969.

Crites, J. O. *Career maturity inventory*. Monterey, Calif.: CTB/McGraw-Hill, 1973.

Deutsch, M., Taleporos, E., & Victor, J. A brief synopsis of an initial enrichment program in early childhood. In S. Ryan (Ed.), *A report on longitudinal evaluations of preschool programs* (Vol. 1). Washington, D.C.: Office of Child Development, Department of Health, Education, and Welfare, Children's Bureau (DHEW Publication No. OHD 74-24), 1974.

Dunn, L. M. *Manual for the Peabody Picture Vocabulary Test*. Minnesota: American Guidance Service, 1959.

Goodenough, F. L. *Measurement of intelligence by drawings*. New York: World Book, 1962.

Gray, S. W., & Klaus, R. A. The Early Training Project: A seventh year report. *Child Development*, 1970, *41*, 909–924.

Harrington, M. *The other America: Poverty in the United States*. New York: Macmillan, 1962.

Hawkes, Nigel. Tracing Burt's descent to scientific fraud. *Science*, August 17, 1979, *205*, 673–675.

Honzig, M. P., Macfarlane, J. W., & Allen, L. The stability of mental test performance between two and 18 years. *Journal of Experimental Education*, 1948, *4*, 309–324.

Hunt, J. McV. *Intelligence and experience*. New York: Ronald Press, 1961.

Jackson, D. N. *Personality Research Form Manual*. Goshen, N.Y.: Research Psychologists Press, 1974.

Jensen, A. R. How much can we boost IQ and scholastic achievement? *Harvard Educational Review*, 1969, reprint series No. 2, 1–23.

Kagan, J. Reflection-impulsivity and reading ability in primary grade school. *Child Development*, 1965, *36*, 609–628.

Kamin, L. J. *The science and politics of IQ*. Potomac, Maryland: Lawrence Earlbaum Associates, 1974.

Karnes, M. B., Hodgins, A. S., & Teska, J. A. *Research and development program on preschool disadvantaged children* (Vol. 1). Final Report, Bureau of Research, Office of Education, U.S. Department of Health, Education, and Welfare, Project No. 5-1811, Contract No. OE 6-10-235, May 1969.

Loevinger, J. *Measuring ego development: Construction and use of a sentence completion test*. San Francisco: Jossey-Bass, 1970.

Miller, L. B., Dyer, J. L. et al. *Experimental variation of Head Start curricula: A comparison of current approaches*. Progress Report No. 9, Research Grant CG 8199, Office of Economic Opportunity. Louisville, Ky.: University of Louisville, 1971.

Piaget, J. *The moral judgment of the child* (M. Gabain, trans.). New York: Harcourt, Brace & World, 1932.

Piers, E. V., & Harris, D. B. Age and other correlates of self-concept in children. *Journal of Educational Psychology*, 1964, *55*, No. 2, 91–95.

Seltzer, A. R., & Beller, E. K. *Judgments of time and moral development in lower class children*. Presented at the biennial meeting of the Society for Research in Child Development, Santa Monica, Calif., March 1969.

Terman, L. M., & Merrill, M. A. *Stanford–Binet Intelligence Scale*. Boston: Houghton Mifflin Company, 1960.

Weikart, D. P. *Early childhood special education for intellectually subnormal culturally different children*. Paper prepared for the National Leadership Institute in Early Childhood Development, Washington, D.C., October 1971.

Wellman, B. L. Iowa studies on the effect of schooling. *Yearbook National Sociological Studies in Education*, 1940, *39*, 377–399.

12

The IDS Program: An Experiment in Early and Sustained Enrichment

Martin Deutsch, Cynthia P. Deutsch, Theresa J. Jordan, Richard Grallo
New York University

Introduction

In 1961, after several years of pilot testing and associated investigations, the Institute for Developmental Studies (IDS) established an early childhood enrichment program that was a forerunner of what later became the national Head Start effort and a pilot program for Follow-Through. The IDS program, which was to serve some 1200 children as well as their parents and teachers throughout its 7-year duration, addressed the cognitive growth and social and emotional adjustment of minority children from poverty backgrounds. It was implemented in New York's Harlem community and extended beyond the school setting into homes and neighborhood centers.

The IDS early enrichment program emerged from a series of preliminary research activities and field observations that were directed at uncovering antecedents of the school and social difficulties that have been disproportionately common in the majority of urban areas throughout the United States. These initial efforts corroborated the view that developmental processes are interactional in nature, and that even at the prekindergarten and kindergarten stages, a child's competencies, coping skills, and socioemotional adjustment are the products of a history of encounters with the social world. Academic and interpersonal behavior patterns, as well as developmental lags in these areas, appeared to be both initiated and maintained by reinforcement from a variety of sources in the child's increasingly complex environment, including home and school.

To provide children the opportunity to acquire essential concepts and skills in a consistently supportive environment, a mutually reinforcing cycle of school, community, and family structures was conceived. Within the context of these integrated elements, IDS provided enrichment experiences to enhance children's basic cognitive and perceptual skills in areas such as using language to encode experience, discriminating relevant from irrelevant auditory and visual stimulation, and developing adaptive and realistic self-perceptions and motivational orientations. The program brought 4-year-old children into special classes in their neighborhood schools and continued to work with these youngsters and their families through the third-grade year. Curriculum reformulation, teacher and parent training, and special community outreach services were central to the IDS efforts, which constituted a pioneering venture into early, systematic, and sustained enrichment.

Throughout its duration, the IDS program constituted experimental and comparison groups through random selection and assignment of children from a pool of families who opted for participation in special educational programs. The existence of these initially equivalent groups provided the foundation for program evaluations, as well as investigations of more general issues in child and adolescent development. For a subsample of these children, IDS has generated an information base that spans the period from age 4 through adolescence and includes complementary parent and sibling data. In recent years, a number of these youngsters have become parents themselves. In these cases, attempts have been made to expand the data base to encompass information regarding a third generation of inner-city families.

As program participants enter middle and late adolescence and confront the expanded role responsibilities associated with adulthood, investigations have begun to focus on the long-term effects of early intervention on psycho-social adjustment and the quality of later life. To obtain a holistic view of the lives of program participants and a perspective on the role of early enrichment in these youngsters' development, a series of case studies has been generated. These case studies suggest that the effects of early enrichment should not be assessed in a static framework that yields a kind of "stop motion" view of the life process but rather as one element in widely differing and evolving life contexts. Through case studies, an attempt has been made to identify the life events that have either supported or attenuated initial positive effects of enrichment. These case studies are perhaps of optimal value when viewed against the backdrop of early evaluation results (Deutsch, Taleporos, & Victor, 1974) and in conjunction with emerging psychometric studies (Jordan, 1981). Evidence regarding the value of the intervention for coping with new situations and generalizing beyond narrowly defined academic skills will continue to accumulate as program participants attempt to meet the demands of their adolescent and adult lives.

THEORETICAL AND HISTORICAL FOUNDATIONS

The IDS early childhood enrichment program evolved from a series of pilot studies and field observations in inner-city settings that suggested that preschool experiences could be used to stimulate children's cognitive growth and to contribute to the development of a more satisfying life. Deutsch's (1965a) position regarding the essential malleability of the child and Hunt's (1961) rejection of the notion of intelligence fixed at birth set the theoretical parameters for an intervention program that would provide perceptual, conceptual, and language enrichment as an antidote for restriction of early experiences.

During the initial phases of the IDS program, Deutsch (1965a) suggested that a range of behavioral deficiencies can result from repeated exposure to poverty environments that limit the child's opportunities to generate cognitive systems for interpreting and mediating life events. Restriction of locomotion in crowded home settings (Lewis, 1961), fewer meaningful auditory "signals" and more noise (Deutsch, 1965b), and minimal social interaction with verbally mature individuals (John & Goldstein, 1964) appeared to characterize the early lives of substantial numbers of inner-city minority youngsters. Opportunities for developing adaptive and realistic perceptions of one's own competencies and attributes were attenuated by a host of environmental conditions. For example, many children involved in the IDS program had never viewed themselves in a full-length mirror or in a photograph or had anyone respond to them in a relevant verbal exchange.

Children from low socioeconomic inner-city backgrounds have been described as exhibiting such educationally related problems as deficits in basic cognitive skills, lack of reading readiness, difficulty with mathematical calculations, inadequate problem-solving skills, and related motivational and attitudinal difficulties (Barbe, 1967; Reissman, 1976). With the Civil Rights movements of the 1960s, enhancing the school performance and cognitive skills of inner-city minority youngsters evolved into an issue of national attention and concern (Doll & Hawkins, 1971; Gordon & Wilkerson, 1966; Reissman, 1976; Witty, 1967). Simultaneously, considerable discrepancy emerged regarding the causes of these youngsters' achievement problems and the appropriate strategies for reversing the limiting effects of poverty backgrounds (Bloom, Davis, & Hess, 1965).

Early attempts to explain the low achievement syndrome of inner-city youngsters focused largely on the role of innate ability in determining cognitive performance, a tradition with roots in the conceptual frameworks of Darwin, Galton, Cattell, and Hall. During a period of much emphasis on heritability and fixed intelligence, the IDS program advocated the position that intellectual growth is in large measure a product of environmental encounters that shape and limit the ability to learn. This perspective carried with it the expectation that intelligence could be altered through appropriate modifications of learning environments (Hunt, 1961). Furthermore, the child's cognitive capacity was considered most malleable or amenable to change during the earliest years (C. P. Deutsch, 1964; M. Deutsch, 1964; Skeels, 1965; Skeels, Updergraff, Wellman, & Williams, 1938; Stoddard, 1946; Stoddard & Wellman, 1940). Consequently, the IDS program targetted its enrichment strategies to the very young child.

The recent work of Feuerstein (1979, 1980) provides an updated, international body of support for the "modifiability," flexibility, or plasticity of the human cognitive system anticipated in the IDS program. Proceeding beyond the frameworks of Piaget, Feuerstein's work presents a view of intellectual development as a clearly interactive phenomenon: According to Feuerstein, mediating mechanisms must be operative in order for events to be transformed into experiences and perceptions that fit meaningfully into the child's cognitive grid. Environmental deprivation consists of situations in which essential mediation fails to occur as a result of poverty, pathology, or social or cultural disintegration. This deprivation may take the form of insufficient adult direction and support for understanding life events, or a physical environment that presents a severe deficit of stimuli to be mediated. In this system, the interposition of an external "mediator" temporarily takes the place of underdeveloped cognitive systems and guides the child in the development of structures that enable him/her to assimilate incoming stimuli.

The body of research and theory that has attempted to identify the antecedents of learning and achievement problems in inner-city youngsters has emphasized the role of self-perceptions, as well as basic cognitive abilities, in accounting for differences in performance. Since the work of Cooley (1956) and Mead (1934), self-concept has been thought to develop through the individual's interaction with the environment: Self-views and self-evaluations are acquired as a result of life experiences, with the "data" from social interaction assuming primary importance (Cooley, 1956; James, 1980; Sullivan, 1953; Yamamoto, 1972). A link between self-perceptions and school performance derives empirical support from numerous studies (Bledsoe, 1967; Campbell, 1967; Irwin, 1967; Rosenberg, 1965; Sears & Sherman, 1964). Successful students have been shown to regard themselves favorably, and to be self-confident and self-accepting (Brunkan & Skeni, 1966; Gowan, 1960; Williams & Cole, 1968), whereas low-achievers have been found to perceive themselves as generally unacceptable and inadequate (Combs, 1963).

The IDS program incorporated a self-perception component that was designed to facilitate the process of self-definition, as well as to provide "mediation of competence" (Feuerstein, 1980)—enabling children to correctly perceive/evaluate their own abilities and successes. Contrary to positions held by numerous self-concept theorists, the IDS program sought to enhance self-perceptions through skills development (Bereiter & Englemann, 1966), rather than provide children with positive views of self unsupported by evidence from the domains of school or social functioning. The IDS program encouraged youngsters in the construction of maximally positive "selves," and attempted to counter passivity and feelings of helplessness. Current investigations of the relative merits of skills development versus self-enhancement approaches lend support to the importance of emphasizing skills mastery: For example, Calsyn and Kenny's (1977) causal analysis strongly suggests that self-concept is largely the effect rather than the initiator of achievement in children.

SITE AND SAMPLES

The children described in this report attended IDS early enrichment classes in Central and East Harlem. (Although IDS program classes were also housed in several of the regular public schools on the Lower East Side and the Upper West Side of Manhattan, the most comprehensive program existed in Central and East Harlem.) Each of the host schools had several IDS as well as several non-IDS classrooms at each grade level except prekindergarten. Because the city of New York Board of Education did not sponsor regular prekindergarten classes in these schools at that time, the only prekindergarten groups that existed were IDS program classes.

The larger Harlem community of the 1960s was too diverse to describe simply or to characterize as a homogeneous unit. In general, however, the Institute's staff found that families involved in this program lived in conditions of economic deprivation—in crowded and unsafe housing, and in areas characterized by high drug addiction rates, low employment rates, and inadequate health facilities.

Particularly during the late 1960s, the Harlem community in which the Institute operated was marked by a heightened awareness of political, social, and educational issues that were related to the educational welfare of children. Community members began to work toward increased control of their own institutions, including the public school districts (efforts that were successful in some areas). Community support for the IDS early enrichment program reflected this heightened awareness of children's educational needs and the attempt to take positive action in this area.

The Original Sample

The IDS program involved both male and female black youngsters who ranged in age from 4 to 9 years. Both experimental and comparison participants were from low-SES backgrounds.

Each year, a new pool of participants was formed, consisting of youngsters whose parents expressed an interest and willingness to have their child placed in the program. From this pool of volunteers, children were randomly assigned to experimental and control groups. Each child in the pool met a set of selection criteria that ensured both that the appropriate population was being served by the program and that the children involved were essentially homogeneous with regard to relevant background dimensions. These criteria consisted of:

1. The child met the New York age requirement for admission to public school kindergarten in September of the following year.
2. The parent was willing to assume responsibility for bringing the child to school.
3. Both child and parent(s) were English-speaking.

4. The child was in generally good physical condition. He or she had no serious orthopedic difficulties, nor any obvious abnormalities in hearing or vision.

5. The child had no serious emotional disturbances or behavior problems that could be detected at the time of observation.

6. The child was in the low-socioeconomic (SES) classification, as defined by the Institute's SES scale. (This scale uses the amount of education and the occupational status of the family's chief breadwinner as its criteria for SES classification.)

An active recruiting program had been established in the community, and was especially instrumental in obtaining youngsters in the early stages of the program's operation. As the program became known in the community, an increasing number of parents volunteered their children for participation. The number of Institute classes in operation could not accommodate all the families who had volunteered to participate in the program. Approximately one-third of the group who volunteered but had not been selected for experimental treatment constituted the initial control group. This third was randomly selected from the total N and was equivalent to the experimental group in parental motivation and desire for the child to participate in an enrichment program. For research purposes, this group was identified as consisting of self-selected control subjects (thereafter referred to as the ''Css group''). The experimental group was given enriched schooling from prekindergarten through the third grade, whereas the Css group first encountered formal schooling in the regular kindergartens (or, in some cases, first grades) of the New York public school systems.

At various points in the program's duration, other sets of comparison groups were formed. The children in these groups were not recruited for participation in the IDS program, but simply began school when a corresponding experimental (E) and Css group was entering the same grade level. One such group (designated ''Ck'') entered school at kindergarten and had no prekindergarten experience. A second group entered school in the first grade and had no kindergarten or prekindergarten experience (designated ''C-1''). Finally, children in a third group entered school in the first grade, but had irregular amounts of preschool training. (This was the ''C-123'' group.)

Experimental youngsters in the first group (or ''wave'') of children described in this chapter were admitted to the IDS prekindergarten classes in 1963. (Prior to this, since 1961, there had been preparatory classes established on a nonexperimental basis.) Starting in September of 1963, and in each successive fall for 7 years, a new group or wave of children began the enrichment program at the prekindergarten level. The number of experimental classes constituted in any one year varied for a number of reasons, including the level at which the program was funded to operate. Normally, each of the IDS prekindergarten classrooms began with 17 children. Table 12.1 provides a breakdown of the program participants and various control groups.

TABLE 12.1
Breakdown of Participants in Original IDS Program

				Wave				
Treatment Group	1	2	3	4	5	6	7	Total
Exper.	63	73	88	88	74	56	41	483
Css	45	52	54	40	—	—	—	191
Ck	40	62	70	56	43	30	—	301
C-1	30	74	47	32	—	—	—	183
C-123	—	—	—	—	56	39	40	135
							Grand Total:	1,293

Original Sample: 1963–1969

Note: Exper. = Experimental Group; Css = Control—Self Selected; Ck = Control—First school year is kindergarten; C-1 = Control—First school year is 1st grade; C-123 = Control—First school year is 1st grade with some pre-school.

Follow-Up Investigations

Despite the high mobility of Harlem's youth and the ever-changing nature of its neighborhoods, IDS has maintained contact with a sample of the early enrichment experimental and comparison youngsters. To locate participants during the years subsequent to the program's operation, IDS utilized both radio and printed media to announce the search for youngsters, as well as an extensive networking system (youngsters locating other youngsters). The task of locating participants was complicated by the rapid disintegration of many low-SES neighborhoods in New York City: Site visits often revealed that a pile of rubble had taken the place of a block of housing or that a vacant building remained where an operating school had recently been situated. The rapid shifts in available housing, aggravated by high arson rates, rendered mail or telephone contact virtually useless, as most participants had experienced a series of relocations during the period following the IDS program.

Between 1976 and 1978, the first follow-up investigation of program participants was conducted. Of several hundred experimental and comparison youngsters who were located, IDS staff were able to interview and test 108. In addition, 83 parents were intensively interviewed during this period. In 1979 and 1980–1981, two more follow-up interviews were obtained from a subsample of youngsters, as well as projective and self-report measures. These data were combined with early childhood information collected when the IDS program was in operation, as well as with test results from 1976, to develop case histories of 28 youngsters.

Insights obtained from the development of these case studies were instrumental in the design of the current follow-up investigation in which 154 participants to date have been interviewed and tested. Although a substantial number of original youngsters have been located for this investigation, maintaining contact with the participants is becoming increasingly complex because their mobility has been enhanced with transitions to adulthood and by such events as marriage and entry into the armed services.

DESIGN AND METHODOLOGICAL APPROACH

Program Outline and Description

The IDS early enrichment program proceeded from a body of literature that had identified four areas critical for a successful school experience and in which significant differences existed between middle-class and disadvantaged children. These areas consisted of: (1) accuracy and precision in perceptual discrimination; (2) facility with language tasks, including verbal expression; (3) mastery of key concepts on which later learning was predicated; and (4) development of realistic and maximally positive self-concepts. A working assumption was that the "hidden curriculum of the middle-class home" was responsible for the differential between the two groups of youngsters in that it provided essential early experiences on which later facility and achievement in these areas depended.

The IDS early enrichment program was designed to address these areas, spanning both academic skills and affective domains of the learner, and to provide experiences that would facilitate development. The program recognized the interrelatedness of what appeared to be prerequisite skills and approached the task of enrichment in a manner that reflected the structure of these attributes. Skills in perceptual discrimination, for example, underlie the ability to separate relevant from irrelevant stimuli in an environment of impinging stimuli. This, in turn, underlies the ability to extract important information from the environment (Gibson, 1965). Such discrimination skills, in both auditory and visual modalities, are also necessary conditions for the successful acquisition of language and the attainment of a number of key concepts (Piaget, 1936/1952).

Without sufficient incorporation of language (involving adequate vocabulary, reading comprehension, knowledge of grammar, ability to spell, and ability to listen), a child lacks many tools necessary for entrance into the adult social context, which is a "world mediated by meaning" and a world where most meaning is conveyed through language. Attainment of key concepts is also necessary for successful negotiation of the school curriculum, and for later entry into the adult social context, wherein experience is organized according to concepts such as time and place, size and shape, and causality and responsibility. Failure to attain such concepts (and there are many of them) keeps an individual on the level of concrete data, preventing the grasping of higher-order relationships between disparate sets of data and creating what Feuerstein (1979, 1980) calls an "episodic grasp of reality."

Finally, the attainment of self-concepts that are both realistic and maximally positive ensures that the child will possess sound evidence regarding his or her competencies and supports the child in continued and proactive efforts toward self-development (Jordan & Merrifield, 1981).

Program Components

A strong in-classroom program of educational enrichment characterized the IDS experimental treatment. This component was designed to incorporate educational strategies that would address very basic skill levels and to emphasize proficiency in those areas most necessary for later learning. The goals were to help children acquire a degree of proficiency with academic skills and to develop both independence and a sense of confidence as learners.

The IDS program modified and adapted educational materials, curriculum, and physical arrangement of the classrooms. In addition, it provided for individual assessments of children's strengths and weaknesses and initiated small-group instruction. Consistent with this emphasis, each child was encouraged to proceed at his or her own pace, in accordance with individual needs and abilities. Activities were paced so that each child could proceed from task to task at the rate most comfortable and reinforcing for him or her, though the goal of task mastery was maintained for every child. Matching child abilities with methods of instruction, recently identified as an aptitude by treatment approach (Bracht, 1969; Cronbach & Snow, 1977; Snow, Federico, & Montague, 1980), constituted an attempt to recognize individual differences and to maximize individual potentials.

From prekindergarten through third grade, the IDS program paid special attention to the order and mode of presentation of curriculum materials and educational activities. For each new task, children first encountered activities that engaged them on the most basic skill levels and then proceeded sequentially through levels of increasing complexity and differentiation. A variety of skills was integrated into many activities during the school day in order to maximize transfer of learning and opportunity for reinforcement. For example, size discrimination tasks were introduced at lunchtime, when foods and containers served as "educational materials," as well as during game or activity time, when children made use of different size blocks and related games and toys to solve size-related problems.

A series of support components coexisted with the in-classroom enrichment. First, the IDS program instituted a staffing pattern that was unique at the time, consisting of teachers, assistant teachers, curriculum specialists, and supervisors whose work was coordinated by a curriculum director. Both teachers and assistant teachers were directly involved in the in-classroom educational enrichment. Assistants, who for the most part were individuals with at least some college experience, were further trained by IDS staff to take an active teaching role.

During the course of the program, in-service training was provided on an ongoing basis to all supervisory and teaching staff: Curriculum specialists and outside resource people worked closely with teachers and supervisors, as well as with assistant teachers, in a program of in-service training. In workshops and conferences, the performance of teachers and pupils was discussed and analyzed. These meetings provided a vehicle for eliciting feedback on the appropriateness of the current curriculum and allowed for the introduction and exploration of new ideas, methods, and materials.

Additionally, a small number of teachers was assigned to each supervisor, who supported teaching staff in new activities and demonstrated new suggestions by actually working with children and introducing materials into the classrooms. These supervisors met periodically with each other and with other IDS research and curriculum staff to engage in a detailed and ongoing formative assessment procedure. The results of this formative assessment were employed to "fine tune" the program as it proceeded, as well as to provide the evaluation staff with preliminary indications of the effectiveness of the program in various areas.

In addition, the program involved parents in the education of their children. This involvement was developed and maintained through home visits made by teachers and assistant teachers, with a view to establishing a positive working relationship between home and school and to allow the teacher to learn more about the child in the context of a home setting. For prekindergarten children, these home visits had the additional effect of easing the initial adjustment to school. The Parent Center, established by IDS in 1966 in the neighborhood settlement house of a local church, was used extensively as a site where an IDS social worker could assist parents with problems relating to housing, welfare, health, and education. Special community aides were added to the personnel complement of the program and served to direct parents with problems to appropriate governmental agencies and to assist them in handling the required procedures. These aides also provided parents with the service of escorting young children to school.

The evaluation component of the IDS early enrichment program also provided a kind of support element that assessed, on an ongoing basis, the effectiveness of the various segments of the intervention and identified the specific learning disabilities to which the disadvantaged child was especially prone, their etiology, and possible treatment and preventive measures.

More extensive descriptions of the various components of the IDS program are available elsewhere (Deutsch, Taleporos, & Victor, 1974; IDS Report, 1966; IDS Report, 1967; Jordan, Frankel-Fein, Hogg, & Grallo, 1981).

Specific Enrichment Strategies and Techniques

Following is a brief sampling of specific aspects of the program curriculum, as it addressed the major areas of language acquisition, perceptual discrimination, concept attainment, and the development of adaptive self-concepts. Although some of the IDS early enrichment strategies and techniques later became accepted practice in the mainstream of American education, they constituted new and innovative ideas at the time when they were introduced into the public schools. That numerous specific practices associated with the IDS program have been widely integrated into contemporary education (e.g., an in-school breakfast program for children) provides corroboration of this program's impact on school-related policy and practice.

Language acquisition was viewed as the result of successfully negotiating a sequence of subtasks, the mastery of each in turn leading to competencies on which more sophisticated skills could be based. Self-awareness of emerging language skills was fostered by a program of targeted teacher-given feedback and positive reinforcement of specific language abilities. Initial phases of the reading curriculum were designed to follow a carefully constructed sequence of combining phonemic elements to build word recognition and comprehension skills in an individualized manner that would allow each child to proceed according to his or her own pace. The Stern reading program formed the initial basis for reading instruction; later, the Sullivan language-based materials were included as a core element.

As part of the efforts to stimulate language acquisition and reading, IDS employed special equipment to supplement printed materials traditionally used in the classroom. One such device was the *Listening Center,* a semipartitioned area containing a tape recorder[1] and several sets of earphones. As many as six children could use the center at the same time: Each child worked individually with a set of earphones, preventing distraction and interference from classroom noises. Special tapes were recorded by Institute teachers, supervisors, and curriculum specialists.

Throughout the language curriculum, the *Listening Center* was employed as a major means of reinforcing auto-instructional and small group learning activities. Children were introduced to the device in prekindergarten. The first tapes presented to the child were prepared by his or her own familiar classroom teacher, in order to provide a speech model and to facilitate attention to the strange equipment. Later, children recorded their own voices and played back the sounds they produced themselves. In addition to stimulating an interest in language (from perceptual as well as semantic viewpoints), the technique was another aspect of the attempt to assist the child to construct a total image of himself or herself.

---

[1]At the time the program was in operation, only large, heavy tape recorders that needed house current were available.

After kindergarten, the Center was employed in both the reading and mathematics curricula.

Another technique used in the prereading and language curriculum was the *Language Master,* a type of tape recorder that recorded and played back a length of tape fixed on a laminated card. The card also had room for pictures and/or symbols. One set of cards used in the program presented the teacher's voice on the tape first, after which the child recorded his or her own voice on the same short tape. In this way, the child was able to compare his or her speech patterns and sentence structures with the teacher's. It also permitted simultaneous perception of associated auditory and visual stimuli to help the child grasp relationships between sounds and symbols: in Chall's terms, to help him or her "break the code" (1967). In addition, the ability to record and hear their own voices provided children with yet another opportunity for self-definition through contrasts and comparisons with significant others. Both these devices were complementary to a program that consistently encouraged children to name things and to attend to, to generate, and to reproduce both oral and written language and that maximized opportunities for children to make perceptual discriminations, to attain various types of higher-order concepts, and to arrive at realistic and positive self-concepts.

Children's interests in games and puzzles were tapped by the *Letter Form Board.* Introduced in the prekindergarten to enhance both perceptual discrimination and language development, this tool consisted of solid three-dimensional letters that fit into matching spaces. The Board was shaped like an easel, with capital letters on one side and lowercase letters on the other. Constructed with precision, no letter could be fit into a portion of another letter's space. Making use of Piagetian stage theory, IDS curriculum specialists attempted to provide a language-related learning opportunity that would be meaningful to children at a concrete level of development. Through the *Letter Form Board,* the alphabet was introduced to children as a sensorimotor experience. In order to complete the formboard, the child was required to make a number of perceptual discriminations, while at the same time gaining experience with letters appropriate to his or her own stage of development. In addition, other games such as *Language Lotto* and ·*Matrix Games*[2] were developed, studied, and employed as vehicles for enhancing language development, perceptual discrimination, and concept attainment.

Lunch time and snack time were also used to provide children with opportunities for making perceptual discriminations, for naming and describing objects, and for attaining higher-order concepts. For example, the "Cognitive Cookie Curriculum" was developed for use during snack time. In this approach,

---

[2]*Language Lotto* and the *Matrix Games* were developed by Dr. L. Gotkin of the Institute after years of work with game procedures as a medium for teaching young children who have difficulties with language and learning. Both have been published by Appleton-Century-Crofts.

cookies were used as educational materials—as highly reinforcing objects that could be manipulated, felt, tasted, seen, heard, smelled, classified, and even constructed (i.e., baked). Children were never given just "cookies"; instead, they were given round ones, square ones, large ones, small ones, vanilla or chocolate, iced or plain, etc. Children were encouraged to describe and classify cookies of different shapes, textures, and tastes and were assisted in reproducing cookies of various shapes by baking new batches. Through baking activities, children were encouraged to display their competencies in producing a concrete product; the actual tasting of this achievement provided an opportunity for experiencing this competence.

Throughout the program, efforts were made to help each child understand himself or herself as a unique being. This process began with the gradual integration of the child into the classroom environment so that he/she would feel comfortable. Later, children were introduced to the camera, which was maintained as a standard piece of classroom equipment. Pictures were taken of each child at different times during the year, and were affixed to each of the children's "cubbies,"[3] along with a written label of the child's name. A special point was made to greet each child by name each day, and to incorporate the children's names in a variety of songs, games, and other activities. A full-length mirror was placed in the doll and dress-up corner, so that each child could see what he or she looked like. (For many children, this was the first time they had seen themselves in a mirror.) Thus, various sets of data (some visual, some auditory, some linguistic) were used to identify each child as a unique person, with numerous attributes. Children were invited to synthesize these sets of data to form maximally positive and realistic self-concepts.

As indicated earlier, another way in which children's positive self-concepts were fostered was to divide larger tasks into smaller units that could easily be mastered, so that a series of small successes could be built. For example, a variety of reasons can account for a child's inability to respond when the teacher holds up a red circle and asks, "What is this?". The child might not have understood the type of response necessary or might not possess the specific language required to answer the question or the conceptual ability to respond to it adequately. However, if the task were subdivided and meaningful cues and associations provided, the child might be able to generate a correct answer on some level. For example, the teacher might ask, "Is this a red circle or a green circle?" thus defining the task in simple color terms and providing the specific language necessary for answering the original question. Or, the teacher might place the red circle against a piece of red paper and ask, "Is this the same color or a different color?" thus further reducing the task to one of its more elementary

---

[3]"Cubbies" were small storage spaces set aside in each classroom. Each child had one of these spaces for his or her own materials.

components and maximizing the possibility for a correct response to be given. Through such elementary success experiences, both competence and self-confidence were nurtured.

Creative dramatics was another way in which children were encouraged to discover and clarify their own feelings and to define themselves through oral and nonverbal expression. It provided the child with an opportunity to ''try on'' and elaborate different roles. In addition, the practice was employed to foster language and conceptual skills, to teach inference making and problem solving, and to develop imaginative thinking.

Early in the IDS program, it became evident to field staff that a significant contingent of youngsters arrived at school lethargic and listless and unable to participate fully in any of these and other educational activities. Inquiries into this problem revealed that many children had no breakfast before coming to school. The IDS program worked with school personnel to incorporate a recognition of the importance of nutrition early in the day and succeeded in instituting the first in-school breakfast program for youngsters.

Measuring Instruments

Throughout the duration of the IDS early enrichment program, a series of cognitive, personality, life experience, and demographic measures were obtained for both experimental and comparison youngsters (Table 12.2). Interviews with parents, siblings, teachers, and other school personnel augmented this data base and provided a context of expectations and perceptions of significant others associated with each of the children involved in the evaluation efforts.

As indicated earlier, cognitive development and evidence of competence in educational tasks constituted a major focus of this curriculum and were reflected in an emphasis on problem solving, concept formation, and language mastery. Consequently, academic progress of both experimental and comparison youngsters was continually monitored as children progressed through the program, from prekindergarten through third grade. For this purpose, standardized and IDS-developed tests were used, as well as a number of observation procedures and informal rating systems.

During the period of the program's operation, several sources of qualitative data became available. Such information—including unsolicited letters written to IDS regarding its program, anecdotal records, notes from informal conversations with parents, IDS field supervisors' reports, and observations and discussions that occurred at the third-grade graduation ceremony—provided an additional resource that was not analyzed during the initial phases of program evaluation but was drawn upon subsequently in the development of case studies of participants.

TABLE 12.2
Measuring Instruments Used in Original Evaluations

General Area	Relevant Measures
Personality	Brown Self-Concept Scale*
Cognitive Skills/Abilities	Cloze Technique
	Early Childhood Inventories*
	Gates-McKillop Reading Diagnostic Test
	Illinois Test of Psycholinguistic Abilities
	Lorge-Thorndike
	Metropolitan Achievement Test
	Orientation Scale*
	Peabody Picture Vocabulary Test (PPVT)
	Reading Prognosis Test
	Stanford-Binet
	Stern Reading Test
	Verbal Survey Language Tests
	Wechsler Intelligence Scale for Children (WISC)
Life Experience Patterns	Behavior Rating Scale*
	Child Screening Interview*
	Location Activity Material Inventory*
	Teacher Observation Scale*
Parental Expectations	Encouragement of Intellectual Abilities*
	Parent's Aspiration for Child*
Demographic Characteristics	Deprivation Index*
	Home Interview*
	SES Index*

*Index, scale, interview, or portion of interview developed at the Institute for Developmental Studies.

Data Collection Procedures

The ability and achievement instruments that were used in the program's original evaluation research were administered according to standardized procedures provided by test publishers and were given on either an individual or group basis in compliance with the requirement of each particular test. The evaluation design provided for yearly measurement of ability and achievement, a model that was closely adhered to during the first 5 years of the program's operation (subsequently, funding constraints interfered with the continuation of an extensive testing program).

Indices of demographic status, parental expectations, and ancillary life experiences were obtained shortly after youngsters volunteered for program participation. Because these data were intended to provide a contextual framework, rather than information regarding program impact, retesting along these dimensions was not included in the evaluation efforts.

A final category of data, self-perception information, was collected at several points during the program's duration but not according to a regular, yearly schedule.

Trained IDS proctors administered all instruments except the Metropolitan Achievement Tests, which were teacher-given. Because minority researchers were few in number at the time of these investigations, the IDS proctors were predominantly white and of middle-class backgrounds.

Data Analysis

Because random selection and assignment of participants were utilized to constitute experimental and comparison groups, initial investigations were treated as experimental studies within an analysis of variance framework.

Results of data analyses presented in the following section represent program effects for the first four waves of children. These waves were provided with the full 5-year complement of the IDS program, whereas groups entering later proceeded through only a portion of the program prior to its termination.

FOLLOW-UP INVESTIGATIONS

Measuring Instruments

Table 12.3 contains a listing of measurement instruments that have been used in the three sets of follow-up investigations (1976–1978; 1979; 1980–1981) conducted to date by IDS.

Data regarding academic progress of experimental and comparison participants were obtained through a combination of interview protocols, standardized tests of verbal skills, and school records where available. Increased attention to participants' assessments of themselves in relation to their achievements is reflected in the addition of self-concept scales to the test battery. Parent interviews, a family environment scale, and segments of the interviews conducted with participants were used to gather information regarding each youngster's home and family context, support system, and parent's expectations.

Data Collection Procedures

All interviewing and testing of participants for the follow-up investigations was conducted on an individual basis at private IDS offices; no group testing procedures were used. Standardized tests were administered according to appropriate procedures provided by the test publishers; interviews were administered according to a set of prescribed probes. Both black and white, male and female proctors were used in this research, but no race or sex effects on participant responses were indicated. Participants received compensation for the time spent

TABLE 12.3
Measuring Instruments Used in Follow-Up Investigations

1976–1978	
	Parent Follow-Up Interview*
	Participant School Records
	Wechsler Scales (Wechsler Adult Intelligence Scale or Wechsler Intelligence Scale for Children-Revised)
	Youth Interview for Developmental Continuity**
1979	
	Consortium Biographical Youth Interview**
	Iowa Language Usage Test (subsection)
	Moos and Moos Family Environment Scale
	Orientation Scale*
	Rotter Incomplete Sentences (selected stems)
1980–1981	
	Consortium Biographical Youth Interview** (adapted)
	Intellectual Achievement Responsibility Scale
	Need for Academic Competence Scale
	Rosenberg Self-Esteem Scale
	Self-Concept of Academic Ability Scale
	Wechsler Adult Intelligence Scale (vocabulary and similarities subtests)
	Work Self-Concept Scale*

*Developed at the Institute for Developmental Studies.
**Developed by the Consortium for Longitudinal Studies.

in research activities at IDS, as well as for transportation between home and testing site.

Prior to each testing session, the participant was informed that alphanumeric codes would be assigned to the response materials and that he or she would be anonymous in resulting research reports. Because the 1980–1981 follow-up study involved an extensive testing/interview package, order of presentation was randomized to counteract seriation effects.

Interviewing of participants' parents in the 1976–1978 follow-up investigation was done by telephone and preceeded by a brief explanation of IDSs purposes in conducting this research.

Data Analysis

Case studies were developed by two IDS clinicians, using data from the original program evaluations and both 1976–1978[4] and 1979 follow-up investigations.

_____

[4]Data collected during the 1976–1978 follow-up investigation are currently undergoing further analysis.

Demographic data, interview information, results of standardized tests, school records, and parent and sibling interviews were used to generate a holistic view of each participant's life course and the role of the IDS early enrichment program in this context.

Current investigations (1980–1981) employ a complement of both large-scale linear techniques (e.g., multiple regression, discriminant analysis) and non-linear, nonparametric methods (e.g., profile and cluster analysis) to address a set of long-term evaluation questions and to study intensively the longitudinal development of naturally occurring subgroups of individuals.

FINDINGS

Research Objectives

The initial evaluation studies that ran concurrently with the IDS early enrichment program were designed to determine whether the strategies employed in this experiment were effective in enhancing educational achievement and related personality traits, such as self-perceptions, of inner-city minority children. In particular, the initial investigations attempted to evaluate the effectiveness of a program that provided early and sustained in-school enrichment, as well as family and community support structures to augment classroom experiences and to facilitate the application of newly acquired skills beyond the school setting.

Follow-up investigations have been designed to determine whether initial gains associated with program participation have been maintained subsequent to the enrichment experience and to identify possible "sleeper effects" that might not have emerged previously. In the 1976–1978 and 1979 investigations, emphasis was placed on determining the role of early enrichment in the context of individual lives and to identify personal attributes and other life experiences that have worked to support or attenuate the value of the enrichment experience. The availability of support structures and the nature of personal barriers to achievement were of particular concern. Imbedded in these efforts was the attempt to generate descriptive and heuristic information regarding the interactions of the enrichment experience with larger social forces.

Current IDS research efforts represent a synthesis of both initial evaluation results and findings from the 1976–1978 and 1979 follow-ups, in that they are designed to examine program effects in interaction with other life forces, as these occur in relatively homogeneous subgroups of youngsters. The issue of long-term differences between experimental and comparison participants evolved into the more targeted question: Along which dimensions and for which individuals have there been persistent, positive effects of early enrichment? This more targeted approach is also being used to investigate a series of alternate developmental paths that characterize participants' transitions to autonomy and competence.

Results

Selected Original Findings: Evaluation of Program Effectiveness

The results that follow have been obtained from original evaluations of the first four waves of children who participated in the IDS early enrichment program as members of either experimental or comparison groups. As discussed earlier, these participant groups were provided the full 5 years of enrichment, from prekindergarten through third grade.

Throughout the original evaluation, significant experimental/comparison group differences were found on a variety of achievement, aptitude, and personality tests, including:

Stanford–Binet Intelligence Scale
Peabody Picture Vocabulary Test
Lorge–Thorndike Intelligence Test (Nonverbal battery, Level I)
Metropolitan Achievement Tests (Reading and arithmetic subsections)
Reading Prognosis Test
Illinois Test of Psycholinguistic Abilities
Brown/IDS Self-Concept Scale

The nature of some of these instruments, as well as an uneven funding pattern for evaluation efforts, precluded consistent yearly measurement with each of these tests. Results of the Stanford–Binet (S–B) and Peabody Picture Vocabulary Test (PPVT), which were administered regularly at the close of the program year, are reported here to provide a partial view of program effects.

Tables 12.4 and 12.5 present means and standard deviations on the S–B and PPVT for each wave of experimental and comparison participants prior to their entering the program and at the close of the prekindergarten, kindergarten, and third-grade year. Inspection of these tables suggests that, along the dimensions tapped by these tests, experimental and comparison participants were fairly similar prior to entry into the IDS program but diverged sharply after each of the preschool years.

Analysis of variance procedures applied to these data (Table 12.6) provide evidence that significant differences emerged between experimental and comparison groups after participation in the preschool components of the IDS program. Examination of experimental and comparison group means (Tables 12.4 and 12.5) indicate that the direction of these differences is, as hypothesized, in favor of the experimental groups. (The extremely high p-values associated with these differences ensure that significance would be maintained if the Bonferroni–Ryan Technique were used to correct for the application of a series of significance tests.) Evidence of program effects after third grade was found in

TABLE 12.4
Mean Stanford-Binet Scores for First Four Waves of Children at Each
Administration*

Prekindergarten

	E			Css		
Wave	N	$\bar{X}$	SD	N	$\bar{X}$	SD
1	31	96.19	11.62	15	96.53	14.89
2	70	93.07	11.27	34	92.94	12.57
3	88	91.63	11.53	48	90.31	14.54
4	86	91.28	12.63	32	89.25	12.73
Total	275	92.40	11.86	129	91.46	13.68

Post-Prekindergarten

	E			Css			Ck		
Wave	N	$\bar{X}$	SD	N	$\bar{X}$	SD	N	$\bar{X}$	SD
1	62	100.19	12.33	40	91.90	14.50			
2	62	98.89	9.69	45	91.29	12.52	58	88.19	12.44
3	67	100.76	10.75	34	92.76	11.41	66	92.91	10.73
4	69	96.96	12.06	23	92.70	9.71	56	90.00	14.71
Total	260	99.17	11.30	142	92.04	12.36	180	90.48	12.71

Post-Kindergarten

	E			Css			Ck			C_1	
Wave	N	$\bar{X}$	SD	N	$\bar{X}$	SD	N	$\bar{X}$	SD	N	$\bar{X}$
1	43	103.58	14.02	29	92.07	14.65	26	92.23	13.55	30	85.53
2	39	94.72	12.75	26	94.54	13.77	37	90.73	13.40	74	80.82
3	55	101.91	12.39	23	90.52	19.72	61	94.84	13.45	47	87.64
4	52	99.85	13.94	20	95.20	11.65	53	91.19	12.19	32	84.69
Total	189	100.24	13.54	98	93.00	15.13	177	92.50	13.09	183	84.02

Third Grade

	E			Css			Ck			C_1	
Wave	N	$\bar{X}$	SD	N	$\bar{X}$	SD	N	$\bar{X}$	SD	N	$\bar{X}$
1	32	97.63	12.78	12	93.92	11.62	13	94.00	11.90	17	94.29
2	21	91.76	14.92	13	91.23	13.26	19	86.32	10.87	26	84.81
3	29	99.28	12.31	12	93.58	16.22	30	93.43	15.33	20	90.65
Total	82	96.71	13.38	37	92.86	13.98	62	91.37	13.64	63	89.22

Key: E = Experimental, Css = Comparison (Self-Selected); Ck = Comparison (First school year is kindergarten); C1 = Comparison (First school year is first grade)

*Source: Deutsch, Taleporos & Victor (1974).

TABLE 12.5
Mean PPVT IQ Scores for First Four Waves of Children at Each
Administration*

Prekindergarten

	E			Css		
Wave	N	$\bar{X}$	SD	N	$\bar{X}$	SD
1	32	75.16	16.08	16	70.44	18.13
2	69	68.73	16.24	32	67.72	17.95
3	87	66.87	14.02	50	62.64	13.73
4	84	66.81	13.86	30	64.93	13.56
Total	272	68.29	14.92	128	65.42	15.48

Post-Prekindergarten

	E			Css			Ck		
Wave	N	$\bar{X}$	SD	N	$\bar{X}$	SD	N	$\bar{X}$	SD
1	62	85.85	17.95	40	75.25	17.95	39	76.08	17.
2	63	81.46	18.91	47	71.77	20.57	57	69.09	20.
3	69	81.41	17.55	36	68.51	16.69	70	75.06	17.
4	71	78.45	20.22	23	74.52	16.74	56	71.55	19.
Total	265	81.67	18.80	146	72.38	18.38	222	72.82	19.

Post-Kindergarten

	E			Css			Ck			C_1	
Wave	N	$\bar{X}$	SD	N	$\bar{X}$	SD	N	$\bar{X}$	SD	N	$\bar{X}$
1	43	90.36	15.67	33	83.36	18.16	34	87.38	14.75	30	77.77
2	38	88.66	17.05	26	84.15	17.56	38	78.82	20.49	73	73.37
3	55	87.25	13.83	25	74.84	22.34	62	82.89	17.27	47	76.62
4	52	87.19	16.85	20	80.50	14.26	53	76.47	17.08	31	68.06
Total	188	88.22	15.72	104	80.96	18.55	187	81.06	17.80	181	74.03

Third Grade

	E			Css			Ck			C_1	
Wave	N	$\bar{X}$	SD	N	$\bar{X}$	SD	N	$\bar{X}$	SD	N	$\bar{X}$
1	31	90.39	12.88	12	86.25	17.71	13	86.15	10.55	17	84.71
2	21	90.95	12.68	13	84.15	14.55	21	89.19	14.37	25	83.28
3	30	96.40	14.40	13	84.92	9.39	30	94.07	17.72	22	87.91
Total	82	92.73	13.56	38	85.08	13.83	64	90.86	15.55	64	85.25

Key: E = Experimental, Css = Comparison (Self-Selected); Ck = Comparison (First School year is kindergarten); C_1 = Comparison (First school year is first grade).

*Source: Deutsch, Taleporos & Victor (1974)

TABLE 12.6
Selected Analysis of Variance Results from Initial Program
Evaluation*

Stanford-Binet	
Testing Period	*F Ratio for Treatment*
Pre-Prekindergarten	non-significant
Post-Prekindergarten	31.82 (p = .0001)
Post-Kindergarten	31.52 (p = .0001)
Post Third Grade	non-significant

Peabody Picture Vocabulary Test	
Testing Period	*F Ratio for Treatment*
Pre-Prekindergarten	non-significant
Post-Prekindergarten	14.83 (p = .0001)
Post-Kindergarten	16.33 (p = .0001)
Post Third Grade	3.36 (p = .02)

*Source: Deutsch, Taleporos & Victor (1974).
Note: Corresponding N's are provided in Tables 5 and 6.

PPVT scores but not in the S–B. However, on this latter measure, both experimental and comparison children performed significantly better than age peers from the same urban area and schools (Deutsch, Taleporos, & Victor, 1974), a finding that might reflect the spread of IDS program techniques into comparison group classrooms. Analyses of variance also indicate that experimental and comparison participants did not differ significantly on these two tests prior to program participation, attesting to the initial equivalence of these groups.

In addition to the quantitative aspects of the evaluation, interview and anecdotal data were collected from administrators, teaching personnel, parents, and older siblings of program participants. At the time that the IDS program operated in the public schools, school administrators expressed favorable opinions about the program, stressing primarily the strength of the IDS educational materials and the expertise of IDS program staff. Teachers and assistant teachers tended to praise the program for assisting children to work in an independent fashion but expressed some difficulty in working with experimental teaching materials that were revised and refined on a yearly basis. They expressed a need for more guidance from program staff to assist in making the required adaptation to new and unfamiliar educational tools and techniques.

These early reports contrast rather sharply with the affect tone of those received from teachers and administrators during the period of children's transitions from experimental to regular public school classrooms. Experimental girls, in particular, were consistently criticized by their teachers for excessive verbosity and curiosity and a level of independence that was seen as incompatible with a traditional classroom routine. Although teachers reported that experimental youngsters were more articulate and more active in the learning process, they regarded these traits as problems rather than assets, especially for females.

Selected Follow-Up Findings: The 1979 Case Studies

The IDS case studies were undertaken primarily to investigate further the group findings in the ongoing longitudinal study: to identify and understand individual life courses in the context of a complex life situation that has been touched by the existence of the special intervention program. Because these case studies are intended to augment the psychometric treatment of group data, and because by definition they are examinations of *individuals*, it would defeat the purpose of the case history approach to attempt to view individuals so studied as a homogeneous group. With that understanding, however, it is possible, in looking over the 28 case histories compiled, to reach some overall generalizations about trends observed. These trends are interesting in themselves but also can serve to generate hypotheses that can be investigated by future research. To that end, the common themes which have emerged from the case studies are listed below.

Common Themes in the Case Histories:

1. Participants reported that among the support structures that had played a central role in providing strength and direction to their families in difficult periods were the church, stable extended family contacts, and long-term parent support programs, including the parent component of the intervention program. Participants viewed these facilities as supports for the family unit, which was then better able to provide encouragement to the school-age child.

2. Those participants who have been most consistent in pursuing educational goals report an early and continuing influence of an interested adult. Such a figure was typically characterized as understanding the steps required for the child to achieve "real-world" goals and as providing guidance and/or moral support in aiding the pursuit of the goals. It did not seem to matter whether this adult was in fact a model for the achievement of the goal or simply a realistically encouraging person: What the participant perceived as critical was the knowledge that someone had faith in his or her ability to achieve.

3. A special case of this "encouraging adult" figure is one or more teachers who were perceived as helpful, caring, and involved. A teacher could not provide the continuity of such encouragement from year to year as other adult figures would, but it would seem that experiences with such teachers provided a

foundation that supported participants in later years. In some instances, dropping out of high school or staying was reported to be directly related to the presence or absence of such early support experiences with teachers.

4. A major area of concern for the participants was continuity of schooling. Although some of the concern can be attributed to the artifact of the context of the interviewing, examination of the life courses of the individuals lends credence to this scholastic involvement as a major theme of their lives. Participants also frequently pointed to an academic achievement or school-related event when asked what they were most proud of in their lives.

5. Both participants and their parents consistently indicated the importance of the information about child development and educational principles that was offered by the early intervention program. Parents' receiving such information apparently contributed to a mutually beneficial cycle, in which an increase in parental confidence enabled them better to encourage children's intellectual, social, and emotional development.

6. Among those participants who became parents in their teens, there is a theme of expressed caring for their children but with little awareness of the need for this caring to be translated into such actions as assuming financial responsibility for the children or concretely planning ways to meet their future needs.

An overall generalization from the case studies and the themes that emerged is that critical links exist among the various domains of an individual's experience and that school-related interventions, if they are to exert sustained effects on the quality of later life, must also take into account the influences of the other primary learning environments that are part of the child's life context, for example, the specific family situation and both the physical and social aspects of the home and neighborhood.

The case study summary that follows offers examples of some of the trends described. The case chosen for presentation has been randomly selected from available IDS case studies. By definition, a single case cannot exemplify all the elements presented in a group of cases, nor is that the reason for its presentation. For purposes of large-scale investigation of many individuals, single case studies can serve a heuristic function designed to guide future research, not to rigidly determine it (Hersen & Barlow, 1976; Kratochwill, 1978). Thus, although the life course of Joan P. and her family context is atypical in some respects, it provides a very good example of the vicissitudes common in the lives of many of the families in the urban inner city, including premature and violent death, and thus offers some insight into the magnitude of external forces whose influence must be taken into account when intervention programs are planned and evaluated. The case of Joan P. also illustrates the concrete way in which individual evaluation and collaboration among teachers in the school context can have a timely influence on the school career of a child whose parents do not have informed understanding of the nature and operation of a curriculum or of the school as an institution.

Abbreviated Case Study: Joan P.

Joan P.'s relationship with the Institute began in 1963, when, at 4 years old, she entered the experimental program. She was interviewed on four occasions between then and 1980, and her mother was interviewed twice. Although Joan can speak about the difficulties and barriers that financial hardship presents for young black men and women, she also speaks very proudly about the hard work that she has invested in following through on her aspiration to pursue a business career.

Joan was born in New York. Her parents were both born and raised in the southern United States and were 30 years old at the time of her birth. Mrs. P. had completed eleventh grade; Mr. P., seventh grade.

At the time of initial home interview for the IDS program in 1963, Mr. P. was working the day shift in a factory, and Mrs. P. worked the night shift as a maid in a hotel. They and their six children were living in a two-bedroom apartment, which was rated by the interviewer as being "very run down," with plaster falling off the walls. Each child shared a bed with one sibling.

When asked what she hoped her 4-year-old daughter would choose to do when she got older, Mrs. P. said, "I hope she'll go through college if she could get a scholarship." She hoped that Joan would become a school teacher or a secretary. Mrs. P. reported that she and her two oldest sons read to Joan at least three times a week and had taught her how to write her name and recite the alphabet. As part of the home interview, Mrs. P. was also asked which things in her life she was most and least satisfied with. Her response was, "I'm most satisfied with my personal health and my job, and least satisfied with the apartment we have and with the amount of money we have to spend." When asked, Mrs. P. stated that she viewed herself most like those people who were "going up in the world."

Joan's preschool and first-grade teachers in the IDS program expressed concern about her highly variable behavior in the classroom. They noted that when Joan was confronted with an anxiety-provoking situation, she became markedly withdrawn and timid. When she seemed comfortable within the setting, she was outgoing and friendly. Both teachers characterized her movements as often slow and lethargic. As a result of these teachers' reports, a psychoeducational assessment was done in the first grade. The results confirmed the teachers' observations that Joan was working below her potential in the academic sphere. More individualized attention was recommended, and the program staff responded by providing a special volunteer companion who spent some time with Joan each week. After this additional intervention, no further educational difficulties were noted.

At the time of Joan's first follow-up interview with the IDS staff, she was 19 years old and attending one of the colleges of the City University of New York, where she was majoring in business. Joan said that she was doing fairly well in school and believed that she had made a good choice of career. Joan perceived herself as doing "a little better than others" in her schoolwork. She was sure that she would want to obtain graduate training and that she would be able to do so. Joan also enjoyed doing volunteer work with a special service club at the college a few times a week.

When asked, Joan stated that she enjoyed listening to music and reading fiction in her spare time. She said that she spent at least 15 hours a week reading for her own enjoyment. She watched very little TV at home.

In order to supplement the financial aid she was receiving to pay for her education, Joan did light chores for some neighbors. This part-time work also allowed her to contribute to her family's income.

When asked what she was most proud of, Joan said, "Graduated from high school." She believed that one of her siblings and her mother really supported her effort toward academic achievement. Without their moral support, she said, she would not have been able to go as far as she had gone in school. Even though her older siblings had all moved out of the family's apartment, they kept in close touch with each other.

Mrs. P. was also interviewed at the time, and she said she was pleased to have an IDS staff member come to her home. Mrs. P. had not been employed for a few years; her major source of income was disability payments. She spoke at length about the importance of Joan's education, saying that she was sure that Joan would complete college and go on to be a business administrator. When asked how she felt about Joan's progress in school, Mrs. P. said, "I'm proud."

Mrs. P. believed that the enrichment program tried to give the children a sense of how important it is to finish school. When asked what she liked best about the program, she said, "The program helped her really want to be something. *It gave her hope*. It gave them something better to look at in comparison to the street."

Two years later, Joan was interviewed again. She stated that she enjoyed speaking with Institute staff because she liked to talk about her school experiences. School was one area in which Joan felt especially proud of her hard work. Despite the family's financial difficulties, Joan was making it through college. She maintained good grades and was involved with many school activities.

At the time of that interview, Joan conveyed a lot of personal information about her life. She spoke openly about suffering two great losses in her childhood. When she was eight, her father was killed. Two years later, her brother, 12 years her senior and a college graduate, was also killed. Joan was not able to discuss with us the circumstances surrounding their deaths. However, as confirmed in interviews with other participants, sudden and violent tragedies happen to many members of the Harlem community. There seems to be some recognition within the family that they must provide a real support for one another when tragedy strikes. For example, Joan stated that she tried to serve as a role model for her four younger siblings, just as her two older brothers did for her. After her eldest brother's death, her other brother became her greatest source of support. She reported that he encouraged her to do well academically and to search for personal happiness in her relationships.

When asked about her school experience, Joan said that she always loved school. Among the favorite teachers she mentioned were two of those she had while in the IDS program. Joan did very well academically in high school and was particularly interested in her business courses. "They were a real challenge."

Joan seemed to be very satisfied with and proud of her college experience. At the time of this latest interview, she was completing her junior year. She hoped to be able to go on for a Master's degree in business, though she was somewhat doubtful about the possibility of doing this. "I'll probably get married along the way and other problems will come up (financial)." She was sure, however, that she would complete her undergraduate work. Joan was making college a learning experience in the social and emotional spheres as well as in the academic areas. She had done tutoring on a volunteer basis for a community group during her high school years, and now cited her volunteer peer counseling work at the college as one of her most important learning experiences. Joan is one of the few subjects who reported that she is registered to vote and actually does so.

Joan's family has had financial difficulties since her early childhood, so all the children began to do odd jobs around the neighborhood to bring home some extra money. In addition to her volunteer work, Joan has been working part-time for pay since her fourteenth birthday. She stated that she has gained some useful skills while in the college work-study program, through which she had the opportunity to work for a number of private accounting firms and to learn how they operate. She believed that these experiences would help her when she began to interview for jobs after graduation. When asked what she hoped to do after she completed her education, she said, "I'd like to be the president of my own accounting firm, but I'll probably end up working for other people." This discrepancy between Joan's aspiration and her expectation did not seem to diminish her sense of optimism and pride. "I'm ambitious and I know how to get along with people; you can go further with qualities like that."

At this latest interview, Joan again spoke at length about how important her mother's and brother's encouragement has been to her. She gave the interviewer an excellent example of how some guidance can help the adolescent to learn more about the importance of the decision-making process. It seems that during her senior year in high school, Joan decided that rather than going on to college she would work so that she and the family could have more money. Her mother, over a 3-month period, sat down with Joan and discussed with her the job prospects that might be available to her with a high school diploma as contrasted with those that might be open to her with a college degree. "If she would have pressured me, I would have rebelled—but the way she did it, I knew she had my interest in mind." After thinking about how much more opportunity she would have with a college degree, she decided to apply to schools.

Joan also commented on the significance of religion in her life. "Religion teaches you respect for God and family; with guidelines like that, you can't go wrong."

As indicated above, the case of Joan P. is not fully representative of the entire set of individual descriptions. But because the subject was so articulate, many themes that can be inferred from some of the other cases were more explicitly identified. The family's vicissitudes were clearly described, and the role of a consistent supportive adult and of a responsive early school program could be observed. The observation and analysis of her behavior in the preschool years that led to a formal assessment and a subsequent individualized intervention provide an example of the importance of early intervention for later school success. This case study also illustrates how youngsters from low-income families in the inner city can acquire and maintain an educational orientation through which they could enter the opportunity structure of the broader society.

Current Investigations

Analyses of data collected in conjunction with the 1980–1981 follow-up investigation have begun to highlight gender-linked trends in the persistence of positive enrichment effects and to suggest more targeted approaches to the study of psychosocial development in the years subsequent to the intervention experience.[5]

First, sex differences have begun to emerge in the relation between treatment and later levels of the achievement and personality variables that the IDS program had been designed to address and enhance. For example, the relation between scores on a set of self-concept measures and early membership in an experimental or comparison group remains significant for late adolescent and young adult males ($R = .35, R^2 = .12, F = 2.80, p = .048$ with $N = 65, df = 3,61$) but not for females (Deutsch & Jordan, 1981; Jordan, 1981).

Second, cluster analyses have identified relatively homogeneous subgroups of participants that transcend categorization by gender or treatment: A combination of self-concept, motivation, and attribution variables has been useful in deriving subgroups of participants within which more precise predictions regarding the attainment of autonomy have been possible (Grallo, 1981).

---

[5]*Note:* These results reflect a partial analysis of 1980–1981 database and are preliminary findings. Further analyses are presently underway.

MEANING OF FINDINGS: DISCUSSION AND IMPLICATIONS

Original evaluations of the IDS enrichment program and associated follow-up investigations provide evidence that early, sustained, and systematic intervention can exert a positive influence on the growth of school-related skills and attributes. The likelihood that these initial gains will persist through adolescence and young adulthood is heavily determined by the interaction of these enhanced skills and attributes with later life experiences and social forces operating in the school, home, and community. A possibly crucial role of complex attribute-by-treatment interactions is suggested by the recent finding that initial gains in such areas as self-perceptions appear to have been maintained only for males, who were more likely than females to receive continued reinforcement for their competencies, curiosity, and independence when they moved into regular classrooms.

Results of initial IDS program evaluations present a challenge to notions of intelligence fixed at birth: Substantial increments in intelligence and aptitude test scores associated with the IDS program argue that appropriate presentation and mediation of stimuli can result in enhanced capability to learn new tasks and acquire new skills. Related achievement and self-concept factors were also malleable during the enrichment period. The IDS effort was successful in that it endowed disadvantaged children with essential tools for coping with educational demands.

Maintaining these advantages was a challenge, however, that was likely to conflict with other realities and social pressures. Case studies of a sample of youngsters involved in the IDS intervention program confirm the notion that the extent to which early enrichment will act as an incentive to later life success depends largely on a host of other social forces that act to support or attenuate its effects. A holistic framework that takes into account differences in life experience patterns and differential availability of support structures becomes essential for assessing the role of early enrichment experiences in later life.

Although similarities in patterns of life experience, and in receptivity to early enrichment, can be identified within certain clusters of participants (e.g., enhanced language skills in experimental youngsters), these clusters do not always correspond to the simple breakdown of experimental and control group membership (e.g., differential persistence of initial self-concept gains). Instead, IDS data often reveal a far more complex and multi-dimensional scatter of individuals and a need to explore interindividual and intraindividual differences that transcend the experimental/control dichotomy. The emerging trends suggest that the acquisition of life-coping skills, and satisfactory transitions into the career force and higher education programs, can be achieved by a variety of different routes, as a result of different patterns of interaction with the social world. The presence or absence of early intervention in an individual's life constitutes only one possible facet of these patterns, a facet whose changing effects can be traced throughout an antecedent sequence of successes and failures in a range of performance areas.

Based on the IDS early enrichment experience, the following is a distillation of some general areas to which future enrichment programs might give special attention. In particular, it appears crucial to assist children in forging clear links between the training offered and its application beyond the experimental setting:

1. Building involvement in social networks. A good deal of vertical mobility in our society is dependent on the fostering of social networks, so providing a strong and stable network would be an important reference model for children.

2. Providing an individual success model. If possible, programs should identify a successful individual with whom the child can identify, communicate, and establish a relationship, and who would be available for multiple years.

3. Developing an awareness of the impact of one's behavior on the lives of others. This could be especially crucial in later parenting functions. From current experience, it appears that young adults are not aware of the implications of family fragmentation, and in fact see an objective trade-off between college or skills training and the maintenance of support or even contact with a child or partner.

4. Planning directions for life. This is critical in order to avoid a solely reactive mode of living and extreme vulnerability to social pressure.

5. Incorporating a temporal dimension into skills training. Skills in planning and organizing are requisite to successful functioning in a complex world. Because these are critical skills for later life, temporal training should occupy an even more central position than had previously been assumed.

6. Developing attainable life goals and a means of self-evaluation in relation to these goals.

7. Developing processes for acquiring information, for sorting out relevant from irrelevant data, and for incorporating appropriate information into the behavioral system.

OVERALL SUMMARY

The IDS early enrichment program was designed to enhance children's basic cognitive and perceptual skills and to assist in developing positive and realistic self-concepts. Children were provided with the opportunity to acquire these essential skills and concepts within the framework of a consistently supportive environment of school, community, and family. Curriculum reformulation, teacher and parent training, and special community outreach services were central to these efforts.

Initial program evaluations revealed that experimental children performed significantly better then their comparison counterparts on a number of achievement, aptitude, and personality measures. Results from repeated administration of the Stanford–Binet Intelligence Scale and the Peabody Picture Vocabulary Test provide examples of the marked between-groups differences that emerged and the patterns of positive change that characterized the experimental youngsters.

An initial set of follow-up investigations (1976–1978, 1979), conducted when most program participants had entered adolescence, concentrated on the role of early enrichment in the context of individual lives and on general issues in adolescent development. Case studies affirmed that critical links exist among the various domains of an individual's experience and suggested that school-related interventions, if they are to exert sustained effects on the quality of later life, must take into account the influences of other primary learning environments that are part of the child's life context.

The most recent follow-up investigations, currently in progress (1980–1981), investigate issues in psychosocial development as program participants make transitions to adulthood. Preliminary results from these investigations suggest that the persistence of enrichment effects is in part gender-linked and that relatively homogeneous subgroups of individuals, which transcend the experimental/comparison dichotomy, are associated with different developmental paths to autonomy and competence.

Implications for future enrichment programs are offered, with special focus on essential support systems that contribute to maintaining the advantages of early intervention throughout later life.

ACKNOWLEDGMENTS

The IDS early enrichment program received funding from the Office of Education (OE), the Office of Economic Opportunity (OEO), the National Institute of Mental Health (NIMH), the Taconic and Ford Foundations, and the Consortium for Longitudinal Studies.

REFERENCES

Baltes, P. B., & Nesselroade, J. F. Cultural change and adolescent personality development: An application of longitudinal sequences. *Developmental Psychology,* 1972, 7(3), 244–256.

Barbe, W. B. Identification and diagnosis of the needs of the educationally retarded and disadvantaged. In P. A. Witty (Ed.), *The educationally retarded and disadvantaged: The sixty-sixth yearbook of the National Society for the Study of Education.* Chicago: University of Chicago Press, 1967.

Bereiter, C., & Engelmann, S. *Teaching disadvantaged children in the preschool.* Englewood Cliffs, N.J.: Prentice-Hall, 1966.

Bledsoe, J. Self-concept of children and their intelligence, achievement, interests, and anxiety. *Childhood Education*, 1967, *43*, 436–438.

Bloom, B. S., Davis, A., & Hess, R. *Compensatory education for cultural deprivation.* New York: Holt, Rinehart & Winston, 1965.

Bracht, G. H. The relationship of treatment tasks, personological variables, and dependent variables to aptitude-treatment interactions. *The Review of Educational Research,* 1970, *4*, 627–745.

Brown, B. *The assessment of self-concept among four-year-old Negro and white children: A comparative study using the Brown IDS Self-Concept Referents Test.* Paper presented t the meeting of the Eastern Psychological Association, New York, 1966.

Brunkan, R. J., & Skeni, F. Personality characteristics of ineffective, effective, and efficient readers. *Personnel and Guidance Journal,* 1966, *44*, 837–844.

Calsyn, R. J., & Kenny, D. A. Self-concept of ability of perceived evaluation of others: Cause or effect of academic achievement. *The Journal of Educational Psychology,* 1977, *69*, 136–145.

Campbell, P. B. School and self-concept. *Educational Leadership,* 1967, *24*, 510–515.

Chall, J. F. *Learning to read: The great debate. An inquiry into the science, art, and ideology of old and new methods of teaching children to read. 1910–1965.* New York: McGraw-Hill, 1967.

Cronbach, L. J., & Snow, R. E. *Aptitudes and instructional methods.* New York: Irvington, 1977.

Combs, C. F. A study of the relationship between certain perceptions of self and scholastic underachievement in academically capable high school boys. (Doctoral Dissertation, Syracuse University, 1963). *Dissertation Abstracts International,* 1963, *24*, 620. (University Microfilms No. 63-51034)

Cooley, C. H. *Human nature and the social order.* New York: Free Press, 1956.

Deutsch, C. P. Auditory discrimination and learning: Social factors. *The Merrill–Palmer Quarterly,* 1964, *10*(3), 277–296.

Deutsch, M. Facilitating development in the pre-school child: Social and psychological perspectives. *The Merrill–Palmer Quarterly,* 1964, *10*(3), 249–263.

Deutsch, M. *Social intervention and the malleability of the child.* Fourth Annual School of Education Lecture. Ithaca, N.Y.: Cornell University, 1965. (a)

Deutsch, M. The role of social class in language development and cognition. *American Journal of Orthopsychiatry,* 1965, *35*, 78–87. (b)

Deutsch, M., & Jordan, T. J. *Self-concept and the growth of competence: A nineteen-year longitudinal study.* Paper presented at the Eastern Educational Research Association Conference, Philadelphia, March 1981.

Deutsch, M., Taleporos, E., & Victor, J. A brief synopsis of an initial enrichment program in early childhood. In S. Ryan (Ed.), *A report on longitudinal evaluations of preschool programs* (Vol. 1). Washington, D.C.: Office of Child Development, Department of Health, Education, and Welfare, Children's Bureau (DHEW Publication No. OHD 74-24), 1974.

Doll, R. C., & Hawkins, M. *Educating the disadvantaged.* New York: AMS Press, 1971.

Dunn, L. M. *Peabody Picture Vocabulary Test.* Minneapolis: American Guidance Service, 1959, 1965.

Durost, W. M., Bixler, H. H., Wrightstone, J. W., Prescott, G. A., & Balow, I. H. *Metropolitan Achievement Tests: Mathematics Tests.* New York: Harcourt Brace Javonovich,

Durost, W. M., Bixler, H. H., Wrightstone, J. W., Prescott, G. A., & Balow, I. H. *Metropolitan Achievement Tests: Reading Tests.* New York: Harcourt Brace Javonovich,

Feuerstein, R. *The dynamic assessment of retarded performers: The learning potential assessment device, theory, instruments, and techniques.* Baltimore: University Park Press, 1979.

Feuerstein, R. *Instrumental enrichment: An intervention program for cognitive modifiability.* Baltimore: University Park Press, 1980.

Gates, A. I., & MacGinitie, W. H. *Gates-McKillop Reading Diagnostic Test.* New York: Teachers College Press, 1965.

Gibson, E. J. *Perceptual development.* New York: Academic Press, 1965.

Gordon, E. W., & Wilkerson, D. A. *Compensatory education for the disadvantaged.* New York: College Entrance Examination Board, 1966.

Gowan, J. C. Factors of achievement in high school and college. *Journal of Counseling Psychology,* 1960, *7,* 91–95.

Grallo, R. Learning and employability: Profiles for achievement. In T. Jordan (Chair), *Culture, conflict, and the growth of competence: A twenty-year longitudinal study.* Symposium presented at the meeting of the American Psychological Association, Los Angeles, 1981.

Hersen, M., & Barlow, D. H. *Single case experimental designs.* Elmsford, N.Y.: Pergamon Press, 1976.

Hunt, J. McV. *Intelligence and experience.* New York: Ronald Press, 1961.

Institute for Developmental Studies (Theresa M. Miller, Ed.). *Proceedings of a presentation to the Division of Early Childhood and Elementary Education by the Institute for Developmental Studies, November 28, 1966.* New York: New York University School of Education.

Institute for Developmental Studies (Theresa M. Miller, Ed.). *Proceedings #2 of a presentation to the Division of Early Childhood and Elementary Education by the Institute for Developmental Studies, February 24, 1967.* New York: New York University School of Education.

Irwin, F. S. Sentence completion responses and scholastic success or failure. *Journal of Counseling Psychology,* 1967, *14,* 269–271.

James, W. *Principles of psychology* (2 vols.). New York: Holt, 1890.

John, V. P., & Goldstein, L. S. The social context of language acquisition. *The Merrill–Palmer Quarterly,* 1964, *10*(3), 265–275.

Jordan, T. J. Long-term latent effects of early enrichment on later life-span development. In T. Jordan (Chair), *Culture, conflict, and the growth of competence: A twenty-year longitudinal study.* Symposium presented at the meeting of the American Psychological Association, Los Angeles, 1981.

Jordan, T. J., Frankel-Fein, R., Hogg, L., & Grallo, R. *Inner-city adolescents: A nineteen-year longitudinal perspective.* Symposium presented at the Eastern Educational Research Association Conference, Philadelphia, March 1981.

Jordan, T. J., & Merrifield, P. E. Self-concepting: Another aspect of aptitude? In M. D. Lynch, A. A. Norem-Hebeisen, & K. Gergen (Eds.), *Self-concept: Advances in theory and research.* Cambridge, Mass.: Ballinger, 1981.

Keniston, K. *The uncommitted: Alienated youth in American society.* New York: Dell, 1960.

Kirk, S. A., McCarthy, J. J., & Kirk, W. D. *Illinois Test of Psycholinguistic Abilities.* Chicago: University of Illinois Press, 1961, 1968.

Kratochwill, T. R. *Single subject research: Strategies for evaluating change.* New York: Academic Press, 1978.

Lewis, O. *The children of Sanchez.* New York: Random House, 1961.

Lorge, I., Thorndike, R. L., & Hagen, E. *Lorge–Thorndike Intelligence Tests.* Boston: Houghton Mifflin Co.,

Mead, G. H. *Mind, self, and society.* Chicago: University of Chicago Press, 1934.

Moos, R. H., & Moss, B. *Family environment scale.* Palo Alto, Calif.: Consulting Psychologists Press, 1974.

Muuss, R. E. Adolescent development and the secular trend. *Adolescence,* 1970, *5,* 267–284.

Nesselroade, J. R., & Baltes, P. B. (Eds.). *Longitudinal research in the study of behavior and development.* New York: Academic Press, 1979.

Piaget, J. *The origins of intelligence in children.* New York: International Univerities Press, 1952. (Originally published 1936).

Reissman, F. *The inner-city child.* New York: Harper & Row, 1976.

Rosenberg, M. *Society and the adolescent self-image.* Princeton: Princeton University Press, 1965.

Runyan, W. M. A stage-state analysis of the life course. *Journal of Personality and Social Psychology,* 1980, *38*(6), 951–962.

Sears, P. S., & Sherman, V. S. *In pursuit of self-esteem.* Belmont, Calif.: Wadsworth, 1964.

Skeels, H. M. Some preliminary findings of three follow-up studies on the effects of adoption of children from institutions. *Children,* 1965, *12,* 33–34.

Skeels, H. M., Updergraff, R., Wellman, B. L., & Williams, H. M. *A study of environmental stimulation: An orphanage preschool project.* University of Iowa Study of Child

Snow, R. E., Federico, P. A., & Montague, W. E. *Aptitude learning and instruction* (Vols. 1 & 2). Hillsdale, N.J.: Lawrence Erlbaum Associates, 1980.

Stoddard, G. D. *The meaning of intelligence.* New York: Macmillan, 1946.

Stoddard, B. D., & Wellman, B. L. Environment and the I.Q. *Yearbook of the National Society of Studies for Education,* 1940, *39*(2), 405–442.

Sullivan, H. S. *The interpersonal theory of psychiatry.* New York: Norton, 1953.

Terman, L. M., & Merrill, M. A. *Stanford–Binet Intelligence Scale (Form L-M).* Boston: Houghton Mifflin, 1960.

Tyrone, R. C., & Bailey, D. E. *Cluster analysis.* New York: McGraw-Hill, 1970.

Wechsler, D. *Wechsler Adult Intelligence Scale.* New York: The Psychological Corporation, 1955.

Wechsler, D. *Wechsler Intelligence Scale for Children.* New York: The Psychological Corporation, 1949.

Wechsler, D. *Wechsler Intelligence Scale for Children-Revised.* New York: The Psychological Corporation,

Williams, R. L., & Cole, S. Self-concept and school adjustment. *Personnell and Guidance Journal,* 1968, *46,* 478–481.

Witty, P. A. (Ed.). *The educationally retarded and disadvantaged: The sixty-sixth yearbook of the National Society for the Study of Education.* Chicago: University of Chicago Press, 1967.

Yamamoto, K. *The child and his image.* Boston: Houghton Mifflin, 1972.

13 Pooled Analyses: Findings Across Studies

Jacqueline M. Royce
University of Minnesota-Duluth

Richard B. Darlington
Cornell University

Harry W. Murray
Syracuse University

Introduction

The Consortium for Longitudinal Studies was formed to study the long-term effects of early education programs for children of low-income families. In 1975, Consortium investigators agreed on important core constructs to be studied with common instruments. They also delegated to an independent analytic group in Ithaca, New York,[1] the tasks of instrument design, coordination of data collection, and the conduct of pooled analyses. Each project site sent its raw data to Ithaca. In this chapter the Ithaca group describes the results of our multisample, metaanalytic treatment of these data. We were not involved in any of the original studies; the analytic and interpretive material reported here are solely the work and responsibility of the Ithaca group. In some instances our analytic decisions and their consequences differ from those of the individual investigators.

The Sample of Studies

Every early intervention study that had a specific curriculum, focused on children of low-income families, was completed prior to 1969, and had an original

---

[1]The Foundation for Human Service Studies, in Ithaca, New York (henceforth called the Ithaca group).

sample in excess of 100 subjects was invited to join the Consortium. The investigators of all but one of the 15 eligible studies accepted this invitation. Thus, this is not a sample of preschool programs but rather is essentially the whole population of large-scale preschool intervention studies conducted in the United States during the 1960s. Results of the pooled study are generalizable in the same sense as a thorough literature review is generalizable—it summarizes the best available information.

The early-childhood education programs described in this volume differed in several ways—children's ages, program duration, parental involvement, curriculum type, and delivery system (in the home or in a center setting). Despite variations, the Consortium projects were similar to one another in many ways. All were research projects with carefully planned, well-run, and carefully monitored programs. Baseline data were collected on the children participating in the programs and, in most cases, control or comparison groups were used for the evaluation of program effectiveness. All programs shared the goal of enhancing children's cognitive development; many programs had noncognitive goals as well.

Research Questions and Conceptual Framework

Each Consortium project stands alone as an independent, self-contained study. We did not intend that the pooled assessments would summarize these richly diverse studies; rather we addressed questions about common patterns of long-term effects across the different programs.

Our main research questions concerned the overall effectiveness of early education programs. For instance, what difference, if any, did the programs make on a child's intelligence and achievement test scores and success (or failure) in school? Did the programs produce changes in the children's goals and aspirations, motivations, and feelings toward themselves and their school environment? Did the programs affect parental goals and aspirations for their children? As subjects reached young adulthood, did program participants have higher rates of high school graduation or employment than did the controls?

A corollary set of questions asked if these programs, in general, were more effective for certain subgroups of children than for others. For example, did family background variables affect how much a child benefited from an early education program? Did the brightest (or least bright) children benefit most? Did early education programs decrease the likelihood of school failure more for boys or for girls?

To answer these questions, data on age-appropriate outcome measures were collected at each follow-up. The outcome measures were selected to indicate individuals' adaptations to their own social and psychological environments. For example, we collected data on whether a person repeated a grade level in school or whether later, as young adults, they were employed—outcome measures that are concrete, independent, and consequential.

ith the complexities of describing and understanding real
ntexts, we used a variety of conceptual frameworks. We
iterature in the areas of black studies, life course, social
field, and status   inment research (Baltes, Reese, & Lipsitt, 1980; Blau &
Duncan, 1967; Boykin, Jackson, & Yates, 1979; Erikson, 1963; Kellam,
Branch, Agrawal, & Ensminger, 1975; Martin & Martin, 1978; Sewel, Hauser &
Featherman, 1976; Sameroff, 1976; Stack, 1974; Walberg & Marjoribanks,
1976).

SITES AND POOLED ANALYSIS SAMPLES

Sites

The programs were carried out in rural and urban sites in the Northeast, Southeast, and the Midwest. By 1976, the subjects had dispersed to hundreds of
communities throughout the United States. Indeed, several were located abroad.
This dispersion played a significant role in our analytic decisions, as we sought
to assure comparability of indicators across sites.

Original and Follow-Up Samples: Longitudinal Design

The overall longitudinal design of the pooled analysis consisted of four phases
(waves) of data collected that yielded four "samples": Wave 1 original samples
(3 months to 5 years of age) are the preprogram data collected independently by
the projects; Wave 2 follow-up samples (5 to 10 years of age) are based on
postprogram data collected independently prior to 1976; Wave 3 follow-up samples (10 to 19 years of age) are based on the 1976 collaborative Consortium data;
and Wave 4 follow-up samples (14 to 21 years of age) are based on the 1980
collaborative Consortium data.

The number of cases in the overall Consortium data collection effort are
shown in Table 13.1. These totals represent the number of cases sent to Ithaca by
the individual projects at each wave. All of these cases, however, were not used
in the pooled analyses because data were missing for certain variables or because
particular groups within projects were excluded for reasons discussed in the
following. Thus, the numbers in our pooled analysis tables may differ from those
reported in the chapters of individual investigators. Further, this table includes
two projects, Woolman and Deutsch, which collected common data but were not
included in the pooled analysis due to the incompatability of their research
designs with the overall design of the pooled analysis (for analyses, see Woolman & Deutsch et al., this volume).

Wave 1—Original Samples. The original studies were variously conducted
between 1961 and 1969. Each investigator independently selected subjects, as-

TABLE 13.1
Number of Cases with Original Data and Follow-up Data in 1976
and 1980 with Birth Year and Age at Latest Follow-up[a]

Project	Subject Birth Year(s)	Original Sample (Wave 1)	1976 Follow-up Sample (Wave 3)	1980 Follow-up Sample (Wave 4)	Age at Latest Follow-up[b] (Years)
Beller	1959	170	126	122	21
Deutsch	1958-66	1097	97	24[c]	22
Gordon/Jester	1966-67	309	107	99	13-14
Gray	1958	92	77	86	21
Karnes	1961-63	268[d]	168	213	18-19
Levenstein	1966-67	250	186	46[c]	13-14
Miller	1964	271	141	172	16
Palmer	1964	309	228	219	15
Weikart	1958-62	123	123	123	19
Woolman	1966-68	611	611	—[c]	10-11
Zigler	1962-64	156	144	—[c]	12-13
Totals		3656	2008	1104	

[a] Follow-up sample n is the number of cases with data on at least one instrument. All groups are included.

[b] Follow-ups were conducted over several years so that age at latest follow-up varies depending on when follow-up took place.

[c] Deutsch collected 24 case studies; Woolman and Zigler did not collect data in 1980 follow-up; Levenstein collected data on one program and one control group only.

[d] Total includes "original" data on post-hoc controls.

signed them to program or control groups, and collected preprogram measures. All investigators used low-income family background as a selection requirement, and each collected baseline data.

In addition to their unique inquiries, a common pool of data was collected by the majority of the projects and was available for the analyses described in this chapter. This pool included Stanford–Binet and Peabody Picture Vocabulary Test (PPVT) IQ scores and such demographic data as sex, ethnicity, mother's education, family size (number of siblings), household SES, and family structure (one or two parents). The original sample was based on data sent to Ithaca for 3656 study participants (see Table 13.1).

Wave 2—Early Postprogram Samples. Samples for the second wave were based on postprogram follow-up data that were collected independently by each investigator prior to 1976. The common pool of data included Stanford–Binet and PPVT tests collected at various (usually annual) intervals by the projects. It should be noted that what we consider the second wave of data collection was actually several waves from the standpoint of the individual projects. The number of annual follow-ups ranged from two to seven and generally extended until the children were 8–10 years old. Approximately 2107 study participants had IQ assessments from Wave 2 that were available for pooled analyses (see Consortium, 1977, Vol. 2, and other chapters, this volume). The decrease in total sample size was due primarily to two projects that did not have data available for Wave 2 (Woolman and Zigler). Most other projects also tested fewer participants for Wave 2 compared to Wave 1. In early 1976, the first two waves of data were sent to Ithaca where they were checked for accuracy and consistency and then recoded into a common format.

Wave 3—1976 Consortium Follow-Up Samples.   The first collaborative follow-up began in 1976 and ended in the fall of 1977. It included four instruments: the School Record Form, the 1976 Youth Interview, the 1976 Parent Interview, and the age-appropriate Weschler Intelligence Scale. In the 1976 follow-up, data on at least one instrument were collected for 2008 subjects from eleven projects (see Table 13.1). The largest sample, the Deutsch project, originally included over 1000 children, but budgetary and time constraints permitted data collection for only about 100 cases in the 1976 follow-up.[2]

Wave 4—1980 Consortium Follow-Up Samples.   The second collaborative follow-up began in the fall of 1979 and ended in the fall of 1981. Wave 4 samples were based on data collected with two common instruments: the 1980 School Data Form and the 1980 Youth Interview. A total of 1104 study participants provided data on at least one instrument (see Table 13.1).[3]

Demographic Characteristics of the Follow-Up Samples

In these analyses we concentrate on the characteristics of the 1976 and 1980 samples.

The original samples can be generally characterized as black (94%) and from low-income families, in which the mothers had completed an average of 10.3

---

[2]According to Deutsch, it became more costly in both time and money to locate subjects in New York City than it would have been in many other areas of the country as a result of extremely high population turnover, burned out neighborhoods, school closings, and vandalism of records. Once location was achieved, making contact with subjects was also costly.

[3]Two investigators, Woolman and Zigler, did not participate in the 1980 Consortium follow-up. Other changes in the samples were: the Deutsch project concentrated on a limited number of case studies and Levenstein collected school data on two of her original groups (see Deutsch et al. and Levenstein et al., this volume). In three projects the 1980 samples were larger than the 1976 samples. In 1980, Gray was able to collect data on all but six study participants, and Karnes located and tested a control group (young people who had been screened with her original sample but had not participated in Karnes' preschool programs; see Karnes et al., this volume). Beller found and interviewed a larger number of respondents in 1980 than he was able to locate in 1976.

years of education, and the average head of household was a semiskilled or unskilled worker (Consortium, 1977, 1981). Sixty-two percent of the children lived in two-parent families. Among the original samples, the Gray and Weikart samples had the lowest mother's educational level (9.0 and 9.4 years, respectively), the lowest Hollingshead SES (69.3 and 68.2, respectively), and the greatest number of siblings (3.7 and 4.0, respectively). Weikart's sample had the lowest mean preprogram IQ test score (79). With these exceptions, the original samples came from similar backgrounds. The follow-up samples were similar to the original samples. Characteristics of the 1976 sample are summarized in Table 13.2.

The median background characteristics of the 1980 follow-up sample for eight projects (Beller, Gordon/Jester, Gray, Karnes, Levenstein, Miller, Palmer, and Weikart) differ only slightly from the median background characteristics of the same projects in 1976. The only substantial change between the 1976 and 1980 samples was that the 1980 sample included a higher average percentage of control subjects (38%) than the 1976 sample (26%) due to the creation of a post hoc control group in the Karnes project.

Attrition: Program/Control Differences

A serious hazard in longitudinal research is that of attrition, the loss of subjects over time. We conducted extensive studies of attrition in the Consortium data (Consortium, 1977, 1978, 1981). Recovery rates for the Consortium projects included in 1976 analyses ranged from 35% to 100%, with a median recovery rate of 74%. For the 1980 pooled analyses, the recovery rate ranged from 31% to 100%, with a median recovery rate of 79% (see Table 13.3). For school competence analyses described in this report, we were able to include data for 79% of the original sample in eight projects. For labor market and educational attainment analyses reported here, we were able to include interview data from 90% of the original subjects in the Gray sample, 56% of the original Beller sample, and 69% of the original Karnes sample.

Attrition was mainly due to inability to locate or test subjects or to budgetary constraints on data collection. Less than 3% of the subjects who were contacted refused to participate in either 1976 or 1980. There were no significant differences in recovery rates between program and control children.

Recovered subjects were compared to those not recovered on four background variables—pretest IQ score, mother's education, Hollingshead SES (all measured at time of program entry), and IQ score at age 6—to determine if any differences existed between the follow-up program and control samples. This resulted in over 300 significance tests for each follow-up. From these analyses, we concluded that attrition was random and that the follow-up program and control samples were equivalent. We are reasonably sure that our findings are not due to initial program/control differences, to nonequivalent attrition in program and control groups, or to selective attrition.

TABLE 13.2
Background Characteristics of the 1976 Follow-up Sample

Project (n)	% Program	% Black	% Female	Mean Ed. of Mother	Mean SES	Mean Pretest IQ	Mean No. Siblings
Beller (126	38.1	89.7	50.0	10.5	60.8	90.9	3.1
Deutsch (97)	64.9	100.0	50.5	10.3	63.2	92.0	3.9
Gordon (107)	77.6	94.4	53.3	9.9	65.1	—[a]	2.6
Gray (77)	46.8	100.0	55.8	9.2	69.5	87.7	4.0
Karnes (168)	100.0	64.9	51.2	10.1	64.0	92.3	3.4
Levenstein (186)	71.5	95.2	46.2	10.5	64.0	93.6	2.6
Miller (141)	77.3	92.2	53.9	10.7	64.0	—	3.2
Palmer (228)	78.9	100.0	0.0	11.2	58.2	92.2	2.4
Weikart (123)	47.2	100.0	41.5	9.4	68.2	79.0	4.0
Woolman (611)	31.8	—	43.0	—	—	—	
Zigler (144)	54.2	89.1	44.2	11.1	—	—	3.0
Median	64.9	94.8	50.0	10.4	64.0	92.0	3.2

Note. Last four columns are absed on somewhat less than total sample size for most projects. Mean education of mother is grades completed. SES is Hollingshead Index of Social Position, ranging from 11 to 77, 61 to 77 indicates lowest social position. Beller retrospectively collected mother's education, SES, and sibling data for 1976 follow-up sample only.

[a] Data not available.

TABLE 13.3

Follow-up Samples as a Percent of Original Sample by Project[a]

(Pooled Analysis Groups Only)

	1976 Follow-Up			1980 Follow-Up		
Project (n)	Program %(n)	Control %(n)	Total %(n)	Program %(n)	Control %(n)	Total %(n)
Beller (112)	66.1 (39)	66.0 (35)	66.1 (74)	74.6 (44)	69.8 (37)	72.3 (81)
Gordon/Jester (309)	34.3 (83)	35.8 (24)	34.6 (107)	30.6 (74)	34.3 (23)	31.4 (97)
Gray (65)	81.8 (36)	90.5 (19)	84.6 (55)	93.2 (41)	100 (21)	95.4 (62)
Karnes (140)	83.6 (97)	–	83.6 (97)	87.9 (102)	79.2 (19)	86.4 (121)
Levenstein (250)	73.1 (133)	77.9 (53)	74.4 (186)	100 (20)	86.7 (26)	92 (46)
Miller (248)	50.9 (109)	52.9 (18)	51.2 (127)	62.6 (134)	64.7 (22)	62.9 (156)
Palmer (309)	74.4 (180)	71.6 (48)	73.8 (228)	69.4 (168)	76.1 (51)	70.9 (219)
Weikart (123)	100 (58)	100 (65)	100 (123)	100 (65)	100 (58)	100 (123)
Zigler (156)	94.1 (79)	90.3 (65)	92.3 (144)	–	–	–
Median	74.4 (814)	74.8 (327)	74.4 (1141)	81.3 (648)	77.7 (257)	79.4 (905)

Note. Figures in parentheses indicate number of cases in each sample. – indicates data not available.
[a] Definition of original sample is based on groups used for pooled analyses in this report. The groups are as follows: Beller - first grade controls excluded; Gray - distal controls excluded; Karnes - Five Approaches sample and post hoc controls, 1976 figures exclude post hoc controls; Levenstein - full sample in 1976, 1980 figures based on one cohort only; Miller - post hoc controls excluded; Gordon/ Jester, Palmer, and Weikart - full sample; Zigler - middle SES controls excluded. Individual investigators may use other definitions of groups for their analyses (see other chapters, this volume).

Pooled data
methods

METHODS

......................d in the pooled analyses involved techniques from meta-, secondary, and primary analysis.

Meta-analysis refers to a set of techniques that statistically combines the results of individual studies (Glass, McGaw, & Smith, 1981). It has been described as a quantitative analog to literature reviews (Cook & Levitan, 1980). The present study is metaanalytic in two respects. First, it pools results from a number of research projects; second, its basis for generalizability is based on the available pool of studies rather than a random sample of any population. Unlike other metaanalyses, we did not work solely with published materials but rather went back to the original raw data of these studies.

This approach had two important effects. First, it allowed us to specify the research question to be analyzed and thus to reduce measurement and specification error. Second, it allowed us to include in each analysis only those studies that were appropriate to the particular research question.

Secondary analysis refers to the reanalysis of data collected by a previous investigator in order to answer new questions or to apply different analytic techniques to the data. Our analyses were secondary in that we were reanalyzing data collected by Consortium members for their own research purposes.

Primary analysis is the original analysis of data in a research study. Our analyses were primary in the sense that the post-1975 data collection was undertaken by the principal investigators in cooperation with the Ithaca team, and much of the data was collected using instruments designed by the Ithaca investigators for purposes of the pooled analyses.

Data Collection Procedures

Waves 1 and 2 Data Collection.   The preceding chapters in this volume describe the procedures used to collect the original baseline and early postprogram data. The common pool of 60 variables that make up Waves 1 and 2 data consisted primarily of IQ test scores and family background variables.

Waves 3 and 4 Data Collection: Instruments and Procedures.   The 1976 and 1980 interviews and school record instruments for Waves 3 and 4 were developed and pretested by Ithaca research staff in consultation with Consortium investigators and their staffs. The four common 1976 instruments were the school record form, parent and youth interviews, and the Wechsler Intelligence Scale. The 1976 School Record Form contained information on the child's academic history, grades, and achievement test scores. The 1976 Parent and Youth Interviews contained demographic and attitude questions that formed the basis for the noncognitive outcome measures. The revised form of the Wechsler Intelligence Scale (WISC-R) was administered.

In 1980 the two common instruments were a school data form and a youth interview. The 1980 School Data Form consisted of three sections. Part A covered year-by-year information about the student's school career such as progress through the grades, assignment to special education, absences, suspensions, honors, and dropout date(s) and reasons. Part B was designed to collect detailed information on the children who received psychological evaluations, such as diagnoses, reasons for recommending special services, and teacher impressions. Part C provided a suggested interview for gathering information from school administrators on school district policies regarding special education placement, grade retention, and programs for dropout prevention and pregnant students.

The 1980 Youth Interview was primarily a post high school interview. It focused on education, employment, and family formation. Additional items included questions on job satisfaction, attitudes toward work, educational and vocational aspirations and expectations, sources of income, desired and expected family size, stresses and supports during childhood, self-esteem, and life priorities.

The Ithaca staff trained supervisors at each project site and coordinated data collection to ensure comparability across project sites. We prepared video tapes to train interviewers at the field sites and maintained frequent contact with field supervisors.

In 1976, 30% of the interviewers were black and 51% were male. In 1980, 18% of the interviewers were black and 26% were male. In 1976 and in 1980, over 80% of the respondents showed moderate to high interest in the interview.

Reliability tests of office coding of the interview responses yielded 98% agreement. (The procedures used to reduce errors in data collection and processing are presented in detail in the 1977–1981 Consortium reports.)

Outcome Measures

In selecting outcome measures, we concentrated on measures that were meaningfully related to the goals of the program and that were feasible to collect. The theoretical constructs that we have attempted to assess, the measures that we selected to assess these constructs, and the sources of data for measures discussed in this report are shown in Table 13.4.

The background demographic variables listed in Table 13.4 were used primarily as covariates. We also examined the role of background factors in questions related to differential program effectiveness. Our measures of family size (number of siblings) and family structure (father presence) as well as mother's educational level provide, of course, only broad differentiation among families.

Under the theoretical construct of developed abilities, we grouped together two types of cognitive ability test scores—IQ scores and achievement scores. Both intelligence tests and achievement tests sample children's cognitive abilities, but they also draw on prior learning and experience and tap attributes such as test-taking skills, motivation, and ability to play the role of student. The adjective *developed* expresses the *learned* attributes that IQ and achievement tests measure in addition to "ability" (Anastasi, 1980).

As shown in Table 13.4, for this report we analyzed Stanford–Binet IQ test scores measured before the programs began and at ages 5 through 10 years of age. The Wave 3 IQ instrument was the Wechsler Intelligence Scale. For achievement test indicators of developed abilities, we used the available achievement test data. These included the Iowa, Metropolitan, Wide Range, California, and Stanford Achievement Tests for grades 3 through 6.

School competence and educational attainment constructs were the school outcome variables. School competence was operationalized as never receiving one or more years of special education services, never retained in grade, and a composite variable termed *meeting school requirements* (combining special education placement and retention data). Educational attainment was operationalized as high school completion.

The 1976 and 1980 interviews assessed a variety of social–psychological attributes. For pooled analyses, we concentrated on the construct achievement orientation. As used here, this includes motivation and those values, attitudes, and goals that seemed related to success in school and work. The sources of data for this construct were the 1976 and 1980 interview questions on educational and occupational aspirations and the 1976 question on pride in accomplishments. Items related to early labor market experiences from the 1980 post high-school interviews were used to define occupational status. (For additional analyses, see other Consortium reports and Rosché, 1979.)

Techniques of Parallel and Pooled Analyses

Our basic analytic approach for each outcome measure was to determine the difference between the program and control groups within each project. The significance level (*p* value) was converted to a standard score (*z* score), and the standard scores of all projects were pooled (Mosteller & Bush, 1954). This technique assures that each study has equal weight and that each program group is compared with its own control.

Techniques for Parallel Project Analyses.   The primary research question in this study was: Did program participation have an effect on later outcomes (the main effect of early education)? The corollary question was: Did program participation affect one type of child more than another (the differential effect of early education)? For both questions, program attendance was viewed simply as a yes/no dichotomous variable (i.e., program versus control) regardless of the program variation the child may have received. For example, although children in the Miller project experienced a Montessori, DARCEE, Bereiter–Engelman,

TABLE 13.4
Constructs and Sources of Data[a]

Construct	Measure	Source of Data	Wave of Data Collection[b]	Age (Years)[c]	Project Sites in Pooled Analyses[d]
Background Demographics	Mother's education Two-parents Number of siblings Sex, race, SES	Entry Parent Interview	Wave 1	Birth to 5	All
Developed Abilities	Intelligence Test Scores Preprogram IQ Postprogram IQ 1976 IQ	Stanford-Binet Stanford-Binet WISC, WISC-R	Wave 1 Wave 2 Wave 3	3-5 5-10 10-19	All All (except Karnes) All (except Beller, Karnes)
Developed Abilities	Achievement Tests	1976 School Record Form	Wave 3	8-11	All (except Karnes)
School Competence	Special Education Placement	1980 School Data Form	Wave 4	6-19	All
School Competence	Grade Retention	1980 School Data Form	Wave 4	6-19	All (plus Zigler)

Achievement Orientation	Child's Pride in Activity Mother/Child Occupational Aspirations	1976 Youth/Parent Interviews	Wave 3	10-19	All (except Karnes, Levenstein)
	Youth Occupational Aspirations	1980 Youth Interview	Wave 4	18-22	Beller, Gray, Karnes
Educational Attainment	High School Completion	1980 School Data Form and Youth Interview	Wave 4	18-22	Beller, Gray, Karnes
Early Occupational Status	Items from Interview	1980 Youth Interview	Wave 4	18-22	Beller, Gray, Karnes

[a] For reports on additional constructs, data on file, and analyses, see Consortium 1977, 1978; Lazar et al., 1982.

[b] Data Collection Waves: Wave 1 preprogram data - 1962-69; Wave 2 postprogram follow-ups 1963-75; Wave 3-First Consortium Follow-up 1976-77; Wave 4 - Second Consortium Follow-up 1979-81.

[c] Indication of age to which measure applies.

[d] All sites for purposes of this report refers to Beller, Gordon/Jester, Gray, Karnes, Levenstein, Miller, Palmer, Weikart; other results reported separately where appropriate.

or traditional curriculum, we grouped them together as *program*. For some projects, the children designated *control* were randomly assigned to control group status before the program began; for other projects, the comparison children were recruited from a similar population (e.g., from first-grade classrooms that the program children were attending; for details, see Murray, Royce, Lazar, & Darlington, in press; Royce, Murray, Lazar, & Darlington, 1982). Both control and comparison children were coded as *control*. For projects with multiple comparison groups, we deleted any group or groups that we considered not appropriate for the pooled research questions (e.g., Gray's distal controls, Beller's first-grade group).[4]

For most of the outcome measures, analyses were performed twice—once using the simplest possible technique and again using multiple regression to control for background variables. Each technique compensated for a disadvantage of the other.

The simpler techniques (e.g., cross-tabulation, t tests) were used because multiple regression often reduced the sample size (and, therefore, the power) due to missing data on covariates. Multiple regression, on the other hand, helped to ensure that any program/control differences on outcome measures were not attributable to any slight differences in background characteristics.

The simpler techniques varied by outcome measure. For the school performance outcomes (special education, retention, and meeting school requirements), cross-tabulation of an outcome variable with program status (program versus control) were performed. Chi-squares were unadjusted for continuity as recommended by Camilli and Hopkins (1978). For the IQ score outcomes, t tests were performed to compare program and control groups. The significance tests reported are two-tailed in all cases.

A basic multiple regression equation was used to evaluate the effect of program on outcomes while controlling for a number of background characteristics measured at entry to each project. These included sex, preprogram Binet IQ score, number of siblings, family structure (as measured by father presence or absence), and mother's education (number of grades completed). In addition to these variables, in those projects whose subjects included white and black children, ethnicity was included in analyses of school performance outcomes. Certain of these variables were omitted for some projects due to missing data or known problems on a particular variable.

The basic multiple regression equation was: Outcome = constant + preprogram IQ + sex + mother's education + siblings + father's presence + program/

---

[4]All groups within projects are included in the totals in Table 13.1 and Table 13.2, but only the groups that were included in the pooled analyses appear in the other tables in this chapter (see note on Table 13.3; for details, see Lazar et al. 1982).

control status.[5] The effect of program on an outcome was evaluated by the significance level and by the size of the regression coefficient for the program versus control variable. The significance level indicates whether the program effect was greater than expected by chance, when controlling for all other independent variables. The magnitude of the coefficient estimates the effect of program on the outcome measure when the other independent variables have been statistically controlled, and this allows the reader to judge whether the effect of program is "educationally significant" regardless of its statistical significance.

When several dependent variables were analyzed and consequently many significance tests performed, some results might be significant by chance alone. To correct for this possibility, we have used the Bonferroni/Ryan technique, which involves multiplying the significance level of each result by the number of significance tests performed in that analysis, to arrive at a corrected significance level. This procedure and the others described in this section are conservative; they maximize our confidence in the results to be reported in the next section.

Techniques for Pooling Results.   The significance levels for program effect were pooled across projects using the pooled z technique described in Mosteller and Bush (1954).[6] The technique is directional, so that negative effects tend to cancel out positive effects. This method tests the presence of an overall "average" effect in the Consortium projects.

Because an overall significant result might be due to a single project, we checked the robustness of our results by deleting, one by one, the projects that had the most significant results in the analysis at hand. Each time a deletion was made, we recomputed the pooled z on the remaining projects to see if the overall results were still significant. We are highly confident of results that stood up to one or more such deletions. Tests for robustness are reported for all analyses that included more than three project sites.

---

[5]Coding of dependent variables for basic multiple regression equations were as follows: IQ test scores and achievement test scores were coded as continuous variables; school competence, high school completion, and employment were coded as dummy variables (regular classroom = 1, high school completion = 1, employed = 1). Coding for the independent variables was as follows: preprogram IQ score (continuous variable, Stanford-Binet except PPVT for Levenstein); mother's education at program entry (continuous variable, number of grades completed); number of siblings at program entry (continuous variable); family structure at program entry (dummy variable, two-parent = 1); sex (dummy variable, female = 1); program versus control status (dummy variable, program = 1). For Beller, family background information was gathered retrospectively as part of the 1976 interview. For dichotomous dependent variables, we used regression rather than logit analysis because we have previously found identical results with both methods when testing for main effects in our data set.

[6]The significance level p is converted to a z score with the sign corresponding to the direction of the effect. A pooled z is computed as follows: $z = \Sigma z_i / \sqrt{k}$, where z_i is the z score from project i and k is the number of projects. The significance level of the pooled z is the pooled significance level.

For regression coefficients we typically report the median coefficient across projects. In most or all cases this value appears to closely approximate other possible average values, such as a mean or a trimmed mean. When averaging six or more values, we used trimmed means to minimize the effects of extremes by deleting the projects for which the differences were highest and lowest.

FINDINGS

We present our findings in a developmental sequence to simplify the reader's task. We start with the relationship of early education to test scores in the early grades and then to the 1976 indicators of achievement orientation. The third section describes the outcomes of preschool attendance on several measures of school competence and their relation to background variables. The fourth section summarizes our findings in relation to attitudes, achievement, and labor market participation of the subjects.

Effects on Developed Abilities: IQ and Achievement Scores

Intelligence Test Scores.   Although controversial, IQ scores are good predictors of scholastic achievement and provide a uniform basis for assessing cognitive performance (for discussion, see Lazar, Darlington, Murray, Royce, & Snipper, 1982). The issue of culture fairness of IQ scores is not relevant here because 94% of our sample was black and almost all were from low-income families. Further we were not concerned with the absolute magnitude of the scores, only the differences between mean program and control scores. In addition, intelligence tests were collected by all Consortium investigators prior to their collaboration and are among the few repeated measures held in common. Finally, Consortium data on intelligence tests allow us to replicate other research on the persistence of IQ score gains.

Pretest and early posttest Stanford–Binet scores were used to examine the duration of IQ score effects. We pooled the intelligence test results on the basis of elapsed time after the program's termination: immediately after the program, 1 year, 2 years, and 3 or 4 years after the program ended. The results for the two analytic techniques (regression and simpler techniques) were quite similar; only the pooled results for the regression technique are reported here.

The conclusion that a well-run, cognitively oriented early education program will increase the IQ scores of low-income children by the end of the program is one of the least disputed results in education evaluation. Consortium early education programs replicated those findings as shown in the first column of Table 13.5. The pooled results for seven projects were highly significant ($p < .001$)

TABLE 13.5
Effect of Early Education on Stanford-Binet IQ when Background
Variables and Pretest IQ are Controlled, by Number of Years
After Program
(Unstandardized Regression Coefficients for
Program/Control Status)

Project	Posttest	1 Year After	2 Years After	3 or 4 Years After
Beller	7.42**	4.32*	5.33**	6.68**
	(109)	(105)	(101)	(96)
Gordon/Jester	3.47	5.59*	5.27*	5.34**
	(196)	(186)	(187)	(179)
Gray	12.52**	4.15	.92	.741
	(54)	(52)	(49)	(49)
Levenstein	7.87**	4.46	15.30**	6.80[a]*
	(134)	(102)	(79)	(61)
Miller	7.42**	0.31	1.15	-3.45
	(227)	(216)	(206)	(189)
Palmer	4.68*	5.26**		
	(278)	(253)		
Weikart	10.27**	4.22*	3.96*	.37
	(121)	(120)	(119)	(117)
Median IQ Difference (All Projects)	7.42	4.32	4.62	3.04
Pooled z	8.535	4.569	4.826	3.130
Pooled p	$<$.001	$<$.001	$<$.001	.002

Note: The basic equation is: IQ Score = Constant + Pretest IQ Score + Mother's Education + Father Presence + Number of Siblings + Sex + *Program/Control Status.*
Pretest IQ not included for Gordon, Miller, or Palmer. PPVT is pretest IQ for
Levenstein. Sample size is in parentheses below the unstandardized regression coefficients for program/control status.
[a] Based on WISC IQ
*$p <$.05
**$p <$.01

and robust. The median early education regression coefficient, which indicates
the program/control IQ point difference, was 7.42 IQ points.

How long did these IQ score differences remain significant? For both 1 and 2
years after the early education program, the pooled results were both significant
and robust ($p <$ .001). The median program coefficient was 4.32 IQ points for 1
year after and 4.62 points for 2 years after program completion. The results
clearly indicated that the average effect of the program lasted for at least 2 years
after the end of the program.

Results for the "3 or 4 years after" category were still statistically significant
but somewhat weaker. The pooled results were significant ($p =$ .002) but not
robust ($p =$ .081). The median program coefficient was 3.04. Thus, it appears

that the Consortium projects produced relative gains in IQ scores that were significant for up to 3 or 4 years after the program.

The second IQ analysis examined whether program children had an IQ score advantage as they started school. (For children in the Gordon/Jester, Levenstein, and Palmer projects, this was several years after program completion.) In a separate analysis of the projects listed in Table 13.5, we pooled Stanford–Binet IQ test scores at 6 years of age, approximately the age of entry into regular school (Royce, 1979; Consortium, 1978). Controlling for background variables, the pooled program effect was highly significant and robust at age 6 ($p < .001$). The median program/control difference was 5.80 points. Moreover, when we pooled results for the five projects with preprogram IQ scores, the program/control difference remained highly significant and robust even when the equation included preprogram IQ score as well as background variables.

To complete our picture of the effects of early education on intelligence test scores over time, we examined the latest available IQ test scores. The Wechsler Intelligence Scale for Children (revised version for most projects) was administered during the 1976 follow-up when the mean ages of the children in the various projects ranged from 10 years (Gordon/Jester and Levenstein) to 17 years (Gray). The shortest follow-up time was 7 years after program graduation and the longest was 10 years. The WISC-R yielded three IQ scores—full-scale, performance, and verbal. All three were utilized in regression analyses. The results for the WISC-R analyses were not pooled across projects because they represented scores of children at different ages and at differing number of years after program graduation.

Results on the WISC-R analyses were generally nonsignificant, although the Palmer and Levenstein projects showed some program/control differences. Palmer's program children at age 12 had significantly higher scores on performance IQ. Levenstein's program children at age 10 scored significantly higher than did her 1972 control group on full-scale, verbal, and performance IQ score.

In summary, early education programs produced an increase in children's IQ scores that lasted for several years after the program. The size of the effect appeared to decrease, from a median IQ score difference of 7.42 points at immediate posttest to a median difference of about 3 points when measured 3 or 4 years after the program. The program children started first grade with a significant advantage over control children, 5.80 IQ points on the average. The effect was not permanent, however; by 1976 there were no significant program/control differences on WISC scores in most Consortium projects.

Achievement Test Scores.   Although data were not available for all projects at all grades, we were able to look at mathematics and reading subtest scores at several grades across projects. The effectiveness of the program was tested with multiple regression equations using child's sex, age (and square of age), and pretest IQ as covariates. At grade 3, program graduates performed significantly better than controls on both math and reading subtests when the results were pooled across four projects (pooled $p = .002$ for math, pooled $p = .008$ for reading). Only the math finding was robust, however. At grades 4 and 5, pooled results showed program graduates to be significantly higher than controls on math but not on reading (grade 4 math scores, pooled $p = .030$ across six projects; grade 5 math, pooled $p = .040$ across five projects). The math results for these grades, however, were not robust. The pooled results of program/control comparisons for grade 6 were not significant for either subtest. In sum, there are some indications that program children did better than controls on math tests through grade 5 (Lazar et al., 1982).

Effects on Achievement Orientation at 1976 Follow-Up

In addition to cognitive goals, Consortium programs had noncognitive goals such as enhancing children's self-esteem, increasing achievement motivation, and facilitating school adjustment. Unfortunately, prior to the formation of the Consortium, there were no measures of noncognitive outcomes common to all Consortium projects. Items from the 1976 Consortium parent and youth interviews provided the first common noncognitive measures available for pooled analyses.

Child's Achievement Orientation.   In both program and control groups, the aspirations of these low-income, predominantly black children were quite high. Most children aspired to white-collar jobs, even though their parents were largely semiskilled or unskilled workers. They planned to attend and complete college, although their parents had, typically, not completed high school. In 1976 (at 10 to 19 years of age), there were no differences between program and control children's educational or occupational aspirations, their employment experiences, or their leisure activities. There were, however, program/control differences in one area of achievement orientation—pride in accomplishments related to school or work.

When asked to ''tell me something you've done that made you feel proud of yourself,'' program children were far more likely to give achievement-related answers than were control children ($p = .003$, see Koretz, 1978). Program children were more likely to respond with school or work achievements, whereas controls were more likely to respond with altruistic behavior or to say they were not proud of anything. This finding was robust and significant after correction for multiple comparisons. The program effect was especially strong among older girls (15–19 years of age).

Occupational Aspirations.   When asked in 1976, ''What kind of job would you like (your child) to have later in life?'', mothers of program children consistently named occupations that were higher than the occupations the children themselves hoped for. This was not true for mothers of control children. We termed the difference between a mother's and a child's aspirations a discrepancy score. The program/control differences in discrepancy scores were significant (p = .006) across the six projects with these data (Beller, Gordon/Jester, Gray, Levenstein, Palmer, Weikart). This finding was robust and significant after correcting for multiple comparisons. There was also a tendency for program mothers to have higher aspirations for their children than did control mothers (p = .065; see Koretz, 1978, and Lazar et al., 1982, for more details on noncognitive effects).

Self-Evaluations.   When asked in 1976 to rate their overall school performance on a scale from 1 (much better than others in your class) to 5 (much worse than others in your class), the overall mean rating for program and control groups combined was 2.7, indicating that most of the children believed they were doing somewhat better than average in school. Across all projects, there were no program/control differences on this variable, although in projects with youth above the age of 13 at follow-up (Beller, Gray, Weikart), program children evaluated themselves higher than did control children (p = .039; not significant after correction for multiple comparisons).

Effects on School Competence

A basic goal of all early childhood programs is to improve later competence in school through the provision of sequenced cognitive and noncognitive experiences.

In their school careers, the study participants faced social and behavioral demands as well as strictly academic ones. As Boocock (1972) has suggested, to be a successful student involves learning to play a specific role in a complex institution. Success in meeting school requirements (which may be seen as successfully playing the role of student) often foreshadows success in later educational, occupational, and economic roles. In this section, we summarize our analyses of actual school performance.

We examined progression through the school system as a measure of the children's competence in adapting to the situational demands of their schools. Normal progression through the grades indicated that children were meeting their school's basic requirements. Two categories of failure to progress normally were coded: ever placed in special classes (i.e., educable mentally retarded, learning disabled, and emotionally disturbed classes but not speech, hearing, or orthopedically impaired classes) and ever retained in grade. Although these two practices vary across school districts, they reflect each school's judgment that the student has not met school expectations. Therefore, they can be considered to have a common meaning across project sites although the actual criteria used or services provided may have varied.

Because school districts of some projects relied mainly on special education placement whereas school districts of others relied more heavily on grade retention, a composite variable was constructed. This variable, met versus did not meet school's requirements for adequate performance, was operationalized as never/ever retained in grade, never/ever assigned to special education, or both.

In earlier reports, based on data that were available in 1976, we reported that early education had a strong and significant but less striking effect on grade retention (Darlington, Royce, Snipper, Murray, & Lazar, 1980; Lazar et al., 1982; Royce, 1979). These analyses were based on data that were available at one time point for each project—the latest grade only. This meant that, for the various projects, grade levels ranged from fifth through twelfth grade in a given 1976 pooled analyses. The program group for each project site was, of course, only compared to its control group of the same age, and the results were then pooled across project sites.

By contrast, in the 1980 follow-up, the availability of detailed year-by-year school information gave us much more flexibility and precision for pooled analysis. We were able to examine results at specific grade levels across projects, to extend our pooled analyses to higher grade levels, and to add additional cases for some projects (see Footnote 3, p. 415). These new data made it possible to study the effects of early education at each school grade, both at the individual project level and pooled (average) project level.

We summarize here school competence analyses pooled across projects at two selected grade levels—seventh and twelfth grades (for details and site-specific analyses, see Rossiter, 1981). Seventh grade was selected because that was the latest grade available for the largest number of projects. Eight project sites provided yearly school data from kindergarten through seventh grade (Beller, Gordon/Jester, Gray, Karnes, Levenstein, Miller, Palmer, and Weikart).[7] The Beller, Gray, Karnes, and Weikart projects provided school data through twelfth grade as well.

Results at Seventh Grade. Looking first at chi-square results for special education assignment, we found significant differences between the program and control groups at seventh grade (see Table 13.6). All projects reported an equal

---

[7]The various school competence tables include different numbers of projects because of special considerations in the data. Zigler, in 1976, collected data on retentions but not on special education placements. Palmer collected special education data in 1980; however, only 2.4% of the program sample and 2% of the control sample were assigned to special education classes ($p = .845$). Because of this extremely low rate we did not pool Palmer's special education results with the other seven projects. For Palmer's sample, the retention results were pooled with the other results in Table 13.7; Palmer's results shown in Table 13.8 include both special education placements and retention.

The Gordon/Jester control sample proved to be too small for meaningful retention analyses. This problem arose because our operationalization of "ever retained" excluded from retention analysis anyone who had been assigned previously to special education by a given grade. By this definition, only four Gordon/Jester control children remained in the analysis after third grade. For Weikart, rather than yearly data, information was available at the grade 7 and grade 12 levels only.

TABLE 13.6
Percent of Students Placed in Special Education Classes
as of 7th Grade, Program vs. Control

Project	Chi-Square Results			Regression Results[a]	
	Program % (n)	Control % (n)	p	Coefficient	p
Beller	0.0 (44)	5.6 (36)	.113	.053	.115
Gordon/Jester	24.6 (61)	66.7 (12)	.004	.414	.047
Gray	2.4 (41)	23.8 (21)	.007	.219	.007
Karnes	21.6 (97)	33.3 (18)	.283	.086	.435
Levenstein	20.0 (20)	20.0 (25)	.999	.027	.831
Miller	12.5 (120)	15.0 (20)	.757	.046	.587
Weikart	31.0 (58)	44.6 (65)	.122	.115	.178
Average or median[b] (Total n)	14.5 (441)	34.9 (197)		.086	
		Pooled $z = 3.81^c$		Pooled $z = 3.45^c$	
		Pooled $p < .001$		Pooled $p = .001$	

Note. All p values are two-tailed. See Rossiter, 1981, for details.

[a] The basic equation is: School Competence = Constant + Preprogram IQ + Mother's Education + Father Present + Sibs + Sex + Race + *Program*. Preprogram IQ not included for Gordon/Jester, Miller, Palmer. Program coefficient is the unstandardized regression coefficient for program/control status.

[b] For chi-square results, average percentages were computed by trimmed means of logits as described in Methods section. For regression results, median program regression coefficient was computed.

TABLE 13.7
Percent of Students Retained in Grade as of 7th Grade,
Program vs. Control

Project	Chi-Square Results			Regression Results[a]	
	Program % (n)	Control % (n)	p	Program Coefficient	p
Beller	9.1 (44)	13.9 (36)	.499	.057	.422
Gray	47.5 (40)	55.6 (18)	.570	.022	.866
Karnes	12.9 (85)	35.7 (14)	.032	.133	.217
Levenstein	0.0 (16)	14.3 (21)	.115	.147	.121
Miller	9.7 (113)	15.8 (19)	.428	.044	.597
Palmer	30.2 (159)	52.0 (50)	.005	.216	.004
Weikart	14.9 (47)	12.5 (40)	$(.747)^a$	.020	$(.795)^a$
Zigler	26.6 (65)	32.3 (79)	.452	—	—
Average or median[b] (Total n)	19.8 (569)	32.0 (277)		.057	
		Pooled $z = 3.40$		Pooled $z = 2.80$	
		Pooled $p = .001$		Pooled $p = .005$	

Note. All p values are two-tailed. See Rossiter, 1981, for details.

[a] Parentheses surrounding p value indicate that controls have a lower retention rate.

[b] For chi-square results, average percentages were computed by trimmed means of logits as described in Methods section. For regression results, median program regression coefficient was computed.

or lower rate of special education placements among program than control children. Averaging across projects, as described in the methods section on p. 426, we found the average rate of such placement to be 14.5% for program children and 34.9% for control children. The difference was highly significant (pooled z = 3.81, pooled $p < .001$), and remained robust when two projects were removed from the pooling (pooled $p = .043$, without Gordon/Jester and Gray).

The use of multiple regression procedures confirmed the results. The program regression coefficients and p values for each project are shown in the last two columns of Table 13.6. The regression results for special education placement were statistically significant and highly robust.

Chi-square results for the second indicator of school competence, grade retention, are shown in Table 13.7. Across the eight projects with appropriate data, the average rate of grade retention was 19.8% in the program group and 32.0% in the control group. The pooled results across projects revealed that program children were significantly less likely to be retained in grade than controls (pooled $z = 3.40$, pooled $p = .001$). The finding remained robust (pooled $p = .012$) after deleting the project with the strongest result.[8]

Controlling for the covariates (Table 13.7, last column), early education reduced retention in grade across eight projects (pooled $z = 2.80$, $p = .005$). This result was not robust, however (pooled $z = .072$, after removing Karnes).

The chi-square results for the composite school competence variable—ability to meet school requirements—were strong and robust at seventh grade (see Table 13.8). Across the eight projects, the average rate of failure to meet school requirements was 44.6% in the control group but only 29.5% in the program group. This result was statistically significant across projects (pooled $z = 3.87$, $p < .001$) and very robust ($p = .002$ after deleting the strongest result from the pooled z; $p = .006$ after deleting the two strongest projects).

Regression analysis confirmed these results. With background variables controlled, preschool graduates were significantly more likely to meet their schools' requirements for adequate performance as of seventh grade (pooled $z = 3.40$ across eight projects, $p = .001$). Again this strong finding was robust even after deleting the two strongest projects (pooled $z = 2.29$, pooled $p = .011$). Regres-

---

[8]Smaller numbers were included in retention analyses than special education analyses since subjects were removed from consideration for retention once they had been assigned to special education. However, if they had been retained previous to special education assignment, they continued to be recorded as ever having been retained. Although fewer children could be included in analysis for retention, those who were included came from a pool of students whose school difficulties were not judged to require special education placement.

For Palmer, pretest IQ was not included as a covariate because a large portion of the sample was not pretested due to the young age of certain subjects (Lazar et al., 1982; Palmer, this volume). However, when Palmer's pretest IQ was included as a covariate, the results were essentially identical to those reported on Table 13.7 in the text. That is, with pretest IQ controlled for Palmer ($N = 127$), program coefficient = .247, $p = .004$.

TABLE 13.8

Percent of Students Who Failed to Meet School Requirements as of
7th Grade (Placed in Special Education Classes or Retained in
Grade), Program vs. Control

	Chi-Square Results			Regression Results	
Project	Program % (n)	Control % (N)	p	Program Coefficient	p
Beller	9.1 (44)	16.2 (37)	.332	.107	.208
Gordon/Jester	52.5 (61)	66.7 (12)	.366	.088	.705
Gray	48.8 (41)	61.9 (21)	.327	.088	.475
Karnes	27.5 (102)	50.0 (18)	.056	.132	.256
Levenstein	20.0 (20)	30.8 (26)	.410	.129	.330
Miller	19.7 (127)	27.3 (22)	.418	.075	.448
Palmer	31.1 (161)	52.9 (51)	.005	.217	.004
Weikart	31.0 (58)	46.2 (65)	.086	.131	.128
Average or median[a] (Total n)	29.5 (614)	44.6 (252)	–	.118	
		Pooled z = 3.87		Pooled z = 3.40	
		Pooled p < .001		Pooled p = .001	

Note. All p values are two-tailed. See Rossiter, 1981, for details.

[a]For chi-square results, average percentages were computed by trimmed means of logits
as described in Methods section. For regression results, median program regression coefficient was computed.

sion results on the special education variable and the composite variable should
be viewed as educationally significant as well as statistically significant. The
magnitude of the early education effect is indicated by the value of the unstandardized regression coefficient. For example, for Gray, 23.8% of the control children and 2.4% of the program children were assigned to special education
classrooms—a difference of 21.4% (see Table 13.6). When background factors
were controlled, the value of 21.4% changes slightly to 21.9%. The corresponding program/control difference on special education placement for the median
project was 8.6% (Table 13.6, Karnes project). For the composite variable, in
the median project, the program/control difference was 11.8% after controlling
for background factors (see Table 13.8).

Cumulative Effects: Kindergarten Through Seventh Grade. How long-lasting are the effects of preschool programs on measures of school competence—
never placed in special education programs or retained in grade? If the effects are
short-lived, then it might be argued that they were caused by the teachers'
knowledge that a child had attended preschool. Believing that preschool provides
good preparation for elementary school could cause a teacher to make special
allowances for that child's inadequate school performance.

To investigate this argument, from kindergarten through seventh grade, we determined whether children were meeting school requirements at the end of each grade. We also examined the effects of preschool programs on special education placements alone and on retention alone. For each of these three measures, we used regression analysis. The pooled p values yielded by these analyses are shown in Table 13.9.

Suppose the effects of preschool were short-lived—either because they were caused by teacher expectations, as mentioned above, or because the direct effects on children did not last. If this were the case, we would expect the differences between preschool and comparison groups to be most significant in the early grades and to fade thereafter. That is, the p values should be numerically small in the early grades and rise thereafter. Inspection of Table 13.9 shows that just the opposite was found. In Table 13.9 there are 21 opportunities to compare a given p value with the comparable p value for the preceding year (the value just above it in Table 13.9). Twenty of these 21 comparisons show the p values declining (becoming more significant) with time; the one exception is between kindergarten and first grade on the composite measure. We concluded that the effects of preschool are not short-lived.

Effects on Type and Length of Special Education Placements.   In a related analysis of program effectiveness, Schruben (1982) performed an in-depth as-

TABLE 13.9
Effect of Early Education on School Competence,
Kindergarten through 7th Grade
(Pooled p values)

Grade Level	Special Education pooled p	Retention pooled p	Special Education or Retention pooled p
K	$(.973)^a$	(.877)	(.524)
1	.436	(.475)	(.808)
2	.421	(.314)	(.408)
3	.191	.374	.392
4	.179	.190	.267
5	.124	.025	.043
6	.059	.011	.035
7	.004	.003	.002

Note. Pooled program/control comparisons controlling for background variables for Beller, Gray, Gordon/Jester, Karnes, Miller, Levenstein, and Palmer project sites. Year-by-year data not available for Weikart. Gray excluded from kindergarten analysis; Gordon/Jester excluded from retention analyses. See footnote, Table 13.6, for basic regression equation. For details, see Rossiter, 1981.

[a] Parentheses indicate that the results favor the controls.

sessment of special education placements for one sample with especially detailed data. Most Gordon/Jester study participants were in eighth grade at the 1980 follow-up. Their schools offered learning disability (LD), educable retardation (EMR), and emotional/behavior remediation classes as well as speech and hearing remediation. As of eighth grade, only half of the students who received special education services remained in some type of special classes for the rest of their schooling; the others returned full-time to regular classrooms for their subsequent school years. For example, the average stay in learning disability classes was 3.5 years. About one-fourth of the special education students had more than one type of special education placement; in particular, learning disability and emotional remediation placements overlapped.

Examination of the long-term effectiveness of the Gordon/Jester early education program on specific types of special education placements showed significant program/control differences on "ever in EMR" placements ($p = .006$) and "ever in learning disability" placements ($p = .028$) but not on emotional/behavioral placements.

There were also statistically significant group differences in the number of years of remediation, both EMR and major academic (an aggregate category which includes EMR, LD placements, and grade retentions). Control subjects averaged 3.08 years in major academic placements compared to 1.23 years for program participants. In retardation remediation, controls averaged 1.25 years compared to .2 years for program subjects. The significant program group advantage on the extent of retardation remediation remained in regression analysis ($p = .002$) that controlled for subjects' sex, race, mother's education, and number of siblings. Regression results showed a nearly significant program effect ($p = .052$) on the extent of major academic remediation when the same background variables were controlled.

Results at Twelfth Grade.   Participants in four projects were old enough to have records through the end of high school by the 1980 follow-up. When we repeated chi-square and regression analyses with grade 12 school competence data, the program/control differential remained significant. The chi-square analyses presented in Table 13.10 show that preschool attendance was associated with better school performance for all three dependent variables.

Regression analysis confirmed these long-term findings for special education (pooled $p = .001$) and the composite variable (pooled $p = .002$). Both results were robust after deleting the strongest result (pooled $p = .019$ for special education, pooled $p = .017$ for the composite variable). Grade retention results, however, did not reach statistical significance after background variables were controlled (pooled $p = .060$).

The preschool program effects proved to be educationally meaningful for a substantial number of students and their school districts (Table 13.10). The median regression coefficient for special education assignment was .189 at grade

TABLE 13.10
Students Placed in Special Education Classes or
Retained as of 12th Grade
(Program vs. Control)

| | Special Education Placements | | | | |
| | Chi-Square Results | | | Regression Results | |
Project (n)	% Program	% Control	p	Prog. Coefficient[a]	p
Beller (80)	4.5	5.6	.837	.018	.752
Gray (62)	4.9	28.6	.008	.231	.009
Karnes (115)	32.3	63.2	.011	.244	.039
Weikart (123)	32.8	49.2	.064	.147	.095
Average or Median[b]	13.4	30.8		.189	
N = 380	Pooled z = 3.62, Pooled p < .001			Pooled z = 3.34, Pooled p = .001	
	Retention				
Beller (78)	38.1	52.8	.194	.236	.080
Gray (58)	57.5	61.1	.796	.016	.906
Karnes (88)	26.3	58.3	.025	.204	.148
Weikart (86)	15.2	20.0	.560	.037	.657
Average or Median[b]	32.5	47.0		.121	
N = 310	Pooled z = 2.19, Pooled p = 0.29			Pooled z = 1.88, Pooled p = .060	

(continued)

TABLE 13.10 (Continued)

Special Education Placements

	Special Education Placement or Retention				
Beller (81)	40.9	54.1	.238	.218	.098
Gray (62)	58.5	66.7	.534	.077	.523
Karnes (121)	44.1	73.7	.018	.267	.028
Weikart (123)	32.8	50.8	.044	.162	.065
Average or Median [b]	43.9	61.8		.190	
N = 387	Pooled z = 3.09, Pooled p = .002			Pooled z = 3.17, Pooled p = .002	

Note. All p values are two-tailed. For regression equation, see footnote, Table 13.6

[a] Program coefficient is unstandardized regression coefficient for program/control status.

[b] For chi-square results, average percentages were computed by trimmed means of logits described in Methods section. For regression results, median program regression coefficient was computed.

12, an 18.9% assignment differential in favor of the program group. For failure to meet school requirements, the median regression differential was 19.0% in favor of the program group.

Year-by-year school competence data were avilable through grade 12 for students in the Beller, Gray, and Karnes projects. For both chi-square and regression results, pooled statistical significance was achieved at grade 4 for special education placement (pooled $p = .049$) and became progressively stronger through grade 12 (pooled $p = .004$, controlling for background variables; Rossiter, 1981). Retention results for the three projects reached significance beginning at grade 7 (pooled $p = .037$) and remained significant through grade 11 (pooled $p = .052$, controlling for background variables). Chi-square results were significant from sixth through twelfth grade.

The composite variable, special education placement and/or grade retention, revealed a similar effect for the three projects. Statistical significance and marked program/control differentials were attained at every grade from grade 7 (pooled $p = .047$, controlling for background) through the end of high school (twelfth grade pooled $p = .009$).

Summary of School Competence Findings.   Systematic analyses of school competence on a year-by-year basis demonstrated a substantial and significant program effect on special education placement and retention (and on the combination of the two). These program effects increased throughout the elementary and junior high school years. For the four projects with high school data, the effect was significant through grade 12 for special education and the composite variable but leveled off somewhat for grade retention.

Although the statistical power of four projects is less than that of eight, these essentially independent studies had similar effects. Both the seventh and twelfth grade results are consistent with the conclusion that children benefited from early education programs and that this benefit was not due to initial program/control differences.

Effects on Educational Attainment

Having demonstrated a long-term educational impact of early childhood programs, we extended our analyses to a later criterion of educational effectiveness—educational outcome and as an important intermediate aspect of the general status-attainment process. The important relationship between educational attainment and occupational success has been extensively documented.

Educational attainment is usually operationalized as number of grades completed or highest degree attained. Due to the ages and economic status of these samples, we selected high school completion. Unfortunately, only four projects (Beller, Gray, Karnes, and Weikart) had subjects old enough for such analyses at

TABLE 13.11
Percent of Subjects who Completed High School, Program vs. Control

Project	Chi-Square Results			Regression Results[a]	
	Program % (n)	Control % (n)	p	Program Coefficient	p
Beller	65.1 (43)	62.2 (37)	.784	.041	.743
Gray	68.3 (41)	52.4 (21)	.220	.180	.166
Karnes	67.4 (92)	52.9 (17)	.251	.122	.365
Weikart	57.8 (51)	42.2 (52)	.031	.199	.042
Average or median[b] (Total n)	64.8 (237)	52.5 (127)		.151	
		Pooled z = 2.40		Pooled z = 2.32	
		Pooled p = .016		Pooled p = .020	

Note. Students still in high school are excluded; Weikart results are tentative pending further data collection on remainder of cases.

[a] Basic equation is: High School Completion = Constant + Pretest IQ + Mother's Education + Father Present + Sibs + Sex + Race + *Program*. Program coefficient is unstandardized regression coefficient for program/control status.

[b] For chi-square results, average percentages were computed by trimmed means of logits as described in Methods section. For regression results, median program regression coefficient was computed.

the time of this study.[9] Young people with high school equivalency degrees were considered to be high school graduates.

The overall high school completion rates ranged from 42% to 68% (see Table 13.11). In all four projects, program participants were more likely to complete high school than were controls. The pooled result was significant in both cross-tabulation (pooled p = .016) and multiple regression analyses (pooled p = .020).

The magnitude of the program effect was substantial and educationally meaningful for three of the projects. When background factors were controlled, the program/control difference for the median project was 15% (see Chang, 1981, for additional analyses).

The effects of the background variables on high school completion are of interest from a developmental perspective. Females, across projects, had a higher rate of high school completion than males. Mother's education was also

---

[9]The sample for high school completion analyses included 103 of the 123 participants in the Weikart study (84%). Information on the graduation status of the remainder of the Weikart sample was incomplete. At the 1980 follow-up, 12 Karnes students were still attending high school because of grade retentions or other reasons (e.g., resumed schooling after childbirth). Since it was not clear whether these students would eventually graduate, we excluded them from the high school completion analysis.

positively related to high school completion. There was no evidence that pretest IQ score, number of siblings, or two-parent family structure were significantly related to high school completion.

There are several reasons for concluding that preschool programs increased the rate of high school graduation. First, our direct test of this hypothesis on four projects yielded a significant result. Second, the result reported in Table 13.11 is more significant than the result for grade 7, when the grade 7 result is calculated using just the four projects in Table 13.11. It is therefore reasonable to guess that by the time the children in all eight projects have reached graduation age, the pooled results for high school graduation will be of at least the size as the results for grade 7, which were significant and highly robust. (The same argument suggests that the results for meeting school requiremets by twelfth grade, as in Table 13.10, will also ultimately become significant and highly robust, because the pooled p of .002 in Table 13.10 is much smaller than the pooled p of .061 for the same four projects in Table 13.8.)

Differential Effects on Educational Outcomes

Along with questions of main effects, we asked a corollary set of questions about the differential effectiveness of Consortium programs for subgroups of children with various background characteristics. We investigated whether preschool programs had different effects for male compared to female program participants, for children with differing preprogram IQ scores, and for participants from various family backgrounds (two- versus one-parent family structure, different number of siblings, and different levels of mother's educational attainment).

Overall, there was no evidence that the "average" preschool program had different effects on children with different background characteristics (for details on IQ score and school competence analyses, see Royce, Snipper, Murray, & Nelson, 1980; for year-by-year school competence analyses, see Rossiter, 1981; for high school completion analyses, see Chang, 1981).

Several caveats need to be mentioned in interpreting this lack of findings. First, we tested only two-factor interactions and they were not significant. Second, as discussed earlier, our measures of family background provided only broad categorizations of families that may not capture all the relevant distinctions among families. The other subject attributes—sex and preprogram IQ test scores—are less problematic measures. We do not consider these findings conclusive; rather we present the results as a stimulus for further research.

Differential Program Effects.   Educational investigators have long been concerned with the development of optimal curricula for preschool children and for low-income children. Indeed, several of the studies represented in the Consortium were originally designed to compare the effectiveness of different curricula and different settings. We were able to address three sets of questions related to curricular structure and content, using school outcomes as indicators of effectiveness.

First, we asked whether the setting of the intervention made a difference. Included in these studies are home-based and center-based programs and some that combined home and center interventions. We found no clear difference in school outcomes related to the setting of the intervention. Further, we found that parents were equally positive about both settings and gave reasons for their satisfaction that indicated that they clearly understood the advantages and disadvantages of each (Hubbell, 1978; Consortium, 1977, 1978).

Secondly, we asked whether any of the curricula represented in these studies were more or less effective than the others (Koretz, Vopava, & Darlington, 1978). This question, which has theoretical, practical, and commercial significance, was of considerable interest to many practitioners, because virtually every commonly used curricular model is represented in these data. We found no significant differences in later school outcomes related to curricula. All the curricula were successful in reducing school failure. On achievement tests, we did find small differences in the directions one would expect: The more verbally focused programs had graduates with somewhat higher reading scores and the more conceptually focused had graduates with higher arithmetic scores. However, these differences were so small that they were neither statistically nor educationally significant. It may be that finer-grained outcome measures or measures of social learning would find differential effects, but the present indicators did not. It appears that a variety of curricula are equally effective in preparing children for school and that any of the tested curricula is better than no preschool program at all.

At a third level of specificity, we identified structural characteristics of each treatment—for example, length of day, child/adult ratio, and number of home visits. Unfortunately, these variables were too highly interrelated to enable us to disentangle their individual effects. For example, all the infant programs were home-based, so that age and setting were inextricably confounded with each other. Although the combination of such structural confounding with some variables and limited variance for others made it impossible to evaluate specific program characteristics with these data, there was one cluster of variables that appeared to merit future investigation. The data suggest that program effectiveness can be enhanced by a combination of the following characteristics:

1. Intervention begun as early as possible.
2. Services provided to the parents as well as to the child.
3. Frequent home visits.
4. Involvement of the parents in the instruction of the child.
5. As few children per teacher as possible.

Effects on Occupational Attainment

We investigated whether young people 19–22 years of age, who had preschool experiences more than 15 years earlier, differed in any measurable ways from their counterparts who had no preschool experiences. Three projects with samples beyond the age of normal high school completion (Beller, Gray, and Karnes) collected extensive interview data in 1980. The interview items covered many aspects of the current life situations of study participants, including data on further education, household composition, use of governmental services, and labor market status. Only analyses related to labor market experiences are summarized in any detail here (for other analyses and further detail see Henderson, 1981; Nigro, 1981; Staszewski, 1981; Wickham-Crowley, 1981).

Labor Market Participation. We examined three traditional measures of labor market participation: unemployment rate (the number currently seeking employment divided by the number employed plus the number currently seeking employment); labor force participation rates (number of employed plus unemployed divided by total sample); and employment/population ratio (number of employed divided by total sample). There were no program/control differences within projects or when results were pooled on any of the three labor market measures. Nor did we find program/control differences on other labor market measures (e.g., earnings, hours worked, or type of job) or on other outcomes such as measures of public assistance utilization or posthigh school educational experiences. We also examined the mechanisms and intervening processes by which preschool programs might affect occupational attainment indirectly.

Intervening Factors. We hypothesized that two important antecedents of employment would be high school completion and school competence. There is an extensive literature that documents the value of high school credentials to prospective employers, particularly for low-income minority youths such as ours. Success in meeting school requirements indicates academic ability as well as certain social and behavioral attributes, such as the ability to adapt to an expected role.

Employment data for three samples were available to test our hypotheses. The total sample for the employment analyses was 192 youths who were no longer in high school. The dependent variable, currently employed, was coded dichotomously, based on youth interview data.

Our analyses examined two indirect paths from preschool to employment— through the mediating variables of school competence (never assigned to special education and never retained) and high school completion. The link between preschool program participation and school competence was documented in Tables 13.8 and 13.10. The link from school competence to employment was also confirmed. For all three samples, a higher percentage of those who met school requirements as of grade 12 were holding jobs compared to those who failed to meet these school requirements. For the median project, 66% of the students who had met school requirements were employed compared to 41% of the students who had not. The differences for the Beller and Gray samples were statistically significant ($p = .028$ and $p = .020$, respectively), and the pooled chi-square result for the three sites was highly significant (pooled $z = 3.38$; pooled $p = .001$). This result remained significant after controlling for background factors (pooled $z = 3.24$; pooled $p = .001$). The median regression coefficient was .262, indicating a 26.2% difference in employment rates.

In looking at the role of high school completion as a mediating variable, we found that preschool attendance and school competence were significant antecedents of high school completion (see Table 13.11). The final link in the chain was the path from high school completion to employment. We found in these three samples (as has been found in most other studies) that high school credentials influenced to a great extent whether or not a person was employed in 1980, regardless of that person's background characteristics (sex, preprogram IQ score, and family background) and preschool participation (pooled $z = 3.41$, pooled $p = .001$).

After finding that employment was strongly related to both high school completion and to school competence, we sought to establish whether one factor played a more important role in employment than the other.

We found that the association between employment and high school graduation was significant after controlling for school competence at grade 12, background variables, and preschool attendance (pooled $z = 2.11$; pooled $p = .035$). We also found that the association between employment and school competence was statistically significant regardless of high school graduation, background factors, and preschool attendance (pooled $z = 2.09$; pooled $p = .036$). Both factors were equally important. This means that among young people who have high school degrees, those who have progressed through school without repeating a grade or receiving any special education services have a better chance of being employed than do high school graduates from the same background who did not meet this standard. Given the strong preschool effect on school competence established earlier with eight samples and the preschool effect on high school completion documented with the four oldest samples, this strengthens the argument that there is an important indirect effect of preschool on labor market outcomes.

When we separated the effects of the two components of school competence—special education assignments and grade retentions—we found that grade retentions had stronger effects than special education on later outcomes. That is, young people who received one or more years of special education services were just as likely to finish high school and to report that they had a job in 1980 as youths who never received special education services. Retention as of grade 12 was a better predictor of later outcomes than retention as of grade 9. Those young people who finished high school without ever repeating a grade were significantly more likely to obtain a high school diploma (pooled $z = 5.91$, pooled $p < .001$) and were also more likely to be employed (pooled $z = 3.14$, pooled $p = .002$) than were young people from the same background who had repeated one or more grades. However, high school completion was more strongly associated with employment than was grade retention as of grade 12.

Another factor found to have an influence on employment was gender in all three samples. Females had significantly lower employment rates than males, even if they had high school credentials and had never been retained or received special educational services.

From these findings we conclude that preschool programs help children do better in their later (as well as earlier) school careers, and that children with better school careers fare better in the job market.

Composite Measure of Educational/Occupational Status.   According to specialists in life course studies, transition points in life, such as early labor market experiences, require that the individual face new tasks, adopt new roles, and integrate a new identity. At each developmental stage individuals are required to perform certain social tasks for which there are specific criteria for success and failure (Kellam et al., 1975; Bronfenbrenner, 1979). How well an individual adapts to society's expectations at each developmental stage has been termed social competence (Scarr, 1981; Zigler & Trickett, 1978). In the spirit of this theoretical approach, we created a social competency measure for the Consortium study. The educational and labor market information contained in our data base could be categorized in a number of ways; the dichotomous global variable "social adaptation to mainstream society" represents one of those ways. The indicators selected for this dependent variable reflect some of the major values identified as important in American society. This variable is consistent with Williams' (1970) analysis of the value placed on personal achievement, success, and work in American society and Rokeach's (1973) finding that black and white Americans hold quite similar values toward work. While clearly a value statement, we believe the outcome measure "social adaptation to mainstream society" represents activities that are deemed important by most segments of the population.

Study participants were coded as "adapting to mainstream society" at the 1980 follow-up if interview data indicated that they were: in an educational program of any type (including high school); in the military; employed with weekly earnings of at least $50 (and did not list public assistance as their main source of income); temporarily laid off; or living with a working spouse/companion. The remainder of the sample was coded as not adapting to mainstream society because they were unemployed (i.e., seeking employment); not in the labor force (i.e., out of work and not seeking employment); in prison; or were nonstudents receiving public assistance as the major source of income.

As in the employment analyses, three samples with 1980 interview data were included in this analysis (Beller, Gray, and Karnes), with one difference. Young people still in high school were included and coded as adapting to mainstream society; this yielded a greater number of subjects in this analysis ($N = 219$) than in the preceding employment analysis (Nigro, 1981). We did not find significant program/control differences in this measure but, as in the employment analysis, there were significant relationships between adapting to mainstream society and the intervening variables that were linked to preschool attendance—school competence at grade 12 and high school completion. In general, young people who were never retained and never in special education were adapting to mainstream society significantly more often than were their peers from the same background who had school failure experiences (pooled $p = .001$). The difference between the two school competence groups was substantial after controlling for background factors (26.5%).

When we tested simultaneously the role of school competence and high school graduation on the measure of transition to adult status, both variables were positively associated with our criterion measure of adaptation to mainstream society (pooled p of .044 and .041, respectively). Therefore, not just graduation alone but the fact of having progressed normally through school was significantly related to later life events. Again, as in the preschool/employment analyses, it is plausible to conclude that an indirect relationship between preschool attendance and social adaptation to mainstream society exists through mediating factors such as school competence and high school graduation. The impact of high school graduation on "adapting to mainstream society" is probably understated because all high school students were coded as if they had not graduated from high school, a coding that would attenuate the observed relationship.

Summary of Occupational Attainment Effects.   Preschool program participation for three of the oldest samples had long-term effects on school competence through ninth and twelfth grades after background factors were considered. School competence at grades 9 and 12 in turn affected the likelihood of high school graduation, and both of these academic measures were significant predictors of whether or not a young person was employed.

Although preschool had a significant effect on both special education placement and grade retention, retention played a stronger role in dropping out of high school and later employment than did special education placement. Preschool apparently had a similar indirect effect on the global outcome measure "social adaptation to mainstream society" through the intervening variables.

Effects on Achievement Orientation at 1980 Follow-Up

Our developmental model of status attainment has thus far largely ignored the social and psychological variables that shape an individual's behaviors, motivations, and values (Fishbein & Ajzen, 1975). The model has also omitted external factors, such as the ways schools and classrooms are organized and structured (e.g., tracking procedures and differing school quality), and the labor market conditions that determine opportunities above and beyond an individual's personal characteristics (see Karabel & Halsey, 1977; Rutter, Maughan, Martimore, & Ouston, 1979). We do not have the empirical data to include these factors in our model. However, we do have data for analyses of "achievement orientation"—achievement motivation and the attitudes, values, and goals that are empirically related to success in school and work.

Data sources for the theoretical construct, achievement orientation, were items from the 1976 and 1980 interviews. Although recognizing that data from interviews should be interpreted cautiously, we performed analyses designed to fill out the social-psychological aspects of our model. These analyses aid our understanding of the mechanisms by which preschool can have long-term effects.

Educational and Occupational Aspirations/Expectations.   A number of studies have documented the relationship of aspirations to subsequent educational and occupational attainment (e.g., Alexander, Eckland, & Griffin, 1975; Sewell & Hauser, 1975; Tucker, Jackson, & Jennings, 1979). Consortium interviews in 1980 assessed a variety of social-psychological attributes, including educational and occupational aspirations and expectations.

Analyses summarized here examined the effects of preschool participation on educational and occupational aspirations in early adulthood for the Beller, Gray, and Karnes samples ($n = 219$; for details, see Bur, 1981). For purposes of multivariate analyses, both educational aspirations and expectations were coded into four categories: high school diploma, vocational/technical school, or less; one to three years of college; four-year college degree; or graduate or professional training. The occupational aspiration and expectation responses were dichotomously coded—blue-collar versus white-collar worker.[10]

---

[10]The dependent variable of educational aspirations was based on responses to the following question on the 1980 interview: "If you could go as far as you would like to go in school, how far would that be?" This question was immediately followed by a question on educational expectations: "How far do you think you will really be able to go in school?" Responses to both questions were classified by the interviewer into a seven-point educational scale (see Consortium, 1981).

The dependent variables of occupational aspirations and expectations were based on responses to two questions: "Now think about the future for a moment—like 5 or 10 years from now. Ideally, if you could choose, what kind of work would you like to be doing in the future?" and "Now imagine it is 1989, ten years from now. What kind of job do you think you will actually have?" Interviewers recorded verbatim responses that were later coded in Ithaca into the Duncan SEI (Socioeconomic Index of Occupational Status, see Hauser & Featherman, 1977) and the Hollingshead Occupational Scale (Hollingshead, 1957).

Summing across projects, 73% of the young people aspired to some college education and 59% aspired to a 4-year college degree or higher. Only 7% aspired to vocational or technical careers. Educational expectations were slightly lower than aspirations (e.g., 66% expected to attain at least some college education). For occupational aspirations, 66% aspired to white-collar jobs, and most (60%) expected to achieve their goal.

We found that preschool participation was associated with higher occupational aspirations and expectations, but not with higher educational aspirations or expectations. Young people with preschool experiences aspired to white-collar jobs rather than blue-collar jobs to a greater degree than did their peers without preschool (pooled z = 2.26; pooled p = .024, after controlling for sex, preprogram IQ score, and family background). Both Beller and Karnes samples yielded significant program/control differences (p = .038 and p = .050, respectively).

Preschool participation was also strongly associated with the expectation of attaining a white-collar rather than a blue-collar job in the future (pooled z = 2.73; pooled p = .006, after sex, preprogram IQ score, and family background factors were controlled). The program/control differences were 32.3%, 22.2%, and 11.3% for Beller, Gray, and Karnes, respectively.

We then asked whether this effect of preschool programs on youths' later occupational expectations could be explained by any effect of preschool programs on special education placement rates or on the rate of youths staying at home to care for their own children. Even after controlling for these two factors as well as family background, preschool participants still expected to attain white-collar jobs more often than controls (pooled z = 2.54; pooled p = .011). School competence at grade 9 was also strongly related to white-collar job expectations after controlling for preschool attendance and background (pooled p = .01).

Thus preschool had an indirect as well as a direct effect on occupational expectations. Young people who had no history of school problems expected white-collar jobs; their peers who had school problems expected to be working in blue-collar jobs. Preschool also influenced these expectations—the young people who had preschool experiences expected to attain a white-collar job even if they had had school problems.

Looking to the future, we have some evidence that higher aspirations in our samples may in the long run be associated with more education and better jobs. Educational and occupational aspirations reported in the 1976 interviews were significant predictors of subsequent educational attainment in 1980. Moreover, among employed men and women, higher educational aspirations in 1976 were significantly associated with holding jobs of higher status in 1980 as measured on the Duncan SEI (Wickham-Crowley, 1981).

Effects of Achievement Orientation in 1976 on Later Outcomes.   We were particularly interested in the long-term effects of achievement orientation because we had previously documented a strong relationship between preschool programs and 1976 achievement orientation.[11]

We found that pride in achievement-related accomplishments (reported in 1976) was significantly associated with a number of concurrent and subsequent outcomes, such as school course marks, 1976 educational and occupational aspirations, school competence at grade 12, and high school completion.[12]

Additionally, 1976 achievement orientation had significant positive effects on three subsequent outcomes (all measured in 1980)—employment status, educational attainment, and educational expectations for the future. We found that young people who had earlier expressed pride in achievement-related accomplishments were significantly more likely to be employed in 1980 ($p = .002$, after controlling for sex, preprogram IQ score, and family background variables, $N = 176$). The results remained significant after controlling for the effects of course marks during school ($p = .008$), and even after we considered 1980 educational attainment along with background factors and course marks ($p = .019$; see Wickham-Crowley, 1981).

The effect of early achievement orientation on later educational attainment was also significant. Young people who were proud of school, work, or sports achievements in 1976 had completed more years of schooling as of 1980, compared to their counterparts from the same background who had expressed pride in nonachievement related activities ($p = .013$, after controlling for sex, preprogram IQ score, and family background).

There was a positive relationship between achievement-related attitudes and educational expectations—highly motivated young people expected that they would really be able to attain their college goals ($p < .05$, after controlling for background factors, $N = 193$; see Bur, 1981).

Summary of Achievement Orientation Findings.   It was found that preschool attendance was significantly associated with higher occupational aspirations and

---

[11]In the achievement-oriented categories were school- and job-related achievements, sports achievements, competitive success, awards, and skill development. In the residual category were good behavior, altruistic acts, self-assertion, finding money, getting married and bearing children, moving out on one's own, going to church, interpersonal relations, and vague generalizations ("nothing" or "everything"). These categories were not meant to imply "better" or "worse" responses, but only intended to tap personality variables that could influence performance in school or in the labor market. As reported earlier, compared to controls, program participants were significantly more likely to give achievement-related reasons for being proud of themselves in 1976, and this program effect was especially strong among older girls.

[12]Because of the temporal overlap of these measures, it is more appropriate to refer to the association as a correlation rather than a predictive relationship. We cannot assume a cause/effect relationship because for many Beller and Gray study participants, the 1976 interview took place after they had graduated or dropped out of school (Chang, 1981).

We did not find program/control differences using the Beller and Gray samples that were appropriate for testing for program effects. 1976 achievement orientation data were available for Beller and Gray program and control groups, but only for the Karnes program group.

expectations in young adulthood. Preschool graduates aspired to and expected to attain white-collar rather than blue-collar jobs.

Additionally, we found that 1976 achievement orientation was significantly related to a number of concurrent and subsequent outcomes, and was itself correlated with preschool attendance. Measured in adolescence, 1976 achievement orientation was correlated with school course marks, school competence, 1976 educational and occupational aspirations, and high school completion. When we considered 1976 achievement orientation as a predictor of later outcomes, we found that pride in achievement-related accomplishments was significantly related to three 1980 outcomes—employment status, educational attainment, and educational expectations for the future.

We conclude that preschool has direct effects on achievement orientation. We also have evidence that preschool indirectly affects other outcomes such as employment status, educational attainment, and educational expectations.

SUMMARY OF FINDINGS

The main research questions addressed in the Consortium metaanalysis concerned the overall effectiveness of early childhood education programs. Corollary questions examined the differential effectiveness of programs and the mechanisms or processes by which early education affected later outcomes. To assess the long-term impact of early education, we selected both standardized tests and a variety of outcome measures of educational and social adaptation that were appropriate for each age group.

When evaluated over a 15-year period, early education had significant effects in five areas: developed abilities in early to middle childhood, school competence in middle childhood and adolescence, attitudes toward achievement in adolsecence, educational attainment in late adolescence, and occupational attitudes in early adulthood. For the sixth outcome area, occupational attainment in early adulthood, indirect preschool effects were found. The significant direct and indirect preschool effects are summarized in Table 13.12 and Fig. 13.1.

Effects on Developed Abilities

Indicators of developed abilities—IQ test scores and achievement test scores—revealed significant program/control differences in the early school years. On Stanford–Binet IQ test scores, we found significant and robust differences 1 year and 2 years after the early education program ended, and significant but not robust differences 3 or 4 years after the program. At immediate posttest, the median program/control difference was 7.42 IQ points.

Program children started first grade with a significant IQ score advantage over control children—5.80 points on the average. The IQ score effect was not perma-

TABLE 13.12

Effects of Early Childhood Programs Listing of Significant Results[a]

Construct Dependent Variable	Age or Grade	N	No. of Projects	Program/ Control Difference[b]	p value (2-tailed)
Developed Abilities					
Stanford-Binet Intelligence Test					
IQ test score	immediate posttest	1119	7	7.42	$<.001*$
IQ test score	1 year after	1034	7	4.32	$<.001*$
IQ test score	2 years after	741	6	4.62	$<.001*$
IQ test score	3 or 4 years after	691	6	3.04	.002
IQ test score	School entry (age 6)	730	7	5.80	$<.001*$
Achievement test scores					
mathematics	grade 3	351	4	—	.002*
reading	grade 3	361	4	—	.008
mathematics	grade 4	369	6	—	.030
mathematics	grade 5	325	5		.040
1976 Achievement Orientation[c]					
Pride in activity (youth)	10-19 years	537	6	13.7%	.003*
Mother/child occupational aspiration (Discrepancy score)	10-19 years	372	6	.68[d]	.006*
Self-evaluation of school performance	15-19 years	215	3	.22[d]	.039
School Competence					
Special education placement	grade 7	638[e]	7	8.6%	.001*
Retained in grade	grade 7	846[e]	8	5.7%	.005*
Aggregate (special ed. or retained)	grade 7	866[e]	8	11.8%	.001*
Special education placement	grade 12	380[e]	4	18.9%	.001*
Aggregate (special ed. or retained)	grade 12	387[e]	4	19.0%	.002*

(continued)

TABLE 13.12 (Continued)

Construct Dependent Variable	Age or Grade	N	No. of Projects	Program/ Control Difference[b]	p value (2-tailed)
Educational Attainment					
High school degree	18 + years	364	4	15.1%	.020
1980 Achievement Orientation					
Occupational Aspirations	19-22 years	187	3	—	.024
Occupational Expectations	19-22 years	168	3	—	.006
Indirect Effects[f]					
High school completion/school competence	grade 9	192	3	—	.001
High school completion/school competence	grade 12	192	3	—	<.001
High school completion/retention	grade 9	192	3	—	<.001
High school completion/retention	grade 12	192	3	—	<.001
1980 Employment/school competence	grade 12	192	3	—	.001
1980 Employment/retention	grade 12	192	3	—	.002
1980 Employment/H.S. diploma	19 + years	192	3	—	.001
1980 Adaptation mainstream soc./school competence	grade 12	190	3	—	.001
1980 Adaptation mainstream soc./H.S. diploma	19 + years	190	3	—	.001
1980 Occup. Aspiration/school competence	grade 9	188	3	—	<.05
1980 Occup. Expectation/school competence	grade 9	165	3	—	.01
1980 Employment/1976 Achievement Orientation	16-19 years	176	3	—	.002

1980 Education Attainment/					
1976 Achievement Orientation	16-19 years	176	3	—	.013
1980 Education Expectations/					
1976 Achievement Orientation	16-19 years	193	3	—	<.05

[a] Regression results controlling for preprogram IQ score, sex, family background at program entry (mother's educational level, two-parent family structure, number of siblings). For exceptions, see text.

[b] Program/control difference based on median unstandardized regression coefficient across projects; e.g., IQ points, percent difference. For analyses with 3 projects, see text.

[c] Chi-square results rather than regression results.

[d] For aspirations, program/control difference is median discrepancy on Hollingshead occupational scale; for self-evaluation, median difference on 5-point scale.

[e] N for chi-square analyses; regression N is slightly less.

[f] Dependent variable/predictor. School competence = aggregate never placed in special education classes or never retained. All results reported here are regression analyses controlling for background variables listed in footnote a (total effects).

*Results are robust after strongest result is deleted from pooled analysis. Robustness not tested when only 3 projects were pooled.

453

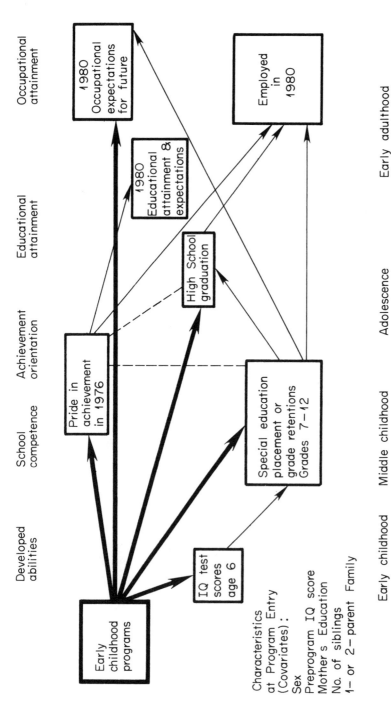

Developed
abilities

School
competence

Achievement
orientation

Educational
attainment

Occupational
attainment

Early childhood Middle childhood Adolescence Early adulthood

FIG. 13.1 Effects of Early Childhood Education Programs: Diagram showing network of direct and indirect program effects suggested by data, significant paths only.

Note: Solid lines represent significant program effects on outcomes after controlling for child background characteristics at program entry. Wide solid lines represent direct program effects; fine solid lines are indirect effects. Dotted lines indicate that time of measurement overlaps for some cases, so that causal ordering is not implied.

Characteristics
at Program Entry
(Covariates):
Sex
Preprogram IQ score
Mother's Education
No. of siblings
1- or 2- parent Family

nent; by 1976, when the youths were 10 to 19 years of age, there were no program/control differences on WISC scores in most Consortium projects. In the analyses of achievement test scores,we found that program children performed better than their controls, particularly in mathematics, in grades 3–6.

1976 Achievement Orientation

The early education experience was also associated with positive attitudes toward achievement in the 1976 follow-up, and particularly so for young women 15–19 years of age. There were no program/control differences on educational or occupational aspirations in adolescence, but older program graduates (15–19 years of age) rated themselves higher on school performance than did their peers who had no preschool experience.

Mothers of program graduates had consistently higher occupational aspirations for their children than the children had for themselves in middle childhood or adolescence, whereas control mothers and children did not show this discrepancy.

School Competence Effects

Systematic analysis of school competence on a year-by-year basis demonstrated substantial and significant program effects on special education placement and retention (as well as on the combination of the two).

As of grade 7, for eight samples, early education graduates were significantly less likely to have been placed in special education classes or to have been retained in grade. The results were highly robust for special education placements and the combined category, meeting school requirements (i.e., never placed in special education or retained). All the differences were educationally meaningful.

Increasing program/control differences were found through grade 7, with progressively higher percentages of control children failing to meet school requirements at each grade level. Statistically significant program/control differences were reached at grade 6 for special education placement, and at grade 5 for retentions and for the combined school competence measure. As of grade 12, the program effect remained highly significant and robust for special education placements and the combined school competence variable but leveled off for grade retention.

Both the grade 7 and grade 12 results are consistent with the conclusion that children benefited from early education programs—in being more likely to meet the schools' basic requirements for adequate performance, be that avoiding special education placement or grade failure—and that this finding was not due to initial program/control differences in ability, sex, ethnicity, or early family background.

Educational Attainment Effects

Program participants were significantly more likely to obtain a high school diploma than were their controls. The magnitude of the program effect was substantial and educationally meaningful—averaging a 15% differential.

Investigation of predictors of high school graduation showed that the relationships between high school graduation and school competence at grade 9 and at grade 12 were highly significant. Those who met school requirements by grade 9 tended to obtain a high school diploma, particularly those who were never retained.

Differential Effects

We also considered the possibility that certain subgroups of children benefited more from program attendance than others. These corollary questions of differential effectiveness were investigated with three dependent variables: IQ test scores, school competence measures, and high school completion. Overall, there was no evidence that the average preschool program had different effects for children from differing backgrounds (two- versus one-parent family structure, differing number of siblings, differing levels of mother's educational attainment), or for children with differing preprogram IQ test scores, or male versus female program participants.

1980 Achievement Orientation

Preschool attendance was significantly associated with higher occupational aspirations and expectations for the posthigh school samples. Preschool graduates aspired to white-collar jobs rather than blue-collar jobs and expected to attain their occupational choice. We found no evidence that attending preschool had effects on either educational aspirations or expectations.

Indirect Preschool Effects

Although we did not find significant direct effects of preschool participation on employment, we found indirect links through school competence measures and high school completion. We concluded that preschool programs helped children to do better in their later school careers, and that children with better school records are faring much better on the job market.

We found evidence of additional indirect links between preschool and later outcomes through the intervening variable of 1976 achievement orientation. Pride in achievement-related accomplishments was influenced by early childhood programs and was in turn a significant predictor of three outcomes in early adulthood (reported in 1980)—employment status, educational attainment, and educational expectations for the future. Achievement orientation in late adolescence was also highly correlated with school competence and high school completion that translated into later occupational and educational attainment.

These findings are discussed in Chapter 14.

ACKNOWLEDGMENTS

In addition to our colleagues mentioned in the general acknowledgments, we wish to thank all those whose work contributed to the pooled analysis. Those who made professional-level contributions to this analysis included Bettie Applewhite, Charles Bur, Chia-Ying Chang, Reginald Gougis, Clarence Henderson, Daniel Koretz, Judith Nelson, Georgia Nigro, Donald Poe, Marilyn Rosché, Caleb Rossiter, Ann Schruben, Reuben Snipper, James Staszewski, Merlene Vassall, Patrick Vitale, Judy Vopava, Jennifer Wartik, Timothy Wickham-Crowley, and Agelia Ypelaar.

We also thank the young people who participated in these studies. We wish them a good life.

REFERENCES

Alexander, K. L., Eckland, B. K., & Griffin, L. J. The Wisconsin model of socioeconomic achievement: A replication. *American Journal of Sociology, 1975, 81,* 324–342.

Anastasi, A. Genuine distinctions and implied pseudodistinctions. In W. Schrader (Ed.), *Measuring achievement: Progress over a decade. New directions for testing and measurement.* San Francisco: Jossey–Bass, 1980 (No. 5).

Baltes, P. B., Reese, H. W., & Lipsitt, L. P. Life-span developmental psychology. *Annual Review of Psychology, 1980, 31,* 65–110.

Blau, P., & Duncan, O. D. *The American occupational structure.* New York: Wiley, 1967.

Boocock, S. S. *An introduction to the sociology of learning.* New York: Houghton Mifflin, 1972.

Boykin, A. W., Jackson, J. S., & Yates, J. F. (Eds.). *Research directions of black psychologists.* New York: Russell Sage, 1979.

Bronfenbrenner, U. *The ecology of human development.* Cambridge, Mass.: Harvard University Press, 1979.

Bur, C. Determinants of aspirations and expectations. In *Persistence of preschool effects: Status, stress, and coping skills.* Final Report Technical Papers, Grant No. 90C-1311(03), to the Administration for Children, Youth and Families, Office of Human Development Services, DHSS, 1981.

Camilli, G., & Hopkins, K. Applicability of chi-square to 2×2 contingency tables with small expected cell frequencies. *Psychological Bulletin, 1978, 85*(1), 163–167.

Chang. C. D. *Evaluating the long-term effects of preschool programs on the educational attainment of children from low-income families.* Unpublished doctoral dissertation, Cornell University, 1981.

Consortium for Longitudinal Studies. *Lasting effects after preschool.* Final report, Grant No. 90C-1311, to Administration for Children, Youth and Families, Office of Human Development Services. DHEW Publication No. (OHDS) 79-30178. Washington, D.C.: U.S. Government Printing Office, 1978.

Consortium for Longitudinal Studies. *Persistence of preschool effects: Status, stress and coping skills.* Final Report Technical Papers, Grant No. 90C-1311(03), to the Administration for Children, Youth and Families, Office of Human Development Services, DHHS, 1981.

Consortium on Developmental Continuity. *The persistence of preschool effects: A long-term follow-up of fourteen infant and preschool programs* (2 vols.). Final Report, Grant No. 18-76-07843, to the Administration for Children, Youth and Families, Office of Human Development Services. DHEW Publication No. (OHDS)78-30130. Washington, D.C.: U.S. Government Printing Office, 1977.

Cook, T. D., & Levitan, L. C. Reviewing the literature: A comparison of traditional methods with meta-analysis. *Journal of Personality,* 1980, *48*(4), 449–472.

Darlington, R. B., Royce, J. M., Snipper, A. S., Murray, H. W., & Lazar, I. Preschool programs and later school competence of children from low-income families. *Science,* April 1980, *208,* 202–204.

Erikson, E. H. *Childhood and society.* New York: Norton, 1963.

Fishbein, M., & Ajzen, I. *Belief attitude, intention and behavior: An introduction to theory and research.* Reading, Mass: Addison-Wesley, 1975.

Glass, G. V., McGaw, B., & Smith, M. L. *Meta-analysis in social research.* Beverly Hills, Calif: Sage, 1981.

Hauser, W. H., & Featherman, D. *The process of stratification: Trends and analyses.* New York: Academic Press, 1977.

Henderson, C. C. Preschool effects on employment. In *Persistence of preschool effects: Status, stress, and coping skills.* Final Report Technical Papers, Grant No. 90C-1311(03), to the Administration for Children, Youth and Families, Office of Human Development Services, DHSS, 1981.

Hollingshead, A. B. *Two factor index of social position.* New York: Wiley, 1957.

Hubbell, V. R. Differential effects of three early childhood intervention delivery systems (Doctoral dissertation, Cornell University, 1978). *Dissertation Abstracts International,* 1978, *39,* 413B. (University Microfilms No. 7809729).

Karabel, J. F., & Halsey, A. H. Educational research: A review and an interpretation. In J. Karabel & A. Halsey (Eds.), *Power and ideology in education.* New York: Oxford University Press, 1977.

Kellam, S. G., Branch, J. D., Agrawal, K. C., & Ensminger, M. E. *Mental health and going to school: The Woodlawn program of assessment, early intervention, and evaluation.* Chicago: University of Chicago Press, 1975.

Koretz, D. M. Long-term non-cognitive effects of seven infant and preschool intervention programs (Doctoral dissertation, Cornell University, 1978). *Dissertation Abstracts International,* 1979, *39,* 3590 B. (University Microfilms No. 7902279).

Koretz, D. M., Vopava, J., & Darlington, R. *Matching early education programs to children: Some methodological limitations.* Paper presented at the American Association for the Advancement of Science, Washington, D.C., February 15, 1978.

Lazar, I., Darlington, R., Murray, H., Royce, J., & Snipper, A. Lasting effects of early education. *Monographs of the Society for Research in Child Development,* 1982, *47* (1–2, Serial No. 194).

Martin, E. P., & Martin, J. M. *The black extended family.* Chicago: University of Chicago Press, 1978.

Mosteller, F., & Bush, R. R. Selected quantitative techniques. In G. Lindzey (Ed.), *Handbook of Social Psychology* (Vol. 1). Reading, Mass.: Addison-Wesley, 1954.

Murray, H. W., Royce, J. M., Lazar, I., & Darlington, R. B. A follow-up of participants in early childhood programs. In S. A. Mednick & M. Harway (Eds.), *Longitudinal research in the United States.* Boston: Martinus Nijhoff, in press.

Nigro, G. Preschool effects on adapting to mainstream society. In *Persistence of preschool effects: Status, stress, and coping skills.* Final Report Technical Papers, Grant No. 90C-1311(03), to the

Administration for Children, Youth and Families, Office of Human Development Services, DHSS, 1981.

Rokeach, M. *The nature of human values*. New York: Free Press, 1973.

Rosché, M. *Early intervention and later use of child welfare services*. Unpublished master's thesis, Cornell University, 1979.

Rossiter, C. Early education effects on nonstandard progression in school. In *Persistence of preschool effects: Status, stress, and coping skills*. Final Report Technical Papers, Grant No. 90C-1311(03), to the Administration for Children, Youth and Families, Office of Human Development Services, DHSS, 1981.

Royce, J. The long-term effects of background characteristics and early education programs on later school outcomes. (Doctoral dissertation, Cornell University, 1979). *Dissertation Abstracts International, 1979, 39,* 6638A-6639A. (University Microfilms No. 7910773).

Royce, J. M., Murray, H. W., Lazar, I., & Darlington, R. B. Studying program outcomes. In B. Spodek (Ed.), *Handbook of research on early childhood education*. Free Press/Macmillan, 1982

Royce, J. M., Snipper, R., Murray, H. W., & Nelson, J. *Differential effectiveness of early education: Testing for long-term interactive effects*. Paper presented at the meeting of the American Educational Research Association, Boston, April 1980.

Rutter, M., Maughan, B., Martimore, P., & Ouston, J. *Fifteen thousand hours: Secondary schools and their effects on children*. Cambridge, Mass.: Harvard University Press, 1979.

Sameroff, A. J. Early influences on development: Fact or fancy? In S. Chess and A. Thomas (Eds.), *Annual progress in child psychiatry and child development*. New York: Bruner/Mazel, 1976.

Scarr, S. Testing for children: Assessment and the many determinants of intellectual competence. *American Psychologist, 1981, 36*(10), 1159–1166.

Schruben, A. *Public school remediations as outcomes in evaluating compensatory preschool*. Unpublished master's thesis, Cornell University, 1982.

Sewell, W. H., & Hauser, K. M. *Education, occupation and earnings: Achievement in the early career*. New York: Academic Press, 1975.

Sewell, W. H., Hauser, R. M., & Featherman, D. (Eds.). *Schooling and achievement in American society*. New York: Academic Press, 1976.

Stack, C. *All our kin*. New York: Harper & Row, 1974.

Staszewski, J. Predicting labor market success from background and school achievement variables: Canonical variate analyses. In *Persistence of preschool effects: Status, stress, and coping skills*. Final Report Technical Papers, Grant No. 90C-1311(03), to the Administration for Children, Youth and Families, Office of Human Development Services, DHSS, 1981.

Tucker, M. B., Jackson, J. S., & Jennings, R. M. Occupational expectations and dropout propensity in urban high school students. In A. W. Boykin, A. J. Franklin, & J. F. Yates (Eds.), *Research directions of black psychologists*. New York: Russell Sage, 1979.

Walberg, H. I., & Marjoribanks, K. Family environments and cognitive development: Twelve analytic models. *Review of Educational Research, 1976, 46*(4), 527–551.

Wickham-Crowley, T. The transition to adulthood: Preschool programs, higher education, and labor market experience. In *Persistence of preschool effects: Status, stress, and coping skills*. Final Report Technical Papers, Grant No. 90C-1311(03), to the Administration for Children, Youth and Families, Office of Human Development Services, DHSS, 1981.

Williams, R. M., Jr. *American society: A sociological interpretation* (3rd ed.). New York: Knopf, 1970.

Zigler, E., & Trickett, P. K. IQ, social competence, and evaluation of early childhood education programs. *American Psychologist, 1978, 33,* 789–798.

14 Discussion and Implications of the Findings

Irving Lazar
Cornell University

SUMMARY OF FINDINGS

Independently and collectively, the major studies of early intervention with low-income children reported in this volume clearly demonstrated positive effects of these programs throughout childhood and the adolescent years.

Using conservative analytic techniques and controlling for potentially confounding background variables, analyses across studies yielded substantial and significant findings. Before discussing the implications of these findings, we summarize them.

Findings for Subjects

1. Preschool programs increase individual scores on standard intelligence tests, and these increases remain statistically significant for a three- to four-year period after the preschool experience.

2. During most of the elementary school years, arithmetic and reading achievement scores of program graduates are higher than those of controls.

3. Preschool graduates are less likely to be placed in special education or remedial classes than are their controls; they are more likely to meet the ordinary requirements of the schools and to graduate from high school.

4. Preschool graduates have higher self-esteem and value achievement more than their controls. Their parents have higher occupational aspirations for them than do control parents—or the children themselves. The program graduates have higher occupational aspirations and expectations than do their controls, and these are predictive of their actual attainments.

461

5. Indirectly, the preschool experience increased labor market participation in late adolescence and the early adult years.

Findings for Programs

Represented in these studies are all the major preschool curricula or their immediate precursors: home-based, center-based, and combination programs; programs that began at various ages, that lasted over various periods of time, and that differed in intensity and varied in the prior training of staffs. Using the molar outcome indicators of school competence and completion, we found that these programs were effective in producing program/control differences. We can conclude that any well-designed, professionally supervised program to stimulate and socialize infants and young children from poor minority families will be efficacious. It is certainly possible that finer-grained outcome measures might reveal differential effectiveness of the programs, settings, durations, and intensities.

The findings that suggest that stimulation stimulates, that success breeds more success, and that children learn when taught are not surprising. All of these programs were effective, and none were more or less effective than the others as measured by our school outcome indicators.

Findings for Subgroups

Various educators have suggested that children from different kinds of families would benefit differentially from preschool experiences. Our analyses did not find that any of the background descriptors differentiated children in terms of the school outcomes. Children from both one- and two-parent families benefited; only children, oldest, middle and youngest children benefited; children whose mothers worked outside the home did as well as those whose mothers stayed home all day. Briefly, regardless of their backgrounds, low-income children enrolled in these programs more often met school expectations than did the children who were not.

IMPLICATIONS OF THE FINDINGS

Why should a brief exposure to an organized educational program in the early years of life have such far-reaching and long-lasting effects? It seems hardly likely that a preschool education could somehow "inoculate" a child against school failure. Yet the findings reported in Chapter 13, despite the conservative treatment of these data, are quite clear. The low-income, mostly black children who participated in this diverse range of programs and curricula were more likely to succeed in school than were similar children who did not have any of those experiences. They also felt better about themselves, had more realistic vocational expectations, and were prouder of their achievements than were the nonparticipants (Koretz, 1978). The complex analyses reported earlier in this volume make it clear that these findings are not a fluke—not due to an accident of sampling or bias or some artifact. The independence of the separate studies makes these findings highly reliable. Indeed, few examples of this kind of multiple and independent replication exist anywhere in the social sciences.

Although the data hint at the processes that link early education to later school achievement and from there to participation in the labor force, we can really only speculate as to what processes are responsible. Although several complex explanations are possible, we prefer to suggest a fairly simple explanation.

What may have happened could be illustrated as follows:

Little Sue comes home from preschool able to do things her mother had never seen 3-year-olds able to do. Mother approves of Sue's accomplishments, which encourages Sue to further accomplishment. Her apparently "high" achievement raises Mother's hopes and expectations for the child, which serve as further stimulus to "do well."

Susie, in turn, much prefers the activities at preschool than her usual fare at home and demands that her family play similar games with her. To the extent that they can, even more educational stimulation is added to the positive reinforcement for increased intellectual and social skills.

Better able to function in a group, more confident of herself, and receiving both rewards and higher expectations from home, Susie conforms more successfully to the demands of the public school than she might have otherwise and is positively rewarded by the teacher.

So, we can speculate, there begins a system of mutual reinforcement between the parent and child, the teacher and child, and the combination that "teaches" that academic success is valuable. It is this continuing mutual reinforcement that could be responsible for the long-term effects: a reinforcement system that is started by the child's participation in a systematic program of cognitive and social stimulation and enrichment and that changes parental aspirations for the child. This "feedback loop" can be initiated as easily in a home-based program as at a center-based preschool.

This speculation is appealing to us because:

1. It would account for the "success" of all the curricula represented in these studies. They all "worked."

2. It would account for the commonly found performance differences between middle- and lower-class children. Middle-class parents value education and have high aspirations and expectations for their children.

3. It would explain the shift to achievement orientation among the experimental children.

4. It explains why "earlier is better"—and why parental involvement is associated with success.

5. It would account for the finding that preschool attendance is related to high school completion, independent of ability or social class or family structure.

These data do not permit a test of this explanation. Most of the studies were designed and carried out before research and theory began to focus on the importance of the parent–child interaction in cognitive development. We must await the completion of newer longitudinal studies that collect such information and for new research to document the process to test these ideas or to develop better ones.

However, we do not need to wait for new research to put these findings to work. They have clear implications for public policy and practice today.

The first clear implication is that a well-designed and well-run program for very young children pays off in later effects—and indeed appears to pay for itself in the savings which accrue from the reduction of costs for special education classes.

A second implication is that closer contact between home and school and greater involvement of parents in the education of their children are probably more important than educational administrators had generally realized.

Still another implication is that the search for the "perfect" curriculum is probably futile. What is important is that there is a curriculum with specific goals and a real assurance that the teachers are carrying out the curriculum. All the widely used preschool curricula are represented in these studies, and all of them were effective, as far as these outcomes are concerned. To be sure, different curricular foci produced slightly different achievement levels in the academic areas related to their foci—but all of them were related to positive overall outcomes.

A principal area in which these findings could be applied is day care for young children.

With few exceptions, state regulation of day care has been limited to concerns for physical safety, space, and sanitation. These studies suggest that, at minimal additional cost, a systematic educational program could be introduced into both home-based and center-based day care. One of the many findings not reported here because of space limitations demonstrated that programs were equally effective whether the teacher was the child's parent, a paraprofessional, or a professional, as long as in-service training and supervision were also provided (Consortium, 1977). With all day care now subsidized by tax money—either directly or through tax deductions—it would seem that the public interest would best be served if these expenditures also served to reduce later educational costs and to increase the probability of graduation from high school.

The same findings suggest a possible value in training potential and new parents in ways to educate their own infants and preschool children. Ira Gordon's manuals for parents were a start in that direction, but only a few communities have picked up on that beginning.

Perhaps the most important implication of these studies is that they have demonstrated that the provision of appropriate services can mitigate the depressing effects of poverty on cognitive and social development. The children in these studies did not reach the achievement levels of affluent children—but it would be foolish to expect that brief intellectual stimulation could fully counteract the economic, housing, nutritional, and cultural barriers our society imposes upon poor black families.

We would like to call a different set of implications to the reader's attention. This study is unusual in a number of important ways.

First of all, this is a collaborative study—not a "team" or group study but a real collaboration, in that each of the studies were independently designed and conducted; each investigator could—and did—publish independently, and all managed their own budgets and hired their own staffs. What these independent, and otherwise competing, senior investigators did that was very special was to agree to entrust their original raw data to a single independent analytic group, to agree to collect common data in addition to the data unique to their own studies, and to turn these new data over to the central analytic team. Without these agreements, it would have been impossible to have a credible number of independent replications of tests of preschool experience's long-term effects on the performance of children from poor families; and the issue would still be in the realm of speculation rather than having, essentially, been settled by these consistent findings.

A second unusual characteristic of this research was the combination of secondary analyses of already existing data with a set of new prospective studies. By using existing studies as a base, the research was shortened by at least 12 years— and saved the millions of dollars that would have been necessary otherwise. Indeed, if the original interventions had not already been conducted, it is unlikely that support for so many studies could have been found in 1975.

A third unusual characteristic is the administrative and fiscal structure that was necessary in order to carry out the studies since 1975. Because none of the investigators could predict in advance how many of their original subjects would be located, nor where they would be found, nor how many would be willing to participate, it was necessary to create a structure that permitted the rapid transfer of money to investigators as their subjects were found. This required finding—or creating—a trustee organization that would receive and distribute funds and be willing to forego the reimbursement of its own indirect costs. Because, under most circumstances, universities could not waive such costs without endangering their other grants, new administrative machinery had to be developed to carry out this study. One benefit of this structure-building activity was that the collaborating institutions were able to waive all or most of their indirect costs, thus making grant monies directly available to the research.

The problems in organizing and administering such a consortium are formidable; however, in a time of shrinking resources, it provides a cost-effective way to address significant problems that cannot be financed otherwise. We hope our example will inspire other investigators to consider adopting—and improving upon—the model this research represents.

These studies do not address a number of questions of importance to both practitioners and scientists. The questions these studies addressed were those of the 1960s. New knowledge since then has raised new questions that await future research. Further, the studies pose some new questions. For example, what is the minimum length and intensity of intervention that will produce optimal effects?

Although these studies varied considerably in both length and intensity, it is not possible from this set of studies to really separate length and intensity from each other or from age, format, or foci of the interventions. The diversity of data made it impossible to look with any depth across studies at socioemotional variables, but those individual studies addressing such variables found them to be important. We speculate that changes in familial values were crucial components of the effects but have only suggestive data on values held by the parents afterwards, and none prior to the intervention.

We cannot pose all the questions that need to be raised, nor would a long list be useful. We can, however, remind the reader that many of the most important questions to be raised when we consider influences on development require longitudinal studies. Longitudinal research requires an unusual level of persistence and is almost impossible to support. Few grant agencies are willing to make a 15- or 20-year commitment to a single study—and yet children will continue to grow at a rate of only 1 year during each 12 months.

Perhaps, if we are sufficiently insistent, our society will one day be willing to make long-range investments in our children and in the quest for ways to improve their ability to succeed in life.

Epilogue:
We Never Promised You A Rose Garden, But One May Have Grown Anyhow

Lois-ellin Datta
National Institute of Education

Much has been made of the early climate of optimism about early childhood programs and how programs were evaluated in light of these dreams rather than what many development psychologists see as a more interactive, complex, and contingent reality.[1] Zigler and Anderson (1979) write:

> The first inklings of the misunderstandings that were to plague Head Start in the next decade came in May 1965, at the ceremony in the White House Rose Garden launching the first Head Start summer program. Surrounded by the experts who had helped design the program, and with their apparent endorsement, President Johnson announced that the eight-week summer program would ensure that "thirty million man years—the combined lifespan of these youngsters—will be spent productively and rewardingly, rather than wasted in tax-supported institutions or in welfare-supported lethargy." To the public, Head Start appeared to be a quick, two-month program to make poor children smart, while to the planners, and those in the program, it was but the beginning of a long cooperative effort of teachers, health care professionals, and parents to make children physically healthy and socially competent [p. 16].

Zigler and Anderson concluded that the climate of euphoria about the use of environmental enrichment to change children's lives now is gone; they might have added that with it is gone a climate of policy enthusiasm for early childhood education.

Another chapter in knowledge about the long-term effects of early childhood programs has been written here. The authors of the Consortium studies, although

---

[1]Opinions expressed are the author's in her private capacity.

467

varying in their beliefs about how large a difference early childhood programs alone might make, nonetheless boldly designed the research in such a way that a test could be made of whether the Rose Garden rhetoric was right.

What claims now may be made on public policy as a result of the Consortium studies? At least three are offered by the researchers themselves: modest, contingent, and strong. In identifying the claims, the focus is on what the authors seem to regard as the policy implications of their own data or of the Consortium data. This is susceptible to personal style in such matters. One author, for example, might claim only that the data justify further research, whereas others might regard the same data as justifying initiation of preschool services to all low-income children. In the discussion, the relation between the claim and the data supporting it are considered; beginning with their conclusions, this chapter focuses on the policy implications of the authors' *own* views.

Levenstein, O'Hara, and Madden make the fewest policy claims, arguing that although there are on average benefits of early intervention, their work shows most clearly that their program can be implemented and maternal behavior affected. Miller and Bizzell, in a similarly cautious vein, emphasize the interaction of particular types of children and particular experiences in preschools. They recommend further research to identify crucial program components, to learn how to match children to programs, and to trace the links between early aptitudes and later school success. Woolman, whose data are limited to immediate effects and retention-in-grade information at the fifth–sixth grades, claims only that ". . . the fact that the outcomes supported the hypotheses does suggest that additional work to test the underlying assumptions is justified, [p. 295]" and that his Micro-Social approach appears to offer a useful supplement to existing day care and Head Start programs. Gray, Ramsey, and Klaus remind us that there is no royal road either to geometry or to solving the problems of the coming generation of those now living in poverty.

Most of the researchers emphasize that early intervention has had some durable, important consequences, particularly, according to Karnes, Shwedel, and Williams, in avoiding the stigma of placement in special education. Beller, whose data were particularly extensive in the area of social-emotional development as long as 13 years after preschool participation, urged awaiting corroboration of the social-emotional findings through replications. He concluded that both length of preschool and preschool-versus-no-preschool showed a magnitude and range of relationships larger than he and his colleagues had expected. Other researchers stress continuity of development, arguing that early intervention helps but the limiting effects of environment—which continues—cannot be broken by early intervention alone (Deutsch, Deutsch, Jordan, & Grallo; Jester & Guinagh).

Schweinhart and Weikart claim meaningful, lasting effects of early intervention, effects powerful enough to break the cycle of poverty. Seitz and her colleagues emphasize the remarkable occurrence of some lasting effects at almost every stage, although they warn that continued attention to motivation and to later school quality are needed for capacity to be realized. And Palmer (this volume), most strongly of all, concludes that the Harlem study showed that a minimal intervention (45 hours of one-to-one teaching at ages 2 and 3) provided substantial benefits and durable effects more than a decade later: ''Perhaps the so-called inoculation hypothesis is more valid than is presently supposed [p. 234].'' The pooled analyses for the Consortium emphasize the durability and long-term significance of effects of the early interventions.

To a certain extent, these distinctions are exaggerated. Schweinhart and Weikart do not discount the effects of postprogram experiences, and Gray (1982) is encouraged by the extent of the immediate benefits, taking a ''strong, modest'' position as far as the pooled results are concerned. Also, there is some reason in matters of public policy to waffle: The lethal consequence of overpromising and underdelivering has become almost a cliche. Indeed, this series of studies could be considered as a way to decide upon promises that might be reasonable for early childhood education.[2]

The next sections of this chapter analyze the modest, contingent, and strong positions: Which, if any, seems most justified by the data reported in this book?

Modest Policy Claims

Gray et al. observe:

> After participation in a carefully designed program, our young people showed a gradual waning in achievement test performance, . . . such declines suggest that, important as our findings of relatively enduring effects may be, they are at best only a start, albeit a consequential one, on the serious educational and social problems that will be encountered by young people who have grown up in poverty [pp. 66–67].

Miller and Bizzell, noting the long and complex causal pattern relating early childhood programs to middle school achievement, which they have as yet imperfectly described due to methodological barriers, further observe: ''It is therefore difficult to know to what extent these programs (in Louisville) as a whole had beneficial effects. For the most part, none of them succeeded in raising school performance at the middle school level to national norms. At seventh grade, on the average, about 16% were at or above the 50th percentile [p. 197].'' Levenstein et al. observed: ''They (the results) do, however, offer good evidence that the desired maternal behavior can be successfully modeled in

---

[2]Several Consortium members planned long-term follow-up from the start (e.g., Gray, Weikart). The intent of the Consortium members was to work forward from theory to expectations to program design to evaluation. Their readers, however, may find these evaluations, like others, useful in defining reasonable promises for the future.

the program. The best evidence derived from this program indicates short-term effects on IQ [p. 261].''

To Woolman, the observations of the children during and immediately postprogram "clearly indicated that young children can rapidly learn to view themselves as members of a society in a classroom context and will learn those skills that society has established as necessary [p. 295].'' These comments summarize the researchers' bases for an encouraging but modest report. Pertinent data follow:

Intelligence.   As noted in the Consortium pooled analyses, "The conclusions that a well-run, cognitively oriented early education program will increase the IQ scores of low-income children by the end of the program is one of the least disputed results in educational evaluation (Royce, Darlington, & Murray, this volume, p. 426).'' This conclusion is consistent also with individual Consortium studies. With two exceptions (Jester and Guinagh; Seitz, Apfel, Rosenbaum, & Zigler), the short-term gains on measures of intelligence (generally noted up to 3 years after program participation) later showed: (1) loss for both participant and comparison groups; and (2) the differences between the groups were reduced. In Schweinhart and Weikart's sample, children from both groups when last tested had intelligence test scores no higher than when they started—80 on the Wechsler, indicating levels of performance at the margin of normal capacity. A similar pattern was reported by Gray and her colleagues: at the last follow-up, intelligence test scores were low for both participant and comparison groups and between-group differences were negligible.

Scholastic Achievement.   Unlike the intelligence test data, the primary reason for modesty in the scholastic achievement data is not overall fade-out of differences once predominant but the generally low levels of achievement. Schweinhart and Weikart's data are illustrative: Although the participant and nonparticipant differences are sustained, the percentiles (against national norms) when the children were tested last were about 35 for the participants and about 25 for the controls. Similar data are reported by Gray et al.: 21st percentile in mathematics, 34th percentile in English, 32nd percentile in reading for participant and nonparticipant groups. Miller and Bizzell also found no notable differences between experimental and control groups and reported a decline in percentiles over all the experimental groups, with final levels in both reading and mathematics about the 25th percentile.

These findings need to be interpreted carefully. First, the percentiles are against national norms—not norms for urban areas where average performance is typically lower than the national norms, and that big city schools use to report such data. Second, it is probable that conclusions about individual pupil progress or program effectiveness are limited unless one knows the overlap between the text (or what was taught) and what was tested. It has been found, for example, that the most widely used elementary texts in mathematics have about 30% overlap among each other on what is taught at a given grade level. Some third-grade texts will include fractions and others will not. Some will teach long division and others will not. There is a range of about 20% to 50% overlap between what texts (and teachers) teach and what standardized achievement tests measure. When achievement data are reanalyzed taking into account the congruence of what is taught (the skill, such as long division, not specific items) and what is tested, considerable differences in conclusions about pupil progress and program effectiveness emerge in comparison to conclusions taken without regard to text/test congruence. In the Consortium studies, the absolute levels of the percentiles can be interpreted as a probable underestimate of actual learning because text/teacher/test congruences across many years of schooling are not known. The congruence issue should affect, of course, participant and comparison groups equally, but caution should be taken in interpreting absolute levels.

One could ask why some groups seem to do well on achievement tests despite the congruence effects: the answer is as yet unclear. Some teachers may be more attentive to the range of skills tested, and there may be systematic differences among schools in the extent to which they emphasize drill and practice on the mechanics of mathematics and reading (on which most children do well) in contrast to problem solving, interpretive, and analytic skills (where the differences among children become most pronounced). However, without further information on the reasons for the still quite low percentiles, ''modest'' interpretations of the findings have considerable justification: the possibility cannot be ruled out that congruences among texts/teaching and tests are high but the Consortium children are not learning as much as needed. Also, Palmer reports that the benefits of his program were clearest for the middle-income participants versus low-income controls and that the gap between middle-income and low-income children was undiminished before, during, after, and long after the intervention. This flags another concern for interpretation of the achievement findings, remarkable as the range and durability of some effects are.

Conclusions. The ''modest'' claims seek funds for continued investigation of the potential of the specific early childhood programs of some researchers in early childhood education. These claims are based on the reliability of the IQ findings and on the encouraging patterns of participant and nonparticipant differences across many years and a range of measures. In some instances (Levenstein et al.; Woolman), the modesty of the claims reflects uncertainties due to design limitations the researchers could not avoid, rather than the modesty of the effects. The bid is made, however, for more research on the particular program rather than generically.

Contingent Policy Claims

Jester and Guinagh write:

> Gordon believed it would be possible to combine a quality intervention program designed to break the poverty cycle with quality research. . . . There is no question regarding the initial issue: the poverty cycle cannot be broken by a project such as this. . . . It is clear, however, that intervention . . . can result in reliable performance differences as long as eight years after the end of intervention. . . . some of the underlying reason is due to changes in the mothers that . . . enhanced the children's school performance. . . . We also know that no matter what the effect of the program, the environmental forces will continue to modify the children as they grow older [pp. 130–131].

Deutsch et al. conclude:

> These case studies affirmed that critical links exist among various domains of an individual's experience and suggested that school-related interventions, if they are to exert sustained effects on the quality of later life, must take into account the influences of other primary learning environments that are part of the child's life context . . . the persistence of enrichment effects is in part gender linked; . . . relatively homogeneous subgroups of individuals, which transcend the experimental/comparison dichotomy, are associated with different developmental paths to autonomy and competency [p. 407].

Karnes, Schwedel and Williams, although emphasizing that early intervention can prevent a sizable number of children from being placed in special classes, and that a high quality preschool program can bring about significant improvements for several years in language and intellectual functions without sacrificing social development, conclude:

> Children need advocates . . . within the school to ensure that adequate supportive services are provided before serious deficiencies in critical academic areas become evident . . . the critical components of a preschool program that facilitate high levels of lasting child progress still need to be delineated; techniques need to be developed to match both children and teachers to preschool programs; acquiring skills in preschool is not enough to ensure school success [p. 166].

This position emphasizes that although there were overall benefits (such as reduced placement is special education), there also were strong interactions of individual characteristics, program characteristics, and postprogram experience that, in the words of Deutsch et al., were more important than program participation per se. What were these?

Program Duration.   Levenstein et al., comparing long-term effects for children who had been in the program for 1 year versus 2 years, reported that reading and mathematics achievement beyond the third grade were linear functions of the amount of treatment received. Jester and Guinagh found a similar effect: participation in a 2- to 3-year program, which also included parent teaching and follow-up, had better results than participation in the short-term, home learning center approach. Beller's data showed a linear effect with regard to durability and range of effects among children who entered school at nursery, kindergarten, and first grades: the earlier and the longer, the better.

Program Characteristics.   Several researchers reported interactions primarily in terms of subgroup effects of different types of preschool programs.

Miller and Bizzell found that whereas the more structured preschool programs initially seemed more effective relative to other types of programs and to comparison children, by the eighth grade the Montessori program seemed particularly beneficial. More children who had participated in these programs were at or above the 50th percentile on reading and mathematics scores. Karnes et al.'s results were similar to those reported by Miller and Bizzell. In the immediate impact and early follow-up studies, the most structured programs of their comparative study seemed most effective. In the middle grades, long-term effects among programs did not differ reliably. By early high school, the impact ratings among the programs were either nonsignificant or reversed the conclusions of the early comparisons. In the pooled analyses of Royce, Darlington, and Murray, there were no clear-cut curricular or structural effects. What emerged as worth further investigation was a cluster of factors: starting early, involvement of both parents and children, home visits, and the opportunity for several adults to work closely with no more than three or four children each.

Gender.   Several researchers report gender effects: Gray et al. found greater impact on females at the high school level in grade point average, personal social adjustment, and realism of occupational and educational aspirations. In the Miller and Bizzell study, males were more susceptible than females to program effects: For example, males attending Montessori programs had higher WISC verbal IQs in the follow-up and higher scores on measures of reading and mathematics. Seitz et al. report durable effects for Wave 1 boys on a measure of general information. The Wave 2 cohort (which they believed to be more typical of inner-city children) showed greater durability of effects for females than for males, including greater mathematics achievement for the females who had participated in Follow Through in comparison to non-Follow Through females 6 years after the program ended.

Interpretations of these interactions—with length of participation, with type of program, and with gender—are provided most analytically by Seitz et al., who systematically rule out selection biases and the effects of small Ns, and seem able to link the effects to special learning opportunities and the differential stresses on inner-city girls and boys.

Conclusions. The contingency of later development on both early and subsequent experience is discussed by Jester and Guinagh, although they do not present analyses of such contingencies. Deutsch et al., through their case studies, feel they isolated two factors that regardless of early experience contribute to life success. These are: (1) support structures that include program-related parent components but that also can be provided by the church and the extended family; and (2) the enabling influence of interested adults who care about a child's pursuit of education, which included but were not limited to teachers.

These studies are as yet incomplete: how the contingencies may work is sketched in only lightly. The conclusion of most of the researchers, however, is that chances of later success are raised by preschool but that how much, for whom, how long, and on what measures is dependent, in ways yet to be specified, on the characteristics of the preschool program, the child's circumstances, community supports and opportunities, and later school experiences.

Although all the authors emphasize that some effects seem durable regardless of the great variety of subsequent school experiences, they seem also to emphasize the contingent nature of these durable results. Such a conclusion lays claim to broader territory than the more modest conclusion. It would include a claim for further inquiry into the improvement of preschool programs to maximize the short-term beneficial effects. In addition, the contingent conclusion would aim at both learning about, and trying to improve, the postprogram factors to capitalize on the impetus given by the early programs: better support systems, more contact with adults who believe in the children (Deustch et al.), and expansion of school programs with high standards of excellence that use the children's fullest learning potential (Seitz et al.). Gray has characterized this as a strong, modest position. She writes (1982), "There's clear and consistent evidence of a difference of considerable importance in the real-life outcomes for the children studied . . . a fine crop of daisies, as it were. If one wants a rose, one had better invest more funds and effort in initial planting and in continued care."

Strong Policy Claims

The strong position—that with quality programs, there are notable, durable, cost-beneficial effects of early intervention—is stated unequivocally only by Schweinhart and Weikart. They write:

> If early intervention programs demonstrate returns to society on investment, they ought to win the support of public and private investors concerned about the society. Early intervention programs cost money and are directed at families with-

out enough money to pay for them. If early intervention programs are to exist, they need the support of investors. The Perry Preschool program did demonstrate substantial return to society on its investment [pp. 91–92].

A position almost as strong is taken by Palmer, who believes the extent and duration of impact from a very early intensive intervention (one-on-one teaching sessions) is consistent with the not often accepted inoculation hypothesis: The right intervention at the right time can prevent later academic problems. Although the other researchers certainly report what might a decade ago have been considered surprising evidence of durable effects, they are more cautious in their conclusions. Some (Jester & Guinagh; Deutsch et al.) clearly believe in the strong interactions of early and later life opportunities. Others (Seitz et al.) may believe this also, but are more likely: (1) to emphasize that for their study, important outcomes—life success—have not yet been analyzed; and (2) to identify postprogram failures among schools in providing opportunities for children to prosper to the limits of their potential, than they are to claim such durable and impressive returns overriding the current variety of life chances.

On what evidence are the strong claims based, and what related evidence do other researchers provide?

Schweinhart and Weikart's case is based primarily on nontest variables. They note that improved cognitive ability was shown by IQ differences in kindergarten and first grade, but these were not sustained. They report greater school achievement lasting up to the eighth grade, but these are the differences between the 35th percentile for the participants and the 25th percentile for the controls. One group is doing better than the other; the participant group is not achieving at levels that offer much hope for later academic success.

The most compelling evidence seems rather to be in the variables that originally were the targets of the war on poverty—not IQ or higher grade point averages, but higher rates of school completion and what these mean in terms of later chances for employment and self-sufficiency. Schweinhart and Weikart write:

Greater commitment to schooling was shown by a higher value placed on schooling by teenagers and by several other aspects of commitment to schooling. Reinforcement of a more positive student role for children who attended preschool was represented by more highly rated social development in elementary school, fewer years spent receiving special educational services throughout their years in the public schools, and greater satisfactions and aspirations by parents with regard to the schooling of their children. Decreased antisocial behavior at school by children who attended preschool was indicated by more favorably rated classroom conduct and personal behavior during elementary school and by teenagers' reports of being kept after school less often. Decreased delinquent behavior was shown by lower frequencies of self-reported delinquent behavior and serious delinquent behavior . . . economic analysis of the Perry Preschool Project revealed that the undiscounted economic benefits for two years of preschool were 248% of the cost [pp. 99–100].

Confirming evidence is included in some other reports, although only in four studies were the children old enough to collect posthigh school data.

Placement in Special Education and Retention in Grade.   Almost all projects reported lower incidence of placement in special education and, for school systems that did not practice social promotion, lower incidence of retention in grade. Although legislation requiring a handicapped child's placement in the least restrictive environment (PL 94–142) may be considered a more direct way to reduce placement in special education than is preschool, reconsideration of the least restrictive environment is underway. Legal ways to increase the intellectual homogeneity of the classroom may be sought as schools strive to increase excellence of outcomes. Programs that reduce—not promise to, but actually do reduce—later need for placement in special education as well as for retention in grade thus are important alternatives for decision makers to consider. The result that seems most pronounced across the Consortium studies is exactly this effect.

Life Success.   On measures of life success, only few researchers have reported as yet on long-term effects. Several researchers began later and do not yet have data on high school graduation, teenage pregnancy, incidence of delinquency, career planning, and similar measures. Gray et al., however, found that 60% of the participants but only 48% of the comparisons completed high school at all. Among the girls, 60% of the controls but only 40% of the participants became pregnant while in high school. Of those who became pregnant, 86% of the participant group but only 18% of the comparison group completed high school.

With the exception of Schweinhart and Weikart, none of the individual Consortium members have analyzed the long-term, life-success indicators of the effects of early intervention in great detail. The most extensive analyses, enabled by pooling data across the four posthigh school studies (Beller; Gray et al.; Karnes et al.; Schweinhart & Weikart) are those of the overall Consortium (Royce, Darlington, & Murray). They traced a path of indirect or contingent influence from preschool participation to long-term economic and social effects. In these analyses the long-term status was considered good if the young adult was enrolled in high school or postsecondary education, was employed in military service, was married and raising a family, or had been employed and was seeking work. This was contrasted to an unfavorable status: the young adult was unemployed and not seeking work, had never been employed, had dropped out of school, was in prison, or was receiving public assistance. Reliably, participation in preschool was likely to lead to normal progress in promotions, which was likely to lead to high school graduation. Students who progressed normally through school and who were high school graduates, in turn, were more likely to achieve "good" economic and social status. A mediating pathway also could be traced between preschool and high school completion. Children who attended preschool were more likely to emphasize academic achievement and be oriented to academic achievement; children with an academic achievement orientation were more likely to have high occupational aspirations. Children with high occupational aspirations in turn were more likely to complete high school.

Summary

How might the different claims be viewed? The modest claims—for funds for further investigation of the long-term potential of early educational opportunities and for development of the next generation of programs based on the findings from the pioneering studies—seem readily supported. Immediate effects are found, to notable degrees, for all the projects; there are a wide range and variety of long-term effects, albeit scattered across projects; and based on the patterns of findings, selections could be made of promising approaches for additional research.

The contingent claims—that preschool does have beneficial effects, but the preschool experience alone cannot do the job—probably would find widespread support. The Consortium studies could be close to a final, accurate assessment of, in Gray's words, "how much difference the little makes." Many of the Consortium children were eligible for compensatory education assistance, although it is not known which received what additional services or the quality of the programs. There is as yet no evidence that more and longer post-preschool opportunities would be that much better, or enough, but the Consortium data are consistent with policy supporting both early and continuing access to high quality education.

The evidence for strong claims, however, may merit most policy attention. Only those early childhood programs attracting wide audiences, such as *Sesame Street*, or those that are beloved as a good thing for poor children, such as Head Start, have survived, and not on the basis of evaluations alone. There are no new experimental programs underway today, no second or third generation of projects in which well-supported first-rate attempts are made to have a long-term effect on children's life chances. The country largely has abandoned the hypothesis that if reducing poverty is a national goal, early intervention is a serious contender for policy attention. We may have backed away, as a nation, from the cause of poor children because we feel so powerless to do something effective directly to better their life chances.

The findings from the Longitudinal Consortium studies force reconsideration. There is, to be sure, much unanswered about what accounts for the long-term effects noted.[3] The probable links among preschool participation, reduced likelihood of placement in special education or being held back a grade, and increased likelihood of favorable long-term outcomes among high school graduates whose school progress was normal are well-defined in the Royce, Darlington, and Murray analyses. But how preschool acts to influence these likelihoods is speculative: improved adjustment to the structured school situation? an increase in parental belief in their child's learning capacities leading to increased parental readiness to prevent special educational placement or retention in grade? some enabling effects of the early intellectual head start that helped the children stand out a bit more and receive greater amounts of instruction from their teachers? There are also some uncertainties about the data themselves. All of the long-term outcome findings (employment, education, military service, marriage, and child rearing) are based on self-reports. Incidence of delinquency, for example, could not be checked against police records in this study, nor employment history with prior or present employers. And neither this book nor others since Steiner (1976) attempt policy analyses of the social costs and benefits of alternative ways of helping improve the life chances of low-income children.

One could argue such analyses should wait until the long-term followup data from all the studies are in. But to disprove the negative case—there are no notable, long-term benefits of early childhood intervention—only one strong instance is needed. Researchers have been cautious for many years in looking at outcomes such as school completion and labor force participation as an associate of early childhood programs. Only Weikart and his colleagues have dared cost-benefit analyses, albeit not to the total enthusiasm of some economists.

The Consortium analyses suggest, however, there is within our reach not necessarily the only way or even the best way of breaking the cycle of poverty, but *a* way, a way that works with returns most economists rarely dream of. Those concerned with child development have not promised us a rose garden, but one may have grown.

One policy implication of the strong position is that the time is now to articulate what a next generation of early childhood programs would look like, building on those that seem to have defied the odds. Which children would be eligible—those, following Steiner's argument and the Schweinhart and Weikart precedent, for whom community consensus and need argue most strongly? What services would they receive, under what auspices? Would the curriculum be

---

[3]A detailed methodological critique of the study is not available. Its dissemination through years of presentations at academic meetings and other public forums has given the Consortium researchers opportunities to examine alternative hypotheses and to confirm the reliability of statistical results across different analytic approaches. These opportunities, perhaps the excellence of the study itself as seen by other researchers or perhaps the generally cautious interpretations offered by most Consortium members, seem associated with what otherwise might be a remarkable lack of published critical analyses.

structured, as the early returns suggested; or more cognitively oriented, as the later returns may indicate? For how long should the children participate, if we are serious about expecting the returns on investment Schweinhart and Weikart report: a few hours a day for 6 to 8 months, or at least two full, intensively programmed years? How would they be supported and administered to assure the quality of staffing and continuity of supervision apparently associated with the returns on investment: what incentives might be provided, how might tax credits be used, what combination of private and public administration might be most feasible and appropriate?

One bouquet of roses may not make a rose garden. It is not too early, however, to address the policy questions of the strong position.

REFERENCES

Gray, S. Personal communication, May 21, 1982.
Steiner, G. Y. *The children's cause*. Washington, D.C.: Brookings Institute, 1976.
Zigler, E., & Anderson, K. An idea whose time had come: The intellectual and political climate. In E. Zigler & J. Valentine (Eds.), *Project Head Start: A legacy of the war on poverty*. New York: Free Press, 1979.

Author Index

481

Reagan, R., 27, *30*
Rees, A., 203, 207, *236*
Reese, H. W., 413, *457*
Reid, J. H., 6, *30*
Reissman, F., 141, *169,* 379, *409*
Research for Better Schools, Inc., 285, *297*
Richardson, H., 113, *132*
Richmond, J. B., 19, 22, 23, *30*
Riessman, F., 106, *132,* 141, *169*
Rist, R. C., 88, *100*
Roberta, J., 253, *263*
Roberts, A. O. H., 302, *331*
Robinson, D., 265, *297*
Rodriguez, J. F., 265, *297*
Rogers, L., 79, *101*
Rokeach, M., 445, *459*
Root, M., 358, *375*
Rosché, M., 423, *459*
Rosenbaum, L. K., 315, 322, *332*
Rosenberg, M., 18, *30,* 46, *68,* 380, *409*
Rosenthal, R., 261, *263*
Rosman, B. L., 45, 55, *68*
Rosnow, R. L., 261, *263*
Rossiter, C., 431, 432, 434, 435, 439, 441, *459*
Roth, J. A., 280, *297*
Rotter, J. B., 55, *68*
Royce, J. M., 302, 303, *331,* 422, 424, 426, 428, 429, 430, 431, 441, *458, 459*
Ruopp, R., 79, *100*
Rusk, R. R., 2, *30*
Russell, J. A., 148, *169*
Rutter, M., 447, *459*
Ryan, S., 302, *332*
Ryan, W., 11, *30*

S

Salter, R., 172, *198*
Sameroff, A. J., 37, *68,* 413, *459*
Sapir, E., 239, *263*
Sarri, R. S., 80, 89, *101*
Scarr, S., 445, *459*
Schaefer, E., 80, *101,* 120, 127, 128, *132,* 235, *263*
Schafer, W. E., 80, 89, *101*
Schaie, K., 253, *263*
Schiller, J., 106, *132*
Schruben, A., 435, *459*
Schweinhart, L. J., 46, *68,* 75, 77, 82, 85, 87, 89, 90, 92, 97, 100, *101*

Sears, P. S., 380, *410*
Seitz, V., 302, 307, 310, 314, 315, 322, 326, 329, *332*
Sellin, T., 91, *101*
Seltzer, A. R., 344, *376*
Sequin, E., 221, *236*
Sewell, W. H., 265, *297,* 413, 447, *459*
Shaw, L. B., 265, *297*
Sherman, V. S., 380, *410*
Shipman, V. C., 10, *29,* 141, *168,* 239, *263*
Siegel, R., 222, 231, *236*
Skeels, H. M., 5, 6, *30,* 204, *236,* 379, *410*
Skeni, F., 380, *408*
Slaughter, D., 182, *198*
Smith, H., 265, *296*
Smith, M., 106, *132*
Smith, M. L., 419, *458*
Smith, M. S., 21, *30,* 302, *332*
Snipper, A. S., 302, 303, *331,* 422, 424, 426, 429, 430, 431, *458*
Snipper, R., 441, *459*
Snow, R. E., 380, 385, *408, 410*
Southern, M. L., 171, *199*
Spicker, H. H., 171, *198*
Spitz, R. A., 6, *30,* 204, *236*
Sprigle, H. A., 171, *199*
Stack, C., 413, *459*
Stafford, F., 95, *100*
Stallings, J., 302, 330, *332*
Staszewski, J., 443, *459*
Steinberg, L. D., 372, *375*
Steiner, G., 17, 18, *30,* 478, *479*
Stern, C., 182, *199*
Stipek, D. J., 19, 22, 23, *30*
Stoddard, B. D., 379, *410*
Stoddard, G. D., 379, *410*
Stoneburner, R. L., 151, *168*
Strickland, B. R., 148, *169*
Strickland, G., 313, *331*
Sullivan, H. S., 380, *410*
Sundquist, J. L., 18, *30*
Sunley, R., 238, *263*

T

Taleporos, E., 369, *376,* 378, 386, 395, 396, 397, 398, *408*
Terman, L. M., 80, 82, *101,* 120, *132,* 143, *169,* 343, *376,* 391, *410*
Teska, J. A., 133, 134, 139, 144, 151, *168, 169,* 172, *198,* 369, *376*

Subject Index